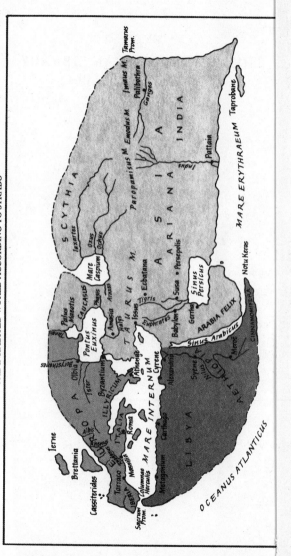

THE INHABITED WORLD ACCORDING TO STRABO

THE LOEB CLASSICAL LIBRARY

FOUNDED BY JAMES LOEB

EDITED BY

G. P. GOOLD

STRABO

I

LCL 49

STRABO

GEOGRAPHY

BOOKS 1-2

WITH AN ENGLISH TRANSLATION BY

HORACE LEONARD JONES

BASED ON THE UNFINISHED VERSION OF
JOHN ROBERT SITLINGTON STERRETT

HARVARD UNIVERSITY PRESS
CAMBRIDGE, MASSACHUSETTS
LONDON, ENGLAND

First published 1917
Reprinted 1931, 1948, 1960, 1969, 1989, 1997

LOEB CLASSICAL LIBRARY® is a registered trademark
of the President and Fellows of Harvard College

ISBN 0-674-99055-2

*Printed in Great Britain by St Edmundsbury Press Ltd,
Bury St Edmunds, Suffolk, on acid-free paper.
Bound by Hunter & Foulis Ltd, Edinburgh, Scotland.*

CONTENTS

LIST OF THE BOOKS OF
THE GEOGRAPHY OF STRABO

Showing their place in the volumes of this
edition and in the edition of Casaubon of 1620

LIST OF THE BOOKS

PREFACE

PROFESSOR JOHN ROBERT SITLINGTON STERRETT, the
eminent scholar who was originally chosen by the
Editors of the Loeb Classical Library to prepare this
edition of Strabo, died suddenly on June 15, 1914.
His many friends and colleagues in the world of
scholarship were greatly disappointed that he was
thus prevented from bringing to a happy completion
a task which would have been a fitting consummation
of a long and notable career. In accordance with a
desire he expressed to me shortly before his death,
and at the invitation of the Editors, I have ventured,
not without misgivings, to carry on the work from
the point where his labours ceased.

The Introduction and the Bibliography remain
substantially as they were left by Professor Sterrett;
and the translation of the first two books, contained
in Volume I., not only is indebted to him for much of
its diction, but reveals in other elements of style
many traces of his individuality. Nevertheless the

present version, a fairly literal one perhaps, is so remote from the free rendering of Professor Sterrett, above all in the technical passages, that it would be unjust to hold him responsible for any mistakes or infelicities which the reader may now detect. The Editors, it is true, at first requested me merely to revise and see through the press the first two books as Professor Sterrett had left them, and then to proceed independently with the remaining fifteen; yet upon a closer examination of his work both they and I decided that to revise it for publication would be impossible without destroying its quality and aim, at all events for a new translator of the whole. The Editors then decided, in view of the purposes of the Loeb Library and for the sake of unity in the work as a whole, to proceed as the title-page indicates; and hence, in order to avoid the danger of attributing to Professor Sterrett a method of interpretation for which he should not be held accountable, the present translator has been forced to assume all the responsibility from the beginning—for the first two books as well as the rest.

In constituting the Greek text I have tried to take into account the work that has been done by scholars, not only since the appearance of Meineke's edition, but prior to that edition as well. The map

PREFACE

of The Inhabited World according to Strabo (drawn by Mr. L. A. Lawrence of Cornell University) is adapted partly from the *Orbis Terrarum secundum Strabonem* of C. Müller and partly from that of W. Sieglin.

I wish to acknowledge my great indebtedness to my colleagues, Professor Lane Cooper and Professor Joseph Quincy Adams, of Cornell University, for their criticism of the translation; and also to Professor Ora M. Leland, for assistance in technical problems related to astronomy. But above all, I desire to record an incalculable debt of gratitude to my lamented friend, Professor Sterrett, who, in the relation first of teacher and later of colleague, was to me, as to many others, an unfailing source of inspiration and encouragement.

H. L. J.

April, 1916.

INTRODUCTION

WHAT is known about Strabo must be gleaned from his own statements scattered up and down the pages of his Geography; this is true not merely of his lineage, for we also learn much by inference concerning his career and writings. Dorylaus, surnamed Tacticus or the General, is the first of the maternal ancestors of Strabo to be mentioned by him, in connexion with his account of Cnossus (10. 4. 10). This Dorylaus was one of the officers and friends of Mithridates Euergetes, who sent him on frequent journeys to Thrace and Greece to enlist mercenary troops for the royal army. At that time the Romans had not yet occupied Crete, and Dorylaus happened to put in at Cnossus at the outbreak of a war between Cnossus and Gortyna. His prestige as a general caused him to be placed in command of the Cnossian army; his operations resulted in a sweeping victory for Cnossus, and great honours were heaped upon him in consequence. At that juncture Euergetes was assassinated at Sinope, and as Dorylaus had nothing to hope for from the widowed queen and young children of the dead king, he cast in his lot permanently with the Cnossians. He married at

Cnossus, where were born his one daughter and two sons, Lagetas and Stratarchas. Their very names indicate the martial proclivities of the family. Stratarchas was already an aged man when Strabo saw him. Mithridates, surnamed Eupator and the Great, succeeded to the throne of Euergetes at the early age of eleven years. He had been brought up with another Dorylaus, who was the nephew of Dorylaus the general. When Mithridates had become king, he showed his affection for his playmate Dorylaus, by showering honours upon him, and by making him priest of Ma at Comana Pontica—a dignity which caused Dorylaus to rank immediately after the king. But not content with that, Mithridates was desirous of conferring benefactions upon the other members of his friend's family. Dorylaus, the general, was dead, but Lagetas and Stratarchas, his sons, now grown to manhood, were summoned to the court of Mithridates. "The daughter of Lagetas was the mother of my mother," says Strabo. As long as fortune smiled on Dorylaus, Lagetas and Stratarchas continued to fare well; but ambition led Dorylaus to become a traitor to his royal master; he was convicted of plotting to surrender the kingdom to the Romans, who, it seems, had agreed to make him king in return for his treasonable service. The details of the sequel are not known; for all that Strabo thinks it worth while to say is that the two men went down into obscurity and discredit along with Dorylaus (10. 4. 10). These ancestors of Strabo

were Greeks, but Asiatic blood also flowed in his
veins. When Mithridates annexed Colchis, he
realized the importance of appointing as governors of
the province only his most faithful officials and
friends. One of these governors was Moaphernes,
the uncle of Strabo's mother on her father's side
(11. 2. 18). Moaphernes did not attain to this exalted
station until towards the close of the reign of
Mithridates, and he shared in the ruin of his royal
master. But other members of the family of Strabo
escaped that ruin; for they foresaw the downfall of
Mithridates, and sought cover from the impending
storm. One of them was Strabo's paternal grandfather, Aeniates by name (if the conjecture of Ettore
Pais be accepted). Aeniates had private reasons for
hating Mithridates, and, besides that, Mithridates
had put to death Tibius, the nephew of Aeniates,
and Tibius' son Theophilus. Aeniates therefore
sought to avenge both them and himself; he treason-
ably surrendered fifteen fortresses to Lucullus, who
made him promises of great advancement in return
for this service to the Roman cause. But at this
juncture Lucullus was superseded by Pompey, who
hated Lucullus and regarded as his own personal
enemies all those who had rendered noteworthy
service to his predecessor. Pompey's hostility to
Aeniates was not confined to the persecution of him
in Asia Minor; for, when he had returned to Rome
after the termination of the war, he prevented the
Senate from conferring the honours promised by

Lucullus to certain men in Pontus, on the ground that
the spoils and honours should not be awarded by
Lucullus, but by himself, the real victor. And so it
came about that Strabo's grandfather failed of the
reward of his treason (12. 3. 13). A further proof of
the existence of Asiatic blood in the veins of Strabo
is the name of his kinsman Tibius; for, says Strabo,
the Athenians gave to their slaves the names of
the nations from which they came, or else the names
that were most current in the countries from which
they came; for instance, if the slave were a Paph-
lagonian, the Athenians would call him Tibius
(7. 3. 12). Thus it appears that Strabo was of
mixed lineage, and that he was descended from
illustrious Greeks and Asiatics who had served the
kings of Pontus as generals, satraps, and priests of
Ma. But by language and education he was
thoroughly Greek.

Strabo was born in Amasia in Pontus in 64 or 63
B.C. (the later date being the year of Cicero's
consulate). It is plain that his family had managed
to amass property, and Strabo must have inherited
considerable wealth; for his fortune was sufficient
to enable him to devote his life to scholarly pursuits
and to travel somewhat extensively. His education
was elaborate, and Greek in character. When he
was still a very young man he studied under Aristo-
demus in Nysa near Tralles in Caria (14. 1. 48)
His parents may have removed from Amasia to
Nysa in consequence of the embarrassing conditions

brought about by the victories of Pompey, the enemy of their house; but the boy may have been sent to study in Nysa before the overthrow of Mithridates the Great; and, if so, he was probably sent thither because one of his kinsmen held high office in the neighbouring Tralles. Ettore Pais points out that, when Mithridates the Great ordered the killing of the Roman citizens in Asia, Theophilus, a Captain in service in Tralles, was employed by the Trallians to do the killing. It seems probable that this Theophilus was the kinsman of Strabo, and the same person who was afterwards executed by Mithridates, an execution that caused Strabo's paternal grandfather to betray the king and desert to Lucullus.

In 44 B.C. Strabo went to Rome by way of Corinth. It was at Rome that he met Publius Servilius, surnamed Isauricus, and that general died in 44 B.C. (This was also the year of the death of Caesar.) Strabo was nineteen or twenty years old at the time of his first visit to Rome. In connexion with his account of Amisus (12. 3. 16) we read that Strabo studied under Tyrannion. That instruction must have been received at Rome; for in 66 B.C. Lucullus had taken Tyrannion as a captive to Rome, where he gave instruction, among others, to the two sons of Cicero. It is Cicero (*Ad Att.* 2. 6. 1) who tells us that Tyrannion was also a distinguished geographer, and he may have guided Strabo into the paths of geographical study. It was probably also at Rome that Strabo had the good fortune to attend

the lectures of Xenarchus (14. 5. 4), the Peripatetic philosopher; for he tells us that Xenarchus abandoned Seleucia, his native place, and lived in Alexandria, Athens, and Rome, where he followed the profession of teacher. He also tells us that he "Aristotelized" along with Boëthus (the Stoic philosopher of Sidon), or, in other words, under Xenarchus in Rome (16. 2. 24). Strabo knew Poseidonius (7. fr. 60, quoted from Athenaeus 14. 75. p. 657), and it has been argued from that statement that Poseidonius, too, was one of Strabo's teachers. But in spite of the fact that his teachers were Peripatetics, there can be no doubt that he was himself an adherent of Stoicism. He confesses himself a Stoic (7. 3. 4); he speaks of "our Zeno" (1. 2. 34); again, he says: "For in Poseidonius there is much inquiry into causes and much imitating of Aristotle—precisely what our School avoids, on account of the obscurity of the causes" (2. 3. 8). Stephanus Byzantius calls him "the Stoic philosopher." Strabo lets his adherence to Stoicism appear on many occasions, and he even contrasts the doctrines of Stoicism with those of the Peripatetic School. What had brought about his conversion cannot be ascertained. It may have been due to Athenodorus; for in his account of Petra he says that it is well-governed, and "my friend Athenodorus, the philosopher, has spoken to me of that fact with admiration" (16. 4. 21). This philosopher-friend was the Stoic Athenodorus, the teacher and friend of Augustus. Strabo makes his

xviii

position in regard to the popular religion quite clear in several passages; he insists that while such religion is necessary in order to hold the illiterate in check, it is unworthy of the scholar. "For in dealing with a crowd of women, at least, or with any promiscuous mob, a philosopher cannot influence them by reason or exhort them to reverence, piety, and faith; nay, there is need of religious fear also, and this cannot be aroused without myths and marvels. For thunderbolt, aegis, trident, torches, snakes, thyrsus-lances,—arms of the gods—are myths, and so is the entire ancient theology" (1. 2. 8). In speaking of the supposed religiosity of the Getans (7. 3. 4) he quotes Menander to the effect that the observances of public worship are ruining the world financially, and he gives a somewhat gleeful picture of the absence of real religion behind those same observances of public worship. Yet Strabo had a religion, and even though he believed that causes are past finding out, he nevertheless believed in Providence as the great First Cause. He sets forth the Stoic doctrine of "conformity to nature" at some length in speaking of Egypt (17. 1. 36), and he also adverts to it in his account of the river-system of France (4. 1. 14).

As for his political opinions, he seems to have followed Polybius in his profound respect for the Romans, with whom, apparently, he is in entire sympathy; he never fails to show great admiration, not only for the political grandeur of the Roman

INTRODUCTION

Empire, but for its wise administration as well; he is convinced of the necessity of a central monarchial power: "The excellence of the government and of the Roman Emperors has prevented Italy (which has often been torn by civil war from the very time when it became subject to Rome), and even Rome itself, from proceeding further in the ways of error and corruption. But it would be difficult for the Romans to govern so vast an empire in any other way than by entrusting it to one person—as it were, to a father. And certainly at no other period have the Romans and their allies enjoyed such perfect peace and prosperity as that which the Emperor Augustus gave them from the very moment when he was clothed with autocratic power, a peace which Tiberius, his son and successor, continues to give them at the present moment; for he makes Augustus the pattern in his policy and administration; and Germanicus and Drusus, the sons of Tiberius, who are now serving in the government of their father, also make Augustus their pattern" (6. 4. 2). And he constantly takes the Roman point of view. For instance, in leading up to his account of the destruction of Corinth by Mummius, he tells us that the Corinthians had perpetrated manifold outrages on the Romans; he does indeed mention the feeling of pity to which Polybius gave expression in telling of the sack of Corinth, and says that Polybius was horrified at the contempt shown by the Roman soldiery for the sacred offerings and the masterpieces

of art; "for Polybius says he personally saw how paintings had been thrown to the ground and saw the soldiers playing dice on them." But Strabo gives us to understand that his own private feeling is that the Corinthians were merely paying for the many insults they had heaped on the Romans (8. 6. 23). He is equally dispassionate in telling of the Roman conquest of his own native country (12. 3. 33). He seems to be thoroughly Roman at heart; for the Romans have united the world under one beneficent administration (1. 1. 16); by the extinction of the pirates the Roman peace has brought prosperity, tranquillity, security to commerce, and safety of travel (3. 2. 5; 14. 3. 3; 16. 2. 20); a country becomes prosperous just as soon as it comes under the Roman sway (3. 3. 8), which opens up means of intercommunication (2. 5. 26); friendship and alliance with Rome mean prosperity to the people possessing them (3. 1. 8; 4. 1. 5); so does the establishment of a Roman colony in any place (6. 3. 4).

We have seen that Strabo went to Rome in 44 B.C., and that he was nineteen or twenty years old at that time. He made several other journeys to Rome: we find him there in 35 B.C.; for that is the date of the execution of Selurus (6. 2. 6), which Strabo witnessed. He was then twenty-nine years old. He was in Rome about 31 B.C.; for he saw the painting of Dionysus by Aristeides (one of those paintings seen by Polybius at the sack of Corinth) in the temple of Ceres in Rome, and he adds: "But

recently the temple was destroyed by fire, and the painting perished " (8. 6. 23). It is known from Dio Cassius (50. 10) that the temple of Ceres was burned in 31 B.C. He was thirty-two or thirty-three years old at that time. We know of still another journey to Rome : " I landed on the island of Gyaros, where I found a small village inhabited by fishermen ; when we sailed from the island, we took on board one of those fishermen who had been sent on a mission to Augustus (who was then at Corinth, on his way [from Egypt] to celebrate his triumph after his victory at Actium). On the voyage we questioned this fisherman, and he told us that he had been sent to ask for a diminution of the tribute " (10. 5. 3). Here we find Strabo journeying from Asia Minor, by way of the island of Gyaros and Corinth, and the clear inference is that he was on his way to Rome at the time. This was in 29 B.C., and Strabo was thirty-four or thirty-five years old. Augustus had just founded Nicopolis in honour of his victory at Actium (7. 7. 6), and it is not unlikely that Strabo visited the new city on that voyage. In 25 and 24 B.C. he is in Egypt, and accompanies Aelius Gallus up the Nile, proceeding as far as Syene and the frontiers of Ethiopia (2. 5. 12). At that time he was thirty-nine years old. He was still in Egypt when Augustus was in Samos in 20 B.C. (14. 1. 14). He was then forty-four years old Accordingly he lived for more than five years in Alexandria, and we may infer that it was in the

Alexandrian library that he made from the works of his predecessors those numerous excerpts with which his book is filled. We find him again in Rome about 7 B.C.; for in his description of Rome he mentions buildings that were erected after 20 B.C., the last of them being the portico of Livia, which was dedicated in 7 B.C. (5. 3. 8). This was perhaps his final visit to Rome, and he was then fifty-six or fifty-seven years old. It seems that he lived to be eighty-four years old, for he chronicles the death of Juba in 21 A.D., but the last twenty-six or twenty-seven years of his life were spent far from Rome, and probably in his native Amasia. His residence at this remote place made it impossible for him to follow the course of recent political events and to incorporate them in the revised edition of his book.

Strabo thought that he had travelled much. He says : " Now I shall tell what part of the land and sea I have myself visited and concerning what part I have trusted to accounts given by others by word of mouth or in writing. I have travelled westward from Armenia as far as the coasts of Tyrrhenia opposite Sardinia, and in the direction of the South I have travelled from the Euxine Sea as far as the frontiers of Ethiopia. And you could not find another person among the writers on Geography who has travelled over much more of the distances just mentioned than I ; indeed, those who have travelled more than I in the western regions have not covered as much ground in the east, and those who have travelled

more in the eastern countries are behind me in the western countries; and the same holds true in regard to the regions towards the South and North" (2. 5. 11). And yet it cannot be said that he was a great traveller; nor can it be said that he travelled for the purpose of scientific research—the real reason for his journeys will presently appear. He saw little even of Italy, where he seems to have followed without much deviation the roads Brindisi-Rome, Rome-Naples-Puteoli, and Rome-Populonia. It does not appear that he lived for any very long stretch of time at Rome; and it cannot be maintained with positiveness that in Greece he saw any place other than Corinth—-not even Athens, strange as this may seem. In the South and the East his travels were more extensive: in the South he visited the Nile valley as far as the frontiers of Ethiopia; he was at Comana Aurea for some time; he saw the river Pyramus, Hierapolis in Phrygia, Nysa in Caria, and Ephesus; he was acquainted with Pontus; he visited Sinope, Cyzicus, and Nicaea; he travelled over Cilicia and much of Caria, visiting Mylasa, Alabanda, Tralles, and probably also Synnada, Magnesia, Smyrna, the shores of the Euxine, and Beirut in Syria. Though we may not limit the places he saw to the places actually mentioned as having been seen by him, still it is clear that his journeys were not so wide as we should have expected in the case of a man who was travelling in the interest of science.

Ettore Pais seems to make good his contention that

the work of Strabo was not written by a man who
was travelling on his own account and for scientific
reasons, but by one who seized every occasion to
study what circumstances and the pleasure of others
gave him an opportunity of knowing. He contends,
further, that it was for the sake of others that
Strabo made his journeys; that he was instructor and
politician, travelling perhaps with, and certainly in
the interest of, persons of the most exalted rank;
that he was the teacher and guide of eminent men.
Strabo never fails to mention the famous scholars and
teachers who were born in the East—the list is a
long one; and we are fain to believe that he occupied a similar social position. He insists that his
Geography is political: The greater part of Geography subserves the uses of states and their rulers;
Geography as a whole is intimately connected with
the functions of persons in positions of political
leadership (1. 1. 16); Geography is particularly useful in the conduct of great military undertakings
(1. 1. 17); it serves to regulate the conduct and
answer the needs of ruling princes (1. 1. 18). Pre-
sumably it was with just such people that he travelled.
But Pais joins issue with Niese and others in their
contention that the men with whom and in whose
interest he travelled were Romans, and he makes out
a good case when he argues that Strabo wrote his
Geography in the interest of Pythodoris, Queen of
Pontus. Even the great respect shown by Strabo
for Augustus, Rome, and Tiberius is to be explained

by the circumstances in which he found himself; for subject-princes had to be obsequious to Rome, and as for Pythodoris, she owed her throne to Augustus fully as much as to Polemon. It was good business, therefore, that necessitated the retouching of the book and the insertion in it of the many compliments to Tiberius—all of which were added after the accession of that prince, and for fear of him, rather than out of respect for him.

The question as to when and where Strabo wrote his geographical work has long been a burning one in circles interested in Strabo criticism. Niese seemed to settle the question, when he maintained that Strabo wrote his Historical Geography at Rome, at the instigation of Roman friends who occupied exalted positions in the political world of Rome; and that he acted as the companion of those friends, accompanying one of them, Aelius Gallus, from Rome to Egypt, and returning with him to Rome; and further that it was at Rome that he wrote his Geography, between the years 18 and 19 A.D. In the main, scholars had accepted the views of Niese, until Pais entered the field with his thesis that Strabo wrote his work, not at the instigation of politicians at Rome, but from the point of view of a Greek from Asia Minor, and in the interest of Greeks of that region; that the material for the Geography was collected at Alexandria and Rome, but that the actual writing of the book and the retouching of it at a later period were done at Amasia, far from Rome—

a fact which accounts for his omissions of events, his errors, his misstatements, his lack of information concerning, and his failure to mention, occurrences that would surely have found a place in his book if it had been written in Rome; it accounts, too, for the surprising fact that Strabo's Geography was not known to the Romans—not even to Pliny—although it was well-known in the East, for Josephus quotes from it.

To go somewhat more minutely into this question, it may be stated that Strabo mentions Tiberius more than twenty times, but the events he describes are all connected with the civil wars that occurred after the death of Caesar and with the period in the life of Augustus that falls between the Battle of Actium (in 31 B.C.) and 7 B.C. He rarely mentions events in the life of Augustus between 6 B.C. and 14 A.D., and, as he takes every opportunity to praise Augustus and Tiberius, such omissions could not be accounted for if he wrote his Geography about 18 A.D. The conclusion reached by Pais is that Strabo wrote the book before 5 B.C. and shortly after 9 B.C., or, in other words, about 7 B.C. Such matters as the defeat of Varus and the triumph of Germanicus were not contained in the original publication of the work, and were inserted in the revised edition, which was made about the year 18 A.D. The list of the Roman provinces governed by the Roman Senate, on the last page of the book, was written between 22 B.C. and 11 B.C., and Strabo himself says that it was

antiquated; it was retouched about 7 B.C., not at Rome, but far from Rome. The facts are similar in the mention he makes of the liberality of Tiberius to the cities of Asia Minor that had been destroyed by earthquakes; in the case of the coronation of Zeno as king of Armenia Major (18 A.D.), and in the case of the death of Juba, which occurred not later than 23 A.D., Strabo made no use of the map of Agrippa—an omission with which he has been reproached—for the very good reason that the map of Agrippa had not been completed in 7 B.C.

If Strabo first published his Geography in 7 B.C., it appeared when he was fifty-six or fifty-seven years old, at a time when he was still in full possession of all his physical and mental powers. But if we say, with Niese and his followers, that the work was written between 18 and 19 A.D., we thereby maintain that Strabo began to write his Geography when he had passed the eighth decade of his life. He himself compares his book to a colossal statue, and it is incredible that he could have carried out such a stupendous work after having passed his eightieth year.

Strabo is so well-known as a geographer that it is often forgotten that he was a historian before he was a geographer. Indeed it may be believed that he is a geographer because he had been a historian, and that the material for his Geography was collected along with that for his Historical Sketches, which comprised forty-seven books (see

1. 1. 22–23, and 2. 1. 9, and footnotes). But his Geography alone has come down to us. In this connexion it will be useful to read Strabo's own account of his Historical Sketches and his Geography: "In short, this book of mine should be generally useful —useful alike to the statesman and to the public at large—as was my work on *History*. In this work, as in that, I mean by 'statesman,' not the man who is wholly uneducated, but the man who has taken the round of courses usual in the case of freemen or of students of philosophy. For the man who has given no thought to virtue and to practical wisdom, and to what has been written about them, would not be able even to form a valid opinion either in censure or in praise; nor yet to pass judgment upon the matters of historical fact that are worthy of being recorded in this treatise. And so, after I had written my *Historical Sketches*, which have been useful, I suppose, for moral and political philosophy, I determined to write the present treatise also; for this work itself is based on the same plan, and is addressed to the same class of readers, and particularly to men of exalted stations in life. Furthermore, just as in my *Historical Sketches* only the incidents in the lives of distinguished men are recorded, while deeds that are petty and ignoble are omitted, so in this work also I must leave untouched what is petty and inconspicuous, and devote my attention to what is noble and great, and to what contains the practically useful, or memorable, or

entertaining. Now just as in judging of the merits
of colossal statues we do not examine each individual
part with minute care, but rather consider the
general effect and endeavour to see ir the statue as
a whole is pleasing, so should this book of mine be
judged. For it, too, is a colossal work, in that it
deals with the facts about large things only, and
wholes, except as some petty thing may stir the
interest of the studious or the practical man. I
have said thus much to show that the present work
is a serious one and one worthy of a philosopher "
(1. 1. 22–23).

The Geography of Strabo is far more than a
mere geography. It is an encyclopaedia of information concerning the various countries of the
Inhabited World as known at the beginning of the
Christian era; it is an historical geography; and,
as Dubois and Tozer point out, it is a philosophy of
geography.

BIBLIOGRAPHY

TEXT

A. Baumeister : In Fleckeisen's *Jahrb. f. Philol.* 1857, 347.
Th. Bergk : In *Philologus*, 1870, 679.
    ,,   In *Rhein. Mus.* 1882, 298.
    ,,   *Emendat. Onomatolog.* Halle, 1859.
    ,,   In *Neue Jahrbücher*, 1860, 416.
G. N. Bernadakis : *Symbolae criticae, vel censura Cobeti emendationum in Strabonem.* Leipzig, 1877.
G. N. Bernadakis : *Zu Strabon.* In *Neue Jahrbücher*, 1876, 504.
G. Bernhardy : *Analecta in Geographos Graecorum minores.* Halle, 1850.
F. Bücheler : *Conjectanea.* In *Neue Jahrbücher*, 1875, 305.
C. Bursian : *Geographie von Griechenland.* Leipzig, 1862–72.
P. Cascorbi : *Observationes Strabonianae.* Greifswald, 1879.
C. G. Cobet : *Miscellanea critica quibus continentur observationes criticae in scriptores Graecos praesertim Homerum et Demosthenem. Ad Strabonem,* pp. 104 ff., 169 ff., 206 ff. Also in *Mnemosyne*, 1876, 79 ff., 176 ff.
C. G. Cobet : *Syllabus Errorum,* in *Mnemosyne*, 1876, 213.
A. Corais : Σημειώσεις εἰς τὰ Στράβωνος Γεωγραφικά. Paris, 1819.
E. Curtius : *Peloponnesus.* Gotha, 1851–52.
    ,,   In *Zeitschrift f. Alterthumswissenschaft*, 1852.
A. Dederich : In Fleckeisen's *Jahrb. f. Philol.* 1879, 66.
M. G. Demitsas : Κριτικαὶ Διορθώσεις εἰς Στράβωνα. In Ἀθήναιον, 1879, 415.
L. Dindorf : In *Neue Jahrbücher*, 1869, 11 and 124.
W. Dittenberger : On Ὀμβρικοί in the first article on *Ethnica und Verwandtes.* In *Hermes*, 1906, 87. On Θρᾳκικά. In *Hermes*, 1907, 195.
A. Forbiger : *Strabo's Erdbeschreibung übersetzt und durch Anmerkungen erläutert.* Stuttgart, published at intervals after 1856 (1905–1908).

BIBLIOGRAPHY

C. **Frick**: Jahresbericht. In Bursian's *Jahresbericht*, 1880, 536.

C. **Frick**: *Zur troischen Frage.* In *Neue Jahrbücher*, 1876, 289 ff.

J. **Geffcken**: *Saturnia Tellus.* In *Hermes*, 1892, 381.

C. G. **Groskurd**: *Strabons Erdbeschreibung.* 4 vols. Berlin and Stettin, 1831.

P. F. J. **Gosselin**: The Notes signed "G" in the Translation of de la Porte du Theil, Corais, and Letronne.

A. von **Gutschmid**: In *Neue Jahrbücher*, 1861, 204, and 1873, 418.

F. **Haase**: *Emendationes faciles.* Breslau, 1858.

R. **Hercher**: In *Philologus*, 1852, 553.

P. **Hirschfeld**: *Die Abkunft des Mithridates von Pergamon* (on Strabo 625 C.). In *Hermes*, 1879, 474.

A. **Jacob**: *Curae Strabonianae.* In *Revue de Philologie*, 1912, 148. It also contains a Collation for Book IV. of the Paris MSS. A C and *s*.

H. **Kallenberg**: *Straboniana. Beiträge zur Textkritik und Erklärung.* In *Rhein. Mus.* 1912, 174.

L. **Kayser**: Review of Meineke's Edition and of his *Vindiciae Strabonianae*, in *Neue Jahrbücher f. Philol.* 1854, 258, 273.

L. **Kayser**: Review of Cobet's *Variae lectiones.* In *Neue Jahrbücher*, 1856, 166.

A. **Kirchhoff**: In *Hermes*, 1866, 420.

C. **Kontos**: In *Bull. de Corr. Hell.* 1877, 60, and 1878, 236.

H. **Kothe**: In *Neue Jahrbücher*, 1888, 826.

G. **Kramer**: *Strabonis Geographica recensuit commentario critico instruxit.* 3 vols. Berlin, 1844.

G. L. **Kriegk**: *Ueber die thessalische Ebene.* In *Neue Jahrbücher*, 1859, 231 ff.

R. **Kunze**: *Zu Griechischen Geographen.* In *Rhein. Mus.* 1901, 333.

G. M. **Lane**: *Smyrnaeorum res gestae et antiquitates.* Göttingen, 1851.

C. A. **Lobeck**: In *Königsberger Ind. Lect.* 1828.

M. **Lüdecke**: *De fontibus quibus usus Arrianus Anabasin composuit.* In *Leipziger Studien*, **xi**. 14 (on Strabo 70 C.).

I. N. **Madvig**: *Adversaria critica ad scriptores graecos. Ad Strabonem*: I., 520. Havn, 1871.

BIBLIOGRAPHY

A. Meineke: *Strabonis Geographica recognovit.* **3** vols. Leipzig, 1866. The *Praefatio* contains merely a statement of the points in which his text differs from that of Kramer.

A. Meineke: *Vindiciarum Straboniarum liber.* Berlin, 1852. Contains much that Meineke did not insert in his text.

C. Meltzer: In *Fleckeisen's Jahrb. f. Philol.* 1873, 193.

L. Mercklin: *Zu Strabo* (v. 230). In *Philologus*, 1863, 134.

E. Meyer: *Forschungen zur alten Geschichte.* Halle A/S, 1892.

E. Meyer: *Nochmals der* ΛΟΓΟΣ *des Königs Pausanias.* In *Hermes*, 1907, 134.

P. Meyer: *Straboniana.* Grimma, 1889–1890.

A. Miller: *Emendationum in Strabonis librum I. specimen.* Bamberg, 1858.

A. Miller: In *Eos*, 1865, 25.

    „   In *Blätter für bayr. Gymn.* 1874, 145 and 1878, 259.

A. Miller: *Die Alexandergeschichte nach Strabo.* I. Theil. Würzburg, 1852.

C. Müller: *Index variae lectionis* to the Müller-Dübner Edition.

C. Müller: In *Philologus*, 1876, 74; 1877, 78. In *Philol. Anzeiger*, 1873, 507.

B. Niese: *Emendationes Strabonianae.* Marburg, 1878.

L. Pareti: *Di un lucgo Straboniano su Regio.* In *Atene e Roma*, 1913, 14 ff.

L. Paul: *Das Druidenthum.* In *Neue Jahrbücher*, 1892, 786.

N. Piccolos: In *Philologus*, 1860, 727.

L. Rademacher: *Observationum et lectionum variarum specimen.* In *Jahrbücher*, 1895, 248.

M. Rostowzew: Πυθόλαος (Strabo xvi. 4, 14 f.). In *Archiv. f. Philol.* v. 1–2, 181.

L. Ross: *Reisen auf den Inseln des griechischen Meeres.* Stuttgart and Halle, 1845-49-52.

L. Ross: *Reisen im Peloponnesus.* Berlin, 1841.

G. Rucca: *Interpretazione di un luogo di Strabone.* Napoli, 1850.

L. Spengel: In *Münchner Gelehrte Anzeigen*, **1845**, 633 and 1848, 145.

A. Schäfer: In *Philologus*, 1872, 184.

BIBLIOGRAPHY

H. Schrader : In *Neue Jahrbücher*, 1868, 226.

G. Schultze : *Varia.* In *Hermes*, 1893, 31.

A. Tardieu : In his *Translation of Strabo.*

W. Tomaschek : *Miscellen aus der alten Geographie.* In *Zeitschrift f. österr. Gymn.* 1867, 691.

T. Tosi : In *Studi italiani di filologia classica*, 17, 463.

H. F. Tozer : *Selections from Strabo.* Oxford, 1893.

T. G. Tucker : *Emendations in Strabo and Plutarch's Moralia.* In *Classical Quarterly*, 1909, 99.

T. Tyrwhitt : *Coniecturae in Strabonem.* Erlangen, 1788.

L. Urlichs : In *Rhein. Mus. f. Philol.* 1856, 465.

A. Vogel : *Jahresberichte in Philologus*, 1880, 326, and 1881, 309, 508.

U. von Wilamowitz-Moellendorff : *Griechisches Lesebuch.* Short selections from Strabo.

U. v. Wilamowitz-Moellendorff : *Parerga.* In *Hermes*, 1878, 168.

MANUSCRIPTS

Strabo was not much read in antiquity : in a sense he was discovered in Byzantine times ; copies of his work were rare, and apparently at one time the only manuscript extant was the so-called archetype, from which all the manuscripts now extant are descended. This seems clear because all the mistakes, the changes in the text, the transposed sentences, all the gaps, particularly the great gap at the end of the seventh book, are reproduced in all the manuscripts. The modern editions, beginning with that of G. Kramer, are based on the Paris manuscript No. 1397 for the first nine books (it contains no more), while books 10 to 17 are based on the Vatican manuscript No. 1329, on the Epitome Vaticana, and on the Venetian manuscript No. 640. But the Epitome, which goes back to the end of the tenth century, was based on a manuscript which still contained the end of Book VII.

J. Groeger : *Quaestiones Eustathianae. De codicibus Strabonis Herodoti Arriani ab Eustathio in commentario ad Dionysii periegesin usurpatis.* Trebnitz, 1911.

G. Kramer : *Commentatio critica de codicibus, qui Strabonis geographia continent, manu scriptis.* Berlin, 1845. And also in the Preface to his large edition, pp. 10–83.

BIBLIOGRAPHY

A. Jacob: *Curae Strabonianae.* In *Revue de Philologie*, 1912, 170.

E. Röllig: *De codicibus Strabonianis qui libros I–IX continent.* Halle, 1885.

FRAGMENTS

G. Cozza-Luzi: *Dell' antico codice della geografia di Strabone scoperto nei palinsesti della badia di Grottoferrata.* Rome, 1875.

G. Cozza-Luzi: *Del piu antico testo della geografia di Strabone nei frammenti scoperti in membrane palinseste.* Rome, 1884–98.

G. Cozza-Luzi: *Frammenti della geografia di Strabone.* In *Studi in Italia*, vii. 1.

D. Detlefsen: In *Berl. philol. Wochenschrift*, 1885, 1122.

R. Hansen: In *Philologische Rundschau*, v. 517.

G. Kramer: *Fragmenta libri VII. e codd. prim. ed.* Berlin, 1843.

G. Kramer: *Zu Strabo. Handschrift aus Grottoferrata.* In *Hermes*, 1876, 375.

R. Kunze: *Strabobruchstücke bei Eustathius und Stephanus Byzantius.* In *Rhein. Mus.* 1903, 126.

R. Kunze: *Unbeachtete Strabofragmente.* In *Rhein. Mus.* 1902, 437.

P. Otto: *Strabonis Ἱστορικῶν Ὑπομνημάτων fragmenta conlegit et enarravit adjectis quaestionibus Strabonianis.* In *Leipziger Studien* xi. Suppl. 1889, 1.

I. Partsch: In *Deutsche Litteratur-Zeitung*, 1885, 646.

V. Strazzula: *Dopo le Strabone Vaticano del Cozza-Luzi.* Messina, 1901.

G. L. F. Tafel: *Fragmenta nov. curis emend. et illustr.* Tübingen, 1844.

A. Vogel: In *Philologischer Anzeiger*, 1886, 103.

" *Zu Strabo.* In *Hermes*, 1884 (vol. 42), 539.

The Epitome is best found in C. Müller's *Geographi Graeci Minores*, 88, 529.

LANGUAGE

O. Birke: *De particularum μή et οὐ usu Polybiano Dionysiaco Diodoreo Straboniano.* Leipzig, 1907.

BIBLIOGRAPHY

P. Cascorbi: *Observationes Strabonianae.* Göttingen, 1879.

C. G. Cobet: *Syllabus errorum.* In *Mnemosyne*, 1876, 213.

H. Kallenberg: *Straboniana, Beiträge zur Textkritik und Erklärung.* In *Rhein. Mus.* 1912, 174.

J. Keim: *Sprichwörter und parömiographische Ueberlieferung bei Strabo.* Tübingen, 1909.

H. Schindler: *De Diodori Siculi et Strabonis enuntiationum relativarum attractione. Pars Prior: De admissa attractione.* Frankenstein (Silesia), 1909.

On the Sources from which Strabo drew

G. Beloch: *Le fonti di Strabone nelle descrizione della Campania.* Rome, 1882.

H. Berger: *Die geographischen Fragmente des Hipparch.* Leipzig, 1869.

H. Berger: *Die geographischen Fragmente des Eratosthenes.* Leipzig, 1880.

H. Berger: *Geschichte der wissenschaftlichen Erdkunde der Griechen.* 1887–93.

G. Bernhardy: *Eratosthenica.* Berlin, 1822.

R. Däbritz: *De Artemidoro Strabonis auctore capita tria.* Leipzig, 1905.

A. Dederich: *Zu Strabon und Suetonius.* In *Neue Jahrb. f. Philol.* 1879, 66.

M. Dubois: *Examen de la Géographie de Strabon.* Paris, 1891.
  ,,   *Strabon et Polybe.* In *Revue des Études Grecques,* 1891, 343.

W. Fabricius: *Theophanes aus Mytilene und Quintus Dellius als Quelle der Geographie des Strabo.* Strassburg, 1888.

J. Groeger: *Quaestiones Eustathianae. De codicibus Herodoti Arriani ab Eustathio in commentario ad Dionysii periegesin usurpatis.* Trebnitz, 1911.

A. H. L. Heeren: *De fontibus Geographicorum Strabonis commentationes duae.* Göttingen, 1825.

F. Hennicke: *De Strabonis Geographiae fide, ex fontium unde hausit auctoritate aestimanda.* Göttingen, 1791.

U. Höfer: *Eine gemeinsame Quelle Strabons und des sog. Skymnos.* Saarbrücken, 1901.

G. Hunrath: *Die Quellen Strabo's im sechsten Buche.* Cassel, 1879.

BIBLIOGRAPHY

G. Hunrath: In *Bursian's Jahresbericht*, 1879, 311, and 1880, 93.

A. Klotz: *Caesarstudien, nebst einer Analyse der strabonischen Beschreibung von Gallien und Brittanien.* Leipzig and Berlin, 1910.

A. Miller: *Strabo's Quellen über Gallien und Brittanien.* Regensburg, 1878.

K. J. Neumann: *Strabons Quellen im elften Buche.* I. Kaukasien. Leipzig, 1881.

K. J. Neumann: *Strabons Landeskunde von Kaukasien. Eine Quellenuntersuchung. Besondere Abdruck aus dem dreizehnten Supplb. des Jahrb. f. class. Philol.* Leipzig, 1883.

B. Niese: *Apollodor's Commentar zum Schiffskataloge als Quelle Strabo's.* In *Rhein. Mus. f. Philol.* 1877, 267.

A. Oddo: *Gl'Hypomnemata Historica di Strabone come fonte di Appiano.* Palermo, 1901.

G. D. Ohling: *Quaestiones Posidonianae ex Strabone conlectae.* Göttingen, 1908.

E. Pais: *Straboniana. Contributo allo studio delle fonti della storia e della amministrazione romana.* In *Rivista di Philologia classica*, 1887, 97.

E. Schweder: *Beiträge zur Kritik der Chorographie des Augustus.* Erster Theil. Kiel, 1878.

E. Schweder: *Ueber die gemeinsame Quelle der geographischen Darstellung des Mela und Plinius.* In *Philologus*, 1887, 278.

F. Sollima: *Le fonti di Strabone nella geografia della Sicilia.* Messina, 1897.

C. Steinbrück: *Die Quellen des Strabo im fünften Buche seiner Erdbeschreibung.* Halle, 1909.

A. Vogel: *De fontibus quibus Strabo in libro quinto decimo conscribendo usus sit.* Göttingen, 1874.

A. Vogel: *Strabons Quellen für das IX. Buch.* In *Philologus*, 1884 (vol. 43), 405.

H. Wilkens: *Quaestiones de Strabonis aliorumque rerum gallicarum auctorum fontibus.* Marburg, 1886.

R. Zimmermann: *Quibus auctoribus Strabo in libro tertio Geographicorum conscribendo usus sit, quaeritur.* Pars Prior. Halle, 1883.

R. Zimmermann: *Posidonius und Strabo.* In *Hermes*, 1888, 103.

BIBLIOGRAPHY

STUDIES ON STRABO

D. Bartolini : *Pro Strabone*. In *Ateneo Veneto*, March, 1884.

E. Beretta : *Solution de problèmes historiques. Les Cités Mystérieuses de Strabon dans la région Cavare (Comtat Venaissin) l'Isaros et l'Isar*. Lyons, 1907.

P. H. Bidder : *De Strabonis studiis homericis capita selecta*. Gedani, 1889.

Bisciola, *An Lib. XVII. geographiae Strabonis sint an Stratonis*. Cologne, 1618.

H. Bötger : *Wohnsitze der Deutschen nach Strabo*. Stuttgart, 1877.

H. Butzer : *Ueber Strabos Geographica, insbesondere über Plan und Ausführung des Werkes und Strabos Stellung zu seinen Vorgängern*. Frankfurt a. M., 1887.

A. Calogiera : *Nuova raccolta d'opusculi scientifici e filologici*. On Strabo in Vol. 18. Venice, 1755.

E. Castorchis : Περὶ τῶν ἐν Ναυπλίᾳ παναρχαίων τάφων καὶ τῶν αὐτόθι ὑπὸ Στράβωνος μνημονευομένων λαβυρίνθων. In 'Αθήναιον, 1879, 515.

E. Curtius : *Strabo über den Seebund von Kalauria*. In *Hermes*, 1876, 385.

H. Diels : *Herodot und Hecataios*. In *Hermes*, 1887, 443.

W. Dörpfeld : *Zum Elaitischen Golf*. In *Hermes*, 1911, 444.

A. Enmann : *Geographische Homerstudien in Pausanias*. In *Neue Jahrbücher*, 1884, 497.

L. Erhardt : *Der Auszug der Cimbern bei Strabo*. In *Philologus*, 1893, 557.

H. Fischer : *Ueber einige Gegenstände der alten Geographie bei Strabo, als Beitrag zur Geschichte der alten Geographie*. Erster Theil. Wernigerode, 1879. Zweiter Theil. Wernigerode, 1892-93.

C. Frick : *Der χωρογραφικὸς πίναξ des Strabo*. In *Neue Jahrbücher*, 1881, 650.

J. Geffcken : *Die Gründung von Tarent*. In *Neue Jahrbücher*, 1893, 177.

W. Gell : *The Itinerary of Greece, with a Commentary on Pausanias and Strabo*. London, 1810.

P. Giovio (P. Jovius) : *Libellus de legatione Basilii Magni Principis Moschoviae*, etc. On the Rhipaean Mountains. Rome, 1525.

BIBLIOGRAPHY

A. Gronovius : *Varia Geographica*, containing *Animadversiones in Strabonis libros novem.* Leiden, 1739.

A. Häbler : *Die Nord- und Westküsten Hispaniens, ein Beitrag zur Geschichte der alten Geographie.* Leipzig, 1886.

G. Hirschfeld : In *Geogr. Jahrb.* 1888, 253.

G. Hirschfeld : *Die Abkunft des Mithridates von Pergamon.* In *Hermes*, 1878, 474.

E. Hübner : *Egelesta.* In *Hermes*, 1867, 456.

E. Huverstuhl : *Die Lupia des Strabo.* Antwerp, 1910. (See H. Nöthe in *Wochens. f. klass. Philol.* 1911, 345.)

C. W. F. Jacobs : *Was sind σκολιὰ ἔργα beim Strabo?* Leipzig, 1834.

W. Judeich : *Caesar im Orient. Kritische Uebersicht der Ereignisse vom 9 August 48 bis October 47.* Leipzig, 1885.

F. Kähler : *Strabos Bedeutung für die moderne Geographie.* Halle, 1900.

W. Dittenberger : *Methana und Hypata.* In *Hermes*, 1907, 542.

B. Keil : *Zur Pausaniasfrage.* In *Hermes*, 1890, 317.

J. Keim : *Sprichwörter und parömiographische Ueberlieferung bei Strabo.* Tübingen, 1909.

G. Knaack : *Zur Sage von Daidalos und Ikaros.* In *Hermes*, 1902, 598.

U. Köhler : *Der Areopag in Athen.* (On 1. 4. 8.) In *Hermes*, 1872, 92.

E. Kornemann : *Die Diözesen der Provinz Hispania Citerior.* In *Lehmann's Beiträge zur alten Geschichte*, 1884, 323.

W. J. Law : *Some Remarks on the Alpine Passes of Strabo.* London, 1846.

A. Linsmayer : *Der Triumphzug des Germanicus.* München, 1875.

B. de Luca : *Il Lago di Lesina in Strabone e Plinio.* In *Rasseyna Pugliese*, 1900, No. 11.

G. H. L. Lünemann : *Descriptio Caucasi, Gentiumque Caucasiarum, ex Strabone.* Leipzig, 1803.

G. Mair : Παντοῖα. (A). *Pytheas' Fahrten in der Ostsee.* (B). Πλεύμων θαλάσσιος bei Strabo, ii. 104. Marburg, 1907.

E. Meyer : *Forschungen zur alten Geschichte.* Halle A/S, 1892.

E. Meyer : *Nochmals der ΛΟΓΟΣ des Königs Pausanias.* In *Hermes*, 1907, 134.

P. Meyer : *Straboniana.* Grimma, 1890.

BIBLIOGRAPHY

F. Meyer : *Botanische Erläuterungen.* Königsberg, 1852.

H. Middendorf : *Ueber die Gegend der Varusschlacht nach Vellejus und Strabo,* etc. Münster, 1868.

A. Miller : *Der Rückzug des Kraterus aus Indien. Eine Strabonische Studie.* Würzburg (no date).

A. Miller : *Die Alexandergeschichte nach Strabo.* I. Theil. Würzburg, 1882.

B. Niese : *Straboniana. Die Erwerbung der Küsten des Pontus durch Mithridates VI. Sonderabdruck aus dem Rhein. Mus. f. Philol.* 1887, 567.

K. J. Neumann : *Gesammturtheil über die homerische Geographie.* In *Hermes,* 1886, 134.

K. J. Neumann : *Strabons Landeskunde von Kaukasien.* Leipzig, 1883.

K. J. Neumann : *Patrokles und der Oxos.* In *Hermes,* 1884, 165.

P. Otto : *Quaestiones Strabonianae.* In *Leipziger Studien,* ii. Suppl. (vol. 12, 1889), 225.

L. Paul : *Das Druidenthum.* In *Neue Jahrbücher,* 1892, 786.

E. Petersen : Review of Benndorf's *Forschungen in Ephesos.* In *Neue Jahrbücher,* 1906, 713.

A. Philippson : *Zur Geographie der unteren Kaïkos-Ebene in Kleinasien.* In *Hermes,* 1911, 254.

A. J. Reinach : *Delphes et les Bastarnes.* In *Bull. Corr. Hell.* 1910, 249.

H. Rid : *Die Klimatologie in den Geographica Strabos. Ein Beitrag zur physischen Geographie der Griechen.* Kaisersläutern, 1903.

H. Rid : *Klimalehre der alten Griechen nach den Geographica Strabos.* Kaisersläutern, 1904.

W. Ridgeway : *Contributions to Strabo's Geography.* In *Classical Review,* 1888, 84.

C. Robert : *Athena Skiras und die Skirophorien.* In *Hermes,* 1885, 349.

G. Ruge : *Quaestiones Strabonianae.* Leipzig, 1888.

A. Schulten : *Polybius und Posidonius über Iberien und die iberischen Kriege.* In *Hermes,* 1911. 568.

A. Serbin : *Bemerkungen über den Vulkanismus und Beschreibung der den Griechen bekannten vulkanischen Gebiete.* Berlin, 1893.

F. M. Schröter : *Bemerkungen zu Strabo.* Leipzig, 1887.

xl

BIBLIOGRAPHY

E. Schweder: *Beiträge zur Kritik der Chorographie des Augustus.* Kiel, 1878.

E. Schweder: *Ueber den Ursprung und die ursprüngliche Bestimmung des sogenannten Strassennetzes der Peutingerschen Tafel.* In *Philologus*, 1903, 357.

J. Sitzler: *Zu Kallinos und Tyrtaeus.* In *Neue Jahrbücher*, 1880, 358.

L. V. Sybel: *Pausanias und Strabon.* In *Neue Jahrbücher*, 1885, 177.

J. Töpffer: *Astakos.* In *Hermes*, 1896, 124.

G. F. Unger: *Frühlingsanfang.* In *Neue Jahrbücher*, 1890, 393.

E. Wendling: *Zu Posidonius und Varro.* In *Hermes*, 1893, 346.

U. v. Wilamowitz-Moellendorff: *Die Herkunft der Magneten am Maeander.* In *Hermes*, 1895, 177.

U. Wilcken: *Ein Theopompfragment in den neuen Hellanika.* In *Hermes*, 1908, 475.

E. Ziebarth: *Die Strabo-Scholion des Cyriacus von Ankona.* In *Mittheil. des Athen. Instit.* 1898, 196.

EARLY EDITIONS

The *editio princeps* was published by Aldus in Venice in 1516, from a poor manuscript, Par. No. 1395. Then came the folio editions of Basle in 1549 and 1571 by G. Xylander. Xylander's work was revised and supplied with a commentary by Isaac Casaubon in 1587 (folio). In 1620 Casaubon replaced this with his own edition, which was accompanied by Xylander's Latin translation and notes by F. Morrellius. Casaubon's edition did much for the text of the first three books, and Strabo is usually cited by Casaubon's pages (C). Next came the Amsterdam edition by T. J. van Almaloveen in 1707, in two folio volumes. Strabo is sometimes cited by his pages (A). In 1763 Bréquigny published the first three books (quarto) on the basis of a Paris manuscript. In 1796 the Leipzig (octavo) edition was begun: the first volume was revised by J. B. Siebenkees; the five following volumes by C. H. Tzschucke; the seventh volume by F. T. Friedmann. The first six volumes give the text and a revision of Xylander's Latin translation, and the seventh volume contains notes. In 1807 appeared at

BIBLIOGRAPHY

Oxford the edition by T. Falconer in two folio volumes; much criticised. Between the years 1815 and 1819 Corais published the Greek text in three volumes, accompanied by a fourth volume containing valuable notes in Modern Greek.

Modern Editions

A. Corais: Στράβωνος Γεωγραφικῶν Βιβλία Ἑπτακαίδεκα. 4 vols. Paris, 1815.

G. Kramer: *Strabonis Geographica recensuit, commentario critico instruxit.* 3 vols. Berlin, 1844.

A. Meineke: *Strabonis Geographica recognovit.* 3 vols. Leipzig, 1852. Various stereotype reprints since.

C. Müller—F. Dübner: *Strabonis Geographica graece cum versione reficta accedit index variantis lectionis et tabula rerum nominumque locupletissima.* Paris, 1853. Pars prior.

C. Müller—F. Dübner: *Pars altera.* *Apparatu critico indicibus rerum nominumque locupletissimis tabulis aeri incisis quindecim instruxit Carolus Müllerus.* Paris, 1858.

M. Bouquet: *Recueil des historiens des Gaules.* In vol. i. Paris, 1738.

P. Carolides: Γεωγραφικῶν τὰ περὶ Μικρᾶς ᾽Ασίας μετὰ Σημειώσεων ᾽Ερμηνευτικῶν. Athens, 1889.

E. Cougny: *Extraits des auteurs grecs concernant la géographie et l'histoire des Gaules. Texte et traduction nouvelle.* Paris, 1878.

H. F. Tozer: *Selections from Strabo, with an Introduction on Strabo's Life and Works.* Oxford, 1893.

Early Translations

The Latin translation by Guarinus Veronensis and Gregorius Tifernas appeared in Rome in 1472 (folio), more than forty years before the publication of the Aldine Greek text. The translation was made from better manuscripts than that used in the Aldine edition, but these have since perished. The first ten books were translated by Guarinus and the remainder by Tifernas. This translation was revised by J. Andreas

xlii

BIBLIOGRAPHY

(Venice 1480); edited and republished by A. Mancellinus
(Venice 1494); republished 1510; revised by C. Heresbach
(Basle 1523, folio); republished in Basle 1539 (folio); republished by M. Hopper in Lyons 1559 in two volumes;
republished in Amsterdam in 1652 in two volumes; and
the same translation appeared in the Basle edition of 1571
as revised by G. Xylander. The Latin of the translation
was so good that it supplanted, for a time, the Greek text,
but it has now been superseded by the Latin translation in
the Didot edition. The translation of the first six books is
by F. Dübner, and that of the other nine books by
C. Müller. At the suggestion of Napoleon I. the
publication of a translation into French was undertaken
by the French Government with the advice of the *Institut.*
The first fifteen books are by A. Corais and Laporte du
Theil, the sixteenth and seventeenth books are by A.
Letronne; the notes signed "G" are by Gosselin, and are
geographical in nature. The work was published in five
quarto volumes in Paris between the years 1805 and 1819.
The first German translation was made by A. J. Penzel,
Lemgo, 1775–1777. There is an Italian translation by
Ambrosoli, Milan 1834–1835 (I have not been able to
consult it).

TRANSLATIONS (*used by the present translator*)

The Latin Translation in the Müller-Dübner edition.
A. Buonaccivoli: *La geografia di Strabone tradotta in volgare
    Italiano* La prima parte in Venetia, 1662. La seconda
    parte in Ferrara, 1665.
E. Cougny: *Extraits des auteurs grecs concernant la géo-
    graphie et l'histoire des Gaules.* Texte et traduction
    nouvelle publiés pour la Société de l'histoire de France.
    Paris, 1878.
A. Forbiger: *Strabo's Erdbeschreibung übersetzt und durch
    Anmerkungen erläutert.* 4 vols. Stuttgart, 1856–1860.
    Stereotype reprints at intervals since (1905-1908).
C. G. Groskurd: *Strabons Erdbeschreibung in siebenzehn
    Büchern nach berichtigtem griechischen Texte unter
    Begleitung kritischer erklärender Anmerkungen verdeutscht.*
    4 vols. Berlin and Stettin, 1831-1834.

BIBLIOGRAPHY

H. C Hamilton and W. Falconer : *The Geography of Strabo,*
  literally translated. 3 vols. London (Bohn's Classical
  Library. Reprint, 1892-93).
K. Kärcher : *Strabo's Geographie übersetzt.* Stuttgart, 1851.
E. Malgeri : *Il VI. libro della geografia (antica Italia, Sicilia,
  Iapigia) tradotto e commentato.* Traduzione corredata
  di una indice geografico. Palermo, 1897.
de la Porte du Theil, A. Coray, et A. Letronne : *Géographie
  de Strabon, traduite du grec en français.* 5 vols. Paris,
  1805-1819.
G. Sottini : *Geografia dell' Italia antica tradotta e corredata
  di una introduzione e note per uso delle scuole classiche.*
  Pisa, 1882.
A. Tardieu : *Géographie de Strabon.* Traduction nouvelle.
  4 vols. Paris, 1909 (Third Edition).

STRABO'S ORIGIN, BIRTH, LIFE, TEACHERS, TRAVELS, DATE OF COMPOSITION OF HIS WORK

E. H. Bunbury : *History of Ancient Geography,* 1883, ii.
  209.
A. Forbiger : In his *Handbuch der alten Geographie,* i. 302.
G. Fritz : *De Strabone Stoicorum disciplinae addicto.*
  Münster, 1906.
A. Häbler : *Hat Strabo seine Geographie in Rom verfasst?*
  In *Hermes,* 1884, 235.
J. Hasenmüller : *De Strabonis geographi vita.* Bonn, 1863.
E. Meyer : *Geschichte des Königreichs Pontus.* Leipzig,
  1879.
P. Meyer : *Quaestiones Strabonianae.* In *Leipziger Studien,*
  ii. 49.
Th. Mommsen : *Res gestae divi Augusti.* Berlin, 1883.
B. Niese : *Beiträge zur Biographie Strabos.* In *Hermes,*
  1878, 33.
E. Pais : *The Time and Place in which Strabo composed his
  Geography.* In *Ancient Italy* (English translation).
  London, 1908, 379.
E. Pais : *Straboniana.* In *Rivista di Filologia,* 1886, 97.
W. Passow : *De Eratosthenis aetate.* In *Genethliacon
  Gottingense,* 1888, 122.
F. M. Schröter : *De Strabonis itineribus.* Leipzig, 1874.

xliv

BIBLIOGRAPHY

G. Siebelis: *De Strabonis patria, genere, aetate, operis instituto atque ratione qua vet. descripsit Graeciam.* Bautzen, 1828.

E. Stemplinger: *Strabons litterarhistorische Notizen.* München, 1894.

H. F. Tozer: *Selections from Strabo with an Introduction on Strabo's Life and Works.* Oxford, 1893.

C. H. Weller: *The Evidence for Strabo's Travels in Greece.* In *Classical Philology*, 1906, 339 ; see also *A.J.A.* 1906, 84.

RECENT WORK ON STRABO

For work done on Strabo year by year: J. Marouzeau, *L'Année Philologique*, should be consulted.

Three series are now in progress:

W. Aly, *Strabons Geographica in 17 Büchern.* Band IV. *Strabon von Amasea. Untersuchungen über Text, Aufbau, und Quellen der Geographica.* Bonn, 1956. This is the first to be published of several volumes (which will include text, translation, and commentary), and is important.

F. Lasserre, *Strabon, Géographie*, Vol. II (Vol. I not yet published), Books 3 and 4. Text, French translation, and notes. Budé. Paris, 1966. Vol. III, Books 5 and 6, 1967.

F. Sbordone, *S. Geographica.* Vol. I, Books 1 and 2. Rome, 1963.

Note also:

A. Schulten, *Estrabón, Geografía de Iberia.* Edition, translation, and commentary. *Fontes Hispaniae Antiquae* VI. Barcelona, 1952.

Germaine Aujac, *Strabon et la Science de son temps.* Paris, 1966.

J. O. Thomson, *History of Ancient Geography.* Cambridge, 1948, index s. v. Strabo.

BIBLIOGRAPHICAL ADDENDUM (1988)

Editions:

Several, under the editorship of the following, are in progress:

F. Lasserre, G. Aujac, and R. Baladié: Budé edition, Paris 1966 – (Tome I in two parts contains [a] Introduction and Book 1 and [b] Book 2); W. Aly: 1–4, Bonn 1968–; F. Sbordone: 1–6, Rome 1963–

Studies:

W. Aly: *Untersuchungen über Text, Aufbau und Quellen der Geographica: Strabonis Geographica IV*, Bonn 1957

R. Baladié: *Le Péloponnèse de Strabon*, Paris 1980

A. Diller: *The textual tradition of Strabo's Geography*, Amsterdam 1975

General:

D. R. Dicks: *Hipparchus: Geographical Fragments* (edited with commentary), London 1960

G. Sarton: *History of Science: Hellenistic Science and Culture in the Last Three Centuries B.C.* (especially vol. 2, pp. 413–433), Cambridge, Mass. 1959

J. O. Thomson: *A History of Ancient Geography*, Cambridge 1948

THE
GEOGRAPHY OF STRABO

BOOK I

ΣΤΡΑΒΩΝΟΣ ΓΕΩΓΡΑΦΙΚΩΝ

Α΄

I

C 1 1. Τῆς τοῦ φιλοσόφου πραγματείας εἶναι νομίζομεν, εἴπερ ἄλλην τινά, καὶ τὴν γεωγραφικήν, ἣν νῦν προῃρήμεθα ἐπισκοπεῖν. ὅτι δ᾽ οὐ φαύλως νομίζομεν, ἐκ πολλῶν δῆλον. οἵ τε γὰρ πρῶτοι θαρρήσαντες αὐτῆς ἅψασθαι τοιοῦτοι δή τινες[1] ὑπῆρξαν· Ὅμηρός τε καὶ Ἀναξίμανδρος ὁ Μιλήσιος καὶ Ἑκαταῖος, ὁ πολίτης αὐτοῦ, καθὼς καὶ Ἐρατοσθένης φησί· καὶ Δημόκριτος δὲ καὶ
C 2 Εὔδοξος καὶ Δικαίαρχος καὶ Ἔφορος καὶ ἄλλοι πλείους· ἔτι δὲ οἱ μετὰ τούτους, Ἐρατοσθένης τε καὶ Πολύβιος καὶ Ποσειδώνιος, ἄνδρες φιλόσοφοι. ἥ τε πολυμάθεια, δι᾽ ἧς μόνης ἐφικέσθαι τοῦδε τοῦ ἔργου δυνατόν, οὐκ ἄλλου τινός ἐστιν, ἢ τοῦ τὰ θεῖα καὶ τὰ ἀνθρώπεια ἐπιβλέποντος, ὧνπερ τὴν φιλοσοφίαν ἐπιστήμην φασίν. ὡς δ᾽ αὕτως καὶ ἡ ὠφέλεια ποικίλη τις οὖσα, ἡ μὲν πρὸς τὰς πολιτικὰς[2] καὶ τὰς ἡγεμονικὰς πράξεις, ἡ δὲ πρὸς ἐπιστήμην τῶν τε οὐρανίων καὶ τῶν ἐπὶ γῆς καὶ θαλάττης ζῴων καὶ φυτῶν καὶ καρπῶν καὶ τῶν

---

[1] τοιοῦτοι δή τινες, Corais, on MS. authority, for τοιοῦτοί τινες.   [2] τὰς πολιτικάς, Spengel, for τὰ πολιτικά.

THE GEOGRAPHY OF STRABO

BOOK I

I

1. THE science of Geography, which I now propose to investigate, is, I think, quite as much as any other science, a concern of the philosopher; and the correctness of my view is clear for many reasons. In the first place, those who in earliest times ventured to treat the subject were, in their way, philosophers —Homer, Anaximander of Miletus, and Anaximander's fellow-citizen Hecataeus—just as Eratosthenes has already said; philosophers, too, were Democritus, Eudoxus, Dicaearchus, Ephorus, with several others of their times; and further, their successors—Eratosthenes, Polybius, and Poseidonius—were philosophers. In the second place, wide learning, which alone makes it possible to undertake a work on geography, is possessed solely by the man who has investigated things both human and divine—knowledge of which, they say, constitutes philosophy. And so, too, the utility of geography—and its utility is manifold, not only as regards the activities of statesmen and commanders but also as regards knowledge both of the heavens and of things on land and sea, animals, plants, fruits, and everything else to be seen in

ἄλλων, ὅσα ἰδεῖν παρ' ἑκάστοις ἐστί, τὸν αὐτὸν
ὑπογράφει ἄνδρα, τὸν φροντίζοντα τῆς περὶ τὸν
βίον τέχνης καὶ εὐδαιμονίας.

2. Ἀναλαβόντες δὲ καθ' ἕκαστον ἐπισκοπῶμεν
τῶν εἰρημένων ἔτι μᾶλλον. καὶ πρῶτον ὅτι ὀρθῶς
ὑπειλήφαμεν καὶ ἡμεῖς καὶ οἱ πρὸ ἡμῶν, ὧν ἐστι
καὶ Ἵππαρχος, ἀρχηγέτην εἶναι τῆς γεωγραφικῆς
ἐμπειρίας Ὅμηρον· ὃς οὐ μόνον ἐν τῇ κατὰ τὴν
ποίησιν ἀρετῇ πάντας ὑπερβέβληται τοὺς πάλαι
καὶ τοὺς ὕστερον, ἀλλὰ σχεδόν τι καὶ τῇ κατὰ τὸν
βίον ἐμπειρίᾳ τὸν πολιτικόν, ἀφ' ἧς οὐ μόνον
περὶ τὰς πράξεις ἐσπούδασεν ἐκεῖνος, ὅπως ὅτι
πλείστας γνοίη καὶ παραδώσει τοῖς ὕστερον ἐσο-
μένοις, ἀλλὰ καὶ τὰ περὶ τοὺς τόπους τούς τε καθ'
ἕκαστα καὶ τοὺς κατὰ σύμπασαν τὴν οἰκουμένην,
γῆν τε καὶ θάλατταν. οὐ γὰρ ἂν μέχρι τῶν
ἐσχάτων αὐτῆς περάτων ἀφίκετο τῇ μνήμῃ κύκλῳ
περιιών.

3. Καὶ πρῶτον μὲν τῷ ὠκεανῷ περίκλυστον,
ὥσπερ ἐστίν, ἀπέφαινεν αὐτήν· ἔπειτα δὲ τῶν
χωρίων τὰ μὲν ὠνόμαζε, τὰ δὲ ὑπηνίττετο τεκμη-
ρίοις τισί, Λιβύην μὲν καὶ Αἰθιοπίαν καὶ Σιδονίους καὶ Ἐρεμβούς, οὓς εἰκὸς λέγειν Τρωγλοδύτας
Ἄραβας, ῥητῶς λέγων, τοὺς δὲ πρὸς ταῖς ἀνατολαῖς καὶ δύσεσιν αἰνιττόμενος ἐκ τοῦ τῷ ὠκεανῷ
κλύζεσθαι. ἐντεῦθεν γὰρ ἀνίσχοντα ποιεῖ τὸν

---

[1] For Strabo's definition of Libya see 17. 3. 1.

various regions—the utility of geography, I say, presupposes in the geographer the same philosopher, the man who busies himself with the investigation of the art of life, that is, of happiness.

2. But I must go back and consider each one of these points in greater detail; and, first, I say that both I and my predecessors, one of whom was Hipparchus himself, are right in regarding Homer as the founder of the science of geography; for Homer has surpassed all men, both of ancient and modern times, not only in the excellence of his poetry, but also, I might say, in his acquaintance with all that pertains to public life. And this acquaintance made him busy himself not only about public activities, to the end that he might learn of as many of them as possible and give an account of them to posterity, but also about the geography both of the individual countries and of the inhabited world at large, both land and sea; for otherwise he would not have gone to the uttermost bounds of the inhabited world, encompassing the whole of it in his description.

3. In the first place, Homer declares that the inhabited world is washed on all sides by Oceanus, and this is true; and then he mentions some of the countries by name, while he leaves us to infer the other countries from hints; for instance, he expressly mentions Libya,[1] Ethiopia, Sidonians, and Erembians—and by Erembians he probably means Arabian Troglodytes [2]—whereas he only indicates in general terms the people who live in the far east and the far west by saying that their countries are washed by Oceanus. For he makes the sun to

[2] "Cave-dwellers." They lived on the western shores of the Red Sea.

ἥλιον καὶ δυόμενον εἰς τοῦτον, ὡς δ' αὕτως καὶ τὰ
ἄστρα·

ἠέλιος μὲν ἔπειτα νεον προσέβαλλεν ἀρούρας,[1]
ἐξ ἀκαλαρρείταο βαθυρρόου Ὠκεανοῖο.
(Il. 7. 421)

ἐν δ' ἔπεσ' Ὠκεανῷ λαμπρὸν φάος ἠελίοιο,
ἕλκον νύκτα μέλαιναν.[2]
(Il. 8. 485)

καὶ τοὺς ἀστέρας δὲ[3] λελουμένους ἐξ ὠκεανοῦ
λέγειν. (Il. 5. 6)

4. Τῶν δ' ἑσπερίων ἀνδρῶν καὶ τὴν εὐδαιμονίαν
ἐμφανίζει καὶ τὴν εὐκρασίαν τοῦ περιέχοντος,
πεπυσμένος, ὡς ἔοικε, τὸν Ἰβηρικὸν πλοῦτον, ἐφ'
ὃν καὶ Ἡρακλῆς ἐστράτευσε καὶ οἱ Φοίνικες ὕστερον, οἵπερ ἀρχὴν[4] καὶ κατέσχον τὴν πλείστην·
μετὰ δὲ ταῦτα Ῥωμαῖοι. ἐνταῦθα γὰρ αἱ τοῦ
C 3 Ζεφύρου πνοαί. ἐνταῦθα δὲ καὶ τὸ Ἠλύσιον
ποιεῖ πεδίον ὁ ποιητής, εἰς ὃ πεμφθήσεσθαί φησι
τὸν Μενέλαον ὑπὸ τῶν θεῶν·

ἀλλά σ' ἐς Ἠλύσιον πεδίον καὶ πείρατα γαίης
ἀθάνατοι πέμψουσιν, ὅθι ξανθὸς Ῥαδάμανθυς,
τῇ περ ῥηΐστη βιοτὴ πέλει·
οὐ νιφετός, οὔτ' ἄρ χειμὼν πολύς,
ἀλλ' αἰεὶ Ζεφύροιο λιγὺ πνείοντος[5] ἀήτας
Ὠκεανὸς ἀνίησι.
(Od. 4. 563)

5. Καὶ αἱ τῶν μακάρων δὲ νῆσοι πρὸ τῆς
Μαυρουσίας εἰσὶ τῆς ἐσχάτης πρὸς δύσιν, καθ'

---

[1] ἀρούρας, the reading of B, for ἀρούραις.
[2] Meineke deletes both quotations; C. Müller, Cobet,
approving; A. Miller defends the quotations.
[3] δέ, Cobet inserts, after ἀστέρας.

rise out of Oceanus and to set in Oceanus; and he refers in the same way to the constellations: "Now the sun was just beating on the fields as he climbed heaven from the deep stream of gently-flowing Oceanus." "And the sun's bright light dropped into Oceanus, drawing black night across the earth." And he declares that the stars also rise from Oceanus "after having bathed in Oceanus."

4. As for the people of the west, Homer makes plain that they were prosperous and that they lived in a temperate climate—doubtless having heard of the wealth of Iberia,[1] and how, in quest of that wealth, Heracles invaded the country, and after him the Phoenicians also, the people who in earliest times became masters of most of the country (it was at a later date that the Romans occupied it). For in the west the breezes of Zephyrus blow; and there it is that Homer places the Elysian Plain itself, to which he declares Menelaus will be sent by the gods: "But the deathless gods will convey thee to the Elysian Plain and the ends of the earth, where is Rhadamanthys of the fair hair, where life is easiest. No snow is there, nor yet great storm; but always Oceanus sendeth forth the breezes of the clear-blowing[2] Zephyrus."

5. And, too, the Islands of the Blest[3] lie to the westward of most western Maurusia,[4] that is, west

---

[1] What is now Portugal and Spain.
[2] See page 107.
[3] Strabo has in mind the Canary Islands.
[4] That is, Morocco, approximately.

---

[4] ἀρχήν, A. Miller transposes, from its position after τὴν πλείστην, and makes it the adverb.
[5] λιγὺ πνείοντος, Sterrett, for λιγυπνείοντας.

ὃ μέρος συντρέχει καὶ τῷ[1] τῆς Ἰβηρίας τὸ ταύτης πέρας· ἐκ δὲ τοῦ ὀνόματος δῆλον, ὅτι καὶ ταύτας ἐνόμιζον εὐδαίμονας διὰ τὸ πλησιάζειν τοιούτοις χωρίοις.

6. Ἀλλὰ μὴν ὅτι γε καὶ οἱ Αἰθίοπες ἐπὶ τῷ ὠκεανῷ ἔσχατοι, δηλοῖ· ὅτι μὲν ἔσχατοι,

Αἰθίοπας, τοὶ διχθὰ δεδαίαται, ἔσχατοι ἀνδρῶν,
(Od. 1. 23)

οὐδὲ τοῦ "διχθὰ δεδαίαται" φαύλως λεγομένου, ὡς δειχθήσεται ὕστερον· ὅτι δ' ἐπὶ τῷ ὠκεανῷ,

Ζεὺς γὰρ ἐς Ὠκεανὸν μετ' ἀμύμονας Αἰθιοπῆας
χθιζὸς ἔβη μετὰ δαῖτα. (Il. 1. 423)

ὅτι δὲ καὶ ἡ πρὸς ταῖς ἄρκτοις ἐσχατιὰ παρω-κεανῖτίς ἐστιν, οὕτως ᾐνίξατο εἰπὼν περὶ τῆς ἄρκτου·

οἴη δ' ἄμμορός ἐστι λοετρῶν Ὠκεανοῖο.
(Il. 18. 489 ; Od. 5. 275)

διὰ μὲν γὰρ τῆς ἄρκτου καὶ τῆς ἁμάξης τὸν ἀρκτικὸν δηλοῖ· οὐ γὰρ ἂν τοσούτων ἀστέρων ἐν τῷ αὐτῷ χωρίῳ περιφερομένων τῷ ἀεὶ φανερῷ οἴηι ἄμμορον εἶπε λοετρῶν ὠκεανοῖο. ὥστ' οὐκ εὖ ἀπειρίαν ἰυτοῦ καταγινώσκουσιν, ὡς μίαν ἄρκτον ἀντὶ δυεῖν εἰδότος· οὐδὲ γὰρ εἰκὸς ἦν πω τὴν ἑτέραν ἠστροθετῆσθαι, ἀλλ' ἀφ' οὗ οἱ Φοί-νικες ἐσημειώσαντο καὶ ἐχρῶντο πρὸς τὸν πλοῦν, παρελθεῖν καὶ εἰς τοὺς Ἕλληνας τὴν διάταξιν ταύτην, ὥσπερ καὶ τὸν Βερενίκης πλόκαμον, καὶ τὸν Κάνωβον, ἐχθὲς καὶ πρῴην κατωνομασμένον

[1] τῷ, Jones inserts.

8

of the region where the end of Maurusia runs close to that of Iberia. And their name shows that because those islands were near to blessed countries they too were thought to be blessed abodes.

6. Furthermore, Homer assuredly makes it plain that the Ethiopians live at the ends of the earth, on the banks of Oceanus: that they live at the end of the earth, when he speaks of "the Ethiopians that are sundered in twain, the farthermost of men" (and indeed the words "are sundered in twain" are not carelessly used, as will be shown later on); and that they live on the banks of Oceanus, when he says "for Zeus went yesterday to Oceanus, unto the noble Ethiopians for a feast." And he has left us to infer that the farthest land in the north is also bounded by Oceanus when he says of the Bear that "She alone hath no part in the baths of Oceanus." That is, by the terms "Bear" and "Wain" he means the "arctic circle"[1]; for otherwise he would not have said of the Bear that "She alone hath no part in the baths of Oceanus," since so many stars complete their diurnal revolutions in that same quarter of the heavens which was always visible to him. So it is not well for us to accuse him of ignorance on the ground that he knew of but one Bear instead of two; for it is likely that in the time of Homer the other Bear had not yet been marked out as a constellation, and that the star-group did not become known as such to the Greeks until the Phoenicians so designated it and used it for purposes of navigation; the same is true of Berenice's Hair and of Canopus, for we know that these two constellations have received

[1] For the meaning of the term "arctic circle" among the ancients, see 2. 2. 2 and footnote.

ἴσμεν,[1] πολλοὺς δ' ἔτι νῦν ἀνωνύμους ὄντας,
καθάπερ καὶ Ἄρατός φησιν (Phaen. 146). οὐδὲ
Κράτης οὖν ὀρθῶς γράφει,

οἶος δ' ἄμμορός ἐστι λοετρῶν

φεύγων τὰ μὴ φευκτά. βελτίων δ' Ἡράκλειτος
καὶ ὁμηρικώτερος, ὁμοίως ἀντὶ τοῦ ἀρκτικοῦ τὴν
ἄρκτον ὀνομάζων· "ἠοῦς καὶ ἑσπέρης[2] τέρματα ἡ
ἄρκτος, καὶ ἀντίον τῆς ἄρκτου οὖρος αἰθρίου
Διός." ὁ γὰρ ἀρκτικός ἐστι δύσεως καὶ ἀνατολῆς
C 4 ὅρος, οὐχ ἡ ἄρκτος. διὰ μὲν δὴ τῆς ἄρκτου, ἣν
καὶ ἄμαξαν καλεῖ καὶ τὸν Ὠρίωνα δοκεύειν φησί
(Od. 5. 274), τὸν ἀρκτικὸν δηλοῖ· διὰ δὲ τοῦ
ὠκεανοῦ τὸν ὁρίζοντα, εἰς ὃν καὶ ἐξ οὗ τὰς δύσεις
καὶ τὰς ἀνατολὰς ποιεῖ.[3] εἰπὼν δὲ αὐτοῦ στρέ-
φεσθαι καὶ ἀμοιρεῖν τοῦ ὠκεανοῦ οἶδεν ὅτι κατὰ
σημεῖον τὸ ἀρκτικώτατον τοῦ ὁρίζοντος γίνεται ὁ
ἀρκτικός. ἀκολούθως δὴ τούτῳ τὸ ποιητικὸν
ἁρμόσαντες τὸν μὲν ὁρίζοντα ὀφείλομεν δέχεσθαι
τὸν ἐπὶ τῆς γῆς οἰκείως τῷ ὠκεανῷ, τὸν δ' ἀρκτικὸν
τῆς γῆς ἁπτόμενον ὡς ἂν πρὸς αἴσθησιν κατὰ τὸ
ἀρκτικώτατον τῆς οἰκήσεως σημεῖον· ὥστε καὶ
τοῦτο τὸ μέρος τῆς γῆς κλύζοιτ' ἂν τῷ ὠκεανῷ

---

[1] ἴσμεν, A. Miller inserts ; A. Vogel approving in part.
[2] ἑσπέρης, Corais, for ἑσπέρος ; Meineke following ;
C. Müller, Cobet, approving.
[3] ποιεῖ, A. Miller, for ποιεῖται ; A. Vogel approving.

their names quite recently, and that there are many
constellations still unnamed, just as Aratus says.
Therefore Crates is not correct, either, when, in
seeking to avoid what needs no avoidance, he alters
the text of Homer so as to make it read, "And the
arctic circle [1] alone hath no part in the baths of
Oceanus." Better and more Homeric is Heracleitus,
who likewise employs "the Bear" for "the arctic
circle": "The Bear forms limits of morning and
evening, and over against the Bear fair breezes blow
from fair skies" [2]; for the arctic circle, and not the
Bear, forms a boundary beyond which the stars neither
rise nor set. Accordingly, by "the Bear," which he
also calls "the Wain" and describes as keeping watch
upon Orion, Homer means the "arctic circle," and
by Oceanus he means the horizon into which he
makes the stars to set and from which he makes them
to rise. And when he says that the Bear makes its
revolution in that region without having a part in
Oceanus, he knows that the arctic circle touches the
most northerly point of the horizon. If we construe
the poet's verse in this way, then we should interpret
the terrestrial horizon as closely corresponding to
Oceanus, and the arctic circle as touching the earth
—if we may believe the evidence of our senses—at
its most northerly inhabited point. And so, in the
opinion of Homer, this part of the earth also is

---

[1] Crates emended Homer's feminine form of the adjective
for "alone" (οἴη) to the masculine form (οἶος), so as to make
it agree with "arctic circle" and not with "Bear."

[2] Heracleitus, with his usual obscurity, divides the heavens
roughly into four quarters, viz.: the Bear (north), morning
(east), evening (west), and the region opposite the Bear
(south). Strabo's interpretation of Heracleitus as regards
the "arctic circle" is altogether reasonable.

κατ᾽ αὐτόν. καὶ τοὺς ἀνθρώπους δὲ οἶδε τοὺς
προσβόρρους¹ μάλιστα, οὓς ὀνομαστὶ μὲν οὐ
δηλοῖ (οὐδὲ γὰρ νῦν που κοινὸν αὐτοῖς ὄνομα
κεῖται πᾶσι), τῇ διαίτῃ δὲ φράζει, νομάδας αὐτοὺς
ὑπογράφων καὶ " ἀγαυοὺς ἱππημολγοὺς γαλακτο-
φάγους ἀβίους² τε" (Il. 13. 5, 6).

7. Καὶ ἄλλως δ᾽ ἐμφαίνει τὸ κύκλῳ περικεῖσθαι
τῇ γῇ τὸν ὠκεανόν, ὅταν οὕτω φῇ ἡ Ἥρα·

εἶμι γὰρ ὀψομένη πολυφόρβου πείρατα γαίης
Ὠκεανόν τε θεῶν γένεσιν. (Il. 14. 200, cf. 301)

τοῖς γὰρ πέρασι πᾶσι συνῆφθαι³ λέγει τὸν ὠκε-
ανόν· τὰ δὲ πέρατα κύκλῳ περίκειται (Il. 18. 607).
ἔν τε τῇ ὁπλοποιίᾳ τῆς Ἀχιλλέως ἀσπίδος κύκλῳ
περιτίθησι τὸν ὠκεανὸν ἐπὶ τῆς ἴτυος. ἔχεται δὲ
τῆς αὐτῆς φιλοπραγμοσύνης καὶ τὸ μὴ ἀγνοεῖν τὰ
περὶ τὰς πλημμυρίδας τοῦ ὠκεανοῦ καὶ τὰς ἀμπώτεις, " ἀψορρόου Ὠκεανοῖο" (Il. 18. 399) λέ-
γοντα⁴ καὶ

τρὶς μὲν γάρ τ᾽ ἀνίησιν ἐπ᾽ ἤματι, τρὶς δ᾽
ἀναροιβδεῖ. (Od. 12. 105)

καὶ γὰρ εἰ μὴ τρίς, ἀλλὰ δίς, τάχα τῆς ἱστορίας
παραπαίσαντος,⁵ ἢ τῆς γραφῆς διημαρτημένης·
ἀλλ᾽ ἥ γε προαίρεσις τοιαύτη. καὶ τὸ "ἐξ ἀκαλαρρείταο" (Il. 7. 422) δὲ ἔχει τινὰ ἔμφασιν τῆς
πλημμυρίδος, ἐχούσης τὴν ἐπίβασιν πραεῖαν καὶ

---

¹ προσβόρρους, Meineke, for προσβορέους; C. Müller approving.   ² Ἄβιοι is a proper name in Homer.
³ συνῆφθαι, Madvig, for συνήθη; Cobet approving.
⁴ λέγοντα, editors before Kramer (who reads λέγοντι);
Meineke restores; C. Müller approving.
⁵ παραπαίσαντος, Cobet, for παραπεσόντος.

washed by Oceanus. Furthermore, Homer knows of the men who live farthest north; and while he does not mention them by name—and even to the present day there is no common term that will embrace them all—he characterises them by their mode of life, describing them as "nomads," and as "proud mare-milkers, curd-eaters, and a resourceless folk."

7. In other ways, too, Homer indicates that Oceanus surrounds the earth, as when Hera says as follows: "For I am going to visit the limits of the bountiful earth, and Oceanus, father of the gods." By these words he means that Oceanus touches all the extremities of the earth; and these extremities form a circle round the earth. Again, in the story of the making of the arms of Achilles, Homer places Oceanus in a circle round the outer edge of the shield of Achilles. It is another proof of the same eagerness for knowledge that Homer was not ignorant about the ebb and flow of the tide of Oceanus; for he speaks of "Oceanus that floweth ever back upon himself," and also says: "For thrice a day she[1] spouts it forth, and thrice a day she sucks it down." For even if it be "twice" and not "thrice"—it may be that Homer really strayed from the fact on this point, or else that there is a corruption in the text[2] —the principle of his assertion remains the same. And even the phrase "gently-flowing" contains a reference to the flood-tide, which comes with a gentle

---

[1] Homer here refers to Charybdis. Strabo himself seems to be doing Homer an injustice by confusing the behaviour of Charybdis with the tides of O anus.

[2] See 1. 2. 16, where Polybius is referred to as making a similar statement.

οὐ τελέως ῥοώδη. Ποσειδώνιος δὲ καὶ ἐκ τοῦ σκοπέλους λέγειν τοτὲ μὲν καλυπτομένους, τοτὲ δὲ γυμνουμένους, καὶ ἐκ τοῦ ποταμὸν φάναι τὸν ὠκεανὸν εἰκάζει τὸ ῥοῶδες αὐτοῦ τὸ περὶ τὰς πλημμυρίδας ἐμφανίζεσθαι (Il. 14. 245). τὸ μὲν οὖν πρῶτον εὖ, τὸ δὲ δεύτερον οὐκ ἔχει λόγον· οὔτε γὰρ ποταμίῳ ῥεύματι ἔοικεν ἡ τῆς πλημμυρίδος ἐπίβασις, πολὺ δὲ μᾶλλον ἡ ἀναχώρησις οὐ τοιαύτη. ὅ τε τοῦ Κράτητος λόγος διδάσκει τι πιθανώτερον. βαθύρρουν μὲν γὰρ καὶ ἄψορρον (Od. 11. 13; 20. 65) λέγει, ὁμοίως δὲ καὶ ποταμὸν C 5 τὸν ὅλον ὠκεανόν· λέγει δὲ καὶ μέρος τοῦ ὠκεανοῦ τι ποταμὸν καὶ ποταμοῖο ῥόον, οὐ τοῦ ὅλου, ἀλλὰ τοῦ μέρους, ὅταν οὕτω φῇ·

αὐτὰρ ἐπεὶ ποταμοῖο λίπεν ῥόον Ὠκεανοῖο
νηῦς, ἀπὸ δ᾽ ἵκετο κῦμα θαλάσσης εὐρυπόροιο.
(Od. 12. 1)

οὐ γὰρ τὸν ὅλον, ἀλλὰ τὸν ἐν τῷ ὠκεανῷ τοῦ ποταμοῦ ῥόον μέρος ὄντα τοῦ ὠκεανοῦ, ὅν φησιν ὁ Κράτης ἀνάχυσίν τινα καὶ κόλπον ἐπὶ τὸν νότιον πόλον ἀπὸ τοῦ χειμερινοῦ τροπικοῦ διήκοντα. τοῦτον γὰρ δύναιτ᾽ ἄν τις ἐκλιπὼν ἔτι εἶναι ἐν τῷ ὠκεανῷ· τὸν δὲ ὅλον ἐκλιπόντα ἔτι εἶναι ἐν τῷ ὅλῳ, οὐχ οἷόν τε. Ὅμηρος δέ γε οὕτω φησί·

"ποταμοῖο λίπεν ῥόον, ἀπὸ δ᾽ ἵκετο κῦμα
θαλάσσης,"

ἥτις οὐκ ἄλλη τίς ἐστιν, ἀλλὰ ὠκεανός. γίνεται οὖν, ἐὰν ἄλλως δέχῃ, ἐκβὰς ἐκ τοῦ ὠκεανοῦ, ἦλθεν εἰς τὸν ὠκεανόν. ἀλλὰ ταῦτα μὲν μακροτέρας ἐστὶ διαίτης.

swell, and not with a violent current. Poseidonius conjectures both from Homer's reference to the head-lands as sometimes covered with the waves and some-times bare, and from his calling Oceanus a river, that by the current of Oceanus Homer is indicating the flow of the tides. The first conjecture of Poseidonius is correct, but the second is unreasonable. For the swell of the tide is not like a stream of a river, and still less so is the ebb. The explanation given by Crates is more plausible. Homer speaks of the whole of Oceanus as "deep-flowing" and "back-flowing," and, likewise, as being a river; he also speaks of a part of Oceanus as a river, or as a "river-stream"; and he is speaking of a part of Oceanus, and not of the whole, when he says: "Now after the ship had left the river-stream of Oceanus, and was come to the wave of the wide sea." Not the whole, I say, but the stream of the river, which stream is in Oceanus, being therefore a part of it; and this stream, Crates says, is a sort of estuary or gulf, which stretches from the winter tropic[1] in the direction of the south pole. Indeed, one might leave this estuary and still be in Oceanus; but it is not possible for a man to leave the whole and still be in the whole. At any rate Homer says: "The ship had left the river-stream, and was come to the wave of the sea," where "the sea" is surely nothing other than Ocean-us; if you interpret it otherwise, the assertion be-comes: "After Odysseus had gone out of Oceanus, he came into Oceanus." But that is a matter to be discussed at greater length.

[1] Strabo placed the "summer tropic" and "winter tropic" respectively at 24° north and south of the equator. They correspond, therefore, pretty closely to our Tropic of Cancer and Tropic of Capricorn.

8. Ὅτι δὲ ἡ οἰκουμένη νῆσός ἐστι, πρῶτον μὲν ἐκ τῆς αἰσθήσεως καὶ τῆς πείρας ληπτέον. πανταχῇ γάρ, ὁπουποτοῦν ἐφικτὸν γέγονεν ἀνθρώποις ἐπὶ τὰ ἔσχατα τῆς γῆς προελθεῖν, εὑρίσκεται θάλαττα, ἣν δὴ καλοῦμεν ὠκεανόν. καὶ ὅπου δὲ τῇ αἰσθήσει λαβεῖν οὐχ ὑπῆρξεν, ὁ λόγος δείκνυσι. τὸ μὲν γὰρ ἑωθινὸν πλευρόν, τὸ κατὰ τοὺς Ἰνδούς, καὶ τὸ ἑσπέριον, τὸ κατὰ τοὺς Ἴβηρας καὶ τοὺς Μαυρουσίους, περιπλεῖται πᾶν ἐπὶ πολὺ τοῦ τε νοτίου μέρους καὶ τοῦ βορείου· τὸ δὲ λειπόμενον ἄπλουν ἡμῖν μέχρι νῦν τῷ μὴ συμμῖξαι μηδένας ἀλλήλοις τῶν ἀντιπεριπλεόντων οὐ πολύ, εἴ τις συντίθησιν ἐκ τῶν παραλλήλων διαστημάτων τῶν ἐφικτῶν ἡμῖν. οὐκ εἰκὸς δὲ διθάλαττον εἶναι τὸ πέλαγος τὸ Ἀτλαντικόν, ἰσθμοῖς διειργόμενον οὕτω στενοῖς τοῖς κωλύουσι τὸν περίπλουν, ἀλλὰ μᾶλλον σύρρουν καὶ συνεχές. οἵ τε γὰρ περιπλεῖν ἐπιχειρήσαντες,[1] εἶτα ἀναστρέψαντες, οὐχ ὑπὸ ἠπείρου τινὸς ἀντιπιπτούσης καὶ κωλυούσης τὸν ἐπέκεινα πλοῦν ἀνακρουσθῆναι φασίν, ἀλλὰ ὑπο ἀπορίας καὶ ἐρημίας, οὐδὲν ἧττον τῆς θαλάττης ἐχούσης τὸν πόρον. τοῖς τε πάθεσι τοῦ ὠκεανοῦ τοῖς περὶ τὰς ἀμπώτεις καὶ τὰς πλημμυρίδας ὁμολογεῖ τοῦτο μᾶλλον· πάντη γοῦν ὁ αὐτὸς τρόπος τῶν[2] μεταβολῶν ὑπάρχει καὶ τῶν αὐξήσεων

---

[1] ἐπιχειρήσαντες, the reading of the MSS., is retained; C. Müller approving. Dübner and Meineke read ἐγχειρήσαντες.

[2] τε, A. Miller deletes, before μεταβολῶν.

8. We may learn both from the evidence of our senses and from experience that the inhabited world is an island; for wherever it has been possible for man to reach the limits of the earth, sea has been found, and this sea we call "Oceanus." And wherever we have not been able to learn by the evidence of our senses, there reason points the way. For example, as to the eastern (Indian) side of the inhabited earth, and the western (Iberian and Maurusian) side, one may sail wholly around them and continue the voyage for a considerable distance along the northern and southern regions; and as for the rest of the distance around the inhabited earth which has not been visited by us up to the present time (because of the fact that the navigators who sailed in opposite directions towards each other never met), it is not of very great extent, if we reckon from the parallel distances that have been traversed by us. It is unlikely that the Atlantic Ocean is divided into two seas, thus being separated by isthmuses so narrow and that prevent the circumnavigation; it is more likely that it is one confluent and continuous sea. For those who undertook circumnavigation, and turned back without having achieved their purpose, say that they were made to turn back, not because of any continent that stood in their way and hindered their further advance, inasmuch as the sea still continued open as before, but because of their destitution and loneliness. This theory accords better, too, with the behaviour of the ocean, that is, in respect of the ebb and flow of the tides; everywhere, at all events, the same principle, or else one that does not vary much, accounts for the changes both of high tide and low

καὶ μειώσεων, ἢ οὐ πολὺ παραλλάττων, ὡς ἂν ἐφ᾽[1]
ἑνὸς πελάγους τῆς κινήσεως ἀποδιδομένης καὶ ἀπὸ
μιᾶς αἰτίας.

9. Ἵππαρχος δ᾽ οὐ πιθανός ἐστιν ἀντιλέγων τῇ
δόξῃ ταύτῃ, ὡς οὔθ᾽ ὁμοιοπαθοῦντος τοῦ ὠκεανοῦ
C 6 παντελῶς, οὔτ᾽, εἰ δοθείη τοῦτο, ἀκολουθοῦντος
αὐτῷ τοῦ σύρρουν εἶναι πᾶν τὸ κύκλῳ πέλαγος
τὸ Ἀτλαντικόν, πρὸς τὸ μὴ ὁμοιοπαθεῖν μάρτυρι
χρώμενος Σελεύκῳ τῷ Βαβυλωνίῳ. ἡμεῖς δὲ τὸν
μὲν πλείω λόγον περὶ τοῦ ὠκεανοῦ καὶ τῶν
πλημμυρίδων εἰς Ποσειδώνιον ἀναβαλλόμεθα καὶ
Ἀθηνόδωρον, ἱκανῶς διευκρινήσαντας[2] τὸν περὶ
τούτων λόγον· πρὸς δὲ τὰ νῦν ἐπὶ τοσοῦτον λέγομεν, ὅτι πρός τε τὴν ὁμοιοπάθειαν οὕτω βέλτιον
νομίσαι· τά τε οὐράνια συνέχοιτ᾽ ἂν κρεῖττον ταῖς
ἐντεῦθεν ἀναθυμιάσεσιν, εἰ πλεῖον εἴη τὸ ὑγρὸν
περικεχυμένον.

10. Ὥσπερ οὖν τὰ ἔσχατα καὶ τὰ κύκλῳ τῆς
οἰκουμένης οἶδε καὶ φράζει σαφῶς ὁ ποιητής,
οὕτω καὶ τὰ τῆς θαλάττης τῆς ἐντός. περιέχει
γὰρ ταύτην ἀπὸ Στηλῶν ἀρξαμένοις Λιβύη τε καὶ
Αἴγυπτος καὶ Φοινίκη, ἑξῆς δὲ ἡ περαία[3] τῆς
Κύπρου, εἶτα Σόλυμοι καὶ Λύκιοι καὶ Κᾶρες,
μετὰ δὲ τούτους ἡ μεταξὺ Μυκάλης καὶ τῆς
Τρῳάδος ἠὼν[4] καὶ αἱ προκείμεναι νῆσοι, ὧν

---

[1] ἐφ᾽, Corais, for ἐπί; C. Müller approving.
[2] διευκρινήσαντας, R. Hercher and Piccolos independently,
for διακρατήσαντας; C. Müller and A. Vogel approving in
part. Corais reads διακροτήσαντας, C. Müller approving;
Kramer διακρατύναντας; Meineke διακριβώσαντας (E. Stemplinger, L. Kayser, approving) or διασαφήσαντας; Madvig
διαιτήσαντας.
[3] περαία, Madvig, for πέριξ.   [4] ἠών, Meineke, for ἠιών.

18

tide,[1] as would be the case if their movements were produced by one sea and were the result of one cause.

9. Hipparchus is not convincing when he con-tradicts this view on the ground, first, that the ocean does not behave uniformly throughout, and, secondly, that, even if this be granted, it does not follow that the Atlantic Ocean runs round the earth in one un-broken circle. In support of his opinion that the ocean does not behave uniformly he appeals to the authority of Seleucus of Babylon. But for a further discussion of the ocean and its tides I refer the reader to Poseidonius and Athenodorus, who have examined the argument on this subject with thoroughness. For my present purpose I merely add that it is better to accept this view of the uniform behaviour of the ocean; and that the farther the mass of water may extend around the earth, the better the heavenly bodies will be held together by the vapours that arise therefrom.[2]

10. Homer, then, knows and clearly describes the remote ends of the inhabited earth and what surrounds it; and he is just as familiar with the regions of the Mediterranean Sea. For if you begin at the Pillars of Heracles,[3] you will find that the Mediterranean Sea is bounded by Libya, Egypt, and Phoenicia, and further on by the part of the continent lying over against Cyprus; then by the territory of the Solymi, by Lycia, and by Caria, and next by the seaboard between Mycale and the Troad, together with the islands adjacent thereto; and all these lands are

[1] See 1. 3. 7. and 1. 3. 12. [2] A doctrine of the Stoics.
[3] See 3. 5. 5 for the different conceptions of what the Pillars were.

ἁπάντων[1] μέμνηται καὶ ἐφεξῆς τῶν περὶ τὴν
Προποντίδα καὶ τοῦ Εὐξείνου[2] μέχρι Κολχίδος
καὶ τῆς Ἰάσονος στρατείας. καὶ μὴν καὶ τὸν
Κιμμερικὸν Βόσπορον οἶδε, τοὺς Κιμμερίους εἰδώς·
οὐ δήπου τὸ μὲν ὄνομα τῶν Κιμμερίων εἰδώς,
αὐτοὺς δὲ ἀγνοῶν, οἳ κατ᾽ αὐτὸν ἢ μικρὸν πρὸ
αὐτοῦ μέχρι Ἰωνίας ἐπέδραμον τὴν γῆν τὴν ἐκ
βοσπόρου πᾶσαν. αἰνίττεται γοῦν καὶ τὸ κλίμα
τῆς χώρας αὐτῶν ζοφῶδες ὄν, καὶ ὥς φησίν,

> ἠέρι καὶ νεφέλῃ κεκαλυμμένοι· οὐδέ ποτ᾽ αὐτοὺς
> Ἥλιος φαέθων ἐπιδέρκεται,[3]
> ἀλλ᾽ ἐπὶ νὺξ ὀλοὴ τέταται. (Od. 11. 15, 19)

γνωρίζει δὲ καὶ τὸν Ἴστρον, μεμνημένος γε[4] Μυσῶν, ἔθνους Θρᾳκίου παροικοῦντος τὸν Ἴστρον.
καὶ μὴν καὶ τὴν ἑξῆς παραλίαν οἶδε, Θρᾳκίαν
οὖσαν, μέχρι Πηνειοῦ, Παίονάς τε ὀνομάζων καὶ
Ἄθω καὶ Ἀξιὸν καὶ τὰς προκειμένας τούτων
νήσους. ἑξῆς δέ ἐστιν ἡ τῶν Ἑλλήνων παραλία
μέχρι Θεσπρωτῶν, ἧς ἁπάσης μέμνηται. καὶ μὴν
καὶ τὰ τῆς Ἰταλίας ἄκρα οἶδε, Τεμέσην καλῶν
καὶ Σικελούς,[5] καὶ τὰ τῆς Ἰβηρίας ἄκρα καὶ τὴν
εὐδαιμονίαν αὐτῶν, ἣν ἀρτίως ἔφαμεν. εἰ δέ τινα
ἐν τοῖς μεταξὺ διαλείμματα φαίνεται, συγγνοίη
τις ἄν· καὶ γὰρ ὁ γεωγραφῶν ὄντως πολλὰ παρ-
ίησι τῶν ἐν μέρει. συγγνοίη δ᾽ ἄν, καὶ εἰ μυθώδη
τινὰ προσπέπλεκται τοῖς λεγομένοις ἱστορικῶς

---

[1] ἁπάντων, Casaubon, for ἁπασῶν; Kramer, Groskurd,
Forbiger, Tardieu, Meineke, following.
[2] τά, Meineke deletes, before μέχρι; C. Müller approving.
[3] ἐπιδέρκεται, C. Müller restores, for the usual reading
καταδέρκεται, from the MSS. of the Odyssey.

mentioned by Homer, as well as those farther on,
about the Propontis and the Euxine Sea as far as
Colchis and the limits of Jason's expedition; more
than that, he knows the Cimmerian Bosporus, because
he knows the Cimmerians—for surely, if he knows
the name of the Cimmerians, he is not ignorant of
the people themselves—the Cimmerians who, in
Homer's own time or shortly before his time, overran the whole country from the Bosporus to Ionia.
At least he intimates that the very climate of their
country is gloomy, and the Cimmerians, as he says, are
" shrouded in mist and in cloud, and never does the
shining sun look upon them, but deadly night is spread
o'er them." Homer also knows of the River Ister,[1]
since he mentions Mysians, a Thracian tribe that
lives on the Ister. More than that, he knows the
sea-board next to the Ister, on the Thracian side, as
far as the Peneus[2] River; for he speaks of Paeonians,
of Athos and Axius,[3] and of their neighbouring
islands. And next comes the sea-board of Greece, as
far as Thesprotia, which he mentions in its entirety.
And yet more, he knows the promontories of Italy
also, for he speaks of Temesa and of Sicily; he also
knows about the headland capes of Iberia, and of the
wealth of Iberia, as I have stated above. If between
these countries there are some countries which he
leaves out, one might pardon him; for the professed
geographer himself omits many details. And we
might pardon the poet even if he has inserted things

---

[1] Danube.   [2] Salambria.   [3] The River Vardar.

---

[4] τοῦ, before Μυσῶν, Kramer deletes; Meineke following.
[5] Reference is made to Od. 1. 184, but that Temesa is in
Cyprus.

21

καὶ διδασκαλικῶς, καὶ οὐ δεῖ μέμφεσθαι. οὐδὲ
C 7 γὰρ ἀληθές ἐστιν, ὅ φησιν Ἐρατοσθένης, ὅτι
ποιητὴς πᾶς στοχάζεται ψυχαγωγίας, οὐ διδα-
σκαλίας· τἀναντία γὰρ οἱ φρονιμώτατοι τῶν περὶ
ποιητικῆς τι φθεγξαμένων πρώτην τινὰ λέγουσι
φιλοσοφίαν τὴν ποιητικήν. ἀλλὰ πρὸς Ἐρατοσθένη μὲν αὖθις ἐροῦμεν διὰ πλειόνων, ἐν οἷς καὶ
περὶ τοῦ ποιητοῦ πάλιν ἔσται λόγος.

11. Νυνὶ δὲ ὅτι μὲν Ὅμηρος τῆς γεωγραφίας
ἦρξεν, ἀρκείτω τὰ λεχθέντα. φανεροὶ δὲ καὶ οἱ
ἐπακολουθήσαντες αὐτῷ ἄνδρες ἀξιόλογοι καὶ
οἰκεῖοι φιλοσοφίας· ὧν τοὺς πρώτους μεθ᾽ Ὅμηρον
δύο φησὶν Ἐρατοσθένης, Ἀναξίμανδρόν τε, Θαλοῦ
γεγονότα γνώριμον καὶ πολίτην, καὶ Ἑκαταῖον
τὸν Μιλήσιον· τὸν μὲν οὖν ἐκδοῦναι πρῶτον
γεωγραφικὸν πίνακα, τὸν δὲ Ἑκαταῖον καταλιπεῖν γράμμα, πιστούμενον ἐκείνου εἶναι ἐκ τῆς
ἄλλης αὐτοῦ γραφῆς.

12. Ἀλλὰ μὴν ὅτι γε δεῖ πρὸς ταῦτα πολυ-
μαθείας εἰρήκασι συχνοί· εὖ δὲ καὶ Ἵππαρχος
ἐν τοῖς πρὸς Ἐρατοσθένη διδάσκει, ὅτι παντί, καὶ
ἰδιώτῃ καὶ τῷ φιλομαθοῦντι, τῆς γεωγραφικῆς
ἱστορίας προσηκούσης ἀδύνατον μεταλαβεῖν [1]
ἄνευ τῆς τῶν οὐρανίων καὶ τῆς τῶν ἐκλειπτικῶν
τηρήσεων ἐπικ ίσεως· οἷον Ἀλεξάνδρειαν τὴν
πρὸς Αἰγύπτῳ, πότερον ἀρκτικωτέρα Βαβυλῶνος
ἢ νοτιωτέρα, λαβεῖν οὐχ οἷόν τε, οὐδ᾽ ἐφ᾽ ὁπόσον
διάστημα, χωρὶς τῆς διὰ τῶν κλιμάτων ἐπισκέ-

[1] μεταλαβεῖν, Capps, for λαβεῖν.

[1] Strabo discusses the point more fully in l. 2. 3.
[2] Hipparchus took as a basis of calculation for latitudes
and longitudes a principal parallel of latitude through the
Pillars of Heracles and the Gulf of Issus, and a principal
meridian through Alexandria. He then drew parallels of

of a mythical nature in his historical and didactic narrative. That deserves no censure; for Eratosthenes is wrong in his contention that the aim of every poet is to entertain, not to instruct; indeed the wisest of the writers on poetry say, on the contrary, that poetry is a kind of elementary philosophy.[1] But later on I shall refute Eratosthenes at greater length, when I come to speak of Homer again.

11. For the moment what I have already said is sufficient, I hope, to show that Homer was the first geographer. And, as every one knows, the successors of Homer in geography were also notable men and familiar with philosophy. Eratosthenes declares that the first two successors of Homer were Anaximander, a pupil and fellow-citizen of Thales, and Hecataeus of Miletus; that Anaximander was the first to publish a geographical map, and that Hecataeus left behind him a work on geography, a work believed to be his by reason of its similarity to his other writings.

12. Assuredly, however, there is need of encyclopaedic learning for the study of geography, as many men have already stated; and Hipparchus, too, in his treatise *Against Eratosthenes*, correctly shows that it is impossible for any man, whether layman or scholar, to attain to the requisite knowledge of geography without the determination of the heavenly bodies and of the eclipses which have been observed; for instance, it is impossible to determine whether Alexandria in Egypt is north or south of Babylon, or how much north or south of Babylon it is, without investigation through the means of the "climata."[2] In

latitude through various well-known places, and thus formed belts of latitude which he called "climata." By means of the solstitial day he determined the width of each "clima," differences of latitude, and so on. But Strabo uses the term primarily in reference to the parallels of latitude themselves.

ψεως· ὁμοίως τὰς πρὸς ἔω προσκεχωρηκυίας[1] ἢ
πρὸς δύσιν μᾶλλον καὶ ἧττον οὐκ ἂν γνοίη τις
ἀκριβῶς, πλὴν εἰ[2] διὰ τῶν ἐκλειπτικῶν ἡλίου
καὶ σελήνης συγκρίσεων. οὗτος δὲ δὴ ταῦτά
φησιν.

13. Ἅπαντες δὲ[3] ὅσοι τόπων ἰδιότητας λέγειν
ἐπιχειροῦσιν οἰκείως προσάπτονται καὶ τῶν οὐρανίων καὶ γεωμετρίας, σχήματα καὶ μεγέθη καὶ
ἀποστήματα καὶ κλίματα δηλοῦντες καὶ θάλπη
καὶ ψύχη καὶ ἁπλῶς τὴν τοῦ περιέχοντος φύσιν.
ἐπεὶ καὶ οἶκον κατασκευάζων οἰκοδόμος ταῦτα ἂν
προορῷτο καὶ πόλιν κτίζων ἀρχιτέκτων, μή τί γε
ὅλην ἐπισκοπῶν τὴν οἰκουμένην ἀνήρ· πολὺ γὰρ
τούτῳ προσήκει μᾶλλον. ἐν μὲν γὰρ τοῖς μικροῖς
χωρίοις τὸ πρὸς ἄρκτους ἢ πρὸς νότον κεκλίσθαι
παραλλαγὴν οὐ πολλὴν ἔχει, ἐν δὲ τῷ παντὶ
κύκλῳ τῆς οἰκουμένης, τὸ[4] πρὸς ἄρκτον μὲν μέχρι
τῶν ὑστάτων ἐστὶ τῆς Σκυθίας ἢ τῆς Κελτικῆς,
μέχρι δὲ τῶν ὑστάτων Αἰθιόπων τὰ πρὸς νότον·
τοῦτο δὲ παμπόλλην ἔχει διαφοράν. ὁμοίως δὲ
καὶ τὸ παρ' Ἰνδοῖς οἰκεῖν ἢ παρ' Ἴβηρσιν· ὧν
C 8 τοὺς μὲν ἑῴους μάλιστα, τοὺς δὲ ἑσπερίους,
τρόπον δέ τινα καὶ ἀντίποδας ἀλλήλοις ἴσμεν.

14. Πᾶν δὲ τὸ τοιοῦτον ἐκ τῆς τοῦ ἡλίου καὶ
τῶν ἄλλων ἄστρων κινήσεως τὴν ἀρχὴν ἔχον καὶ

[1] προσκεχωρηκυίας, Corais, for προπαρακεχωρηκυίας.
[2] εἰ, Corais for ἤ, after πλήν; Meineke following.
[3] δέ, Casaubon inserts, after ἅπαντες.
[4] τὸ πρὸς ἄρκτον μέν, Corais, for πρὸς ἄρκτον μὲν τό.

24

like manner, we cannot accurately fix points that lie
at varying distances from us, whether to the east or
the west, except by a comparison of the eclipses of
the sun and the moon.[1] That, then, is what Hipparchus says on the subject.

13. All those who undertake to describe the
distinguishing features of countries devote special
attention to astronomy and geometry, in explaining
matters of shape, of size, of distances between points,
and of " climata," as well as matters of heat and cold,
and, in general, the peculiarities of the atmosphere.
Indeed, an architect in constructing a house, or an
engineer in founding a city, would make provision for
all these conditions; and all the more would they be
considered by the man whose purview embraced the
whole inhabited world; for they concern him more
than anyone else. Within the area of small countries
it involves no very great discrepancy if a given place
be situated more towards the north, or more towards
the south; but when the area is that of the whole
round of the inhabited world, the north extends to
the remote confines of Scythia and Celtica,[2] and the
south to the remote confines of Ethiopia, and the
difference between these two extremes is very great.
The same thing holds true also as regards a man's
living in India or Iberia; the one country is in the far
east, and the other is in the far west; indeed, they
are, in a sense, the antipodes of each other, as we
know.

14. Everything of this kind, since it is caused by
the movement of the sun and the other stars as well

[1] That is, by a comparison of the observations of the same
eclipse, made from the different points of observation.

[2] France, approximately.

ἔτι τῆς ἐπὶ τὸ μέσον φορᾶς, ἀναβλέπειν ἀναγκάζει
πρὸς τὸν οὐρανὸν καὶ πρὸς τὰ φαινόμενα παρ'
ἑκάστοις ἡμῶν τῶν οὐρανίων· ἐν δὲ τούτοις ἐξαλλάξεις ὁρῶνται παμμεγέθεις τῶν οἰκήσεων. τίς
ἂν οὖν διαφορὰς τόπων ἐκτιθέμενος καλῶς καὶ
ἱκανῶς διδάσκοι, μὴ φροντίσας τούτων μηδενὸς
μηδ' ἐπὶ μικρόν; καὶ γὰρ εἰ μὴ δυνατὸν κατὰ τὴν
ὑπόθεσιν τὴν τοιαύτην ἅπαντα ἀκριβοῦν διὰ τὸ
εἶναι πολιτικωτέραν, τό γε ἐπὶ τοσοῦτον, ἐφ'
ὅσον καὶ τῷ πολιτικῷ παρακολουθεῖν δυνατόν,
προσήκοι ἂν εἰκότως.

15. Ὁ δ' οὕτω μετεωρίσας ἤδη τὴν διάνοιαν
οὐδὲ τῆς ὅλης ἀπέχεται γῆς. φαίνεται γὰρ γε-
λοῖον, εἰ τὴν οἰκουμένην γλιχόμενος σαφῶς ἐξει-
πεῖν τῶν μὲν οὐρανίων ἐτόλμησεν ἅψασθαι καὶ
χρήσασθαι πρὸς τὴν διδασκαλίαν, τὴν δ' ὅλην
γῆν, ἧς μέρος ἡ οἰκουμένη, μήθ' ὁπόση, μήθ'
ὁποία τις, μήθ' ὅπου κειμένη τοῦ σύμπαντος κόσμου, μηδὲν[1] ἐφρόντισε· μηδ', εἰ καθ' ἓν μέρος
οἰκεῖται μόνον τὸ καθ' ἡμᾶς, ἢ κατὰ πλείω, καὶ[2]
πόσα· ὡς δ' αὕτως καὶ τὸ ἀοίκητον αὐτῆς πόσον
καὶ ποῖόν τι καὶ διὰ τί. ἔοικεν οὖν μετεωρο-
λογικῇ τινι πραγματείᾳ καὶ γεωμετρικῇ συνῆφθαι
τὸ τῆς γεωγραφίας εἶδος, τὰ ἐπίγεια τοῖς οὐρα-

---

[1] μηδέν, Corais, for μηθέν; Meineke following; C. Müller
approving.
[2] ἢ, Corais deletes before καὶ πόσα, Meineke following.

as by their tendency towards the centre,[1] compels us to look to the vault of heaven, and to observe the phenomena of the heavenly bodies peculiar to our individual positions ; and in these phenomena we see very great variations in the positions of inhabited places. So, if one is about to treat of the differences between countries, how can he discuss his subject correctly and adequately if he has paid no attention, even superficially, to any of these matters ? For even if it be impossible in a treatise of this nature, because of its having a greater bearing on affairs of state, to make everything scientifically accurate, it will naturally be appropriate to do so, at least in so far as the man in public life is able to follow the thought.

15. Moreover, the man who has once thus lifted his thoughts to the heavens will surely not hold aloof from the earth as a whole ; for it is obviously absurd, if a man who desired to give a clear exposition of the inhabited world had ventured to lay hold of the celestial bodies and to use them for the purposes of instruction, and yet had paid no attention to the earth as a whole, of which the inhabited world is but a part—neither as to its size, nor its character, nor its position in the universe, nor even whether the world is inhabited only in the one part in which we live, or in a number of parts, and if so, how many such parts there are ; and likewise how large the uninhabited part is, what its nature is, and why it is uninhabited. It seems, then, that the special branch of geography represents a union of meteorology[2] and geometry, since it unites terrestrial and celestial phenomena as

[1] See § 20 (following), and footnote.
[2] The Greek word here includes our science of astronomy as well as our science of meteorology.

νίοις συνάπτον εἰς ἕν, ὡς ἐγγυτάτω ὄντα, ἀλλὰ
μὴ διεστῶτα τοσοῦτον,

ὅσον οὐρανός ἐστ᾽ ἀπὸ γαίης. (Π. 8. 16)

16. Φέρε δὴ τῇ τοσαύτῃ πολυμαθείᾳ προσθῶμεν τὴν ἐπίγειον ἱστορίαν, οἷον ζῴων καὶ φυτῶν
καὶ τῶν ἄλλων, ὅσα χρήσιμα ἢ δύσχρηστα φέρει
γῆ τε καὶ θάλασσα· οἶμαι γὰρ ἐναργὲς ἂν γενέσθαι μᾶλλον ὃ λέγω. πάντα γὰρ τὰ τοιαῦτα παρα-
σκευαί τινες εἰς φρόνησιν μεγάλαι·[1] τῷ μαθεῖν
δὲ τῆς χώρας τὴν φύσιν καὶ ζῴων καὶ φυτῶν
ἰδέας προσθεῖναι δεῖ καὶ τὰ τῆς θαλάττης·
ἀμφίβιοι γὰρ τρόπον τινά ἐσμεν καὶ οὐ μᾶλλον
χερσαῖοι ἢ θαλάττιοι.[2] ὅτι δὲ καὶ τὸ ὄφελος
μέγα παντὶ τῷ παραλαβόντι τὴν τοιαύτην ἱστορίαν, ἔκ τε τῆς παλαιᾶς μνήμης δῆλον καὶ ἐκ
τοῦ λόγου. οἱ γοῦν ποιηταὶ φρονιμωτάτους τῶν
ἡρώων ἀποφαίνουσι τοὺς ἀποδημήσαντας πολλαχοῦ καὶ πλανηθέντας· ἐν μεγάλῳ γὰρ τίθενται
τὸ "πολλῶν ἀνθρώπων ἰδεῖν ἄστεα καὶ νόον
γνῶναι" (Od. 1. 3), καὶ ὁ Νέστωρ σεμνύνεται, διότι
τοῖς Λαπίθαις ὡμίλησεν, ἐλθὼν μετάπεμπτος

τηλόθεν ἐξ ἀπίης γαίης· καλέσαντο γὰρ αὐτοί.
(Π. 1. 270)

καὶ ὁ Μενέλαος ὡσαύτως,

Κύπρον Φοινίκην τε καὶ Αἰγυπτίους ἐπαληθεὶς
Αἰθίοπάς θ᾽ ἱκόμην καὶ Σιδονίους καὶ Ἐρεμβοὺς
καὶ Λιβύην,   (Od. 4. 83)

[1] Piccolos reads and punctuates μεγάλαι· τῷ μαθεῖν δὲ τῆς
χώρας τὴν φύσιν καὶ ζῴων καὶ φυτῶν ἰδέας προσθεῖναι δεῖ καὶ τὰ

28

being very closely related, and in no sense separated from each other "as heaven is high above the earth."

16. Well, then, to this encyclopaedic knowledge let us add terrestrial history—that is, the history of animals and plants and everything useful or harmful that is produced by land or sea (this definition will, I think, make clear what I mean by "terrestrial history"). In fact all such studies are important as preliminary helps toward complete understanding. And to this knowledge of the nature of the land, and of the species of animals and plants, we must add a knowledge of all that pertains to the sea; for in a sense we are amphibious, and belong no more to the land than to the sea. That the benefit is great to anyone who has become possessed of information of this character, is evident both from ancient traditions and from reason. At any rate, the poets declare that the wisest heroes were those who visited many places and roamed over the world; for the poets regard it as a great achievement to have "seen the cities and known the minds of many men." Nestor boasts of having lived among the Lapithae, to whom he had gone as an invited guest, "from a distant land afar—for of themselves they summoned me." Menelaus, too, makes a similar boast, when he says: "I roamed over Cyprus and Phoenicia and Egypt, and came to Ethiopians and Sidonians and Erembians and Libya"

τῆς θαλάττης, for μεγάλαι τῷ μαθεῖν τῆς χώρας τὴν φύσιν καὶ ζῴων καὶ φυτῶν ἰδέας. προσθεῖναι δὲ καὶ τὰ τῆς θαλάττης; C. Müller, Sterrett, approving.

[2] A. Miller transposes the words πάντα γὰρ τὰ...ἢ θαλάττιοι to this place from a position before καὶ τὸν Ἡρακλέα (line 9, p. 30); A. Vogel, Sterrett, approving.

προσθεὶς καὶ τὸ ἰδίωμα τῆς χώρας,[1]

ἵνα τ᾽ ἄρνες ἄφαρ κεραοὶ τελέθουσι·
C 9 τρὶς γὰρ τίκτει μῆλα τελεσφόρον εἰς ἐνιαυτον.

ἐπὶ δὲ τῶν Αἰγυπτίων Θηβῶν·

(τῇ πλεῖστα φέρει ζείδωρος ἄρουρα· (Od. 4. 229)
καὶ)

αἵ θ᾽ ἑκατόμπυλοί εἰσι, διηκόσιοι δ᾽ ἀν᾽ ἑκάστην
ἀνέρες ἐξοιχνεῦσι σὺν ἵπποισιν καὶ ὄχεσφιν.
(Il. 9. 383)

καὶ τὸν Ἡρακλέα εἰκὸς ἀπὸ τῆς πολλῆς ἐμπειρίας
τε καὶ ἱστορίας λεχθῆναι

μεγάλων ἐπίστορα ἔργων. (Od. 21. 26)

ἔκ τε[2] δὴ τῆς παλαιᾶς μνήμης καὶ ἐκ τοῦ λόγου
μαρτυρεῖται τὰ λεχθέντα ἐν ἀρχαῖς ὑφ᾽ ἡμῶν.
διαφερόντως δ᾽ ἐπάγεσθαι δοκεῖ μοι πρὸς τὰ
νῦν ἐκεῖνος ὁ λόγος, διότι τῆς γεωγραφίας τὸ
πλέον ἐστὶ πρὸς τὰς χρείας τὰς πολιτικάς. χώρα
γὰρ τῶν πράξεών ἐστι γῆ καὶ[3] θάλαττα, ἣν
οἰκοῦμεν· τῶν μὲν μικρῶν μικρά, τῶν δὲ μεγάλων
μεγάλη· μεγίστη δ᾽ ἡ σύμπασα, ἥπερ ἰδίως
καλοῦμεν οἰκουμένην, ὥστε τῶν μεγίστων πράξεων αὕτη ἂν εἴη χώρα. μέγιστοι δὲ τῶν στρατη-
λατῶν, ὅσοι δύνανται γῆς καὶ θαλάττης ἄρχειν,
ἔθνη καὶ πόλεις συνάγοντες εἰς μίαν ἐξουσίαν
καὶ διοίκησιν πολιτικήν. δῆλον οὖν, ὅτι ἡ γεω-
γραφικὴ πᾶσα ἐπὶ τὰς πράξεις ἀνάγεται τὰς

---

[1] A Miller transposes the words προσθεὶς καὶ τὸ ἰδίωμα τῆς χώρας to this place from a position after τελέθουσι; Sterrett approving.

—and at this point he added the distinctive peculiarity of the country—" where lambs are horned from the birth ; for there the ewes yean thrice within the full circle of a year." And in speaking of Thebes in Egypt, he says that Egypt is the country " where earth the grain-giver yields herbs in plenty" ; and again he says: " Thebes of the hundred gates, whence sally forth two hundred warriors through each, with horses and chariots." And doubtless it was because of Heracles' wide experience and information that Homer speaks of him as the man who " had knowledge of great adventures." And my contention, made at the outset, is supported by reason as well as by ancient tradition. And that other argument, it seems to me, is adduced with especial force in reference to present-day conditions, namely, that the greater part of geography subserves the needs of states ; for the scene of the activities of states is land and sea, the dwelling-place of man. The scene is small when the activities are of small importance, and large when they are of large importance ; and the largest is the scene that embraces all the rest (which we call by the special name of " the inhabited world"), and this, therefore, would be the scene of activities of the largest importance. Moreover, the greatest generals are without exception men who are able to hold sway over land and sea, and to unite nations and cities under one government and political administration. It is therefore plain that geography as a whole has a direct bearing upon the activities of commanders ; for it describes continents

---

² ἔκ τε, Meineke, for ἐκ δέ.
³ ἡ, Corais deletes, before θάλαττα ; Meineke following ; C. Müller approving.

ἡγεμονικάς, διατιθεῖσα ἠπείρους καὶ πελάγη τὰ
μὲν ἐντός, τὰ δὲ ἐκτὸς τῆς συμπάσης οἰκουμένης.
πρὸς τούτους δὲ ἡ διάθεσις, οἷς διαφέρει ταῦτα
ἔχειν οὕτως ἢ ἑτέρως, καὶ γνώριμα εἶναι ἢ μὴ
γνώριμα. βέλτιον γὰρ ἂν διαχειρίζοιεν ἕκαστα,
εἰδότες τὴν χώραν ὁπόση τις καὶ πῶς κειμένη
τυγχάνει καὶ τίνας διαφορὰς ἴσχουσα, τάς τ᾽ ἐν
τῷ περιέχοντι καὶ τὰς ἐν αὐτῇ. ἄλλων δὲ κατ᾽
ἄλλα μέρη δυναστευόντων καὶ ἀπ᾽ ἄλλης ἑστίας
καὶ ἀρχῆς τὰς πράξεις προχειριζομένων καὶ ἐπεκ-
τεινόντων τὸ τῆς ἡγεμονίας μέγεθος, οὐκ ἐπ᾽ ἴσης
δυνατὸν οὔτ᾽ ἐκείνοις ἅπαντα γνωρίζειν οὔτε τοῖς
γεωγραφοῦσιν· ἀλλὰ τὸ μᾶλλον καὶ ἧττον πολὺ
ἐν ἀμφοτέροις καθορᾶται τούτοις. μόλις γὰρ ἂν
τὸ ἐπ᾽ ἴσης πάντ᾽ εἶναι φανερὰ συμβαίη τῆς συμπάσης οἰκουμένης ὑπὸ μίαν ἀρχὴν καὶ πολιτείαν
ὑπηγμένης· ἀλλ᾽ οὐδ᾽ οὕτως, ἀλλὰ τὰ ἐγγυτέρω
μᾶλλον ἂν γνωρίζοιτο. καὶ προσήκοι[1] ταῦτα διὰ
πλειόνων ἐμφανίζειν, ἵν᾽ εἴη γνώριμα· ταῦτα γὰρ
καὶ τῆς χρείας ἐγγυτέρω ἐστίν. ὥστ᾽ οὐκ ἂν εἴη
θαυμαστόν, οὐδ᾽ εἰ ἄλλος μὲν Ἰνδοῖς προσήκοι
χωρογράφος, ἄλλος δὲ Αἰθίοψιν, ἄλλος δὲ
Ἕλλησι καὶ Ῥωμαίοις. τί γὰρ ἂν προσήκοι
C 10 τῷ παρ᾽ Ἰνδοῖς γεω άφῳ καὶ τὰ κατὰ Βοιω-
τοὺς οὕτω φράζειν, ὡς Ὅμηρος·

οἵ θ᾽ Ὑρίην ἐνέμοντο καὶ Αὐλίδα πετρήεσσαν
Σχοῖνόν τε Σκῶλόν τε·   (Π. 2. 496)

ἡμῖν δὲ προσήκει· τὰ δὲ παρ᾽ Ἰνδοῖς οὕτω καὶ
τὰ καθ᾽ ἕκαστα οὐκέτι. οὐδὲ γὰρ ἡ χρεία

---

[1] προσήκοι, C. Müller, on MSS. authority.

and seas—not only the seas inside the limits of the
whole inhabited world, but also those outside these
limits. And the description which geography gives
is of importance to these men who are concerned as to
whether this or that is so or otherwise, and whether
known or unknown. For thus they can manage their
various affairs in a more satisfactory manner, if they
know how large a country is, how it lies, and what
are its peculiarities either of sky or soil. But because different kings rule in different quarters of the
world, and carry on their activities from different
centres and starting-points, and keep extending the
borders of their empires, it is impossible either for
them or for geographers to be equally familiar
with all parts of the world; nay, the phrase "more
or less" is a fault much in evidence in kings
and geographers. For even if the whole inhabited
world formed one empire or state, it would hardly
follow that all parts of that empire would be equally
well known; nay, it would not be true even in that
case, but the nearer regions would be better known.
And it would be quite proper to describe these regions in greater detail, in order to make them
known, for they are also nearer to the needs of the
state. Therefore it would not be remarkable even
if one person were a proper chorographer for the
Indians, another for the Ethiopians, and still another
for the Greeks and Romans. For example, wherein
would it be proper for the Indian geographer to add
details about Boeotia such as Homer gives: "These
were they that dwelt in Hyria and rocky Aulis and
Schoenus and Scolus"? For me these details are proper; but when I come to treat India it is no longer
proper to add such details; and, in fact, utility does

ἐπάγεται· μέτρον δ᾿ αὕτη μάλιστα τῆς τοιαύτης ἐμπειρίας.

17. Καὶ τοῦτο καὶ ἐν μικροῖς ἔνδηλόν[1] ἐστιν, οἷον ἐν τοῖς κυνηγεσίοις. ἄμεινον γὰρ ἂν θηρεύσειέ τις εἰδὼς τὴν ὕλην, ὁποία τις καὶ πόση· καὶ στρατοπεδεῦσαι δὲ καλῶς ἐν χωρίῳ τοῦ εἰδότος ἐστὶ καὶ ἐνεδρεῦσαι καὶ ὁδεῦσαι. ἀλλ᾿ ἐν τοῖς μεγάλοις ἐστὶ τηλαυγέστερον, ὅσῳπερ καὶ τὰ ἆθλα μείζω τὰ τῆς ἐμπειρίας καὶ τὰ σφάλματα τὰ ἐκ τῆς ἀπειρίας. ὁ μέντοι Ἀγαμέμνονος στόλος τὴν Μυσίαν ὡς τὴν Τρῳάδα πορθῶν ἐπαλινδρόμησεν αἰσχρῶς. Πέρσαι δὲ καὶ Λίβυες, τοὺς πορθμοὺς ὑπονοήσαντες εἶναι τυφλοὺς στενωπούς, ἐγγὺς μὲν ἦλθον κινδύνων μεγάλων, τρόπαια δὲ τῆς ἀνοίας[2] κατέλιπον· οἱ μὲν τὸν τοῦ Σαλγανέως τάφον πρὸς τῷ Εὐρίπῳ τῷ Χαλκιδικῷ τοῦ σφαγέντος ὑπὸ τῶν Περσῶν ὡς καθοδηγήσαντος φαύλως ἀπὸ Μαλιέων ἐπὶ τὸν Εὔριπον τὸν στόλον· οἱ δὲ τὸ τοῦ Πελώρου μνῆμα, καὶ τούτου διαφθαρέντος κατὰ τὴν ὁμοίαν αἰτίαν· πλήρης τε ναυαγίων ἡ Ἑλλὰς ὑπῆρξε κατὰ τὴν Ξέρξου στρατείαν, καὶ ἡ τῶν Αἰολέων δὲ καὶ ἡ τῶν Ἰώνων ἀποικία πολλὰ τοιαῦτα πταίσματα παραδέδωκεν. ὁμοίως δὲ καὶ κατορθώματα, ὅπου τι κατορθωθῆναι συνέβη παρὰ τὴν ἐμπειρίαν τῶν τόπων· καθάπερ ἐν τοῖς περὶ Θερμοπύλας στενοῖς ὁ Ἐφιάλτης

[1] ἔνδηλον, Madvig, for μὲν δῆλον.
[2] ἀνοίας, the MSS. reading is restored, for Casaubon's ἀγνοίας; C. Müller approving.

not urge it—and utility above all things is our standard in empirical matters of this kind.

17. The utility of geography in matters of small concern, also, is quite evident; for instance, in hunting. A hunter will be more successful in the chase if he knows the character and extent of the forest; and again, only one who knows a region can advantageously pitch camp there, or set an ambush, or direct a march. The utility of geography is more conspicuous, however, in great undertakings, in proportion as the prizes of knowledge and the disasters that result from ignorance are greater. Thus Agamemnon and his fleet ravaged Mysia in the belief that it was Troy-land, and came back home in disgrace. And, too, the Persians and the Libyans, surmising that the straits were blind alleys, not only came near great perils, but they left behind them memorials of their folly, for the Persians raised the tomb on the Euripus near Chalcis in honour of Salganeus, whom they executed in the belief that he had treacherously conducted their fleet from the Gulf of Malis [1] to the Euripus, and the Libyans erected the monument in honour of Pelorus, whom they put to death for a similar reason [2]; and Greece was covered with wrecks of vessels on the occasion of the expedition of Xerxes; and again, the colonies sent out by the Aeolians and by the Ionians have furnished many examples of similar blunders. There have also been cases of success, in which success was due to acquaintance with the regions involved; for instance, at the pass of Thermopylae it is said that Ephialtes,

[1] Lamia. See 9. 2. 9.
[2] Pelorus tried to conduct the Carthaginians through the Strait of Messina.

λέγεται δείξας τὴν διὰ τῶν ὀρῶν ἀτραπὸν τοῖς
Πέρσαις ὑποχειρίους αὐτοῖς ποιῆσαι τοὺς περὶ
Λεωνίδαν καὶ δέξασθαι τοὺς βαρβάρους εἴσω
Πυλῶν. ἐάσας δὲ τὰ παλαιά, τὴν νῦν Ῥωμαίων
στρατείαν ἐπὶ Παρθυαίους ἱκανὸν ἡγοῦμαι τούτων
τεκμήριον· ὡς δ' αὕτως τὴν ἐπὶ Γερμανοὺς καὶ
Κελτούς, ἐν ἕλεσι καὶ δρυμοῖς ἀβάτοις ἐρημίαις
τε τοπομαχούντων τῶν βαρβάρων καὶ τὰ ἐγγὺς
πόρρω ποιούντων τοῖς ἀγνοοῦσι καὶ τὰς ὁδοὺς
ἐπικρυπτομένων καὶ τὰς εὐπορίας τροφῆς τε καὶ
τῶν ἄλλων.

18. Τὸ μὲν δὴ πλέον, ὥσπερ εἴρηται, περὶ[1] τοὺς
ἡγεμονικοὺς βίους καὶ τὰς χρείας ἐστίν· ἔστι[2] δὲ
καὶ τῆς ἠθικῆς φιλοσοφίας καὶ πολιτικῆς τὸ
πλέον περὶ τοὺς ἡγεμονικοὺς βίους. σημεῖον δέ·
τὰς γὰρ τῶν πολιτειῶν διαφορὰς ἀπὸ τῶν ἡγεμο-
νιῶν διακρίνομεν, ἄλλην μὲν ἡγεμονίαν τιθέντες
C 11 τὴν μοναρχίαν, ἣν καὶ βασιλείαν καλοῦμεν, ἄλλην
δὲ τὴν ἀριστοκρατίαν, τρίτην δὲ τὴν δημοκρατίαν.
τοσαύτας δὲ καὶ τὰς πολιτείας νομίζομεν, ὁμωνύμως καλοῦντες ὡς ἂν ἀπ' ἐκείνων τὴν ἀρχὴν
ἐχούσας τῆς εἰδοποιίας· ἄλλοις[3] γὰρ νόμος τὸ τοῦ
βασιλέως πρόσταγμα, ἄλλοις[3] δὲ τὸ τῶν ἀρίστων,

---

[1] περί, Cobet, for πρός.
[2] τὰς χρείας ἐστίν. ἔστι δὲ καί, Meineke, for τὰς χρείας· ἔτι
δὲ καί; Cobet independently, C. Müller approving.
[3] ἄλλοις, Madvig, for ἄλλος; A. Vogel approving.

---

[1] Under Augustus and Tiberius no Roman army invaded
Parthia, apparently. Strabo must be thinking of the campaign of Crassus or of that of Antony—or of both campaigns.
[2] The campaign of Drusus, apparently, which he carried on
till his death in 9 B.C. But if Niese's theory be accepted as
to the time when Strabo wrote (see *Introduction*, pp. xxiv ff.),

by showing the Persians the pathway across the
mountains, put Leonidas and his troops at their
mercy, and brought the Persians south of Thermopylae. But leaving antiquity, I believe that the
modern campaign of the Romans against the Parthians [1] is a sufficient proof of what I say, and
likewise that against the Germans and the Celts,
for in the latter case the barbarians carried on a
guerilla warfare in swamps, in pathless forests, and
in deserts [2]; and they made the ignorant Romans
believe to be far away what was really near at
hand, and kept them in ignorance of the roads and
of the facilities for procuring provisions and other
necessities.

18. Now just as the greater part of geography, as
I have said, has a bearing on the life and the needs
of rulers, so also does the greater part of the theory
of ethics and the theory of politics have a bearing
on the life of rulers. And the proof of this is the
fact that we distinguish the differences between the
constitutions of states by the sovereignties in those
states, in that we call one sovereignty the monarchy
or kingship, another the aristocracy, and still
another the democracy. And we have a corresponding number of constitutions of states, which we
designate by the names of the sovereignties, because
it is from these that they derive the fundamental
principle of their specific nature; for in one country
the will of the king is law, in another the will of
those of highest rank, and in another the will of the

or if the above reference was inserted in a revised edition
about 18 A.D. (p. xxv), then we might assume that allusion
is made to the destruction of the Roman legions under Varus
in 9 A.D.—to which Strabo refers in 7. 1. 4.

καὶ τὸ τοῦ δήμου. τύπος δὲ καὶ σχῆμα πολιτείας ὁ νόμος. διὰ τοῦτο δὲ καὶ τὸ δίκαιον εἶπόν τινες τὸ τοῦ κρείττονος συμφέρον. εἴπερ οὖν ἡ πολιτικὴ φιλοσοφία περὶ τοὺς ἡγεμόνας τὸ πλέον ἐστίν, ἔστι δὲ καὶ ἡ γεωγραφία περὶ τὰς ἡγεμονικὰς χρείας, ἔχοι ἄν τι πλεονέκτημα καὶ αὐτὴ παρὰ τοῦτο. ἀλλὰ τοῦτο μὲν τὸ πλεονέκτημα πρὸς τὰς πράξεις.

19. Ἔχει δέ τινα καὶ θεωρίαν οὐ φαύλην ἡ πραγματεία, τὴν μὲν τεχνικήν τε καὶ μαθηματικὴν καὶ φυσικήν, τὴν δὲ ἐν ἱστορίᾳ καὶ μύθοις κειμένην, οὐδὲν οὖσι πρὸς τὰς πράξεις· οἷον εἴ τις λέγοι τὰ περὶ τὴν Ὀδυσσέως πλάνην καὶ Μενελάου καὶ Ἰάσονος, εἰς φρόνησιν μὲν οὐδὲν ἂν συλλαμβάνειν δόξειεν, ἣν ὁ πράττων ζητεῖ, πλὴν εἰ καταμίσγοι καὶ τῶν γενομένων ἀναγκαίων τὰ παραδείγματα χρήσιμα· διαγωγὴν δ' ὅμως πορίζοι ἂν οὐκ ἀνελεύθερον τῷ ἐπιβάλλοντι ἐπὶ τοὺς τόπους τοὺς παρασχόντας τὴν μυθοποιίαν. καὶ γὰρ τοῦτο ζητοῦσιν οἱ πράττοντες διὰ τὸ ἔνδοξον καὶ τὸ ἡδύ, ἀλλ' οὐκ ἐπὶ πολύ· μᾶλλον γὰρ σπουδάζουσιν, ὡς εἰκός, περὶ τὰ χρήσιμα. διόπερ καὶ τῷ γεωγράφῳ τούτων μᾶλλον ἢ ἐκείνων ἐπιμελητέον. ὡς δ' αὕτως ἔχει καὶ περὶ τῆς ἱστορίας καὶ περὶ τῶν μαθημάτων· καὶ γὰρ τούτων τὸ χρήσιμον ἀεὶ μᾶλλον ληπτέον καὶ τὸ πιστότερον.

---

[1] The definition ascribed to Thrasymachus, Plato's *Republic*, 1. 12.

[2] Strabo has in mind his theory (which he often takes occasion to uphold) as to the comparative mythical and historical elements in Homer and other poets.

people. It is the law that gives the type and the form of the constitution. And for that reason some have defined "justice" as "the interest of the more powerful."[1] If, then, political philosophy deals chiefly with the rulers, and if geography supplies the needs of those rulers, then geography would seem to have some advantage over political science. This advantage, however, has to do with practice.

19. And yet, a work on geography also involves theory of no mean value, the theory of the arts, of mathematics, and of natural science, as well as the theory which lies in the fields of history and myths[2] —though myths have nothing to do with practice; for instance, if a man should tell the story of the wanderings of Odysseus or Menelaus or Jason, it would not be thought that he was making any contribution to the practical wisdom of his hearers— and that is what the man of affairs demands—unless he should insert the useful lessons to be drawn from the hardships those heroes underwent; still, he would be providing no mean entertainment for the hearer who takes an interest in the regions which furnished the scenes of the myths. Men of affairs are fond of just such entertainment, because the localities are famous and the myths are charming; but they care for no great amount of it, since they are more interested in what is useful, and it is quite natural that they should be. For that reason the geographer, also, should direct his attention to the useful rather than to what is famous and charming. The same principle holds good in regard to history and the mathematical sciences; for in these branches, also, that which is useful and more trustworthy should always be given precedence.

20. Μάλιστα δὲ δοκεῖ, καθάπερ εἴρηται, γεωμετρίας τε καὶ ἀστρονομίας δεῖν τῇ τοιαύτῃ ὑποθέσει. καὶ δεῖ μὲν ὡς ἀληθῶς· σχήματα γὰρ καὶ
κλίματα καὶ μεγέθη καὶ τὰ ἄλλα τὰ τούτοις οἰκεῖα
οὐχ οἷόν τε λαβεῖν καλῶς ἄνευ τῆς τοιαύτης
μεθόδου. ἀλλ᾽ ὥσπερ τὰ περὶ τὴν ἀναμέτρησιν
τῆς ὅλης γῆς ἐν ἄλλοις δεικνύουσιν, ἐνταῦθα δὲ
ὑποθέσθαι δεῖ καὶ πιστεῦσαι τοῖς ἐκεῖ δειχθεῖσιν,
ὑποθέσθαι δεῖ[1] καὶ σφαιροειδῆ μὲν τὸν κόσμον,
σφαιροειδῆ δὲ καὶ τὴν ἐπιφάνειαν τῆς γῆς, ἔτι δὲ
τούτων πρότερον τὴν ἐπὶ τὸ μέσον τῶν σωμάτων
φοράν· αὐτὸ μόνον, εἴ τι[2] τῆς αἰσθήσεως ἢ τῶν
κοινῶν ἐννοιῶν ἐγγύς ἐστιν, εἰ ἄρα, ἐπισημηνά-
μενοι ἐπὶ κεφαλαίῳ μικρά· οἷον ὅτι ἡ γῆ σφαι-
ροειδής, ἐκ μὲν τῆς ἐπὶ τὸ μέσον φορᾶς πόρρωθεν
ἡ ὑπόμνησις καὶ τοῦ ἕκαστον σῶμα ἐπὶ τὸ αὑτοῦ
ἄρτημα νεύειν, ἐκ δὲ τῶν κατὰ πελάγη καὶ τὸν
C 12 οὐρανὸν φαινομένων ἐγγύθεν· καὶ γὰρ ἡ αἴσθησις
ἐπιμαρτυρεῖν δύναται καὶ ἡ κοινὴ ἔννοια. φανερῶς γὰρ ἐπιπροσθεῖ τοῖς πλέουσιν ἡ κυρτότης τῆς
θαλάττης, ὥστε μὴ προσβάλλειν τοῖς πόρρω φέγ-
γεσι τοῖς ἐπ᾽ ἴσον ἐξηρημένοις[3] τῇ ὄψει. ἐξαρθέντα
γοῦν πλέον τῆς ὄψεως ἐφάνη, καίτοι πλέον ἀπο-

---

[1] δεῖ. Groskurd, for δέ. [2] εἴ τι, Madvig. for ἐπί.
[3] Meinecke wrongly emends ἐξηρμένοις to ἐξηρμένοις.

---

[1] See footnote 2, page 22.
[2] Strabo uses the word in its literal sense of "sphere-
shaped," and not in its geometrical sense. The spheroidicity
of the earth in the modern sense appears not to have been
suspected until the seventeenth century. (See 2. 5. 5.)
[3] Strabo here means all the heavenly bodies. According
to his conception, the earth was stationary and all the
heavenly bodies revolved about the earth from east to west,
the heavens having the same centre as the earth. The Greek

20. Most of all, it seems to me, we need, as I have said, geometry and astronomy for a subject like geography; and the need of them is real indeed; for without such methods as they offer it is not possible accurately to determine our geometrical figures, "climata" [1], dimensions, and the other cognate things; but just as these sciences prove for us in other treatises all that has to do with the measurement of the earth as a whole and as I must in this treatise take for granted and accept the propositions proved there, so I must take for granted that the universe is sphere-shaped,[2] and also that the earth's surface is sphere-shaped, and, what is more, I must take for granted the law that is prior to these two principles, namely that the bodies tend toward the centre[3]; and I need only indicate, in a brief and summary way, whether a proposition comes—if it really does—within the range of sense-perception or of intuitive knowledge. Take, for example, the proposition that the earth is sphere-shaped: whereas the suggestion of this proposition comes to us mediately from the law that bodies tend toward the centre and that each body inclines toward its own centre of gravity, the suggestion comes immediately from the phenomena observed at sea and in the heavens; for our sense-perception and also our intuition can bear testimony in the latter case. For instance, it is obviously the curvature of the sea that prevents sailors from seeing distant lights at an elevation equal to that of the eye; however, if they are at a higher elevation than that of the eye, they become visible, even though they be at a

word ἄρτημα, here used figuratively, means a weight suspended by a cord or otherwise. Strabo means that each body is moored, as it were, from its own respective position of suspension to the centre of the earth.

σχόντα αὐτῆς· ὁμοίως δὲ καὶ αὐτὴ μετεωρισθεῖσα
εἶδε τὰ κεκρυμμένα πρότερον. ὅπερ δηλοῖ καὶ ὁ
ποιητής· τοιοῦτον γάρ ἐστι καὶ τὸ

> ὀξὺ μάλα προϊδών, μεγάλου ὑπὸ κύματος
> ἀρθείς.   (Od. 5. 393)

καὶ τοῖς προσπλέουσι δὲ ἀεὶ καὶ μᾶλλον ἀπο-
γυμνοῦται τὰ πρόσγεια μέρη, καὶ τὰ φανέντα ἐν
ἀρχαῖς ταπεινὰ ἐξαίρεται μᾶλλον. τῶν τε οὐρανίων ἡ περιφορὰ ἐναργής ἐστι καὶ ἄλλως καὶ ἐκ τῶν
γνωμονικῶν· ἐκ δὲ τούτων εὐθὺς ὑποτείνει καὶ ἡ
ἔννοια, ὅτι ἐρριζωμένης ἐπ' ἄπειρον τῆς γῆς οὐκ
ἂν ἡ τοιαύτη περιφορὰ συνέβαινε. καὶ τὰ περὶ
τῶν κλιμάτων δὲ ἐν τοῖς περὶ τῶν οἰκήσεων
δείκνυται.

21. Νυνὶ δὲ ἐξ ἑτοίμου δεῖ λαβεῖν ἔνια, καὶ
ταῦθ' ὅσα τῷ πολιτικῷ καὶ τῷ στρατηλάτῃ χρήσιμα. οὔτε γὰρ οὕτω δεῖ ἀγνοεῖν τὰ περὶ τὸν
οὐρανὸν καὶ τὴν θέσιν τῆς γῆς, ὥστ', ἐπειδὰν
γένηται κατὰ τόπους, καθ' οὓς ἐξήλλακταί τινα
τῶν φαινομένων τοῖς πολλοῖς ἐν τῷ οὐρανῷ,
ταράσσεσθαι καὶ τοιαῦτα λέγειν·

> ὦ φίλοι, οὐ γάρ τ' ἴδμεν ὅπῃ[1] ζόφος, οὐδ' ὅπῃ
>   ἠώς,
> οὐδ' ὅπῃ ἥλιος φαεσίμβροτος εἶσ' ὑπὸ γαῖαν,
> οὐδ' ὅπῃ ἀννεῖται·   (Od. 10. 190)

οὔθ' οὕτως ἀκριβοῦν, ὥστε τὰς πανταχοῦ συνανα-
τολάς τε καὶ συγκαταδύσεις καὶ συμμεσουρανή-

---

[1] ὅπῃ—ὅπῃ—ὅπῃ—ὅπῃ, Sterrett, for ὅπη—ὅπη—ὅπη—ὅπη.

greater distance from the eyes; and similarly if the eyes themselves are elevated, they see what was before invisible. This fact is noted by Homer, also, for such is the meaning of the words: " With a quick glance ahead, being upborne on a great wave, [he saw the land very near]." So, also, when sailors are approaching land, the different parts of the shore become revealed progressively, more and more, and what at first appeared to be low-lying land grows gradually higher and higher. Again, the revolution of the heavenly bodies is evident on many grounds, but it is particularly evident from the phenomena of the sun-dial; and from these phenomena our intuitive judgment itself suggests that no such revolution could take place if the earth were rooted to an infinite depth.[1] As regards the " climata "[2], they are treated in our discussion of the Inhabited Districts.

21. But at this point we must assume off-hand a knowledge of some matters, and particularly of all that is useful for the statesman and the general to know. For one should not, on the one hand, be so ignorant of the heavens and the position of the earth as to be alarmed when he comes to countries in which some of the celestial phenomena that are familiar to everybody have changed, and to exclaim: " My friends, lo, now we know not where is the place of darkness, nor of dawning, nor where the sun, that gives light to men, goes beneath the earth, nor where he rises "; nor, on the other hand, need one have such scientifically accurate knowledge as to know what constellations rise and set and pass the

---

[1] This was the doctrine of Xenophanes and Anaximenes. See footnote 2, page 22.

σεις καὶ ἐξάρματα πόλων καὶ τὰ κατὰ κορυφὴν
σημεῖα καὶ ὅσα ἄλλα τοιαῦτα κατὰ τὰς μετα-
πτώσεις τῶν ὁριζόντων ἅμα καὶ τῶν ἀρκτικῶν
διαφέροντα ἀπαντᾷ, τὰ μὲν πρὸς τὴν ὄψιν, τὰ δὲ
καὶ τῇ φύσει, γνωρίζειν ἅπαντα· ἀλλὰ τὰ μὲν
μηδ' ὅλως φροντίζειν, πλὴν εἰ θέας φιλοσόφου
χάριν, τοῖς δὲ πιστεύειν, κἂν μὴ βλέπῃ τὸ διὰ τί·
καὶ γὰρ τοῦτο τοῦ φιλοσοφοῦντος μόνου, τῷ δὲ
πολιτικῷ σχολῆς οὐ τοσαύτης μέτεστιν, ἢ οὐκ ἀεί
οὐ μὴν οὐδ' οὕτως ὑπάρχειν ἁπλοῦν δεῖ τὸν ἐντυγ-
χάνοντα τῇ γραφῇ ταύτῃ καὶ ἀργόν, ὥστε μηδὲ
C 13 σφαῖραν ἰδεῖν, μηδὲ κύκλους ἐν αὐτῇ, τοὺς μὲν
παραλλήλους, τοὺς δ' ὀρθίους πρὸς τούτους, τοὺς
δὲ λοξούς· μηδὲ τροπικῶν τε καὶ ἰσημερινοῦ καὶ
ζῳδιακοῦ θέσιν, δι' οὗ φερόμενος ὁ ἥλιος τρέπεται
καὶ διατάσσει[1] διαφορὰς κλιμάτων τε καὶ ἀνέμων.
ταῦτα γὰρ καὶ τὰ περὶ τοὺς ὁρίζοντας καὶ τοὺς
ἀρκτικοὺς καὶ ὅσα ἄλλα κατὰ τὴν πρώτην ἀγωγὴν
τὴν εἰς τὰ μαθήματα παραδίδοται κατανοήσας
τις ἄλλως πως δύναται παρακολουθεῖν τοῖς
λεγομένοις ἐνταῦθα. ὁ δὲ μηδ' εὐθεῖαν γραμμὴν
ἢ περιφερῆ, μηδὲ κύκλον εἰδώς, μηδὲ σφαιρικὴν
ἐπιφάνειαν ἢ ἐπίπεδον, μηδ' ἐν τῷ οὐρανῷ μηδὲ
τοὺς ἑπτὰ τῆς μεγάλης ἄρκτου ἀστέρας κατα-
μαθών, μηδ' ἄλλο τι τῶν τοιούτων μηδέν, ἢ οὐκ ἂν

---

[1] διατάσσει, Madvig, for διδάσκει.

meridian at the same time everywhere; or as to
know the elevations of the poles, the constellations
that are in the zenith, and all other such changing
phenomena as meet one according as he changes
his horizons and arctic circles,[1] whether those changes
be merely visual, or actual as well. Nay, he should
pay no attention at all to some of these things,
unless it be in order to view them as a philosopher.
But he should take some other things on faith,
even if he does not see a reason for them; for the
question of causes belongs to the student of
philosophy alone, whereas the statesman does not
have adequate leisure for research, or at least not
always. However, the reader of this book should
not be so simple-minded or indifferent as not to have
observed a globe, or the circles drawn upon it, some
of which are parallel, others drawn at right angles
to the parallels, and still others oblique to them;
or, again, so simple as not to have observed the
position of tropics, equator, and zodiac—the region
through which the sun is borne in his course and by
his turning determines the different zones and winds.
For if one have learned, even in a superficial way,
about these matters, and about the horizons and
the arctic circles and all the other matters taught
in the elementary courses of mathematics, he will
be able to follow what is said in this book. If,
however, a man does not know even what a straight
line is, or a curve, or a circle, nor the difference
between a spherical and a plane surface, and if, in
the heavens, he have not learned even the seven
stars of the Great Bear, or anything else of that
kind, either he will have no use for this book, or else

[1] See 2. 2. 2, and footnote.

δέοιτο τῆς πραγματείας ταύτης ἢ οὐχὶ νῦν, ἀλλ'
ἐκείνοις ἐντυχὼν πρότερον, ὧν χωρὶς οὐκ ἂν εἴη
γεωγραφίας οἰκεῖος. οὕτως δὲ καὶ οἱ τοὺς λιμένας
καὶ τοὺς περίπλους καλουμένους πραγματευθέντες
ἀτελῆ τὴν ἐπίσκεψιν ποιοῦνται, μὴ προστιθέντες
ὅσα ἐκ τῶν μαθημάτων καὶ ἐκ τῶν οὐρανίων
συνάπτειν προσῆκε.[1]

22. Ἁπλῶς δὲ κοινὸν εἶναι τὸ σύγγραμμα τοῦτο
δεῖ καὶ πολιτικὸν καὶ δημωφελὲς ὁμοίως, ὥσπερ
τὴν τῆς ἱστορίας γραφήν. κἀκεῖ δὲ πολιτικὸν
λέγομεν οὐχὶ τὸν παντάπασιν ἀπαίδευτον, ἀλλὰ
τὸν μετασχόντα τῆς τε ἐγκυκλίου καὶ συνήθους
ἀγωγῆς τοῖς ἐλευθέροις καὶ τοῖς φιλοσοφοῦσιν·
οὐδὲ γὰρ ἂν οὔτε ψέγειν δύναιτο καλῶς οὔτ'
ἐπαινεῖν, οὐδὲ κρίνειν ὅσα μνήμης ἄξια τῶν γεγο-
νότων, ὅτῳ μηδὲν ἐμέλησεν ἀρετῆς καὶ φρονήσεως
καὶ τῶν εἰς ταῦτα λόγων.

23. Διόπερ ἡμεῖς πεποιηκότες ὑπομνήματα
ἱστορικὰ χρήσιμα, ὡς ὑπολαμβάνομεν, εἰς τὴν
ἠθικὴν καὶ πολιτικὴν φιλοσοφίαν, ἔγνωμεν προσθεῖναι καὶ τήνδε τὴν σύνταξιν· ὁμοειδὴς γὰρ καὶ
αὐτή, καὶ πρὸς τοὺς αὐτοὺς ἄνδρας, καὶ μάλιστα
τοὺς ἐν ταῖς ὑπεροχαῖς. ἔτι δὲ τὸν αὐτὸν τρόπον,
ὅνπερ ἐκεῖ τὰ περὶ τοὺς ἐπιφανεῖς ἄνδρας καὶ
βίους τυγχάνει μνήμης, τὰ δὲ μικρὰ καὶ ἄδοξα

---

[1] The words οὕτως δὲ καὶ . . . συνάπτειν προσῆκε are transposed to this place from the end of § 22 by Meineke, following the suggestion of Corais ; C. Müller approving. Siebenkees
deletes the ἃ before συνάπτειν ; Corais, Meineke, following ;
C. Müller approving.

---

[1] Strabo refers to his historical work (now lost) as his
Historical Sketches and also as his *History*. The work contained both of these, and comprised forty-seven books, cover-

not at present—in fact, not until he has studied those topics without which he cannot be familiar with geography. And so those who have written the treatises entitled *Harbours* and *Coasting Voyages* leave their investigations incomplete, if they have failed to add all the mathematical and astronomical information which properly belonged in their books.

22. In short, this book of mine should be generally useful—useful alike to the statesman and to the public at large—as was my work on *History*.[1] In this work, as in that, I mean by "statesman," not the man who is wholly uneducated, but the man who has taken the round of courses usual in the case of freemen or of students of philosophy. For the man who has given no thought to virtue and to practical wisdom, and to what has been written about them, would not be able even to form a valid opinion either in censure or in praise; nor yet to pass judgment upon the matters of historical fact that are worthy of being recorded in this treatise.

23. And so, after I had written my *Historical Sketches*,[1] which have been useful, I suppose, for moral and political philosophy, I determined to write the present treatise also; for this work itself is based on the same plan, and is addressed to the same class of readers, and particularly to men of exalted stations in life. Furthermore, just as in my *Historical Sketches* only the incidents in the lives of distinguished men are recorded, while deeds that are petty and ignoble are omitted, so in this work

ing the course of events prior to the opening and subsequent to the close of the History of Polybius. The first part was merely an outline of historical events, while the latter part presented a complete history from 146 B.C. to the time of the Empire.

παραλείπεται, κἀνταῦθα δεῖ τὰ μικρὰ καὶ τὰ
ἀφανῆ παραπέμπειν, ἐν δὲ τοῖς ἐνδόξοις καὶ μεγάλοις καὶ ἐν οἷς τὸ πραγματικὸν καὶ εὐμνημόνευτον
καὶ ἡδὺ διατρίβειν. καθάπερ τε[1] καὶ ἐν τοῖς
κολοσσικοῖς ἔργοις οὐ τὸ καθ' ἕκαστον ἀκριβὲς
ζητοῦμεν, ἀλλὰ τοῖς καθόλου προσέχομεν μᾶλλον,
εἰ καλῶς τὸ ὅλον· οὕτως κἂν τούτοις δεῖ ποιεῖσθαι
C 14 τὴν κρίσιν. κολοσσουργία γάρ τις καὶ αὐτή, τὰ
μεγάλα φράζουσα πῶς ἔχει καὶ τὰ ὅλα, πλὴν εἴ
τι κινεῖν δύναται καὶ τῶν μικρῶν τὸν φιλειδήμονα
καὶ τὸν πραγματικόν. ὅτι μὲν οὖν σπουδαῖον τὸ
προκείμενον ἔργον καὶ φιλοσόφῳ πρέπον, ταῦτα
εἰρήσθω.

II

1. Εἰ δὲ πολλῶν προειπόντων ἐπιχειροῦμεν καὶ
αὐτοὶ λέγειν περὶ τῶν αὐτῶν, οὔπω μεμπτέον, ἂν
μὴ καὶ τὸν αὐτὸν τρόπον διελεγχθῶμεν ἐκείνοις
ἅπαντα λέγοντες. ὑπολαμβάνομεν δ' ἄλλων
ἄλλο τι κατορθωσάντων ἄλλο πολὺ μέρος ἔτι τοῦ
ἔργου λείπεσθαι· πρὸς οἷς ἂν καὶ μικρὸν προσ-
λαβεῖν δυνηθῶμεν, ἱκανὴν δεῖ τίθεσθαι πρόφασιν
τῆς ἐπιχειρήσεως. καὶ γὰρ δὴ πολύ τι τοῖς νῦν
ἡ τῶν Ῥωμαίων ἐπικράτεια καὶ τῶν Παρθυαίων
τῆς τοιαύτης ἐμπειρίας προσδέδωκε· καθάπερ τοῖς
προτέροις μέγα τι ἡ Ἀλεξάνδρου στρατεία,[2] ὥς
φησιν Ἐρατοσθένης. ὁ μὲν γὰρ τῆς Ἀσίας

---

[1] τε, Meineke, for γε.
[2] καθάπερ τοῖς προτέροις μέγα τι ἡ Ἀλεξάνδρου στρατεία,
C. Müller, for καθάπερ τοῖς μετὰ τὴν Ἀλεξάνδρου στρατείαν.

also I must leave untouched what is petty and inconspicuous, and devote my attention to what is noble and great, and to what contains the practically useful, or memorable, or entertaining. Now just as in judging of the merits of colossal statues we do not examine each individual part with minute care, but rather consider the general effect and endeavour to see if the statue as a whole is pleasing, so should this book of mine be judged. For it, too, is a colossal work, in that it deals with the facts about large things only, and wholes, except as some petty thing may stir the interest of the studious or the practical man. I have said thus much to show that the present work is a serious one, and one worthy of a philosopher.

II

1. IF I, too, undertake to write upon a subject that has been treated by many others before me, I should not be blamed therefor, unless I prove to have discussed the subject in every respect as have my predecessors. Although various predecessors have done excellent work in various fields of geography, yet I assume that a large portion of the work still remains to be done; and if I shall be able to make even small additions to what they have said, that must be regarded as a sufficient excuse for my undertaking. Indeed, the spread of the empires of the Romans and of the Parthians has presented to geographers of to-day a considerable addition to our empirical knowledge of geography, just as did the campaign of Alexander to geographers of earlier times, as Eratosthenes points out. For Alexander

πολλὴν ἀνεκάλυψεν ἡμῖν καὶ τῶν βορείων τῆς
Εὐρώπης ἄπαντα μέχρι τοῦ Ἴστρου· οἱ δὲ Ῥωμαῖοι τὰ ἑσπέρια τῆς Εὐρώπης ἄπαντα μέχρι [1]
Ἄλβιος ποταμοῦ τοῦ τὴν Γερμανίαν δίχα διαι-
ροῦντος, τά τε πέραν Ἴστρου τὰ μέχρι Τύρα
ποταμοῦ· τὰ δὲ ἐπέκεινα μέχρι Μαιωτῶν καὶ τῆς
εἰς Κόλχους τελευτώσης παραλίας Μιθριδάτης ὁ
κληθεὶς Εὐπάτωρ ἐποίησε γνώριμα καὶ οἱ ἐκείνου
στρατηγοί· οἱ δὲ Παρθυαῖοι τὰ περὶ τὴν Ὑρκανίαν καὶ τὴν Βακτριανὴν καὶ τοὺς ὑπὲρ τούτων
Σκύθας γνωριμωτέρους ἡμῖν ἐποίησαν, ἧττον
γνωριζομένους ὑπὸ τῶν πρότερον· ὥστε ἔχοιμεν
ἄν τι λέγειν πλέον τῶν πρὸ ἡμῶν. ὁρᾶν δ' ἔσται
τοῦτο μάλιστα ἐν τοῖς λόγοις τοῖς πρὸς τοὺς πρὸ
ἡμῶν, ἧττον μὲν τοὺς πάλαι, μᾶλλον δὲ τοὺς μετ'
Ἐρατοσθένη καὶ αὐτὸν ἐκεῖνον· οὓς εἰκὸς ὅσῳπερ
πολυμαθέστεροι τῶν πολλῶν γεγόνασι, τοσούτῳ
δυσελεγκτοτέρους εἶναι τοῖς ὕστερον, ἄν τι πλημ-
μελῶς λέγωσιν. εἰ δ' ἀναγκασθησόμεθά που τοῖς
αὐτοῖς ἀντιλέγειν, οἷς μάλιστα ἐπακολουθοῦμεν
κατὰ τἆλλα,[2] δεῖ συγγνώμην ἔχειν. οὐ γὰρ
πρόκειται πρὸς ἅπαντας ἀντιλέγειν, ἀλλὰ τοὺς
μὲν πολλοὺς ἐᾶν, οἷς μηδὲ ἀκολουθεῖν ἄξιον·
ἐκείνους δὲ διαιτᾶν, οὓς ἐν τοῖς πλείστοις κατωρ-
θωκότας ἴσμεν. ἐπεὶ οὐδὲ πρὸς ἅπαντας φιλο-

---

[1] μέχρι, Meineke, for μέχρις.
[2] κατὰ τἆλλα, Cobet, for κατ' ἄλλα.

---

[1] Danube.　　　[2] Elbe.　　　[3] Dniester.
[4] Sea of Azov.　　[5] Southern Caucasia.

opened up for us geographers a great part of Asia
and all the northern part of Europe as far as the
Ister [1] River; the Romans have made known all the
western part of Europe as far as the River Albis [2]
(which divides Germany into two parts), and the
regions beyond the Ister as far as the Tyras [3]
River; and Mithridates, surnamed Eupator, and his
generals have made known the regions beyond the
Tyras as far as Lake Maeotis [4] and the line of coast
that ends at Colchis [5]; and, again, the Parthians have
increased our knowledge in regard to Hyrcania and
Bactriana, and in regard to the Scythians who live
north of Hyrcania and Bactriana, all of which
countries were but imperfectly known to the earlier
geographers. I therefore may have something more
to say than my predecessors. This will become
particularly apparent in what I shall have to say in
criticism of my predecessors, but my criticism has
less to do with the earliest geographers than with
the successors of Eratosthenes and Eratosthenes
himself. For it stands to reason that because
Eratosthenes and his successors have had wider
knowledge than most geographers, it will be corres-
pondingly more difficult for a later geographer to
expose their errors if they say anything amiss. And
if I shall, on occasion, be compelled to contradict
the very men whom in all other respects I follow
most closely, I beg to be pardoned; for it is not my
purpose to contradict every individual geographer,
but rather to leave the most of them out of
consideration— men whose arguments it is unseemly
even to follow—and to pass upon the opinion of
those men whom we recognize to have been correct
in most cases. Indeed, to engage in philosophical

σοφεῖν ἄξιον, πρὸς Ἐρατοσθένη δὲ καὶ Ἵππαρχον καὶ Ποσειδώνιον[1] καὶ Πολύβιον καὶ ἄλλους τοιούτους καλόν.

C 15   2. Πρῶτον[2] δ' ἐπισκεπτέον Ἐρατοσθένη, παρατιθέντας ἅμα καὶ τὴν Ἱππάρχου πρὸς αὐτὸν ἀντιλογίαν. ἔστι δ' ὁ Ἐρατοσθένης οὔθ'[3] οὕτως εὐκατατρόχαστος, ὥστε μηδ' Ἀθήνας αὐτὸν ἰδεῖν φάσκειν, ὅπερ Πολέμων ἐπιχειρεῖ δεικνύναι· οὔτ' ἐπὶ τοσοῦτον πιστός, ἐφ' ὅσον παρεδέξαντό τινες, καίπερ πλείστοις ἐντυχών, ὡς εἴρηκεν αὐτός, ἀγαθοῖς ἀνδράσιν. ἐγένοντο γάρ, φησίν, ὡς οὐδέποτε, κατὰ τοῦτον τὸν καιρὸν ὑφ' ἕνα περίβολον καὶ μίαν πόλιν οἱ[4] κατ' Ἀρίστωνα καὶ Ἀρκεσίλαον ἀνθήσαντες φιλόσοφοι. οὐχ ἱκανὸν δ' οἶμαι τοῦτο, ἀλλὰ τὸ κρίνειν καλῶς, οἷς μᾶλλον πειστέον.[5] ὁ δὲ Ἀρκεσίλαον καὶ Ἀρίστωνα τῶν καθ' αὑτὸν ἀνθησάντων κορυφαίους τίθησιν, Ἀπελλῆς τε αὐτῷ πολύς ἐστι καὶ Βίων, ὅν φησι πρῶτον ἀνθινὰ περιβαλεῖν φιλοσοφίαν, ἀλλ' ὅμως πολλάκις εἰπεῖν ἄν τινα ἐπ' αὐτοῦ τοῦτο·

οἵην ἐκ ῥακέων ὁ Βίων.   (Od. 18. 74)

ἐν αὐταῖς γὰρ ταῖς ἀποφάσεσι ταύταις ἱκανὴν ἀσθένειαν ἐμφαίνει τῆς ἑαυτοῦ γνώμης· ἢ τοῦ Ζήνωνος τοῦ Κιτιέως γνώριμος γενόμενος Ἀθήνησι

---

[1] Ἵππαρχον καὶ Ποσειδώνιον, Spengel, for Ποσειδώνιον καὶ Ἵππαρχον; Meineke following.
[2] πρῶτον, Spengel, for πρότερον; Meineke following.
[3] οὔθ', Meineke, for οὐχ.
[4] καί, Xylander deletes, after οἱ; Meineke following.
[5] πειστέον, the correction of the prima manus, Spengel, A. Vogel, prefer, for προσιτέον.

discussion with everybody is unseemly, but it is
honourable to do so with Eratosthenes, Hipparchus,
Poseidonius, Polybius, and others of their type.

2. First, I must consider Eratosthenes, at the
same time setting forth the objections which
Hipparchus urges against the statements of
Eratosthenes. Now Eratosthenes is not so open
to attack as to warrant my saying that he never
saw even Athens, as Polemon undertakes to prove;
nor, on the other hand, is he so trustworthy as some
have been taught to believe that he is—notwith-
standing the fact that he had been associated with
many eminent men, as he himself tells us. "For,"
says he, "philosophers gathered together at this
particular time, as never before within one wall or
one city; I refer to those who flourished in the time
of Ariston and Arcesilaus." But I do not think that
sufficient; what we need is a clear-cut judgment as
to what teachers we should choose to follow. But
he places Arcesilaus and Ariston at the head of the
scholars who flourished in his day and generation;
and Apelles is much in evidence with him, and so is
Bion, of whom he says: "Bion was the first to drape
philosophy in embroidered finery"; and yet he states
that people frequently applied to Bion the words:
"Such a [thigh] as Bion [shews] from out his rags." [1]
Indeed, in these very statements Eratosthenes reveals a serious infirmity in his own judgment; and
because of this infirmity, although he himself
studied in Athens under Zeno of Citium, he makes

[1] The original allusion is to "the old man" Odysseus,
Od. 18. 74.

τῶν μὲν ἐκεῖνον διαδεξαμένων οὐδενὸς μέμνηται,
τοὺς δ' ἐκείνῳ διενεχθέντας καὶ ὧν διαδοχὴ οὐδεμία σῴζεται, τούτους ἀνθῆσαί φησι κατὰ τὸν
καιρὸν ἐκεῖνον. δηλοῖ δὲ καὶ ἡ περὶ τῶν ἀγαθῶν
ἐκδοθεῖσα ὑπ' αὐτοῦ πραγματεία καὶ μελέται καὶ
εἴ τι ἄλλο τοιοῦτο τὴν ἀγωγὴν αὐτοῦ· διότι μέσος
ἦν τοῦ τε βουλομένου φιλοσοφεῖν καὶ τοῦ μὴ
θαρροῦντος ἐγχειρίζειν ἑαυτὸν εἰς τὴν ὑπόσχεσιν
ταύτην, ἀλλὰ μόνον μέχρι τοῦ δοκεῖν προϊόντος, ἢ
καὶ παράβασίν τινα ταύτην ἀπὸ τῶν ἄλλων τῶν
ἐγκυκλίων πεπορισμένου πρὸς ὃ ἀγωγὴν ἢ καὶ
παιδιάν· τρόπον δέ τινα καὶ ἐν τοῖς ἄλλοις ἔστι
τοιοῦτος. ἀλλὰ ἐκεῖνα εἰάσθω·[1] πρὸς δὲ τὰ νῦν
ἐπιχειρητέον, ὅσα δύναιτ' ἄν, ἐπανορθοῦν τὴν
γεωγραφίαν, καὶ πρῶτον ὅπερ ἀρτίως ὑπερε-
θέμεθα.

3. Ποιητὴν γὰρ ἔφη πάντα στοχάζεσθαι ψυχαγωγίας, οὐ διδασκαλίας. τοὐναντίον δ' οἱ παλαιοὶ
φιλοσοφίαν τινὰ λέγουσι πρώτην τὴν ποιητικήν,
εἰσάγουσαν εἰς τὸν βίον ἡμᾶς ἐκ νέων καὶ διδάσ-
κουσαν ἤθη καὶ πάθη καὶ πράξεις μεθ' ἡδονῆς·
οἱ δ' ἡμέτεροι καὶ μόνον ποιητὴν ἔφασαν εἶναι
τὸν σοφόν. διὰ τοῦτο καὶ τοὺς παῖδας αἱ τῶν
Ἑλλήνων πόλεις πρώτιστα διὰ τῆς ποιητικῆς
παιδεύουσιν, οὐ ψυχαγωγίας χάριν δήπουθεν
ψιλῆς, ἀλλὰ σωφρονισμοῦ· ὅπου γε καὶ οἱ μου-
σικοὶ ψάλλειν καὶ λυρίζειν καὶ αὐλεῖν διδάσκοντες

C 16

---

[1] εἰάσθω, Cobet, for ἐάσθω.

---

[1] The Greek word here used is significant. The *parabasis*
formed a part of the Old Comedy, and was wholly incidental
to the main action of the play.

no mention of any of Zeno's successors, but speaks of those men who dissented from the teachings of Zeno and who failed to establish a school that lived after them as "flourishing" at that particular time. His treatise entitled *On the Good,* also, and his *Studies in Declamation,* and whatever else he wrote of this nature, go to show his tendency, namely, that of the man who is constantly vacillating between his desire to be a philosopher and his reluctance to devote himself entirely to this profession, and who therefore succeeds in advancing only far enough to have the appearance of being a philosopher; or of the man who has provided himself with this as a diversion[1] from his regular work, either for his pastime or even amusement; and in a sense Eratosthenes displays this tendency in his other writings, too. But let this pass; for my present purpose I must correct Eratosthenes' geography as far as possible; and first, on the point which I deferred a while ago.[2]

3. As I was saying, Eratosthenes contends that the aim of every poet is to entertain, not to instruct. The ancients assert, on the contrary, that poetry is a kind of elementary philosophy, which, taking us in our very boyhood, introduces us to the art of life and instructs us, with pleasure to ourselves, in character, emotions, and actions. And our School[3] goes still further and contends that the wise man alone is a poet. That is the reason why in Greece the various states educate the young, at the very beginning of their education, by means of poetry; not for the mere sake of entertainment, of course, but for the sake of moral discipline. Why, even the musicians, when they give instruction in singing, in

[2] Page 23.   [3] See Introduction, page xvi.

μεταποιοῦνται τῆς ἀρετῆς ταύτης· παιδευτικοὶ
γὰρ εἶναί φασι καὶ ἐπανορθωτικοὶ τῶν ἠθῶν.
ταῦτα δ' οὐ μόνον παρὰ τῶν Πυθαγορείων ἀκούειν
ἐστὶ λεγόντων, ἀλλὰ καὶ 'Αριστόξενος οὕτως ἀποφαίνεται. καὶ "Ομηρος δὲ τοὺς ἀοιδοὺς σωφρο-
νιστὰς εἴρηκε, καθάπερ τὸν τῆς Κλυταιμνήστρας
φύλακα,

ᾧ πόλλ' ἐπέτελλεν
'Ατρείδης Τροίηνδε κιὼν εἴρυσθαι ἄκοιτιν,
(Od. 3. 267)

τόν τε Αἴγισθον οὐ πρότερον αὐτῆς περιγενέσθαι,
πρὶν ἢ

τὸν μὲν ἀοιδὸν ἄγων ἐς νῆσον ἐρήμην
κάλλιπεν·
τὴν δ' ἐθέλων ἐθέλουσαν ἀνήγαγεν ὅνδε δόμονδε.
(Od. 3. 270)

χωρὶς δὲ τούτων ὁ 'Ερατοσθένης ἑαυτῷ μάχεται·
μικρὸν γὰρ πρὸ τῆς λεχθείσης ἀποφάσεως ἐναρ-
χόμενος τοῦ περὶ τῆς γεωγραφίας λόγου φησὶν
ἅπαντας κατ' ἀρχὰς φιλοτίμως ἔχειν εἰς τὸ μέσον
φέρειν τὴν ὑπὲρ τῶν τοιούτων ἱστορίαν. "Ομηρον
γοῦν ὑπέρ τε τῶν Αἰθιόπων ὅσα ἐπύθετο κατα-
χωρίσαι εἰς τὴν ποίησιν καὶ περὶ τῶν κατ' Αἴγυπτον καὶ Λιβύην, τὰ δὲ δὴ κατὰ τὴν 'Ελλάδα καὶ
τοὺς σύνεγγυς τόπους καὶ λίαν περιέργως ἐξενηνο-
χέναι, πολυτρήρωνα μὲν τὴν Θίσβην λέγοντα
(Il. 2. 502), 'Αλίαρτον δὲ ποιήεντα (ib. 503),
ἐσχατόωσαν δὲ 'Ανθηδόνα (ib. 508), Λίλαιαν δὲ
πηγῆς ἔπι Κηφισσοῖο (ib. 523), καὶ οὐδεμίαν
προσθήκην κενῶς ἀπορρίπτειν. πότερον οὖν ὁ
ποιῶν ταῦτα ψυχαγωγοῦντι ἔοικεν ἢ διδάσκοντι;

lyre-playing, or in flute-playing, lay claim to this
virtue, for they maintain that these studies tend to
discipline and correct the character. You may hear
this contention made not merely by the Pythagoreans,
but Aristoxenus also declares the same thing. And
Homer, too, has spoken of the bards as disciplinarians
in morality, as when he says of the guardian of
Clytaemnestra : " Whom the son of Atreus as he
went to Troy strictly charged to keep watch over his
wife " ; and he adds that Aegisthus was unable to
prevail over Clytaemnestra until " he carried the
bard to a lonely isle and left him there—while as for
her, he led her to his house, a willing lady with a
willing lover." But, even apart from this, Eratosthenes contradicts himself; for shortly before the
pronouncement above-mentioned, and at the very
beginning of his treatise on geography, he says that
from the earliest times all the poets have been eager
to display their knowledge of geography ; that
Homer, for instance, made a place in his poems for
everything that he had learned about the Ethiopians
and the inhabitants of Egypt and Libya, and that he
has gone into superfluous detail in regard to Greece
and the neighbouring countries, speaking of Thisbe
as the "haunt of doves," Haliartus as " grassy,"
Anthedon as " on the uttermost borders," Lilaea as
" by the springs of Cephisus" ; and he adds that
Homer never lets fall an inappropriate epithet.
Well then, I ask, is the poet who makes use of these
epithets like a person engaged in entertaining, or in

νὴ Δία, ἀλλὰ ταῦτα μὲν οὕτως εἴρηκε, τὰ δ' ἔξω
τῆς αἰσθήσεως καὶ οὗτος καὶ ἄλλοι τερατολογίας
μυθικῆς πεπληρώκασιν. οὐκοῦν ἐχρῆν οὕτως
εἰπεῖν, ὅτι ποιητὴς πᾶς τὰ μὲν ψυχαγωγίας χάριν
μόνον ἐκφέρει, τὰ δὲ διδασκαλίας· ὁ δ' ἐπήνεγκεν,
ὅτι ψυχαγωγίας μόνον, διδασκαλίας δ' οὔ. καὶ
προσπεριεργάζεταί τε,[1] πυνθανόμενος τί συμβάλλεται πρὸς ἀρετὴν ποιητοῦ πολλῶν ὑπάρξαι τόπων ἔμπειρον ἢ στρατηγίας ἢ γεωργίας ἢ ῥητορικῆς
ἢ οἷα δὴ περιποιεῖν αὐτῷ τινες ἐβουλήθησαν; τὸ
μὲν οὖν ἅπαντα ζητεῖν περιποιεῖν αὐτῷ προεκ-
πίπτοντος ἄν τις θείη τῇ φιλοτιμίᾳ, ὡς ἂν εἴ τις,
φησὶν ὁ Ἵππαρχος, Ἀττικῆς εἰρεσιώνης καταρτῴη[2] καὶ ἃ μὴ δύναται φέρειν μῆλα καὶ ὄγχνας,
οὕτως ἐκείνου πᾶν μάθημα καὶ πᾶσαν τέχνην.
τοῦτο μὲν δὴ ὀρθῶς ἂν λέγοις, ὦ Ἐρατόσθενες·
ἐκεῖνα δ' οὐκ ὀρθῶς, ἀφαιρούμενος αὐτὸν τὴν
τοσαύτην πολυμάθειαν καὶ τὴν ποιητικὴν γραώδη
μυθολογίαν ἀποφαίνων, ᾗ δέδοται πλάττειν, φής,[3]
C 17 ὃ ἂν αὐτῇ φαίνηται ψυχαγωγίας οἰκεῖον. ἆρα
γὰρ οὐδὲ τοῖς ἀκρωμένοις τῶν ποιητῶν οὐδὲν
συμβάλλεται πρὸς ἀρετήν; λέγω δὲ τὸ πολλῶν
ὑπάρξαι τόπων ἔμπειρον ἢ στρατηγίας ἢ γεωργίας
ἢ ῥητορικῆς, ἅπερ ἡ ἀκρόασις, ὡς εἰκός, περιποιεῖ.

---

[1] προσπεριεργάζεταί τε, Toup, for προσεξεργάζεταί γε (προσ-
επεργάζεταί γε); Meineke (Vind. 239) approving, but not
inserting.
[2] καταρτῴη, Madvig, for κατηγοροίη; A. Vogel approving.
[3] φής, Groskurd, for φησίν; Forbiger following.

---

[1] The "eiresione" was an olive (or laurel) branch adorned
with the first-fruits of a given land and carried around to
the accompaniment of a song of thanksgiving and prayer.

instructing? "The latter, of course," you reply; "but while these epithets have been used by him for purposes of instruction, everything beyond the range of observation has been filled, not only by Homer but by others also, with mythical marvels." Eratosthenes, then, should have said that "every poet writes partly for purposes of mere entertainment and partly for instruction"; but his words were "mere entertainment and not instruction." And Eratosthenes gives himself quite unnecessary pains when he asks how it contributes to the excellence of the poet for him to be an expert in geography, or in generalship, or in agriculture, or in rhetoric, or in any kind of special knowledge with which some people have wished to "invest" him. Now the desire to "invest" Homer with all knowledge might be regarded as characteristic of a man whose zeal exceeds the proper limit, just as would be the case if a man— to use a comparison of Hipparchus—should hang apples and pears, or anything else that it cannot bear, on an Attic "eiresione"[1]; so absurd would it be to "invest" Homer with all knowledge and with every art. You may be right, Eratosthenes, on that point, but you are wrong when you deny to Homer the possession of vast learning, and go on to declare that poetry is a fable-prating old wife, who has been permitted to "invent"(as you call it) whatever she deems suitable for purposes of entertainment. What, then? Is no contribution made, either, to the excellence of him who hears the poets recited? I again refer to the poet's being an expert in geography, or generalship, or agriculture, or rhetoric, the subjects in which the poet naturally "invests" the hearer with special knowledge.

4. Ἀλλὰ μὴν ταῦτά γε πάντα ὁ ποιητὴς Ὀδυσσεῖ προσῆψεν, ὃν τῶν πάντων μάλιστα ἀρετῇ πάσῃ κοσμεῖ· οὗτος γὰρ αὐτῷ

> πολλῶν ἀνθρώπων ἴδεν ἄστεα καὶ νόον ἔγνω,
> <div align="right">(<i>Od.</i> 1. 3)</div>

οὗτός τε ὁ

> εἰδὼς παντοίους τε δόλους καὶ μήδεα πυκνά.
> <div align="right">(<i>Il.</i> 3. 202)</div>

οὗτος δ᾽ ὁ "πτολίπορθος" ἀεὶ λεγόμενος καὶ τὸ Ἴλιον ἑλὼν

> βουλῇ καὶ μύθοισι καὶ ἠπεροπηίδι τέχνῃ·
> τούτου γ᾽ ἑσπομένοιο καὶ ἐκ πυρὸς αἰθομένοιο
> ἄμφω νοστήσαιμεν,
> <div align="right">(<i>Il.</i> 10. 246)</div>

φησὶν ὁ Διομήδης. καὶ μὴν ἐπί γε τῇ γεωργίᾳ σεμνύνεται· καὶ γὰρ ἐν ἀμητῷ,

> ἐν ποίῃ· δρέπανον μὲν ἐγὼν εὐκαμπὲς ἔχοιμι,
> καὶ δὲ σὺ τοῖον ἔχοις·
> <div align="right">(<i>Od.</i> 18. 368)</div>

καὶ ἐν ἀρότῳ,

> τῷ κέ μ᾽ ἴδοις, εἰ ὦλκα διηνεκέα προταμοίμην.
> <div align="right">(<i>Od.</i> 18. 375)</div>

καὶ οὐχ Ὅμηρος μὲν οὕτω φρονεῖ περὶ τούτων, οὐχὶ δὲ πάντες οἱ πεπαιδευμένοι μάρτυρι χρῶνται τῷ ποιητῇ, ὡς ὀρθῶς λέγοντι, περὶ τοῦ τὴν τοιαύτην ἐμπειρίαν εἰς φρόνησιν συντείνειν μάλιστα.

5. Ἡ δὲ ῥητορικὴ φρόνησίς ἐστι δήπου περὶ λόγους· ἣν ἐπιδείκνυται παρ᾽ ὅλην τὴν ποίησιν Ὀδυσσεὺς ἐν τῇ Διαπείρᾳ, ἐν ταῖς Λιταῖς, ἐν τῇ Πρεσβείᾳ, ἐν ᾗ φησίν· <div align="right">(<i>Il.</i> 2 ; 9 ; 3)</div>

4. Assuredly Homer has attributed all knowledge of this kind, at least, to Odysseus, whom he adorns beyond his fellows with every kind of excellence; for his Odysseus " of many men the towns did see and minds did learn," and he is the man who " is skilled in all the ways of wile and cunning device." Odysseus is continually spoken of as " the sacker of cities " and as the capturer of Troy " by means of his counsels and his persuasiveness and his deceitful arts "; and Diomedes says of him : " But while he cometh with me, even out of burning fire might we both return." More than that, Odysseus prides himself on being a farmer. For instance, with regard to reaping he says : " In the deep grass might the match be, and might I have a crooked scythe, and thou another like it "; and with regard to ploughing : " Then shouldst thou see me, whether or no I would cut a clean furrow unbroken before me." And not only does Homer thus possess wisdom about these matters, but all enlightened men cite the poet as a witness whose words are true, to prove that practical experience of this kind contributes in the highest degree to wisdom.

5. Rhetoric is, to be sure, wisdom applied to discourse ; and Odysseus displays this gift throughout the entire Iliad, in the Trial, in the Prayers, and in the Embassy, where Homer says : " But when

ἀλλ' ὅτε δὴ ὄπα τε μεγάλην ἐκ στήθεος εἵη
καὶ ἔπεα νιφάδεσσιν ἐοικότα χειμερίῃσιν,
οὐκ ἂν ἔπειτ' Ὀδυσῆΐ γ' ἐρίσσειε βροτὸς ἄλλος.
(Π. 3. 221)

τίς ἂν οὖν ὑπολάβοι τὸν δυνάμενον ποιητὴν
εἰσάγειν ῥητορεύοντας ἑτέρους καὶ στρατηγοῦντας
καὶ τὰ ἄλλα ἐπιδεικνυμένους τὰ τῆς ἀρετῆς ἔργα,
αὐτὸν εἶναι τῶν φλυάρων ἕνα καὶ τῶν θαυματο-
ποιῶν, γοητεύειν μόνον καὶ κολακεύειν τὸν ἀκροα-
τὴν δυνάμενον, ὠφελεῖν δὲ μηδέν; προτέραν[1] δ'
οὐδ' ἀρετὴν ποιητοῦ λέγοιμεν ἂν ἡντινοῦν ἄλλην,
ἢ τὴν μιμητικὴν τοῦ βίου διὰ λόγων. πῶς ἂν
οὖν μιμοῖτο ἄπειρος ὢν τοῦ βίου καὶ ἄφρων;
οὐ γὰρ οὕτω φαμὲν τὴν τῶν ποιητῶν ἀρετὴν
ὡσεὶ[2] τεκτόνων ἢ χαλκέων· ἀλλ' ἐκείνη μὲν
οὐδενὸς ἔχεται καλοῦ καὶ σεμνοῦ, ἡ δὲ ποιητοῦ
συνέζευκται τῇ τοῦ ἀνθρώπου, καὶ οὐχ οἷόν τε
ἀγαθὸν γενέσθαι ποιητήν, μὴ πρότερον γενηθέντα
ἄνδρα ἀγαθόν.

6. Τὸ δὲ δὴ καὶ τὴν ῥητορικὴν ἀφαιρεῖσθαι
τὸν ποιητὴν τελέως ἀφειδοῦντος ἡμῶν ἐστι. τί
γὰρ οὕτω ῥητορικόν, ὡς φράσις; τί δ' οὕτω
ποιητικόν; τίς δ' ἀμείνων Ὁμήρου φράσαι; νὴ
Δία, ἀλλ' ἑτέρα φράσις ἡ ποιητική. τῷ γε εἴδει,
ὡς καὶ ἐν αὐτῇ τῇ ποιητικῇ ἡ τραγικὴ καὶ ἡ
κωμική, καὶ ἐν τῇ πεζῇ ἡ ἱστορικὴ καὶ ἡ δικα-
νική· ἆρα γὰρ οὐδ' ὁ λόγος ἐστὶ γενικός, οὗ εἴδη

C 18

---

[1] προτέραν, Meineke, for πότερον; C. Müller approving.
[2] ὡσεί, Corais, for ὡς ἥ; Meineke following; C. Müller approving.

he uttered his great voice from his chest, and words like unto the snowflakes of winter, then could no mortal man contend with Odysseus." Who, then, can assume that the poet who is capable of introducing other men in the rôle of orators, or of generals, or in other rôles that exhibit the accomplishments of excellence, is himself but one of the buffoons or jugglers, capable only of bewitching and flattering his hearer but not of helping him? Nor can we assume that any excellence of a poet whatever is superior to that which enables him to imitate life through the means of speech. How, then, can a man imitate life if he has no experience of life and is a dolt? Of course we do not speak of the excellence of a poet in the same sense as we speak of that of a carpenter or a blacksmith; for their excellence depends upon no inherent nobility and dignity, whereas the excellence of a poet is inseparably associated with the excellence of the man himself, and it is impossible for one to become a good poet unless he has previously become a good man.

6. So, then, to deny the art of rhetoric to Homer is to disregard my position entirely. For what is so much a part of rhetoric as style[1]? And what is so much a part of poetry? And who has surpassed Homer in style[2]? "Assuredly," you answer, "but the style of poetry is different from that of rhetoric." In species, yes; just as in poetry itself the style of tragedy differs from that of comedy, and in prose the style of history differs from that of forensic speech. Well then, would you assert that discourse is not a generic term, either, whose

[1] *Phrasis.*   [2] *Phrazein.*

ὁ ἔμμετρος καὶ ὁ πεζός; ἢ λόγος μέν, ῥητορικὸς
δὲ λόγος οὐκ ἔστι γενικὸς καὶ φράσις καὶ ἀρετὴ
λόγου; ὡς δ᾽ εἰπεῖν, ὁ πεζὸς λόγος, ὅ γε κατε-
σκευασμένος, μίμημα τοῦ ποιητικοῦ ἐστι. πρώτιστα γὰρ ἡ ποιητικὴ κατασκευὴ παρῆλθεν εἰς
τὸ μέσον καὶ εὐδοκίμησεν· εἶτα ἐκείνην μιμού-
μενοι, λύσαντες τὸ μέτρον, τἆλλα δὲ φυλάξαντες
τὰ ποιητικὰ συνέγραψαν οἱ περὶ Κάδμον καὶ
Φερεκύδη καὶ Ἑκαταῖον· εἶτα οἱ ὕστερον, ἀφαι-
ροῦντες ἀεί τι τῶν τοιούτων, εἰς τὸ νῦν εἶδος
κατήγαγον, ὡς ἂν ἀπὸ ὕψους τινός· καθάπερ
ἄν τις καὶ τὴν κωμῳδίαν φαίη λαβεῖν τὴν
σύστασιν ἀπὸ τῆς τραγῳδίας, καὶ τοῦ κατ᾽
αὐτὴν ὕψους καταβιβασθεῖσαν εἰς τὸ λογοειδὲς
νυνὶ καλούμενον. καὶ τὸ ἀείδειν δὲ ἀντὶ τοῦ
φράζειν τιθέμενον παρὰ τοῖς πάλαι ταυτὸ τοῦτο
ἐκμαρτυρεῖ, διότι πηγὴ καὶ ἀρχὴ φράσεως κατε-
σκευασμένης καὶ ῥητορικῆς ὑπῆρξεν ἡ ποιητική.
αὕτη γὰρ προσεχρήσατο τῷ μέλει κατὰ τὰς ἐπι-
δείξεις· τοῦτο δ᾽ ἦν λόγος μεμελισμένος ἢ ᾠδή,[1]
ἀφ᾽ οὗ δὴ ῥαψῳδίαν τ᾽ ἔλεγον καὶ τραγῳδίαν καὶ
κωμῳδίαν. ὥστ᾽ ἐπειδὴ τὸ φράζειν πρώτιστα ἐπὶ
τῆς ποιητικῆς ἐλέγετο φράσεως, αὕτη δὲ μετ᾽ ᾠδῆς
ὑπῆρξε παρ᾽ ἐκείνοις, τὸ ἀείδειν αὐτοῖς τὸ αὐτὸ
τῷ φράζειν.[2] καταχρησαμένων δ᾽ αὐτῶν θατέρῳ

---

[1] λόγος μεμελισμένος ἢ ᾠδή, A. Miller, for ᾠδὴ ἢ λόγος
μεμελισμένος.

[2] αὕτη δὲ μετ᾽ ᾠδῆς ὑπῆρξε παρ᾽ ἐκείνοις, τὸ ἀείδειν αὐτοῖς τὸ
αὐτὸ τῷ φράζειν, Spengel, for αὕτη δὲ μετ᾽ ᾠδῆς, τὸ ἀείδειν
αὐτοῖς τὸ αὐτὸ τῷ φράζειν ὑπῆρξε παρ᾽ ἐκείνοις; C. Müller
approving.

species are metrical discourse and prose discourse? Or, rather, is discourse, in its broadest sense, generic, while rhetorical discourse is not generic, and style excellence of discourse are not?—But prose and discourse—I mean artistic prose—is, I may say, an imitation of poetic discourse; for poetry, as an art, first came upon the scene and was first to win approval. Then came Cadmus, Pherecydes, Hecataeus, and their followers, with prose writings in which they imitated the poetic art, abandoning the use of metre but in other respects preserving the qualities of poetry. Then subsequent writers took away, each in his turn, something of these qualities, and brought prose down to its present form, as from a sublime height. In the same way one might say that comedy took its structure from tragedy, but that it also has been degraded—from the sublime height of tragedy to its present " prose-like " style, as it is called. And further, the fact that the ancients used the verb " sing" instead of the verb "tell"[1] bears witness to this very thing, namely, that poetry was the source and origin of style, I mean ornate, or rhetorical, style. For when poetry was recited, it employed the assistance of song; this combination formed melodic discourse, or "ode"; and from "ode" they began to use the terms rhapsody, tragedy, and comedy. Therefore, since "tell"[1] was first used in reference to poetic "style"[2] and since among the ancients this poetic style was accompanied by song, the term "sing" was to them equivalent to the term "tell"; and then after they had misused the former of these two terms by applying it to prose

[1] *Phrazein.*   [2] *Phrasis.*

καὶ ἐπὶ τοῦ πεζοῦ λόγου, καὶ ἐπὶ θάτερον ἡ κατά-
χρησις διέβη. καὶ αὐτὸ δὲ τὸ πεζὸν λεχθῆναι τὸν
ἄνευ τοῦ μέτρου λόγον ἐμφαίνει τὸν ἀπὸ ὕψους
τινὸς καταβάντα καὶ ὀχήματος εἰς τοὔδαφος.

7. Ἀλλ' οὐδὲ τὰ σύνεγγυς μόνον, ὥσπερ
Ἐρατοσθένης εἴρηκε, καὶ τὰ ἐν τοῖς Ἕλλησιν,
ἀλλὰ καὶ τῶν πόρρω πολλὰ λέγει· καὶ δι' ἀκρι-
βείας Ὅμηρος καὶ μᾶλλόν γε τῶν ὕστερον μυθο-
λογεῖται, οὐ πάντα τερατευόμενος, ἀλλὰ καὶ πρὸς
ἐπιστήμην ἀλληγορῶν ἢ διασκευάζων ἢ δημαγωγῶν ἄλλα τε καὶ τὰ περὶ τὴν Ὀδυσσέως
πλάνην· περὶ ἧς πολλὰ διαμαρτάνει, τούς τ'
ἐξηγητὰς φλυάρους ἀποφαίνων καὶ αὐτὸν τὸν
ποιητήν· περὶ ὧν ἄξιον εἰπεῖν διὰ πλειόνων.

8. Καὶ πρῶτον ὅτι τοὺς μύθους ἀπεδέξαντο
C 19 οὐχ οἱ ποιηταὶ μόνον, ἀλλὰ καὶ αἱ πόλεις
πολὺ πρότερον καὶ οἱ νομοθέται τοῦ χρησίμου
χάριν, βλέψαντες εἰς τὸ φυσικὸν πάθος τοῦ
λογικοῦ ζῴου· φιλειδήμων γὰρ ἄνθρωπος·[1] προοί-
μιον δὲ τούτου τὸ φιλόμυθον· ἐντεῦθεν οὖν
ἄρχεται τὰ παιδία ἀκροᾶσθαι καὶ κοινωνεῖν
λόγων ἐπὶ πλεῖον. αἴτιον δ', ὅτι καινολογία
τίς ἐστιν ὁ μῦθος, οὐ τὰ καθεστηκότα φράζων,
ἀλλ' ἕτερα παρὰ ταῦτα· ἡδὺ δὲ τὸ καινὸν καὶ
ὃ μὴ πρότερον ἔγνω τις· τοῦτο δ' αὐτό ἐστι καὶ

[1] ἄνθρωπος, Meineke, for ἄνθρωπος; Cobet also independently.

discourse, the misuse passed over to the latter term also. And, furthermore, the very fact that non-metrical discourse was termed " pedestrian " indicates its descent from a height, or from a chariot, to the ground.

7. Nor, indeed, is the statement of Eratosthenes true that Homer speaks only of places that are near by and in Greece; on the contrary, he speaks also of many places that are distant; and when Homer indulges in myths he is at least more accurate than the later writers, since he does not deal wholly in marvels, but for our instruction he also uses allegory, or revises myths, or curries popular favour, and particularly in his story of the wanderings of Odysseus; and Eratosthenes makes many mistakes when he speaks of these wanderings and declares that not only the commentators on Homer but also Homer himself are dealers in nonsense. But it is worth my while to examine these points more in detail.

8. In the first place, I remark that the poets were not alone in sanctioning myths, for long before the poets the states and the lawgivers had sanctioned them as a useful expedient, since they had an insight into the natural affections of the reasoning animal; for man is eager to learn, and his fondness for tales is a prelude to this quality. It is fondness for tales, then, that induces children to give their attention to narratives and more and more to take part in them. The reason for this is that myth is a new language to them—a language that tells them, not of things as they are, but of a different set of things. And what is new is pleasing, and so is what one did not know before; and it is just this that makes men eager to

τὸ ποιοῦν φιλειδήμονα. ὅταν δὲ προσῇ καὶ τὸ
θαυμαστὸν καὶ τὸ τερατῶδες, ἐπιτείνει τὴν
ἡδονήν, ἥπερ ἐστὶ τοῦ μανθάνειν φίλτρον. κατ'
ἀρχὰς μὲν οὖν ἀνάγκη τοιούτοις δελέασι χρῆσθαι,
προϊούσης δὲ τῆς ἡλικίας ἐπὶ τὴν τῶν ὄντων
μάθησιν ἄγειν, ἤδη τῆς διανοίας ἐρρωμένης καὶ
μηκέτι δεομένης κολάκων. καὶ ἰδιώτης δὲ πᾶς
καὶ ἀπαίδευτος τρόπον τινὰ παῖς ἐστι φιλομυθεῖ
τε ὡσαύτως· ὁμοίως δὲ καὶ ὁ πεπαιδευμένος
μετρίως· οὐδὲ γὰρ οὗτος ἰσχύει τῷ λογισμῷ,
πρόσεστι δὲ καὶ τὸ ἐκ παιδὸς ἔθος. ἐπεὶ δ' οὐ
μόνον ἡδύ, ἀλλὰ καὶ φοβερὸν τὸ τερατῶδες,
ἀμφοτέρων ἐστὶ τῶν εἰδῶν χρεία πρός τε τοὺς
παῖδας καὶ τοὺς ἐν ἡλικίᾳ· τοῖς τε γὰρ παισὶ
προσφέρομεν τοὺς ἡδεῖς μύθους εἰς προτροπήν,
εἰς ἀποτροπὴν δὲ τοὺς φοβερούς. ἥ τε γὰρ
Λάμια μῦθός ἐστι καὶ ἡ Γοργὼ καὶ ὁ Ἐφιάλτης
καὶ ἡ Μορμολύκη. οἵ τε πολλοὶ τῶν τὰς πόλεις
οἰκούντων εἰς μὲν προτροπὴν ἄγονται τοῖς ἡδέσι
τῶν μύθων, ὅταν ἀκούσωσι τῶν ποιητῶν ἀνδραγα-
θήματα μυθώδη διηγουμένων, οἷον Ἡρακλέους
ἄθλους ἢ Θησέως, ἢ τιμὰς παρὰ θεῶν νεμομένας,
ἢ νὴ Δία ὁρῶσι γραφὰς ἢ ξόανα ἢ πλάσματα
τοιαύτην τινὰ περιπέτειαν ὑποσημαίνοντα μυ-
θώδη· εἰς ἀποτροπὴν δέ, ὅταν κολάσεις παρὰ
θεῶν καὶ φόβους καὶ ἀπειλὰς ἢ διὰ λόγων ἢ διὰ
τύπων ἀοράτων[1] τινῶν προσδέχωνται, ἢ καὶ

---

[1] ἀοράτων, Kramer, Meineke, for ἀόρων, above which ατ is
written in A. See *Classical Journal* 1814, 113.

learn. But if you add thereto the marvellous and
the portentous, you thereby increase the pleasure,
and pleasure acts as a charm to incite to learning.
At the beginning we must needs make use of such
bait for children, but as the child advances in years
we must guide him to the knowledge of facts, when
once his intelligence has become strong and no
longer needs to be coaxed. Now every illiterate and
uneducated man is, in a sense, a child, and, like a
child, he is fond of stories; and for that matter, so
is the half-educated man, for his reasoning faculty
has not been fully developed, and, besides, the
mental habits of his childhood persist in him. Now
since the portentous is not only pleasing, but fear-
inspiring as well, we can employ both kinds of myth
for children, and for grown-up people too. In the
case of children we employ the pleasing myths to
spur them on, and the fear-inspiring myths to deter
them; for instance, Lamia [1] is a myth, and so are
the Gorgon, and Ephialtes,[2] and Mormolyce.[3] Most
of those who live in the cities are incited to emulation
by the myths that are pleasing, when they hear the
poets narrate mythical deeds of heroism, such as the
Labours of Heracles or of Theseus, or hear of
honours bestowed by gods, or, indeed, when they
see paintings or primitive images or works of sculp-
ture which suggest any similar happy issue of fortune
in mythology; but they are deterred from evil
courses when, either through descriptions or through
typical representations of objects unseen, they learn
of divine punishments, terrors, and threats—or even

[1] A familiar female goblin, devourer of children, in the
ancient nursery-legends.
[2] The giant whose eyes were put out by Apollo and
Heracles.   [3] A female goblin.

πιστεύωσι περιπεσεῖν τινας· οὐ γὰρ ὄχλον γε[1]
γυναικῶν καὶ παντὸς χυδαίου πλήθους ἐπαγαγεῖν
λόγῳ δυνατὸν φιλοσόφῳ, καὶ προκαλέσασθαι[2]
πρὸς εὐσέβειαν καὶ ὁσιότητα καὶ πίστιν, ἀλλὰ
δεῖ καὶ[3] δεισιδαιμονίας· τοῦτο δ᾽ οὐκ ἄνευ μυθοποιίας καὶ τερατείας. κεραυνὸς γὰρ καὶ αἰγὶς
καὶ τρίαινα καὶ λαμπάδες καὶ δράκοντες καὶ
θυρσόλογχα, τῶν θεῶν ὅπλα, μῦθοι καὶ πᾶσα
θεολογία ἀρχαϊκή· ταῦτα δ᾽ ἀπεδέξαντο οἱ τὰς
πολιτείας καταστησάμενοι μορμολύκας τινὰς πρὸς
C 20 τοὺς νηπιόφρονας. τοιαύτης δὲ τῆς μυθοποιίας
οὔσης καὶ καταστρεφούσης εἰς τὸ κοινωνικὸν καὶ
τὸ πολιτικὸν τοῦ βίου σχῆμα καὶ τὴν τῶν ὄντων
ἱστορίαν, οἱ μὲν ἀρχαῖοι τὴν παιδικὴν ἀγωγὴν
ἐφύλαξαν μέχρι τῶν τελείων ἡλικιῶν, καὶ διὰ
ποιητικῆς ἱκανῶς σωφρονίζεσθαι πᾶσαν ἡλικίαν
ὑπέλαβον· χρόνοις δ᾽ ὕστερον ἡ τῆς ἱστορίας
γραφὴ καὶ ἡ νῦν φιλοσοφία παρελήλυθεν εἰς
μεσον. αὕτη μὲν οὖν πρὸς ὀλίγους, ἡ δὲ ποιητικὴ
δημωφελεστέρα καὶ θέατρα πληροῦν δυναμένη· ἡ
δὲ δὴ τοῦ Ὁμήρου ὑπερβαλλόντως. καὶ οἱ πρῶτοι δὲ ἱστορικοὶ καὶ φυσικοὶ μυθογράφοι.

9. Ἄτε δὴ πρὸς τὸ παιδευτικὸν εἶδος τοὺς μύθους ἀναφέρων ὁ ποιητὴς ἐφρόντιζε[4] πολὺ μέρος
τἀληθοῦς· "ἐν δ᾽ ἐτίθει" (Il. 18. 541) καὶ ψεῦδος,
τὸ μὲν ἀποδεχόμενος, τῷ δὲ δημαγωγῶν καὶ στρα-
τηγῶν τὰ πλήθη.

---

[1] γε, Meineke, for τε ; C. Müller approving.
[2] προκαλέσασθαι, is retained against Meineke's προσκαλ-
έσασθαι ; A Miller and C. Müller approving.
[3] διά, Cobet deletes, before δεισιδαιμονίας.
[4] ἐφρόντιζε, Cobet, from the margin of A, for ἐφρόντισε.

when they merely believe that men have met with
such experiences. For in dealing with a crowd of
women, at least, or with any promiscuous mob, a
philosopher cannot influence them by reason or
exhort them to reverence, piety and faith; nay, there
is need of religious fear also, and this cannot be
aroused without myths and marvels. For thunderbolt, aegis, trident, torches, snakes, thyrsus-lances,—
arms of the gods—are myths, and so is the entire
ancient theology. But the founders of states gave
their sanction to these things as bugbears wherewith
to scare the simple-minded. Now since this is the
nature of mythology, and since it has come to have
its place in the social and civil scheme of life as well
as in the history of actual facts, the ancients clung
to their system of education for children and applied
it up to the age of maturity; and by means of poetry
they believed that they could satisfactorily discipline
every period of life. But now, after a long time,
the writing of history and the present-day philosophy
have come to the front. Philosophy, however, is for
the few, whereas poetry is more useful to the people
at large and can draw full houses—and this is excep-
tionally true of the poetry of Homer. And the early
historians and physicists were also writers of myths.

9. Now inasmuch as Homer referred his myths
to the province of education, he was wont to pay
considerable attention to the truth. "And he
mingled therein" a false element also, giving his
sanction to the truth, but using the false to win the
favour of the populace and to out-general the masses.

STRABO

ὡς δ' ὅτε τις χρυσὸν περιχεύεται ἀργύρῳ ἀνήρ,
(Od. 6. 232)

οὕτως ἐκεῖνος ταῖς ἀληθέσι περιπετείαις προσετίθει[1] μῦθον, ἡδύνων καὶ κοσμῶν τὴν φράσιν·
πρὸς δὲ τὸ αὐτὸ τέλος τοῦ ἱστορικοῦ καὶ τοῦ τὰ
ὄντα λέγοντος βλέπων. οὕτω δὴ τόν τε Ἰλιακὸν
πόλεμον γεγονότα παραλαβὼν ἐκόσμησε ταῖς
μυθοποιίαις, καὶ τὴν Ὀδυσσέως πλάνην ὡσαύτως·
ἐκ μηδενὸς δὲ ἀληθοῦς ἀνάπτειν κενὴν τερατο-
λογίαν οὐχ Ὁμηρικόν. προσπίπτει γάρ, ὡς εἰκός,
ὡς πιθανώτερον ἂν οὕτω τις ψεύδοιτο, εἰ καταμίσγοι τι καὶ αὐτῶν τῶν ἀληθινῶν·[2] ὅπερ καὶ
Πολύβιός φησι περὶ τῆς Ὀδυσσέως πλάνης ἐπι-
χειρῶν· τοιοῦτο δ' ἐστὶ καὶ τὸ

ἴσκε ψεύδεα πολλὰ λέγων ἐτύμοισιν ὁμοῖα·
(Od. 19. 203)

οὐ γὰρ πάντα, ἀλλὰ πολλά, ἐπεὶ οὐδ' ἂν ἦν
ἐτύμοισιν ὁμοῖα. ἔλαβεν οὖν παρὰ τῆς ἱστορίας
τὰς ἀρχάς. καὶ γὰρ τὸν Αἴολον[3] δυναστεῦσαί
φησι τῶν περὶ τὴν Λιπάραν νήσων, καὶ τῶν
περὶ τὴν Αἴτνην καὶ Λεοντίνην Κύκλωπας καὶ
Λαιστρυγόνας ἀξένους τινάς· διὸ καὶ τὰ περὶ
τὸν πορθμὸν ἀπροσπέλαστα εἶναι τοῖς τότε, καὶ
τὴν Χάρυβδιν καὶ τὸ Σκύλλαιον ὑπὸ λῃστῶν
κατέχεσθαι. οὕτω δὲ καὶ τοὺς ἄλλους τῶν ὑπὸ
Ὁμήρου λεγομένων ἐν ἄλλοις τόποις ἱστοροῦμεν·
οὕτω δὲ καὶ τοὺς Κιμμερίους εἰδὼς οἰκοῦντας

---

[1] προσετίθει, Corais, for προσεπετίθει; Cobet independently.
[2] On the passage οὕτω δὴ... ἀληθινῶν, see R. Zimmermann,
Hermes 23, 125. [3] Αἴολον, Meineke, for Αἴολον.

" And as when some skilful man overlays gold upon silver," just so was Homer wont to add a mythical element to actual occurrences, thus giving flavour and adornment to his style; but he has the same end in view as the historian or the person who narrates facts. So, for instance, he took the Trojan war, an historical fact, and decked it out with his myths; and he did the same in the case of the wanderings of Odysseus; but to hang an empty story of marvels on something wholly untrue is not Homer's way of doing things. For it occurs to us at once, doubtless, that a man will lie more plausibly if he will mix in some actual truth, just as Polybius says, when he is discussing the wanderings of Odysseus. This is what Homer himself means when he says of Odysseus: " So he told many lies in the likeness of truth;" for Homer does not say " all" but "many" lies; since otherwise they would not have been " in the likeness of truth." Accordingly, he took the foundations of his stories from history. For instance, history says that Aeolus was once king over the islands about Lipara, and that the Cyclopes and the Laestrygonians, inhospitable peoples, were lords over the region about Aetna and Leontine; and that for this reason the region about the Strait might not be visited by men of that time, and that Charybdis and the Rock of Scylla were infested by brigands. And from history we learn that the rest of the peoples mentioned by Homer lived in other parts of the world. And, too, it was on the basis of Homer's actual knowledge that the Cimmerians lived

73

τὸν Κιμμερικὸν βόσπορον πρόσβορρον[1] καὶ ζο-
φώδη μετήγαγεν οἰκείως εἰς σκοτεινόν τινα τόπον
τὸν καθ' "Αιδην, χρήσιμον ὄντα πρὸς τὴν μυθοποιίαν τὴν ἐν τῇ πλάνῃ. ὅτι δ' οἶδεν αὐτούς,
οἱ χρονογράφοι δηλοῦσιν, ἢ μικρὸν πρὸ αὐτοῦ
τὴν τῶν Κιμμερίων ἔφοδον ἢ κατ' αὐτὸν ἀναγρά-
φοντες.

C 21   10. Ὡσαύτως[2] καὶ τοὺς Κόλχους εἰδὼς καὶ
τὸν Ἰάσονος πλοῦν τὸν εἰς Αἶαν καὶ τὰ περὶ
Κίρκης καὶ Μηδείας μυθευόμενα καὶ ἱστορούμενα
περὶ τῆς φαρμακείας καὶ τῆς ἄλλης ὁμοιοτροπίας,
συγγενείας τε ἔπλασε τῶν οὕτω διῳκισμένων,
τῆς μὲν ἐν τῷ μυχῷ τοῦ Πόντου, τῆς δ' ἐν τῇ
Ἰταλίᾳ, καὶ ἐξωκεανισμὸν ἀμφοῖν, τάχα καὶ τοῦ
Ἰάσονος μέχρι τῆς Ἰταλίας πλανηθέντος· δείκνυται γάρ τινα[3] καὶ περὶ τὰ Κεραύνια ὄρη καὶ
περὶ τὸν Ἀδρίαν καὶ ἐν τῷ Ποσειδωνιάτῃ κόλπῳ
καὶ ταῖς πρὸ τῆς Τυρρηνίας νήσοις τῆς τῶν Ἀρ-
γοναυτῶν πλάνης σημεῖα. προσέδοσαν δέ τι καὶ
αἱ Κυάνεαι, ἅσπερ Συμπληγάδας καλοῦσι πέτρας
τινές, τραχὺν ποιοῦσαι τὸν διέκπλουν τὸν διὰ τοῦ
Βυζαντιακοῦ στόματος· ὥστε παρὰ μὲν τὴν Αἶαν
ἡ Αἰαίη, παρὰ δὲ τὰς Συμπληγάδας αἱ Πλαγκταί,

---

[1] πρόσβορρον, Madvig, for πρὸς Βορρᾶν.
[2] ὡσαύτως, the reading of the MSS., is retained by Kramer
and Meineke ; C. Müller approving.
[3] σημεῖα after τινα, Meineke deletes, following suggestion
of Müller-Dübner.

about the Cimmerian Bosporus, a gloomy country in the north, that he transferred them, quite appropriately, to a certain gloomy region in the neighbourhood of Hades—a region that suited the purpose of his mythology in telling of the wanderings of Odysseus. The writers of chronicles make it plain that Homer knew the Cimmerians, in that they fix the date of the invasion of the Cimmerians either a short time before Homer, or else in Homer's own time.

10. And likewise it was on the basis of Homer's actual knowledge of the Colchians, of Jason's expedition to Aea, and of the stories of fact and fiction told about Circe and Medea regarding their use of magic potions and their general similarity of character, that he invented a blood-relationship between the two, although they lived so very far apart, the one in the remote recess of the Pontus, and the other in Italy, and also invented a residence for both of them out by Oceanus, though it may be that Jason wandered as far as Italy ; for there are some indications that point to the wanderings of the Argonauts in the region of the Ceraunian Mountains,[1] about the Adriatic Sea,[2] in the Gulf of Poseidonia,[3] and in the islands that lie off Tyrrhenia. And the Cyaneae[4] also, which some call the Symplegades,[5] furnished the poet an additional matter of fact, in that they made the passage through the mouth of the strait at Byzantium very difficult ; so that when we compare the Aeaea of Circe with the Aea of Medea, and Homer's Planctae[6] with the Symplegades,

[1] The Kimara Mountains in Albania.
[2] See 7 5. 9.   [3] Gulf of Salerno.
[4] Dark Blue Rocks.   [5] Clashing Rocks.
[6] Wandering Rocks.

καὶ ὁ δι' αὐτῶν πλοῦς τοῦ Ἰάσονος πιθανὸς ἐφάνη·
παρὰ δὲ τὴν Σκύλλαν καὶ τὴν Χάρυβδιν ὁ διὰ τῶν
σκοπέλων πλοῦς. ἁπλῶς δ' οἱ τότε τὸ πέλαγος
τὸ Ποντικὸν ὥσπερ ἄλλον τινὰ ὠκεανὸν ὑπε-
λάμβανον, καὶ τοὺς πλέοντας ἐκεῖσε ὁμοίως
ἐκτοπίζειν ἐδόκουν, ὥσπερ τοὺς ἔξω Στηλῶν ἐπὶ
πολὺ προϊόντας· καὶ γὰρ μέγιστον τῶν καθ'
ἡμᾶς ἐνομίζετο, καὶ διὰ τοῦτο κατ' ἐξοχὴν ἰδίως
πόντον προσηγόρευον, ὡς ποιητὴν Ὅμηρον. ἴσως
οὖν καὶ διὰ τοῦτο μετήνεγκε τὰ ἐκ τοῦ Πόντου
πρὸς τὸν ὠκεανὸν ὡς εὐπαράδεκτα διὰ τὴν
κατέχουσαν δόξαν. οἶμαι δὲ καὶ τῶν Σολύμων
τὰ ἄκρα τοῦ Ταύρου τὰ περὶ τὴν Λυκίαν ἕως
Πισιδίας κατεχόντων τὰ ὑψηλότατα, καὶ τὰς ἀπὸ
τῆς μεσημβρίας ὑπερβολὰς ἐπιφανεστάτας παρε-
χόντων τοῖς ἐντὸς τοῦ Ταύρου, καὶ μάλιστα τοῖς
περὶ τὸν Πόντον, καθ' ὁμοιότητά τινα καὶ τούτους
ἐξωκεανισθῆναι· φησὶ γὰρ ἐπὶ τοῦ πλέοντος ἐν τῇ
σχεδίᾳ,

> τὸν δ' ἐξ Αἰθιόπων ἀνιὼν κρείων Ἐνοσίχθων
> τηλόθεν ἐκ Σολύμων ὀρέων ἴδεν.   (Od. 5. 282)

τάχα δὲ καὶ τοὺς μονομμάτους Κύκλωπας ἐκ
τῆς Σκυθικῆς ἱστορίας μετενήνοχε· τοιούτους γάρ

---

[1] Draw a north and south line from the poet's point of
observation (near the Black Sea) through the Solyman
Mountains and through Egypt to the Ethiopians on Oceanus
south of Egypt. Then draw a north and south line from
Odysseus' point of observation (on his raft, west of Greece)
to the Ethiopians living on Oceanus due south of the raft.
Homer transfers the Solymi and their mountains from his
own due-south line of vision to an analogous position on
Odysseus' due-south line of vision. Just as these mountains,

Jason's voyage through the Planctae was clearly plausible also; and so was Odysseus' passage between the Rocks, when we think of Scylla and Charybdis. Again, the men of Homer's day, in general, regarded the Pontic Sea as a kind of second Oceanus, and they thought that those who voyaged thither got beyond the limits of the inhabited world just as much as those who voyaged far beyond the pillars of Heracles; the Pontic Sea was thought to be the largest of the seas in our part of the world, and for that reason they applied to this particular sea the term "The Pontus," just as they spoke of Homer as "The Poet." Perhaps it was for that very reason that Homer transferred to Oceanus things that were true of the Pontus, in the belief that such a change would prove acceptable because of the prevailing notions in regard to the Pontus. And I think that since the Solymi occupied the loftiest peaks of the Taurus Range, I mean the peaks about Lycia as far as Pisidia, and since their country presented to people who lived north of the Taurus Range, and particularly to those who lived about the Pontus, the most conspicuous altitudes on the south—for this reason, on the strength of a certain similarity of position, these people too were transferred to the position out by Oceanus; for in speaking of Odysseus sailing on his raft he says : " Now the lord, the shaker of the earth, on his way from the Ethiopians espied Odysseus from afar, from the mountains of the Solymi." [1] Perhaps Homer also borrowed his idea of the one-eyed Cyclopes from the history of Scythia ;

to Homer, arose on the northern border of the Mediterranean, so to Odysseus they arose on the northern border of Oceanus. Strabo again refers to this on page 127.

τινας τοὺς Ἀριμασπους φασιν, οὓς ἐν τοῖς Ἀρι-
μασπείοις ἔπεσιν ἐνδέδωκεν Ἀριστέας ὁ Προκον-
νήσιος.

11. Δεῖ δὲ ταῦτα προϋποθέμενον σκοπεῖν, τί
λέγουσιν οἱ φήσαντες περὶ Σικελίαν ἢ Ἰταλίαν
γενέσθαι τῷ Ὀδυσσεῖ τὴν πλάνην καθ᾽ Ὅμηρον·[1]
ἔστι γὰρ ἀμφοτέρως τοῦτο δέξασθαι, καὶ βέλτιον
καὶ χεῖρον. βέλτιον μέν, ἂν οὕτω δέχηταί τις,
ὅτι πεισθεὶς ἐκεῖ τὴν πλάνην τῷ Ὀδυσσεῖ γενέσθαι, λαβὼν ἀληθῆ ταύτην τὴν ὑπόθεσιν ποιη-
C 22 τικῶς διεσκεύασε· τοῦτο γὰρ οἰκείως ἂν λέγοιτο
περὶ αὐτοῦ, καὶ οὐ μόνον γε περὶ Ἰταλίαν, ἀλλὰ
καὶ μέχρι τῶν ἐσχάτων τῆς Ἰβηρίας ἐστὶν εὑρεῖν
ἴχνη τῆς ἐκείνου πλάνης καὶ ἄλλων πλειόνων.
χεῖρον δέ, ἐάν τις καὶ τὴν διασκευὴν ὡς ἱστορίαν
δέχηται, ἐκείνου ὠκεανὸν καὶ Ἅδην καὶ Ἡλίου
βόας καὶ παρὰ θεαῖς ξενίας καὶ μεταμορφώσεις
καὶ μεγέθη Κυκλώπων καὶ Λαιστρυγόνων καὶ
μορφὴν Σκύλλης καὶ διαστήματα πλοῦ καὶ ἄλλα
πλείω τοιαῦτα τερατογραφοῦντος φανερῶς. οὔτε
δὲ πρὸς τοῦτον ἄξιον ἀντιλέγειν, οὕτω φανερῶς
καταψευδόμενον τοῦ ποιητοῦ, καθάπερ οὐδ᾽, εἰ
φαίη, τοῦτον τὸν τρόπον γενέσθαι τὸν εἰς τὴν
Ἰθάκην κατάπλουν τοῦ Ὀδυσσέως καὶ τὴν μνη-
στηροφονίαν καὶ τὴν ἐπὶ τοῦ ἀγροῦ συστᾶσαν
μάχην τοῖς Ἰθακησίοις πρὸς αὐτόν· οὔτε πρὸς
τὸν δεξάμενον οἰκείως προσπλέκεσθαι δίκαιον.

[1] ἢ μὴ γενέσθαι, Meineke deletes, after καθ᾽ Ὅμηρον; Forbiger, Kramer, C. Müller approving.

for it is reported that the Arimaspians are a one-
eyed people—a people whom Aristeas of Proconnesus has made known in his Arimaspian Epic.

11. Having made these preliminary remarks, I
must ask what people mean when they affirm that
Homer places the wanderings of Odysseus in the
region of Sicily and Italy? It is possible to accept
this view in two senses, one better and the other
worse. The better is to assume that Homer was
convinced that those regions were the scene of the
wanderings of Odysseus, and that, taking this
hypothesis as fact, he elaborated the story in poetic
fashion. So much may be said with propriety about
Homer; at any rate one may find traces of the wanderings of Odysseus, and of several others, not only
in the region of Italy, but also as far as the extreme
frontiers of Iberia. But the worse is to accept
Homer's elaboration of the story as history also,
because the poet is obviously indulging in marvels
when he tells of Oceanus, Hades, cattle of Helius,
entertainment by goddesses, metamorphoses, huge
Cyclopes and huge Laestrygonians, Scylla's shape,
distances traversed on the voyage, and many other
things of a similar nature. But, on the one hand,
it is not worth while to refute one who so obviously
misinterprets the poet—any more than it would be
if one should contend that the return of Odysseus
to Ithaca, the massacre of the suitors, and the fight
which took place out in the country between the
Ithacans and Odysseus, all happened precisely as
described by the poet; nor, on the other hand, is it
right to quarrel with the man who interprets Homer
in a proper fashion.

12. Ὁ Ἐρατοσθένης δὲ πρὸς ἀμφοτέρας τὰς ἀποφάσεις ἀπήντηκεν οὐκ εὖ. πρὸς μὲν τὴν δευτέραν, ὅτι πειρᾶται διαβάλλειν φανερῶς ψευδῆ καὶ οὐκ ἄξια λόγου διὰ μακρῶν· πρὸς δὲ τὴν προτέραν, ποιητήν τε ἅπαντα ἀποφήνας φλύαρον, καὶ μήτε τόπων ἐμπειρίαν μήτε τεχνῶν πρὸς ἀρετὴν συντείνειν νομίσας· τῶν τε μύθων τῶν μὲν ἐν τόποις οὐ πεπλασμένοις πεφημισμένων, οἷον ἐν Ἰλίῳ καὶ Ἴδῃ καὶ Πηλίῳ, τῶν δὲ ἐν πεπλασμένοις, καθάπερ ἐν οἷς αἱ Γοργόνες ἢ ὁ Γηρυόνης, ταύτης φησὶ τῆς ἰδέας εἶναι καὶ τοὺς κατὰ τὴν Ὀδυσσέως πλάνην λεγομένους, τοὺς δὲ μὴ πεπλάσθαι λέγοντας ἀλλ' ὑποκεῖσθαι ἐξ αὐτοῦ τοῦ μὴ συμφωνεῖν ἐλέγχεσθαι ψευδομένους· τὰς γοῦν Σειρῆνας τοὺς μὲν ἐπὶ τῆς Πελωριάδος καθιδρύειν, τοὺς δὲ ἐπὶ τῶν Σειρηνουσσῶν πλείους ἢ δισχιλίους διεχουσῶν σταδίους· εἶναι δ' αὐτὰς σκόπελον τρικόρυφον διείργοντα τὸν Κυμαῖον[1] καὶ Ποσειδωνιάτην κόλπον. ἀλλ' οὔθ' ὁ[2] σκόπελος οὗτός ἐστι τρικόρυφος, οὔθ' ὅλως κορυφοῦται πρὸς ὕψος, ἀλλ' ἀγκών τις ἔκκειται μακρὸς καὶ στενὸς ἀπὸ τῶν κατὰ Συρρεντὸν[3] χωρίων ἐπὶ τὸν κατὰ Καπρίας πορθμόν, ἐπὶ θάτερα μὲν τῆς ὀρεινῆς τὸ τῶν Σειρήνων ἱερὸν ἔχων, ἐπὶ θάτερα δὲ πρὸς τῷ Ποσειδωνιάτῃ κόλπῳ νησίδια τρία προκείμενα ἔρημα πετρώδη, ἃ καλοῦσι Σειρῆνας· ἐπ' αὐτῷ

---

[1] Κυμαῖον, Meineke, for Κύμαιον; C. Müller approving.
[2] οὔθ' ὁ, Meineke, for οὐδὲ ὁ.
[3] Συρρεντόν, Meineke, for Σύρρεντον; C. Müller approving.

12. Eratosthenes, however, has taken issue with both these answers to my question, and in so doing he is wrong; he is wrong as regards the second answer, in that he attempts to misrepresent things that are obviously fictitious and that do not deserve protracted discussion; and he is wrong as regards the first, because he declares that all poets are dealers in absurdities and thinks their knowledge either of places or of arts does not conduce to virtue. Again, because Homer lays the scenes of his myths not only in non-fictitious places, such as Ilion, Mt. Ida, and Mt. Pelion, but also in fictitious places, such as those in which the Gorgons and Geryon dwell, Eratosthenes says that the places mentioned in the story of the wanderings of Odysseus, also, belong to the category of fiction, and that the persons who contend that they are not fictitious but have a foundation in fact, stand convicted of error by the very fact that they do not agree among themselves; at any rate, that some of them put the Sirens on Cape Pelorias,[1] while others put them more than two thousand stadia distant on the Sirenussae, which is the name given to a three-peaked rock that separates the Gulf of Cumae [2] from the Gulf of Poseidonia.[3] But neither does this rock have three peaks, nor does it run up into a peak at all; instead it is a sort of elbow that juts out, long and narrow, from the territory of Surrentum to the Strait of Capreae, with the sanctuary of the Sirens on one side of the hilly headland, while on the other side, looking towards the Gulf of Poseidonia, lie three uninhabited rocky little islands, called the Sirens, and on the Strait of Capreae itself

---

[1] Cape Faro, Sicily.   [2] Bay of Naples.
[3] Gulf of Salerno.

δὲ τῷ πορθμῷ τὸ Ἀθήναιον, ὥπερ ὁμωνυμεῖ καὶ ὁ ἀγκὼν αὐτός.

13. Ἀλλ' οὐδ'[1] εἰ μὴ συμφωνοῦσιν οἱ τὴν ἱστορίαν τῶν τόπων παραδιδόντες εὐθὺς ἐκβάλλειν δεῖ τὴν σύμπασαν ἱστορίαν· ἀλλ' ἔσθ' ὅτε καὶ πιστοῦσθαι τὸ καθόλου μᾶλλόν ἐστιν. οἷον λέγω, ζητουμένου, εἰ κατὰ Σικελίαν καὶ Ἰταλίαν ἡ πλάνη γέγονε, καὶ εἰ αἱ Σειρῆνες ἐνταῦθά που λέγονται, ὁ μὲν φήσας ἐν τῇ Πελωριάδι πρὸς τὸν ἐν ταῖς Σειρηνούσσαις διαφωνεῖ, ἀμφότεροι δὲ πρὸς τὸν περὶ Σικελίαν καὶ Ἰταλίαν λέγοντα οὐ διαφωνοῦσιν, ἀλλὰ καὶ μείζω πίστιν παρέχουσιν, ὅτι, καίπερ μὴ τὸ αὐτὸ χωρίον φράζοντες, ὅμως οὐκ ἐκβεβήκεσάν γε τοῦ κατὰ τὴν Ἰταλίαν ἢ Σικελίαν. ἐὰν δὲ προσθῇ τις, ὅτι ἐν Νεαπόλει Παρθενόπης δείκνυται μνῆμα, μιᾶς τῶν Σειρήνων, ἔτι πλείων προσεγένετο πίστις, καίτοι τρίτου τινὸς λεχθέντος τούτου τοῦ τόπου. ἀλλ' ὅτι ἐν τούτῳ τῷ κόλπῳ, τῷ ὑπὸ Ἐρατοσθένους λεχθέντι Κυμαίῳ, ὃν ποιοῦσιν αἱ Σειρηνοῦσσαι, καὶ ἡ Νεάπολις ἵδρυται, βεβαιοτέρως πιστεύομεν τὸ περὶ τούτους τοὺς τόπους γεγονέναι τὰς Σειρῆνας· οὔτε γὰρ τὸν ποιητὴν ἀκριβῶς ἕκαστα πυθέσθαι, οὔθ' ἡμεῖς παρ' ἐκείνου ζητοῦμεν τὸ ἀκριβές· οὐ μὴν οὐδ' οὕτως ἔχομεν ὡς ὑπολαμβάνειν, καὶ μηδὲν

---

[1] οὐδ', Meineke, for οὔτ'.

---

[1] That is, Cape Minerva.

is situated the sanctuary of Athene, from which the elbow takes its name.[1]

13. However, even if those who hand down to us our knowledge of the regions under consideration do not agree among themselves, we should not on that account set aside the entire body of that knowledge; indeed there are times when the account as a whole is all the more to be accepted for this reason. For example, suppose the question is raised whether the wanderings took place in the regions of Sicily and Italy, and whether the Siren Rocks are anywhere thereabouts: the man who places the Siren Rocks on Cape Pelorias is in disagreement with the man who places them on the Sirenussae, but neither disagrees with the man who says that the Siren Rocks are placed in the neighbourhood of Sicily and Italy; nay, they even add to the credibility of the third witness, because, though they do not name the self-same spot for the Rocks, yet, at all events, they have not gone beyond the regions of Italy and Sicily for them. Then, if some one adds that a monument of Parthenope, one of the Sirens, is shown in Neapolis, we have still further proof, although a third site has been introduced into the discussion. Furthermore, the fact that Neapolis also lies on this gulf (called by Eratosthenes the gulf of Cumae), which is formed by the Sirenussae, induces us to believe all the more firmly that the Sirens were in the neighbourhood of these places; for we do not demand of the poet that he should have inquired accurately into every detail, nor do we in our School demand scientific accuracy in his statements; yet, even so, we surely are not entitled to assume that Homer composed the story of the

πεπυσμένον περὶ τῆς πλάνης, μήθ' ὅπου μήθ'
ὅπως γεγένηται, ῥαψῳδεῖν.

14. Ἐρατοσθένης δὲ Ἡσίοδον μὲν εἰκάζει πεπυσμένον περὶ τῆς Ὀδυσσέως πλάνης, ὅτι κατὰ
Σικελίαν καὶ Ἰταλίαν γεγένηται, πιστεύσαντα τῇ
δόξῃ μὴ μόνον τῶν ὑφ' Ὁμήρου λεγομένων μεμνῆσθαι, ἀλλὰ καὶ Αἴτνης καὶ Ὀρτυγίας, τοῦ πρὸς
Συρακούσαις νησίου, καὶ Τυρρηνῶν· Ὅμηρον δὲ
μήτε εἰδέναι ταῦτα, μήτε βούλεσθαι ἐν γνωρίμοις
τόποις ποιεῖν τὴν πλάνην. πότερον οὖν Αἴτνη
μὲν καὶ Τυρρηνία γνώριμα, Σκύλλαιον δὲ καὶ
Χάρυβδις καὶ Κίρκαιον καὶ Σειρηνοῦσσαι οὐ πάνυ;
ἢ καὶ Ἡσιόδῳ μὲν ἔπρεπε μὴ φλυαρεῖν, ἀλλὰ ταῖς
κατεχούσαις δόξαις ἀκολουθεῖν, Ὁμήρῳ δὲ "πᾶν,
ὅ τι κὲν[1] ἐπ' ἀκαιρίμαν γλῶσσαν ἴῃ, κελαδεῖν;"
χωρὶς γὰρ τῶν λεχθέντων περὶ τοῦ τύπου τῆς
πρεπούσης Ὁμήρῳ μυθοποιίας, καὶ τὸ πλῆθος
τῶν συγγραφέων τῶν ταὐτὰ θρυλούντων καὶ
τῆς κατὰ τοὺς τόπους ἐπιχωριαζούσης φήμης
διδάσκειν δύναται, διότι ταῦτα οὐ ποιητῶν πλάσ-
ματά ἐστιν οὐδὲ συγγραφέων, ἀλλὰ γεγενημένων
ἴχνη καὶ προσώπων καὶ πράξεων.

15. Καὶ Πολύβιος δ' ὀρθῶς ὑπονοεῖ τὰ περὶ τῆς
πλάνης. τὸν γὰρ Αἴολον,[2] τὸν προσημάναντα[3]
τοὺς ἔκπλους ἐν τοῖς κατὰ τὸν πορθμὸν τόποις
ἀμφιδρόμοις οὖσι καὶ δυσέκπλοις διὰ τὰς παλιρ-

---

[1] κέν, Cobet, for ἄν; and γλῶσσαν (which Meineke inserts)
for γλῶτταν, in keeping with the proverb attributed to
Pindar. See Bergk's note on *Fr. Adesp.* 86 A.

wanderings without any inquiry at all, either as to
where or as to how they occurred.

14. But Eratosthenes conjectures that Hesiod
learned by inquiry that the scene of the wanderings
of Odysseus lay in the region of Sicily and Italy,
and, adopting this belief, mentioned not only the
places spoken of by Homer, but also Aetna, Ortygia
(the little island next to Syracuse), and Tyrrhenia;
and yet he contends that Homer knew nothing
about these places and had no intention of placing
the wanderings in any known regions. Now were
Aetna and Tyrrhenia well-known places, but Scyllaeum, Charybdis, Circaeum, and the Sirenussae
wholly unknown? Or was it the proper thing for
Hesiod not to talk nonsense and to follow prevailing
opinions, but the proper thing for Homer to " give
utterance to every thought that comes to his in-
opportune tongue "? For apart from what I have
said concerning the type of myth which it was
proper for Homer to employ, most of the writers
who discuss the same topics that Homer discusses,
and also most of the various local traditions, can
teach us that these matters are not fictions of poets
nor yet of prose writers, but are traces of real persons
and events.

15. Polybius also entertains correct views in
regard to the wanderings of Odysseus, for he says
that Aeolus, the man who taught navigators how to
steer a course in the regions of the Strait of Messina,
whose waters are subject to a constant ebb and
flow and are difficult to navigate on account of the

---

² Αἰόλον, Meineke, for Αἴολον.
³ προσημάναντα, A. Miller, for προσημαίνοντα.

ροίας, ταμίαν τε εἰρῆσθαι τῶν ἀνέμων καὶ βασιλέα νενομίσθαι φησί· καὶ [1] καθάπερ Δαναὸν μέν, τὰ ὑδρεῖα τὰ ἐν Ἄργει παραδείξαντα, Ἀτρέα δέ, τοῦ ἡλίου τὸν ὑπεναντίον τῷ οὐρανῷ δρόμον, μάντεις τε καὶ ἱεροσκοπουμένους ἀποδείκνυσθαι βασιλέας· C 24 τούς θ' ἱερέας τῶν Αἰγυπτίων καὶ Χαλδαίους καὶ Μάγους, σοφίᾳ τινὶ διαφέροντας τῶν ἄλλων, ἡγεμονίας καὶ τιμῆς τυγχάνειν παρὰ τοῖς πρὸ ἡμῶν· οὕτω δὲ καὶ τῶν θεῶν ἕνα ἕκαστον, τῶν χρησίμων τινὸς εὑρετὴν γενόμενον, τιμᾶσθαι. ταῦτα δὲ προοικονομησάμενος οὐκ ἐᾷ τὸν Αἴολον [2] ἐν μύθου σχήματι ἀκούεσθαι, οὐδ' ὅλην τὴν Ὀδυσσέως πλάνην· ἀλλὰ μικρὰ μὲν προσμεμυθεῦσθαι καθάπερ καὶ τῷ Ἰλιακῷ πολέμῳ, τὸ δ' ὅλον περὶ Σικελίαν καὶ τῷ ποιητῇ πεποιῆσθαι καὶ τοῖς ἄλλοις συγγραφεῦσιν, ὅσοι τὰ ἐπιχώρια [3] λέγουσι τὰ περὶ τὴν Ἰταλίαν καὶ Σικελίαν. οὐκ ἐπαινεῖ δὲ οὐδὲ τὴν τοιαύτην τοῦ Ἐρατοσθένους ἀπόφασιν, διότι φησὶ τότ' ἂν εὑρεῖν τινα, ποῦ Ὀδυσσεὺς πεπλάνηται, ὅταν εὕρῃ τὸν σκυτέα τὸν συρράψαντα τὸν τῶν ἀνέμων ἀσκόν. καὶ τοῦτο δ' οἰκείως εἰρῆσθαι τοῖς συμβαίνουσι περὶ τὸ Σκύλλαιον καὶ τὴν θήραν τῶν γαλεωτῶν τὸ ἐπὶ τῆς Σκύλλης·

αὐτοῦ δ' ἰχθυάᾳ σκόπελον περιμαιμώωσα
δελφῖνάς τε κύνας τε, καὶ εἴ ποθι μεῖζον ἕλῃσι
κῆτος.   (Od. 12. 95)

τοὺς γὰρ θύννους ἀγεληδὸν φερομένους παρὰ τὴν

[1] καί, Meineke inserts, before καθάπερ.
[2] Αἴολον, Meineke, for Αἴολον.
[3] τὰ ἐπιχώρια, Corais, for τὰ περιχώρια; Cobet τἀπιχώρια independently.

reverse currents, has been called lord of the winds
and regarded as their king; and just as Danaüs,
because he discovered the subterranean reservoirs
of water in Argos, and Atreus, because he discovered
that the sun revolves in a direction opposite to the
movement of the heavens, both of them being seers
and diviners, were appointed kings; and just as the
priests of the Egyptians, the Chaldaeans, and the
Magi, because they excelled their fellows in knowledge of some kind or other, attained to leadership
and honour among the peoples before our times;
so, says Polybius, each one of the gods came to
honour because he discovered something useful to
man. Having said this much by way of preamble,
Polybius insists that we shall not interpret Aeolus
as a myth, nor yet the wanderings of Odysseus, as
a whole; but that insignificant elements of myth
have been added by the poet, just as had already
been done in the case of the Trojan War, and that
the scene of the whole story has been laid in the
neighbourhood of Sicily by Homer as well as by
all the other writers who deal with local matters
pertaining to Italy and Sicily. Neither does
Polybius approve of this sort of declaration from
Eratosthenes : "You will find the scene of the
wanderings of Odysseus when you find the cobbler
who sewed up the bag of the winds." And the
description of Scylla by the poet, says Polybius, is in
agreement with what takes place off the Scyllaean
Rock and in the hunting of the "galeotae" : "And
there she fishes, swooping round the rock, for
dolphins or for dog-fish, or whatso greater beast she
may anywhere take." For when the tunny-fish,
Polybius goes on to say, as they swim along in

87

Ἰταλίαν, ἐπειδὰν ἐμπέσωσι καὶ κωλυθῶσι τῆς
Σικελίας ἅψασθαι, περιπίπτειν τοῖς μείζοσι τῶν
ζῴων, οἷον δελφίνων καὶ κυνῶν καὶ ἄλλων κητω-
δῶν· ἐκ δὲ τῆς θήρας αὐτῶν πιαίνεσθαι τοὺς
γαλεώτας, οὓς καὶ ξιφίας λέγεσθαι καὶ κύνας
φησί. συμβαίνειν γὰρ ταὐτὸν ἐνθάδε καὶ κατὰ
τὰς ἀναβάσεις τοῦ Νείλου καὶ τῶν ἄλλων ὑδάτων,
ὅπερ ἐπὶ πυρὸς καὶ ὕλης ἐμπιπραμένης· ἀθροιζό-
μενα γὰρ τὰ θηρία φεύγειν τὸ πῦρ ἢ τὸ ὕδωρ, καὶ
βορὰν γίνεσθαι τοῖς κρείττοσι.

16. Ταῦτα δ' εἰπὼν διηγεῖται τῶν γαλεωτῶν
θήραν, ἢ συνίσταται περὶ τὸ Σκύλλαιον· σκοπὸς
γὰρ ἐφέστηκε κοινὸς ὑφορμοῦσιν ἐν δικώποις
σκαφιδίοις πολλοῖς, δύο καθ' ἕκαστον σκαφίδιον,
καὶ ὁ μὲν ἐλαύνει, ὁ δ' ἐπὶ τῆς πρῴρας ἕστηκε δόρυ
ἔχων· σημήναντος δὲ[1] τοῦ σκοποῦ τὴν ἐπιφάνειαν
τοῦ γαλεώτου (φέρεται δὲ τὸ τρίτον μέρος ἔξαλον
τὸ ζῷον) συνάψαντός τε[2] τοῦ σκάφους ὁ μὲν
ἔπληξεν ἐκ χειρός, εἶτ' ἐξέσπασεν ἐκ τοῦ σώματος
τὸ δόρυ χωρὶς τῆς ἐπιδορατίδος· ἀγκιστρώδης τε
γάρ ἐστι καὶ χαλαρῶς ἐνήρμοσται τῷ δόρατι ἐπίτηδες, καλώδιον δ' ἔχει μακρὸν ἐξημμένον. τοῦτ'
ἐπιχαλῶσι τῷ τρωθέντι τέως, ἕως ἂν κάμῃ σφα-
δάζον καὶ ὑποφεῦγον· τότε δ' ἕλκουσιν ἐπὶ τὴν
γῆν, ἢ εἰς τὸ σκάφος ἀναλαμβάνουσιν, ἐὰν μὴ
μέγα ᾖ τελέως τὸ σῶμα. κἂν ἐκπέσῃ δὲ εἰς τὴν
θάλατταν τὸ δόρυ, οὐκ ἀπόλωλεν· ἔστι γὰρ πη-
κτὸν ἔκ τε δρυὸς καὶ ἐλάτης, ὥστε βαπτιζομένου

---

[1] δέ, A. Miller inserts, as it is written in A "prima manu"
above σημήναντος.

[2] τε, A. Miller, for δέ.

schools by the coast of Italy, meet with the current
from the strait and are prevented from reaching
Sicily, they fall a prey to the larger sea-animals,
such as dolphins, dog-fish and cetaceans in general;
and the "galeotae" (which are called both sword-
fish and dog-fish) grow fat from the chase of the
tunny-fish.   Indeed, the same thing occurs here, and
at the rise of the Nile and other rivers, as happens
when there is a conflagration or a forest fire, namely,
the assembled animals attempt to escape the fire or
the flood and become prey of animals more powerful
than themselves.

16. After making this statement Polybius goes on
to describe the hunting of the "galeotae," which
takes place off the Scyllaean Rock : one man on the
look-out acts for all the fishermen, who lie in wait
in many two-oared skiffs, two men in each skiff, one
rowing and the other standing in the bow with
his spear poised in hand.   And when the man on
the look-out signals the appearance of the "galeotes"
(the creature swims along with a third of its body
out of the water), and when the skiff draws near it,
the man in the bow strikes the fish at close range,
and then withdraws the spear-shaft, leaving the
spear-head in the body of the fish ; for the spear-head
is barbed and loosely attached to the spear-shaft on
purpose, and has a long line fastened to it.   They
pay out this line to the wounded fish until he
becomes tired out by his struggles and his attempts
at escape ; then they tow him to the shore, or take
him aboard the skiff—unless he be of enormous size.
If the spear-shaft fall into the water, it is not lost;
for it is made of both oak and pine wood, so that

τοῦ δρυΐνου βάρει μετέωρον εἶναι τὸ λοιπὸν καὶ
C 25 εὐανάληπτον. συμβαίνειν δέ ποτε καὶ τιτρώσκε-
σθαι διὰ τοῦ σκαφιδίου τὸν κωπηλάτην διὰ τὸ
μέγεθος τοῦ ξίφους τῶν γαλεωτῶν καὶ τὸ τὴν
ἀκμὴν τοῦ ξίφους[1] συαγρώδη εἶναι καὶ δηκτηρίαν.[2]
ἔκ τε δὴ τῶν τοιούτων εἰκάζοι τις ἄν, φησί, περὶ
Σικελίαν γενέσθαι τὴν πλάνην κατὰ τὸν Ὅμηρον,
ὅτι τῇ Σκύλλῃ προσῆψε τὴν τοιαύτην θήραν, ἣ
μάλιστ᾿ ἐπιχώριός ἐστι τῷ Σκυλλαίῳ· καὶ ἐκ τῶν
περὶ τῆς Χαρύβδεως λεγομένων ὁμοίων τοῖς τοῦ
πορθμοῦ πάθεσι. τὸ δὲ

     τρὶς μὲν γάρ τ᾿ ἀνίησιν,   (Od. 12. 105)

ἀντὶ τοῦ δίς, γραφικὸν εἶναι ἁμάρτημα ἢ ἱστο-
ρικόν.

17. Καὶ τὰ ἐν τῇ Μήνιγγι δὲ τοῖς περὶ τῶν
Λωτοφάγων εἰρημένοις συμφωνεῖν. εἰ δέ τινα μὴ
συμφωνεῖ, μεταβολὰς αἰτιᾶσθαι δεῖν ἢ ἄγνοιαν ἢ
καὶ ποιητικὴν ἐξουσίαν, ἣ συνέστηκεν ἐξ ἱστορίας
καὶ διαθέσεως καὶ μύθου. τῆς μὲν οὖν ἱστορίας
ἀλήθειαν εἶναι τέλος, ὡς ἐν Νεῶν καταλόγῳ τὰ
ἑκάστοις τόποις συμβεβηκότα λέγοντος τοῦ ποιητοῦ, τὴν μὲν πετρήεσσαν, τὴν δὲ ἐσχατόωσαν
πόλιν, ἄλλην δὲ πολυτρήρωνα, τὴν δ᾿ ἀγχίαλον·
τῆς δὲ διαθέσεως ἐνέργειαν εἶναι τὸ τέλος, ὡς ὅταν
μαχομένους εἰσάγῃ· μύθου δὲ ἡδονὴν καὶ ἔκπλη-

---

[1] ξίφους, Sterrett, for ζώου.
[2] δηκτηρίαν, Madvig, for τὴν θήραν; Sterrett following.

although the oaken end sinks because of its weight, the rest stays afloat and is easily recovered. It sometimes happens, says Polybius, that the man who rows the skiff is wounded through the bottom of the boat because of the great size of the sword of the " galeotae " and because the edge of the sword is sharp and biting like the wild boar's tusk. So, from such facts as these, Polybius concludes, one may conjecture that the wanderings of Odysseus took place in the neighbourhood of Sicily according to Homer, inasmuch as Homer attributed to Scylla that sort of fish-hunting which is most characteristic of Scyllaeum; and also from Homer's statements in regard to Charybdis, which correspond to the behaviour of the waters of the Strait. But the use of the word " thrice " instead of " twice " in the statement " for thrice a day she spouts it forth " is either an error of a copyist or an error of fact.

17. Furthermore, the facts about Meninx,[1] continues Polybius, agree with what Homer says about the Lotus-Eaters. But if there be some discrepancy we must ascribe it to the changes wrought by time, or to ignorance, or to poetic license—which is compounded of history, rhetorical composition, and myth. Now the aim of history is truth, as when in the Catalogue of Ships the poet mentions the topographical peculiarities of each place, saying of one city that it is " rocky," of another that it is " on the uttermost border," of another that it is the " haunt of doves," and of still another that it is " by the sea "; the aim of rhetorical composition is vividness, as when Homer introduces men fighting; the aim of myth is to please and

---

[1] The Island of Jerba, off the northern coast of Africa.

ξιν. τὸ δὲ πάντα πλάττειν οὐ πιθανόν, οὐδ᾽
Ὁμηρικόν· τὴν γὰρ ἐκείνου ποίησιν φιλοσόφημα
πάντας νομίζειν, οὐχ ὡς Ἐρατοσθένης φησί, κελεύων μὴ κρίνειν πρὸς τὴν διάνοιαν τὰ ποιήματα,
μηδ᾽ ἱστορίαν ἀπ᾽ αὐτῶν ζητεῖν. πιθανώτερόν τε τὸ

ἔνθεν δ᾽ ἐννῆμαρ φερόμην ὀλοοῖς ἀνέμοισιν
(Od. 9. 82)

ἐν βραχεῖ διαστήματι δέχεσθαι (οἱ γὰρ ὀλοοὶ οὐκ
εὐθύδρομοι) ἢ ἐξωκεανίζειν, ὡς ἂν οὐρίων πνεόν-
των συνεχῶς. συνθεὶς δὲ τὸ διάστημα τὸ ἐκ
Μαλεῶν ἐπὶ Στήλας σταδίων δισμυρίων καὶ δισχιλίων πεντακοσίων, εἰ, φησί, τοῦτο θείημεν ἐν
ταῖς ἐννέα ἡμέραις διηνύσθαι ἰσοταχῶς, ἑκάστης
ἂν ἡμέρας ὁ πλοῦς συμβαίνοι σταδίων δισχιλίων
πεντακοσίων. τίς οὖν ἱστόρηκεν ἐκ Λυκίας ἢ Ῥόδου δευτεραῖόν τινα ἀφιγμένον εἰς Ἀλεξάνδρειαν,
ὄντος τοῦ διαστήματος σταδίων τετρακισχιλίων;
πρὸς δὲ τοὺς ἐπιζητοῦντας, πῶς τρὶς εἰς Σικελίαν
ἐλθὼν οὐδ᾽ ἅπαξ διὰ τοῦ πορθμοῦ πέπλευκεν
Ὀδυσσεύς, ἀπολογεῖται, διότι καὶ οἱ ὕστερον
ἔφευγον ἅπαντες τὸν πλοῦν τοῦτον.

18. Τοιαῦτα μὲν εἴρηκεν. ἔστι δὲ τἆλλα μὲν
C 26 εὖ λεγόμενα· ὅταν δ᾽ ἀνασκευάζῃ τὸν ἐξωκεανισμόν,[1] καὶ πρὸς ἀκριβῆ μέτρα τὸν τῶν ἡμερῶν
πλοῦν ἀνάγῃ καὶ διαστήματα, ὑπερβολὴν οὐκ

---

[1] ἐξωκεανισμόν, the old reading, is retained for the ἐξωκεανι-
ζόμενον of Kramer and Meineke; C. Müller approving.

to excite amazement. But to invent a story out-right is neither plausible nor like Homer; for everybody agrees that the poetry of Homer is a philosophic production—contrary to the opinion of Eratosthenes, who bids us not to judge the poems with reference to their thought, nor yet to seek for history in them. And Polybius says it is more plausible to interpret the poet's words, "Thence for nine whole days was I borne by baneful winds," as applying to a restricted area (for baneful winds do not maintain a straight course), than to place the incident out on Oceanus, as though the phrase had been "fair winds continually blowing." Now, if we reckon the distance from Cape Malea to the Pillars of Heracles at twenty-two thousand five hundred stadia, and if, says Polybius, we suppose that this distance was traversed at an even speed for those nine days, the distance covered each day would be two thousand five hundred stadia. But where do we find it recorded that anyone ever arrived at Alexandria from Lycia or Rhodes on the second day, though the distance is only four thousand stadia? And to those who ask the further question how it came about, if Odysseus touched Sicily three times, that he never once sailed through the Strait, Polybius replies that it was for the same reason that all later navigators have avoided that passage.

18. Such are the words of Polybius, and what he says is in the main correct. But when he demolishes the argument that places the wanderings of Odysseus on Oceanus, and when he reduces the nine days' voyage and the distances covered thereon to exact measurements, he reaches the height of

93

ἀπολείπει τῆς ἀνομολογίας. ἅμα μὲν γὰρ παρατίθησι τὰ τοῦ ποιητοῦ ἔπη·

ἔνθεν δ' ἐννῆμαρ φερόμην ὀλοοῖς ἀνέμοισιν,
(Od. 9. 82)

ἅμα δ' ἐπικρύπτεται· καὶ γὰρ ταῦτα τοῦ ποιητοῦ,

αὐτὰρ ἐπεὶ ποταμοῖο λίπεν ῥόον Ὠκεανοῖο
νηῦς,   (Od. 12. 1)

καὶ τὸ

νήσῳ ἐν Ὠγυγίῃ, ὅθι τ' ὀμφαλός ἐστι θαλάσσης·
(Od. 1. 50)

καὶ ὅτι ἐνταῦθα οἰκεῖ Ἄτλαντος θυγάτηρ· καὶ τὸ περὶ τῶν Φαιάκων,

οἰκέομεν δ' ἀπάνευθε πολυκλύστῳ ἐνὶ πόντῳ
ἔσχατοι· οὐ δέ τις ἄμμι βροτῶν ἐπιμίσγεται
ἄλλος.   (Od. 6. 204)

ταῦτα γὰρ πάντα φανερῶς ἐν τῷ Ἀτλαντικῷ πελάγει πλαττόμενα δηλοῦται.[1] ὁ δὲ ταῦτ' ἐπικρυπτόμενος τὰ φανερῶς λεγόμενα ἀναιρεῖ. τοῦτο μὲν οὖν οὐκ εὖ· τὸ δὲ περὶ Σικελίαν καὶ Ἰταλίαν γεγονέναι τὴν πλάνην ὀρθῶς, καὶ ὑπὸ τῶν τοπικῶν τὰ[2] τοῦ ποιητοῦ βεβαιοῦται. ἐπεὶ τίς ἔπεισε ποιητὴς ἢ συγγραφεὺς Νεαπολίτας μὲν λέγειν μνῆμα Παρθενόπης τῆς Σειρῆνος, τοὺς δὲ ἐν Κύμῃ καὶ Δικαιαρχείᾳ[3] καὶ Οὐεσουίῳ Πυριφλεγέθοντα καὶ Ἀχερουσίαν λίμνην καὶ νεκυομαντεῖον τὸ ἐν τῷ Ἀόρνῳ καὶ Βάιον καὶ Μισηνὸν τῶν Ὀδυσσέως ἑταίρων τινάς; οὕτω δὲ καὶ τὰ

---

[1] δηλοῦται, Meineke, for δηλοῦνται.

inconsistency. For at one moment he quotes the words of the poet: "Thence for nine whole days was I borne by baneful winds"; and at another moment he suppresses statements. For Homer says also: "Now after the ship had left the river-stream of Oceanus"; and "In the island of Ogygia, where is the navel of the sea," going on to say that the daughter of Atlas lives there; and again, regarding the Phaeacians, "Far apart we live in the wash of the waves, the farthermost of men, and no other mortals are conversant with us." Now all these incidents are clearly indicated as being placed in fancy in the Atlantic Ocean; but Polybius by suppressing them destroys what the poet states in express terms. In so doing he is wrong; but he is right in placing the wanderings in the neighbourhood of Sicily and Italy; and the words of the poet are confirmed by the geographical terms of those regions. For what poet or prose writer ever persuaded the Neapolitans to name a monument after Parthenope the Siren, or the people of Cumae, of Dicaearchia,[1] and of Vesuvius, to perpetuate the names of Pyriphlegethon, of the Acherusian Marsh, of the oracle of the dead at Lake Avernus, and of Baius and Misenus, two of the companions of Odysseus? The same question may be asked regarding Homer's stories of the

[1] Puteoli.

---

[2] τῶν τοπικῶν τά, C. Müller inserts.
[3] Δικαιαρχείᾳ, Meineke, for Δικαιαρχίᾳ.

περὶ Σειρηνούσσας καὶ τὰ περὶ τὸν πορθμὸν καὶ
Σκύλλαν καὶ Χάρυβδιν καὶ Αἴολον· ἅπερ οὔτ᾽
ἀκριβῶς ἐξετάζειν δεῖ οὔτ᾽ ἄρριζα καὶ ἀνέστια
ἐᾶν, ἀληθείας μηδὲν προσαπτόμενα μηδ᾽ ὠφελείας
ἱστορικῆς.

19. Καὶ αὐτὸς δὲ ὑπονοήσας τοῦτο ὁ Ἐρατοσθένης, ὑπολάβοι τις ἄν, φησί, τὸν ποιητὴν
βούλεσθαι μὲν ἐν τοῖς προσεσπερίοις τόποις τὴν
πλάνην τῷ Ὀδυσσεῖ ποιεῖν, ἀποστῆναι δ᾽ ἀπὸ
τῶν ὑποκειμένων, τὰ μὲν οὐκ ἀκριβῶς πεπυσμένον,
τὰ δὲ οὐδὲ προελόμενον οὕτως, ἀλλ᾽ ἐπὶ τὸ δεινό-
τερον καὶ τὸ τερατωδέστερον ἕκαστα ἐξάγειν.
τοῦτο μὲν αὐτὸ εὖ, τὸ δ᾽ οὗ χάριν τοῦτ᾽ ἐποίει
κακῶς δεξάμενος· οὐ γὰρ φλυαρίας, ἀλλ᾽ ὠφελείας
χάριν. ὥστε δίκαιός ἐστιν ὑπέχειν λόγον καὶ
περὶ τούτου καὶ διότι φησὶ τὰ πόρρω τερατολο-
γεῖσθαι μᾶλλον διὰ τὸ εὐκατάψευστον. πολλο-
στὸν γὰρ μέρος ἐστὶ τὰ πόρρω τερατολογούμενα
τῶν ἐν τῇ Ἑλλάδι καὶ ἐγγὺς τῆς Ἑλλάδος· οἷα
δὴ τὰ κατὰ τοὺς Ἡρακλέους ἄθλους καὶ Θησέως
καὶ τὰ ἐν Κρήτῃ καὶ Σικελίᾳ μυθευόμενα καὶ ταῖς
ἄλλαις νήσοις, καὶ τὰ περὶ τὸν Κιθαιρῶνα καὶ
Ἑλικῶνα καὶ Παρνασσὸν καὶ Πήλιον καὶ τὴν
C 27 Ἀττικὴν ὅλην καὶ Πελοπόννησον· οὐδείς τε ἐκ
τῶν μύθων ἄγνοιαν αἰτιᾶται τῶν μυθοποιῶν. ἔτι
δέ, ἐπεὶ οὐ πάντα μυθεύουσιν, ἀλλὰ πλείω προσ-
μυθεύουσι, καὶ μάλιστα Ὅμηρος, ὁ ζητῶν τί οἱ

Sirenussae, the Strait, Scylla, Charybdis, and Aeolus—stories which we should neither scrutinize rigorously, nor set aside as baseless and as without local setting, having no claim to truthfulness or to utility as history.

19. Eratosthenes himself had a suspicion of this, for he says one may suppose that the poet wished to place the wanderings of Odysseus in the far west, but abandoned his purpose, partly because of his lack of accurate information, and partly because he had even preferred not to be accurate but rather to develop each incident in the direction of the more awe-inspiring and the more marvellous. Now Eratosthenes interprets rightly what Homer actually did, but wrongly his motive in doing it; for Homer's object was not to indulge in empty talk, but to do useful service. It is therefore right that Eratosthenes should submit to examination both on this point and on his assertion that far distant places are made the scenes of Homer's marvellous stories because of the fact that it is safer to fabricate about them. For his stories of marvels whose scenes are laid in distant places are very few in number in comparison with those laid in Greece or in countries near Greece; as such I may mention the stories about the labours of Heracles and Theseus, and the myths whose scenes are laid in Crete and Sicily and in the other islands, and on Cithaeron, Helicon, Parnassus, Pelion, and in various places in Attica or in the Peloponnesus. No one accuses the myth-makers of ignorance because of the myths they create; furthermore, since the poets, and Homer in particular, do not narrate pure myths simply but more often use mythical elements as additions to fact, the man who investigates what

97

παλαιοὶ προσμυθεύουσιν οὐ ζητεῖ, εἰ τὰ προσ-
μυθευόμενα ὑπῆρξεν ἤ ἐστιν, ἀλλὰ καὶ μᾶλλον,
οἷς προσμυθεύεται τόποις ἢ προσώποις, περὶ
ἐκείνων ζητεῖ τἀληθές· οἷον τὴν Ὀδυσσέως πλάνην, εἰ γέγονε, καὶ ποῦ.

20. Τὸ δ' ὅλον οὐκ εὖ τὸ τὴν Ὁμήρου ποίησιν
εἰς ἓν συνάγειν τῇ τῶν ἄλλων ποιητῶν καὶ μηδὲν
αὐτῷ πρεσβεῖον ἀπονέμειν[1] εἴς τε τἆλλα καὶ εἰς
αὐτὰ τὰ νῦν προκείμενα, τὰ τῆς γεωγραφίας. καὶ
γὰρ εἰ μηδὲν ἄλλο, τόν γε Τριπτόλεμον τὸν
Σοφοκλέους ἢ τὸν ἐν ταῖς Βάκχαις ταῖς Εὐρι-
πίδου πρόλογον ἐπελθόντα καὶ παραβαλόντα τὴν
Ὁμήρου περὶ τὰ τοιαῦτα ἐπιμέλειαν, ῥᾴδιον ἦν
αἰσθέσθαι τὴν ἐπιπολαίαν τήνδε διαφοράν.[2] ὅπου
γὰρ χρεία τάξεως ὧν μέμνηται τόπων, φυλάττει
τὴν τάξιν Ὅμηρος[3] ὁμοίως μὲν τῶν Ἑλληνικῶν,
ὁμοίως δὲ τῶν ἄπωθεν·

Ὄσσαν ἐπ' Οὐλύμπῳ μέμασαν θέμεν, αὐτὰρ
   ἐπ' Ὄσσῃ
Πήλιον εἰνοσίφυλλον.   (Od. 11. 315)

Ἥρη δ' ἀΐξασα λίπεν ῥίον Οὐλύμποιο,
Πιερίην δ' ἐπιβᾶσα καὶ Ἠμαθίην ἐρατεινὴν
σεύατ' ἐφ' ἱπποπόλων Θρῃκῶν ὄρεα νιφόεντα·
ἐξ Ἀθόω δ' ἐπὶ πόντον.   (Il. 14. 225)

καὶ ἐν τῷ Καταλόγῳ τὰς μὲν πόλεις οὐκ ἐφεξῆς

---

[1] καὶ μηδὲν αὐτῷ πρεσβεῖον ἀπονέμειν, A. Miller transposes
to this place from a position after γεωγραφίας.

[2] ῥᾴδιον ἦν αἰσθέσθαι τὴν ἐπιπολαίαν τήνδε διαφοράν, A. Miller,
for ῥᾴδιον εἶναι θέσθαι τὴν ἐπιβολὴν ἢ τὴν διαφοράν; A. Vogel
approving, but suggesting the omission of τήνδε.

[3] Ὅμηρος, A. Miller inserts.

mythical additions the ancients make does not seek
to discover whether the additions were once true or
are true to-day, but rather seeks to discover the
truth in regard to the places to which, or the
persons to whom, these mythical elements are
added; for instance, in regard to the wanderings
of Odysseus, whether they took place and, if so,
where.

20. Generally speaking, it is wrong to place
the poetry of Homer on the same level with that
of other poets, and to decline to rank him above
them in any respect, and particularly in the
subject that now occupies our attention, namely,
geography. For if you did no more than go
over the *Triptolemus* of Sophocles or the prologue
to the *Bacchae* of Euripides, and then compare
Homer's care with respect to geographical matters,
it would be easy for you to perceive this difference,
which lies on the surface. Indeed, wherever there
is need of an orderly sequence in the places he
mentions, Homer is careful to preserve that order,
not only in regard to places in Greece, but equally
in regard to those beyond the limits of Greece:
"They strove to pile Ossa on Olympus, and on
Ossa Pelion with the trembling forest leaves";
"And Hera, rushing down, left the peak of Olympus,
and touched on Pieria and pleasant Emathia, and
sped over the snowy hills of the Thracian horsemen;
and she went from Athos across the sea." In the
Catalogue of Ships he does not, indeed, mention
the cities in their order, for that was not necessary,

λέγει· οὐ γὰρ ἀναγκαῖον· τὰ δὲ ἔθνη ἐφεξῆς.
ὁμοίως δὲ καὶ περὶ τῶν ἄπωθεν·

> Κύπρον Φοινίκην τε καὶ Αἰγυπτίους ἐπαληθεὶς
> Αἰθίοπάς θ᾽ ἱκόμην καὶ Σιδονίους καὶ Ἐρεμβοὺς
> καὶ Λιβύην. (Od. 4. 83)

ὅπερ καὶ Ἵππαρχος ἐπισημαίνεται. οἱ δ᾽, ἐφ᾽
ὧν τάξεως χρεία, ὁ μὲν τὸν Διόνυσον ἐπιόντα τὰ
ἔθνη φράζων, ὁ δὲ τὸν Τριπτόλεμον τὴν κατα-
σπειρομένην γῆν, τὰ μὲν πολὺ διεστῶτα συν-
άπτουσιν ἐγγύς, τὰ δὲ συνεχῆ διασπῶσι·

> λιπὼν δὲ Λυδῶν τὰς πολυχρύσους γύας
> Φρυγῶν τε Περσῶν θ᾽ ἡλιοβλήτους πλάκας
> Βάκτριά τε τείχη, τήν τε δύσχειμον χθόνα
> Μήδων ἐπελθὼν Ἀραβίαν τ᾽ εὐδαίμονα.
>   (Eur. Bacch. 13)

τοιαῦτα δὲ καὶ ὁ Τριπτόλεμος ποιεῖ. κἂν τοῖς
κλίμασι δὲ κἂν τοῖς ἀνέμοις διαφαίνει τὸ πολυ-
μαθὲς τὸ περὶ τὴν γεωγραφίαν Ὅμηρος, ἐν ταῖς
τοποθεσίαις λέγων ἅμα καὶ ταῦτα πολλαχοῦ.

C 28   αὐτὴ δὲ χθαμαλὴ πανυπερτάτη εἰν ἁλὶ κεῖται
> πρὸς ζόφον· αἱ δέ τ᾽ ἄνευθε πρὸς ἠῶ τ᾽ ἠέλιόν τε.
>   (Od. 9. 25)

> δύω δέ τέ οἱ θύραι εἰσίν,
> αἱ μὲν πρὸς Βορέαν,
> αἱ δ᾽ αὖ πρὸς Νότον. (Od. 13. 109)

> εἴτ᾽ ἐπὶ δεξί᾽ ἴωσι πρὸς ἠῶ τ᾽ ἠέλιόν τε,
> εἴτ᾽ ἐπ᾽ ἀριστερὰ τοί γε ποτὶ ζόφον. (Il. 12. 239)

---

[1] Strabo does not mean to attribute to Homer a knowledge
of "climata" in the technical sense as employed by Hipparchus (see footnote 2, page 22), but merely a knowledge of

but he does mention the peoples in their order.
And so in case of the peoples remote from Greece:
"I roamed over Cyprus and Phoenicia and Egypt,
and reached the Ethiopians and Sidonians and Erembians and Libya"; Hipparchus also noted this
fact. But Sophocles and Euripides, even where
there is need of orderly sequence—the latter when
he describes the visits of Dionysus to the various
peoples, and the former when he tells of Triptolemus
visiting the earth that is being sown with seed—both
poets, I say, bring near together regions that are
very widely separated, and separate those that are
contiguous: "I have left behind me," says Dionysus, "the gold-bearing glades of Lydia and of
Phrygia, and I have visited the sun-stricken plains
of Persia, the walled towns of Bactria, the wintry
land of the Medes, and Arabia the Blest." And
Triptolemus does the same sort of thing. Again, in
the case of the "climata"[1] and of the winds, Homer
displays the breadth of his geographical knowledge;
for in marking the sites of places he often touches
upon both these points too: "Now Ithaca lies low,
uppermost on the sea-line toward the darkness, but
those others face the dawning and the sun"[2]; "Two
gates there are, the one set toward the north wind,
but the other toward the south"; "Whether they
fare to the right, to the dawn and to the sun, or to
the left, to darkness." In point of fact, Homer

the general principle involved—the inclination of the earth's
surface.

[2] Strabo would take this passage as referring to Ithaca's
geographical position, not its topography. Thus "low"
would mean "next to the mainland"; and "uppermost,"
"farthest up on the earth's surface." And "darkness,"
according to Strabo, means "north," not "south." See § 28
following; and 10. 2. 12.

καὶ μὴν τὴν ἄγνοιάν γε τῶν τοιούτων τελειαν
ἡγεῖται σύγχυσιν τῶν ἀπάντων·

ὦ φίλοι, οὐ γάρ τ' ἴδμεν, ὅπη ζόφος, οὐδ' ὅπη
ἠώς,
οὐδ' ὅπη ἤελιος.   (Od. 10. 190)

κἀνταῦθα δ' εἰπόντος εὖ τοῦ ποιητοῦ,

Βορέης καὶ Ζέφυρος, τώ τε Θρηκηθεν ἄητον,
                (Il. 9. 5)

οὐκ εὖ δεξάμενος ὁ αὐτὸς συκοφαντεῖ, ὡς καθόλου
λέγοντος, ὅτι ὁ Ζέφυρος ἐκ Θρᾴκης πνεῖ, ἐκείνου
λέγοντος οὐ καθόλου, ἀλλ' ὅταν κατὰ τὴν Θρᾳκίαν θάλασσαν συμπέσωσι περὶ τὸν Μέλανα
κόλπον αὐτοῦ τοῦ Αἰγαίου μέρος οὖσαν. ἐπι-
στροφὴν γὰρ λαμβάνει πρὸς νότον ἀκρωτηριά-
ζουσα ἡ Θρᾴκη, καθ' ἃ συνάπτει τῇ Μακεδονίᾳ,
καὶ προπίπτουσα εἰς τὸ πέλαγος, τοὺς Ζεφύρους
ἐντεῦθεν πνέοντας ἀποφαίνει τοῖς ἐν Θάσῳ καὶ
Λήμνῳ καὶ Ἴμβρῳ καὶ Σαμοθράκῃ καὶ τῇ περὶ
αὐτὰς θαλάττῃ, καθάπερ καὶ τῇ Ἀττικῇ ἀπὸ
τῶν Σκειρωνίδων πετρῶν, ἀφ' ὧν καὶ Σκείρωνες
καλοῦνται οἱ Ζέφυροι, καὶ μάλιστα οἱ Ἀργέσται.
οὐκ ἐνόησε δὲ τοῦτο Ἐρατοσθένης, ὑπενόησε δ'
ὅμως. αὐτὸς γοῦν ἐξηγεῖται τὴν ἐπιστροφήν, ἣν
λέγω, τῆς χώρας· ὡς καθόλου οὖν δέχεται, εἶτ'
ἀπειρίαν αἰτιᾶται τοῦ ποιητοῦ, ὡς τοῦ Ζεφύρου
μὲν ἀπὸ τῆς ἑσπέρας πνέοντος καὶ τῆς Ἰβηρίας
τῆς δὲ Θρᾴκης ἐκεῖσε μὴ διατεινούσης. πότερον
οὖν τὸν Ζέφυρον ἀγνοεῖ ἀπὸ ἑσπέρας πνέοντα;

regards ignorance of these matters as tantamount
to utter confusion in all particulars: "My friends,
lo, we know not where is the place of darkness
or of dawning, nor where the sun." In still another
passage Homer is accurate when he speaks of "the
north wind and the west wind that blow from
Thrace"; but Eratosthenes puts a false interpretation
upon these words and falsely accuses the poet, as
though he were making the universal statement
that the west wind blows from Thrace; whereas
Homer is not speaking in a universal sense, but
refers to the time when these two winds meet in
the Gulf of Melas [1] upon the Thracian Sea, which
is a part of the Aegean itself. For Thrace, running
out into a promontory at the point where Thrace
borders on Macedonia, takes a turn towards the
south, and, thus projecting into the sea, gives the
impression to the people in Thasos, Lemnos, Imbros,
Samothrace, and on the sea that lies round about
those islands, that the west winds actually blow
from Thrace; precisely as, for Attica, they seem
to come from the Scironian Rocks; and it is from
these that the west winds, and particularly the
north-west winds, get their name "Scirones." But
Eratosthenes did not perceive this, though he
suspected it; at any rate he himself describes the
turn of the coast which I have mentioned. In any
case, he interprets Homer's verse as a universal
statement, and then charges the poet with ignorance,
on the ground that, while the west wind blows from
the west and from Iberia, Thrace does not extend
so far west. Now is Homer really unaware that
the west wind blows from the west? But Homer

[1] Gulf of Saros.

ἀλλ' ὅταν οὕτω φῇ, φυλάττει τὴν οἰκείαν αὐτοῦ
τάξιν·

> σὺν δ' Εὖρός τε Νότος τε πέσον Ζέφυρός τε
> δυσαὴς
> καὶ Βορέης·　　　　　　　　　　　(Od. 5. 295)

ἢ τὴν Θράκην οὐκ οἶδε μὴ προπίπτουσαν πέρα[1]
τῶν Παιονικῶν καὶ Θετταλικῶν ὁρῶν; ἀλλὰ καὶ
ταύτην τὴν κατὰ τοὺς Θρᾷκας καὶ τὴν ἐφεξῆς[2]
εἰδὼς καὶ εὖ[3] κατονομάζων τήν τε παραλίαν καὶ
τὴν μεσόγαιαν Μάγνητας μέν τινας καὶ Μαλιεῖς
καὶ τοὺς ἐφεξῆς Ἕλληνας καταλέγει μέχρι Θεσπρωτῶν, ὁμοίως δὲ καὶ τοῖς Παίοσι τοὺς ὁμό-
ρους Δόλοπας καὶ Σελλοὺς περὶ Δωδώνην μέχρις
Ἀχελώου, Θρακῶν δ' οὐ μέμνηται περαιτέρω.
εὐεπιφόρως δὲ ἔχει πρὸς τὴν ἐγγυτάτην καὶ γνω-
ριμωτάτην ἑαυτῷ θάλατταν, ὡς καὶ ὅταν φῇ·

C 29
> κινήθη δ' ἀγορὴ ὡς κύματα μακρὰ θαλάσσης
> πόντου Ἰκαρίοιο.　　　　　　　　(Il. 2. 144)

21. Εἰσὶ δέ τινες, οἵ φασιν εἶναι δύο τοὺς
κυριωτάτους ἀνέμους, Βορέαν καὶ Νότον, τοὺς
δὲ ἄλλους κατὰ μικρὰν ἔγκλισιν διαφέρειν· τὸν
μὲν ἀπὸ θερινῶν ἀνατολῶν Εὖρον, χειμερινῶν
δὲ Ἀπηλιώτην· δύσεων δὲ θερινῶν μὲν Ζέφυρον,
χειμερινῶν δὲ Ἀργέστην. τοῦ δὲ δύο εἶναι τοὺς
ἀνέμους ποιοῦνται μάρτυρας Θρασυάλκην τε καὶ
τὸν ποιητὴν αὐτὸν τῷ τὸν μὲν Ἀργέστην τῷ Νότῳ
προσνέμειν·

> ἀργεστᾶο Νότοιο,　　　　　　　　(Il. 11. 306)

---

[1] πέρα, Cobet, for πέραν.
[2] κατὰ τοὺς Θρᾷκας καὶ τὴν ἐφεξῆς, A. Miller, for ἐφεξῆς κατὰ
τοὺς Θρᾷκας.　　　[3] εὖ, T. G. Tucker, for οὐ.

keeps it in its own proper place when he says:
"The east wind and the south wind clashed, and the
stormy west and the north." Or is he unaware that
Thrace does not extend westward beyond the
mountains of Paeonia and Thessaly? But he knows
and correctly names the Thracian country as well as
the country contiguous to it, both the sea-coast and
the interior; and while he lists Magnesians, Malians,
and the Hellenes next after them as far as the
Thesprotians, and likewise the Dolopians and Sellans
about Dodona, next neighbours to the Paeonians, as
far as Acheloüs, yet he mentions no Thracians further
west. And besides, Homer has a special fondness
for the sea that lies nearest his home and is best-
known to him, as is shown when he says: "And
the assembly swayed like high waves of the Icarian
deep."

21. There are some writers who say that there are
only two principal winds, Boreas and Notus; and
that the rest of the winds differ from these only
by a slight variation of direction—Eurus blowing
from the direction of summer sunrise,[1] Apeliotes
from the direction of winter sunrise,[2] Zephyrus from
the direction of summer sunset,[3] Argestes from the
direction of winter sunset.[4] And to prove that there
are only two winds they adduce the testimony
of Thrasyalces[5] and of Homer himself, on the
ground that Homer assigns Argestes to Notus in
the phrase "of Argestes Notus," and Zephyrus to

---

[1] North-east.   [2] South-east.   [3] North-west.
[4] South-west.   [5] See 17. 1. 5.

τὸν δὲ Ζέφυρον τῷ Βορέᾳ·

Βορέης καὶ Ζέφυρος, τώ τε Θρήκηθεν ἄητον.

(Il. 9. 5)

φησὶ δὲ Ποσειδώνιος, μηδένα οὕτως παραδεδω-
κέναι τοὺς ἀνέμους τῶν γνωρίμων περὶ ταῦτα, οἷον
Ἀριστοτέλη, Τιμοσθένη, Βίωνα τὸν ἀστρολόγον·
ἀλλὰ τὸν μὲν ἀπὸ θερινῶν ἀνατολῶν Καικίαν, τὸι
δὲ τούτῳ κατὰ διάμετρον ἐναντίον Λίβα, ἀπὸ
δύσεως ὄντα χειμερινῆς· πάλιν δὲ τὸν μὲν ἀπὸ
χειμερινῆς ἀνατολῆς Εὖρον, τὸν δ' ἐναντίον Ἀρ-
γέστην· τοὺς δὲ μέσους Ἀπηλιώτην καὶ Ζέφυρον.
τὸν δὲ ποιητὴν δυσαῆ μὲν Ζέφυρον λέγειν τὸν ὑφ'
ἡμῶν καλούμενον Ἀργέστην, λίγα δὲ πνέοντα
Ζέφυρον τὸν ὑφ' ἡμῶν Ζέφυρον, ἀργέστην δὲ
Νότον τὸν Λευκόνοτον· οὗτος γὰρ ὀλίγα τὰ νέφη
ποιεῖ, τοῦ λοιποῦ Νότου ὀλεροῦ [1] πως ὄντος·

ὡς ὁπότε Ζέφυρος νέφεα στυφελίξῃ
ἀργεστᾶο Νότοιο, βαθείῃ λαίλαπι τύπτων.

(Il. 11. 305)

τὸν γὰρ δυσαῆ Ζέφυρον νῦν λέγει, ὃς εἴωθε δια-
σκιδνάναι τὰ ὑπὸ τοῦ Λευκόνοτου συναγόμενα
ἀσθενῆ ὄντα, ἐπιθέτως τοῦ Νότου νῦν ἀργέστου
λεγομένου. ταῦτα μὲν δὴ ἐν ἀρχῇ τοῦ πρώτου
τῶν γεωγραφικῶν εἰρημένα τοιαύτην τινὰ τὴν
ἐπανόρθωσιν ἔχει.

22. Ἐπιμένων δὲ τοῖς περὶ Ὁμήρου ψευδῶς
ὑποληφθεῖσι καὶ ταῦτά φησιν, ὅτι οὐδὲ τὰ τοῦ
Νείλου στόματα οἶδε πλείω ὄντα οὐδ' αὐτὸ
τοὔνομα, Ἡσίοδος δὲ οἶδε· μέμνηται γάρ. τὸ μὲν

---

[1] ὀλεροῦ, Kramer suggests, for ὅλου Εὔρου, but does not
insert. Meineke inserts; C. Müller, A. Vogel approving.

Boreas in the verse: "Boreas and Zephyrus that blow from Thrace." But Poseidonius says that none of the recognised authorities on these matters, such as Aristotle, Timosthenes, and Bion the astrologer, have taught any such doctrine about the winds; rather do they maintain that Caecias is the name of the wind that blows from the direction of summer sunrise, while Lips is the name of the wind that blows diametrically opposite to Caecias from the direction of winter sunset; and again, that Eurus is the name of the wind that blows from the direction of winter sunrise, while Argestes is its opposite; and that the winds that lie between these are Apeliotes and Zephyrus. They say further that when Homer speaks of "the boisterous Zephyrus" he means what we call Argestes; that Homer's "clear-blowing Zephyrus" is what we call Zephyrus, and that Homer's "Argestes Notus" is our Leuconotus; for Leuconotus causes very few clouds, while Notus proper is somewhat cloudy: "Even as when Zephyrus driveth the clouds of Argestes Notus, smiting with deep storm." Homer here means "the boisterous Zephyrus," which usually scatters the thin clouds assembled by Leuconotus; for in this passage "Argestes" is applied to "Notus" as an epithet. Such, then, are the corrections that must be made to the remarks of Eratosthenes at the beginning of the first chapter of his Geography.

22. But, persisting in his false assumptions, Eratosthenes says that Homer does not even know that there are several mouths of the Nile, nor yet does he know the real name of the river, though Hesiod knows, for he mentions it. Now, as to the

οὖν ὄνομα εἰκὸς μήπω λέγεσθαι κατ' αὐτόν· τὰ δὲ
στόματα εἰ μὲν ἦν ἀφανῆ καὶ ὀλίγοις γνώριμα,
ὅτι πλείω καὶ οὐχ ἕν, δοίη τις ἂν μὴ πεπύσθαι
αὐτόν· εἰ δὲ τῶν κατ' Αἴγυπτον τὸ γνωριμώτατον
καὶ παραδοξότατον καὶ μάλιστα πάντων μνήμης
ἄξιον καὶ ἱστορίας ὁ ποταμὸς καὶ ἦν καὶ ἔστιν,
ὡς δ' αὕτως αἱ ἀναβάσεις αὐτοῦ καὶ τὰ στόματα,
τίς ἂν ἢ τοὺς ἀγγέλλοντας αὐτῷ ποταμὸν Αἴγυ-
C 30 πτον καὶ χώραν καὶ Θήβας Αἰγυπτίας καὶ Φάρον
ὑπολάβοι μὴ γνωρίζειν ταῦτα, ἢ γνωρίζοντας μὴ
λέγειν, πλὴν εἰ μὴ διὰ τὸ γνώριμον; ἔτι δ'
ἀπιθανώτερον, εἰ τὴν μὲν Αἰθιοπίαν ἔλεγε καὶ
Σιδονίους καὶ Ἐρεμβοὺς καὶ τὴν ἔξω θάλασσαν
καὶ τὸ διχθὰ δεδάσθαι τοὺς Αἰθίοπας, τὰ δ' ἐγγὺς
καὶ γνώριμα μὴ ᾔδει.[1] εἰ δὲ μὴ ἐμνήσθη τούτων,
οὐ τοῦτο σημεῖον τοῦ ἀγνοεῖν (οὐδὲ γὰρ τῆς αὐτοῦ
πατρίδος ἐμνήσθη οὐδὲ πολλῶν ἄλλων) ἀλλὰ
μᾶλλον τὰ λίαν γνώριμα ὄντα φαίη τις ἂν δόξαι
μὴ[2] ἄξια μνήμης εἶναι πρὸς τοὺς εἰδότας.

23. Οὐκ εὖ δὲ οὐδὲ τοῦτο προφέρουσιν αὐτῷ τὸ
περὶ τῆς νήσου τῆς Φαρίας, ὅτι φησὶ πελαγίαν,
ὡς κατ' ἄγνοιαν λέγοντι. τοὐναντίον γὰρ κἂν
μαρτυρίῳ χρήσαιτό τις τούτῳ πρὸς τὸ μὴ ἀγνο-
εῖσθαι μηδὲν ὑπὸ τοῦ ποιητοῦ τῶν εἰρημένων

---

[1] ᾔδει, Jones inserts.
[2] τὰ λίαν γνώριμα ὄντα φαίη τις ἂν δόξαι μή, Meineke, for
τοῦ λίαν ἢ γνώριμα ὄντα φαίη δόξειν.

name, it is likely that in Homer's time it was not yet in use; but as to the mouths, if the fact that there were several, and not one only, was unnoticed or known to only a few, one might grant that Homer had not heard of it. But if the river was then, as it still is, the best-known and most marvellous thing in Egypt and decidedly the most worthy of mention and of historical record—and the same applies to its inundations and its mouths— who could ever assume either that those who brought to Homer the story of the River " Aegyptus " and the country " Aegyptus," and Egyptian Thebes, and Pharos, did not know about these mouths, or that if they knew, did not tell about them—except for the reason that they were already well known ? But it is more incredible still that he mentioned Ethiopia, Sidonians, Erembians, the sea beyond,[1] and the fact that the Ethiopians are "sundered in twain," and yet did not know about what was near at hand and well known. The fact that he did not mention them is no sign that he did not know about them— he does not mention his own native country, either, nor many other things—but rather would one say that Homer thought the best-known facts were not worth mentioning to those who already knew them.

23. Equally unjust is the reproach they cast upon Homer in the matter of the island of Pharos, because he says that it is "in the open sea"—as though he said this in ignorance. On the contrary, one might use that statement as bearing witness to the fact that not one of the things which we have just been talking about regarding Egypt was un-

---

[1] The Atlantic Ocean.

STRABO

ἀρτίως περὶ τὴν Αἴγυπτον. γνοίης δ᾽ ἂν οὕτως·
ἀλαζὼν δὴ πᾶς ὁ πλάνην αὑτοῦ διηγούμενος·
τούτων δ᾽ ἦν καὶ ὁ Μενέλαος, ὃς ἀναβεβηκὼς
μέχρις Αἰθιόπων ἐπέπυστο τὰς ἀναβάσεις τοῦ
Νείλου καὶ τὴν χοῦν, ὅσην ἐπιφέρει τῇ χώρᾳ, καὶ
τὸν πρὸ τῶν στομάτων πόρον, ὅσον ἤδη προσχώ-
σας τῇ ἠπείρῳ προστέθεικεν, ὥστε εἰκότως ὑπὸ
τοῦ Ἡροδότου καὶ τὴν ὅλην Αἴγυπτον τοῦ ποταμοῦ δῶρον λέγεσθαι· κἂν εἰ μὴ¹ τὴν ὅλην, τήν γε
ὑπὸ τῷ Δέλτα, τὴν κάτω χώραν προσαγορευο-
μένην. ἱστόρησε δὲ καὶ τὴν Φάρον πελαγίαν
οὖσαν τὸ παλαιόν· προσεψεύσατο δὴ καὶ τὸ
πελαγίαν εἶναι, καίπερ μηκέτι πελαγίαν οὖσαν.
ὁ δὲ ταῦτα διασκευάζων ὁ ποιητὴς ἦν· ὥστ᾽ ἐκ
τούτων εἰκάζειν, ὅτι καὶ τὰς ἀναβάσεις ᾔδει καὶ
τὰ στόματα τοῦ Νείλου.

24. Ἡ δ᾽ αὐτὴ ἁμαρτία καὶ περὶ τοῦ ἀγνοεῖν
τὸν ἰσθμὸν τὸν μεταξὺ τοῦ Αἰγυπτίου πελάγους
καὶ τοῦ Ἀραβίου κόλπου καὶ περὶ τοῦ ψευδῶς
λέγεσθαι

Αἰθίοπας, τοὶ διχθὰ δεδαίαται ἔσχατοι ἀνδρῶν·
(Od. 1. 23)

καὶ γὰρ τοῦτο ἐκείνου λέγοντος καλῶς, ἐπιτιμῶσιν
οἱ ὕστερον οὐκ εὖ. τοσούτου γὰρ δεῖ τοῦτ᾽ ἀληθὲς
εἶναι, τὸ ἀγνοεῖν Ὅμηρον τὸν ἰσθμὸν τοῦτον, ὥστε
ἐκεῖνον μέν φημι μὴ εἰδέναι μόνον, ἀλλὰ καὶ ἀπο-
φαίνεσθαι ἄντικρυς, τοὺς δὲ γραμματικοὺς μηδὲ

¹ τε, Corais deletes, after μή; Meineke following; C. Müller,
A. Miller, approving.

known to the poet. You might convince yourself of
it in the following way : Everybody who tells the
story of his own travels is a braggart ; to this class
belonged Menelaus, who had ascended the Nile as
far as Ethiopia, and had heard about the inundations
of the Nile and the quantity of alluvial soil which
the river deposits upon the country, and about the
large extent of territory off its mouths which the
river had already added to the continent by silting
—so that Herodotus [1] was quite right in saying that
the whole of Egypt is "a gift of the River Nile";
and even if this is not true of the whole of Egypt,
it certainly is true of the part embraced by the
Delta, which is called Lower Egypt ; and Menelaus
was told that the island of Pharos had been "in the
open sea" in ancient times; so he falsely added that
it was still "in the open sea," although it was no
longer "in the open sea." However, it was the poet
who elaborated this story, and therefore from
it we may conjecture that Homer knew about
the inundations of the Nile and about its mouths as
well.

24. The same mistake is made by those who say that
Homer is not acquainted with the isthmus that lies
between the Egyptian Sea and the Arabian Gulf, and
that he is in error when he speaks of "the Ethiopians
that are sundered in twain, the farthermost of men."
Men of later times are wrong when they censure
Homer for saying that, for it is correct. Indeed, the
reproach that Homer is ignorant of this isthmus is
so far from being true, that I affirm not only that he
knows about it, but that he describes it in express
terms, and that the grammarians beginning with

[1] Herod. 2. 5.

STRABO

λέγοντος ἐκείνου αἰσθάνεσθαι ἀπὸ Ἀριστάρχου
ἀρξαμένους[1] καὶ Κράτητος τῶν κορυφαίων ἐν τῇ
ἐπιστήμῃ ταύτῃ. εἰπόντος γὰρ τοῦ ποιητοῦ·

Αἰθίοπας, τοὶ διχθὰ δεδαίαται ἔσχατοι ἀνδρῶν,
(Od. 1. 23)

περὶ τοῦ ἐπιφερομένου ἔπους διαφέρονται, ὁ μὲν
Ἀρίσταρχος γράφων,

οἱ μὲν δυσομένου Ὑπερίονος, οἱ δ᾽ ἀνιόντος,
(Od. 1. 24)

ὁ δὲ Κράτης,

ἠμὲν δυσομένου Ὑπερίονος, ἠδ᾽ ἀνιόντος,
(Od. 1. 24)

C 31 οὐδὲν διαφέρον πρὸς τὴν ἑκατέρου ὑπόθεσιν
οὕτως ἢ ἐκείνως γράφειν. ὁ μὲν γάρ, ἀκολουθῶν
τοῖς μαθηματικῶς λέγεσθαι δοκοῦσι, τὴν διακεκαυμένην ζώνην κατέχεσθαί φησιν ὑπὸ τοῦ ὠκεα-
νοῦ· παρ᾽ ἑκάτερον δὲ ταύτης εἶναι τὴν εὔκρατον,
τήν τε καθ᾽ ἡμᾶς καὶ τὴν ἐπὶ θάτερον μέρος.
ὥσπερ οὖν οἱ παρ᾽ ἡμῖν Αἰθίοπες οὗτοι λέγονται
οἱ πρὸς μεσημβρίαν κεκλιμένοι παρ᾽ ὅλην τὴν
οἰκουμένην ἔσχατοι τῶν ἄλλων παροικοῦντες τὸν
ὠκεανόν, οὕτως οἴεται δεῖν καὶ πέραν τοῦ ὠκεανοῦ
νοεῖσθαί τινας Αἰθίοπας ἐσχάτους τῶν ἄλλων
τῶν ἐν τῇ ἑτέρᾳ εὐκράτῳ, παροικοῦντας τὸν αὐτὸν
τοῦτον ὠκεανόν· διττοὺς δὲ εἶναι καὶ διχθὰ δεδάσθαι ὑπὸ τοῦ ὠκεανοῦ. προσκεῖσθαι δὲ τὸ

ἠμὲν δυσομένου Ὑπερίονος, ἠδ᾽ ἀνιοντος,
(Od. 1. 24)

ὅτι τοῦ Ζωδιακοῦ κατὰ κορυφὴν ὄντος ἀεὶ τῷ ἐν

---

[1] ἀρξαμένους, H. Kallenberg inserts, after Ἀριστάρχου. It is
inserted in the margin of q "secunda manu" after Κράτητος.

112

Aristarchus and Crates, the leading lights in the
science of criticism, even though Homer speaks of
it, do not perceive that he does. The poet says:
"the Ethiopians that are sundered in twain, the
farthermost of men." About the next verse there is
a difference of opinion, Aristarchus writing: "abiding
some where Hyperion sets, and some where he rises";
but Crates: "abiding both where Hyperion sets and
where he rises." Yet so far as the question at
issue is concerned, it makes no difference whether
you write the verse one way or the other. For
Crates, following the mere form of mathematical
demonstration, says that the torrid zone is
"occupied"[1] by Oceanus and that on both sides of
this zone are the temperate zones, the one being
on our side, while the other is on the other side of
it. Now, just as these Ethiopians on our side of
Oceanus, who face the south throughout the whole
length of the inhabited world, are called the most
remote of the one group of peoples, since they dwell
on the shores of Oceanus, so too, Crates thinks, we
must conceive that on the other side of Oceanus
also there are certain Ethiopians, the most remote
of the other group of peoples in the temperate
zone, since they dwell on the shores of this same
Oceanus; and that they are in two groups and are
"sundered in twain" by Oceanus. Homer adds the
words, "abiding both where Hyperion sets and
where he rises," because, inasmuch as the celestial
zodiac always lies in the zenith above its corresponding

---

[1] For the purposes of demonstration Crates identified the
limits of Oceanus with those of the torrid zone, an assumption which was not strictly true.

τῇ γῇ Ζωδιακῷ, τούτου δ' οὐκ ἐκβαίνοντος ἔξω
τῆς Αἰθιόπων ἀμφοῖν τῇ λοξώσει, ἀνάγκη καὶ τὴν
πάροδον τοῦ ἡλίου πᾶσαν ἐν τῷ πλάτει τούτῳ
νοεῖσθαι, καὶ τὰς ἀνατολὰς καὶ τὰς δύσεις συμβαίνειν ἐνταῦθα ἄλλας ἄλλοις καὶ κατ' ἄλλα ἢ
ἄλλα σημεῖα. εἴρηκε μὲν οὕτως, ἀστρονομικώ-
τερον νομίσας· ἦν δὲ καὶ ἁπλούστερον εἰπεῖν
αὐτὸ σώζοντα τὸ οὕτω διῃρῆσθαι δίχα τοὺς
Αἰθίοπας, ὡς εἴρηται· ὅτι ἀφ' ἡλίου ἀνιόντος
μέχρι δύσεως ἐφ' ἑκάτερα παρήκουσι[1] τῷ ὠκεανῷ
Αἰθίοπες. τί οὖν διαφέρει πρὸς τὸν νοῦν τοῦτον
ἢ οὕτως εἰπεῖν, ὥσπερ αὐτὸς γράφει, ἢ ὡς Ἀρίσταρχος,

οἱ μὲν δυσομένου Ὑπερίονος, οἱ δ' ἀνιόντος;

(Od. 1. 24)

καὶ γὰρ τοῦτ' ἐστι καὶ πρὸς δύσιν καὶ πρὸς
ἀνατολὴν ἐφ' ἑκάτερα τοῦ ὠκεανοῦ οἰκεῖν. ὁ δ'
Ἀρίσταρχος ταύτην μὲν ἐκβάλλει τὴν ὑπόθεσιν,
δίχα δὲ μεμερισμένους οἴεται λέγεσθαι τοὺς καθ'
ἡμᾶς Αἰθίοπας, τοὺς τοῖς Ἕλλησι πρὸς μεσημβρίαν ἐσχάτους. τούτους δὲ μὴ μεμερίσθαι δίχα,
ὥστε εἶναι δύο Αἰθιοπίας, τὴν μὲν πρὸς ἀνατολήν,
τὴν δὲ πρὸς δύσιν· ἀλλὰ μίαν μόνην, τὴν πρὸς
μεσημβρίαν κειμένην τοῖς Ἕλλησιν, ἱδρυμένην
δὲ κατ' Αἴγυπτον. τοῦτο δὲ ἀγνοοῦντα τὸν ποιητήν, ὥσπερ καὶ τὰ ἄλλα ὅσα εἴρηκεν Ἀπολλό-

---

[1] παρήκουσι, the reading of AC*hi* MSS., Madvig apparently
prefers to παροικοῦσι.

terrestrial zodiac and inasmuch as the latter does not by reason of its obliquity[1] extend outside the territory of the two Ethiopias, we must conceive that the entire revolution of the sun takes place within the width of this celestial zone, and that his risings and his settings take place herein, appearing differently to different peoples, and now in this sign and now in that. Such, then, is the explanation of Crates, who conceives of the matter rather as an astronomer; but he might have put it more simply— still saving his point that this was the sense in which the Ethiopians are " sundered in twain," as Homer has stated—namely, by declaring that the Ethiopians stretch along both shores of Oceanus from the rising to the setting of the sun. What difference, I say, does it make with respect to this thought whether we read the verse as Crates writes it, or as Aristarchus does—" abiding some where Hyperion sets and some where he rises " ? For this, too, means that Ethiopians live on both sides of Oceanus, both towards the west and towards the east. But Aristarchus rejects this hypothesis of Crates, and thinks that the people referred to as divided " in twain " are the Ethiopians in our part of the world, namely, those that to the Greeks are most remote on the south ; but he thinks these are not so divided " in twain " that there are two Ethiopias, the one lying towards the east and the other towards the west, but that there is just one, the one that lies south of the Greeks and is situated along Egypt ; and he thinks that the poet, ignorant of this fact, just as he was ignorant of those other matters which

[1] Compare " the obliquity of the ecliptic "—which is now about $23\frac{1}{2}°$.

δωρος ἐν τῷ περὶ Νεῶν καταλόγου δευτέρῳ, καταψεύσασθαι τῶν τόπων τὰ μὴ ὄντα.

25. Πρὸς μὲν οὖν Κράτητα μακροῦ λόγου δεῖ, καὶ ἴσως οὐδὲν ὄντος πρὸς τὰ νῦν. Ἀριστάρχου δὲ τοῦτο μὲν ἐπαινοῦμεν,[1] διότι τὴν Κρατήτειον ἀφεὶς ὑπόθεσιν, δεχομένην πολλὰς ἐνστάσεις, περὶ τῆς καθ᾽ ἡμᾶς Αἰθιοπίας ὑπονοεῖ γεγονέναι τὸν λόγον· τὰ δ᾽ ἄλλα ἐπισκοπῶμεν. καὶ πρῶτον ὅτι καὶ αὐτὸς μικρολογεῖται μάτην περὶ τῆς γραφῆς. καὶ γὰρ ἂν ὁποτέρως[2] γράφηται, δύ-
C 32 ναται ἐφαρμόττειν τοῖς νοήμασιν αὐτοῦ. τί γὰρ διαφέρει λέγειν ἢ οὕτως, "δύο εἰσὶ καθ᾽ ἡμᾶς Αἰθίοπες, οἱ μὲν πρὸς ἀνατολάς, οἱ δὲ πρὸς δύσεις," ἢ οὕτως, "καὶ γὰρ πρὸς ἀνατολὰς καὶ πρὸς δύσεις"; ἔπειθ᾽ ὅτι ψευδοῦς προΐσταται δόγματος. φέρε γὰρ τὸν ποιητὴν ἀγνοεῖν μὲν τὸν ἰσθμόν, τῆς δὲ κατ᾽ Αἴγυπτον Αἰθιοπίας μεμνῆσθαι, ὅταν φῇ·

Αἰθίοπας, τοὶ διχθὰ δεδαίαται·   (Od. 1. 23)

πῶς οὖν; οὐ διχθὰ δεδαίαται οὕτως, ἀλλ᾽ ἀγνοῶν οὕτως εἴρηκεν ὁ ποιητής; πότερ᾽ οὐδ᾽ ἡ Αἴγυπτος, οὐδ᾽ οἱ Αἰγύπτιοι ἀπὸ τοῦ Δέλτα ἀρξάμενοι μέχρι πρὸς Συήνην ὑπὸ τοῦ Νείλου δίχα διῄρηνται,

οἱ μὲν δυσομένου Ὑπερίονος, οἱ δ᾽ ἀνιόντος;
(Od. 1. 24)

τί δ᾽ ἄλλο ἢ Αἴγυπτός ἐστι πλὴν ἢ[3] ποταμία,[4] ἣν ἐπικλύζει τὸ ὕδωρ; αὕτη δ᾽ ἐφ᾽ ἑκάτερα τοῦ

---

[1] ἐπαινοῦμεν, Cobet, for ἐπαινῶμεν.
[2] ὁποτέρως, Corais, for ὡς ἑτέρως; C. Müller approving.
[3] πλὴν ἤ, Corais, for πλὴν ἡ; Groskurd, Forbiger following.

Apollodorus has mentioned in the second book of
his work entitled " On the Catalogue of Ships,"
told what was not true about the regions in
question.

25. To reply to Crates would require a long discourse, which would perhaps be irrelevant to my
present purpose. As for Aristarchus, I approve of
him in this, that he rejects the hypothesis of Crates,
which is open to many objections, and inclines to
the view that the words of Homer have reference to
our Ethiopia. But let us examine Aristarchus on the
other points ; and, in the first place, take the fact
that he too indulges in a petty and fruitless discussion
of the text. For if the verse be written in either of
the two ways, it can fit his thought on the subject.
For what difference does it make whether we say :
" On our side of Oceanus there are two groups of
Ethiopians, some in the east and some in the west,"
or, " both in the east and in the west " ? In the
second place, take the fact that Aristarchus champions
a false doctrine. Well, let us suppose that the poet
is ignorant of the existence of the isthmus, but is
referring to the Ethiopia on the confines of Egypt
when he speaks of " Ethiopians that are sundered in
twain." What then ? Are they not thus " sundered
in twain " ? And did the poet make that statement
in ignorance ? Is not Egypt also, are not the
Egyptians also, from the Delta up to Syene, "sundered
in twain " by the Nile, "some where Hyperion sets
and some where he rises " ? What is Egypt but a
river valley, which the water floods ? And this valley

---

[4] νῆσος, after ποταμία, Kramer wishes to delete ; Meineke
deletes ; Forbiger following ; C. Müller approving.

ποταμοῦ κεῖται πρὸς ἀνατολὴν καὶ δύσιν. ἀλλὰ
μὴν ἡ Αἰθιοπία ἐπ᾽ εὐθείας ἐστὶ τῇ Αἰγύπτῳ καὶ
παραπλησίως ἔχει πρός τε τὸν Νεῖλον καὶ τὴν
ἄλλην φύσιν τῶν τόπων. καὶ γὰρ αὕτη στενή τέ
ἐστι καὶ μακρὰ καὶ ἐπίκλυστος. τὰ δ᾽ ἔξω τῆς
ἐπικλύστου ἔρημά τε καὶ ἄνυδρα καὶ σπανίως
οἰκεῖσθαι δυνάμενα, τὰ μὲν πρὸς ἔω, τὰ δὲ πρὸς
δύσιν κεκλιμένα. πῶς οὖν οὐχὶ καὶ δίχα διῄρηται;
ἢ τοῖς μὲν τὴν Ἀσίαν ἀπὸ τῆς Λιβύης διαιροῦσιν
ἀξιόλογον τοῦθ᾽ ὅριον ἐφάνη ὁ Νεῖλος, μῆκος
μὲν ἀνατείνων ἐπὶ τὴν μεσημβρίαν πλειόνων
ἢ μυρίων σταδίων, πλάτος δέ, ὥστε καὶ νήσους
ἀπολαμβάνειν μυριάνδρους, ὧν μεγίστη ἡ Μερόη,
τὸ βασίλειον καὶ μητρόπολις τῶν Αἰθιόπων·
αὐτὴν δὲ τὴν Αἰθιοπίαν οὐχ ἱκανὸς ἦν διαιρεῖν
δίχα; καὶ μὴν οἵ γε ἐπιτιμῶντες τοῖς τὰς ἠπείρους
τῷ ποταμῷ διαιροῦσι τῶν ἐγκλημάτων τοῦτο
μέγιστον προφέρουσιν αὐτοῖς, ὅτι τὴν Αἴγυπτον
καὶ τὴν Αἰθιοπίαν διασπῶσι καὶ ποιοῦσι τὸ μέν
τι μέρος ἑκατέρας αὐτῶν Λιβυκόν, τὸ δ᾽ Ἀσιατι-
κόν· ἢ εἰ μὴ βούλονται τοῦτο ἢ οὐ διαιροῦσι τὰς
ἠπείρους, ἢ οὐ τῷ ποταμῷ.

26. Χωρὶς δὲ τούτων ἐστὶ καὶ ἄλλως διαιρεῖν
τὴν Αἰθιοπίαν. πάντες γὰρ οἱ παραπλεύσαντες
τῷ ὠκεανῷ τὴν Λιβύην, οἵ τε ἀπὸ τῆς Ἐρυθρᾶς
καὶ οἱ ἀπὸ τῶν Στηλῶν, μέχρι ποσοῦ προελθόντες

lies on both sides of the river, toward the east and toward the west. But Ethiopia lies directly beyond Egypt and it is analogous to Egypt in its relation both to the Nile and the other physical characteristics of the regions in question. For it, too, is narrow, long, and subject to inundations; and its parts that lie beyond the territory subject to inundations are desert, without water, and habitable only in spots, both on the east and on the west. Of course, then, Ethiopia also is "sundered in twain." Or, again, did the Nile seem important enough for those who were drawing a boundary-line between Asia and Libya to serve as that boundary-line (since in length it stretches toward the south for more than ten thousand stadia, and is of such width that it contains islands with many thousands of inhabitants, the largest of which is Meroë, the residence of the King and the metropolis of the Ethiopians) and yet was not important enough to "sunder" Ethiopia itself "in twain"? And furthermore, the critics of the men who make the River Nile the boundary-line between the continents bring this against them as their most serious charge, that they dismember Egypt and Ethiopia, and that they reckon one part of each country to Libya and one part to Asia; or that, if they do not wish such dismemberment, then either they do not divide the continents at all, or else do not make the river the boundary-line.

26. But Ethiopia may be divided in still another way, quite apart from this. For all those who have made coasting-voyages on the ocean along the shores of Libya, whether they started from the Red Sea or from the Pillars of Heracles, always turned back, after they had advanced a certain distance, because

εἶτα ἀνέστρεψαν ὑπὸ πολλῶν ἀποριῶν κωλυό-
μενοι, ὥστε καὶ πίστιν κατέλιπον τοῖς πολλοῖς,
ὡς τὸ μεταξὺ διείργοιτο ἰσθμῷ· καὶ μὴν σύρρους
ἡ πᾶσα Ἀτλαντικὴ θάλασσα, καὶ μάλιστα ἡ
κατὰ μεσημβρίαν. ἅπαντες δὲ οὗτοι τὰ τελευταῖα
χωρία, ἐφ᾽ ἃ πλέοντες ἦλθον, Αἰθιοπικὰ προση-
C 33 γόρευσαν καὶ ἀπήγγειλαν οὕτως. τί οὖν ἄλογον,
εἰ καὶ Ὅμηρος ὑπὸ τοιαύτης ἀκοῆς ἀχθεὶς δίχα
διῄρει, τοὺς μὲν πρὸς ἀνατολὴν λέγων, τοὺς δὲ
πρὸς δύσιν, τῶν μεταξὺ οὐ γινωσκομένων, εἴτε
εἰσὶν εἴτε μὴ εἰσίν; ἀλλὰ μὴν καὶ ἄλλην τινὰ
ἱστορίαν εἴρηκεν παλαιὰν Ἔφορος, ᾗ οὐκ ἄλογον
ἐντυχεῖν καὶ Ὅμηρον. λέγεσθαι γάρ φησιν ὑπὸ
τῶν Ταρτησσίων Αἰθίοπας τὴν Λιβύην ἐπελθόντας
μέχρι Δύρεως[1] τοὺς μὲν αὐτοῦ μεῖνα͵, τοὺς δὲ καὶ
τῆς παραλίας κατασχεῖν πολλήν· τεκμαίρεται
δ᾽ ἐκ τούτου καὶ Ὅμηρον εἰπεῖν οὕτως·

Αἰθίοπας, τοὶ διχθὰ δεδαίαται ἔσχατοι ἀνδρῶν.
(Od. 1. 23)

27. Ταῦτά τε[2] δὴ πρὸς τὸν Ἀρίσταρχον λέγοι
ἄν τις καὶ πρὸς τοὺς ἀκολουθοῦντας αὐτῷ, καὶ
ἄλλα τούτων ἐπιεικέστερα, ἀφ᾽ ὧν τὴν πολλὴν
ἄγνοιαν ἀφαιρήσεται τοῦ ποιητοῦ. φημὶ γὰρ
κατὰ τὴν τῶν ἀρχαίων Ἑλλήνων δόξαν, ὥσπερ
τὰ πρὸς βορρᾶν μέρη τὰ γνώριμα ἑνὶ ὀνόματι
Σκύθας ἐκάλουν ἢ Νομάδας, ὡς Ὅμηρος, ὕστερον
δὲ καὶ τῶν πρὸς ἑσπέραν γνωσθέντων Κελτοὶ καὶ

---

[1] Δύρεως, C. Müller, for δύσεως.
[2] τε, Corais, for δέ; Meineke following; C. Müller approving.

they were hindered by many perplexing circumstances, and consequently they left in the minds of most people the conviction that the intervening space was blocked by an isthmus; and yet the whole Atlantic Ocean is one unbroken body of water, and this is particularly true of the Southern Atlantic. All those voyagers have spoken of the last districts to which they came in their voyagings as Ethiopic territory and have so reported them. Wherein, then, lies the absurdity, if Homer, too, was misled by a report of this character and divided the Ethiopians into two groups, placing the one group in the east and the other in the west, since it was not known whether the intervening people really existed or not? Furthermore, Ephorus mentions still another ancient tradition, and it is not unreasonable to believe that Homer also had heard it. Ephorus says the Tartessians report that Ethiopians overran Libya as far as Dyris,[1] and that some of them stayed in Dyris, while others occupied a great part of the sea-board; and he conjectures it was from this circumstance that Homer spoke as he did: "Ethiopians that are sundered in twain, the farthermost of men."

27. These arguments one might urge in reply to Aristarchus and his followers, and also others still more convincing, and thus set the poet free from the charge of gross ignorance. I maintain, for example, that in accordance with the opinion of the ancient Greeks—just as they embraced the inhabitants of the known countries of the north under the single designation "Scythians" (or "Nomads," to use Homer's term) and just as later, when the inhabitants of the west also were discovered, they were called

[1] The barbarian name for the Atlas mountains. See 17. 3. 2.

Ἴβηρες ἢ μικτῶς Κελτίβηρες καὶ Κελτοσκύθαι προσηγορεύοντο, ὑφ' ἓν ὄνομα τῶν καθ' ἕκαστα ἐθνῶν ταττομένων διὰ τὴν ἄγνοιαν, οὕτω τὰ μεσημβρινὰ πάντα Αἰθιοπίαν καλεῖσθαι τὰ πρὸς ὠκεανῷ. μαρτυρεῖ δὲ τὰ τοιαῦτα. ὅ τε γὰρ Αἰσχύλος ἐν Προμηθεῖ τῷ λυομένῳ φησὶν οὕτω·

> φοινικόπεδόν τ' ἐρυθρᾶς ἱερὸν
> χεῦμα θαλάσσης,
> χαλκομάραυγόν[1] τε παρ' Ὠκεανῷ
> λίμναν παντοτρόφον Αἰθιόπων,
> ἵν' ὁ παντόπτας Ἥλιος αἰεὶ
> χρῶτ' ἀθάνατον κάματόν θ' ἵππων
> θερμαῖς ὕδατος
> μαλακοῦ προχοαῖς ἀναπαύει.

(*fr.* 192, Nauck)

παρ' ὅλον γὰρ τὸ μεσημβρινὸν κλίμα τοῦ ὠκεανοῦ ταύτην πρὸς τὸν ἥλιον ἴσχοντος τὴν χρείαν καὶ τὴν σχέσιν, παρ' ὅλον καὶ τοὺς Αἰθίοπας τάττων φαίνεται. ὅ τ' Εὐριπίδης ἐν[2] τῷ Φαέθοντι τὴν Κλυμένην δοθῆναί φησι

> Μέροπι τῆσδ' ἄνακτι γῆς,
> ἣν ἐκ τεθρίππων ἁρμάτων πρώτην χθόνα
> Ἥλιος ἀνίσχων χρυσέᾳ βάλλει φλογί·
> καλοῦσι δ' αὐτὴν γείτονες μελάμβροτοι
> Ἕω φαεννὰς Ἡλίου θ' ἱπποστάσεις. (*fr.* 771)

νῦν μὲν δὴ κοινὰς ποιεῖται τὰς ἱπποστάσεις τῇ τε Ἠοῖ καὶ τῷ Ἡλίῳ, ἐν δὲ τοῖς ἑξῆς πλησίον αὐτὰς φησιν εἶναι τῇ οἰκήσει τοῦ Μέροπος· καὶ ὅλῃ γε τῇ δραματουργίᾳ τοῦτο παραπέπλεκται, οὐ δή που τῆς κατ' Αἴγυπτον ἴδιον ὄν, μᾶλλον δὲ τῆς

C 34

"Celts" and "Iberians," or by the compound words "Celtiberians" and "Celtiscythians," the several peoples being classed under one name through ignorance of the facts—I maintain, I say, that just so, in accordance with the opinion of the ancient Greeks, all the countries in the south which lie on Oceanus were called "Ethiopia." And there is the following testimony to this statement. Aeschylus, in his *Prometheus Unbound*, speaks thus: "The sacred flood of the Red Sea with its bed of scarlet sands, and the mere on the shore of Oceanus that dazzles with its gleam of brass¹ and furnishes all nourishment to Ethiopians, where the Sun, who sees all things, gives rest to his tired steeds and refreshes his immortal body in warm outpourings of soft water." For since Oceanus renders this service and maintains this relation to the sun along the whole southern belt, Aeschylus obviously places the Ethiopians also along this whole belt. And Euripides, in his *Phaëthon*, says that Clymene was given "to Merops, the king of this country which is the first country that the Sun, as he rises in his chariot and four, strikes with his golden flame. And the swarthy men who dwell upon the confines of that country call it the bright stables of Dawn and Sun." In² this passage Euripides assigns the stables jointly to Dawn and Sun, but in what immediately follows he says that these stables are near to the dwelling of Merops, and indeed this is woven into the whole structure of the play, not, I am sure, because it is a peculiarity of the Ethiopia which lies next to Egypt, but rather

---

¹ χαλκομάραυγον, G. Herrmann, for χαλκοκέραυνον.
² ἐν, Meineke, for ἐπί.

παρ' ὅλον τὸ μεσημβρινὸν κλίμα διηκούσης
παραλίας.

28. Μηνύει δὲ καὶ Ἔφορος τὴν παλαιὰν περὶ
τῆς Αἰθιοπίας δόξαν, ὅς φησιν ἐν τῷ περὶ τῆς
Εὐρώπης λόγῳ, τῶν περὶ τὸν οὐρανὸν καὶ τὴν γῆν
τόπων εἰς τέτταρα μέρη διῃρημένων, τὸ πρὸς τὸν
ἀπηλιώτην Ἰνδοὺς ἔχειν, πρὸς νότον δὲ Αἰθίοπας,
πρὸς δύσιν δὲ Κελτούς, πρὸς δὲ βορρᾶν ἄνεμον
Σκύθας. προστίθησι δ', ὅτι μείζων ἡ Αἰθιοπία
καὶ ἡ Σκυθία· δοκεῖ γάρ, φησί, τὸ τῶν Αἰθιόπων
ἔθνος παρατείνειν ἀπ' ἀνατολῶν χειμερινῶν μέχρι
δυσμῶν, ἡ Σκυθία δ' ἀντίκειται τούτῳ, ὅτι δ' ὁ
ποιητὴς ὁμόλογος τούτοις, καὶ ἐκ τῶνδε δῆλον,
ὅτι ἡ μὲν Ἰθάκη κεῖται

"πρὸς ζόφον" (ὅπερ ἐστὶ πρὸς ἄρκτον) "αἱ δέ
τ' ἄνευθε πρὸς ἠῶ τ' ἠέλιόν τε," (Od. 9. 26)

ὅλον τὸ νότιον πλευρὸν οὕτω λέγων· καὶ ἔτι,
ὅταν φῇ·

εἴτ' ἐπὶ δεξί' ἴωσι πρὸς ἠῶ τ' ἠέλιόν τε,
εἴτ' ἐπ' ἀριστερά τοί γε ποτὶ ζόφον ἠερόεντα.
(Il. 12. 239)

καὶ πάλιν·

ὦ φίλοι, οὐ γάρ τ' ἴδμεν, ὅπῃ ζόφος, οὐδ' ὅπῃ
ἠώς,
οὐδ' ὅπῃ ἠέλιος φαεσίμβροτος εἶσ' ὑπὸ γαῖαν,
οὐδ' ὅπῃ ἀννεῖται. (Od. 10. 190)

περὶ ὧν λέγεται καὶ ἐν τοῖς περὶ τῆς Ἰθάκης
λόγοις σαφέστερον. ὅταν οὖν φῇ·

Ζεὺς γὰρ ἐς Ὠκεανὸν μετ' ἀμύμονας Αἰθιοπῆας
χθιζὸς ἔβη, (Il. 1. 423)

because it is a peculiarity of the sea-board that stretches along the entire southern belt.

28. Ephorus, too, discloses the ancient belief in regard to Ethiopia, for in his treatise *On Europe* he says that if we divide the regions of the heavens and of the earth into four parts, the Indians will occupy that part from which Apeliotes blows, the Ethiopians the part from which Notus blows, the Celts the part on the west, and the Scythians the part from which the north wind blows.[1] And he adds that Ethiopia and Scythia are the larger regions; for it is thought, he says, that the nation of the Ethiopians stretches from the winter sunrise to sunset,[2] and that Scythia lies directly opposite in the north. That Homer is in agreement with this view is also clear from his assertion that Ithaca lies " toward the darkness "— that is, of course, toward the north—" but those others face the dawning and the sun "; by which he means the whole country on the southern side. And again this is clear when he says: " Whether they fare to the right, to the dawn and to the sun, or to the left, to mist and darkness"; and from this passage too : " My friends, lo, now we know not where is the place of darkness or of dawning, nor where the sun that gives light to men goes beneath the earth, nor where he rises." But about all these passages I shall speak more fully in my account of Ithaca.[3] And so, when Homer says, " For Zeus went yesterday to Oceanus, unto the noble Ethiopians," we

---

[1] On the winds, see page 105.
[2] That is, on the due east and west line drawn from the south-east point of the sky to the south-west point.
[3] See 10. 2. 11 f.

κοινότερον δεκτέον καὶ τὸν ὠκεανὸν τὸν καθ᾽
ὅλον τὸ μεσημβρινὸν κλίμα τεταμένον καὶ τοὺς
Αἰθίοπας· ᾧ γὰρ ἂν τόπῳ τοῦδε τοῦ κλίματος
προσβάλῃς τὴν διάνοιαν, καὶ ἐπὶ τῷ ὠκεανῷ ἔσῃ
καὶ ἐπὶ τῇ Αἰθιοπίᾳ. οὕτω δὲ λέγει καὶ τὸ

> τὸν δ᾽ ἐξ Αἰθιόπων ἀνιὼν
> τηλόθεν ἐκ Σολύμων ὀρέων ἴδεν,   (Od. 5. 282)

ἴσον τῷ ἀπὸ μεσημβρινῶν τόπων, Σολύμους λέγων
οὐ τοὺς ἐν τῇ Πισιδίᾳ, ἀλλ᾽, ὡς ἔφην πρότερον,
πλάσας[1] τινὰς ὁμωνύμους, τοὺς ἀναλόγως ἔχοντας
πρός τε τὸν πλέοντα ἐν τῇ σχεδίᾳ καὶ τοὺς ἐκεῖ
μεσημβρινούς, ὡς ἂν Αἰθίοπας, ὡς οἱ Πισιδικοὶ
πρός τε τὸν Πόντον καὶ τοὺς ὑπὲρ τῆς Αἰγύπτου
Αἰθίοπας. οὕτω δὲ καὶ τὸν περὶ τῶν γεράνων
λόγον κοινὸν ποιούμενός φησιν·

> αἵ τ᾽ ἐπεὶ οὖν χειμῶνα φύγον καὶ ἀθέσφατον
> ὄμβρον,
> C 35   κλαγγῇ ταί γε πέτονται ἐπ᾽ Ὠκεανοῖο ῥοάων,
> ἀνδράσι Πυγμαίοισι φόνον καὶ κῆρα φέρου-
> σαι.   (Il. 3. 4)

οὐ γὰρ ἐν μὲν τοῖς κατὰ τὴν Ἑλλάδα τόποις
ὁρᾶται φερομένη ἡ γέρανος ἐπὶ τὴν μεσημβρίαν,
ἐν δὲ τοῖς κατὰ τὴν Ἰταλίαν ἢ Ἰβηρίαν οὐδαμῶς
ἢ τοῖς κατὰ τὴν Κασπίαν καὶ Βακτριανήν. κατὰ
πᾶσαν οὖν τὴν μεσημβρινὴν παραλίαν τοῦ ὠκεανοῦ παρατείνοντος, ἐφ᾽ ἅπασαν δὲ καὶ χειμο-
φυγούντων, δέχεσθαι δεῖ καὶ τοὺς Πυγμαίους
μεμυθευμένους κατὰ πᾶσαν. εἰ δ᾽ οἱ ὕστερον ἐπὶ

---

[1] πλάσας, A. Miller, for πλάσαι.

must understand both words in a more general sense, "Oceanus" meaning the body of water that extends along the entire southern belt, and the "Ethiopians" meaning the people along the same extent; for upon whatever point of this belt you fix your attention, you will be both on Oceanus and in Ethiopia. And this is the meaning also of the words: "On his way from the Ethiopians he espied Odysseus from afar, from the mountains of the Solymi"—which is equivalent to saying "from the regions of the south"; for he does not mean the Solymi in Pisidia, but, as I said before,[1] he invents a people of the same name whom he depicts as occupying the same position relatively to the sailor on his raft and the people to the south of him (who would be the Ethiopians) as the Pisidians occupy relatively to the Pontus and to the Ethiopians that lie beyond Egypt. And in like manner Homer puts his assertion about the cranes in general terms: "When they flee from the coming of winter and sudden rain, and fly with clamour toward the streams of Oceanus, bearing slaughter and doom to the Pygmy men." For it is not the case that the crane is seen migrating toward the south only in Greek lands, and never in Italy or Iberia, or in the regions of the Caspian Sea and Bactriana. Since, then, Oceanus stretches along the entire southern sea-board, and since the cranes migrate in winter to this entire sea-board, we must admit that the Pygmies also are placed by mythology along the entire extent of that sea-board. And if

[1] See page 77 and footnote.

τοὺς κατ' Αἴγυπτον Αἰθίοπας[1] μόνους μετήγαγον καὶ τὸν περὶ τῶν Πυγμαίων λόγον, οὐδὲν ἂν εἴη πρὸς τὰ πάλαι. καὶ γὰρ Ἀχαιοὺς καὶ Ἀργείους οὐ πάντας μὲν νῦν φαμεν τοὺς στρατεύσαντας ἐπὶ Ἴλιον, Ὅμηρος δὲ καλεῖ πάντας. παραπλήσιον δέ ἐστιν ὃ λέγω καὶ περὶ τῶν δίχα διῃρημένων Αἰθιόπων, ὅτι δεῖ δέχεσθαι τοὺς παρ' ὅλην διατείνοντας τὴν ὠκεανῖτιν ἀφ' ἡλίου ἀνιόντος μέχρι ἡλίου δυομένου. οἱ γὰρ οὕτω λεγόμενοι Αἰθίοπες δίχα διῄρηνται φυσικῶς τῷ Ἀραβίῳ κόλπῳ, ὡς ἂν μεσημβρινοῦ κύκλου τμήματι ἀξιολόγῳ, ποταμοῦ δίκην ἐν μήκει σχεδόν τι καὶ πεντακισχιλίων σταδίων ἐπὶ τοῖς μυρίοις, πλάτει δ' οὐ πολὺ τῶν χιλίων μείζονι τῷ μεγίστῳ· πρόσεστι δὲ τῷ μήκει καὶ τὸ τὸν μυχὸν τοῦδε τοῦ κόλπου διέχειν τῆς κατὰ Πηλούσιον θαλάσσης τριῶν ἢ τεττάρων ἡμερῶν ὁδόν, ἣν ἐπέχει ὁ ἰσθμός. καθάπερ οὖν οἱ χαριέστεροι τῶν διαιρούντων τὴν Ἀσίαν ἀπὸ τῆς Λιβύης ὅρον εὐφυέστερον ἡγοῦνται τοῦτον τῶν ἠπείρων ἀμφοῖν τὸν κόλπον, ἢ τὸν Νεῖλον (τὸν μὲν γὰρ διήκειν παρ' ὀλίγον παντελῶς ἀπὸ θαλάττης ἐπὶ θάλατταν, τὸν δὲ Νεῖλον πολλαπλάσιον ἀπὸ τοῦ ὠκεανοῦ διέχειν, ὥστε μὴ διαιρεῖν τὴν Ἀσίαν πᾶσαν ἀπὸ τῆς Λιβύης)· τοῦτον ὑπολαμβάνω τὸν τρόπον κἀγὼ τὰ μεσημβρινὰ μέρη πάντα καθ' ὅλην τὴν οἰκουμένην δίχα διῃρῆσθαι νομίσαι τὸν ποιητὴν τῷ κόλπῳ τούτῳ.[2] πῶς οὖν ἠγνόει τὸν ἰσθμόν, ὃν οὗτος ποιεῖ πρὸς τὸ Αἰγύπτιον πέλαγος;

[1] ὕστερον ἐπὶ τοὺς κατ' Αἴγυπτον Αἰθίοπας, Madvig, for ὕστερον τοὺς Αἰθίοπας ἐπὶ τοὺς κατ' Αἴγυπτον.

[2] τούτῳ, is omitted in the Dübner edition without an apparent reason.

men of later generations restricted the story about
the Pygmies to the Ethiopians next to Egypt alone,
that would have no bearing on the facts in ancient
times. For nowadays we do not use the terms
" Achaeans" and " Argives" of all who took part in
the expedition against Troy, though Homer so uses
them. Now what I contend in the case of the
Ethiopians that are "sundered in twain" is similar
to this, namely, that we must interpret " Ethiopians"
as meaning that the Ethiopians extend along the
whole sea-board of Oceanus from the rising to the
setting sun. For the Ethiopians that are spoken of
in this sense are " sundered in twain " naturally by
the Arabian Gulf (and this would constitute a considerable part of a meridian circle) as by a river,
being in length almost fifteen thousand stadia, and
in width not much more than one thousand stadia,
I mean at its greatest width ; and to the length we
must add the distance by which the head of this
gulf is separated from the sea at Pelusium, a journey
of three or four days—the space occupied by the
isthmus. Now, just as the abler of the geographers
who separate Asia from Libya regard this gulf as a
more natural boundary-line between the two continents than the Nile (for they say the gulf lacks but
very little of stretching from sea to sea, whereas the
Nile is separated from Oceanus by many times that
distance, so that it does not separate Asia as a whole
from Libya), in the same way I also assume that the
poet considered that the southern regions as a whole
throughout the inhabited world were " sundered in
twain " by this gulf. How, then, can the poet have
been ignorant of the isthmus which the gulf forms
with the Egyptian [1] Sea?

[1] Mediterranean.

29. Καὶ γὰρ δὴ καὶ τελέως ἄλογον, εἰ τὰς μὲν Αἰγυπτίους Θήβας ᾔδει σαφῶς, αἳ διέχουσι τῆς καθ᾽ ἡμᾶς θαλάττης σταδίους μικρὸν ἀπολείποντας ἀπὸ τῶν τετρακισχιλίων,[1] τὸν δὲ μυχὸν τοῦ Ἀραβίου κόλπου μὴ ᾔδει, μηδὲ τὸν ἰσθμὸν τὸν κατ᾽ αὐτόν, πλάτος ἔχοντα οὐ πλειόνων ἢ χιλίων σταδίων. πολὺ δ᾽ ἂν ἀλογώτερον δόξειεν, εἰ τὸν μὲν Νεῖλον ᾔδει ὁμωνύμως τῇ τοσαύτῃ χώρᾳ λεγόμενον, τὴν δ᾽ αἰτίαν μὴ ἑώρα τούτου· μάλιστα γὰρ ἂν προσπίπτοι τὸ ῥηθὲν ὑφ᾽ Ἡρο-

C 36 δότου, διότι δῶρον ἦν ἡ χώρα τοῦ ποταμοῦ καὶ διὰ τοῦτο ἠξιοῦτο τοῦ αὐτοῦ ὀνόματος. ἄλλως τε τῶν παρ᾽ ἑκάστοις ἰδίων ταῦτ᾽ ἐστὶ γνωριμώτατα, ἃ καὶ παραδοξίαν ἔχει τινά, καὶ ἐν τῷ φανερῷ πᾶσιν ἐστί· τοιοῦτον δ᾽ ἐστὶ καὶ ἡ τοῦ Νείλου ἀνάβασις καὶ ἡ πρόσχωσις τοῦ πελάγους. καὶ καθάπερ οἱ προσαχθέντες πρὸς τὴν Αἴγυπτον οὐδὲν πρότερον ἱστοροῦσι περὶ τῆς χώρας, ἢ τὴν τοῦ Νείλου φύσιν, διὰ τὸ τοὺς ἐπιχωρίους μήτε καινότερα τούτων λέγειν ἔχειν πρὸς ἄνδρας ξένους, μήτ᾽ ἐπιφανέστερα περὶ τῶν παρ᾽ αὐτοῖς (τῷ γὰρ ἱστορήσαντι περὶ τοῦ ποταμοῦ κατάδηλος καὶ ἡ χώρα γίνεται πᾶσα, ὁποία τίς ἐστιν), οὕτω καὶ οἱ πόρρωθεν ἀκούοντες οὐδὲν πρότερον ἱστοροῦσι τούτου. προστίθει οὖν τούτῳ καὶ τὸ φιλείδημον τοῦ ποιητοῦ καὶ τὸ φιλέκδημον, ὅπερ αὐτῷ μαρτυροῦσιν ὅσοι τὸν βίον ἀναγράφουσι, καὶ ἐξ αὐτῶν δὲ λαμβάνεται τῶν ποιημάτων πολλὰ παραδείγματα τοῦ τοιούτου. οὗτος μὲν οὖν ἐκ πλεόνων ἐλέγχεται καὶ εἰδὼς καὶ λέγων ῥητῶς

---

[1] τετρακισχιλίων, Gosselin, for πεντακισχιλίων; Groskurd, Forbiger following; C. Müller approving.

29. And indeed it is in the highest degree unreasonable that the poet had accurate knowledge
about Thebes in Egypt, which is distant from the
Mediterranean Sea but a trifle less than four thousand
stadia, and yet had no knowledge about the head of the
Arabian Gulf, or about the adjoining isthmus, whose
width is not more than one thousand stadia; but it
would seem to be much more unreasonable that he
knew the Nile bore the same name as the vast
country Aegyptus and yet did not see the reason
therefor; for the thought which has been expressed
by Herodotus [1] would occur to one at once, namely,
that the country was "a gift of the river" and laid
claim for this reason to the same name as the river.[2]
Moreover, those peculiarities of each several country
which are in some way marvellous are most widely
known, and manifest to everybody; such is the case
with the rising of the Nile as also the silting up
of the sea. And just as those who visit Egypt learn
no fact concerning the country before they learn the
nature of the Nile, because the natives cannot tell
foreigners anything more novel or more remarkable
about their country than these particulars (for the
nature of the entire country becomes quite clear to
one who has learned about the river), so also those
who hear about the country at a distance learn this
fact before anything else. To all this we must add
the poet's fondness for knowledge and for travel, to
which all who have written on his life bear witness;
and one may find many illustrations of such a pre-
dilection in the poems themselves. And so it is
proved, on many grounds, that Homer both knows
and expressly says what is to be said, and that he

---

[1] Herod. 2. 5.   [2] Compare 15. 1. 16.

τὰ ῥητὰ καὶ σιγῶν τὰ λίαν ἐκφανῆ ἢ ἐπιθέτως λέγων.

30. Θαυμάζειν δὲ δεῖ τῶν Αἰγυπτίων καὶ Σύρων, πρὸς οὓς νῦν ἡμῖν ὁ λόγος, εἰ μηδ' ἐκείνου λέγοντος τὰ παρ' αὐτοῖς ἐπιχώρια συνιᾶσιν, ἀλλὰ καὶ ἄγνοιαν αἰτιῶνται, ᾗ αὐτοὺς ἐνόχους δείκνυσιν ὁ λόγος. ἁπλῶς δὲ τὸ μὴ λέγειν οὐ τοῦ μὴ εἰδέναι σημεῖόν ἐστιν· οὐδὲ γὰρ τὰς τροπὰς τοῦ Εὐρίπου λέγει, οὐδὲ τὰς Θερμοπύλας, οὐδ' ἄλλα πλείω τῶν γνωρίμων παρὰ τοῖς Ἕλλησιν, οὐ μὴν ἠγνόει γε. ἀλλὰ καὶ λέγει, οὐ δοκεῖ δὲ τοῖς ἐθελοκωφοῦσιν· ὥστε ἐκείνους αἰτιατέον. ὁ ποιητὴς τοίνυν διιπετέας καλεῖ τοὺς ποταμούς, οὐ τοὺς χειμάρρους μόνους, ἀλλὰ καὶ πάντας κοινῶς, ὅτι πληροῦνται πάντες ἀπὸ τῶν ὀμβρίων ὑδάτων· ἀλλὰ τὸ κοινὸν ἐπὶ τῶν κατ' ἐξοχὴν ἴδιον γίνεται. ἄλλως γὰρ ἂν τὸν χειμάρρουν ἀκούοι τις διιπετῆ καὶ ἄλλως τὸν ἀέναον· ἐνταῦθα δὲ διπλασιάζει πως ἡ ἐξοχή. καὶ καθάπερ εἰσί τινες ὑπερβολαὶ ἐπὶ ὑπερβολαῖς, ὡς τὸ κουφότερον εἶναι φελλοῦ σκιᾶς, δειλότερον δὲ λαγὼ Φρυγός, ἐλάττω δ' ἔχειν γῆν τὸν ἀγρὸν ἐπιστολῆς Λακωνικῆς· οὕτως ἐξοχὴ ἐπὶ ἐξοχῇ συντρέχει ἐπὶ τοῦ διιπετῆ τὸν Νεῖλον λέγεσθαι. ὁ μὲν γὰρ χειμάρρους ὑπερ-

---

[1] Compare 1. 2. 3.

[2] Aristarchus and Crates, respectively.

[3] That is, "heaven-fed" in the former case is used in the literal sense of the Greek word, "heaven-fallen," and applies

keeps silent about what is too obvious to mention, or else alludes to it by an epithet.[1]

30. But I must express my amazement at the Egyptians and Syrians,[2] against whom I am directing this argument, that they do not understand Homer even when he tells them about matters in their own countries, and yet actually accuse him of ignorance —a charge to which my argument shows that they themselves are subject. In general, silence is no sign of ignorance; for neither does Homer mention the refluent currents of the Euripus, nor Thermopylae, nor yet other things in Greece that are well-known, though assuredly he was not ignorant of them. However, Homer also speaks of things well-known, though those who are wilfully deaf do not think so; and therefore the fault of ignorance is theirs. Now the poet calls the rivers "heaven-fed"—not merely the winter torrents, but all rivers alike—because they are all replenished by the rains. But the general epithet becomes particular when applied to things in relation to their pre-eminence. For one would interpret "heaven-fed" in one way of the winter torrent and in quite another way of the ever-flowing stream; and in the latter case the pre-eminence is, one may say, twofold.[3] And just as there are cases of hyperbole on hyperbole— for example, "lighter than the shadow of a cork," "more timid than a Phrygian[4] hare," "to own a farm smaller than a Laconian letter"—just so there is a parallel case of pre-eminence on pre-eminence when the Nile is spoken of as being "heaven-fed." For while the winter torrent surpasses the other specifically to precipitate descent; in the latter case the epithet has reference to volume and duration.

[4] The Phrygian slave was a proverbial coward.

βέβληται τοὺς ἄλλους ποταμοὺς τῷ διιπετὴς
εἶναι· ὁ δὲ Νεῖλος καὶ τοὺς χειμάρρους ἐπὶ τοσοῦτον πληρούμενος καὶ πλήθους καὶ χρόνου.
ὥστ' ἐπεὶ καὶ γνώριμον ἦν τὸ πάθος τοῦ ποταμοῦ
C 37 τῷ ποιητῇ, ὥσπερ[1] παραμεμυθήμεθα, καὶ κέχρηται τῷ ἐπιθέτῳ τούτῳ κατ' αὐτοῦ, οὐκ ἄλλως
δεκτέον ἢ ὡς εἰρήκαμεν. τὸ δὲ πλείοσι στόμασιν
ἐκδιδόναι κοινὸν καὶ πλειόνων, ὥστ' οὐκ ἄξιον
μνήμης ὑπέλαβε, καὶ ταῦτα πρὸς εἰδότας· καθάπερ οὐδ' Ἀλκαῖος, καίτοι φήσας ἀφῖχθαι καὶ
αὐτὸς εἰς Αἴγυπτον. αἱ δὲ προσχώσεις καὶ ἐκ
τῶν ἀναβάσεων μὲν δύνανται ὑπονοεῖσθαι, καὶ ἐξ
ὧν δὲ εἶπε περὶ τῆς Φάρου. ὁ γὰρ ἱστορῶν αὐτῷ
περὶ τῆς Φάρου, μᾶλλον δὲ ἡ κοινὴ φήμη, διότι
μὲν τότε τοσοῦτον ἀπεῖχεν ἀπὸ τῆς ἠπείρου, ἐφ'[2]
ὅσον φησί, δρόμον νεὼς ἡμερήσιον, οὐκ ἂν εἴη
διατεθρυλημένη ἐπὶ τοσοῦτον ἐψευσμένως. ὅτι
δ' ἡ ἀνάβασις καὶ αἱ προσχώσεις τοιαῦταί τινες,
κοινότερον πεπύσθαι εἰκὸς ἦν· ἐξ ὧν συνθεὶς ὁ
ποιητής, ὅτι πλέον ἢ τότε ἀφειστήκει τῆς γῆς ἡ
νῆσος κατὰ τὴν Μενελάου παρουσίαν, προσέθηκε
παρ' ἑαυτοῦ πολλαπλάσιον διάστημα τοῦ μυθώδους χάριν. αἱ δὲ μυθοποιίαι οὐκ ἀγνοίας[3]
σημεῖα[4] δήπου, οὐδὲ[5] τὰ περὶ τοῦ Πρωτέως καὶ

[1] ὥσπερ, A. Miller, for ὡς; A. Vogel approving.
[2] ἐφ', Capps inserts.
[3] χάριν, Corais deletes, after ἀγνοίας; Meineke, Forbiger,
following; C. Müller approving.
[4] σημεῖα, is retained, against the σημεῖον of Corais and
Meineke. γάρ, after σημεῖα, Groskurd deletes; Forbiger
following; C. Müller approving.
[5] γάρ, after οὐδέ, Groskurd deletes; Forbiger following;
C. Müller approving.

rivers in respect of being "heaven-fed," the Nile, when at its flood, surpasses even the winter torrents to just that extent, not only in the amount of its flood but also in the duration thereof. And so, since the behaviour of the river was known to the poet, as I have urged in my argument, and since he has applied this epithet to it, we cannot interpret it in any other way than that which I have pointed out. But the fact that the Nile empties its waters through several mouths is a peculiarity it shares with several other rivers, and therefore Homer did not think it worthy of mention, particularly in addressing people who knew the fact; just as Alcaeus does not mention those mouths, either, although he affirms that he too visited Egypt. But the matter of the silting may be inferred not only from the risings of the river but also from what Homer says about Pharos. For the man who told Homer about Pharos—or rather, I should say, the common report that it was so and so far from the mainland—this report, I say, would not have got abroad falsified to such an extent as the distance which Homer gives, namely, a day's run for a ship; but as for the rising and silting, it is reasonable to suppose that the poet learned as a matter of common knowledge that they were such and such; and concluding from these facts that at the time of the visit of Menelaus the island was more distant from the mainland than it was in his own times, he added a distance many times as great on his own responsibility for the sake of the fabulous element. Moreover, the fabulous creations are not, I take it, a sign of ignorance—not even those stories about Proteus and the Pygmies,

τῶν Πυγμαίων, οὐδ᾽ αἱ τῶν φαρμάκων δυνάμεις,
οὐδ᾽ εἴ τι ἄλλο τοιοῦτον οἱ ποιηταὶ πλάττουσι·
οὐ γὰρ κατ᾽ ἄγνοιαν τῶν τοπικῶν λέγεται, ἀλλ᾽
ἡδονῆς καὶ τέρψεως χάριν. πῶς οὖν καὶ ἄνυδρον
οὖσαν φησὶν ὕδωρ ἔχειν;

ἐν δὲ λιμὴν εὔορμος, ὅθεν τ᾽ ἀπὸ νῆας ἐΐσας
ἐς πόντον βάλλουσιν ἀφυσσάμενοι μέλαν ὕδωρ.
(Od. 4. 358)

ἀλλ᾽ οὔτε τὸ ὑδρεῖον ἐκλιπεῖν ἀδύνατον, οὔτε τὴν
ὑδρείαν ἐκ τῆς νήσου γενέσθαι φησίν, ἀλλὰ τὴν
ἀναγωγὴν μόνην διὰ τὴν τοῦ λιμένος ἀρετήν, τὸ
δ᾽ ὕδωρ ἐκ τῆς περαίας ἀρύσασθαι παρῆν, ἐξομο-
λογουμένου πως τοῦ ποιητοῦ δι᾽ ἐμφάσεως, ὅτι
πελαγίαν εἶπεν οὐ πρὸς ἀλήθειαν, ἀλλὰ πρὸς
ὑπερβολὴν καὶ μυθοποιίαν.

31. Ἐπεὶ δὲ καὶ τὰ περὶ τῆς πλάνης τῆς
Μενελάου λεχθέντα συνηγορεῖν δοκεῖ τῇ ἀγνοίᾳ
τῇ περὶ τοὺς τόπους ἐκείνους, βέλτιον ἴσως ἐστί,
τὰ ἐν τοῖς ἔπεσι τούτοις ζητούμενα προεκθεμένους
ἅμα ταῦτά τε διαστεῖλαι καὶ περὶ τοῦ ποιητοῦ
ἀπολογήσασθαι καθαρώτερον. φησὶ δὴ πρὸς
Τηλέμαχον ὁ Μενέλαος θαυμάσαντα τὸν τῶν
βασιλείων κόσμον·

ἦ γὰρ πολλὰ παθὼν καὶ πόλλ᾽ ἐπαληθεὶς
ἠγαγόμην ἐν νηυσί, καὶ ὀγδοάτῳ ἔτει ἦλθον,
Κύπρον Φοινίκην τε καὶ Αἰγυπτίους ἐπαληθείς,
Αἰθίοπάς θ᾽ ἱκόμην καὶ Σιδονίους καὶ Ἐρεμβοὺς
καὶ Λιβύην.
(Od. 4. 81)

C 38 ζητοῦσι δέ, πρὸς τίνας ἦλθεν Αἰθίοπας, πλέων

nor the potent effects of magic potions, nor any other such inventions of the poets; for these stories are told, not in ignorance of geography, but in order to give pleasure and enjoyment. How does it come, then, that Homer says that Pharos has water, when it is without water: "And therein is a good haven, whence men launch the well-proportioned ships into the deep when they have drawn a store of black water"? Now, in the first place, it is not impossible that the source of the water has dried up; and, in the second place, Homer does not say that the water came from the island, but merely that the launching of the ships took place thence—on account of the excellence of the harbour; but the water itself may have been drawn from the opposite mainland, since, in a way, the poet by implication confesses that, when he applied the term "in the open sea" to Pharos, he did not use it in a literal sense, but as an hyperbolical or mythical statement.

31. Now, since it is thought that Homer's account of the wanderings of Menelaus, also, argues for ignorance of those countries on his part, it is perhaps better to make a preliminary statement of the questions called forth by those poems, and then at once to separate these questions and thus speak more clearly in defence of the poet. Menelaus says, then, to Telemachus, who has marvelled at the decorations of the palace: "Yea, after many a woe and wanderings manifold, I brought my wealth home in ships, and in the eighth year came hither. I roamed over Cyprus and Phoenicia and Egypt, and came to Ethiopians, Sidonians, Erembians, and to Libya." Now they ask to what Ethiopians he came in thus

ἐξ Αἰγύπτου· οὔτε γὰρ ἐν τῇ καθ᾽ ἡμᾶς θαλάττῃ
οἰκοῦσί τινες Αἰθίοπες, οὔτε τοῦ Νείλου τοὺς
καταράκτας ἦν διελθεῖν ναυσί· τίνες τε οἱ Σι-
δόνιοι· οὐ γὰρ οἵ γε ἐν Φοινίκῃ· οὐ γὰρ ἂν τὸ
γένος προθεὶς τὸ εἶδος ἐπήνεγκε· τίνες τε οἱ
Ἐρεμβοί; καινὸν γὰρ τὸ ὄνομα. Ἀριστόνικος μὲν
οὖν ὁ καθ᾽ ἡμᾶς γραμματικὸς ἐν τοῖς περὶ τῆς
Μενελάου πλάνης πολλῶν ἀναγέγραφεν ἀνδρῶν
ἀποφάσεις περὶ ἑκάστου τῶν ἐκκειμένων κεφα-
λαίων· ἡμῖν δ᾽ ἀρκέσει κἂν ἐπιτέμνοντες λέγωμεν.
οἱ μὲν δὴ πλεῦσαι φήσαντες εἰς τὴν Αἰθιοπίαν,
οἱ μὲν περίπλουν διὰ τῶν[1] Γαδείρων μέχρι τῆς
Ἰνδικῆς εἰσάγουσιν, ἅμα καὶ τὸν χρόνον τῇ πλάνῃ
συνοικειοῦντες, ὅν φησιν, ὅτι ὀγδοάτῳ ἔτει ἦλθον·
οἱ δὲ διὰ τοῦ ἰσθμοῦ τοῦ κατὰ τὸν Ἀράβιον
κόλπον· οἱ δὲ διὰ τῶν διωρύγων τινός. οὔτε δ᾽ ὁ
περίπλους ἀναγκαῖος, ὃν Κράτης εἰσάγει, οὐχ ὡς
ἀδύνατος εἴη ἄν[2] (καὶ γὰρ ἡ Ὀδυσσέως πλάνη
ἂν ἦν[3] ἀδύνατος), ἀλλ᾽ ὅτι οὔτε πρὸς τὰς ὑποθέσεις τὰς μαθηματικὰς χρήσιμος, οὔτε πρὸς τὸν
χρόνον τῆς πλάνης. καὶ γὰρ ἀκούσιοι διατριβαὶ
κατέσχον αὐτὸν ὑπὸ δυσπλοίας, φήσαντος ὅτι
ἀπὸ ἑξήκοντα νεῶν πέντε ἐλείφθησαν αὐτῷ, καὶ
ἑκούσιοι χρηματισμοῦ χάριν· φησὶ γὰρ ὁ Νέστωρ·

> ὡς ὁ μὲν ἔνθα πολὺν βίοτον καὶ χρυσὸν ἀγείρων
> ἠλᾶτο ξὺν νηυσί·
>
> (Od. 3. 301)
>
> Κύπρον Φοινίκην τε καὶ Αἰγυπτίους ἐπαλη-
> θείς.
> (Od. 4. 83)

[1] διὰ τῶν, Madvig, for τῶν διά; A. Vogel approving.
[2] εἴη ἄν, Sterrett, for εἶναι, adapting the suggestion in
Madvig's conjecture.
[3] ἂν ἦν, B. Niese inserts, before ἀδύνατος.

sailing from Egypt (for no Ethiopians live in the Mediterranean Sea, nor was it possible for ships to pass the cataracts of the Nile); and who the Sidonians are (for they are certainly not those that live in Phoenicia, since he would not have put the genus first and then brought in the species); and who the Erembians are (for that is a new name). Now Aristonicus, the grammarian of our own generation, in his book *On the Wanderings of Menelaus,* has recorded opinions of many men on each one of the points set forth; but for me it will be sufficient to speak briefly on these questions. Of those who say that Menelaus "sailed" to Ethiopia, some propose a coasting-voyage by Gades as far as India, making his wanderings correspond exactly to the time which Homer gives: "In the eighth year I came back"; but others propose that he sailed across the isthmus that lies at the head of the Arabian Gulf, while still others propose that he sailed through one of the canals of the Nile. But, in the first place, Crates' theory of a coasting-voyage is unnecessary—not that such a voyage would be impossible (for the wanderings of Odysseus would have been impossible), but because it serves no purpose either as regards Crates' mathematical hypotheses or as regards the time consumed in the wanderings. For Menelaus was detained against his will because of the difficulties of sailing (he himself says that out of sixty ships only five were left to him), and he also made intentional stops for the sake of trafficking. For Nestor says: "Thus Menelaus, gathering much substance and gold, was wandering there with his ships"; [to which Menelaus adds:] "having roamed over Cyprus and Phoenicia and Egypt." Again, the

ὅ τε διὰ τοῦ ἰσθμοῦ πλοῦς ἢ τῶν διωρύγων λεγόμενος μὲν ἠκούετο ἂν ἐν μύθου σχήματι, μὴ
λεγόμενος δὲ περιττῶς καὶ ἀπιθάνως εἰσάγοιτο ἄν.
ἀπιθάνως δὲ λέγω, ὅτι πρὸ τῶν Τρωικῶν οὐδεμία
ἦν διῶρυξ· τὸν δὲ ἐπιχειρήσαντα ποιῆσαι
Σέσωστριν ἀποστῆναί φασι, μετεωροτέραν ὑπο-
λαβόντα τὴν τῆς θαλάσσης ἐπιφάνειαν. ἀλλὰ
μὴν οὐδ' ὁ ἰσθμὸς ἦν πλόϊμος· ἀλλ' εἰκάζει ὁ
Ἐρατοσθένης οὐκ εὖ. μὴ γάρ πω τὸ ἔκρηγμα τὸ
κατὰ τὰς Στήλας γεγονέναι νομίζει· ὥστε ἐνταῦθα[1]
συνάπτειν τὴν εἴσω θάλασσαν τῇ ἐκτὸς[2] καὶ
καλύπτειν τὸν ἰσθμὸν μετεωροτέραν οὖσαν, τοῦ δ'
ἐκρήγματος γενομένου ταπεινωθῆναι καὶ ἀνακα-
λύψαι τὴν γῆν τὴν κατὰ τὸ Κάσιον καὶ τὸ
Πηλούσιον μέχρι τῆς Ἐρυθρᾶς. τίνα οὖν ἔχομεν
ἱστορίαν περὶ τοῦ ἐκρήγματος τούτου, διότι πρὸ
τῶν Τρωικῶν οὔπω ὑπῆρχεν; ἴσως δ' ὁ ποιητὴς
ἅμα μὲν τὸν Ὀδυσσέα ταύτῃ διεκπλέοντα εἰς τὸν
ὠκεανὸν πεποίηκεν, ὡς ἤδη ἐκρήγματος γεγονότος,
ἅμα δὲ εἰς τὴν Ἐρυθρὰν τὸν Μενέλαον ἐκ τῆς
Αἰγύπτου ναυστολεῖ, ὡς οὔπω γεγονότος. ἀλλὰ
καὶ τὸν Πρωτέα εἰσάγει λέγοντα αὐτῷ,

> ἀλλά σ' ἐς Ἠλύσιον πεδίον καὶ πείρατα γαίης
> ἀθάνατοι πέμψουσι.   (Od. 4. 563)

C 39

---

[1] Groskurd inserts μή before συνάπτειν (Kramer, Meineke,
Forbiger, Dübner-Müller following), thus referring ἐνταῦθα
to the Pillars; A. Vogel shows that ἐνταῦθα refers to the
Isthmus and that μή is wrong.
[2] Groskurd writes τὴν ἔσω θάλασσαν τῇ ἐκτὸς for τὴν ἔξω
θάλασσαν τῇ ἐντός; Dübner-Müller, Forbiger following.
Meineke, too, follows except that he writes εἴσω for ἴσω;
A. Vogel approving.

voyage through the isthmus or one of the canals
would, if Homer mentioned such a voyage, be
interpreted as a kind of fiction ; but since he does
not mention such a voyage it would be gratuitous
and absurd for one to propose it. It would be absurd,
I repeat, since before the Trojan War there was no
canal ; and the person who undertook to build one—
I mean Sesostris[1]—is said to have abandoned the
undertaking because he supposed the level of the
Mediterranean Sea was too high. Furthermore, the
isthmus was not navigable either, and Eratosthenes'
conjecture is wrong. For he thinks that the breaking
of the channel at the Pillars of Heracles had not yet
taken place and that in consequence the Mediterranean Sea, since it was of a higher level, joined
the exterior sea at the isthmus and covered it, but
after the breaking of the channel took place at the
Pillars, the Mediterranean Sea was lowered and thus
exposed the land about Casium and Pelusium, as far
as the Red Sea. Now what historical information
have we regarding this break at the Pillars to the
effect that it did not yet exist before the Trojan
War ? But perhaps—you will say—the poet has
represented Odysseus as sailing through the strait
at the Pillars into the ocean (as though a channel
were already in existence) at the same time that he
conveys Menelaus by ship from Egypt into the Red
Sea (as though a channel were not yet in existence) !
Furthermore, Homer brings in Proteus as saying to
Menelaus : " Nay, the deathless gods will convey
thee to the Elysian Plain and to the end of the

---

[1] See 17. 1. 25 ; also Herodotus, 2. 158, and 4. 39.

ποῖα οὖν; καὶ ὅτι ἑσπέριόν τινα λέγει τόπον
τοῦτον ἔσχατον, ὁ Ζέφυρος παρατεθεὶς δηλοῖ·

ἀλλ' αἰεὶ Ζεφύροιο λιγὺ πνείοντος ἀήτας
Ὠκεανὸς ἀνίησι. (*Od.* 4. 567)

ταῦτα γὰρ αἰνίγματος πλήρη.

32. Εἰ δ' οὖν καὶ σύρρουν ποτὲ ὑπάρξαντα τὸν
ἰσθμὸν τοῦτον ὁ ποιητὴς ἱστορήκει, πόσῳ μείζονα
ἂν ἔχοιμεν πίστιν τοῦ τοὺς Αἰθίοπας διχθὰ
διῃρῆσθαι, πορθμῷ τηλικούτῳ διειργομένους; τίς
δὲ καὶ χρηματισμὸς παρὰ τῶν ἔξω καὶ κατὰ τὸν
ὠκεανὸν Αἰθιόπων; ἅμα μὲν γὰρ θαυμάζουσι τοῖ
κόσμου τῶν βασιλείων οἱ περὶ Τηλέμαχον τὸ
πλῆθος, ὅ ἐστι

χρυσοῦ τ' ἠλέκτρου τε καὶ ἀργύρου ἠδ' ἐλέφαντος. (*Od.* 4. 73)

τούτων δ' οὐδενὸς πλὴν ἐλέφαντος εὐπορία παρ'
ἐκείνοις ἐστίν, ἀπορωτάτοις τῶν ἁπάντων οὖσι
τοῖς πλείστοις καὶ νομάσι. νὴ Δία, ἀλλ' ἡ Ἀραβία
προσῆν καὶ τὰ μέχρι τῆς Ἰνδικῆς· τούτων δ' ἡ
μὲν εὐδαίμων κέκληται μόνη τῶν ἁπασῶν, τὴν δέ,
εἰ καὶ μὴ ὀνομαστὶ καλοῦσιν οὕτως,[1] ὑπολαμ-
βάνουσί γε καὶ ἱστοροῦσιν, ὡς εὐδαιμονεστάτην·
τὴν μὲν οὖν Ἰνδικὴν οὐκ οἶδεν Ὅμηρος, εἰδὼς δὲ
ἐμέμνητο ἄν·[2] τὴν δ' Ἀραβίαν, ἣν εὐδαίμονα
προσαγορεύουσιν οἱ νῦν,[3] τότε δ' οὐκ ἦν πλουσία,
ἀλλὰ καὶ αὐτὴ ἄπορος καὶ ἡ πολλὴ αὐτῆς

---

[1] καλοῦσιν οὕτως, with a comma after οὕτως, A. Miller, for
καλοῦσιν, οὕτως; A. Vogel approving.
[2] Keelhoff deletes εἰδὼς δὲ ἐμέμνητο ἄν as a marginal gloss.
[3] Meineke, Cobet delete Groskurd's οἶδε μέν (which Kramer,
Dübner-Müller, Forbiger follow) after οἱ νῦν.

earth." What end of the earth, pray? Why, the citing of "Zephyrus" shows that he means by this remote region a place somewhere in the west: "But always Oceanus sendeth forth the breezes of the clear-blowing Zephyrus." Really, these matters are full of puzzling questions.

32. If, however, the poet had heard that this isthmus was once submerged, should we not have all the greater reason for believing that the Ethiopians, since they were separated by so great a strait, were really "sundered in twain"? And how could Menelaus have gotten treasures from the remote Ethiopians who lived along Oceanus? For at the moment when they marvelled at the ornaments themselves in the palace of Menelaus, Telemachus and his companions marvelled at the great quantity of them—"of gold and of amber and of silver and of ivory"; but with the exception of ivory, there is no great store of any of these things among those people, most of whom are the poorest of all peoples and are wandering shepherds. "Very true," you say; "but Arabia and the regions as far as India belonged to them; and though Arabia alone of all these countries has the name 'Blest,' India is supposed and reported to be in the highest degree 'blest,' even though people do not so call it by name." Now as to India, Homer did not know of it (for had he known of it, he would have mentioned it); but he did know the Arabia which is to-day called "Blest." [1] In his time, however, it was not rich, and not only was the country itself without resources but most of it was occupied by

[1] That is, Arabia Felix, east of the Red Sea. Strabo defines it in 16. 3. 1.

σκηνιτῶν ἀνδρῶν· ὀλίγη δ' ἡ ἀρωματοφόρος, δι'
ἣν καὶ τοῦτο τοὔνομα εὕρετο ἡ χώρα διὰ τὸ καὶ
τὸν φόρτον εἶναι τὸν τοιοῦτον ἐν τοῖς παρ' ἡμῖν
σπάνιον καὶ τίμιον. νυνὶ μὲν οὖν εὐποροῦσι καὶ
πλουτοῦσι διὰ τὸ καὶ τὴν ἐμπορίαν εἶναι πυκνὴν
καὶ δαψιλῆ, τότε δ' οὐκ εἰκός. αὐτῶν δὲ χάριν
τῶν ἀρωμάτων ἐμπόρῳ μὲν καὶ καμηλίτῃ γένοιτ'
ἄν τις ἐκ τῶν τοιούτων φορτίων εὐπορία· Μενελάῳ
δὲ λαφύρων ἢ δωρεῶν ἔδει παρὰ βασιλέων καὶ
δυναστῶν, ἐχόντων τε ἃ δώσουσι καὶ βουλομένων
διδόναι διὰ τὴν ἐπιφάνειαν αὐτοῦ καὶ εὔκλειαν.
οἱ μὲν οὖν Αἰγύπτιοι καὶ οἱ πλησίον Αἰθίοπες
καὶ Ἄραβες οὔθ' οὕτω τελέως ἄβιοι, οὔτ' ἀνήκοοι
τῆς τῶν Ἀτρειδῶν δόξης, καὶ μάλιστα διὰ τὴν
κατόρθωσιν τοῦ Ἰλιακοῦ πολέμου, ὥστ' ἐλπὶς ἦν
C 40 τῆς ἐξ αὐτῶν ὠφελείας· καθάπερ ἐπὶ τοῦ θώρακος
τοῦ Ἀγαμέμνονος λέγεται,

  τόν ποτέ οἱ Κινύρης δῶκε ξεινήιον εἶναι·
  πεύθετο γὰρ Κύπρονδε μέγα κλέος. (Π. 11. 20)

καὶ δὴ καὶ τὸν πλείω χρόνον τῆς πλάνης λεκτέον
μὲν ἐν τοῖς κατὰ Φοινίκην καὶ Συρίαν καὶ
Αἴγυπτον καὶ Λιβύην γενέσθαι καὶ τὰ περὶ
Κύπρον χωρία καὶ ὅλως τὴν καθ' ἡμᾶς παραλίαν
καὶ τὰς νήσους· καὶ γὰρ ξένια παρὰ τούτοις καὶ
τὸ βίᾳ καὶ τὸ ἐκ λεηλασίας πορίσασθαι, καὶ
μάλιστα παρὰ τῶν συμμαχησάντων τοῖς Τρωσίν,
ἐντεῦθεν ἦν. οἱ δ' ἐκτὸς καὶ πόρρω βάρβαροι

[1] The Troglodytes on the western side of the Arabian
Gulf (1. 1. 3).   [2] See 16. 2. 21.   [3] See 16. 2. 1.

dwellers in tents. The part of Arabia that produces
the spices is small; and it is from this small territory that the country got the name of "Blest,"
because such merchandise is rare in our part of the
world and costly. To-day, to be sure, the Arabs
are well to do and even rich, because their trade is
extensive and abundant, but it is not likely to have
been so in Homer's time. So far as the mere spices
are concerned, a merchant or camel-driver might
attain to some sort of wealth by trafficking in them,
whereas Menelaus needed booty or presents from
kings or dynasts who had not only the means to
give, but also the good-will to make him presents
because of his distinction and fame. The Egyptians,
however, and the neighbouring Ethiopians and
Arabs,[1] were not wholly destitute of the means of
livelihood, as were the other Ethiopians, nor wholly
ignorant of the fame of the sons of Atreus, particularly in view of the successful issue of the Trojan
War, and hence Menelaus might hope for profit from
them. Compare what Homer says of the breastplate
of Agamemnon: "The breastplate that in time past
Cinyras gave him for a guest-gift; for afar in Cyprus
did Cinyras hear the mighty tale." Furthermore, we
must assert that Menelaus' time in his wanderings was
spent mostly in the regions about Phoenicia,[2] Syria,[3]
Egypt, and Libya, and in the countries round Cyprus,
and, generally speaking, along the Mediterranean
sea-board and among the islands. For Menelaus
might procure guest-gifts among these peoples
and also enrich himself from them by violence and
robbery, and more particularly from those who had
been allies of the Trojans. But the barbarians that
lived outside these regions or at a distance could

οὐδεμίαν τοιαύτην ὑπηγόρευον ἐλπίδα. εἰς οὖν
τὴν Αἰθιοπίαν ἀφῖχθαι λέγεται ὁ Μενέλαος, οὐχ
ὅτι εἰς τὴν Αἰθιοπίαν τῷ ὄντι ἀφῖκτο, ἀλλ' ὅτι[1]
μέχρι τῶν ὅρων τῶν πρὸς Αἰγύπτῳ. τάχα μὲν
γὰρ καὶ πλησιαίτεροι ἦσαν ταῖς Θήβαις οἱ τότε
ὅροι, ἀλλὰ καὶ οἱ νῦν πλησίον εἰσίν, οἱ κατὰ
Συήνην καὶ τὰς Φίλας· ὧν ἡ μὲν τῆς Αἰγύπτου
ἐστίν, αἱ δὲ Φίλαι κοινὴ κατοικία τῶν Αἰθιόπων
καὶ τῶν Αἰγυπτίων. ὁ οὖν εἰς Θήβας ἀφιγμένος
εἰ καὶ μέχρι τῶν ὅρων ἀφῖκτο ἢ καὶ περαιτέρω
τῶν Αἰθιόπων, καὶ ταῦτα τῇ βασιλικῇ ξενίᾳ
χρώμενος, οὐδὲν ἄλογον. οὕτω δὲ καὶ Κυκλώπων
εἰς γαῖαν ἀφῖχθαί φησιν ὁ Ὀδυσσεύς, μέχρι τοῦ
σπηλαίου προεληλυθὼς ἀπὸ θαλάττης· ἐπ' ἐσχα-
τιᾶς γὰρ ἱδρῦσθαί που λέγει. καὶ εἰς Αἰολίαν δὲ
καὶ Λαιστρυγόνας καὶ τοὺς ἄλλους, ὅπου ποτὲ
καὶ καθωρμίσατο, ἐκεῖσέ φησιν ἀφῖχθαι. καὶ ὁ
Μενέλαος οὖν οὕτως εἰς Αἰθιοπίαν ἧκεν, οὕτω δὲ
καὶ εἰς Λιβύην, ὅτι προσέσχε τόποις τισίν· ἀφ'
οὗ καὶ ὁ κατὰ τὴν Ἀρδανίδα[2] λιμὴν τὴν ὑπὲρ
Παραιτονίου Μενέλαος καλεῖται.

33. Εἰ δὲ Φοίνικας εἰπὼν ὀνομάζει καὶ Σιδονίους, τὴν μητρόπολιν αὐτῶν, σχήματι συνήθει
χρῆται, ὡς

Τρῶάς τε καὶ Ἕκτορα νηυσὶ πέλασσε·

(Il. 13. 1)

---

[1] εἰς τὴν Αἰθιοπίαν τῷ ὄντι ἀφῖκτο, ἀλλ' ὅτι, Casaubon inserts ;
Forbiger, Sterrett, following ; Kramer approving.
[2] Ἀρδανίδα, Kramer, for Ἀρδανίαν.

prompt in him no such expectations. Now Homer says that Menelaus "came to" Ethiopia, not meaning that [he really came into Ethiopia, but that] he reached its frontier next to Egypt. For perhaps at that time the frontier was still nearer Thebes [1] (though to-day it is quite near)—I mean the frontier that runs by Syene and Philae. Of these towns the former belongs to Egypt, but Philae is inhabited alike by Ethiopians and Egyptians. Accordingly, when Menelaus came to Thebes, it need not cause surprise if he also came as far as the frontier of the Ethiopians or even farther, especially since he was enjoying the hospitality of the king of Thebes.[2] And it is in the same sense that Odysseus says he "came to" the country of the Cyclopes, although he did not get any further away from the sea than the cave; for he says that the cave lay "on the edge"[3] of the country, I believe; and again in referring to the country of Aeolus, to the Laestrygonians and the rest—wherever, I say, he so much as came to anchor, he says he "came to" the country. It is in this sense, therefore, that Menelaus "came to"[4] Ethiopia and in this sense to Libya, too, namely, that he "touched at" certain points; and it is from his having touched there that the harbour at Ardanis above Paraetonium[5] is called "Menelaus."

33. Now if Homer, in speaking of the Phoenicians, mentions Sidonians also, who occupy the Phoenician metropolis, he is but employing a familiar figure of speech, as when he says: "Now Zeus, when he had brought the Trojans and Hector to the ships"; and,

[1] See 17. 1. 46.   [2] *Od.* 4. 126.   [3] *Od.* 9. 182.
    [4] *Od.* 4. 84.   [5] Now, Baretoun.

καὶ

οὐ γὰρ ἔτ᾽ Οἰνῆος μεγαλήτορος υἱέες ἦσαν,
οὐδ᾽ ἄρ᾽ ἔτ᾽ αὐτὸς ἔην, θάνε δὲ ξανθὸς Μελέ-
αγρος·   (Il. 2. 641)

καὶ "'Ἴδην δ᾽ ἵκανεν" καὶ "Γάργαρον·" (Il. 8. 47)
καὶ " οἱ δ᾽ Εὔβοιαν ἔχον" καὶ "Χαλκίδα τ᾽ Εἰρέ-
τριάν τε·" (Il. 2. 536).

καὶ Σαπφώ·

ἤ σε Κύπρος ἤ Πάφος ἤ πάνορμος.[1]

καίτοι καὶ ἄλλο τι ἦν τὸ ποιῆσαν, καίπερ ἤδη
μνησθέντα τῆς Φοινίκης, ἰδίως πάλιν καὶ τὴν
Σιδόνα συγκαταλέξαι. πρὸς μὲν γὰρ τὸ τὰ ἐφεξῆς
ἔθνη καταλέξαι ἱκανῶς εἶχεν οὕτως εἰπεῖν,

Κύπρον Φοινίκην τε καὶ Αἰγυπτίους ἐπαληθεὶς
Αἰθίοπάς θ᾽ ἱκόμην·   (Od. 4. 83)

C 41 ἵνα δ᾽ ἐμφήνῃ καὶ τὴν παρὰ τοῖς Σιδονίοις ἀποδημίαν, καλῶς εἶχεν εἴτ᾽ ἀναλαβεῖν εἴτε καὶ
παραλαβεῖν, ἣν ἐπὶ πλέον γενομένην ἐμφαίνει[2]
διὰ τῶν ἐπαίνων τῆς παρ᾽ αὐτοῖς εὐτεχνίας καὶ
τοῦ τὴν Ἑλένην προεξενῶσθαι τοῖς ἀνθρώποις
μετὰ Ἀλεξάνδρου· διόπερ παρὰ τῷ Ἀλεξάνδρῳ
πολλὰ τοιαῦτα ἀποκείμενα λέγει·

ἔνθ᾽ ἔσαν οἱ πέπλοι παμποίκιλοι, ἔργα γυναικῶν
Σιδονίων, ἃς αὐτὸς Ἀλέξανδρος θεοειδὴς
ἤγαγε Σιδονίηθεν
τὴν ὁδόν, ἣν Ἑλένην περ ἀνήγαγε· (Il. 6. 289)

---

[1] ἤ πάνορμος, Casaubon, for ἤ Πάνορμος; Corais, Groskurd,
following.

"For the sons of great-hearted Oeneus were no more, neither did he still live, and the golden-haired Meleager was dead"; and, "So fared he to Ida" and "to Gargaros"; and, "But they possessed Euboea" and "Chalcis and Eretria"; and likewise Sappho, in the verse: "Either Cyprus or Paphos of the spacious harbour holds thee." And yet there was another reason which induced Homer, although he had already mentioned Phoenicia, to repeat Phoenicia in a special way—that is, to add Sidon to the list. For merely to list the peoples in their proper order it was quite enough to say: "I roamed over Cyprus and Phoenicia and Egypt, and came to Ethiopia." But in order to suggest also the sojourn of Menelaus among the Sidonians, it was proper for Homer to repeat as he did, or even add still more than that; and he suggests that this sojourn was of long duration by his praise of their skill in the arts and of the hospitality formerly extended to Helen and Paris by these same people. That is why he speaks of many Sidonian works of art stored up in the house of Paris—"where were her embroidered robes, the work of Sidonian women, whom godlike Alexandros himself brought from Sidon, that journey wherein he brought back Helen to his home"; and in the

---

² The reading of the MSS. is: ἀποδημίαν τὴι ἐπὶ πλέον γενομένην ἐμφαίνει διὰ τῶν ἐπαίνων τῆς παρ' αὐτοῖς εὐτυχίας, καλῶς εἶχεν εἴτ' ἀναλαβεῖν εἴτε καὶ παραλαβεῖν εὐτεχνίας καί. As a result of the conjectures of Casaubon and Corais it appears in the editions of Kramer and Dübner as: ἀποδημίαν τὴν ἐπὶ πλέον γενομένην, καλῶς εἶχεν εἴτ' ἀναλαβεῖν εἴτε καὶ παραλαβεῖν· ἐμφαίνει [δὲ] διὰ τῶν ἐπαίνων τῆς παρ' αὐτοῖς εὐ-τυχίας [καὶ] εὐτεχνίας καί. Spengel, Meineke, C. Müller, Cobet, delete εὐτεχνίας [καί], and with this as a basis Madvig reads as given in the text above.

καὶ παρὰ τῷ Μενελάῳ· λέγει γὰρ πρὸς Τηλέμαχον,

δώσω τοι κρητῆρα τετυγμένον· ἀργύρεος δὲ
ἐστὶν ἅπας, χρυσῷ δ' ἐπὶ χείλεα κεκράανται.
ἔργον δ' Ἡφαίστοιο· πόρεν δέ ἑ Φαίδιμος¹ ἥρως
Σιδονίων βασιλεύς, ὅθ' ἑὸς δόμος ἀμφεκάλυψε
κεῖσέ με νοστήσαντα. (ᴗα. 4. 615 ; Od. 15. 115)

δεῖ δὲ δέξασθαι πρὸς ὑπερβολὴν εἰρημένον τὸ
Ἡφαίστου ἔργον, ὡς λέγεται Ἀθηνᾶς ἔργα τὰ
καλὰ καὶ Χαρίτων καὶ Μουσῶν. ἐπεὶ ὅτι γε οἱ
ἄνδρες ἦσαν καλλίτεχνοι, δηλοῖ τὸν κρατῆρα
ἐπαινῶν, ὃν ὁ Εὔνεως ἔδωκεν ἀντὶ Λυκάονος· φησὶ
γάρ,

κάλλει ἐνίκα πᾶσαν ἐπ' αἶαν
πολλόν· ἐπεὶ Σιδόνες πολυδαίδαλοι εὖ ἤσκησαν,
Φοίνικες δ' ἄγον ἄνδρες. (Il. 23. 742)

34. Περὶ δὲ τῶν Ἐρεμβῶν πολλὰ μὲν εἴρηται,
πιθανώτατοι δ' εἰσὶν οἱ νομίζοντες τοὺς Ἄραβας
λέγεσθαι. Ζήνων δ' ὁ ἡμέτερος καὶ γράφει
οὕτως·

Αἰθίοπάς θ' ἱκόμην καὶ Σιδονίους Ἄραβάς τε.
(Od. 4. 84)

τὴν μὲν οὖν γραφὴν οὐκ ἀνάγκη κινεῖν, παλαιὰν
οὖσαν· αἰτιᾶσθαι δὲ βέλτιον τὴν τοῦ ὀνόματος
μετάπτωσιν, πολλὴν καὶ ἐπιπολαίαν οὖσαν ἐν
πᾶσι τοῖς ἔθνεσιν. ἀμέλει δὲ καὶ ποιοῦσί τινες
παραγραμματίζοντες. ἄριστα δ' ἂν δόξειεν εἰπεῖν
ὁ Ποσειδώνιος, κἀνταῦθα ἀπὸ τῆς τῶν ἐθνῶν
συγγενείας καὶ κοινότητος ἐτυμολογῶν. τὸ γὰρ

¹ Φαίδιμος, Sterrett, for φαίδιμος.

house of Menelaus too, for Menelaus says to Telemachus: "I will give thee a mixing-bowl beautifully wrought; it is all of silver, and the lips thereof are finished with gold, the work of Hephaestus; and the hero Phaedimus, the king of the Sidonians, gave it me, when his house sheltered me on my coming thither." But the expression "the work of Hephaestus" must be regarded as a case of hyperbole, just as beautiful things are spoken of as "works of Athene," or of the Graces, or of the Muses. For Homer makes it clear that the Sidonians were makers of beautiful works of art, by the praise he bestows on the bowl which Euneos gave as a ransom for Lycaon; his words are: "In beauty it was far the best in all the earth, for artificers of Sidon wrought it cunningly, and men of the Phoenicians brought it."

34. Much has been said about the Erembians; but those men are most likely to be correct who believe that Homer meant the Arabians. Our Zeno[1] even writes the text accordingly: "And I came to the Ethiopians and Sidonians and Arabians." However, it is not necessary to change the reading, for it is old. It is better to lay the confusion to the change of their name, for such change is frequent and noticeable among all nations, than to change the reading—as in fact some do when they emend by changing certain letters. But it would seem that the view of Poseidonius is best, for here he derives an etymology of the words from the kinship of the peoples and their common characteristics.

[1] See Introduction, page xvi.

τῶν Ἀρμενίων ἔθνος καὶ τὸ τῶν Σύρων καὶ Ἀράβων πολλὴν ὁμοφυλίαν ἐμφαίνει, κατά τε τὴν
διάλεκτον καὶ τοὺς βίους καὶ τοὺς τῶν σωμάτων
χαρακτῆρας, καὶ μάλιστα καθὸ πλησιόχωροί εἰσι.
δηλοῖ δ᾽ ἡ Μεσοποταμία ἐκ τῶν τριῶν συνεστῶσα
τούτων ἐθνῶν· μάλιστα γὰρ ἐν τούτοις ἡ ὁμοιότης
διαφαίνεται. εἰ δέ τις παρὰ τὰ κλίματα γίνεται
διαφορὰ τοῖς προσβόρροις ἐπὶ πλέον πρὸς τοὺς
μεσημβρινοὺς καὶ τούτοις πρὸς μέσους τοὺς
C 42 Σύρους,[1] ἀλλ᾽ ἐπικρατεῖ γε τὸ κοινόν. καὶ οἱ
Ἀσσύριοι δὲ καὶ οἱ Ἀριανοὶ καὶ οἱ Ἀραμμαῖοι[2]
παραπλησίως πως ἔχουσι καὶ πρὸς τούτους καὶ
πρὸς ἀλλήλους. εἰκάζει γε δὴ καὶ τὰς τῶν ἐθνῶν
τούτων κατονομασίας ἐμφερεῖς ἀλλήλαις εἶναι.
τοὺς γὰρ ὑφ᾽ ἡμῶν Σύρους καλουμένους ὑπ᾽ αὐτῶν
τῶν Σύρων Ἀριμαίους[3] καὶ Ἀραμμαίους καλεῖ-
σθαι· τούτῳ δ᾽ ἐοικέναι τοὺς Ἀρμενίους καὶ τοὺς
Ἄραβας καὶ Ἐρεμβούς, τάχα τῶν πάλαι Ἑλλήνων οὕτω καλούντων τοὺς Ἄραβας, ἅμα καὶ τοῦ
ἐτύμου συνεργοῦντος πρὸς τοῦτο. ἀπὸ γὰρ τοῦ εἰς
τὴν ἔραν ἐμβαίνειν τοὺς Ἐρεμβοὺς ἐτυμολογοῦσιν
οὕτως οἱ πολλοί, οὓς μεταλαβόντες οἱ ὕστερον
ἐπὶ τὸ σαφέστερον Τρωγλοδύτας ἐκάλεσαν· οὗτοι
δέ εἰσιν Ἀράβων οἱ ἐπὶ θάτερον μέρος τοῦ Ἀραβίου κόλπου κεκλιμένοι, τὸ πρὸς Αἰγύπτῳ καὶ
Αἰθιοπίᾳ. τούτων δ᾽ εἰκὸς μεμνῆσθαι τὸν ποιητὴν καὶ πρὸς τούτους ἀφῖχθαι λέγειν τὸν Μενέλαον, καθ᾽ ὃν τρόπον εἴρηται καὶ πρὸς τοὺς

---

[1] Σύρους, A. Miller, for ὅρους; A. Vogel approving.
[2] Several MSS., including A, have καὶ οἱ Ἀρμένιοι after
Ἀριανοί. Groskurd reads Ἀραμαῖοι. For this Sterrett reads
Ἀραμμαῖοι, which has MS. authority.
[3] Ἀριμαίους, Groskurd, for Ἀρμενίους.

For the nation of the Armenians and that of the Syrians
and Arabians betray a close affinity, not only in their
language, but in their mode of life and in their bodily
build, and particularly wherever they live as close
neighbours. Mesopotamia, which is inhabited by
these three nations, gives proof of this, for in the
case of these nations the similarity is particularly
noticeable. And if, comparing the differences of
latitude, there does exist a greater difference between
the northern and the southern people of Mesopotamia
than between these two peoples and the Syrians in
the centre, still the common characteristics prevail.
And, too, the Assyrians, the Arians, and the Arammaeans display a certain likeness both to those just
mentioned and to each other. Indeed, Poseidonius
conjectures that the names of these nations also are
akin ; for, says he, the people whom we call Syrians
are by the Syrians themselves called Arimaeans and
Arammaeans ; and there is a resemblance between
this name and those of the Armenians, the Arabians
and the Erembians, since perhaps the ancient Greeks
gave the name of Erembians to the Arabians, and
since the very etymology of the word "Erembian"
contributes to this result. Most scholars, indeed, derive the name "Erembian" from *eran embainein,*[1]
a name which later peoples changed to "Troglodytes[2]"
for the sake of greater clearness. Now these
Troglodytes are that tribe of Arabians who live on
the side of the Arabian Gulf next to Egypt and
Ethiopia. It was natural for the poet to mention
these Erembians and to say that Menelaus " came to "
them, in the same sense in which he says that
Menelaus "came to" the Ethiopians (for they too

[1] To go into the earth.   [2] Cave-dwellers.

Αἰθίοπας· τῇ γὰρ Θηβαΐδι καὶ οὗτοι πλησια-
ζουσιν· ὅμως[1] οὐκ ἐργασίας οὐδὲ χρηματισμοῦ
χάριν τούτων ὀνομαζομένων (οὐ πολὺ γὰρ ἦν
τοῦτο), ἀλλὰ τοῦ μήκους τῆς ἀποδημίας καὶ τοῦ
ἐνδόξου· ἔνδοξον γὰρ τοσοῦτον ἐκτοπίσαι. τοιοῦτον δὲ καὶ τὸ

πολλῶν ἀνθρώπων ἴδεν ἄστεα, καὶ νόον ἔγνω·
(Od. 1. 3)

καὶ τὸ

ἦ γὰρ πολλὰ παθὼν καὶ πόλλ' ἐπαληθεὶς
ἠγαγόμην.   (Od. 4. 81)

Ἡσίοδος δ' ἐν Καταλόγῳ φησὶ

καὶ κούρην Ἀράβοιο, τὸν Ἑρμάων ἀκάκητα
γείνατο καὶ Θρονίη, κούρη Βήλοιο ἄνακτος.
fr. 23 (45)

οὕτω δὲ καὶ Στησίχορος λέγει. εἰκάζειν οὖν ἐστιν,
ὅτι ἀπὸ τούτου καὶ ἡ χώρα Ἀραβία ἤδη τότε
ὠνομάζετο· κατὰ δὲ τοὺς ἥρωας τυχὸν ἴσως οὔπω.
35. Οἱ δὲ πλάττοντες Ἐρεμβοὺς ἴδιόν τι ἔθνος
Αἰθιοπικὸν καὶ ἄλλο Κηφήνων καὶ τρίτον Πυγμαίων καὶ ἄλλα μυρία ἧττον ἂν πιστεύοιντο,
πρὸς τῷ μὴ ἀξιοπίστῳ καὶ σύγχυσίν τινα ἐμφαί-
νοντες τοῦ μυθικοῦ καὶ ἱστορικοῦ σχήματος.
ὅμοιοι δ' εἰσὶ τούτοις καὶ οἱ Σιδονίους ἐν τῇ κατὰ
Πέρσας θαλάττῃ διηγούμενοι, ἢ ἄλλοθί που τοῦ
ὠκεανοῦ, καὶ τὴν τοῦ Μενελάου πλάνην ἐξωκεα-
νίζοντες· ὁμοίως δὲ καὶ τοὺς Φοίνικας. τῆς δ'
ἀπιστίας αἴτιον οὐκ ἐλάχιστόν ἐστι τὸ ἐναντιοῦ-
σθαι ἀλλήλοις τοὺς λέγοντας· οἱ μὲν γὰρ καὶ

[1] ὅμως, Corais, for ὁμοίως.

are near the territory of Thebes); however, they were mentioned not on account of their handicraft nor yet on account of the profit Menelaus made among them (for that could not amount to much), but on account of the length of his sojourn among them and the fame of having visited them; for it was a famous thing to have travelled so far abroad. This is the meaning of: " Many were the men whose towns he saw and whose mind he learnt "; and of : " Yea, and after many woes and wanderings manifold, I brought [my wealth home in ships]." Hesiod in his Catalogue speaks of " the daughter of Arabus, the son of guileless Hermaon [1] and of Thronia the daughter of king Belus." And Stesichorus says the same thing. Therefore, we may conjecture that at the time of Hesiod and Stesichorus the country was already called Arabia from this " Arabus," although it may be that it was not yet so called in the times of the heroes.

35. Those scholars who invent the explanation that the Erembians are some particular Ethiopian tribe, or, again, a tribe of Cephenians, or thirdly, a tribe of Pygmies—or a host of other tribes—are less deserving of credence, since in addition to the incredibility of their theories they betray a tendency to confound myth and history. Like them are the writers who tell of Sidonians on the Persian Gulf, or somewhere else on Oceanus, and who place the wanderings of Menelaus, and likewise place the Phoenicians, out in Oceanus. And not the least reason for not believing them is the fact that they contradict one another. For some of them say that

[1] Hermes.

τοὺς Σιδονίους τοὺς καθ' ἡμᾶς ἀποίκους εἶναι τῶν
ἐν τῷ ὠκεανῷ φασι, προστιθέντες καὶ διὰ τί
Φοίνικες ἐκαλοῦντο, ὅτι καὶ ἡ θάλαττα ἐρυθρά·
οἱ δ' ἐκείνους τούτων. εἰσὶ δ' οἳ καὶ τὴν Αἰθιο-
C 43 πίαν εἰς τὴν καθ' ἡμᾶς Φοινίκην μετάγουσι, καὶ
τὰ περὶ τὴν Ἀνδρομέδαν ἐν Ἰόπῃ συμβῆναί
φασιν· οὐ δήπου κατ' ἄγνοιαν τοπικὴν καὶ τούτων
λεγομένων, ἀλλ' ἐν μύθου μᾶλλον σχήματι· καθάπερ καὶ τῶν παρ' Ἡσιόδῳ καὶ τοῖς ἄλλοις ἃ
προφέρει ὁ Ἀπολλόδωρος, οὐδ' [1] ὃν τρόπον παρατίθησι τοῖς Ὁμήρου ταῦτα εἰδώς. τὰ μὲν γὰρ
Ὁμήρου, τὰ περὶ τὸν Πόντον καὶ τὴν Αἴγυπτον,
παρατίθησιν ἄγνοιαν αἰτιώμενος, ὡς λέγειν μὲν
τὰ ὄντα βουλομένου, μὴ λέγοντος δὲ τὰ ὄντα,
ἀλλὰ τὰ μὴ ὄντα ὡς ὄντα κατ' ἄγνοιαν. Ἡσιόδου
δ' οὐκ ἄν τις αἰτιάσαιτο ἄγνοιαν, Ἡμίκυνας
λέγοντος καὶ Μακροκεφάλους καὶ Πυγμαίους·
οὐδὲ γὰρ αὐτοῦ Ὁμήρου ταῦτα μυθεύοντος, ὧν
εἰσι καὶ οὗτοι οἱ Πυγμαῖοι, οὐδ' Ἀλκμᾶνος
Στεγανόποδας ἱστοροῦντος, οὐδ' Αἰσχύλου Κυνο-
κεφάλους καὶ Στερνοφθάλμους καὶ Μονομμάτους,
ὅπου γε οὐδὲ τοῖς πεζῇ συγγράφουσιν ἐν ἱστορίας
σχήματι προσέχομεν περὶ πολλῶν, κἂν μὴ ἐξο-
μολογῶνται τὴν μυθογραφίαν. φαίνεται γὰρ
εὐθύς, ὅτι μύθους παραπλέκουσιν ἑκόντες, οὐκ

---

[1] οὐδ', Corais, for οὔθ'; Meineke following.

---

[1] *Phoen* means "red."
[2] For example, by Sophocles or Euripides.
[3] These quotations are from works now lost, though
Aeschylus refers to certain one-eyed men in *Prometheus* 804
also.

even the Sidonians who are our neighbours are
colonists from the Sidonians on Oceanus, and they
actually add the reason why our Sidonians are
called Phoenicians,[1] namely, because the colour of
the Persian Gulf is "red"; but others hold that
the Sidonians on Oceanus are colonists from our
Phoenicia. And there are some who transfer
Ethiopia also to our Phoenicia, and who say that
the adventure of Andromeda took place in Joppa,
though the story is surely not told in ignorance of
its local setting[2] but rather in the guise of myth;
and the same is true of the stories that Apollodorus
cites from Hesiod and the other poets without even
realising in what way he is comparing them with the
stories in Homer. For he compares what Homer
says about the Pontus and Egypt and charges him
with ignorance, on the ground that, though he
wanted to tell the truth, he did not do so, but in
his ignorance stated as true what was not true.
Yet no one could charge Hesiod with ignorance
when he speaks of "men who are half-dog," of
"long headed men" and of "Pygmies"; no more
should one charge Homer with ignorance when he
tells these mythical stories of his, one of which is
that of these very Pygmies; nor Alcman when he
tells about "web-footed men"; nor Aeschylus when
he speaks of "dog-headed men," or of "men with
eyes in their breasts," or of "one-eyed men"[3];
since, at all events, we do not pay much attention
to prose writers, either, when they compose stories
on many subjects in the guise of history, even
if they do not expressly acknowledge that they
are dealing in myths. For it is self-evident that
they are weaving in myths intentionally, not through

ἀγνοίᾳ τῶν ὄντων, ἀλλὰ πλάσει τῶν ἀδυνάτων
τερατείας καὶ τέρψεως χάριν· δοκοῦσι δὲ κατ'
ἄγνοιαν, ὅτι μάλιστα καὶ πιθανῶς τὰ τοιαῦτα
μυθεύουσι περὶ τῶν ἀδήλων καὶ τῶν ἀγνοουμένων.
Θεόπομπος δὲ ἐξομολογεῖται φήσας ὅτι καὶ
μύθους ἐν ταῖς ἱστορίαις ἐρεῖ, κρεῖττον ἢ ὡς
Ἡρόδοτος καὶ Κτησίας καὶ Ἑλλάνικος καὶ οἱ τὰ
Ἰνδικὰ συγγράψαντες.

36. Περὶ δὲ τῶν τοῦ ὠκεανοῦ παθῶν εἴρηται
μὲν ἐν μύθου σχήματι· καὶ γὰρ τούτου στοχάζεσθαι δεῖ τὸν ποιητήν. ἀπὸ γὰρ τῶν ἀμπώτεων
καὶ τῶν πλημμυρίδων ἡ Χάρυβδις αὐτῷ μεμύ-
θευται, οὐδ' αὐτὴ παντάπασιν Ὁμήρου πλάσμα
οὖσα, ἀλλ' ἀπὸ τῶν ἱστορουμένων περὶ τὸν Σικελικὸν πορθμὸν διεσκευασμένη. εἰ δὲ δὶς τῆς
παλιρροίας γινομένης καθ' ἑκάστην ἡμέραν καὶ
νύκτα ἐκεῖνος τρὶς εἴρηκε,

τρὶς μὲν γάρ τ' ἀνίησιν ἐπ' ἤματι, τρὶς δ' ἀναροιβδεῖ,   (Od. 12. 105)

λέγοιτ' ἂν καὶ οὕτως· οὐ γὰρ κατ' ἄγνοιαν τῆς
ἱστορίας ὑποληπτέον λέγεσθαι τοῦτο, ἀλλὰ τραγῳδίας χάριν καὶ φόβου, ὃν ἡ Κίρκη πολὺν τοῖς
λόγοις προστίθησιν ἀποτροπῆς χάριν, ὥστε καὶ
τὸ ψεῦδος παραμίγνυσθαι. ἐν αὐτοῖς γοῦν τοῖς
ἔπεσι τούτοις εἴρηκε μὲν οὕτως ἡ Κίρκη·

τρὶς μὲν γάρ τ ἀνίησιν ἐπ' ἤματι, τρὶς δ'
ἀναροιβδεῖ

ignorance of the facts, but through an intentional invention of the impossible, to gratify the taste for the marvellous and the entertaining. But they give the impression of doing this through ignorance, because by preference and with an air of plausibility they tell such tales about the unfamiliar and the unknown. Theopompus expressly acknowledges the practice when he says that he intends to narrate myths too in his History—a better way than that of Herodotus, Ctesias, Hellanicus, and the authors of the Histories of India.[1]

36. What Homer says about the behaviour of Oceanus is set forth in the guise of a myth (this too is a thing the poet must aim at); for he borrowed the myth of Charybdis from the ebb and flow of the tides; though even Charybdis herself is not wholly an invention of Homer, for she was dressed up by him in accordance with what had been told him about the Strait of Sicily. And suppose that by the words, " For thrice a day she spouts it forth, and thrice a day she sucks it down," Homer does affirm that the refluent tide comes in three times within the course of each day and night (although it comes in but twice), he might be permitted to express it in this way; for we must not suppose that he used these words in ignorance of the facts, but for the sake of the tragic effect and of the emotion of fear upon which Circe plays largely in what she says to Odysseus in order to terrify him; and for that reason she mingled the false with the true. At any rate, in these very lines Circe has said : " For thrice a day she spouts it forth and thrice a day she sucks it

---

[1] Deïmachus, Megasthenes, Onesicritus, Nearchus and others. See 2. 1. 9.

δεινόν· μὴ σύ γε κεῖθι τύχοις, ὅτε ῥοιβδήσειε·
οὐ γάρ κεν ῥύσαιτό σ' ὑπὲκ κακοῦ οὐδ' Ἐνο-
σίχθων.   (Od. 12. 105)

καὶ μὴν παρέτυχέ τε τῇ ἀναρροιβδήσει ὁ Ὀδυσσεὺς καὶ οὐκ ἀπώλετο, ὥς φησιν αὐτός·

C 44   ἡ μὲν ἀνερροίβδησε θαλάσσης ἁλμυρὸν ὕδωρ·
       αὐτὰρ ἐγώ, ποτὶ μακρὸν ἐρινεὸν ὑψόσ' ἀερθείς,
       τῷ προσφὺς ἐχόμην, ὡς νυκτερίς. (Od. 12. 431)

εἶτα περιμείνας τὰ ναυάγια καὶ λαβόμενος πάλιν
αὐτῶν σώζεται, ὥστ' ἐψεύσατο ἡ Κίρκη. ὡς οὖν
τοῦτο, κἀκεῖνο τὸ "τρὶς μὲν γάρ τ' ἀνίησιν ἐπ'
ἤματι" ἀντὶ τοῦ δίς, ἅμα καὶ τῆς ὑπερβολῆς τῆς
τοιαύτης συνήθους πᾶσιν οὔσης, τρισμακαρίους
καὶ τρισαθλίους λεγόντων· καὶ ὁ ποιητής·

            τρισμάκαρες Δαναοί,   (Od. 5. 306)
καὶ
            ἀσπασίη τρίλλιστος,   (Π. 8. 488)
καὶ
            τριχθά τε καὶ τετραχθά.   (Π. 3. 363)

ἴσως δ' ἄν τις καὶ ἀπὸ τῆς ὥρας τεκμήραιτο, ὅτι
ὑπαινίττεταί πως τὸ ἀληθές· μᾶλλον γὰρ ἐφαρμόττει[1] τῷ δὶς γενέσθαι τὴν παλίρροιαν κατὰ τὸν
συνάμφω χρόνον, τὸν ἐξ ἡμέρας καὶ νυκτός, ἢ τῷ
τρίς, τὸ[2] τοσοῦτον χρόνον μεῖναι τὰ ναυάγια
ὑποβρύχια, ὀψὲ δὲ ἀναβληθῆναι ποθοῦντι καὶ
συνεχῶς προσισχομένῳ τοῖς κλάδοις·

       νωλεμέως δ' ἐχόμην, ὄφρ' ἐξεμέσειεν ὀπίσσω
       ἱστὸν καὶ τρόπιν αὖτις, ἐελδομένῳ δέ μοι ἦλθον[3]
       ὄψ'· ἦμος δ'[4] ἐπὶ δόρπον ἀνὴρ ἀγορῆθεν ἀνέστη,

---

[1] ἐφαρμόττει, Corais following kno, for ἐφαρμόττοι.

down—a terrible sight! Never mayest thou be there when she sucks the water, for none might save thee from thy bane, not even the Earth-Shaker." Yet Odysseus later on was present when she "sucked it down," and he did not perish; as he himself says: "Now she had sucked down the salt sea-water, but I was swung up on high to a tall fig-tree, whereto I clung like a bat." Then waiting for the pieces of wreckage and laying hold of them again, he saved himself on them; and so Circe lied. And as she lied in this statement, so she lied in that other statement, "for thrice a day she spouts it forth," instead of "twice a day," although it is true, at the same time, that this kind of hyperbole is familiar to everybody—as, for instance, when we say "thrice-blessed" and "thrice-wretched." The poet himself says: "Thrice-blessed those Danaäns"; and again: "Welcome, thrice-prayed for"; and yet again: "Into three, yea, into four pieces." Perhaps one might infer also from the time involved that Homer is, in a way, hinting at the truth; for the fact that the pieces of wreckage remained so long engulfed and were only tardily cast up for Odysseus, who was longing for them and constantly clinging to the limbs of the tree, better suits the assumption that the refluent tide came in twice, rather than thrice, during the twofold period, consisting of a day and a night: "Steadfastly I clung," he says, "till she should vomit forth mast and keel again; and late they came to my desire. At the hour when a man rises up from the assembly and goes to supper,

---

[2] τό before τοσοῦτον, Corais inserts, following g; Madvig independently.

[3] ἦλθον, Sterrett, for ἦλθεν. [4] δ', Sterrett, for τ'.

κρίνων νείκεα πολλὰ δικαζομένων αἰζηῶν,
καὶ τότε δή μοι δοῦρα Χαρύβδιος ἐξεφαάνθη.

(Od. 12. 437)

πάντα γὰρ ταῦτα χρόνου τινὸς ἔμφασιν ἀξιολόγου
δίδωσι, καὶ μάλιστα τὸ τὴν ἑσπέραν ἐπιτεῖναι,
μὴ κοινῶς εἰπόντα, ἡνίκα ὁ δικαστὴς ἀνίσταται,
ἀλλ' ἡνίκα κρίνων νείκεα πολλά, ὥστε βραδῦναι
πλέον τι. καὶ ἄλλως δὲ οὐ πιθανὴν ἂν ὑπέτεινε
τῷ ναυαγῷ τὴν ἀπαλλαγήν, εἰ, πρὶν ἀποσπασ-
θῆναι πολύ,[1] αὐτίκα εἰς τοὐπίσω παλίρρους
μετέπιπτεν.

37. Ἀπολλόδωρος δὲ ἐπιτιμᾷ Καλλιμάχῳ,
συνηγορῶν τοῖς περὶ τὸν Ἐρατοσθένη, διότι,
καίπερ γραμματικὸς ὤν, παρὰ τὴν Ὁμηρικὴν
ὑπόθεσιν καὶ τὸν ἐξωκεανισμὸν τῶν τόπων, περὶ
οὓς τὴν πλάνην φράζει, Γαῦδον καὶ Κόρκυραν
ὀνομάζει. ἀλλ' εἰ μὲν μηδαμοῦ γέγονεν ἡ πλάνη,
ἀλλ' ὅλον πλάσμα ἐστὶν Ὁμήρου τοῦτο, ὀρθὴ ἡ
ἐπιτίμησις· ἤ, εἰ γέγονε μέν, περὶ ἄλλους δὲ
τόπους, ἔδει[2] λέγειν εὐθὺς καὶ περὶ τίνας,
ἐπανορθούμενον ἅμα τὴν ἄγνοιαν. μήτε δὲ ὅλου
πλάσματος εἶναι πιθανῶς λεγομένου, καθάπερ
ἐπεδείκνυμεν, μήτ' ἄλλων τόπων κατὰ πίστιν
μείζω δεικνυμένων, ἀπολύοιτ' ἂν τῆς αἰτίας ὁ
Καλλίμαχος.

---

[1] καί, Corais deletes, before αὐτίκα; Groskurd, Forbiger, following.   [2] ἔδει, Corais, for δεῖ.

---

[1] That is, three times a day.

the arbiter of many quarrels of the young men that plead their cases, at that hour the timbers came forth to view from out Charybdis." All this gives the impression of a considerable lapse of time, and particularly the fact that the poet prolongs the time to the evening, for he does not merely say in general terms, " at the hour when the judge rises up," but he adds " arbiter of many quarrels " ; hence he had been detained somewhat longer than usual. And another consideration: the means of escape which the poet offers the shipwrecked Odysseus would not be plausible, if each time, before he was carried far away by the tide, he was immediately thrown back by the refluent tide.[1]

37. Apollodorus, agreeing with Eratosthenes and his school, censures Callimachus, because, though a scholar, Callimachus names Gaudos [2] and Corcyra as scenes of the wanderings of Odysseus, in defiance of Homer's fundamental plan, which is to transfer to Oceanus the regions in which he describes the wanderings as taking place. But if the wanderings never took place anywhere, and if this is wholly a fiction of Homer's, then Apollodorus' censure is just. Or if the wanderings did take place, but in other regions, then Apollodorus should have said so at the outset and should have told in what regions they took place, thus at once correcting the ignorant view of Callimachus. But since the story cannot with plausibility be called wholly a fiction, as I have shown above,[3] and since no other places are pointed out that have a greater claim to our credence, Callimachus might be absolved from censure.

[2] The island of Gozo, south of Sicily, which Callimachus makes the Isle of Calypso.   [3] 1. 2. 9 ff.

C 45   38. Οὐδ' ὁ Σκήψιος δὲ Δημήτριος εὖ, ἀλλὰ
καὶ τῷ Ἀπολλοδώρῳ τῶν ἁμαρτιῶν ἐνίων αἴτιος
ἐκεῖνος κατέστη. πρὸς γὰρ Νεάνθη τὸν Κυζικηνὸν
φιλοτιμοτέρως ἀντιλέγων, εἰπόντα ὅτι οἱ Ἀργο-
ναῦται πλέοντες εἰς Φᾶσιν τὸν ὑφ' Ὁμήρου καὶ
τῶν ἄλλων ὁμολογούμενον πλοῦν, ἱδρύσαντο τὰ
τῆς Ἰδαίας μητρὸς ἱερὰ περὶ Κύζικον, ἀρχήν
φησι μηδ' εἰδέναι τὴν εἰς Φᾶσιν ἀποδημίαν τοῦ
Ἰάσονος Ὅμηρον. τοῦτο δ' οὐ μόνον τοῖς ὑφ'
Ὁμήρου λεγομένοις μάχεται, ἀλλὰ καὶ τοῖς ὑπ'
αὐτοῦ. φησὶ γὰρ τὸν Ἀχιλλέα Λέσβον μὲν
πορθῆσαι καὶ ἄλλα χωρία, Λήμνου δ' ἀποσχέσθαι
καὶ τῶν πλησίον νήσων διὰ τὴν πρὸς Ἰάσονα καὶ
τὸν υἱὸν Εὔνεων συγγένειαν τὸν[1] τότε τὴν νῆσον
κατέχοντα. πῶς οὖν ὁ ποιητὴς τοῦτο μὲν ᾔδει,
διότι συγγενεῖς ἢ ὁμοεθνεῖς ἢ γείτονες ἢ ὁπωσοῦν
οἰκεῖοι ὑπῆρχον ὅ τε Ἀχιλλεὺς καὶ ὁ Ἰάσων
(ὅπερ οὐδαμόθεν ἄλλοθεν, ἀλλ' ἐκ τοῦ Θετταλοὺς
ἀμφοτέρους εἶναι συνέβαινε, καὶ τὸν μὲν Ἰώλκιον,
τὸν δ' ἐκ τῆς Φθιώτιδος Ἀχαιίδος ὑπάρχειν),
τοῦτο δ' ἠγνόει, πόθεν ἐπῆλθε[2] τῷ Ἰάσονι,
Θετταλῷ καὶ Ἰωλκίῳ ὑπάρχοντι, ἐν μὲν τῇ
πατρίδι μηδεμίαν καταλιπεῖν διαδοχήν, Λήμνου
δὲ καταστῆσαι κύριον τὸν υἱόν; καὶ Πελίαν μὲν
ᾔδει καὶ τὰς Πελιάδας καὶ τὴν Ἄλκηστιν[3] τὴν
ἀρίστην αὐτῶν, καὶ τὸν υἱὸν αὐτῆς

Εὔμηλον, τὸν ὑπ' Ἀδμήτῳ τέκε δῖα γυναικῶν
Ἄλκηστις, Πελίαο θυγατρῶν εἶδος ἀρίστη·
(Il. 2. 714)

[1] τόν, H. Kallenberg inserts, before τότε.
[2] ἐπῆλθε, Cobet, for ἦλθε; Bernadakis, A. Vogel, approving.
[3] τὴν Ἄλκηστιν, Kramer inserts.

38. Nor is Demetrius of Scepsis right; on the contrary, he is the cause of some of the mistakes of Apollodorus. For in his excessive eagerness to refute the statement of Neanthes of Cyzicus that the Argonauts erected the sanctuary of the Idaean Mother [1] in the neighbourhood of Cyzicus when they were sailing to Phasis [2] on the voyage which is admitted by Homer and other writers, Demetrius says that Homer knew absolutely nothing about the voyage of Jason to Phasis. Now this is opposed not only to Homer's statements but to the statements made by Demetrius himself. For Demetrius says that Achilles sacked Lesbos and other places, but spared Lemnos and the islands adjacent thereto on account of his kinship with Jason and with Jason's son Euneos who at that time possessed the island of Lemnos. Now how comes it that the poet knew this, namely, that Achilles and Jason were kinsmen or fellow-countrymen, or neighbours, or friends in some way or other (a relationship that could not be due to any other fact than that both men were Thessalians, and that one was born in Iolcus and the other in Achaean Phthiotis), and yet did not know what had put it into the head of Jason, a Thessalian and an Iolcan, to leave no successor on the throne of of his native country, but to establish his son as lord of Lemnos? And did he know about Pelias and the daughters of Pelias, and about Alcestis, the noblest of them, and about her son " Eumelus, whom Alcestis, fair among women, bare to Admetus, Alcestis that was most beauteous to look upon of the daughters of Pelias," and yet, as regards the

---

[1] Cybele. See 10. 3. 12–13.
[2] See 11. 2. 16–18.

τῶν δὲ περὶ τὸν Ἰάσονα συμβάντων καὶ τὴν
Ἀργὼ καὶ τοὺς Ἀργοναύτας, τῶν μὲν ὁμολογου-
μένων παρὰ πᾶσιν ἀνήκοος ἦν, ἐν δὲ τῷ ὠκεανῷ
τὸν παρ' Αἰήτου πλοῦν ἔπλαττεν, ἀρχὴν μηδεμίαν
ἐξ ἱστορίας λαβών;

39. Ὡς μὲν γὰρ ἅπαντες λέγουσιν, ὅ τε[1] ἐξ ἀρχῆς πλοῦς ὁ[2] ἐπὶ Φᾶσιν ἔχει πιθανόν τι, τοῦ Πελίου
στείλαντος, καὶ ἡ ἐπάνοδος καὶ ἡ ἐν τῷ παράπλῳ
νήσων ὁσηδὴ ἐπικράτεια καὶ νὴ Δία ἡ ἐπὶ πλέον
γενηθεῖσα πλάνη, καθάπερ καὶ τῷ Ὀδυσσεῖ καὶ
τῷ Μενελάῳ, ἐκ τῶν ἔτι νῦν δεικνυμένων καὶ
πεπιστευμένων, ἔτι δὲ[3] ἐκ τῆς Ὁμήρου φωνῆς.
ἥ τε γὰρ Αἶα δείκνυται περὶ Φᾶσιν πόλις· καὶ
ὁ Αἰήτης πεπίστευται βασιλεῦσαι τῆς Κολχίδος,
καὶ ἔστι τοῖς ἐκεῖ τοῦτ' ἐπιχώριον τοὔνομα. ἥ τε
Μήδεια φαρμακὶς ἱστορεῖται, καὶ ὁ πλοῦτος τῆς
ἐκεῖ χώρας ἐκ τῶν χρυσείων καὶ ἀργυρείων καὶ
σιδηρείων καὶ χαλκείων[4] δικαίαν τινὰ ὑπαγορεύει
πρόφασιν τῆς στρατείας, καθ' ἣν καὶ Φρίξος
πρότερον ἔστειλε τὸν πλοῦν τοῦτον· καὶ ἔστιν
ὑπομνήματα τῆς ἀμφοῖν στρατείας, τό τε Φρίξειον
τὸ ἐν τοῖς μεθορίοις τῆς τε Κολχίδος καὶ τῆς
Ἰβηρίας, καὶ τὰ Ἰασόνεια, ἃ πολλαχοῦ καὶ τῆς
Ἀρμενίας καὶ τῆς Μηδίας καὶ τῶν πλησιοχώρων
C 46   αὐταῖς τόπων δείκνυται. καὶ μὴν καὶ περὶ

---

[1] ὅ τε ἐξ ἀρχῆς πλοῦς, Corais, for ὅτι ἐξ ἀρχῆς ὁ πλοῦς;
Madvig approving.
[2] ὁ, H. Kallenberg inserts, before ἐπὶ Φᾶσιν.
[3] ἔτι δέ, Madvig, for ἐστίν.
[4] σιδηρείων καὶ χαλκείων δικαίαν, A. Miller, for σιδηρείων καὶ
δικαίαν; A. Vogel approving.

adventures of Jason and the Argo and the Argonauts, had never heard of the things that are agreed upon by everybody, but invented the voyage away from Aeëtes' country and placed it on Oceanus, without any foundation for his story in history?

39. For, as all admit, the original voyage to Phasis ordered by Pelias, the return voyage, and the occupation, however considerable, of islands on the coasting-voyage thither, contain an element of plausibility, as do also, I am sure, the wanderings which carried Jason still further—just as there is an element of plausibility in the wanderings of both Odysseus and Menelaus—as evidenced by things still to this day pointed out and believed in, and by the words of Homer as well. For example, the city of Aea is still shown on the Phasis, and Aeëtes is believed to have ruled over Colchis, and the name Aeëtes [1] is still locally current among the people of that region. Again, Medea the sorceress is a historical person; and the wealth of the regions about Colchis, which is derived from the mines of gold, silver, iron, and copper, suggests a reasonable motive for the expedition, a motive which induced Phrixus also to undertake this voyage at an earlier date. Moreover, memorials of both expeditions still exist: the sanctuary of Phrixus, [2] situated on the confines of Colchis and Iberia, and the sanctuaries of Jason, which are pointed out in many places in Armenia and Media and in the countries adjacent thereto. More than that, it is

[1] Aeëtes was a patronym of a dynasty of Colchian kings. See Xenophon, *Anab.* 5. 6. 37.

[2] On this sanctuary and Iberia (east of Colchis) see 11. 2. 18.

Σινώπην καὶ τὴν ταύτῃ[1] παραλίαν καὶ τὴν Προποντίδα καὶ τὸν Ἑλλήσποντον μέχρι τῶν κατὰ τὴν Λῆμνον τόπων λέγεται πολλὰ τεκμήρια τῆς τε Ἰάσονος στρατείας καὶ τῆς Φρίξου· τῆς δ' Ἰάσονος καὶ τῶν ἐπιδιωξάντων Κόλχων καὶ μέχρι τῆς Κρήτης καὶ τῆς Ἰταλίας καὶ τοῦ Ἀδρίου, ὧν ἔνια καὶ ὁ Καλλίμαχος ἐπισημαίνεται, τοτὲ μὲν

Αἰγλήτην Ἀνάφην τε Λακωνίδι γείτονα Θήρῃ

λέγων ἐν ἐλεγείᾳ, ἧς ἡ ἀρχή·[2]

Ἄρχμενος, ὡς ἥρωες ἀπ' Αἰήταο Κυταίου,
αὖτις ἐς ἀρχαίην ἔπλεον Αἱμονίην·

τοτὲ δὲ περὶ τῶν Κόλχων,

οἱ μὲν ἐπ' Ἰλλυριοῖο[3] πόρου σχάσσαντες ἐρετμὰ
λᾶα πάρα ξανθῆς Ἁρμονίης τάφιον[4]

ἄστυρον ἐκτίσσαντο, τό κεν[5] Φυγάδων τις ἐνίσποι
Γραικός, ἀτὰρ κείνων γλῶσσ' ὀνόμηνε Πόλας.

τινὲς δὲ καὶ τὸν Ἴστρον ἀναπλεῦσαί φασι μέχρι πολλοῦ τοὺς περὶ τὸν Ἰάσονα, οἱ δὲ καὶ μέχρι τοῦ Ἀδρίου· οἱ μὲν κατὰ ἄγνοιαν τῶν τόπων, οἱ δὲ καὶ ποταμὸν Ἴστρον ἐκ τοῦ μεγάλου Ἴστρου τὴν ἀρχὴν ἔχοντα ἐκβάλλειν εἰς τὸν Ἀδρίαν φασί· τἆλλα[6] δὲ οὐκ ἀπιθάνως οὐδ' ἀπίστως λέγοντες.

40. Τοιαύταις δή τισιν ἀφορμαῖς ὁ ποιητὴς χρησάμενος τὰ μὲν ὁμολογεῖ τοῖς ἱστορουμένοις,

---

[1] ταύτῃ, Meineke (Vind. 4), for ταύτης; A. Vogel approving.
[2] ἐν ἐλεγείᾳ, ἧς ἡ ἀρχή·, Meineke (Vind. 5) inserts, after λέγων; Forbiger, C. Müller, Tardieu, following.
[3] Ἰλλυριοῖο, Meineke, for Ἰλλυρικοῖο; C. Müller approving.
[4] τάφιον, Bentley, for ὄφιος; Meineke following.
[5] τό κεν, Corais, for τὸ μέν; Meineke following.
[6] τἆλλα, Groskurd, for τά; Forbiger approving.

said that there are many evidences of the expeditions
of Jason and of Phrixus in the neighbourhood of
Sinope and the adjacent sea-board and also about
the Propontis and the Hellespont as far as the
regions about Lemnos. And there are traces of
the expedition of Jason, and of the Colchians who
pursued him, as far as Crete and Italy and the
Adriatic Sea, some of which Callimachus notes when
he says, "Aegletes[1] and Anaphe hard by Laconian
Thera,[2]" in an elegy whose opening words are,
"At the outset I shall sing how the heroes sailed
back from the kingdom of Aeëtes of Cytaea to
ancient Haemonia.[3]" In another place Callimachus
speaks about the Colchians, who "stayed their oars
in the Sea of Illyria beside the tomb-stone of blonde
Harmonia, and there built a little city, which a
Greek would call 'the city of the exiles,' but which
their language has named Polae.[4]" Some say
that Jason and his companions even sailed up the
Ister[5] a considerable distance, while others say that
he ascended as far as the Adriatic Sea; the former
make their statement in ignorance of these regions,
whereas the latter make the assertion that a river
Ister branches off from the great Ister and empties
into the Adriatic Sea; but apart from this, what
they say is neither improbable nor incredible.

40. Accordingly, it is by availing himself of some
such basis of fact that Homer tells his story,
agreeing in some respects with matters of history,

---

[1] "The radiant one," epithet of Apollo. To save the
Argonauts he caused the island of Anaphe, now Nanfi, to
rise from the sea. The Argonauts erected a temple there
to "Apollo Aegletes." [2] In Cyrene. See 8. 3. 19.
[3] Thessaly. See 9. 5. 23. [4] See 5. 1. 9. [5] Danube.

προσμυθεύει δὲ τούτοις, ἔθος τι φυλάττων καὶ
κοινὸν καὶ ἴδιον. ὁμολογεῖ μέν, ὅταν τὸν[1] Αἰήτην
ὀνομάζῃ, καὶ τὸν Ἰάσονα καὶ τὴν Ἀργὼ λέγῃ,
καὶ παρὰ τὴν Αἶαν[2] τὴν Αἰαίην πλάττῃ, καὶ τὸν
Εὔνεων ἐν Λήμνῳ καθιδρύῃ, καὶ ποιῇ τῷ Ἀχιλλεῖ
φίλην τὴν νῆσον, καὶ παρὰ τὴν Μήδειαν τὴν
Κίρκην φαρμακίδα ποιῇ

> αὐτοκασιγνήτην ὀλοόφρονος Αἰήταο·
>
> (Od. 10. 137)

προσμυθοποιεῖ δὲ τὸν ἐξωκεανισμὸν τὸν κατὰ τὴν
πλάνην συμβάντα τὴν ἀπ᾽ ἐκείνου τοῦ πλοῦ. ἐπεὶ
κἀκεῖνο, ὑποκειμένων μὲν τούτων, εὖ λέγεται,

> Ἀργὼ πασιμέλουσα,   (Od. 12. 70)

ὡς ἐν γνωρίμοις τόποις καὶ εὐανδροῦσι τῆς ναυστολίας γενομένης· εἰ δ᾽, ὥσπερ ὁ Σκήψιός
φησι παραλαβὼν μάρτυρα Μίμνερμον, ὃς ἐν τῷ
ὠκεανῷ ποιήσας τὴν οἴκησιν τοῦ Αἰήτου πρὸς
ταῖς ἀνατολαῖς ἐκτὸς πεμφθῆναί φησιν ὑπὸ τοῦ
Πελίου τὸν Ἰάσονα καὶ κομίσαι τὸ δέρος, οὔτ᾽ ἂν
ἡ ἐπὶ τὸ δέρος ἐκεῖσε πομπὴ πιθανῶς λέγοιτο εἰς
ἀγνῶτας καὶ ἀφανεῖς τόπους οὖσα,[3] οὔθ᾽ ὁ δι᾽
ἐρήμων καὶ ἀοίκων καὶ καθ᾽ ἡμᾶς τοσοῦτον ἐκτε-
τοπισμένων πλοῦς οὔτ᾽ ἔνδοξος οὔτε πασιμέλων.

C 47   (οὐδέ κοτ᾽ ἂν μέγα κῶας ἀνήγαγεν αὐτὸς
Ἰήσων
ἐξ Αἴης, τελέσας ἀλγινόεσσαν ὁδόν,

---

[1] τόν, Corais inserts, before Αἰήτην.
[2] τὴν Αἶαν, Corais inserts before τὴν Αἰαίην (or τὸν Αἰήτην);
Kramer, Forbiger, Meineke, following.
[3] οὖσα, B. Niese inserts, after τόπους.

170

but adding to them an element of myth, thus adhering to a custom that is not only his own but one common to poets. He agrees with history when he uses the name of "Aeëtes,"[1] when he tells of Jason and the Argo, when, with "Aea" in mind, he invents "Aeaea,"[2] when he establishes Euneos in Lemnos, when he makes the island of Lemnos beloved of Achilles, and when, with Medea in mind, he makes the sorceress Circe "own sister to the baleful Aeëtes." But he adds an element of myth when he transfers to Oceanus the wanderings that follow the voyage to Aeëtes' country. For if the facts above-mentioned be assumed, then the words, "the Argo that is in all men's minds," are also properly used, inasmuch as the expedition is supposed to have taken place in well-known and populous regions. But if the facts were as Demetrius of Scepsis maintains, on the authority of Mimnermus (Mimnermus places the home of Aeëtes in Oceanus, outside the inhabited world in the east, and affirms that Jason was sent thither by Pelias and brought back the fleece), then, in the first place, the expedition thither in quest of the fleece would not sound plausible (since it was directed to unknown and obscure countries), and in the second place, the voyage through regions desolate and uninhabited and so out-of-the-way from our part of the world would be neither famous nor "in all men's minds." Mimnermus says : "Never would Jason himself have brought back the great fleece from Aea, accomplishing his mind-racking journey and fulfilling the

[1] *Od.* 12. 70.
[2] *Od.* 11. 70 ; 12. 3. Homer's "Aeaea" (home of Circe) was an invention based upon "Aea," which he actually knew. Strabo alludes to the same thing in 1. 2. 10.

STRABO

ὑβριστῇ Πελίῃ τελέων χαλεπηρὲς ἄεθλον,
  οὐδ' ἂν ἐπ' Ὠκεανοῦ καλὸν ἵκοντο ῥόον·
καὶ ὑποβάς,

Αἰήταο πόλιν, τόθι τ' ὠκέος Ἠελίοιο
  ἀκτῖνες χρυσέῳ κείαται ἐν θαλάμῳ
Ὠκεανοῦ παρὰ χείλεσ', ἵν' ᾤχετο θεῖος Ἰήσων.)[1]

III

1. Οὐδὲ τοῦτ' εὖ Ἐρατοσθένης, ὅτι ἀνδρῶν οὐκ
ἀξίων μνήμης ἐπὶ πλέον μέμνηται, τὰ μὲν ἐλέγχων,
τὰ δὲ πιστεύων καὶ μάρτυσι χρώμενος αὐτοῖς,
οἷον Δαμάστῃ καὶ τοιούτοις ἄλλοις. καὶ γὰρ εἴ τι
λέγουσιν ἀληθές, οὐ μάρτυσί γε ἐκείνοις χρηστέον
περὶ αὐτοῦ, οὐδὲ πιστευτέον διὰ τοῦτο· ἀλλ' ἐπὶ
τῶν ἀξιολόγων ἀνδρῶν μόνων τῷ τοιούτῳ τρόπῳ
χρηστέον, οἳ πολλὰ μὲν εἰρήκασιν εὖ, πολλὰ δὲ
καὶ παραλελοίπασιν ἢ οὐχ ἱκανῶς ἐξεῖπον, οὐδὲν
δ' ἐψευσμένως. ὁ δὲ Δαμάστῃ χρώμενος μάρτυρι
οὐδὲν διαφέρει τοῦ καλοῦντος μάρτυρα τὸν Βεργαῖον ἢ τὸν Μεσσήνιον Εὐήμερον καὶ τοὺς ἄλλους,
οὓς αὐτὸς εἴρηκε διαβάλλων τὴν φλυαρίαν. καὶ
τούτου δ' ἕνα τῶν λήρων αὐτὸς λέγει, τὸν μὲν

[1] These lines are regarded as a marginal note by Kramer, Meineke, C. Müller.

[1] Since Antiphanes of Berga, in Thrace, was the typical romancer, "Bergaean" became a proverbial epithet for writers of his type. It is not known whether Euhemerus was from Messene in Sicily, or from Messene in the Peloponnesus. He made extensive journeys by order of Cassander, King of Macedonia (316–297 B.C.). In his work on "Sacred

difficult task for insolent Pelias, nor would they have come even to the fair stream of Oceanus"; and further on he says: "To the city of Aeëtes, where the rays of the swift Sun lie in a chamber of gold beside the lips of Oceanus, whither glorious Jason went."

III

1. ERATOSTHENES is wrong on this point too, that he makes mention at too great length of men who do not deserve mention, censuring them in some things, while in other things he believes them and uses them as authorities—for instance, Damastes and others of his type. For even if there is an element of truth in what they say, we should not on that account use them as authorities, or believe them, either; on the contrary, we should use in such a way only men of repute—men who have been right on many points, and who, though they have omitted many things, or treated them inadequately, have said nothing with false intent. But to use Damastes as an authority is no whit better than to cite as authorities the "Bergaean"—or rather the Messenian—Euhemerus [1] and the other writers whom Eratosthenes himself cites, in order to ridicule their absurdities. Eratosthenes himself tells us one of the absurd stories of Damastes, who assumes that the

History" he gave a fanciful account of his travels, and, on the basis of various inscriptions which he said he saw, attempted to rationalize the whole system of Greek mythology.

Ἀράβιον κόλπον λίμνην ὑπολαμβάνοντος εἶναι,
Διότιμον δὲ τὸν Στρομβίχου πρεσβείας Ἀθηναίων
ἀφηγούμενον διὰ τοῦ Κύδνου ἀναπλεῦσαι ἐκ τῆς
Κιλικίας ἐπὶ τὸν Χοάσπην ποταμόν, ὃς παρὰ τὰ
Σοῦσα ῥεῖ, καὶ ἀφικέσθαι τεσσαρακοσταῖον εἰς
Σοῦσα· ταῦτα δ' αὐτῷ διηγήσασθαι αὐτὸν τὸν
Διότιμον. εἶτα θαυμάζειν [1] εἰ τὸν Εὐφράτην καὶ
τὸν Τίγριν ἦν δυνατὸν διακόψαντα τὸν Κύδνον εἰς
τὸν Χοάσπην ἐκβαλεῖν.

2. Οὐ μόνον δὲ ταῦτ' ἄν τις ἐπισημήναιτο, ἀλλ'
ὅτι καὶ περὶ τῶν πόντων [2] οὐδὲ καθ' ἑαυτόν πω
γνώριμα εἶναι φήσας [3] τὰ καθ' ἕκαστα ἀκριβο-
λογούμενα, καὶ κελεύσας ἡμῖν μὴ ῥᾳδίως τοῖς
τυχοῦσι πιστεύειν, καὶ τὰς αἰτίας διὰ μακρῶν
ἀποδούς, δι' ἃς οὐδενὶ [4] πιστευτέον μυθολογοῦντι
περὶ τῶν κατὰ τὸν Πόντον καὶ τὸν Ἀδρίαν,
αὐτὸς ἐπίστευσε τοῖς τυχοῦσι. τοιγάρτοι τὸν μὲν
Ἰσσικὸν κόλπον ἐπίστευσεν ἑωθινώτατον τῆς καθ'
ἡμᾶς θαλάττης σημεῖον, τοῦ κατὰ Διοσκουριάδα
τὴν ἐν τῷ τοῦ Πόντου μυχῷ σχεδόν τι καὶ
τρισχιλίοις σταδίοις ἑωθινωτέρου ὄντος καὶ κατ'
αὐτὸν ἐκ τοῦ σταδιασμοῦ οὗ φησι· τοῦ τε
Ἀδρίου καὶ τὰ ἀρκτικὰ καὶ τὰ ἔσχατα διεξιὼν
οὐδενὸς ἀπέχεται μυθώδους. πεπίστευκε δὲ καὶ
περὶ τῶν ἔξω στηλῶν Ἡρακλείων πολλοῖς
μυθώδεσι, Κέρνην τε νῆσον καὶ ἄλλους τόπους

---

[1] On θαυμάζειν see H. Berger (*Die geog. Frag. des Erat.*, p.
44) and C. Frick (Bursian's *Jahresb.* 1880, p. 552).

[2] πόντων, Kramer conjectures, for τόπων; C. Müller,
Forbiger, Tardieu, following.

[3] φήσας, A. Miller, for φησί; A. Vogel approving.

[4] οὐδενί, A. Miller, for οὐδέ; and μυθολογοῦντι, for μεθ' ὃ
λέγει ὅτι, for which Siebenkees' οἷον appears in the editions.

Arabian Gulf is a lake, and that Diotimus, the son of Strombichus, sailed, at the head of an embassy of the Athenians, from Cilicia up the Cydnus River to the Choaspes River, which flows by Susa, and reached Susa on the fortieth day; and Eratosthenes says that Damastes was told all this by Diotimus himself. And then, Eratosthenes adds, Damastes wonders whether it was really possible for the Cydnus River to cut across the Euphrates and the Tigris and to empty into the Choaspes.

2. Not only might one disapprove of Eratosthenes for telling such a story, but also for this reason : after admitting that the exact details about the seas were not yet known even in his own time, and although he bids us not to be too ready to accept the authority of people at haphazard, and although he gives at length the reasons why we should believe no one who writes mythical tales about the regions along the Euxine and the Adriatic, yet he himself accepted the authority of people at haphazard. So, for example, he believed that the Gulf of Issus is the most easterly point of the Mediterranean ; whereas the point at Dioscurias in the extreme corner of the Euxine Sea is farther east by almost three thousand stadia, even according to Eratosthenes himself, if we follow the reckoning by stadia which he gives. And when he describes the northernmost and extreme parts of the Adriatic Sea there is nothing fabulous about them from which he holds aloof. And he has also given credence to many fables about the regions beyond the Pillars of Heracles, mentioning an island named Cerne and other countries which are

175

C 48 ὀνομάζων τοὺς μηδαμοῦ νυνὶ δεικνυμένους, περὶ
ὧν μνησθησόμεθα καὶ ὕστερον. εἰπών τε τοὺς
ἀρχαιοτάτους πλεῖν μὲν[1] κατὰ λῃστείαν ἢ ἐμπορίαν, μὴ πελαγίζειν δέ, ἀλλὰ παρὰ γῆν, καθάπερ
τὸν Ἰάσονα, ὅνπερ καὶ μέχρι τῆς Ἀρμενίας καὶ
Μηδίας ἐκ τῶν Κόλχων στρατεῦσαι ἀφέντα τὰς
ναῦς, ὕστερόν φησι τὸ παλαιὸν οὔτε τὸν Εὔξεινον
θαρρεῖν τινα πλεῖν, οὔτε παρὰ Λιβύην καὶ Συρίαν
καὶ Κιλικίαν. εἰ μὲν οὖν τοὺς πάλαι τοὺς πρὸ
τῆς ἡμετέρας λέγει μνήμης, οὐδὲν ἐμοὶ μέλει περὶ
ἐκείνων λέγειν, οὔτ' εἰ ἔπλεον, οὔτ' εἰ μή. εἰ δὲ
περὶ τῶν μνημονευομένων, οὐκ ἂν ὀκνήσαι τις
εἰπεῖν ὡς οἱ παλαιοὶ μακροτέρας ὁδοὺς φανοῦνται
καὶ κατὰ γῆν καὶ κατὰ θάλατταν τελέσαντες τῶν
ὕστερον, εἰ χρὴ προσέχειν τοῖς λεγομένοις· οἷον
Διόνυσος καὶ Ἡρακλῆς καὶ αὐτὸς ὁ Ἰάσων, ἔτι δ'
οἱ ὑπὸ τοῦ ποιητοῦ λεγόμενοι, Ὀδυσσεὺς καὶ
Μενέλαος. καὶ Θησέα δὲ καὶ Πειρίθουν μακρὰς
εἰκός ἐστι στρατείας ὑπομείναντας καταλιπεῖν
δόξαν περὶ ἑαυτῶν ὡς εἰς Ἅιδου καταβάντας, τοὺς
δὲ Διοσκούρους ἐπιμελητὰς τῆς θαλάσσης λεχθῆναι καὶ σωτῆρας τῶν πλεόντων. ἥ τε Μίνω
θαλαττοκρατία θρυλεῖται καὶ ἡ Φοινίκων ναυτιλία,
οἳ καὶ τὰ ἔξω τῶν Ἡρακλείων στηλῶν ἐπῆλθον
καὶ πόλεις ἔκτισαν κἀκεῖ καὶ περὶ τὰ μέσα τῆς
Λιβύης παραλίας μικρὸν τῶν Τρωικῶν ὕστερον.
Αἰνείαν δὲ καὶ Ἀντήνορα καὶ Ἐνετοὺς καὶ ἁπλῶς

---

[1] μέν, Bernhardy, Groskurd, B. Niese, for καί; Forbiger,
A. Vogel, approving.

nowhere pointed out to-day—matters about which I shall speak later on. And although Eratosthenes has said that the earliest Greeks made voyages for the sake of piracy or of commerce, not, indeed, in the open sea, but along the coast—as did Jason, who actually abandoned his ships and, starting from the Colchians, penetrated as far as Armenia and Media —he says later on that in ancient times no one had the courage to sail on the Euxine Sea, or along Libya, Syria, or Cilicia. Now if by "the ancients" he means those who lived in the times of which we of to-day have no records, then I am in no wise concerned to speak about them, as to whether they made voyages or not. But if he means men who are mentioned in history, then one would not hesitate to affirm that the ancients will be shown to have made longer journeys, both by land and by sea, than have men of a later time, if we are to heed what tradition tells us: for instance, Dionysus, and Heracles, and Jason himself; and, again, Odysseus and Menelaus, whose stories are narrated by the poet. And again, it is doubtless because Theseus and Pirithous had the hardihood to make such long journeys as they made that they left behind them the reputation of having gone down to Hades, and that the Dioscuri were called "guardians of the sea" and "saviours of sailors." Again, the maritime supremacy of Minos is far-famed, and so are the voyages of the Phoenicians, who, a short time after the Trojan War, explored the regions beyond the Pillars of Heracles and founded cities both there and in the central parts of the Libyan sea-board. As to Aeneas, Antenor, and the Enetians, and, in a word,

τοὺς ἐκ τοῦ Τρωικοῦ πολέμου πλανηθέντας εἰς πᾶσαν τὴν οἰκουμένην ἄξιον μὴ τῶν παλαιῶν ἀνθρώπων νομίσαι; συνέβη γὰρ δὴ τοῖς τότε Ἕλλησιν ὁμοίως καὶ τοῖς βαρβάροις διὰ τὸν τῆς στρατείας χρόνον ἀποβαλεῖν τά τε ἐν οἴκῳ καὶ τῇ στρατείᾳ πορισθέντα· ὥστε μετὰ τὴν τοῦ Ἰλίου καταστροφὴν τούς τε νικήσαντας ἐπὶ λῃστείαν τραπέσθαι διὰ τὰς ἀπορίας, καὶ πολὺ μᾶλλον τοὺς ἡττηθέντας καὶ περιγενομένους ἐκ τοῦ πολέμου. καὶ δὴ καὶ πόλεις ὑπὸ τούτων πλεῖσται κτισθῆναι λέγονται κατὰ πᾶσαν τὴν ἔξω τῆς Ἑλλάδος παραλίαν, ἔστι δ᾽ ὅπου καὶ τὴν μεσόγαιαν.

3. Εἰπὼν δὲ καὶ αὐτός, ὁπόσον προὔβη τὰ τῆς οἰκουμένης εἰς γνῶσιν τοῖς μετ᾽ Ἀλέξανδρον καὶ κατ᾽ αὐτὸν ἤδη, μεταβέβηκεν ἐπὶ τὸν περὶ τοῦ σχήματος λόγον, οὐχὶ περὶ τοῦ τῆς οἰκουμένης, ὅπερ ἦν οἰκειότερον τῷ περὶ αὐτῆς λόγῳ, ἀλλὰ τοῦ τῆς συμπάσης γῆς· δεῖ μὲν γὰρ καὶ τούτου μνησθῆναι, μὴ ἀτάκτως δέ. εἰπὼν οὖν, ὅτι σφαιροειδὴς ἡ σύμπασα, οὐχ ὡς ἐκ τόρνου δέ, C 49 ἀλλ᾽ ἔχει τινὰς ἀνωμαλίας, ἐπιφέρει τὸ πλῆθος τῶν ἐν μέρει μετασχηματισμῶν αὐτῆς, οἳ συμβαίνουσιν ἔκ τε ὕδατος καὶ πυρὸς καὶ σεισμῶν καὶ ἀναφυσημάτων καὶ ἄλλων τοιούτων, οὐδ᾽ ἐνταῦθα τὴν τάξιν φυλάττων. τὸ μὲν γὰρ σφαιροειδὲς περὶ ὅλην τὴν γῆν ἀπὸ τῆς τοῦ ὅλου ἕξεως συμβαίνει, οἱ δὲ τοιοῦτοι μετασχηματισμοὶ τὴν

---

[1] See note 2, page 40.

the survivors of the Trojan War that wandered forth
into the whole inhabited world—is it proper not to
reckon them among the men of ancient times? For
it came about that, on account of the length of the
campaign, the Greeks of that time, and the barbarians as well, lost both what they had at home and
what they had acquired by the campaign; and so,
after the destruction of Troy, not only did the
victors turn to piracy because of their poverty, but
still more the vanquished who survived the war.
And, indeed, it is said that a great many cities were
founded by them along the whole sea-coast outside
of Greece, and in some places in the interior also.

3. Now after Eratosthenes has himself told what
great advances in the knowledge of the inhabited
world had been made not only by those who came
after Alexander but by those of Alexander's own
times, he passes to his discussion of the shape of the
world, not indeed of the inhabited world—which
would have been more appropriate to his discussion
of that subject—but of the earth as a whole; of
course, one must discuss that point too, but not out
of its proper place. And so, after he has stated
that the earth as a whole is spheroidal [1]—not spheroidal indeed as though turned by a sphere-lathe, but
that it has certain irregularities of surface—he proceeds to enumerate the large number of its successive
changes in shape—changes which take place as the
result of the action of water, fire, earthquakes,
volcanic eruptions, and other similar agencies; and
here too he does not preserve the proper order.
For the spheroidal shape that characterises the earth
as a whole results from the constitution of the universe, but such changes as Eratosthenes mentions do

μὲν ὅλην γῆν οὐδὲν ἐξαλλάττουσιν (ἐν γὰρ τοῖς μεγάλοις ἐναφανίζεται τὰ οὕτω μικρά), τῆς δὲ οἰκουμένης διαθέσεις ἑτέρας καὶ ἑτέρας τινὰς ἀπεργάζονται, καὶ τὰς προσεχεῖς αἰτίας ἄλλας καὶ ἄλλας ἔχουσι.

4. Μάλιστα δέ φησι ζήτησιν παρασχεῖν, πῶς ἐν δισχιλίοις καὶ τρισχιλίοις ἀπὸ θαλάττης σταδίοις κατὰ τὴν μεσόγαιαν ὁρᾶται πολλαχοῦ κόγχων καὶ ὀστρέων καὶ χηραμύδων πλῆθος καὶ λιμνοθάλατται, καθάπερ φησὶ περὶ τὸ ἱερὸν τοῦ Ἄμμωνος καὶ τὴν ἐπ᾽ αὐτὸ[1] ὁδὸν τρισχιλίων σταδίων οὖσαν· πολλὴν γὰρ εἶναι χύσιν ὀστρέων, ἅλας τε καὶ νῦν ἔτι εὑρίσκεσθαι πολλούς, ἀναφυσήματά τε θαλάττης εἰς ὕψος ἀναβάλλειν, πρὸς ᾧ καὶ ναυάγια θαλαττίων πλοίων δείκνυσθαι, ἃ ἔφασαν διά του[2] χάσματος ἐκβεβράσθαι, καὶ ἐπὶ στυλιδίων ἀνακεῖσθαι δελφῖνας ἐπιγραφὴν ἔχοντας Κυρηναίων θεωρῶν. ταῦτα δ᾽ εἰπὼν τὴν Στράτωνος ἐπαινεῖ δόξαν τοῦ φυσικοῦ, καὶ ἔτι Ξάνθου τοῦ Λυδοῦ. τοῦ μὲν Ξάνθου λέγοντος ἐπὶ Ἀρταξέρξου γενέσθαι μέγαν αὐχμόν, ὥστ᾽ ἐκλιπεῖν ποταμοὺς καὶ λίμνας καὶ φρέατα· αὐτόν τε ἰδεῖν[3] πολλαχῇ πρόσω ἀπὸ τῆς θαλάττης λίθους τε κογχυλιώδεις[4] καὶ ὄστρακα[5] κτενώδεα καὶ χηραμύδων τυπώματα καὶ λιμνοθάλατταν[6] ἐν Ἀρμενίοις καὶ Ματιηνοῖς καὶ ἐν Φρυγίᾳ τῇ κάτω,

---

[1] ἐπ᾽ αὐτό, A. Miller, for ἐπ᾽ αὐτῷ, and Cascorbi's ἐπ᾽ αὐτοῦ.

[2] διά του, Corais, for διὰ τοῦ.

[3] ἰδεῖν, Corais on the authority of ghno, for εἰδέναι; Cobet independently; Bernadakis, A. Vogel, approving.

[4] λίθους τε κογχυλιώδεις, the old reading of the editors on the authority of B is retained by Corais, for the λίθον τε καὶ κογχυλιώδη of 1A; Kramer, Meineke, Müller-Dübner, following, but omitting the καί.

not in any particular alter the earth as a whole (changes so insignificant are lost in great bodies), though they do produce conditions in the inhabited world that are different at one time from what they are at another, and the immediate causes which produce them are different at different times.

4. Eratosthenes says further that this question in particular has presented a problem : how does it come about that large quantities of mussel-shells, oyster-shells, scallop-shells, and also salt-marshes are found in many places in the interior at a distance of two thousand or three thousand stadia from the sea— for instance (to quote Eratosthenes) in the neighbourhood of the temple of Ammon and along the road, three thousand stadia in length, that leads to it ? At that place, he says, there is a large deposit of oyster-shells, and many beds of salt are still to be found there, and jets of salt-water rise to some height ; besides that, they show pieces of wreckage from seafaring ships which the natives said had been cast up through a certain chasm, and on small columns dolphins are dedicated that bear the inscription : "Of Sacred Ambassadors of Cyrene." Then he goes on to praise the opinion of Strato, the physicist, and also that of Xanthus of Lydia. In the first place he praises the opinion of Xanthus, who says that in the reign of Artaxerxes there was so great a drought that the rivers, lakes, and wells dried up ; that far from the sea, in Armenia, Matiene, and Lower Phrygia, he himself had often seen, in many places, stones in the shape of a bivalve, shells of the pecten order, impressions of scallop-shells, and a

---

⁵ ὄστρακα, Madvig, for τά.
⁶ λιμνοθάλατταν, Meineke, for λιμνοθάλασσαν.

ὧν ἕνεκα πείθεσθαι τὰ πεδία ποτὲ θάλατταν
γενέσθαι. τοῦ δὲ Στράτωνος ἔτι μᾶλλον ἁπτο-
μένου τῆς αἰτιολογίας, ὅτι φησὶν οἴεσθαι τὸν
Εὔξεινον μὴ ἔχειν πρότερον τὸ κατὰ Βυζάντιον
στόμα, τοὺς δὲ ποταμοὺς βιάσασθαι καὶ ἀνοῖξαι
τοὺς εἰς αὐτὸν ἐμβάλλοντας, εἶτ’ ἐκπεσεῖν τὸ
ὕδωρ εἰς τὴν Προποντίδα καὶ τὸν Ἑλλήσποντον.
τὸ δ’ αὐτὸ συμβῆναι καὶ περὶ τὴν καθ’ ἡμᾶς
θάλατταν· καὶ γὰρ ἐνταῦθα τὸν κατὰ Στήλας
ἐκραγῆναι πόρον, πληρωθείσης ὑπὸ τῶν ποταμῶν
τῆς θαλάττης, κατὰ δὲ τὴν ἔκρυσιν ἀνακαλυφθῆναι
τὰ τεναγώδη πρότερον. φέρει δ’ αἰτίαν, πρῶτον
μὲν ὅτι τῆς ἔξω θαλάττης καὶ τῆς ἐντὸς τοὔδαφος
ἕτερόν ἐστιν, ἔπειθ’ ὅτι καὶ νῦν ἔτι ταινία τις
ὕφαλος διατέτακεν ἀπὸ τῆς Εὐρώπης ἐπὶ τὴν
C 50 Λιβύην, ὡς ἂν μὴ μιᾶς οὔσης πρότερον τῆς τε
ἐντὸς καὶ τῆς ἐκτός. καὶ βραχύτατα μὲν εἶναι τὰ
περὶ τὸν Πόντον, τὸ δὲ Κρητικὸν καὶ Σικελικὸν
καὶ Σαρδῷον πέλαγος σφόδρα βαθέα. τῶν γὰρ
ποταμῶν πλείστων καὶ μεγίστων ῥεόντων ἀπὸ
τῆς ἄρκτου καὶ τῆς ἀνατολῆς, ἐκεῖνα μὲν ἰλύος
πληροῦσθαι, τὰ ἄλλα δὲ μένειν βαθέα. διὸ καὶ
γλυκυτάτην εἶναι τὴν Ποντικὴν θάλατταν, τάς τ’
ἐκρύσεις γίνεσθαι εἰς οὓς ἐγκέκλιται τόπους τὰ
ἐδάφη. δοκεῖν δὲ κἂν χωσθῆναι τὸν Πόντον ὅλον
εἰς ὕστερον, ἂν μένωσιν αἱ ἐπιρρύσεις τοιαῦται·
καὶ γὰρ νῦν ἤδη τεναγίζειν τὰ ἐν ἀριστερᾷ τοῦ
Πόντου, τόν τε Σαλμυδησσὸν καὶ τὰ καλούμενα

---

[1] Western side.   [2] See 7. 6. 1.

salt-marsh, and therefore was persuaded that these plains were once sea. Then Eratosthenes praises the opinion of Strato, who goes still further into the question of causes, because Strato says he believes the Euxine Sea formerly did not have its outlet at Byzantium, but the rivers which empty into the Euxine forced and opened a passage, and then the water was discharged into the Propontis and the Hellespont. The same thing, Strato says, happened in the Mediterranean basin also; for in this case the passage at the Pillars was broken through when the sea had been filled by the rivers, and at the time of the outrush of the water the places that had hitherto been covered with shoal-waters were left dry. Strato proposes as a cause of this, first, that the beds of the Atlantic and the Mediterranean are on different levels, and, secondly, that at the Pillars even at the present day a submarine ridge stretches across from Europe to Libya, indicating that the Mediterranean and the Atlantic could not have been one and the same formerly. The seas of the Pontus region, Strato continues, are very shallow, whereas the Cretan, the Sicilian, and the Sardinian Seas are very deep; for since the rivers that flow from the north and east are very numerous and very large, the seas there are being filled with mud, while the others remain deep; and herein also is the reason why the Pontus is sweetest, and why its outflow takes place in the direction of the inclination of its bed. Strato further says it is his opinion that the whole Euxine Sea will be silted up at some future period, if such inpourings continue; for even now the regions on the left side [1] of the Pontus are already covered with shoal waters; for instance, Salmydessus,[2] and

Στήθη ὑπὸ τῶν ναυτικῶν τὰ περὶ τὸν Ἴστρον καὶ
τὴν Σκυθῶν ἐρημίαν. τάχα δὲ[1] καὶ τὸ τοῦ Ἄμμωνος ἱερὸν πρότερον ἐπὶ τῆς θαλάττης ὂν ἐκρύσεως
γενομένης νῦν ἐν τῇ μεσογαίᾳ κεῖσθαι. εἰκάζει
τε τὸ μαντεῖον εὐλόγως ἐπὶ τοσοῦτον γενέσθαι
ἐπιφανές τε καὶ γνώριμον ἐπὶ θαλάττῃ ὄν· τόν τε
ἐπὶ πολὺ οὕτως ἐκτοπισμὸν ἀπὸ τῆς θαλάττης
οὐκ εὔλογον ποιεῖν τὴν νῦν οὖσαν ἐπιφάνειαν καὶ
δόξαν· τήν τε Αἴγυπτον τὸ παλαιὸν θαλάττῃ
κλύζεσθαι μέχρι τῶν ἑλῶν τῶν περὶ τὸ Πηλούσιον,
καὶ τὸ Κάσιον ὄρος καὶ τὴν Σιρβωνίδα λίμνην·
ἔτι γοῦν καὶ νῦν κατὰ τὴν Αἴγυπτον τῆς ἁλμυρίδος
ὀρυττομένης ὑφάμμους καὶ κογχυλιώδεις εὑρίσκεσθαι τοὺς βόθρους, ὡς ἂν τεθαλαττωμένης τῆς
χώρας καὶ τοῦ τόπου παντὸς τοῦ περὶ τὸ Κάσιον
καὶ τὰ Γέρρα καλούμενα τεναγίζοντος, ὥστε
συνάπτειν τῷ τῆς Ἐρυθρᾶς κόλπῳ· ἐνδούσης δὲ
τῆς θαλάττης ἀνακαλυφθῆναι, μεῖναι δὲ τὴν
Σιρβωνίδα λίμνην, εἶτ’ ἐκραγῆναι καὶ ταύτην,
ὥστε ἑλώδη γενέσθαι. ὡς δ’ αὔτως καὶ τῆς
καλουμένης Μοίριδος[2] λίμνης τοὺς αἰγιαλοὺς
αἰγιαλοῖς[3] θαλάττης μᾶλλον ἢ ποταμοῦ προσεοι-
κέναι. τὸ μὲν οὖν ἐπικλύζεσθαί ποτε πολὺ μέρος
τῶν ἠπείρων ἐπὶ καιρούς τινας καὶ πάλιν ἀνακα-
λύπτεσθαι δοίη τις ἄν· ὡς δ’ αὔτως καὶ τὸ τοῖς
ἐδάφεσιν ἀνώμαλον εἶναι τὴν γῆν ἅπασαν τὴν νῦν
ὕφαλον, καθάπερ γε νὴ Δία καὶ τὴν ἔξαλον,
ἐν ᾗ οἰκοῦμεν, τοσαύτας[4] δεχομένην, ὅσας αὐτὸς

[1] δέ, Corais, for δή.
[2] καλουμένης Μοίριδος, Corais, for Ἁλμυρίδος.
[3] αἰγιαλοῖς, Corais inserts, after αἰγιαλούς; Meineke following; C. Müller, A. Vogel, approving.
[4] τε, Meineke deletes, after τοσαύτας; A. Miller approving.

the land at the mouth of the Ister, which sailors
call "the Breasts," and the desert of Scythia[1];
perhaps too the temple of Ammon was formerly on
the sea, but is now situated in the interior because
there has been an outpouring of the sea. Strato
conjectures that the oracle of Ammon with good
reason became so distinguished and so well-known as
it is if it was situated on the sea, and that its
present position so very far from the sea gives no
reasonable explanation of its present distinction
and fame; and that in ancient times Egypt was
covered by the sea as far as the bogs about Pelusium,
Mt. Casius, and Lake Sirbonis; at all events, even
to-day, when the salt-lands in Egypt are dug up, the
excavations are found to contain sand and fossil-shells,
as though the country had been submerged beneath
the sea and the whole region round Mt. Casius and
the so-called Gerrha had once been covered with
shoal water so that it connected with the Gulf of the
Red Sea; and when the sea retired, these regions
were left bare, except that the Lake Sirbonis
remained; then the lake also broke through to the
sea, and thus became a bog. In the same way,
Strato adds, the beaches of the so-called Lake
Moeris[2] more nearly resemble sea-beaches than
river-banks. Now one may admit that a great part
of the continents was once covered by water for
certain periods and was then left bare again; and in
the same way one may admit also that the whole
surface of the earth now submerged is uneven, at the
bottom of the sea, just as we might admit, of course,
that the part of the earth above water, on which we
live, is subject to all the changes mentioned by

[1] See 7. 4. 5.　　[2] Birket-el-Kerun. See 17. 1. 35.

Ἐρατοσθένης εἴρηκε μεταβολάς· ὥστε πρός γε τὸν Ξάνθου λόγον οὐδὲν ἂν ἔχοι τις προσφέρειν ἄτοπον.

5. Πρὸς δὲ τὸν Στράτωνα λέγοιτ' ἄν, ὅτι πολλῶν αἰτίων ὄντων ἀφεὶς ταῦτα τὰ μὴ ὄντα αἰτιᾶται. πρώτην γὰρ αἰτίαν φησίν, ὅτι τῆς ἐντὸς θαλάττης καὶ τῆς ἐκτὸς οὐ ταὐτὸν τὸ ἔδαφος καὶ ὁ βυθός. πρὸς γὰρ τὸ μετεωρίζεσθαι ταύτην C 51 καὶ ταπεινοῦσθαι καὶ ἐπικλύζειν τόπους τινὰς καὶ ἀναχωρεῖν ἀπ' αὐτῶν οὐ τοῦτό ἐστιν αἴτιον, τὸ[1] ἄλλα καὶ ἄλλα ἐδάφη τὰ μὲν ταπεινότερα εἶναι τὰ δὲ ὑψηλότερα, ἀλλὰ τὸ αὐτὰ τὰ[2] ἐδάφη ποτὲ μὲν μετεωρίζεσθαι, ποτὲ δ' αὖ ταπεινοῦσθαι καὶ συνεξαίρειν ἢ συνενδιδόναι τὸ πέλαγος· ἐξαρθὲν μὲν γὰρ ἐπικλύσαι ἄν, ταπεινωθὲν δὲ ἀναδράμοι ἂν εἰς τὴν ἀρχαίαν κατάστασιν. εἰ γὰρ[3] οὕτω, δεήσει πλεονασμῷ τῆς θαλάττης αἰφνιδίῳ γενομένῳ τὴν ἐπίκλυσιν συμβαίνειν, καθάπερ ἐν ταῖς πλημμυρίσιν[4] ἢ ταῖς ἀναβάσεσι τῶν ποταμῶν, τοτὲ μὲν ἐπενεχθέντος ἑτέρωθεν, τοτὲ δ' αὐξηθέντος τοῦ ὕδατος. ἀλλ' οὔθ' αἱ αὐξήσεις ἀθρόαι καὶ αἰφνίδιοι οἰδαίνονται,[5] οὔθ' αἱ πλημμυρίδες τοσοῦτον ἐπιμένουσι χρόνον, οὐδ' ἄτακτοί εἰσιν, οὔτε κατὰ τὴν ἡμετέραν ἐπικλύζουσι θάλατταν, οὐδ' ὅπου ἔτυχε. λοιπὸν οὖν αἰτιᾶσθαι τὸ ἔδαφος

---

[1] τό, Corais inserts, before ἄλλα καὶ ἄλλα; Meineke following; C. Müller approving.

[2] αὐτὰ τά, Sterrett, for τὰ αὐτά.

[3] Sterrett deletes the οὐχ inserted by Kramer before οὕτω; Meineke, C. Müller, Forbiger, following Kramer.

[4] ἐν ταῖς πλημμυρίσιν, omitted by the type-setters in the edition of Kramer, and left uncorrected in the edition of Meineke. [5] οἰδαίνονται, C. Müller, for δύνανται.

Eratosthenes himself; and therefore, so far as the argument of Xanthes is concerned, one cannot bring against it any charge of absurdity.

5. Against Strato, however, one might urge that, although there are many real causes of these changes, he overlooks them and suggests causes that do not exist; for he says their primary cause is that the beds of the Mediterranean Sea and of the Atlantic Ocean are not on the same level, and that their depth is not the same. But I reply that the cause of the rising and the falling of the sea, of its inundation of certain tracts of country, and of its subsequent retirement from them, is not to be sought for in the varying levels of the beds of the sea, in that some are lower and others higher, but in the fact that the beds of the sea themselves sometimes rise, and, on the other hand, sometimes sink, and in the fact that the sea rises or recedes along with its beds; for when the sea is lifted up, it will overflow, and when it is lowered, it will subside to its former level. Indeed, if what Strato says is true, then the overflow will necessarily follow every sudden increase in the volume of the sea; for instance, at every high tide of the sea or whenever the rivers are at their flood— in the one case the water having been brought in from other parts of the sea, in the other case the volume of water having been increased. But neither do the increases from the rivers come on all at the same time and suddenly and thus cause a swelling of the sea, nor do the tides persist long enough to do so (they are not irregular, either), nor do they cause inundations either on the Mediterranean Sea or anywhere else. Therefore, it remains for us to find the cause in the floor of the sea, either that which under-

ἢ τὸ τῇ θαλάττῃ ὑποκείμενον ἢ τὸ ἐπικλυζόμενον,
μᾶλλον δὲ τὸ ὕφαλον. πολὺ γὰρ εὐκινητότερον
καὶ μεταβολὰς θάττους δέξασθαι δυνάμενον τὸ
ἔνυγρον· καὶ γὰρ τὸ πνευματικὸν τὸ πάντων τῶν
τοιούτων αἴτιον πλέον ἐνταῦθα. ἀλλ᾽, ὡς ἔφην,
τῶν τοιούτων ἀπεργαστικόν ἐστι παθῶν τὸ αὐτὰ
τὰ¹ ἐδάφη ποτὲ μὲν ἐξαίρεσθαι ποτὲ δὲ ὑφίζησιν
λαμβάνειν, οὐ τὸ τὰ μὲν εἶναι ὑψηλὰ τὰ δὲ ἥττον·
ὁ δὲ τοῦτο λαμβάνει, νομίζων ὅπερ ἐπὶ τῶν
ποταμῶν συμβαίνει, τοῦτο καὶ ἐπὶ τῆς θαλάττης
ἀπαντᾶν, τὸ ἀπὸ τῶν μετεώρων τόπων εἶναι τὴν
ῥύσιν. οὐδὲ γὰρ ἂν τοῦ κατὰ Βυζάντιον ῥοῦ τὸ
ἔδαφος ᾐτιᾶτο, λέγων ὑψηλότερον τὸ τοῦ Εὐξείνου
ἢ τὸ τῆς Προποντίδος καὶ τοῦ ἑξῆς πελάγους, ἅμα
καὶ αἰτίαν προστιθείς· ἀπὸ γὰρ τῆς ἰλύος τῆς
ἀπὸ τῶν ποταμῶν καταφερομένης πληροῦσθαι
τὸν βυθὸν καὶ βραχὺν γίνεσθαι, διὰ τοῦτο δὲ καὶ
ῥεῖν εἰς τὰ ἐκτός. τὸν δ᾽ αὐτὸν λόγον καὶ ἐπὶ τὴν
ἡμετέραν θάλατταν σύμπασαν μεταφέρει πρὸς
τὴν ἐκτός, ὡς καὶ ταύτης μετεωρότερον τοὔδαφος
ποιούσης τοῦ ὑποκειμένου τῷ Ἀτλαντικῷ πελάγει·
καὶ γὰρ αὕτη ἐκ πολλῶν ποταμῶν πληροῦται,
καὶ τὴν ὑποστάθμην τῆς ἰλύος δέχεται τὴν ἀνάλογον. ἐχρῆν οὖν καὶ τὸν εἴσρουν ὅμοιον γίνεσθαι
τῷ κατὰ Βυζάντιον τὸν κατὰ Στήλας καὶ τὴν
Κάλπην. ἀλλὰ τοῦτο μὲν ἐῶ· ἐροῦσι γὰρ κἀκεῖ

¹ αὐτὰ τά, Sterrett restores, the reading of the MSS.,
against the τὰ αὐτά of Corais and subsequent editors.

¹ The Rock of Gibraltar. See 3. 5. 5.
² That is, the current of the Mediterranean should be
toward the Atlantic just as that of the Euxine is toward

lies the sea or that which is temporarily flooded, but
preferably the submarine floor. For the floor that is
saturated with water is far more easily moved and is
liable to undergo more sudden changes; for the air-
element, which is the ultimate cause of all such
occurrences, is greater there. But, as I have said,
the immediate cause of such occurrences is that the
beds of the sea themselves are sometimes elevated
and sometimes undergo a settling process, and not
that some of the beds are high, while others are less
so. Strato, however, assumes this, believing that
what happens in the case of rivers occurs also in the
case of the sea, namely, that the flow is away from
the high places; otherwise, he would not have
suggested that the bed is the cause of the current at
Byzantium, saying that the bed of the Euxine is
higher than that of the Propontis and the sea next
after the Propontis, and at the same time adding
the reason, namely, that the deeps of the Euxine are
being filled up by the mud which is carried down
from the rivers, and are becoming shallow, and that,
on this account, the current is outward. He applies
the same reasoning to the Mediterranean Sea as a
whole as compared with the Atlantic Ocean, since,
in his opinion, the Mediterranean Sea is making its
bed higher than that which lies beneath the Atlantic
Ocean; for the Mediterranean Sea, too, is being
filled up with silt from many rivers, and is receiving
a deposit of mud similar to that of the Euxine Sea.
It should also be true, then, that the inflow at the
Pillars and Calpe[1] is similar to the inflow at
Byzantium.[2] But I pass this point by, for people

the Aegean, and the amount of the two inflows should be
proportional to the deposits received.

τοῦτο συμβαίνειν, περισπᾶσθαι δὲ ὑπὸ τῶν ἀμπώτεων καὶ τῶν πλημμυρίδων καὶ ἐπικρύπτεσθαι.

6. Ἐκεῖνο δὲ πυνθάνομαι, τί ἐκώλυε, πρὶν
ἀνεῳγέναι τὸ στόμα τὸ κατὰ Βυζάντιον, ταπεινότερον ὂν τὸ τοῦ Εὐξείνου ἔδαφος τοῦ τῆς Προ-
C 52 ποντίδος καὶ τῆς ἑξῆς θαλάττης πληρωθῆναι
ὑπὸ τῶν ποταμῶν, εἴτε θάλατταν οὖσαν καὶ
πρότερον εἴτε λίμνην μείζω τῆς Μαιώτιδος; εἰ
γὰρ τοῦτο συγχωροῖτο, προσερήσομαι καὶ τοῦτο·
ἆρά γε ἡ ἐπιφάνεια τοῦ ὕδατος ἐκείνου καὶ τοῦ
τῆς Προποντίδος οὐχ οὕτως εἶχεν, ὥστε, μέχρι
μὲν ἡ αὐτὴ ἦν, μὴ βιάζεσθαι πρὸς ἔκρυσιν διὰ
τὴν ἐξ ἴσης ἀντέρεισιν καὶ θλῖψιν, ἐπειδὴ δὲ
ὑπερεπόλασεν ἡ ἐντός, βιάσασθαι καὶ ἀπερᾶσαι
τὸ πλεονάζον· ἐκ δὲ τούτου γενέσθαι σύρρουν τὸ
ἔξω πέλαγος τῷ ἐντός, καὶ τὴν αὐτὴν ἐπιφάνειαν
ἐκείνῳ λαβεῖν, εἴτε θαλαττίῳ εἴτε λιμναίῳ μὲν
πρότερον ὄντι, θαλαττίῳ δὲ ὕστερον, διὰ τὴν μίξιν
καὶ τὴν ἐπικράτειαν; εἰ γὰρ καὶ τοῦτο δώσουσιν,
ἡ μὲν ἔκρυσις οὐκ ἂν κωλύοιτο ἡ νῦν, οὐκ ἀπὸ
ὑπερτέρου δὲ ἐδάφους οὐδὲ ἐπικλινοῦς, ὅπερ ἠξίου
Στράτων.

7. Ταῦτα δὲ δεῖ[1] μεταφέρειν καὶ ἐπὶ τὴν ὅλην
τὴν καθ᾽ ἡμᾶς θάλατταν καὶ τὴν ἐκτός, μὴ ἐν τοῖς
ἐδάφεσι καὶ ταῖς ἐπικλίσεσιν αὐτῶν τὴν αἰτίαν
τοῦ ἔκρου τιθεμένους, ἀλλ᾽ ἐν τοῖς ποταμοῖς· ἐπεὶ

---

[1] δεῖ, Corais inserts; Groskurd, Meineke, Forbiger,
Dübner-Müller, following; A. Vogel, L. Kayser, approving.

will say that the same thing does occur here, but that the inflow is lost in the ebb and flow of the tides and thus escapes observation.

6. But what I wish to learn is this: supposing the bed of the Euxine Sea was lower[1] than that of the Propontis and of the sea next after the Propontis before the opening of the outlet at Byzantium, what was there to prevent the Euxine from being filled up by the rivers, whether it was previously a sea or merely a lake greater than Lake Maeotis? If this point be conceded, then I shall go on to ask this question too: Is it not true that the water-levels of the Euxine and the Propontis were such that, so long as they remained the same, there could be no straining for an outflow, for the reason that resistance and pressure were equal, but that, as soon as the inner sea reached a higher level, it set up a strain and discharged its excess water? And is not this the reason why the outer sea became confluent with the inner sea and why it assumed the same level as the inner sea— regardless of whether the latter was originally a sea or once a lake and later a sea—simply because of its mingling with the inner sea and prevailing over it? For if this point be granted as well as the first, the outflow that now takes place would go on just the same, but it would not be away from a higher sea-bed, or from a sloping one, as Strato contended.

7. Now we must apply these principles to the whole of the Mediterranean Sea and to the Atlantic Ocean, finding the cause of the outflow not in their beds, nor in the sloping of their beds, but in the rivers. For according to Strato and

---

[1] Strabo has assumed (§ 4 preceding) that the bed was higher.

οὐκ ἀπίθανον κατ' αὐτούς, οὐδ' εἰ τὴν ὅλην θάλατταν τὴν ἡμετέραν λίμνην πρότερον εἶναι
συνέβαινε, πληρουμένην ὑπὸ τῶν ποταμῶν, ἐπι-
πολάσασαν ἐκπεσεῖν ἔξω διὰ τῶν κατὰ Στήλας
στενῶν, ὡς ἐκ καταράκτου· ἐπαυξομένην δ' ἀεὶ
καὶ μᾶλλον ἐκείνην[1] τὴν θάλατταν σύρρουν
γενέσθαι ὑπ' αὐτῆς τῷ χρόνῳ καὶ συνδραμεῖν εἰς
μίαν ἐπιφάνειαν, ἐκθαλαττωθῆναι δὲ ταύτην[2] διὰ
τὴν ἐπικράτειαν. οὐ φυσικὸν δ' ὅλως τὸ[3] τοῖς
ποταμοῖς εἰκάζειν τὴν θάλατταν· οἱ μὲν γὰρ
φέρονται κατὰ ἐπικλινὲς ῥεῖθρον, ἡ δὲ ἀκλινὴς
ἕστηκεν. οἱ δὲ πορθμοὶ ῥευματίζονται κατ' ἄλλον
τρόπον, οὐ διὰ τὸ τὴν ἰλὺν τὴν ἐκ τῶν ποταμῶν
προσχοῦν τὸν τοῦ πελάγους βυθόν. ἡ γὰρ
πρόσχωσις περὶ αὐτὰ συνίσταται τὰ στόματα
τῶν ποταμῶν, οἷον περὶ μὲν τὰ τοῦ Ἴστρου τὰ
λεγόμενα Στήθη καὶ ἡ Σκυθῶν ἐρημία καὶ ὁ
Σαλμυδησσός, καὶ ἄλλων χειμάρρων συνεργούντων
πρὸς τοῦτο, περὶ δὲ τὰ τοῦ Φάσιδος ἡ Κολχικὴ
παραλία, δίαμμος καὶ ταπεινὴ καὶ μαλακὴ οὖσα,
περὶ δὲ τὸν Θερμώδοντα καὶ τὸν Ἴριν ὅλη Θεμί-
σκυρα, τὸ τῶν Ἀμαζόνων πεδίον, καὶ τῆς Σιδηνῆς
τὸ πλέον· οὕτω δὲ καὶ ἐπὶ τῶν ἄλλων. ἅπαντες
γὰρ μιμοῦνται τὸν Νεῖλον, ἐξηπειροῦντες τὸν πρὸ
αὐτῶν πόρον, οἱ μὲν μᾶλλον, οἱ δὲ ἧττον· ἧττον
μὲν οἱ μὴ πολλὴν καταφέροντες τὴν ἰλύν, μᾶλλον
δὲ οἱ πολλήν τε καὶ μαλακόγειον χώραν ἐπιόντες
καὶ χειμάρρους δεχόμενοι πολλούς, ὧν ἐστι καὶ

[1] ἐκείνην, Forbiger inserts.
[2] ταύτην, Forbiger inserts; improving on Groskurd's
ἐκείνην.
[3] τό, Corais, for οὔτε; Groskurd, Meineke, Forbiger, following; C. Müller approving.

Eratosthenes, it is not improbable that our whole
Mediterranean Sea (even granting that in former
times it was a lake) became flooded by the rivers,
overflowed, and poured its waters out through the
narrows at the Pillars as over a waterfall; and that
the Atlantic Ocean, swollen ever more and more,
was finally made confluent by it, and united with it
on one sea-level; and that thus the Mediterranean
basin was turned into a sea because the Atlantic
prevailed over it. It is wholly contrary to physical
science,[1] however, to liken the sea to rivers; for the
rivers are carried down a sloping course, whereas
the sea has no slope. But the current through the
straits is accounted for by another principle, and is not
due to the fact that the mud carried down by the
rivers silts up the deeps of the sea. For this silting
up occurs only at the very mouths of the rivers, as
for example the so-called "Breasts" at the mouth
of the Ister, the Scythian desert, and Salmydessus—
where other violent streams also contribute to this
result; and, at the mouths of the Phasis, the Colchian
seaboard, which is sandy, low-lying and soft; and, at
the mouths of the Thermodon and the Iris, the
whole of Themiscyra, that plain of the Amazons,
and the most of Sidene. The same is true of the
other rivers also; for they all imitate the Nile in
that they keep converting the channel just in front
of them into land, some to a greater and others to a
less extent; to a less extent those that do not bring
down much mud, but to a greater extent those that
flow for a great distance through a country with a soft
soil and have many torrents as tributaries. To the

[1] On page 181 Strabo has referred to Strato as "the
physicist."

ὁ Πύραμος ὁ τῇ Κιλικίᾳ πολὺ μέρος προσθείς, ἐφ'
οὗ καὶ λόγιον ἐκπέπτωκέ τι τοιοῦτον·

C 53   ἔσσεται ἐσσομένοις, ὅτε Πύραμος ἀργυροδίνης[1]
ἠϊόνα προχόων[2] ἱερὴν ἐς Κύπρον ἵκηται.

ἐκ μέσων γὰρ τῶν τῆς Καταονίας πεδίων ἐνεχθεὶς
πλωτὸς καὶ διεκπαισάμενος διὰ τῶν τοῦ Ταύρου
στενῶν εἰς τὴν Κιλικίαν ἐκδίδωσιν εἰς τὸν πρὸ
ταύτης τε καὶ τῆς Κύπρου πόρον.

8. Αἴτιον δὲ τοῦ μὴ φθάνειν τὴν χοῦν εἰς τὸ
πέλαγος προϊοῦσαν τὴν ὑπὸ τῶν ποταμῶν κατα-
φερομένην τὸ τὴν θάλατταν ἀνακόπτειν αὐτὴν
εἰς τοὐπίσω, παλιρροοῦσαν φύσει. ἔοικε γὰρ τοῖς
ζῴοις, καὶ καθάπερ ἐκεῖνα συνεχῶς ἀναπνεῖ τε
καὶ ἐκπνεῖ, τὸν αὐτὸν τρόπον καὶ αὐτὴ ἐξ αὑτῆς
τε καὶ εἰς ἑαυτὴν συνεχῶς παλινδρομικήν τινα
κινουμένη κίνησιν. δῆλον[3] δὲ τῷ ἐπὶ τοῦ αἰγιαλοῦ
ἑστῶτι κατὰ τὴν κυμάτωσιν· ἅμα γὰρ κλύζονται
οἱ πόδες καὶ γυμνοῦνται καὶ πάλιν κλύζονται,
καὶ τοῦτο συνεχῶς. τῷ δὲ κλύδωνι καὶ κῦμα
ἐπιτρέχει, ὅ,[4] κἂν γαληνότατον ᾖ, ἐπιφερόμενον
ἔχει τινὰ βίαν πλείω, καὶ ἀπορρίπτει πᾶν τὸ
ἀλλότριον εἰς τὴν γῆν,

πολλὸν δὲ παρὲξ ἅλα φῦκος ἔχευε.   (Il. 9. 7)

μᾶλλον μὲν οὖν ἐν ἀνέμῳ συμβαίνει τοῦτο, ἀλλὰ

---

[1] ἀργυροδίνης, Meineke, for εὐρυοδίνης ; C. Müller, L. Kayser,
approving   [2] προχόων, Sterrett, for προχέων.
[3] δῆλον, Casaubon, for δηλοῖ ; Siebenkees, Corais, Meineke,
Forbiger, following ; C. Müller, L. Kayser, approving.
[4] ὅ, Casaubon inserts, after ἐπιτρέχει ; Groskurd, Meineke,
Forbiger, following ; Corais, C. Müller, approving.

latter class belongs the Pyramus, which has added much land to Cilicia, and it is to this fact that the following oracle refers: "Men that are yet to be will experience this at the time when the Pyramus of the silvery eddies shall silt up its sacred sea-beach and come to Cyprus." The Pyramus, making its course as a navigable stream from the midst of the plains of Cataonia, and then breaking a passage for itself into Cilicia through the gorges of the Taurus Mountains, empties into the strait that lies between Cilicia and Cyprus.

8. Now the reason why the alluvium brought down by the rivers does not reach the open sea in its forward course[1] is that the sea, which is naturally refluent, drives it back again ; for the sea is like animated beings, and, just as they inhale and exhale their breath unremittingly, so in like manner the sea too is subject to a certain recurrent motion that proceeds from itself and returns to itself unremittingly. This is apparent to any one who stands on the beach at the time when the waves break ; for no sooner are one's feet washed than they are left bare by the waves, and then again they are washed, and this goes on unremittingly. And close upon the wash comes a wave also, which, however gentle it may be, possesses a certain increase of power as it rushes in, and casts all foreign matter out upon the land—" and casteth much tangle out along the sea." Now while this takes place to a greater extent when there is wind, yet it occurs

---

[1] It has to prepare the way for itself gradually. The following illustration concerning the action of the *waves* does not mean that the alluvium cannot eventually build its way over the whole bottom of the sea—a possibility admitted by Strabo in § 9.

καὶ ἐν νηνεμίᾳ καὶ ἐν ἀπογαίοις πνεύμασιν· οὐδὲν
γὰρ ἧττον ἐπὶ γῆν φέρεται τὸ κῦμα ὑπεναντίως
τῷ ἀνέμῳ, ὡς ἂν ἰδίαν τινὰ τῆς θαλάττης κίνησιν
συγκινούμενον αὐτῇ.   Τοιοῦτον δὲ καὶ τὸ

ἀμφὶ δέ τ᾽ ἄκρας
κυρτὸν ἐὸν κορυφοῦται, ἀποπτύει δ᾽ ἁλὸς ἄχ-
νην·   (Π. 4. 425)

καὶ τὸ

ἠϊόνες βοόωσιν ἐρευγομένης ἁλὸς ἔξω.[1]   (Π.17.265)

9. Ἡ μὲν οὖν ἔφοδος τοῦ κύματος ἔχει τινὰ
βίαν, ὥστ᾽ ἀπωθεῖσθαι τὸ ἀλλότριον.   καὶ δὴ καὶ
κάθαρσίν τινα τῆς θαλάττης ταύτην φασί, καθ᾽
ἣν καὶ τὰ νεκρὰ σώματα καὶ τὰ ναυάγια εἰς γῆν
ἐκκυμαίνεται. ἡ δ᾽[2] ἀναχώρησις οὐκ ἔχει τοσαύτην βίαν, ὥστε νεκρὸν ἢ ξύλον ἢ τὸ κουφότατον,
φελλόν, ὑπὸ τοῦ κύματος εἰς γῆν ἀναβληθέντα
ἐκ τῶν πλησίον αὐτῆς τόπων εἰς τὸ πέλαγος
προπεσεῖν ὑπολειφθέντα ὑπὸ τοῦ κύματος.[3]   οὕτω
δὴ καὶ τὴν χοῦν καὶ τὸ σὺν αὐτῇ τεθολωμένον
ὕδωρ ἐκκυμαίνεσθαι συμβαίνει, καὶ τοῦ βάρους
ἅμα συνεργοῦντος, ὥστε θᾶττον κατενεχθῆναι
πρὸς τὴν γῆν κάτω, πρὶν εἰς τὸ πρόσω πελαγίσαι.
καὶ γὰρ ἡ τοῦ ποταμοῦ βία παύεται, μικρὸν
προελθοῦσα τοῦ στόματος.   οὕτω μὲν οὖν ἐνδέ-

---

[1] The words Τοιοῦτον . . . ἁλὸς ἔξω are deleted by Meineke
on the ground that they prove the contrary of what the
writer desires; C. Müller approving.

[2] δ᾽, Meineke, for τ᾽.

[3] The MSS. have ὥστε νεκρὸν . . . ὑπὸ τοῦ κύματος εἰς γῆν
ἀναβληθῆναι, οὕτω δὲ καὶ τῶν πλησίον αὐτῆς τόπων εἰς τὸ πέλαγος
προσπεσεῖν ὑποληφθέντων ὑπὸ τοῦ κύματος, without meaning.
Attempts at a reconstitution of the passage have been made

both when there is a calm and when the winds blow from the land; for the wave is carried to the land none the less even against the wind, as though it were subject, along with the sea itself, to the sea's own motion. This is what Homer means when he says: "And goeth with arching crest about the promontories, and speweth the foaming brine afar," and "The shores cry aloud as the salt sea belches forth."

9. Accordingly, the onset of the wave has a power sufficient to expel foreign matter. They call this, in fact, a "purging [1]" of the sea—a process by which dead bodies and bits of wreckage are cast out upon the land by the waves. But the ebb has not power sufficient to draw back into the deep sea a corpse, or a stick of wood, or even that lightest of substances, a cork (when once they have been cast by the wave upon the land) from the places on the shore that are near the sea, where they have been stranded by the waves. And so it comes about that both the silt and the water fouled by it are cast out by the waves, the weight of the silt coöperating with the wave, so that the silt is precipitated to the bottom near the land before it can be carried forward into the deep sea; in fact, even the force of the river ceases just a short distance beyond the mouth. So, then, it is possible

---

[1] *Catharsis*: commonly used of (1) the purification of the soul by sacrifice, or (2) the purging effect of tragedy upon the emotions, or (3) as a medical term for various bodily discharges.

---

by Kramer, Groskurd, Meineke, C. Müller, A. Miller, Madvig, and A. Vogel. That by A. Vogel has been adopted and placed into the text above. But none is really satisfactory.

χεται προσχωσθῆναι τὸ πέλαγος πᾶν, ἀπὸ τῶν αἰγιαλῶν ἀρξάμενον, ἂν συνεχεῖς ἔχῃ τὰς ἐκ τῶν ποταμῶν ἐπιρρύσεις. Τοῦτο δ' ἂν συμβαίη, κἂν τοῦ Σαρδονίου πελάγους βαθύτερον ὑποθώμεθα

C 54 τὸν Πόντον, ὅπερ λέγεται τῶν ἀναμετρηθέντων βαθύτατον, χιλίων που ὀργυιῶν, ὡς Ποσειδώνιός φησι.

10. Τὴν μὲν οὖν τοιαύτην αἰτιολογίαν ἧττον ἄν τις ἀποδέξαιτο· μᾶλλον δ' ἀπὸ τῶν φανερωτέρων καὶ τῶν καθ' ἡμέραν τρόπον τινὰ ὁρωμένων ἀναπτέον τὸν λόγον. καὶ γὰρ κατακλυσμοὶ . . .[1] καὶ σεισμοὶ καὶ ἀναφυσήματα καὶ ἀνοιδήσεις[2] τῆς ὑφάλου γῆς μετεωρίζουσι καὶ τὴν θάλατταν, αἱ δὲ συνιζήσεις ταπεινοῦσιν αὐτήν. οὐ γὰρ μύδροι μὲν ἀνενεχθῆναι δύνανται καὶ μικραὶ νῆσοι, μεγάλαι δ' οὔ· οὐδὲ νῆσοι μέν, ἤπειροι δ' οὔ. ὁμοίως δὲ καὶ συνιζήσεις καὶ μικραὶ καὶ μεγάλαι γένοιντ' ἄν, εἴπερ καὶ χάσματα καὶ καταπόσεις χωρίων καὶ κατοικιῶν, ὡς ἐπὶ Βούρας τε καὶ Βιζώνης καὶ ἄλλων πλειόνων, ὑπὸ σεισμοῦ γενέσθαι φασί· καὶ τὴν Σικελίαν οὐδέν τι μᾶλλον ἀπορρῶγα τῆς Ἰταλίας εἰκάζοι τις ἄν, ἢ ἀναβληθεῖσαν ὑπὸ τοῦ Αἰτναίου πυρὸς ἐκ βυθοῦ συμμεῖναι· ὡσαύτως δὲ καὶ τὰς Λιπαραίων νήσους καὶ Πιθηκούσσας.

[1] A. Miller points out that something has fallen out after or before κατακλυσμοί, because it is absurd to say κατακλυσμοὶ . . . μετεωρίζουσι καὶ τὴν θάλατταν, and the statement contradicts the argument of the paragraph above.

[2] ἀνοιδήσεις, Meineke, for ἀποιδήσεις; Forbiger, C. Müller, A. Miller, Tozer, following.

for the sea, beginning at its beaches, to be entirely
silted up, if it receives the inflow from the rivers
uninterruptedly. And this would be the result
even if we assume that the Euxine Sea is deeper
than the Sea of Sardinia, which is said to be the
deepest of all the seas that have been sounded—
about one thousand fathoms, as Poseidonius states.

10. However, one might be rather disinclined to
accept such an explanation, and so it is necessary for
me to bring my discussion into closer connection
with things that are more apparent to the senses
and that, so to speak, are seen every day. Now
deluges [as we have seen, are caused by upheavals
of the bed of the sea]; and earthquakes, volcanic
eruptions, and upheavals of the submarine ground
raise the sea, whereas the settling of the bed of
the sea lowers the sea. For it cannot be that
burning masses may be raised aloft, and small
islands, but not large islands; nor yet that islands
may thus appear, but not continents. And in a
similar way settlings in the bed of the sea, both
great ones and small, may also occur, if it be
true, as people say, that yawning abysses and en-
gulfments of districts and villages have been caused
by earthquakes—as happened in the case of Bura
and Bizone and several other places; and as for
Sicily, one might conjecture that it is not so much
a piece broken away from Italy as that it was cast
up from the deeps by the fire of Aetna and remained
there[1]; and the same is true both of the Lipari
Islands and the Pithecussae.

---

[1] But compare 6. 1. 6, where Strabo discusses this subject
again and leaves a different impression.

11. Ὁ δ᾽ οὕτως ἡδύς ἐστιν, ὥστε καὶ μαθη-
ματικὸς ὢν οὐδὲ τὴν Ἀρχιμήδους βεβαιοῖ δόξαν,
ὅτι φησὶν ἐκεῖνος ἐν τοῖς περὶ τῶν ὀχουμένων,
παντὸς ὑγροῦ καθεστηκότος καὶ μένοντος τὴν
ἐπιφάνειαν σφαιρικὴν εἶναι, σφαίρας ταὐτὸ κέν-
τρον ἐχούσης τῇ γῇ. ταύτην γὰρ τὴν δόξαν
ἀποδέχονται πάντες οἱ μαθημάτων πως ἁψά-
μενοι. ἐκεῖνος δὲ τὴν ἐντὸς θάλατταν, καίπερ
μίαν οὖσαν, ὥς φησιν, οὐ νομίζει ὑπὸ μίαν ἐπιφάνειαν τετάχθαι, ἀλλ᾽ οὐδ᾽ ἐν[1] τοῖς σύνεγγυς
τόποις. καὶ μάρτυράς γε τῆς τοιαύτης ἀμα-
θίας ἀρχιτέκτονας ἄνδρας ποιεῖται, καίτοι[2] τῶν
μαθηματικῶν καὶ τὴν ἀρχιτεκτονικὴν μέρος τῆς
μαθηματικῆς ἀποφηναμένων. φησὶ γὰρ καὶ Δη-
μήτριον διακόπτειν ἐπιχειρῆσαι τὸν τῶν Πελοπον-
νησίων ἰσθμὸν πρὸς τὸ παρασχεῖν διάπλουν
τοῖς στόλοις, κωλυθῆναι δ᾽ ὑπὸ τῶν ἀρχιτεκτόνων
ἀναμετρησάντων καὶ ἀπαγγειλάντων μετεωροτέραν τὴν ἐν τῷ Κορινθιακῷ κόλπῳ θάλατταν τῆς
κατὰ Κεγχρεὰς εἶναι, ὥστε, εἰ διακόψειε τὸ
μεταξὺ χωρίον, ἐπικλυσθῆναι ἂν ἅπαντα τὸν
περὶ Αἴγιναν πόρον καὶ αὐτὴν τὴν[3] Αἴγιναν καὶ[4]
τὰς πλησίον νήσους, καὶ μηδὲ τὸν διάπλουν ἂν
γενέσθαι χρήσιμον. διὰ δὲ τοῦτο καὶ τοὺς εὐρί-

---

[1] ἐν, Corais inserts.
[2] καίτοι, Corais, for καί, following B and t.
[3] τὴν, Cobet inserts, before Αἴγιναν (Corais reads καὶ τὴν
Αἴγιναν, omitting αὐτήν, as in editions before Kramer).
[4] αὐτάς, before τάς, Kramer prefers to delete; Meineke
deletes; C. Müller approving.

11. But Eratosthenes is so simple that, although he is a mathematician, he will not even confirm the doctrine of Archimedes, who, in his treatise *On Floating Bodies* says that the surface of every liquid body at rest and in equilibrium is spherical, the sphere having the same centre as the earth[1]—a doctrine that is accepted by every one who has studied mathematics at all. And so, although Eratosthenes himself admits that the Mediterranean Sea is one continuous sea, yet he does not believe that it has been brought under a law of one continuous surface, even in places that lie close together. And as authorities for such an ignorant opinion as this he summons engineers, although the mathematicians have declared that engineering is a branch of mathematics. For he says that Demetrius, too, attempted to cut through the Isthmus of Corinth in order to provide a passage for his fleets, but was prevented by the engineers, after they had taken measurements and reported to him that the sea in the Corinthian Gulf was higher than at Cenchreae, so that, if he should cut through the intervening land, the whole strait about Aegina, Aegina itself, and the neighbouring islands would be submerged, and the canal would not be useful, either. And Eratosthenes says that this is the reason why the narrow straits have

---

[1] Chapter 1, Theorem 2: "Of every liquid body perfectly at rest, the surface is spheroidal and has the same centre as the earth." Archimedes says "spheroidal," and not "spherical" as Strabo quotes him; but Archimedes used his term in the literal and not the geometrical sense, and the term is equivalent to "spherical" when it is applied to "a liquid body perfectly at rest." Compare the use of "spheroidal" by Strabo himself on page 41.

πους ῥοώδεις εἶναι, μάλιστα δὲ τὸν κατὰ Σικελίαν
πορθμόν, ὅν φησιν ὁμοιοπαθεῖν ταῖς κατὰ τὸν
ὠκεανὸν πλημμυρίσι τε καὶ ἀμπώτεσι· δὶς [1] γὰρ
μεταβάλλειν τὸν ῥοῦν ἑκάστης ἡμέρας καὶ νυκτός,
καὶ [2] καθάπερ τὸν ὠκεανὸν δὶς μὲν πλημμυρεῖν,
C 55 δὶς δὲ ἀναχωρεῖν. τῇ μὲν οὖν πλημμυρίδι ὁμολογεῖν τὸν ἐκ τοῦ Τυρρηνικοῦ πελάγους εἰς τὸ
Σικελικὸν καταφερόμενον ὡς ἂν ἐκ μετεωροτέρας
ἐπιφανείας, ὃν δὴ καὶ κατιόντα ὀνομάζεσθαι,
ὁμολογεῖν δ' ὅτι καὶ κατὰ τὸν αὐτὸν καιρὸν
ἄρχεταί τε καὶ παύεται καθ' ὃν αἱ πλημμυρίδες·
ἄρχεται μὲν γὰρ περὶ τὴν ἀνατολὴν τῆς σελήνης
καὶ τὴν δύσιν, λήγει δ' ὅταν συνάπτῃ τῇ μεσου-
ρανήσει ἑκατέρα, τῇ τε ὑπὲρ γῆς καὶ τῇ ὑπὸ γῆς·
τῇ δὲ [3] ἀμπώτει τὸν ἐναντίον, ὃν [4] ἐξιόντα καλεῖσθαι, ταῖς μεσουρανήσεσι τῆς σελήνης ἀμφοτέραις
συναρχόμενον,[5] καθάπερ αἱ ἀμπώτεις, ταῖς δὲ
συνάψεσι ταῖς πρὸς τὰς ἀνατολὰς καὶ δύσεις
παυόμενον.

12. Περὶ μὲν οὖν τῶν πλημμυρίδων καὶ τῶν
ἀμπώτεων εἰρήκασιν ἱκανῶς Ποσειδώνιός τε καὶ
Ἀθηνόδωρος· περὶ δὲ τῆς τῶν πορθμῶν παλιρροίας, ἐχόντων καὶ αὐτῶν φυσικώτερον λόγον ἢ [6]
κατὰ τὴν νῦν ὑπόθεσιν, τοσοῦτον εἰπεῖν ἀπόχρη,
ὅτι οὔθ' [7] εἷς τρόπος τοῦ ῥοώδεις εἶναι τοὺς

---

[1] τε, Meineke deletes, before γάρ ; C. Müller approving.
[2] καί, Corais inserts, before καθάπερ.
[3] δέ, Corais, for τε ; Groskurd, following ; C. Müller
approving.   [4] ὅν, Corais inserts ; all following.
[5] συναρχόμενον, Madvig, for ἐναρχόμενον.
[6] ἤ, Corais inserts, before κατά, and punctuates after
ὑπόθεσιν ; Meineke following ; C. Müller approving.
[7] οὔθ', Corais, for οὐδέ ; Meineke, C. Müller, approving.

strong currents, and in particular the strait off
Sicily, which, he declares, behaves in a manner
similar to the flow and the ebb of the ocean; for
the current changes twice within the course of
every day and night, and like the ocean, it floods
twice a day and falls twice a day. Now corresponding to the flood-tide, he continues, is the
current that runs down from the Tyrrhenian Sea
to the Sicilian Sea as though from a higher water-
level—and indeed this is called the "descending"
current—and this current corresponds to the flood-
tides in that it begins and ends at the same time
that they do, that is, it begins at the time of the
rising and the setting of the moon, and it stops
when the moon attains either meridian, namely,
the meridian above the earth or that below the
earth; on the other hand, corresponding to the
ebb-tide is the return-current—and this is called
the "ascending" current—which begins when the
moon attains either meridian, just as the ebbs do,
and stops when the moon attains the points of her
rising and setting.

12. Now Poseidonius and Athenodorus have satisfactorily treated the question of the flow and ebb
of the tides; but concerning the refluent currents
of straits, which also involve a discussion that goes
deeper into natural science than comports with the
purpose of the present work, it is sufficient to say
that neither does one principle account for the
straits' having currents, the principle by which

πορθμούς, ὅ γε κατ᾽ εἶδος· οὐ γὰρ ἂν ὁ μὲν
Σικελικὸς δὶς ἑκάστης ἡμέρας μετέβαλλεν, ὡς
οὗτός φησιν, ὁ δὲ Χαλκιδικὸς ἑπτάκις, ὁ δὲ κατὰ
Βυζάντιον οὐδὲ μετέβαλλεν, ἀλλὰ διετέλει τὸν
ἔκρουν μόνον ἔχων τὸν ἐκ τοῦ Ποντικοῦ πελάγους
εἰς τὴν Προποντίδα, ὡς δὲ Ἵππαρχος ἱστορεῖ, καὶ
μονάς ποτε ἐποιεῖτο· οὔτ᾽ εἰ τρόπος εἷς εἴη, ταύτην
ἂν ἔχοι τὴν αἰτίαν, ἥν φησιν ὁ Ἐρατοσθένης, ὅτι
ἡ ἐφ᾽ ἑκάτερα θάλαττα ἄλλην καὶ ἄλλην ἐπιφάνειαν ἔχει· οὐδὲ γὰρ ἐπὶ τῶν ποταμῶν τοῦτο
γένοιτ᾽ ἄν, εἰ μὴ καταράκτας ἔχοιεν· ἔχοντες δὲ
οὐ παλιρροοῦσιν, ἀλλ᾽ ἐπὶ τὸ ταπεινότερον ἀεὶ
φέρονται. καὶ τοῦτο δὲ συμβαίνει διὰ τὸ κεκλι-
μένον εἶναι τὸ ῥεῦμα καὶ τὴν ἐπιφάνειαν αὐτοῦ.
πελάγους δὲ τίς ἂν φαίη κεκλιμένην ἐπιφάνειαν;
καὶ μάλιστα κατὰ τὰς σφαιροποιούσας ὑποθέσεις
τὰ τέτταρα σώματα, ἃ δὴ καὶ στοιχεῖα φαμέν.
ὥστ᾽ οὐχ ὅτι παλιρροοῦντας, ἀλλ᾽ οὐδὲ καθεστῶ-
τας καὶ μένοντας, συρροίας μὲν ἐν αὐτοῖς οὔσης,
μὴ μιᾶς δὲ ἐπιφανείας, ἀλλὰ τῆς μὲν ὑψηλοτέρας,
τῆς δὲ ταπεινοτέρας.[1] οὐ γὰρ ὥσπερ ἡ γῆ κατὰ
ἕξιν ἐσχημάτισται στερεὰ οὖσα, ὥστε καὶ κοι-
λάδας ἔχειν συμμενούσας καὶ ἀναστήματα, οὕτω
καὶ τὸ ὕδωρ, ἀλλ᾽ αὐτῇ τῇ κατὰ τὸ βάρος ῥοπῇ τὴν

---

[1] The editors transfer ὥστ᾽ οὐχ . . . ταπεινοτέρας to a position before πελάγους. Jones follows both reading and order
of the MSS.

they are classified as straits (for if that were the
case, the Strait of Sicily would not be changing its
current twice a day, as Eratosthenes says it does,
but the strait of Chalcis seven times a day, while
the strait at Byzantium makes no change at all
but continues to have its outflow only from the
Pontus into the Propontis, and, as Hipparchus reports,
even stands still sometimes), nor, if one principle
should account for the currents, would the cause
be what Eratosthenes alleges it to be, namely, that
the two seas on the sides of a strait have different
levels. Indeed this would not be the case with the
rivers either, except when they have cataracts;
but since they have cataracts, they are not refluent,
but run continuously toward the lower level. And
this, too, results on account of the fact that the
stream and its surface are inclined. But who would
say that a sea-surface is inclined? And particularly
in view of the hypotheses by which the four bodies
(which, of course, we also call "elements"[1]) are
made spheres. And so not only is a strait not
refluent, but it is also not subject to standing still
without any current at all, since, although there is a
confluence therein of two seas, yet there is not
merely one level, but two of them, one higher, the
other lower. The case of the water, indeed, is not
the same as that of the earth, which, being solid
in character, has taken shape accordingly; and
therefore it has hollows that keep their shape, and
elevations as well; but the water, through the mere

---

[1] A Pythagorean doctrine: "The bodies of the four elements" (water, earth, air, and fire) "are spherical, fire only
excepted, whose figure is conical" (Plutarch, *De Placitis
Philosophorum* 1. 14).

ὄχησιν ἐπὶ τῆς γῆς ποιεῖται, καὶ τοιαύτην λαμβάνει τὴν ἐπιφάνειαν, οἵαν ὁ Ἀρχιμήδης φησίν.

13. Ἐπιφέρει δὲ τοῖς περὶ τοῦ Ἄμμωνος καὶ
τῆς Αἰγύπτου ῥηθεῖσιν, ὅτι δοκοίη καὶ τὸ Κάσιον
ὄρος περικλύζεσθαι θαλάττῃ, καὶ πάντα τὸν
τόπον, ὅπου νῦν τὰ καλούμενα Γέρρα καθ᾽ ἕκαστα,[1]
τεναγίζειν συνάπτοντα τῷ τῆς Ἐρυθρᾶς κόλπῳ,
συνελθούσης δὲ τῆς θαλάττης ἀποκαλυφθῆναι.
τὸ δὴ τεναγίζειν τὸν λεχθέντα τόπον συνάπτοντα
C 56 τῷ τῆς Ἐρυθρᾶς κόλπῳ, ἀμφίβολόν ἐστιν· ἐπειδὴ
τὸ συνάπτειν σημαίνει καὶ τὸ σύνεγγυς καὶ
τὸ ψαύειν, ὥστε, εἰ ὕδατα εἴη, σύρρουν εἶναι
θάτερον θατέρῳ. ἐγὼ μὲν οὖν δέχομαι[2] τὸ
συνεγγίζειν τὰ τενάγη τῇ Ἐρυθρᾷ θαλάττῃ, ἕως
ἀκμὴν ἐκέκλειστο τὰ κατὰ τὰς Στήλας στενά,
ἐκραγέντων δὲ τὴν ἀναχώρησιν γενέσθαι, ταπεινω-
θείσης τῆς ἡμετέρας θαλάττης διὰ τὴν κατὰ τὰς
Στήλας ἔκρυσιν. Ἵππαρχος δὲ ἐκδεξάμενος τὸ
συνάπτειν ταὐτὸν τῷ σύρρουν γενέσθαι τὴν ἡμετέραν θάλατταν τῇ Ἐρυθρᾷ διὰ τὴν πλήρωσιν,
αἰτιᾶται τί δή ποτε οὐχὶ τῇ κατὰ τὰς Στήλας
ἐκρύσει μεθισταμένη ἐκεῖσε ἡ καθ᾽ ἡμᾶς θάλαττα
συμμεθίστα καὶ τὴν σύρρουν αὐτῇ γενομένην τὴν

---

[1] τέ, after ἕκαστα, Corais omits ; so Meineke.
[2] καί, Corais deletes, after δέχομαι ; A. Miller approving.

[1] A little town in Egypt between Pelusium and Mt.
Casius ; not the Arabian Gerrha.

influence of gravity, rides upon the earth and
assumes the sort of surface which Archimedes says it
does.

13. Eratosthenes adds to what he has said about
Ammon and Egypt his opinion that Mt. Casius
was once washed by the sea, and also that all the
region where the so-called Gerrha[1] now is, was in
every part covered with shoal-water since it was
connected with the gulf of the Red Sea, and that it
became uncovered when the seas[2] came together.
Now it is ambiguous to say that the region mentioned
was covered with shoal-water since it was connected
with the gulf of the Red Sea, for "to be connected
with" means either "to come near to" or "to touch";
so that, if we were referring to bodies of water, the
phrase would mean, in the latter sense, that one
body of water is confluent with another. My interpretation, however, is that the shoal-waters "came
near to" the Red Sea as long as the narrows at the
Pillars of Heracles were still closed, and that after
the narrows had been broken through, the retirement of the shoal-water took place because the level
of the Mediterranean Sea had been lowered by the
outflow at the Pillars. But Hipparchus, interpreting
the phrase "to be connected with" to be the same
thing as "to become confluent with," that is, that
our Mediterranean Sea "became confluent with"
the Red Sea because of its being filled up with
water, finds fault by asking why in the world it is
that, at the time when our Mediterranean Sea,
because of the outflow of its waters at the Pillars,
underwent its change in that direction, it did not
also cause the Red Sea, which had become confluent

[2] The Atlantic and the Mediterranean.

Ἐρυθράν, καὶ ἐν τῇ αὐτῇ διέμεινεν ἐπιφανείᾳ,
μὴ ταπεινουμένῃ· καὶ γὰρ κατ' αὐτὸν Ἐρατοσθένη τὴν ἐκτὸς θάλατταν ἅπασαν σύρρουν
εἶναι, ὥστε καὶ τὴν ἑσπέριον καὶ τὴν Ἐρυθρὰν
θάλατταν μίαν εἶναι. τοῦτο δ' εἰπὼν ἐπιφέρει
τὸ ἀκόλουθον, τὸ τὸ αὐτὸ ὕψος ἔχειν τήν τε ἔξω
Στηλῶν θάλατταν καὶ τὴν Ἐρυθρὰν καὶ ἔτι τὴν
ταύτῃ γεγονυῖαν σύρρουν.

14. Ἀλλ' οὔτ' εἰρηκέναι τοῦτό φησιν Ἐρατοσθένης, τὸ σύρρουν γεγονέναι κατὰ τὴν πλήρωσιν
τῇ Ἐρυθρᾷ, ἀλλὰ συνεγγίσαι μόνον, οὔτ'
ἀκολουθεῖν τῇ μιᾷ καὶ συνεχεῖ θαλάττῃ τὸ αὐτὸ
ὕψος ἔχειν καὶ τὴν αὐτὴν ἐπιφάνειαν, ὥσπερ
οὐδὲ τὴν καθ' ἡμᾶς, καὶ νὴ Δία τὴν κατὰ τὸ
Λέχαιον καὶ τὴν περὶ Κεγχρεάς. ὅπερ καὶ αὐτὸς
ὁ Ἵππαρχος ἐπισημαίνεται ἐν τῷ πρὸς αὐτὸν
λόγῳ· εἰδὼς οὖν τὴν δόξαν αὐτοῦ τοιαύτην ἰδίᾳ
τι πρὸς αὐτὸν λεγέτω, καὶ μὴ ἐξ ἑτοίμου
λαμβανέτω, ὡς ἄρα ὁ φήσας μίαν εἶναι τὴν ἔξω
θάλατταν σύμφησι καὶ ὅτι μία ἐστὶν αὐτῆς ἡ
ἐπιφάνεια.

15. Ψευδῆ δ' εἶναι φήσας τὴν ἐπὶ τοῖς δελφῖσιν
ἐπιγραφὴν Κυρηναίων θεωρῶν αἰτίαν ἀποδίδωσιν
οὐ πιθανήν, ὅτι ἡ μὲν τῆς Κυρήνης κτίσις ἐν
χρόνοις φέρεται μνημονευομένοις, τὸ δὲ μαντεῖον
οὐδεὶς μέμνηται ἐπὶ θαλάττῃ ποτὲ ὑπάρξαν. τί

---

[1] That is, the gulfs of Corinth and Aegina, west and east,
respectively, of the Isthmus of Corinth.
[2] That is at the oracle of Ammon. See page 181.
[3] The dolphin was to the Greeks the symbol of a seaport
town. It would seem to us that the ambassadors from
Cyrene set up the dolphin as a symbol of their own town,

with it, to make the same change, and why in the
world the Red Sea continued at the same level
instead of being lowered with the Mediterranean?
For, says he, even according to Eratosthenes himself
the whole exterior sea is confluent, and consequently
the western sea and the Red Sea form one sea.
After saying this, Hipparchus adds his corollary:
that the Sea outside the Pillars, the Red Sea, and
the Mediterranean Sea, too, which has become confluent with the Red Sea, all have the same level.

14. But Eratosthenes replies to this that he has not
said that the confluence with the Red Sea took place
at the time the Mediterranean Sea had become filled,
but merely that the Mediterranean Sea had come
near to it; and, besides, that it does not follow from
the notion of one continuous sea that it has the same
height and the same level—just as the Mediterranean
has not, and as most assuredly its waters at Lechaeum
and those about Cenchreae [1] have not. This very
point Hipparchus himself makes in his book against
Eratosthenes; since, then, he knows that such is the
opinion of Eratosthenes, let him give some argument
of his own against Eratosthenes, and let him not
assume off-hand that, forsooth, if a man says the
exterior sea is one, he at the same time affirms also
that its level is everywhere the same.

15. Again, when Hipparchus says that the inscription on the dolphins,[2] made by sacred ambassadors
of Cyrene, is false, he gives an unconvincing reason
when he says that although the founding of Cyrene
falls within historical times, yet no historian has
recorded that the oracle was ever situated on a sea.[3]

and that it had no bearing on the question whether or not
the oracle of Ammon was once on the seashore.

γὰρ εἰ μηδεὶς μὲν ἱστορεῖ, ἐκ δὲ τῶν τεκμηρίων,
ἐξ ὧν εἰκάζομεν παράλιόν ποτε τὸν τόπον γενέσθαι,
οἵ τε δελφῖνες ἀνετέθησαν καὶ ἡ ἐπιγραφὴ
ἐγένετο ὑπὸ Κυρηναίων θεωρῶν; συγχωρήσας δὲ
τῷ μετεωρισμῷ τοῦ ἐδάφους συμμετεωρισθεῖσαν
καὶ τὴν θάλατταν ἐπικλύσαι τοὺς μέχρι τοῦ
C 57   μαντείου τόπους, πλέον τι[1] ἀπὸ θαλάττης
διέχοντας τῶν τρισχιλίων σταδίων, οὐ συγχωρεῖ
τὸν μέχρι τοσούτου μετεωρισμόν, ὥστε καὶ τὴν
Φάρον ὅλην καλυφθῆναι καὶ τὰ πολλὰ τῆς
Αἰγύπτου, ὥσπερ οὐχ ἱκανοῦ ὄντος τοῦ τοσούτου
ὕψους καὶ ταῦτα ἐπικλύσαι. φήσας δέ, εἴπερ
ἐπεπλήρωτο ἐπὶ τοσοῦτον ἡ καθ' ἡμᾶς θάλαττα
πρὶν τὸ ἔκρηγμα τὸ κατὰ Στήλας γενέσθαι, ἐφ'
ὅσον εἴρηκεν ὁ Ἐρατοσθένης, χρῆναι καὶ τὴν
Λιβύην πᾶσαν καὶ τῆς Εὐρώπης τὰ πολλὰ καὶ
τῆς Ἀσίας κεκαλύφθαι πρότερον, τούτοις
ἐπιφέρει, διότι καὶ ὁ Πόντος τῷ Ἀδρίᾳ σύρρους
ἂν ὑπῆρξε κατά τινας τόπους, ἅτε δὴ τοῦ Ἴστρου
ἀπὸ τῶν κατὰ τὸν Πόντον τόπων σχιζομένου καὶ
ῥέοντος εἰς ἑκατέραν τὴν θάλατταν διὰ τὴν θέσιν
τῆς χώρας. ἀλλ' οὔτ' ἀπὸ τῶν κατὰ τὸν Πόντον
μερῶν ὁ Ἴστρος τὰς ἀρχὰς ἔχει, ἀλλὰ τἀναντία
ἀπὸ τῶν ὑπὲρ τοῦ Ἀδρίου ὀρῶν, οὔτ' εἰς ἑκατέραν
τὴν θάλατταν ῥεῖ, ἀλλ' εἰς τὸν Πόντον μόνον,
σχίζεταί τε πρὸς αὐτοῖς μόνον τοῖς στόμασι.
κοινὴν δέ τινα τῶν πρὸ αὐτοῦ τισιν ἄγνοιαν
ταύτην ἠγνόηκεν, ὑπολαβοῦσιν εἶναί τινα ὁμώνυμον τῷ Ἴστρῳ ποταμὸν ἐκβάλλοντα εἰς τὸν
Ἀδρίαν ἀπεσχισμένον αὐτοῦ, ἀφ' οὗ καὶ τὸ γένος

---

[1] τι, T. G. Tucker, for ἤ.

Well, what if no historian does record the fact, and yet, according to the evidence on which we base the conjecture that the region was once coast-land, the dolphins were in fact dedicated and the inscription was engraved by sacred ambassadors of Cyrene? Again, although Hipparchus has admitted that, along with the elevation of the bed of the sea, the sea itself was elevated, and that it inundated the country as far as the oracle, a distance of somewhat more than three thousand stadia from the sea, he does not admit the elevation of the sea to such a point that both the whole island of Pharos and the greater part of Egypt were covered—just as though so high an elevation of the sea were not sufficient to inundate these districts too! And again, after saying that if, before the outbreak of the waters at the Pillars took place, the Mediterranean Sea was really filled to such an extent as Eratosthenes has stated, the whole of Libya and the greater part of Europe and Asia must first have been covered, he adds thereto that the Pontus would then have been confluent with the Adriatic in some places, for the reason that the Ister,[1] as he supposes, branches off from the Pontus regions and thus flows into both seas, on account of the lie of the land. But neither does the Ister rise in the Pontus regions (on the contrary, it rises in the mountains above the Adriatic), nor does it flow into both seas, but into the Pontus alone, and it branches off near its mouths only. However, this mistake of Hipparchus is shared with him by some of his predecessors, who supposed that there was a river of the same name as the Ister, which branched off from it and emptied into the Adriatic, and that the tribe

[1] The Danube.

Ἴστρων,[1] δι' οὗ φέρεται, λαβεῖν τὴν προσηγορίαν, καὶ τὸν Ἰάσονα ταύτῃ ποιήσασθαι τὸν ἐκ τῶν Κόλχων ἀνάπλουν.

16. Πρὸς δὲ τὴν ἀθαυμαστίαν τῶν τοιούτων μετα-βολῶν, οἵας ἔφαμεν αἰτίας εἶναι τῶν ἐπικλύσεων καὶ τῶν τοιούτων παθῶν, οἷα εἴρηται τὰ κατὰ τὴν Σικελίαν καὶ τὰς Αἰόλου νήσους καὶ Πιθηκούσσας, ἄξιον παραθεῖναι καὶ ἄλλα πλείω τῶν ἐν ἑτέροις τόποις ὄντων ἢ γενομένων ὁμοίων τούτοις. ἀθρόα γὰρ τὰ τοιαῦτα παραδείγματα πρὸ ὀφθαλμῶν τεθέντα παύσει τὴν ἔκπληξιν. νυνὶ δὲ τὸ ἄηθες[2] ταράττει τὴν αἴσθησιν καὶ δείκνυσιν ἀπειρίαν τῶν φύσει συμβαινόντων καὶ τοῦ βίου παντός, οἷον εἴ τις λέγοι τὰ[3] περὶ Θήραν καὶ Θηρασίαν νήσους ἱδρυμένας ἐν τῷ μεταξὺ πόρῳ Κρήτης καὶ τῆς Κυρηναίας, ὧν ἡ Θήρα μητρόπολίς ἐστι τῆς Κυρήνης, καὶ τὴν Αἴγυπτον καὶ πολλὰ μέρη τοιαῦτα τῆς Ἑλλάδος. ἀνὰ μέσον γὰρ Θήρας καὶ Θηρασίας ἐκπεσοῦσαι φλόγες ἐκ τοῦ πελάγους ἐφ' ἡμέρας τέτταρας,[4] ὥστε πᾶσαν ζεῖν καὶ φλέγεσθαι τὴν θάλατταν, ἀνεφύσησαν κατ' ὀλίγον ἐξαιρο-μένην ὡς ἂν ὀργανικῶς καὶ συντιθεμένην ἐκ μύδρων νῆσον ἐπέχουσαν δώδεκα σταδίων τὴν περίμετρον.

---

[1] Ἴστρων, Meineke, for Ἴστρον.
[2] νυνὶ δὲ τὸ ἄηθες, Xylander, for νῦν εἰ δὲ τὸ ἀληθές ; editors following.
[3] τά, Groskurd, for τάς; Kramer, Forbiger, Meineke, following.
[4] τέτταρας, Meineke, for τέσσαρας.

of Istrians, through whose territory this Ister flows, got their appellation from it, and that it was by this route that Jason made his return voyage from the land of the Colchians.

16. Now, in order to promote the virtue of not marvelling[1] at such changes as I have declared to be responsible for deluges and for such operations of nature as I have spoken of[2] in the case of Sicily, the islands of Aeolus, and the Pithecussae, it is worth while to set forth still other instances of things similar thereto that exist, or else have taken place, in other regions. For if a large number of such instances are placed in view, they will put a stop to one's amazement. But, as it is, the unfamiliar thing disturbs the senses and shews one's ignorance of natural occurrences and of the conditions of life generally; for instance, suppose one should tell the story of Thera and Therasia (islands situated in the roadstead between Crete and Cyrenaea, the first of which, Thera, is the mother-city of Cyrene), and of Egypt, and of many such places in Greece. For midway between Thera and Therasia fires broke forth from the sea and continued for four days, so that the whole sea boiled and blazed, and the fires cast up an island which was gradually elevated as though by levers and consisted of burning masses— an island with a stretch of twelve stadia in circum-

---

[1] Compare Horace's "Nil admirari" (*Epist.* 6). Also 1. 3. 21 (below); and Cicero, *De Finibus* 5. 8. 23 and 5. 29. 87. The Stoic philosophers attached great importance to the virtue of "marvelling at nothing." Strabo's present purpose is, by heaping up instances of marvellous occurrences, to promote that virtue in the student of geography, and thus to remove doubt and encourage the scientific spirit.

[2] Page 199.

μετὰ δὲ τὴν παῦλαν τοῦ πάθους ἐθάρρησαν
πρῶτοι Ῥόδιοι θαλαττοκρατοῦντες ἐπιπροσ-
πλεῦσαι τῷ τόπῳ, καὶ Ποσειδῶνος Ἀσφαλίου
C 58 ἱερὸν ἱδρύσασθαι κατὰ τὴν νῆσον. ἐν δὲ τῇ
Φοινίκῃ φησὶ Ποσειδώνιος γενομένου σεισμοῦ
καταποθῆναι πόλιν ἱδρυμένην ὑπὲρ Σιδόνος, καὶ
αὐτῆς δὲ Σιδόνος σχεδόν τι τὰ δύο μέρη πεσεῖν,
ἀλλ᾽ οὐκ ἀθρόως, ὥστε μὴ πολὺν φθόρον ἀνθρώπων
γενέσθαι. τὸ δ᾽ αὐτὸ πάθος καὶ ἐπὶ τὴν Συρίαν
ὅλην διέτεινε, μετρίως δέ πως. διέβη δὲ καὶ ἐπί
τινας νήσους τάς τε Κυκλάδας καὶ τὴν Εὔβοιαν,
ὥστε τῆς Ἀρεθούσης (ἔστι δ᾽ ἐν Χαλκίδι κρήνη)
τὰς πηγὰς ἀποτυφλωθῆναι, συχναῖς δ᾽ ἡμέραις
ὕστερον ἀναβλύσαι κατ᾽ ἄλλο στόμιον, μὴ
παύεσθαι δὲ σειομένην τὴν νῆσον κατὰ μέρη,
πρὶν ἢ χάσμα γῆς ἀνοιχθὲν ἐν τῷ Ληλάντῳ πεδίῳ
πηλοῦ διαπύρου ποταμὸν ἐξήμεσε.

17. Πολλῶν δὲ συναγωγὰς ποιησαμένων
τοιαύτας, ἀρκέσει τὰ ὑπὸ τοῦ Σκηψίου Δημητρίου
συνηγμένα οἰκείως παρατεθέντα. μνησθεὶς γὰρ
τῶν ἐπῶν τούτων,

κρουνὼ δ᾽ ἵκανον καλλιρρόω, ἔνθα τε πηγαὶ
δοιαὶ ἀναΐσσουσι Σκαμάνδρου δινήεντος.
ἡ μὲν γάρ θ᾽ ὕδατι λιαρῷ,
ἡ δ᾽ ἑτέρη θέρεϊ προρέει εἰκυῖα χαλάζῃ,

(Π. 22.147)

οὐκ ἐᾷ θαυμάζειν, εἰ νῦν ἡ μὲν τοῦ ψυχροῦ
ὕδατος μένει πηγή, ἡ δὲ τοῦ θερμοῦ οὐχ ὁρᾶται.
δεῖν γάρ φησιν αἰτιᾶσθαι τὴν ἔκθλιψιν τοῦ

ference. After the cessation of the eruption, the Rhodians, at the time of their maritime supremacy, were first to venture upon the scene and to erect on the island a temple in honour of Poseidon Asphalios.[1] And in Phoenicia, says Poseidonius, on the occasion of an earthquake, a city situated above Sidon was swallowed up, and nearly two-thirds of Sidon itself was engulfed too, but not all at once, so that no considerable destruction of human life took place. The same operation of nature extended also over the whole of Syria, but with rather moderate force ; and it also passed over to certain islands, both the Cyclades and Euboea, with the result that the fountains of Arethusa (a spring in Chalcis) were stopped up, though after many days they gushed up at another mouth, and the island did not cease from being shaken in some part or other until a chasm in the earth opened in the Lelantine Plain and vomited forth a river of fiery lava.

17. Though many writers have made collections of such instances, those collected by Demetrius of Scepsis will suffice since they are appropriately cited. For example, he mentions these verses of Homer : " And they came to the two fair-flowing springs, where two fountains rise of deep-eddying Scamander ; the one floweth with warm water, while the other in summer floweth forth like hail " ; and then he does not allow us to marvel if at the present time the spring of cold water is still there, whereas the one of hot water is no longer visible. For, says he, we must lay the cause to the shutting off of the hot

---

[1] Poseidon, "Securer" of travel by sea, and of the foundations of the earth.

θερμοῦ ὕδατος. μιμνήσκεται δὲ πρὸς ταῦτα τῶν
ὑπὸ Δημοκλέους λεγομένων, σεισμούς τινας μεγά-
λους τοὺς μὲν πάλαι περὶ Λυδίαν γενομένους
καὶ Ἰωνίαν μέχρι τῆς Τρῳάδος ἱστοροῦντος,
ὑφ' ὧν καὶ κῶμαι κατεπόθησαν καὶ Σίπυλος
κατεστράφη, κατὰ τὴν Ταντάλου βασιλείαν.
καὶ ἐξ ἑλῶν λίμναι ἐγένοντο, τὴν δὲ Τροίαν
ἐπέκλυσε κῦμα. ἡ δὲ Φάρος ἡ κατ' Αἴγυπτον ἦν
ποτε πελαγία, νῦν δὲ τρόπον τινὰ χερρόνησος
γέγονεν· ὡς δ' αὕτως καὶ Τύρος καὶ Κλαζομεναί.
ἡμῶν δ' ἐπιδημούντων ἐν Ἀλεξανδρείᾳ τῇ πρὸς
Αἰγύπτῳ, περὶ Πηλούσιον καὶ τὸ Κάσιον ὄρος
μετεωρισθὲν τὸ πέλαγος ἐπέκλυσε τὴν γῆν καὶ
νῆσον ἐποίησε τὸ ὄρος, ὥστε πλωτὴν γενέσθαι
τὴν παρὰ τὸ Κάσιον ὁδὸν τὴν ἐς Φοινίκην. οὐδὲν
οὖν θαυμαστόν, οὐδ' εἴ ποτε διαστὰς ὁ ἰσθμὸς ἢ
ἵζημα λαβὼν ὁ διείργων τὸ Αἰγύπτιον πέλαγος
ἀπὸ τῆς Ἐρυθρᾶς θαλάττης ἀποφανεῖ πορθμόν,
καὶ σύρρουν ποιήσει τὴν ἐκτὸς θάλατταν τῇ[1]
ἐντός, καθάπερ ἐπὶ τοῦ κατὰ τὰς Ἡρακλέους
στήλας πορθμοῦ συνέβη. εἴρηται δὲ περὶ τῶν
τοιούτων τινὰ καὶ ἐν ἀρχαῖς τῆς πραγματείας,
ἃ δεῖ συμφέρειν εἰς ἓν καὶ τὴν πίστιν ἰσχυρὰν
κατασκευάζειν τῶν τε τῆς φύσεως ἔργων καὶ τῶν
ἄλλως γινομένων μεταβολῶν.

18. Τόν τε Πειραιᾶ νησιάζοντα πρότερον καὶ
C 59 πέραν τῆς ἀκτῆς κείμενον οὕτως φασὶν ὀνομα-

[1] τῇ, Corais, for τῆς, before ἐντός; Meineke following;
C. Müller approving.

water.[1] And he recalls on this point the words of
Democles, who records certain great earthquakes,
some of which long ago took place about Lydia
and Ionia as far north as the Troad, and by their
action not only were villages swallowed up, but
Mt. Sipylus was shattered—in the reign of Tantalus.
And lakes arose from swamps, and a tidal wave
submerged the Troad. Again, the Egyptian Pharos
was once an island of the sea, but now it has
become, in a sense, a peninsula; and the same is
true of Tyre and Clazomenae. And when I was
residing in Alexandria, in Egypt, the sea about
Pelusium and Mt. Casius rose and flooded the
country and made an island of the mountain, so
that the road by Mt. Casius into Phoenicia became
navigable. Hence it is nothing to marvel at even
if, at some time, the isthmus should be parted
asunder or else undergo a settling process—I mean
the isthmus that separates the Egyptian Sea from
the Red Sea—and thus disclose a strait and make
the outer sea confluent with the inner,[2] just as
happened in the case of the strait at the Pillars of
Heracles. I have already said something about such
things at the beginning of this treatise [3]; and all
these instances must needs contribute to one result,
namely, to fix strong our belief in the works of
nature and also in the changes that are being
brought to pass by other agencies.

18. And as for the Peiraeus, it was because the
Peiraeus was formerly an island and lay "over
against [4]" the mainland, they say, that it got the

---

[1] See 13. 1. 43, where Strabo again refers to these springs.
[2] Compare the Suez Canal. [3] 1. 3. 4. [4] *Peran.*

σθῆναι· ὑπεναντίως δ' ἡ Λευκὰς Κορινθίων τὸν
ἰσθμὸν διακοψάντων νῆσος γέγονεν, ἀκτὴ πρότερον οὖσα· περὶ ταύτης γάρ φασι λέγειν τὸν
Λαέρτην,

οἷος Νήρικον[1] εἶλον ἐϋκτίμενον πτολίεθρον,
ἀκτὴν ἠπείροιο·   (Od. 24. 377)

ἐνταῦθα μὲν δὴ διακοπαὶ χειρότμητοι γεγόνασιν,
ἀλλαχόθι δὲ προσχώσεις ἢ γεφυρώσεις, καθάπερ
ἐπὶ τῆς πρὸς Συρακούσαις νήσου νῦν μὲν γέφυρά
ἐστιν ἡ συνάπτουσα αὐτὴν πρὸς τὴν ἤπειρον,
πρότερον δὲ χῶμα, ὥς φησιν Ἴβυκος, λογαίου
λίθου, ὃν καλεῖ ἐκλεκτόν. Βοῦρα δὲ καὶ Ἑλίκη,
ἡ μὲν ὑπὸ χάσματος, ἡ δ' ὑπὸ κύματος ἠφανίσθη.
περὶ Μεθώνην δὲ τὴν ἐν τῷ Ἑρμιονικῷ κόλπῳ
ὄρος[2] ἑπταστάδιον τὸ ὕψος ἀνεβλήθη γενηθέντος
ἀναφυσήματος φλογώδους, μεθ' ἡμέραν μὲν
ἀπρόσιτον ὑπὸ τοῦ θερμοῦ καὶ τῆς θειώδους
ὀδμῆς, νύκτωρ δ'[3] ἐκλάμπον πόρρω καὶ θερ-
μαῖνον, ὥστε ζεῖν τὴν θάλατταν ἐπὶ σταδίους
πέντε, θολερὰν δ' εἶναι καὶ ἐπὶ εἴκοσι σταδίους,
προσχωσθῆναι δὲ πέτραις ἀπορρῶξι πύργων οὐκ
ἐλάττοσιν. ὑπὸ δὲ τῆς Κωπαΐδος λίμνης ἥ τε

---

[1] Νήρικον, Corais, for Νήριτον ; C, the Epitome, and modern
editors also
[2] ὄρος, Kramer adds, from the Epitome ; Groskurd,
Meineke, Müller-Dübner, following.
[3] εὐῶδες, before ἐκλάμπον, Corais deletes ; Meineke following ; C. Müller approving.

name it has; but contrariwise Leucas, since the
Corinthians cut a canal through the isthmus, has
become an island, although it was formerly a headland. Indeed, it is with reference to Leucas, they
say, that Laertes remarks: "As I was when I took
Nericus, the well-built castle on the headland of the
continent." Here, then, a partition cut by hand has
been made; in other places man has built moles
or bridges—just as, in the case of the island next
to Syracuse, there is at the present time a bridge
which connects it with the mainland, whereas
formerly there was a mole, as Ibycus says, built of
selected stones, which he calls stones "picked out."[1]
Then there are Bura and Helice; Bura disappeared
in a chasm of the earth, and Helice was wiped out
by a wave from the sea.[2] And about Methone in
the Hermionic Gulf[3] a mountain seven stadia in
height was cast up in consequence of a fiery
eruption, and this mountain was unapproachable by
day on account of the heat and the smell of sulphur,
while at night it shone to a great distance and was
so hot that the sea boiled for five stadia and was
turbid even for twenty stadia, and was heaped up
with massive broken-off rocks no smaller than towers.
And again, by Lake Copaïs[4] both Arne and Mideia

---

[1] Ibycus says: "picked out by mortal hands."
[2] Both were in Achaia. The earthquake took place
373 B.C.
[3] We should have expected Strabo to say "Saronic" Gulf.
The form which he elsewhere gives to the Hermionic Gulf
(see 8. 6. 1), making it reach as far north as Aegina and
Epidaurian territory, is strange indeed; but in accordance
with his definition Methone comes within the Hermionic
Gulf.
[4] In Boeotia (Lake Topolia).

Ἄρνη κατεπόθη καὶ Μίδεια, ἃς ὠνόμακεν ὁ ποιητὴς ἐν τῷ Καταλόγῳ·

οἵ τε πολυστάφυλον Ἄρνην ἔχον, οἵ τε Μίδειαν.
(Il. 2. 507)

καὶ ὑπὸ τῆς Βιστονίδος δὲ καὶ τῆς νῦν Ἀφνίτιδος λίμνης ἐοίκασι κατακεκλύσθαι πόλεις τινὲς Θρακῶν· οἱ δὲ καὶ Τρηρῶν, ὡς συνοίκων τοῖς Θραξὶν ὄντων. καὶ ἡ πρότερον δὲ Ἀρτεμίτα λεγομένη μία τῶν Ἐχινάδων νήσων ἤπειρος γέγονε· καὶ ἄλλας δὲ τῶν περὶ τὸν Ἀχελῷον νησίδων τὸ αὐτὸ πάθος φασὶ παθεῖν ἐκ τῆς ὑπὸ τοῦ ποταμοῦ προσχώσεως τοῦ πελάγους, συγχοῦνται δὲ καὶ αἱ λοιπαί, ὡς Ἡρόδοτός[1] φησι. καὶ Αἰτωλικαὶ δέ τινες ἄκραι εἰσὶ νησίζουσαι πρότερον, καὶ ἡ Ἀστερία ἤλλακται, ἣν Ἀστερίδα φησὶν ὁ ποιητής·

ἔστι δέ τις νῆσος μέσση ἁλὶ πετρήεσσα,
Ἀστερίς, οὐ μεγάλη, λιμένες δ' ἐνὶ ναύλοχοι αὐτῇ
ἀμφίδυμοι·
(Od. 4. 844)

νυνὶ δὲ οὐδ' ἀγκυροβόλιον εὐφυὲς ἔχει. ἔν τε τῇ Ἰθάκῃ οὐδέν ἐστιν ἄντρον τοιοῦτον, οὐδὲ Νυμφαῖον, οἷόν φησιν Ὅμηρος· βέλτιον δὲ αἰτιᾶσθαι μεταβολὴν ἢ ἄγνοιαν ἢ κατάψευσιν τῶν τόπων κατὰ τὸ μυθῶδες. τοῦτο μὲν δὴ ἀσαφὲς ὂν

C 60 ἐῶ ἐν κοινῷ σκοπεῖν.

---

[1] Ἡρόδοτος, Corais, for Ἡσίοδος; Meineke, Forbiger, Tozer, Tardieu, following.

were swallowed up, places which have been named by Homer in the Catalogue of Ships: "And they that possess Arne rich in vineyards, and they that possess Mideia." And by Lake Bistonis [1] and by the lake which they now call Aphnitis [2] certain cities of Thracians appear to have been overwhelmed; and some say cities of Trerans also, thinking they were neighbours of the Thracians. And, too, one of the Echinades Islands, which used to be called Artemita, has become part of the continent; and they say that still others of the little islands about the mouth of the Acheloüs have suffered the same change from the silting up of the sea by the river; and the rest of them too, as Herodotus [3] says, are in process of fusion with the continent. Again, there are certain Aetolian promontories which were formerly islands; and Asteria has been changed, which the poet calls Asteris: "Now there is a rocky isle in the mid-sea,[4] Asteris, a little isle; and there is a harbour therein with a double entrance, where ships may lie at anchor." But at the present time it has not even a good anchorage. Further, in Ithaca there is no cave, neither grotto of the Nymphs, such as Homer describes; but it is better to ascribe the cause to physical change rather than to Homer's ignorance or to a false account of the places to suit the fabulous element in his poetry. Since this matter, however, is uncertain, I leave it to the public to investigate.

---

[1] In Thrace (Lake Lagos).
[2] The other name was Dascylitis (see 13. 1. 9). It was in Bithynia; and according to the best authority, it was not the lake now called Maniyas or that called Abullonia, but a third lake which has disappeared. [3] 2. 10.
[4] Asteris lay "midway between Ithaca and rugged Samos," says Homer; but scholars have been unable to identify it.

19. Ἡ δὲ Ἄντισσα νῆσος ἦν πρότερον, ὡς
Μυρσίλος φησί· τῆς δὲ Λέσβου καλουμένης
πρότερον Ἴσσης, καὶ τὴν νῆσον Ἄντισσαν καλεῖσθαι συνέβη· νῦν δὲ τῆς Λέσβου πόλις ἐστίν.
οἱ δὲ καὶ τὴν Λέσβον τῆς Ἴδης ἀπερρωγέναι
πεπιστεύκασι, καθάπερ τὴν Προχύτην καὶ τὴν
Πιθηκοῦσσαν τοῦ Μισηνοῦ, τὰς δὲ Καπρέας τοῦ
Ἀθηναίου, τὴν Σικελίαν δὲ τῆς Ῥηγίνης, τὴν
Ὄσσαν δὲ τοῦ Ὀλύμπου. γεγόνασι δὲ καὶ περὶ
ταῦτα τοιαῦται μεταβολαί. καὶ ὁ Λάδων δὲ ὁ
ἐν Ἀρκαδίᾳ ἐπέσχε ποτὲ τὸ ῥεῦμα. Δοῦρις δὲ
τὰς Ῥάγας τὰς κατὰ Μηδίαν ὠνομάσθαι φησὶν
ὑπὸ σεισμῶν ῥαγείσης τῆς περὶ τὰς Κασπίους
πύλας γῆς, ὥστε ἀνατραπῆναι πόλεις συχνὰς
καὶ κώμας καὶ ποταμοὺς ποικίλας μεταβολὰς
δέξασθαι. Ἴων δὲ περὶ τῆς Εὐβοίας φησὶν ἐν
Ὀμφάλῃ Σατύροις·

> Εὐβοΐδα μὲν γῆν λεπτὸς Εὐρίπου κλύδων
> Βοιωτίας ἐχώρισ’, ἀκτὴν ἐκτεμὼν
> προβλῆτα πορθμῷ.   (fr. 18, Nauck)

20. Δημήτριος δ’ ὁ Καλλατιανὸς τοὺς καθ’
ὅλην τὴν Ἑλλάδα γενομένους ποτὲ σεισμοὺς
διηγούμενος τῶν τε Λιχάδων νήσων καὶ τοῦ
Κηναίου τὰ πολλὰ καταδῦναί φησι, τά τε θερμὰ
τὰ ἐν Αἰδηψῷ καὶ Θερμοπύλαις ἐπὶ τρεῖς ἡμέρας
ἐπισχεθέντα πάλιν ῥυῆναι, τὰ δ’ ἐν Αἰδηψῷ καὶ
καθ’ ἑτέρας ἀναρραγῆναι πηγάς· Ὠρεοῦ δὲ τὸ
πρὸς θαλάττῃ τεῖχος καὶ τῶν οἰκιῶν περὶ ἑπτα-

---

[1] That is, the island *opposite* Issa (Lesbos) was called
Antissa (Anti-Issa).   [2] See 8. 8. 4.

19. Antissa was formerly an island, as Myrsilus says; and since Lesbos was formerly called Issa, it came about that this island was called Antissa[1]; but now Antissa is a city of Lesbos. And some believe that Lesbos itself is a fragment broken off from Mt. Ida, just as Prochyta and Pithecussa from Misenum, Capri from the Promontory of Athene, Sicily from the district of Rhegium, and Ossa from Olympus. And it is a fact that changes of this sort have also occurred in the neighbourhood of these places. And, again, the River Ladon in Arcadia once ceased to flow.[2] Duris says that Rhagae in Media has received its name because the earth about the Caspian Gates had been "rent"[3] by earthquakes to such an extent that numerous cities and villages were destroyed, and the rivers underwent changes of various kinds. Ion says of Euboea in his satyr-drama *Omphale*: "The slender wave of Euripus hath separated the land of Euboea from Boeotia, in that by means of a strait it hath cut a projecting headland away."

20. Demetrius of Callatis, in his account of all the earthquakes that have ever occurred throughout all Greece, says that the greater part of the Lichades Islands[4] and of Cenaeum[5] was engulfed; the hot springs at Aedepsus[6] and Thermopylae, after having ceased to flow for three days, began to flow afresh, and those at Aedepsus broke forth also at another source; at Oreus[7] the wall next to the sea and about

---

[3] The root of the verb here used is *rhag*.
[4] Between Euboea and Locris.
[5] A promontory in north-western Euboea, opposite Locris.
[6] A city in north-western Euboea.
[7] A city in north-eastern Euboea.

κοσίας συμπεσεῖν, Ἐχίνου τε καὶ Φαλάρων καὶ
Ἡρακλείας τῆς Τραχῖνος, τῶν μὲν πολὺ μέρος
πεσεῖν, Φαλάρων δὲ καὶ ἐξ ἐδάφους ἀνατραπῆναι[1]
τὸ κτίσμα. παραπλήσια δὲ συμβῆναι καὶ Λαμι-
εῦσι καὶ Λαρισαίοις· καὶ Σκάρφειαν δ' ἐκ θεμε-
λίων ἀναρριφῆναι, καὶ καταδῦναι σώματα χιλίων
καὶ ἑπτακοσίων οὐκ ἐλάττω, Θρονίους δ' ὑπὲρ
ἥμισυ τούτων· κῦμά τε ἐξαρθὲν τριχῇ, τὸ μὲν
πρὸς Τάρφην[2] ἐνεχθῆναι καὶ Θρόνιον, τὸ δὲ πρὸς
Θερμοπύλας, ἄλλο δὲ εἰς τὸ πεδίον ἕως τοῦ
Φωκικοῦ Δαφνοῦντος. πηγάς τε ποταμῶν ξηραν-
θῆναι πρὸς ἡμέρας τινάς, τὸν δὲ Σπερχειὸν
ἀλλάξαι τὸ ῥεῖθρον καὶ ποιῆσαι πλωτὰς τὰς
ὁδούς, τὸν δὲ Βοάγριον κατ' ἄλλης ἐνεχθῆναι
φάραγγος, καὶ Ἀλόπης δὲ καὶ Κύνου καὶ Ὀποῦν-
τος πολλὰ καταβλαβῆναι μέρη, Οἶον δὲ τὸ ὑπερ-
κείμενον φρούριον πᾶν ἀνατραπῆναι, Ἐλατείας
δὲ τοῦ τείχους καταρραγῆναι μέρος, περὶ δὲ
Ἄλπωνον[3] θεσμοφορίων ὄντων πέντε καὶ εἴκοσι
παρθένους ἀναδραμούσας εἰς πύργον τῶν ἐλλι-
μενίων κατὰ θέαν, πεσόντος τοῦ πύργου, πεσεῖν
καὶ αὐτὰς εἰς τὴν θάλατταν. λέγουσι δὲ καὶ τῆς
C 61 Ἀταλάντης τῆς πρὸς Εὐβοίᾳ τὰ μέσα, ῥήγματος
γενομένου, διάπλουν δέξασθαι μεταξύ, καὶ τῶν
πεδίων ἔνια καὶ μέχρι εἴκοσι σταδίων ἐπικλυ-

---

[1] ἀνατραπῆναι, Meineke restores, for Kramer's ἀναστραφῆναι;
Tozer following ; C. Müller approving.
[2] Τάρφην, Groskurd, for Σκάρφην ; Meineke, Forbiger, Tozer,
following ; C. Müller approving.
[3] Ἄλπωνον, Corais, for Ἄγωνον ; editors following.

seven hundred of the houses collapsed;[1] and as for Echinus and Phalara and Heracleia in Trachis, not only was a considerable portion of them thrown down, but the settlement of Phalara was overturned, ground and all. And, says he, something quite similar happened to the people of Lamia and of Larissa; and Scarphia, also, was flung up, foundations and all, and no fewer than seventeen hundred human beings were engulfed, and over half as many Thronians; again, a triple-headed wave rose up, one part of which was carried in the direction of Tarphe and Thronium, another part to Thermopylae, and the rest into the plain as far as Daphnus in Phocis; fountains of rivers were dried up for a number of days, and the Sphercheius changed its course and made the roadways navigable, and the Boagrius was carried down a different ravine, and also many sections of Alope, Cynus, and Opus were seriously damaged, and Oeum, the castle above Opus, was laid in utter ruin, and a part of the wall of Elateia was broken down, and at Alponus, during the celebration of the Thesmophoria, twenty-five girls ran up into one of the towers at the harbour to get a view, the tower fell, and they themselves fell with it into the sea. And they say, also, of the Atalanta near Euboea that its middle portions, because they had been rent asunder, got a ship-canal through the rent, and that some of the plains were overflowed even as far as twenty stadia, and

---

[1] The places subsequently named in this paragraph—except Atalanta—are all on the mainland of Greece, more or less in proximity to the Euboean Sea.

σθῆναι, καὶ τριήρη τινὰ ἐκ τῶν νεωριων ἐξαρθεῖσαν[1] ὑπερπεσεῖν τοῦ τείχους.

21. Προστιθέασι δὲ καὶ τὰς ἐκ τῶν μεταστάσεων μεταβολὰς ἐπὶ πλέον τὴν ἀθαυμαστίαν ἡμῖν κατασκευάζειν ἐθέλοντες, ἣν ὑμνεῖ Δημόκριτος καὶ οἱ ἄλλοι φιλόσοφοι πάντες· παράκειται γὰρ τῷ ἀθαμβεῖ καὶ ἀταράχῳ καὶ ἀνεκπλήκτῳ· οἷον Ἰβήρων μὲν τῶν ἑσπερίων εἰς τοὺς ὑπὲρ τοῦ Πόντου καὶ τῆς Κολχίδος τόπους μετῳκισμένων (οὓς ὁ Ἀράξης, ὥς φησιν Ἀπολλόδωρος, ἀπὸ τῆς Ἀρμενίας ὁρίζει, Κύρος δὲ μᾶλλον καὶ τὰ ὄρη τὰ Μοσχικά), Αἰγυπτίων δ' εἴς τε Αἰθίοπας καὶ Κόλχους, Ἑνετῶν δ' ἐκ Παφλαγονίας ἐπὶ τὸν Ἀδρίαν. ἅπερ καὶ ἐπὶ τῶν Ἑλληνικῶν ἐθνῶν συνέβη, Ἰώνων καὶ Δωριέων καὶ Ἀχαιῶν καὶ Αἰολέων· οἱ νῦν Αἰτωλοῖς ὅμοροι περὶ τὸ Δώτιον ᾤκουν καὶ τὴν Ὄσσαν μετὰ Περραιβῶν· καὶ αὐτοὶ δὲ Περραιβοὶ μετανάσται τινές. πλήρης δέ ἐστι τῶν τοιούτων παραδειγμάτων ἡ νῦν ἐνεστῶσα πραγματεία. τινὰ μὲν οὖν καὶ πρόχειρα τοῖς πολλοῖς ἐστιν·[2] αἱ δὲ τῶν Καρῶν καὶ Τρηρῶν καὶ Τεύκρων μεταναστάσεις καὶ Γαλατῶν, ὁμοῦ δὲ καὶ τῶν ἡγεμόνων οἱ ἐπὶ πολὺ ἐκτοπισμοί, Μάδυός τε τοῦ Σκυθικοῦ καὶ Τεαρκὼ τοῦ Αἰθίοπος καὶ Κώβου τοῦ Τρηρὸς καὶ Σεσώστριος καὶ

---

[1] ἐξαρθεῖσαν, Madvig, for ἐξαιρεθεῖσαν; Tozer following.
[2] ἐστιν, Meineke, for εἰσιν.

---

[1] Diodorus (12. 59) says that Atalanta was once a peninsula and that it was broken away from the mainland by an earthquake, though he does not refer to the occurrence

that a trireme was lifted out of the docks and cast over the wall.[1]

21. Writers also add the changes resulting from the migrations of peoples, wishing to develop in us, to a still greater extent, that virtue of not marvelling at things (a virtue which is lauded by Democritus and all the other philosophers; for they put it in a class with freedom from dread and from perturbability and from terror).[2] For instance: the migration of Western Iberians[3] to the regions beyond the Pontus and Colchis (regions which are separated from Armenia by the Araxes according to Apollodorus, but rather by the River Cyrus and the Moschican Mountains); and the migration of Egyptians to Ethiopia and Colchis; and that of Enetians[4] from Paphlagonia to the Adriatic. This is what took place in the case of the Greek tribes also—Ionians, Dorians, Achaeans, and Aeolians; and the Aenianians that are now neighbours of the Aetolians used to live about Dotium and Mt. Ossa among the Perrhaebians; and, too, the Perrhaebians themselves are emigrants. And the present treatise is full of such instances. A number of them, to be sure, are matters even of ready knowledge to most people, but the emigrations of the Carians, Trerans, Teucrians, and Galatians, and likewise also the expeditions of the princes to lands far remote (I refer to Madys the Scythian, Tearko the Ethiopian, Cobus the Treran, Sesostris and Psammitichus the

mentioned by Strabo. Both apparently have in mind the earthquake of 426 B.C.

[2] See § 16 above, and the footnote.

[3] That is, "Western" as distinguished from the new, or "Eastern," Iberia beyond the Pontus.

[4] Compare "Venetians"; and see 5. 1. 4.

Ψαμμιτίχου τῶν Αἰγυπτίων καὶ Περσῶν τῶν ἀπὸ
Κύρου μέχρι Ξέρξου οὐχ ὁμοίως ἐν ἑτοίμῳ πᾶσίν
εἰσιν. οἵ τε Κιμμέριοι οὓς καὶ Τρῆρας ὀνομά-
ζουσιν, ἢ ἐκείνων τι ἔθνος, πολλάκις ἐπέδραμον τὰ
δεξιὰ μέρη τοῦ Πόντου καὶ τὰ συνεχῆ αὐτοῖς,
τοτὲ μὲν ἐπὶ Παφλαγόνας, τοτὲ δὲ καὶ Φρύγας
ἐμβαλόντες, ἡνίκα Μίδαν αἷμα ταύρου πιόντα
φασὶν ἀπελθεῖν εἰς τὸ χρεών. Λύγδαμις δὲ τοὺς
αὑτοῦ ἄγων μέχρι Λυδίας καὶ Ἰωνίας ἤλασε καὶ
Σάρδεις εἷλεν, ἐν Κιλικίᾳ δὲ διεφθάρη. πολλάκις
δὲ καὶ οἱ Κιμμέριοι καὶ οἱ Τρῆρες ἐποιήσαντο
τὰς τοιαύτας ἐφόδους· τοὺς δὲ Τρῆρας καὶ Κῶβον
ὑπὸ Μάδνος τὸ τελευταῖον ἐξελαθῆναί φασι τοῦ
τῶν Σκυθῶν[1] βασιλέως. ταῦτα μὲν εἰρήσθω
πρὸς ἅπασαν κοινῇ τὴν περίοδον τῆς γῆς ἔχοντα
οἰκείαν ἱστορίαν.

22. Ἐπάνιμεν δ᾽ ἐπὶ τὰ ἑξῆς, ἀφ᾽ ὧν παρέβημεν.
τοῦ γὰρ Ἡροδότου μηδένας Ὑπερβορείους εἶναι
φήσαντος, μηδὲ γὰρ Ὑπερνοτίους, γελοίαν[2] φησὶν
C 62 εἶναι τὴν ἀπόδειξιν καὶ ὁμοίαν ὁ Ἐρατοσθένης
τῷ σοφίσματι τούτῳ, εἴ τις λέγοι μηδένας εἶναι
ἐπιχαιρεκάκους, μηδὲ γὰρ ἐπιχαιραγάθους· κατὰ
τύχην τε εἶναι καὶ Ὑπερνοτίους· κατὰ γοῦν τὴν
Αἰθιοπίαν μὴ πνεῖν Νότον, ἀλλὰ[3] κατωτέρω.

---

[1] Σκυθῶν, Penzel, Larcher, for Κιμμερίων; Groskurd,
Meineke, Forbiger, following; Kramer, C. Müller, approving.
[2] γελοίαν, Tyrwhitt, for λέγοι ἄν; editors following.
[3] The old reading without καί is restored by Kramer,
Meineke, C. Müller.

Egyptians, and to Persians from Cyrus to Xerxes)
are not likewise matters of off-hand knowledge to
everybody. And those Cimmerians whom they also
call Trerans (or some tribe or other of the Cimmerians) often overran the countries on the right of
the Pontus and those adjacent to them, at one time
having invaded Paphlagonia, and at another time
Phrygia even, at which time Midas drank bull's
blood, they say, and thus went to his doom.
Lygdamis,[1] however, at the head of his own soldiers,
marched as far as Lydia and Ionia and captured
Sardes, but lost his life in Cilicia. Oftentimes both
Cimmerians and Trerans made such invasions as
these; but they say that the Trerans and Cobus
were finally driven out by Madys, the king of the
Scythians. Let these illustrations be given here,
inasmuch as they involve matters of fact which have
a bearing upon the entire compass of the world in
general.

22. I now return to the points next in order,
whence I digressed.[2] First, as for the statement of
Herodotus[3] that there are no Hyperboreans[4] because
there are also no Hypernotians.[5] Eratosthenes says
the argument presented is absurd and like the following quibble: suppose some one should say "There
are none who rejoice over the ills of others because
there are also none who rejoice over the blessings of
others." And, adds Eratosthenes, it so happens that
there are also Hypernotians—at all events, Notus
does not blow in Ethiopia, but farther north. But it

[1] King of the Cimmerians.
[2] At § 16 Strabo digressed from the order of discussion
pursued by Eratosthenes.   [3] Herod. 4. 36.
[4] People who live beyond Boreas (North Wind).
[5] People beyond Notus (South Wind).

θαυμαστὸν δ᾽, εἰ, καθ᾽ ἕκαστον κλίμα πνέοντος
ἀνέμου, καὶ πανταχοῦ τοῦ ἀπὸ μεσημβρίας Νότου
προσαγορευομένου, ἔστι τις οἴκησις ἐν ᾗ τοῦτο
μὴ συμβαίνει. τοὐναντίον γὰρ οὐ μόνον Αἰθιοπία
ἔχοι ἂν τὸν καθ᾽ ἡμᾶς Νότον, ἀλλὰ καὶ ἡ ἀνωτέρω
πᾶσα μέχρι τοῦ ἰσημερινοῦ. εἰ δ᾽ ἄρα, τοῦ
Ἡροδότου τοῦτ᾽ ἐχρῆν αἰτιᾶσθαι, ὅτι τοὺς
Ὑπερβορείους τούτους ὑπέλαβε λέγεσθαι, παρ᾽
οἷς ὁ Βορέας οὐ πνεῖ. καὶ γὰρ εἰ οἱ ποιηταὶ
μυθικώτερον οὕτω φασίν, οἵ γ᾽ ἐξηγούμενοι τὸ
ὑγιὲς ἂν ἀκούσαιεν, Ὑπερβορείους τοὺς βορειο-
τάτους λέγεσθαι.[1] ὅρος δὲ τῶν μὲν βορείων ὁ
πόλος, τῶν δὲ νοτίων ὁ ἰσημερινός· καὶ τῶν
ἀνέμων δ᾽ ὁ αὐτὸς ὅρος.

23. Ἑξῆς δὲ λέγει πρὸς τοὺς φανερῶς πεπλα-
σμένα καὶ ἀδύνατα λέγοντας, τὰ μὲν ἐν μύθου
σχήματι, τὰ δ᾽ ἱστορίας, περὶ ὧν οὐκ ἄξιον
μεμνῆσθαι· οὐδ᾽ ἐκεῖνον ἐχρῆν ἐν ὑποθέσει
τοιαύτῃ φλυάρους ἐπισκοπεῖν. ἡ μὲν οὖν πρώτη
διέξοδος αὐτῷ τῶν ὑπομνημάτων τοιαύτη.

IV

1. Ἐν δὲ τῇ δευτέρᾳ πειρᾶται διόρθωσίν τινα
ποιεῖσθαι τῆς γεωγραφίας, καὶ τὰς ἑαυτοῦ λέγει

---

[1] φασί, after λέγεσθαι, Groskurd deletes; editors following

is a marvellous thing if, although winds blow in every latitude, and although the wind that blows from the south is everywhere called Notus, there is any inhabited place where this is not the case. For, on the contrary, not only might Ethiopia have the same Notus as we have, but even the whole country further south as far as the equator might have it. However that may be, this charge should be laid against Herodotus, that he assumed that by "Hyperboreans" those peoples were meant in whose countries Boreas does not blow. For even if the poets do speak thus, rather mythically, those, at least, who expound the poets should give ear to sound doctrine, namely, that by "Hyperboreans" were meant merely the most northerly [1] peoples. And as for limits, that of the northerly [1] peoples is the north pole, while that of the southerly [2] peoples is the equator; and the winds too have the same limits.

23. Next in order, Eratosthenes proceeds to reply to those whose stories are plainly fictitious and impossible, some of which are in the form of myths, and others in the form of history—persons whom it is not worth while to mention; neither should he, when treating a subject of this kind, have paid heed to persons who talk nonsense. Such, then, is Eratosthenes' course of argument in the First Book of his Commentaries.

IV

1. In his Second Book Eratosthenes undertakes a revision of the principles of geography; and he declares his own assumptions, to which, in turn, it

[1] Literally, "borean."   [2] Literally, "notian."

ὑπολήψεις· πρὸς ἃς πάλιν, εἰ ἔστι τις ἐπανόρθωσις,
πειρατέον προσφέρειν. τὸ μὲν οὖν τὰς μαθηματικὰς ὑποθέσεις εἰσάγειν[1] καὶ φυσικὰς εὖ
λέγεται, καὶ ὅτι εἰ σφαιροειδὴς ἡ γῆ, καθάπερ καὶ
ὁ κόσμος, περιοικεῖται, καὶ τὰ ἄλλα τὰ τοιαῦτα.
εἰ δὲ τηλικαύτη, ἡλίκην αὐτὸς εἴρηκεν, οὐχ
ὁμολογοῦσιν οἱ ὕστεροι, οὐδ᾽[2] ἐπαινοῦσι τὴν
ἀναμέτρησιν· ὅμως δὲ πρὸς τὴν σημείωσιν τῶν
κατὰ τὰς οἰκήσεις ἑκάστας φαινομένων προσχρῆται τοῖς διαστήμασιν ἐκείνοις Ἵππαρχος ἐπὶ
τοῦ διὰ Μερόης καὶ Ἀλεξανδρείας καὶ Βορυσθένους
μεσημβρινοῦ, μικρὸν παραλλάττειν φήσας παρὰ
τὴν ἀλήθειαν. καὶ περὶ τοῦ σχήματος δ᾽ ἐν τοῖς
ἑξῆς διὰ πλειόνων καταδεικνὺς[3] ὅτι σφαιροειδὴς
καὶ ἡ γῆ σὺν τῇ ὑγρᾷ φύσει καὶ ὁ οὐρανός,
ἀλλοτριολογεῖν ἂν δόξειεν· ἀρκεῖ γὰρ τὸ ἐπὶ
μικρόν.

2. Ἑξῆς δὲ τὸ πλάτος τῆς οἰκουμένης ἀφορίζων
φησὶν ἀπὸ μὲν Μερόης ἐπὶ τοῦ δι᾽ αὐτῆς μεσημβ-
C 63 ρινοῦ μέχρι Ἀλεξανδρείας εἶναι μυρίους, ἐνθένδε
εἰς τὸν Ἑλλήσποντον περὶ ὀκτακισχιλίους ἑκατόν,
εἶτ᾽ εἰς Βορυσθένη πεντακισχιλίους, εἶτ᾽ ἐπὶ τὸν
κύκλον τὸν διὰ Θούλης (ἥν φησι Πυθέας ἀπὸ μὲν
τῆς Βρεττανικῆς ἐξ ἡμερῶν πλοῦν ἀπέχειν πρὸς
ἄρκτον, ἐγγὺς δ᾽ εἶναι τῆς πεπηγυίας θαλάττης)

---

[1] εἰσάγειν, Corais, for ἄγειν ; editors following.
[2] οὐδ᾽, Casaubon, for δέ ; editors following.
[3] καταδεικνύς, T. G. Tucker, for (καὶ) δεικνύς.

---

[1] 252,000 stadia in circumference at the equator. See
2. 5. 7.
[2] The Dnieper ; Strabo means, as usual, the mouth of the
river.

there is any further revision to be made, I must
undertake to supply it. Now his introduction of
the principles of mathematics and physics into the
subject is a commendable thing; also his remark
that if the earth is sphere-shaped, just as the universe
is, it is inhabited all the way round; and his other
remarks of this nature. But as to the question
whether the earth is as large as he has said,
later writers do not agree with him; neither do
they approve his measurement of the earth.[1] Still,
when Hipparchus plots the celestial phenomena for
the several inhabited places, he uses, in addition,
those intervals measured by Eratosthenes on the
meridian through Meroë and Alexandria and the
Borysthenes,[2] after saying that they deviate but
slightly from the truth. And, too, in Eratosthenes'
subsequent discussion about the shape of the earth,
when he demonstrates at greater length that not only
the earth with its liquid constituent is sphere-shaped
but the heavens also, he would seem to be talking
about things that are foreign to his subject; for a
brief statement is sufficient.[3]

2. Next, in determining the breadth of the inhabited world, Eratosthenes says that, beginning at
Meroë and measuring on the meridian that runs
through Meroë, it is ten thousand stadia to Alexandria; and thence to the Hellespont about eight
thousand one hundred; then to the Borysthenes five
thousand; then to the parallel circle that runs
through Thule (which Pytheas says is a six days'
sail north of Britain, and is near the frozen sea)

[3] Strabo means that the hypotheses of physics and
astronomy should be accepted at once by geographers.
Compare 2. 5. 2.

ἄλλους ὡς μυρίους χιλίους πεντακοσίους. ἐὰν
οὖν ἔτι προσθῶμεν ὑπὲρ τὴν Μερόην ἄλλους
τρισχιλίους τετρακοσίους, ἵνα τὴν τῶν Αἰγυπτίων
νῆσον ἔχωμεν καὶ τὴν Κινναμωμοφόρον καὶ τὴν
Ταπροβάνην, ἔσεσθαι σταδίους τρισμυρίους ὀκτακισχιλίους.

3. Τὰ μὲν οὖν ἄλλα διαστήματα δεδόσθω αὐτῷ·
ὡμολόγηται γὰρ ἱκανῶς· τὸ δ' ἀπὸ τοῦ Βορυσθένους ἐπὶ τὸν διὰ Θούλης κύκλον τίς ἂν δοίη
νοῦν ἔχων; ὅ τε γὰρ ἱστορῶν τὴν Θούλην Πυθέας
ἀνὴρ ψευδίστατος ἐξήτασται, καὶ οἱ τὴν Βρεττανικὴν καὶ[1] Ἰέρνην ἰδόντες οὐδὲν περὶ τῆς Θούλης
λέγουσιν, ἄλλας νήσους λέγοντες μικρὰς περὶ τὴν
Βρεττανικήν. αὐτή τε ἡ Βρεττανικὴ τὸ μῆκος
ἴσως πώς ἐστι τῇ Κελτικῇ παρεκτεταμένη, τῶν
πεντακισχιλίων σταδίων οὐ μείζων, καὶ τοῖς ἄκροις
τοῖς ἀντικειμένοις ἀφοριζομένη. ἀντίκειται γὰρ
ἀλλήλοις τά τε ἑῷα ἄκρα τοῖς ἑῴοις καὶ τὰ
ἑσπέρια τοῖς ἑσπερίοις, καὶ τά γε ἑῷα ἐγγὺς
ἀλλήλων ἐστὶ μέχρις ἐπόψεως, τό τε Κάντιον καὶ
αἱ τοῦ Ῥήνου ἐκβολαί. ὁ δὲ πλειόνων ἢ δισμυρίων
τὸ μῆκος ἀποφαίνει τῆς νήσου, καὶ τὸ Κάντιον
ἡμερῶν τινων πλοῦν ἀπέχειν τῆς Κελτικῆς φησι·
καὶ τὰ περὶ τοὺς Ὠστιμίους δὲ καὶ τὰ πέραν τοῦ
Ῥήνου τὰ μέχρι Σκυθῶν πάντα κατέψευσται
τῶν τόπων. ὅστις οὖν περὶ τῶν γνωριζομένων

---

[1] καί, Kramer inserts; editors following.

---

[1] Strabo elsewhere speaks of this island as "the island of
the *fugitive* Egyptians." See 2. 5. 14 (and note), 16. 4. 8,
and 17. 1. 2; also Pliny, *Nat. Hist.* 6. 35.

about eleven thousand five hundred more. Accordingly, if we add three thousand four hundred stadia more to the south of Meroë, in order to embrace the Island of the Egyptians,[1] the Cinnamon-producing country, and Taprobane,[2] we shall have thirty-eight thousand stadia.

3. However, with one exception, let all the distances of Eratosthenes be granted him—for they are sufficiently agreed upon; but what man of sense could grant his distance from the Borysthenes to the parallel of Thule? For not only has the man who tells about Thule, Pytheas, been found, upon scrutiny, to be an arch-falsifier, but the men who have seen Britain and Ierne[3] do not mention Thule, though they speak of other islands, small ones, about Britain; and Britain itself stretches alongside of Celtica[4] with a length about equal thereto, being not greater in length than five thousand stadia, and its limits are defined by the extremities of Celtica which lie opposite its own. For the eastern extremity of the one country lies opposite the eastern extremity of the other, and the western extremity of the one opposite the western of the other; and their eastern extremities, at all events, are near enough to each other for a person to see across from one to the other —I mean Cantium[5] and the mouths of the Rhine. But Pytheas declares that the length of Britain is more than twenty thousand stadia, and that Cantium is several days' sail from Celtica; and in his account both of the Ostimians and of what is beyond the Rhine as far as Scythia he has in every case falsified the regions. However, any man who has told such

---

[2] Ceylon.
[4] France, roughly.
[3] Ireland.
[5] Kent.

τόπων τοσαῦτα ἔψευσται, σχολῇ γ' ἂν περὶ τῶν
ἀγνοουμένων παρὰ πᾶσιν ἀληθεύειν δύναιτο.

4. Τὸν δὲ διὰ τοῦ Βορυσθένους παράλληλον τὸν
αὐτὸν εἶναι τῷ διὰ τῆς Βρεττανικῆς εἰκάζουσιν
Ἵππαρχός τε καὶ ἄλλοι ἐκ τοῦ τὸν αὐτὸν εἶναι τὸν
διὰ Βυζαντίου τῷ διὰ Μασσαλίας· ὃν γὰρ λόγον
εἴρηκε Πυθέας[1] τοῦ ἐν Μασσαλίᾳ γνώμονος πρὸς
τὴν σκιάν, τὸν αὐτὸν καὶ Ἵππαρχος κατὰ τὸν
ὁμώνυμον καιρὸν εὑρεῖν ἐν τῷ Βυζαντίῳ φησίν.
ἐκ Μασσαλίας δὲ εἰς μέσην τὴν Βρεττανικὴν οὐ
πλέον τῶν πεντακισχιλίων ἐστὶ σταδίων. ἀλλὰ
μὴν ἐκ μέσης τῆς Βρεττανικῆς οὐ πλέον τῶν
τετρακισχιλίων προελθὼν εὕροις[2] ἂν οἰκήσιμον
ἄλλως πως (τοῦτο δ' ἂν εἴη τὸ περὶ τὴν Ἰέρνην),
ὥστε τὰ ἐπέκεινα, εἰς ἃ ἐκτοπίζει τὴν Θούλην,
οὐκέτ' οἰκήσιμα. τίνι δ' ἂν καὶ στοχασμῷ λέγοι
τὸ ἀπὸ τοῦ διὰ Θούλης ἕως τοῦ διὰ Βορυσθένους
μυρίων καὶ χιλίων πεντακοσίων, οὐχ ὁρῶ.

C 64   5. Διαμαρτὼν δὲ τοῦ πλάτους ἠνάγκασται
καὶ τοῦ μήκους ἀστοχεῖν. ὅτι μὲν γὰρ πλέον ἢ
διπλάσιον τὸ γνώριμον μῆκός ἐστι τοῦ γνωρίμου
πλάτους, ὁμολογοῦσι καὶ οἱ ὕστερον καὶ τῶν
παλαιῶν[3] οἱ χαριέστατοι· λέγω δὲ τὸ[4] ἀπὸ τῶν
ἄκρων τῆς Ἰνδικῆς ἐπὶ τὰ ἄκρα τῆς Ἰβηρίας
τοῦ ἀπ'[5] Αἰθιόπων ἕως τοῦ κατὰ Ἰέρνην κύκλου.

---

[1] Πυθέας, Spengel inserts; Meineke, Forbiger, following;
C. Müller approving.
[2] εὕροις, Ουιαιο for εὕροι; Groskurd, Meineke, Forbiger,
following; C. Müller approving.
[3] παλαιῶν, Corais, for ἄλλων; Groskurd, Meineke, Forbiger,
Tardieu, following; C. Müller approving.
[4] τό, Xylander inserts, before ἀπό; Meineke following;
Kramer, C. Müller, approving.
[5] ἀπ', Meineke inserts.

great falsehoods about the known regions would hardly, I imagine, be able to tell the truth about places that are not known to anybody.

4. The parallel through the mouth of the Borysthenes is conjectured by Hipparchus and others to be the same as that through Britain, from the fact that the parallel through Byzantium is the same as that through Massilia[1]; for as to the relation of the dial-index to the shadow, which Pytheas has given for Massilia, this same relation Hipparchus says he observed at Byzantium, at the same time of the year as that mentioned by Pytheas. But it is not more than five thousand stadia from Massilia to the centre of Britain. Furthermore, if you were to proceed not more than four thousand stadia north from the centre of Britain you would find a region that is inhabitable only after a fashion (which region would be in the neighbourhood of Ierne); and so, as for the regions farther on, far out where Eratosthenes places Thule, you would find places no longer habitable. But by what guesswork Eratosthenes could say that the distance from the parallel through Thule to that through the mouth of the Borysthenes is eleven thousand five hundred stadia, I do not see.

5. And since he entirely missed the breadth of the inhabited world, he has necessarily failed to guess its length also. For, in the first place, that the known length is more than double the known breadth is agreed to by the later writers as well as by the most accomplished of the early writers (I mean the distance from the extremities of India to the extremities of Iberia, double that from Ethiopia up to the parallel that runs by Ierne). Again, after

[1] Marseilles.

ὁρίσας δὲ τὸ λεχθὲν πλάτος, τὸ ἀπὸ τῶν ἐσχάτων
Αἰθιόπων μέχρι τοῦ διὰ Θούλης ἐκτείνει πλέον
ἢ δεῖ τὸ μῆκος, ἵνα ποιήσῃ πλέον ἢ διπλάσιον
τοῦ λεχθέντος πλάτους. φησὶ γοῦν[1] τὸ μὲν τῆς
Ἰνδικῆς μέχρι τοῦ Ἰνδοῦ ποταμοῦ τὸ στενότατον
σταδίων μυρίων ἑξακισχιλίων· τὸ γὰρ ἐπὶ τὰ ἀκρωτήρια τεῖνον τρισχιλίοις εἶναι μεῖζον· τὸ δὲ ἔνθεν
ἐπὶ Κασπίους πύλας μυρίων τετρακισχιλίων, εἶτ'
ἐπὶ τὸν Εὐφράτην μυρίων, ἐπὶ δὲ τὸν Νεῖλον ἀπὸ
τοῦ Εὐφράτου πεντακισχιλίων, ἄλλους δὲ χιλίους
καὶ τριακοσίους[2] μέχρι Κανωβικοῦ στόματος, εἶτα
μέχρι τῆς Καρχηδόνος μυρίους τρισχιλίους πεντακοσίους, εἶτα μέχρι Στηλῶν ὀκτακισχιλίους
τοὐλάχιστον· ὑπεραίρειν δὴ τῶν ἑπτὰ μυριάδων
ὀκτακοσίοις.[3] δεῖν δὲ ἔτι προσθεῖναι τὸ ἐκτὸς
Ἡρακλείων στηλῶν κύρτωμα τῆς Εὐρώπης, ἀντι-
κείμενον μὲν τοῖς Ἴβηρσι, προπεπτωκὸς δὲ πρὸς
τὴν ἑσπέραν, οὐκ ἔλαττον σταδίων τρισχιλίων,
καὶ τὰ ἀκρωτήρια τά τε ἄλλα καὶ τὸ τῶν
Ὠστιμίων, ὃ καλεῖται Κάβαιον, καὶ τὰς κατὰ
τοῦτο νήσους, ὧν τὴν ἐσχάτην Οὐξισάμην φησὶ
Πυθέας ἀπέχειν ἡμερῶν τριῶν πλοῦν. ταῦτα δ'
εἰπὼν τὰ τελευταῖα οὐδὲν πρὸς τὸ μῆκος συν-
τείνοντα προσέθηκε τὰ περὶ τῶν ἀκρωτηρίων καὶ
τῶν Ὠστιμίων καὶ τῆς Οὐξισάμης καὶ ὧν φησι
νήσων· (ταῦτα γὰρ πάντα προσάρκτιά ἐστι καὶ
Κελτικά, οὐκ Ἰβηρικά, μᾶλλον δὲ Πυθέου πλάσματα.) προστίθησί τε τοῖς εἰρημένοις τοῦ μήκους

---

[1] γοῦν, A. Miller, for δ' οὖν.
[2] τριακοσίους, Gosselin, for πεντακοσίους.
[3] ὀκτακοσίοις, Sterrett restores, the reading before Kramer.

Eratosthenes has determined the said breadth, namely, that from extreme Ethiopia up to the parallel of Thule, he extends the length beyond the due measure, in order to make the length more than double the aforesaid breadth. At all events he says that the narrowest part of India up to the river Indus measures sixteen thousand stadia (for the part of India that extends to its capes will increase this length by three thousand stadia); and the distance thence to the Caspian Gates, fourteen thousand; then, to the Euphrates, ten thousand, and from the Euphrates to the Nile five thousand, and on to its Canobic mouth thirteen hundred more; then, to Carthage, thirteen thousand five hundred; then, to the Pillars, at least eight thousand; there is, accordingly, he says, an excess of eight hundred stadia over seventy thousand stadia. We must still add, he says, the bulge of Europe outside the Pillars, which lies over against Iberia and leans westward, reaching not less than three thousand stadia; we must also add all the capes, but in particular that of the Ostimians, called Cabaeum,[1] and the islands about it—the outermost of which, Uxisame,[2] Pytheas says, is a three days' sail distant. And after mentioning these last places, though all of them in their stretch add nothing to the length of the inhabited world, he has added the regions in the neighbourhood of the capes, of the Ostimians, of Uxisame, and of all the islands he names. (In fact, these places all lie towards the north and belong to Celtica, not to Iberia—or rather they are inventions of Pytheas.) And he adds to the

---

[1] Or Gabaeum (Ptol. 2. 8. 1); apparently Pointe du Raz.
[2] Ushant (Ouessant); the Axanthos of Pliny, *Nat. Hist.* 4. 16 (30).

διαστήμασιν ἄλλους σταδίους δισχιλίους μὲν
πρὸς τῇ δύσει, δισχιλίους δὲ πρὸς τῇ ἀνατολῇ,
ἵνα σώσῃ τὸ μὴ[1] πλέον ἢ ἥμισυ τοῦ μήκους τὸ
πλάτος.

6. Παραμυθούμενος δ' ἐπὶ πλέον, ὅτι κατὰ
φύσιν ἐστὶ τὸ ἀπὸ ἀνατολῆς ἐπὶ δύσιν διάστημα
μεῖζον λέγειν, κατὰ φύσιν φησὶν εἶναι ἀπὸ τῆς
ἕω πρὸς τὴν ἑσπέραν μακροτέραν εἶναι τὴν οἰκουμένην, καί[2], καθάπερ εἰρήκαμεν, ὡς οἱ μαθηματικοί,
φησί, κύκλον συνάπτειν, συμβάλλουσαν αὐτὴν
ἑαυτῇ· ὥστ', εἰ μὴ τὸ μέγεθος τοῦ Ἀτλαντικοῦ
πελάγους ἐκώλυε, κἂν πλεῖν ἡμᾶς ἐκ τῆς Ἰβηρίας
εἰς τὴν Ἰνδικὴν διὰ τοῦ αὐτοῦ παραλλήλου τὸ
C 65 λοιπὸν μέρος παρὰ τὸ λεχθὲν διάστημα ὑπὲρ τὸ
τρίτον μέρος ὂν τοῦ ὅλου κύκλου· εἴπερ ὁ δι'
Ἀθηνῶν[3] ἐλάττων ἐστὶν εἴκοσι μυριάδων, ὅπου
πεποιήμεθα τὸν εἰρημένον σταδιασμὸν ἀπὸ τῆς
Ἰνδικῆς εἰς τὴν Ἰβηρίαν. οὐδὲ ταῦτα οὖν εὖ λέγει.
οὗτος γὰρ ὁ λόγος[4] περὶ μὲν τῆς εὐκράτου καὶ

---

[1] μή, Kramer inserts; Forbiger following.
[2] καί, Jones inserts.
[3] The old reading was διὰ Θινῶν; but AC have Θηνῶν.
Kramer rightly reads as above. (cf. readings of MSS. on
1. 4. 6, 2. 1. 1, 2. 1. 2, 2. 1. 5, and 2. 1. 24.)
[4] τά, after λόγος, Corais deletes; Meineke following.

---

[1] The inhabited world is thought of as an arc, which, when
produced, completes a circle. Even Aristotle had discussed
the question whether the inhabited world, in its length,
could be connected by an arc of latitude drawn from Spain
westward to India (*Meteor.* 2. 5. 13).
[2] Eratosthenes means by "the aforesaid distance" his
length of the inhabited world, 77,800 stadia.

aforesaid length-distances still other stadia, namely, two thousand on the west, and two thousand on the east, in order to keep the breadth from being more than half the length.

6. Again, attempting still further to appease us by saying that it is " in accordance with nature " to call the distance from east to west greater, he says it is " in accordance with nature " that from the east to the west the inhabited world is longer, and, " just as I have already stated in the manner of the mathematicians," he says, " it forms a complete circle,[1] itself meeting itself; so that, if the immensity of the Atlantic Sea did not prevent, we could sail from Iberia to India along one and the same parallel over the remainder of the circle, that is, the remainder when you have subtracted the aforesaid distance[2], which is more than a third of the whole circle—if it be true that the circle that runs through Athens, along which I have made the said reckoning of stadia from India to Iberia, is less than two hundred thousand stadia in circuit."[3] However, Eratosthenes is not happy in this statement, either; for although this argument might be used in the

[3] It has been assumed by various scholars that Eratosthenes' parallel of latitude, above referred to, ran 25,450 stadia north of the equator, which would be at 36° 21' 25½". In this case the circumference of this parallel works out to be 202,945 stadia—if we count 700 stadia to the degree, following Eratosthenes' method. But Strabo fails to quote Eratosthenes on one section of the distance (from the equator to the southern limit of the inhabited world), and the 25,450 is reached only by a computation based on a statement of Ptolemy (*Mathematica Syntaxis* 1. 10), wherein Ptolemy refers to Eratosthenes' estimate of the distance between the tropics. That estimate was inaccurate and so is this; but even in his round numbers Eratosthenes is usually close to the truth.

καθ' ἡμᾶς ζώνης λέγοιτ' ἂν κατὰ τοὺς μαθηματι-
κούς, ἧς μέρος ἡ οἰκουμένη ἐστί, περὶ δὲ τῆς
οἰκουμένης—καλοῦμεν γὰρ οἰκουμένην ἣν οἰκοῦμεν
καὶ γνωρίζομεν· ἐνδέχεται δὲ ἐν τῇ αὐτῇ εὐκράτῳ
ζώνῃ καὶ δύο οἰκουμένας εἶναι ἢ καὶ πλείους,[1]
καὶ μάλιστα ἐγγὺς τοῦ δι' Ἀθηνῶν κύκλου
τοῦ διὰ τοῦ Ἀτλαντικοῦ πελάγους γραφομένου.
πάλιν δὲ ἐπιμένων τῇ περὶ τοῦ σφαιροειδῆ τὴν
γῆν εἶναι ἀποδείξει τῆς αὐτῆς ἐπιτιμήσεως ἂν
τυγχάνοι. ὡς δ' αὕτως καὶ πρὸς τὸν Ὅμηρον οὐ
παύεται περὶ τῶν αὐτῶν διαφερόμενος.

7. Ἑξῆς δὲ περὶ τῶν ἠπείρων εἰπὼν γεγονέναι
πολὺν λόγον, καὶ τοὺς μὲν τοῖς ποταμοῖς διαιρεῖν
αὐτάς, τῷ τε Νείλῳ καὶ τῷ Τανάϊδι, νήσους
ἀποφαίνοντας, τοὺς δὲ τοῖς ἰσθμοῖς, τῷ τε μεταξὺ
τῆς Κασπίας καὶ τῆς Ποντικῆς θαλάσσης καὶ τῷ
μεταξὺ τῆς Ἐρυθρᾶς καὶ τοῦ Ἐκρήγματος, τούτους
δὲ χερρονήσους αὐτὰς λέγειν, οὐχ ὁρᾶν φησι, πῶς
ἂν εἰς πρᾶγμά τι[2] καταστρέφοι ἡ ζήτησις αὕτη,
ἀλλὰ μόνον ἔριν διαιτώντων μᾶλλον κατὰ Δημόκριτον εἶναι. μὴ ὄντων γὰρ ἀκριβῶν ὅρων καθάπερ
Κολυττοῦ καὶ Μελίτης, οἷον στηλῶν ἢ περιβόλων,
τοῦτο μὲν ἔχειν φάναι ἡμᾶς, ὅτι τουτὶ μέν ἐστι
Κολυττός, τουτὶ δὲ Μελίτη, τοὺς ὅρους δὲ μὴ
ἔχειν εἰπεῖν. διὸ καὶ συμβαίνειν κρίσεις πολλάκις

---

[1] εἰ, Corais deletes, before καὶ; Kramer, C. Müller
suspecting; Meineke following.
[2] πρᾶγμά τι, Cobet, for πράγματα; A. Miller apparently
approving.

treatment of the temperate zone (that is, our zone)
from the point of view of mathematics (since the
inhabited world is a fraction of the temperate zone),
yet in the treatment of the inhabited world—why[1]
we call "inhabited" the world which we inhabit and
know; though it may be that in this same temperate
zone there are actually two inhabited worlds, or
even more, and particularly in the proximity of the
parallel through Athens that is drawn across the
Atlantic Sea. And again, by dwelling on his demonstration of the spheroidal shape of the earth he might
meet with the same criticism as before. And in the
same way also he does not cease to quarrel with
Homer about the very same things.

7. Next, after saying that there has been much
discussion about the continents, and that some
divide them by the rivers (the Nile and the Tanaïs),
declaring them to be islands, while others divide
them by the isthmuses (the isthmus between the
Caspian and the Pontic Seas, and the isthmus
between the Red Sea and the Ecregma[1]), and that
the latter call the continents peninsulas, Eratosthenes then says that he does not see how this
investigation can end in any practical result, but
that it belongs only to persons who choose to live on
a diet of disputation, after the manner of Democritus; for if there be no accurate boundaries—
take the case of Colyttus and Melite[2]—of stone
posts, for example, or enclosures, we can say only
this, "This is Colyttus," and "That is Melite," but
we should not be able to point out the boundaries;
and this is the reason also why disputes often arise

---

[1] Literally, the "Outbreak"; the outlet of Lake Sirbonis
into the Mediterranean.   [2] Attic demes, or townships.

περὶ χωρίων τινῶν, καθάπερ Ἀργείοις μὲν καὶ
Λακεδαιμονίοις περὶ Θυρέας, Ἀθηναίοις δὲ καὶ
Βοιωτοῖς περὶ Ὠρωποῦ. ἄλλως τε τοὺς Ἕλληνας
τὰς τρεῖς ἠπείρους ὀνομάσαι, οὐκ εἰς τὴν οἰκουμένην ἀποβλέψαντας, ἀλλ' εἴς τε τὴν σφετέραν
καὶ τὴν ἀπαντικρὺ τὴν Καρικήν, ἐφ' ᾗ νῦν Ἴωνες
καὶ οἱ ἑξῆς· χρονῷ δὲ ἐπὶ πλεον προϊόντας ἀεὶ
καὶ πλειόνων γνωριζομένων χωρῶν εἰς τοῦτο
καταστρέψαι τὴν διαίρεσιν. πότερον οὖν οἱ
πρῶτοι διορίσαντες τὰς τρεῖς, ἵνα ἀπὸ τῶν
ἐσχάτων ἄρξωμαι διαιτῶν τὴν ἔριν μὴ κατὰ
Δημόκριτον, ἀλλὰ κατ' αὐτόν, οὗτοι ἦσαν οἱ
πρῶτοι τὴν σφετέραν ἀπὸ τῆς ἀντικειμένης τῆς
τῶν Καρῶν διορίσαι ζητοῦντες; ἢ οὗτοι μὲν τὴν
Ἑλλάδα ἐπενόουν μόνην καὶ τὴν Καρίαν καὶ
ὀλίγην τὴν συνεχῆ, οὔτε δ' Εὐρώπην οὔτε Ἀσίαν
C 66 ὡσαύτως οὔτε Λιβύην, οἱ δὲ λοιποὶ ἐπιόντες
ὅση ἦν ἱκανὴ ὑπογράψαι[1] τὴν τῆς οἰκουμένης
ἐπίνοιαν, οὗτοί εἰσιν οἱ εἰς τρία διαιροῦντες; πῶς
οὖν οὐ τῆς οἰκουμένης ἐποιοῦντο διαίρεσιν; τίς δὲ
τρία μέρη λέγων καὶ καλῶν ἤπειρον ἕκαστον τῶν
μερῶν οὐ προσεπινοεῖ τὸ ὅλον, οὐ τὸν μερισμὸν
ποιεῖται; εἰ δ' ἐπινοεῖ μὲν μὴ τὴν οἰκουμένην,
μέρους δέ τινος αὐτῆς τὸν μερισμὸν ποιοῖτο, τίνος
ἄν τις μέρους τῆς οἰκουμένης μέρος εἶπε τὴν

[1] ὅση ... ὑπογράψαι, Corais, for ὅσην ἱκανοὶ ἐπιγράψαι;
Groskurd, Forbiger, Meineke, following.

244

concerning districts, such as the dispute between
the Argives and the Lacedaemonians about Thyrea,
and between the Athenians and the Boeotians about
Oropus; and the Greeks named the three continents
wrongly, because they did not look out upon the whole
inhabited world, but merely upon their own country
and that which lay directly opposite, namely, Caria,
where Ionians and their immediate neighbours now
live; but in time, ever advancing still further and
becoming acquainted with more and more countries,
they have finally brought their division of the continents to what it now is. The question, then, is
whether the " first men " who divided the three continents by boundaries (to begin with Eratosthenes' last
points, dieting upon disputation, not after the manner
of Democritus, but after that of Eratosthenes) were
those " first men" who sought to divide by boundaries
their own country from that of the Carians, which lay
opposite; or, did the latter have a notion merely of
Greece, and of Caria and a bit of territory that is
contiguous thereto, without having, in like manner,
a notion of Europe or Asia, or of Libya, whereas
the men of subsequent times, travelling over what
was enough of the earth to suggest the notion of the
inhabited world—are these the men, I say, who
made the division into three parts? How, pray,
could they have failed to make a division? And
who, when speaking of three parts and calling each
of the parts a continent, does not at the same time
have a notion of the integer of which he makes his
division into parts? But suppose he does not have
a notion of the inhabited world, but should make
his division of some part of it—of what part of the
inhabited world, I ask, would anyone have said Asia

Ἀσίαν ἢ τὴν Εὐρώπην ἢ ὅλως ἤπειρον; ταῦτα
γὰρ εἴρηται παχυμερῶς.

8. Ἔτι δὲ παχυμερέστερον τὸ φήσαντα μὴ ὁρᾶν,
εἰς τί πραγματικὸν καταστρέφει τὸ τοὺς ὅρους
ζητεῖν, παραθεῖναι τὸν Κολυττὸν καὶ τὴν Μελίτην,
εἶτ' εἰς τἀναντία περιτρέπεσθαι. εἰ γὰρ οἱ περὶ
Θυρεῶν καὶ Ὠρωποῦ πόλεμοι διὰ τὰς τῶν ὅρων
ἀγνοίας ἀπέβησαν, εἰς πραγματικόν τι κατα-
στρέφον τὸ διαχωρίζειν τὰς χώρας· ἢ τοῦτο
λέγει, ὡς ἐπὶ μὲν τῶν χωρίων, καὶ νὴ Δία τῶν
καθ' ἕκαστα ἐθνῶν πραγματικὸν τὸ διορίζειν
ἀκριβῶς, ἐπὶ δὲ τῶν ἠπείρων περιττόν; καίτοι
οὐδὲ ἐνταῦθα ἧττον οὐδέν· γένοιτο γὰρ ἂν καὶ ἐπὶ
τούτων ἡγεμόσι μεγάλοις ἀμφισβήτησις, τῷ μὲν
ἔχοντι τὴν Ἀσίαν, τῷ δὲ τὴν Λιβύην, ὁποτέρου
δή[1] ἐστιν ἡ Αἴγυπτος δηλονότι ἡ κάτω λεγομένη τῆς Αἰγύπτου χώρα. κἂν ἐάσῃ[2] δέ τις
τοῦτο διὰ τὸ σπάνιον, ἄλλως φατέον διαιρεῖσθαι
τὰς ἠπείρους κατὰ μέγαν διορισμὸν καὶ πρὸς τὴν
οἰκουμένην ὅλην ἀναφερόμενον· καθ' ὃν οὐδὲ
τούτου φροντιστέον, εἰ οἱ τοῖς ποταμοῖς διορίσαντες ἀπολείπουσί τινα χωρία ἀδιόριστα, τῶν
ποταμῶν μὴ μέχρι τοῦ ὠκεανοῦ διηκόντων, μηδὲ[3]
νήσους ὡς ἀληθῶς ἀπολειπόντων τὰς ἠπείρους.

9. Ἐπὶ τέλει δὲ τοῦ ὑπομνήματος οὐκ ἐπαι-
νέσας τοὺς δίχα διαιροῦντας ἅπαν τὸ τῶν ἀνθρω-

[1] δή, Meineke, for δ'.
[2] κἂν ἐάσῃ, for κατάνας, Paetz; Forbiger, Meineke, following.
[3] μηδέ, for τὰς μὲν δή, Corais; Groskurd, Meineke, Forbiger, following; Kramer, C. Müller, suspecting.

was a part, or Europe, or a continent in general?—
Indeed these points of his have been crudely stated.

8. Still cruder is it, after he has said that he does
not see what practical result there can be to the
investigation of the boundaries, to cite Colyttus and
Melite, and then turn round to the opposite side of
the question. For if the wars about Thyrea and
Oropus resulted through ignorance of the boundaries,
then the separation of countries by boundaries is a
thing that results in something practical. Or does
Eratosthenes mean this, that in the case of the
districts and, of course, of the several nations it is
practical to divide them by accurate boundaries,
whereas in case of the continents it is superfluous?
And yet, I answer, not even here is it any the less
practical; for there might arise also in case of the
continents a controversy between great rulers, for
example, one ruler who held Asia and another who
held Libya, as to which one of them really owned
Egypt, that is to say, the so-called " Lower" country
of Egypt. Moreover, if anyone dismisses this example
on account of its rarity, at all events it must be
said that the continents are divided according to a
process of grand division which also has relation to
the whole inhabited world. In following that
principle of division we must not worry about this
point, either, namely, that those who have made
the rivers the dividing lines leave certain districts
without dividing lines, because the rivers do not
reach all the way to the ocean and so do not really
leave the continents as islands.

9. Now, towards the end of his treatise—after
withholding praise from those who divide the whole
multitude of mankind into two groups, namely,

πων πλῆθος εἴς τε Ἕλληνας καὶ βαρβάρους, καὶ
τοὺς Ἀλεξάνδρῳ παραινοῦντας τοῖς μὲν Ἕλλησιν
ὡς φίλοις χρῆσθαι, τοῖς δὲ βαρβάροις ὡς πολε-
μίοις, βέλτιον εἶναί φησιν ἀρετῇ καὶ κακίᾳ διαιρεῖν ταῦτα. πολλοὺς γὰρ καὶ τῶν Ἑλλήνων
εἶναι κακοὺς καὶ τῶν βαρβάρων ἀστείους, καθάπερ Ἰνδοὺς καὶ Ἀριανούς, ἔτι δὲ Ῥωμαίους καὶ
Καρχηδονίους, οὕτω θαυμαστῶς πολιτευομένους.
διόπερ τὸν Ἀλέξανδρον, ἀμελήσαντα τῶν παραι-
νούντων, ὅσους οἷόν τ᾽ ἦν ἀποδέχεσθαι τῶν
C 67 εὐδοκίμων ἀνδρῶν καὶ εὐεργετεῖν· ὥσπερ δι᾽
ἄλλο τι τῶν οὕτω διελόντων, τοὺς μὲν ἐν ψόγῳ
τοὺς δ᾽ ἐν ἐπαίνῳ τιθεμένων, ἢ διότι τοῖς μὲν
ἐπικρατεῖ τὸ νόμιμον καὶ τὸ πολιτικὸν[1] καὶ τὸ
παιδείας καὶ λόγων οἰκεῖον, τοῖς δὲ τἀναντία.
καὶ ὁ Ἀλέξανδρος οὖν, οὐκ ἀμελήσας τῶν παραι-
νούντων ἀλλ᾽ ἀποδεξάμενος τὴν γνώμην, τὰ
ἀκόλουθα, οὐ τὰ ἐναντία, ἐποίει, πρὸς τὴν διάνοιαν
σκοπῶν τὴν τῶν ἐπεσταλκότων.

[1] καὶ τὸ πολιτικόν, omitted by Kramer, and also by
Meineke, Dübner-Müller, and Tardieu.

Greeks and Barbarians, and also from those who advised Alexander to treat the Greeks as friends but the Barbarians as enemies—Eratosthenes goes on to say that it would be better to make such divisions according to good qualities and bad qualities; for not only are many of the Greeks bad, but many of the Barbarians are refined—Indians and Arians, for example, and, further, Romans and Carthaginians, who carry on their governments so admirably. And this, he says, is the reason why Alexander, disregarding his advisers, welcomed as many as he could of the men of fair repute and did them favours—just as if those who have made such a division, placing some people in the category of censure, others in that of praise, did so for any other reason than that in some people there prevail the law-abiding and the political instinct, and the qualities associated with education and powers of speech, whereas in other people the opposite characteristics prevail! And so Alexander, not disregarding his advisers, but rather accepting their opinion, did what was consistent with, not contrary to, their advice; for he had regard to the real intent of those who gave him counsel.

BOOK II

I

1. Ἐν δὲ τῷ τρίτῳ τῶν γεωγραφικῶν καθιστά-
μενος τὸν τῆς οἰκουμένης πίνακα γραμμῇ τινι
διαιρεῖ δίχα ἀπὸ δύσεως ἐπ' ἀνατολὴν παραλλήλῳ
τῇ ἰσημερινῇ γραμμῇ. πέρατα δ' αὐτῆς τίθησι
πρὸς δύσει μὲν τὰς Ἡρακλείους στήλας, ἐπ'
ἀνατολῇ δὲ τὰ ἄκρα καὶ ἔσχατα ὄρη τῶν ἀφορι-
ζόντων ὀρῶν τὴν πρὸς ἄρκτον τῆς Ἰνδικῆς πλευράν. γράφει δὲ τὴν γραμμὴν ἀπὸ Στηλῶν διά
τε τοῦ Σικελικοῦ πορθμοῦ καὶ τῶν μεσημβρινῶν
ἄκρων τῆς τε Πελοποννήσου καὶ τῆς Ἀττικῆς,
καὶ μέχρι τῆς Ῥοδίας καὶ τοῦ Ἰσσικοῦ κόλπου.
μέχρι μὲν δὴ δεῦρο διὰ τῆς θαλάττης φησὶν εἶναι
τὴν λεχθεῖσαν γραμμὴν καὶ τῶν παρακειμένων
ἠπείρων (καὶ γὰρ αὐτὴν ὅλην τὴν καθ' ἡμᾶς
θάλατταν οὕτως ἐπὶ μῆκος τετάσθαι μέχρι τῆς
C 68 Κιλικίας), εἶτα ἐπ' εὐθείας πως ἐκβάλλεσθαι
παρ' ὅλην τὴν ὀρεινὴν τοῦ Ταύρου μέχρι τῆς
Ἰνδικῆς· τὸν γὰρ Ταῦρον ἐπ' εὐθείας τῇ ἀπὸ
Στηλῶν θαλάττῃ τεταμένον δίχα τὴν Ἀσίαν
διαιρεῖν ὅλην ἐπὶ μῆκος, τὸ μὲν αὐτῆς μέρος
βόρειον ποιοῦντα, τὸ δὲ νότιον· ὥσθ' ὁμοίως καὶ
αὐτὸν ἐπὶ τοῦ δι' Ἀθηνῶν[1] ἱδρῦσθαι παραλλήλου
καὶ τὴν ἀπὸ Στηλῶν μέχρι δεῦρο θάλατταν.

[1] δι' Ἀθηνῶν, Kramer, for διὰ Θινῶν ; see note 3, page 240.

BOOK II

I

1. IN the Third Book of his Geography Eratosthenes, in establishing the map of the inhabited world, divides it into two parts by a line drawn from west to east, parallel to the equatorial line; and as ends of this line he takes, on the west, the Pillars of Heracles, on the east, the capes and most remote peaks of the mountain-chain that forms the northern boundary of India. He draws the line from the Pillars through the Strait of Sicily and also through the southern capes both of the Peloponnesus and of Attica, and as far as Rhodes and the Gulf of Issus. Up to this point, then, he says, the said line runs through the sea and the adjacent continents (and indeed our whole Mediterranean Sea itself extends, lengthwise, along this line as far as Cilicia); then the line is produced in an approximately straight course along the whole Taurus Range as far as India, for the Taurus stretches in a straight course with the sea that begins at the Pillars, and divides all Asia lengthwise into two parts, thus making one part of it northern, the other southern; so that in like manner both the Taurus and the Sea from the Pillars up to the Taurus lie on the parallel of Athens.

2. Ταῦτα δ' εἰπὼν οἴεται δεῖν διορθῶσαι τὸν ἀρχαῖον γεωγραφικὸν πίνακα. πολὺ γὰρ ἐπὶ τὰς ἄρκτους παραλλάττειν τὰ ἑωθινὰ μέρη τῶν ὁρῶν κατ' αὐτόν, συνεπισπᾶσθαι δὲ καὶ τὴν Ἰνδικὴν ἀρκτικωτέραν ἢ δεῖ[1] γινομένην. πίστιν δὲ τούτου φέρει μίαν μὲν τοιαύτην, ὅτι τὰ τῆς Ἰνδικῆς ἄκρα τὰ μεσημβρινώτατα ὁμολογοῦσι πολλοὶ τοῖς κατὰ Μερόην ἀνταίρειν τόποις, ἀπό τε τῶν ἀέρων καὶ τῶν οὐρανίων τεκμαιρόμενοι, ἐντεῦθεν δ' ἐπὶ τὰ βορειότατα τῆς Ἰνδικῆς τὰ πρὸς τοῖς Καυκασίοις ὄρεσι Πατροκλῆς, ὁ μάλιστα πιστεύεσθαι δίκαιος διά τε τὸ ἀξίωμα καὶ διὰ τὸ μὴ ἰδιώτης εἶναι τῶν γεωγραφικῶν, φησὶ σταδίους μυρίους καὶ πεντακισχιλίους· ἀλλὰ μὴν καὶ τὸ ἀπὸ Μερόης ἐπὶ τὸν δι' Ἀθηνῶν παράλληλον τοσοῦτόν πώς ἐστιν, ὥστε τῆς Ἰνδικῆς τὰ προσάρκτια μέρη συνάπτοντα τοῖς Καυκασίοις ὄρεσιν εἰς τοῦτον τελευτᾶν τὸν κύκλον.

3. Ἄλλην δὲ πίστιν φέρει τοιαύτην, ὅτι τὸ ἀπὸ τοῦ Ἰσσικοῦ κόλπου διάστημα ἐπὶ τὴν θάλατταν τὴν Ποντικὴν τρισχιλίων πώς ἐστι σταδίων πρὸς ἄρκτον ἰόντι καὶ τοὺς περὶ Ἀμισὸν ἢ Σινώπην τόπους, ὅσον καὶ τὸ πλάτος τῶν ὁρῶν λέγεται· ἐκ δὲ Ἀμισοῦ πρὸς τὴν ἰσημερινὴν ἀνατολὴν φερομένῳ πρῶτον μὲν ἡ Κολχίς ἐστιν, ἔπειτα ἡ ἐπὶ τὴν Ὑρκανίαν θάλατταν ὑπέρθεσις καὶ ἡ ἐφεξῆς ἡ ἐπὶ Βάκτρα καὶ τοὺς ἐπέκεινα Σκύθας

---

[1] ἢ δεῖ, Groskurd, for ἤδη.

---

[1] The Greek word meaning "rise opposite to", which Strabo often uses (following Eratosthenes), apparently contains the idea of "lies on the same parallel with the equator."

2. After Eratosthenes has said that, he thinks he must needs make a complete revision of the early geographical map; for, according to it, he says, the eastern portions of the mountains deviate considerably towards the north, and India itself is drawn up along with it, and comes to occupy a more northerly position than it should. As proof of this he offers, first, an argument to this effect: the most southerly capes of India rise opposite to[1] the regions about Meroë, as many writers agree, who judge both from the climatic conditions and from the celestial phenomena; and from the capes on to the most northerly regions of India at the Caucasus Mountains, Patrocles (the man who has particular right to our confidence, both on account of his worthiness of character and on account of his being no layman in geographical matters) says the distance is fifteen thousand stadia; but, to be sure, the distance from Meroë to the parallel of Athens is about that distance; and therefore the northerly parts of India, since they join the Caucasus Mountains,[2] come to an end in this parallel.

3. Another proof which he offers is to this effect: the distance from the Gulf of Issus to the Pontic Sea is about three thousand stadia, if you go towards the north and the regions round about Amisus and Sinope, a distance as great as that which is also assigned to the breadth of the mountains; and from Amisus, if you bear towards the equinoctial sunrise, you come first to Colchis; and then you come to the passage which takes you over to the Hyrcanian[3] Sea, and to the road next in order that leads to Bactra

[2] The Indian Caucasus, now Hindu Kush.
[3] Caspian.

ὁδὸς δεξιὰ ἔχοντι τὰ ὄρη· αὕτη δ' ἡ γραμμὴ διὰ
'Αμισοῦ πρὸς δύσιν ἐκβαλλομένη διὰ τῆς Προποντίδος ἐστὶ καὶ τοῦ Ἑλλησπόντου. ἀπὸ δὲ
Μερόης ἐπὶ τὸν Ἑλλήσποντον οὐ πλείους εἰσὶ
τῶν μυρίων καὶ ὀκτακισχιλίων σταδίων, ὅσοι καὶ
ἀπὸ τοῦ μεσημβρινοῦ πλευροῦ τῆς Ἰνδικῆς πρὸς
τὰ περὶ τοὺς Βακτρίους μέρη, προστεθέντων
τρισχιλίων τοῖς μυρίοις καὶ πεντακισχιλίοις, ὧν
οἱ μὲν τοῦ πλάτους ἦσαν τῶν ὁρῶν, οἱ δὲ τῆς
Ἰνδικῆς.

4. Πρὸς δὲ τὴν ἀπόφασιν ταύτην ὁ Ἵππαρχος
ἀντιλέγει διαβάλλων τὰς πίστεις· οὔτε γὰρ
Πατροκλέα πιστὸν εἶναι, δυεῖν ἀντιμαρτυρούντων
C 69 αὐτῷ Δηιμάχου τε καὶ Μεγασθένους, οἳ καθ' οὓς
μὲν τόπους δισμυρίων εἶναι σταδίων τὸ διάστημά
φασι τὸ ἀπὸ τῆς κατὰ μεσημβρίαν θαλάττης, καθ'
οὓς δὲ καὶ τρισμυρίων· τούτους γε δὴ τοιαῦτα
λέγειν, καὶ τοὺς ἀρχαίους πίνακας τούτοις ὁμολογεῖν. ἀπίθανον δή που νομίζει τὸ μόνῳ δεῖν
πιστεύειν Πατροκλεῖ, παρέντας τοὺς τοσοῦτον ἀντιμαρτυροῦντας αὐτῷ, καὶ διορθοῦσθαι
παρ' αὐτὸ τοῦτο τοὺς ἀρχαίους πίνακας, ἀλλὰ
μὴ ἐᾶν οὕτως, ἕως ἄν τι πιστότερον περὶ αὐτῶν
γνῶμεν.

5. Οἶμαι δὴ πολλὰς ἔχειν εὐθύνας τοῦτον τὸν
λόγον. πρῶτον μὲν ὅτι πολλαῖς μαρτυρίαις
ἐκείνου χρησαμένου, μιᾷ φησι τῇ Πατροκλέους
αὐτὸν χρῆσθαι. τίνες οὖν ἦσαν οἱ φάσκοντες τὰ
μεσημβρινὰ ἄκρα τῆς Ἰνδικῆς ἀνταίρειν τοῖς κατὰ
Μερόην; τίνες δ' οἱ τὸ ἀπὸ Μερόης διάστημα
μέχρι τοῦ δι' Ἀθηνῶν παραλλήλου τοσοῦτον

and to the Scythians on beyond, keeping the mountains on your right; and this line, if produced through Amisus westwards, runs through the Propontis and the Hellespont; and from Meroë to the Hellespont is not more than eighteen thousand stadia, a distance as great as that from the southern side of India to the parts round about the Bactrians, if we added three thousand stadia to the fifteen thousand, some of which belonged to the breadth of the mountains, the others to that of India.

4. As for this declaration of Eratosthenes, Hipparchus contradicts it by throwing discredit on the proofs. In the first place, says he, Patrocles is not trustworthy, since two men bear testimony against him, both Deïmachus and Megasthenes, who say that in some places the distance from the southern sea is twenty thousand stadia and in other places even thirty thousand; so these two men, at least, make such a statement, and the early maps agree with them. It is an incredible thing, of course, he thinks, that we have to trust Patrocles alone, in disregard of those whose testimony is so strong against him, and to correct the early maps throughout as regards the very point at issue, instead of leaving them as they are until we have more trustworthy information about them.

5. Now I think this reasoning of Hipparchus is open to censure on many grounds. In the first place, although Eratosthenes used many testimonies, he says that Eratosthenes uses only one—that of Patrocles. Who, pray, were the men that affirmed that the southern capes of India rose opposite to the regions of Meroë? And who the men that said the distance from Meroë up to the parallel of Athens

λέγοντες; τίνες δὲ πάλιν οἱ τὸ τῶν ὁρῶν πλάτος,
ἢ οἱ τὸ ἀπὸ τῆς Κιλικίας ἐπὶ τὴν Ἀμισὸν τὸ
αὐτὸ τοῦτο λέγοντες; τίνες δὲ οἱ τὸ ἀπὸ Ἀμισοῦ
διὰ Κόλχων καὶ τῆς Ὑρκανίας μέχρι Βακτρίων
καὶ τῶν ἐπέκεινα εἰς τὴν ἑῴαν θάλατταν καθηκόν-
των ἐπ᾽ εὐθείας τε εἶναι λέγοντες καὶ ἐπ᾽ ἰσημερινὰς ἀνατολὰς καὶ παρὰ[1] τὰ ὄρη ἐν δεξιᾷ
ἔχοντι αὐτά; ἢ πάλιν τὸ ἐπὶ τὴν δύσιν ἐπ᾽
εὐθείας ταύτῃ τῇ γραμμῇ, διότι ἐπὶ τὴν Προποντίδα ἐστὶ καὶ τὸν Ἑλλήσποντον; ταῦτα γὰρ ὁ
Ἐρατοσθένης λαμβάνει πάντα ὡς καὶ ἐκμαρτυ-
ρούμενα ὑπὸ τῶν ἐν τοῖς τόποις γενομένων, ἐν-
τετυχηκὼς ὑπομνήμασι πολλοῖς, ὧν εὐπόρει
βιβλιοθήκην ἔχων τηλικαύτην ἡλίκην αὐτὸς
Ἵππαρχός φησι.

6. Καὶ αὐτὴ δὲ ἡ τοῦ Πατροκλέους πίστις ἐκ
πολλῶν μαρτυριῶν σύγκειται, τῶν βασιλέων τῶν
πεπιστευκότων αὐτῷ τηλικαύτην ἀρχήν, τῶν
ἐπακολουθησάντων αὐτῷ, τῶν ἀντιδοξούντων, ὧν
αὐτὸς ὁ Ἵππαρχος κατονομάζει· οἱ γὰρ κατ᾽ ἐκείνων ἔλεγχοι πίστεις τῶν ὑπὸ τούτου λεγομένων
εἰσίν. οὐδὲ τοῦτο δὲ ἀπίθανον τοῦ Πατροκλέους,
ὅτι φησὶ τοὺς Ἀλεξάνδρῳ συστρατεύσαντας ἐπι-
δρομάδην ἱστορῆσαι ἕκαστα, αὐτὸν δὲ Ἀλέξανδρον
ἀκριβῶσαι, ἀναγραψάντων τὴν ὅλην χώραν τῶν
ἐμπειροτάτων αὐτῷ· τὴν δ᾽ ἀναγραφὴν αὐτῷ

---

[1] παρά, Corais, for περί; Groskurd, Forbiger, Meineke
following.

was such a distance ? And who, again, the men that gave the breadth of the Taurus Mountains, or the men that called the distance from Cilicia to the Amisus the same as that of this breadth ? And who said as regards the distance from Amisus, through Colchis and Hyrcania up to Bactria and through the regions beyond Bactria which reach down to the eastern sea, that it was in a straight line and toward the equinoctial east and that it was alongside the mountains which you keep on your right hand ? Or, again, as regards the distance towards the west in a straight course with this line, that it was towards the Propontis and the Hellespont ? Why, Eratosthenes takes all these as matters actually established by the testimony of the men who had been in the regions, for he has read many historical treatises— with which he was well supplied if he had a library as large as Hipparchus says it was.[1]

6. Further, the trustworthiness of Patrocles, itself, rests upon many testimonies ; I refer to the Kings[2] who had entrusted to him such an important office ; to the men who followed him, to the men who oppose him, whom Hipparchus himself names ; for the tests to which those men are subjected are but proofs of the statements of Patrocles. Neither does this statement of Patrocles lack plausibility, namely, that those who made the expedition with Alexander acquired only cursory information about everything, but Alexander himself made accurate investigations, since the men best acquainted with the country had described the whole of it for him ; and this description was later presented to

[1] The library at Alexandria.
[2] Seleucus I. and Antiochus I.

δοθῆναί φησιν ὕστερον ὑπὸ Ξενοκλέους τοῦ γαζοφύλακος.

7. Ἔτι φησὶν ὁ Ἵππαρχος ἐν τῷ δευτέρῳ ὑπο-μνήματι αὐτὸν τὸν Ἐρατοσθένη διαβάλλειν τὴν τοῦ Πατροκλέους πίστιν ἐκ τῆς πρὸς Μεγασθένη διαφωνίας περὶ τοῦ μήκους τῆς Ἰνδικῆς τοῦ κατὰ τὸ βόρειον πλευρόν, τοῦ μὲν Μεγασθένους λέ-γοντος σταδίων μυρίων ἑξακισχιλίων, τοῦ δὲ Πατροκλέους χιλίοις λείπειν φαμένου· ἀπὸ γάρ τινος ἀναγραφῆς σταθμῶν ὁρμηθέντα τοῖς μὲν
C 70 ἀπιστεῖν διὰ τὴν διαφωνίαν, ἐκείνῃ δὲ προσέχειν. εἰ οὖν διὰ τὴν διαφωνίαν ἐνταῦθα ἄπιστος ὁ Πατροκλῆς, καίτοι παρὰ χιλίους σταδίους τῆς διαφορᾶς οὔσης, πόσῳ χρὴ μᾶλλον ἀπιστεῖν ἐν οἷς παρὰ ὀκτακισχιλίους ἡ διαφορά ἐστι, πρὸς δύο καὶ ταῦτα ἄνδρας συμφωνοῦντας ἀλλήλοις, τῶν μὲν λεγόντων τὸ τῆς Ἰνδικῆς πλάτος δισμυ-ρίων σταδίων, τοῦ δὲ μυρίων καὶ δισχιλίων;

8. Ἐροῦμεν δ' ὅτι οὐ ψιλὴν τὴν διαφωνίαν ᾐτιάσατο, ἀλλὰ συγκρίνων πρὸς τὴν ὁμολογίαν καὶ τὴν ἀξιοπιστίαν τῆς ἀναγραφῆς τῶν σταθμῶν. οὐ θαυμαστὸν δέ, εἰ πιστοῦ γίνεταί τι πιστότερον, καὶ εἰ τῷ αὐτῷ ἐν ἑτέροις μὲν πιστεύομεν, ἐν ἑτέροις δ' ἀπιστοῦμεν, ὅταν παρά τινος τεθῇ τι βεβαιότερον. γελοῖόν τε τὸ τὴν παρὰ πολὺ διαφωνίαν ἀπιστοτέρους ποιεῖν νομίσαι τοὺς

Patrocles (so Patrocles says) by Xenocles, Alexander's treasurer.

7. Hipparchus further says, in his Second Book, that Eratosthenes himself throws discredit on the trustworthiness of Patrocles, in consequence of Patrocles' disagreement with Megasthenes about the length of India on its northern side, which Megasthenes calls sixteen thousand stadia, whereas Patrocles affirms that it is a thousand short of that; for, having started from a certain "Itinerary" as basis, Eratosthenes distrusts both of them on account of their disagreement and holds to the "Itinerary." If, then, says Hipparchus, Patrocles is untrustworthy on account of the disagreement at that point, although the discrepancy is only a matter of a thousand stadia, how much more should we distrust him where the discrepancy is a matter of eight thousand stadia, as against two men, and that, too, men who agree with one another; for both of them call the breadth of India twenty thousand stadia, whereas Patrocles calls it twelve thousand?

8. My answer will be that it was not the bare disagreement with Megasthenes that Eratosthenes found fault with, but he found fault when he compared their disagreement with the harmony and trustworthiness of the "Itinerary." Yet we should not be surprised if one thing proves to be more trustworthy than another trustworthy thing, and if we trust the same man in some things, but distrust him in others, whenever greater certainty has been established from some other source. Again, it is ridiculous to think that the amount by which the authorities disagree makes the parties to the disagreement less trustworthy. Why, on

διαφωνοῦντας· τοὐναντίον γὰρ ἐν τῷ παρὰ μικρὸν
συμβαίνειν τοῦτο μᾶλλον ἔοικε, παρὰ μικρὸν γὰρ
ἡ πλάνη συμβαίνει μᾶλλον, οὐ τοῖς τυχοῦσι
μόνον, ἀλλὰ καὶ τοῖς πλέον τι τῶν ἑτέρων φρο-
νοῦσιν· ἐν δὲ τοῖς παρὰ πολὺ ὁ μὲν τυχὼν ἁμάρτοι
ἄν, ὁ δ᾿ ἐπιστημονικώτερος ἧττον ἂν τοῦτο πάθοι·
διὸ καὶ πιστεύεται θᾶττον.

9. Ἅπαντες μὲν τοίνυν οἱ περὶ τῆς Ἰνδικῆς
γράψαντες ὡς ἐπὶ τὸ πολὺ ψευδολόγοι γεγόνασι,
καθ᾿ ὑπερβολὴν δὲ Δηΐμαχος· τὰ δὲ δεύτερα λέγει
Μεγασθένης· Ὀνησίκριτος δὲ καὶ Νέαρχος καὶ
ἄλλοι τοιοῦτοι παραψελλίζοντες ἤδη· καὶ ἡμῖν
δ᾿ ὑπῆρξεν ἐπὶ πλέον κατιδεῖν ταῦτα, ὑπομνηματι-
ζομένοις τὰς Ἀλεξάνδρου πράξεις· διαφερόντως
δ᾿ ἀπιστεῖν ἄξιον Δηϊμάχῳ τε καὶ Μεγασθένει.
οὗτοι γάρ εἰσιν οἱ τοὺς Ἐνωτοκοίτας καὶ τοὺς
Ἀστόμους καὶ Ἄρρινας ἱστοροῦντες, Μονοφθάλ-
μους τε καὶ Μακροσκελεῖς καὶ Ὀπισθοδακτύλους·
ἀνεκαίνισαν δὲ καὶ τὴν Ὁμηρικὴν τῶν Πυγμαίων
γερανομαχίαν, τρισπιθάμους εἰπόντες. οὗτοι δὲ
καὶ τοὺς χρυσωρύχους μύρμηκας καὶ Πᾶνας
σφηνοκεφάλους ὄφεις τε καὶ βοῦς καὶ ἐλάφους
σὺν κέρασι καταπίνοντας· περὶ ὧν ἕτερος τὸν
ἕτερον ἐλέγχει, ὅπερ καὶ Ἐρατοσθένης φησίν.

---

1 Which formed a part of Strabo's *Historical Sketches* (see footnote on page 46). Both Onesicritus and Nearchus accom-

the contrary, this is more likely to be the case where the matter of disagreement is slight; for if the matter of disagreement is but slight, error is more likely to result, not merely among ordinary writers, but even among writers who are somewhat superior to the other class; but where the matters of disagreement are considerable, though the ordinary man would go astray, the more scientific man would be less likely to do so, and for that reason he is more quickly trusted.

9. However, all who have written about India have proved themselves, for the most part, fabricators, but preëminently so Deïmachus; the next in order is Megasthenes; and then, Onesicritus, and Nearchus, and other such writers, who begin to speak the truth, though with faltering voice. I, too, had the privilege of noting this fact extensively when I was writing the "Deeds of Alexander."[1] But especially do Deïmachus and Megasthenes deserve to be distrusted. For they are the persons who tell us about the "men that sleep in their ears," and the "men without mouths," and "men without noses"; and about "men with one eye," "men with long legs," "men with fingers turned backward"; and they revived, also, the Homeric story of the battle between the cranes and the "pygmies," who, they said, were three spans tall. These men also tell about the ants that mine gold and Pans with wedge-shaped heads; and about snakes that swallow oxen and stags, horns and all; and in these matters the one refutes the other, as is stated by Eratosthenes also. For although they

panied Alexander. Strabo alludes to his own stay at the Alexandrian Library.

ἐπέμφθησαν μὲν γὰρ εἰς τὰ Παλίμβοθρα, ὁ μὲν Μεγασθένης πρὸς Σανδρόκοττον, ὁ δὲ Δηίμαχος πρὸς Ἀλλιτροχάδην τὸν ἐκείνου υἱόν, κατὰ πρεσβείαν· ὑπομνήματα δὲ τῆς ἀποδημίας κατέλιπον τοιαῦτα, ὑφ᾽ ἧς δή ποτε αἰτίας προαχθέντες. Πατροκλῆς δὲ ἥκιστα τοιοῦτος· καὶ οἱ ἄλλοι δὲ μάρτυρες οὐκ ἀπίθανοι, οἷς κέχρηται ὁ Ἐρατοσθένης.

10. Εἰ γὰρ ὁ διὰ Ῥόδου καὶ Βυζαντίου μεσημβρινὸς ὀρθῶς εἴληπται, καὶ ὁ διὰ τῆς Κιλικίας καὶ Ἀμισοῦ ὀρθῶς ἂν εἴη εἰλημμένος· φαίνεται γὰρ τὸ παράλληλον ἐκ πολλῶν, ὅταν μηδετέρωσε[1] C 71 σύμπτωσις ἀπελέγχηται.

11. Ὅ τε ἐξ Ἀμισοῦ πλοῦς ἐπὶ τὴν Κολχίδα ὅτι ἐστὶν ἐπὶ ἰσημερινὴν ἀνατολήν, καὶ τοῖς ἀνέμοις ἐλέγχεται καὶ ὥραις καὶ καρποῖς καὶ ταῖς ἀνατολαῖς αὐταῖς· ὡς δ᾽ αὕτως καὶ ἡ ἐπὶ τὴν Κασπίαν ὑπέρβασις καὶ ἡ ἐφεξῆς ὁδὸς μέχρι Βάκτρων. πολλαχοῦ γὰρ ἡ ἐνάργεια καὶ τὸ ἐκ πάντων συμφωνούμενον ὀργάνου πιστότερόν ἐστιν· ἐπεὶ καὶ ὁ αὐτὸς Ἵππαρχος τὴν ἀπὸ Στηλῶν μέχρι τῆς Κιλικίας γραμμήν, ὅτι ἐστὶν ἐπ᾽ εὐθείας καὶ ὅτι ἐπὶ ἰσημερινὴν ἀνατολήν, οὐ πᾶσαν

---

[1] μηδετέρωσε, A. Miller, for μηδετέρως ἤ.

---

[1] Scholars have agreed that something has fallen out of the manuscripts; but the assumption is unnecessary. Strabo here recurs to "the second argument" of Eratosthenes, which was introduced as far back as § 3, and the connection is not at once apparent; but he has just referred to the credibility of "the other witnesses," and, clearly, it was

were sent on an ambassadorial mission to Palimbothra (Megasthenes to Sandrocottus, Deïmachus
to Allitrochades the son of Sandrocottus), still,
as memoirs of their stay abroad, they have left
behind such writings as these, being prompted to do
so by—I know not what cause! Patrocles, however,
is by no means that sort of man. And also the
other witnesses whom Eratosthenes has used are not
lacking in credibility.

10.[1] For instance, if the meridian through Rhodes
and Byzantium has been correctly drawn, then that
through Cilicia and Amisus will have been correctly
drawn too ; for from many considerations the
parallel relation of lines is obvious whenever it is
proved by test that there is no meeting in either
direction.[2]

11. Again, that the voyage from Amisus to Colchis
lies in the direction of the equinoctial east[3] is proved
by the winds, by the seasons, by the crops, and by
the risings of the sun themselves ; and thus, in
the same way, both the pass that leads over to the
Caspian Sea and the road from there on to Bactra.
For in many cases the way things appear to the
sight and the agreement of all the testimony are
more trustworthy than an instrument.[4] Indeed,
even the same Hipparchus, in taking the line from
the Pillars on to Cilicia to be in a straight course
and to be in the direction of the equinoctial east, did

upon "the other witnesses" that Eratosthenes based that
"second argument," as is indicated in §5. Strabo then
proceeds, in § 10, to illustrate the credibility of those
witnesses by defending Eratosthenes on points wherein they
were involved.
    [2] An echo from Greek geometry.
    [3] That is, due east.   [4] Compare § 35 (below).

ὀργανικῶς καὶ γεωμετρικῶς ἔλαβεν, ἀλλ' ὅλην τὴν
ἀπὸ Στηλῶν μέχρι πορθμοῦ τοῖς πλέουσιν ἐπίστευσεν, ὥστ' οὐδ' ἐκεῖνο[1] εὖ λέγει τὸ[2] " ἐπειδὴ
οὐκ ἔχομεν λέγειν οὔθ' ἡμέρας μεγίστης πρὸς τὴν
βραχυτάτην λόγον οὔτε γνώμονος πρὸς σκιὰν ἐπὶ
τῇ παρωρείᾳ τῇ ἀπὸ Κιλικίας μέχρι[3] Ἰνδῶν, οὐδ'
εἰ ἐπὶ παραλλήλου γραμμῆς ἐστιν ἡ λόξωσις,
ἔχομεν εἰπεῖν, ἀλλ' ἐὰν ἀδιόρθωτον, λοξὴν φυλάξαντες, ὡς οἱ ἀρχαῖοι πίνακες παρέχουσι[4]." πρῶτον
μὲν γὰρ τὸ μὴ ἔχειν εἰπεῖν ταὐτόν ἐστι τῷ
ἐπέχειν, ὁ δ' ἐπέχων οὐδ' ἑτέρωσε ῥέπει, ἐὰν δὲ
κελεύων, ὡς οἱ ἀρχαῖοι, ἐκεῖσε ῥέπει. μᾶλλον δ'
ἂν τἀκόλουθον ἐφύλαττεν, εἰ συνεβούλευε μηδὲ
γεωγραφεῖν ὅλως· οὐδὲ γὰρ τῶν ἄλλων ὀρῶν τὰς
θέσεις, οἷον Ἄλπεων καὶ τῶν Πυρηναίων καὶ τῶν
Θρᾳκίων καὶ Ἰλλυρικῶν καὶ Γερμανικῶν, οὕτως
ἔχομεν εἰπεῖν. τίς δ' ἂν ἡγήσαιτο πιστοτέρους
τῶν ὕστερον τοὺς παλαιοὺς τοσαῦτα πλημ-
μελήσαντας περὶ τὴν πινακογραφίαν, ὅσα εὖ[5]
διαβέβληκεν Ἐρατοσθένης, ὧν οὐδενὶ ἀντείρηκεν
Ἵππαρχος;

12. Καὶ τὰ ἑξῆς δὲ πλήρη μεγάλων ἀποριῶν
ἐστιν. ὅρα γάρ, εἰ τοῦτο μὲν μὴ κινοίη τις τὸ τὰ

---

[1] ἐκεῖνο, Scaliger, for ἐκεῖνος; Corais, Meineke, Dübner-
Müller, Groskurd, Forbiger, following.
[2] εὖ λέγει τό, Xylander, for εὐλογεῖτο; Meineke following.
[3] μέχρι, Meineke, for μέχρις.
[4] παρέχουσι, Kramer, for περιέχουσι; Meineke, Forbiger,
Tardieu, following.
[5] εὖ, Corais, for οὐ; editors following.

not depend wholly on instruments and geometrical calculations, but for the whole line from the Pillars on to the Strait[1] he trusted the sailors. So that this statement of his is not good, either, where he says : "Since we cannot tell either the relation of the longest day to the shortest, or of gnomon to shadow, along the mountain-side that runs from Cilicia on to India, neither can we say whether the slant of the mountains lies in a parallel line,[2] but we must leave the line uncorrected, keeping it aslant as the early maps give it." For, in the first place, "cannot tell" is the same thing as to withhold opinion, and the man who withholds opinion also inclines to neither side ; but when Hipparchus bids us leave the line as the ancients give it, he inclines to that side. Rather would he be "keeping" the consistent course, if he also advised us not to treat geography at all ; for we "cannot tell" in that way[3] the positions of the other mountains, either—for instance, the Alps, the Pyrenees, and the Thracian, the Illyrian, and the German Mountains. But who would think the early geographers more trustworthy than those of later times, since in their map-drawing the ancients made all those blunders that Eratosthenes has rightly accused them of and not one of these blunders has been objected to by Hipparchus ?

12. Again, the next remarks of Hipparchus are full of great difficulties. For example, see how many absurdities would arise if one should not disallow the

[1] Of Sicily.

[2] That is, whether the line of these mountains, which in the early maps makes an acute angle to the north with a parallel of latitude, should lie on a parallel. Compare § 2 (above).

[3] That is, by instruments and geometrical calculations.

ἄκρα τῆς Ἰνδικῆς τὰ μεσημβρινὰ ἀνταίρειν τοῖς κατὰ Μερόην, μηδὲ τὸ διάστημα τὸ ἀπὸ Μερόης ἐπὶ τὸ στόμα τὸ κατὰ τὸ Βυζάντιον, ὅτι ἐστὶ περὶ μυρίους σταδίους καὶ ὀκτακισχιλίους, ποιοίη δὲ τρισμυρίων τὸ ἀπὸ τῶν μεσημβρινῶν Ἰνδῶν μέχρι τῶν ὅρων, ὅσα ἂν συμβαίη ἄτοπα. τὸ πρῶτον μὲν γὰρ εἴπερ ὁ αὐτός ἐστι παράλληλος ὁ διὰ Βυζαντίου τῷ διὰ Μασσαλίας (καθάπερ εἴρηκεν Ἵππαρχος πιστεύσας Πυθέᾳ), ὁ δ' αὐτός καὶ μεσημβρινός ἐστιν ὁ διὰ Βυζαντίου τῷ διὰ Βορυσθένους, ὅπερ καὶ αὐτὸ δοκιμάζει ὁ Ἵππαρχος, δοκιμάζει δὲ καὶ τὸ ἀπὸ Βυζαντίου διάστημα ἐπὶ τὸν Βορυσθένη σταδίους εἶναι τρισχιλίους ἑπτα-
C 72 κοσίους, τοσοῦτοι ἂν εἶεν καὶ οἱ ἀπὸ Μασσαλίας ἐπὶ τὸν διὰ Βορυσθένους παράλληλον, ὅς γε διὰ τῆς Κελτικῆς παρωκεανίτιδος ἂν εἴη· τοσούτους γάρ πως διελθόντες συνάπτουσι τῷ ὠκεανῷ.

13. Πάλιν δ' ἐπεὶ τὴν Κινναμωμοφόρον ἐσχάτην ἴσμεν οἰκουμένην πρὸς μεσημβρίαν, καὶ καθ' Ἵππαρχον αὐτὸν ὁ δι' αὐτῆς παράλληλος ἀρχὴ τῆς εὐκράτου καὶ τῆς οἰκουμένης ἐστί, καὶ διέχει τοῦ ἰσημερινοῦ περὶ ὀκτακισχιλίους καὶ ὀκτα-κοσίους σταδίους· ἐπεὶ οὖν φησιν ἀπὸ τοῦ ἰσημερινοῦ τὸν διὰ Βορυσθένους διέχειν τρισ-μυρίους καὶ τετρακισχιλίους σταδίους, εἶεν ἂν λοιποὶ οἱ ἀπὸ τοῦ ὁρίζοντος τὴν διακεκαυμένην

---

[1] See footnote on page 254.

statement that the southern capes of India rise
opposite to [1] the regions of Meroë, or the statement
that the distance from Meroë to the mouth of the
strait at Byzantium is about eighteen thousand stadia,
but yet should make the distance from Southern
India to the mountains thirty thousand stadia. Why,
in the first place, if it be true that the parallel
which runs through Byzantium is the same as that
which runs through Massilia (as Hipparchus has
stated, on the authority of Pytheas), and that the
meridian which runs through Byzantium is the same
as that through the Borysthenes (which very thing,
also, Hipparchus approves), and if he also approves
the statement that the distance from Byzantium to
the Borysthenes is three thousand seven hundred
stadia, then this last number would be the number
of stadia from Massilia to the parallel that runs
through the Borysthenes [2]; which parallel, of course,
would run through the sea-coast of Celtica, for on
going about this number of stadia through Celtica
you reach the ocean.[3]

13. Again, since the Cinnamon-producing Country
is the most remote inhabited country towards the
south, as we know, and since, according to Hipparchus himself, the parallel that runs through it is
the beginning of the temperate zone and of the
inhabited world, and is distant from the equator about
eight thousand eight hundred stadia; and further,
since, as Hipparchus says, the parallel through
the Borysthenes is thirty-four thousand stadia distant from the equator, there would remain twenty-

[2] Strabo frequently refers to the mouth of the Borysthenes
as merely " Borysthenes."
[3] That is, going toward the north.

καὶ τὴν εὔκρατον εἰς τὸν διὰ Βορυσθένους καὶ τῆς Κελτικῆς παρωκεανίτιδος στάδιοι δισμύριοι πεντακισχίλιοι διακόσιοι. ὁ δέ γε ἀπὸ τῆς Κελτικῆς πρὸς ἄρκτον πλοῦς ἔσχατος λέγεται παρὰ τοῖς νῦν ὁ ἐπὶ τὴν Ἰέρνην, ἐπέκεινα μὲν οὖσαν τῆς Βρεττανικῆς, ἀθλίως δὲ διὰ ψύχος οἰκουμένην, ὥστε τὰ ἐπέκεινα νομίζειν ἀοίκητα. οὐ πλέον δὲ τῆς Κελτικῆς τὴν Ἰέρνην διέχειν φασὶ τῶν πεντακισχιλίων, ὥστε περὶ τρισμυρίους εἶεν ἂν ἢ μικρῷ πλείους οἱ πάντες οἱ τὸ πλάτος τῆς οἰκουμένης ἀφορίζοντες.

14. Φέρε δὴ τὴν ἀνταίρουσαν τῇ Κινναμωμοφόρῳ καὶ ἐπὶ τοῦ αὐτοῦ παραλλήλου πρὸς ἔω κειμένην ὑποβῶμεν. αὕτη δ᾽ ἐστὶν ἡ περὶ τὴν Ταπροβάνην· ἡ δὲ Ταπροβάνη πεπίστευται σφόδρα, ὅτι τῆς Ἰνδικῆς πρόκειται πελαγία μεγάλη νῆσος πρὸς νότον· μηκύνεται δὲ ἐπὶ τὴν Αἰθιοπίαν πλέον ἢ πεντακισχιλίους σταδίους, ὥς φασιν, ἐξ ἧς καὶ ἐλέφαντα κομίζεσθαι πολὺν εἰς τὰ τῶν Ἰνδῶν ἐμπόρια καὶ χελώνεια[1] καὶ ἄλλον φόρτον. ταύτῃ δὴ τῇ νήσῳ πλάτος προστεθὲν τὸ ἀνάλογον τῷ μήκει καὶ δίαρμα τὸ ἐπ᾽ αὐτὴν ἐκ τῆς Ἰνδικῆς τῶν μὲν τρισχιλίων σταδίων οὐκ ἂν ἔλαττον ποιήσειε διάστημα, ὅσον ἦν τὸ ἀπὸ τοῦ ὅρου τῆς οἰκουμένης εἰς Μερόην, εἴπερ μέλλει τὰ ἄκρα τῆς Ἰνδικῆς ἀνταίρειν τῇ Μερόῃ· πιθανώτερον δ᾽ ἐστὶ καὶ πλείους τῶν τρισχιλίων τιθέναι. εἰ δὴ τοῦτο προσθείη τις τοῖς τρισμυρίοις, οἷς φησιν

---

[1] χελώνεια, Meineke, for χελώνια.

five thousand two hundred stadia for the distance from the parallel that divides the torrid from the temperate zone to the parallel that runs through the Borysthenes and the sea-coast of Celtica. And yet the voyage from Celtica to the north is nowadays called the remotest voyage to the north; I mean the voyage to Ierne,[1] which island not only lies beyond Britain but is such a wretched place to live in on account of the cold that the regions on beyond are regarded as uninhabitable. And Ierne is not farther from Celtica, they say, than five thousand stadia; so that about thirty thousand stadia all told, or perhaps a few more, would represent the breadth of the inhabited world.

14. Well, then, let us pass on to the country that rises opposite to the Cinnamon-producing Country and lies toward the east on the same parallel. This is the region about Taprobane.[2] We have strong assurance that Taprobane is a large island in the open sea, which lies off India to the south. It stretches lengthwise in the direction of Ethiopia for more than five thousand stadia, as they say; and from it, they say, much ivory is brought to the markets of India, and also tortoise-shell and other merchandise. Now if we assign to this island a breadth that is proportional to its length, and if we add thereto the expanse of the sea between it and India, the sum would be a distance of not less than three thousand stadia — as much as the distance from the border of the inhabited world to Meroë—that is, if the capes of India are to rise opposite to Meroë; but it is more plausible to set down still more than three thousand stadia. So if you should add these three thousand

---

[1] Ireland.　　[2] Ceylon.

ὁ Δηίμαχος μέχρι τῆς εἰς Βακτρίους καὶ Σογδι-
ανοὺς ὑπερθέσεως, ἐκπέσοι ἂν πάντα ταῦτα τὰ
ἔθνη τῆς οἰκουμένης καὶ τῆς εὐκράτου. τίς ἂν οὖν
θαρρήσειε ταῦτα λέγειν, ἀκούων καὶ τῶν πάλαι
καὶ τῶν νῦν τὴν εὐκρασίαν καὶ τὴν εὐκαρπίαν
λεγόντων πρῶτον μὲν τὴν τῶν προσβόρρων
Ἰνδῶν, ἔπειτα δὲ καὶ τὴν ἐν τῇ Ὑρκανίᾳ καὶ τῇ
Ἀρίᾳ καὶ ἐφεξῆς τῇ τε Μαργιανῇ καὶ τῇ Βακ-
τριανῇ; ἅπασαι γὰρ αὗται προσεχεῖς μέν εἰσι
C 73 τῇ βορείῳ πλευρᾷ τοῦ Ταύρου καὶ ἥ γε Βακτριανὴ καὶ πλησιάζει τῇ εἰς Ἰνδοὺς ὑπερθέσει,
τοσαύτῃ δ᾽ εὐδαιμονίᾳ κέχρηνται, ὥστε πάμπολύ
τι ἀπέχειν τῆς ἀοικήτου. ἐν μέν γε τῇ Ὑρκανίᾳ
τὴν ἄμπελον μετρητὴν οἴνου φέρειν φασί, τὴν
δὲ συκῆν μεδίμνους ἑξήκοντα, τὸν δὲ σῖτον ἐκ
τοῦ ἐκπεσόντος καρποῦ τῆς καλάμης πάλιν
φύεσθαι, ἐν δὲ τοῖς δένδρεσι σμηνουργεῖσθαι
καὶ τῶν φύλλων ἀπορρεῖν μέλι, ὅπερ γίνεσθαι
μὲν καὶ τῆς Μηδίας ἐν τῇ Ματιανῇ καὶ τῆς
Ἀρμενίας ἐν τῇ Σακασηνῇ καὶ τῇ Ἀραξηνῇ.
ἀλλ᾽ ἐνταῦθα μὲν οὐκ ἐπ᾽ ἴσης θαυμαστόν,
εἴπερ εἰσὶ νοτιώτεραι τῆς Ὑρκανίας, καὶ εὐκρασίᾳ
διαφέρουσαι τῆς ἄλλης χώρας· ἐκεῖ δὲ μᾶλλον.
ἐν δὲ τῇ Μαργιανῇ τὸν πυθμένα φασὶν εὑρίσκεσθαι τῆς ἀμπέλου πολλάκις δυεῖν ἀνδρῶν
ὀργυιαῖς περιληπτόν, τὸν δὲ βότρυν δίπηχυν.
παραπλησίαν δὲ λέγουσι καὶ τὴν Ἀρίαν, εὐοινίᾳ

stadia to the thirty thousand stadia which Deïmachus gives as the distance to the pass that leads over to Bactriana and Sogdiana, then all these peoples would fall outside the inhabited world and the temperate zone. Who, pray, would venture to maintain this, when he hears men of both ancient and modern times telling about the mild climate and the fertility, first of Northern India, and then of Hyrcania and Aria, and, next in order, of Margiana and Bactriana? For, although all these countries lie next to the northern side of the Taurus Range, and although Bactriana, at least, lies close to the pass that leads over to India, still they enjoy such a happy lot that they must be a very long way off from the uninhabitable part of the earth. In Hyrcania, at any rate, they say that the vine produces one metretes [1] of wine, the fig-tree sixty medimni [2] of figs, the wheat grows again from the waste seed of the stubble-field, bees have their hives in the trees, and honey drips from the leaves; and this is also true of Matiana, a province of Media, and of Sacasene and of Araxene, districts of Armenia. But in the case of the latter districts this is not equally amazing, if it be true that they lie further south than Hyrcania, and are superior to the rest of the country in mildness of climate; but in the case of Hyrcania it is more amazing. And in Margiana, they say, it is oftentimes found that the trunk of the grape-vine can be encircled only by the outstretched arms of two men, and that the cluster of grapes is two cubits long. And they say that Aria also is similar, but that it even excels in good

[1] A little less than nine gallons.
[2] The *medimnus* was about a bushel and a half.

δὲ καὶ ὑπερβάλλειν, ἐν ᾗ γε καὶ εἰς τριγονίαν[1]
παραμένειν ἐν ἀπιττώτοις ἄγγεσι τὸν οἶνον·
πάμφορον δ' εἶναι καὶ τὴν Βακτριανὴν πλὴν
ἐλαίου, πλησίον τῇ Ἀρίᾳ παρακειμένην.

15. Εἰ δὲ καὶ ψυχρὰ μέρη τῶν τόπων τούτων
ἐστίν, ὅσα ὑψηλὰ καὶ ὀρεινά, οὐδὲν δεῖ θαυμάζειν·
καὶ γὰρ ἐν τοῖς μεσημβρινοῖς κλίμασι τὰ ὄρη
ψυχρά ἐστι, καὶ καθόλου τὰ μετέωρα ἐδάφη, κἂν
πεδία ᾖ. τῆς γοῦν Καππαδοκίας τὰ πρὸς τῷ
Εὐξείνῳ πολὺ βορειότερά ἐστι τῶν πρὸς τῷ
Ταύρῳ· ἀλλ' ἡ μὲν Βαγαδαονία,[2] πεδίον ἐξαίσιον
μεταξὺ πῖπτον τοῦ τε Ἀργαίου ὄρους καὶ τοῦ
Ταύρου, σπάνιον εἴ πού τι τῶν καρπίμων δένδρων
φύοι, καίπερ νοτιώτερον τῆς Ποντικῆς θαλάττης
σταδίοις τρισχιλίοις, τὰ δὲ τῆς Σινώπης προάστεια
καὶ τῆς Ἀμισοῦ καὶ τῆς Φαναροίας τὸ πλέον
ἐλαιόφυτά ἐστι. καὶ τὸν Ὦξον δὲ τὸν ὁρίζοντα
τὴν Βακτριανὴν ἀπὸ τῆς Σογδιανῆς οὕτω φασὶν
εὔπλουν εἶναι, ὥστε τὸν Ἰνδικὸν φόρτον ὑπερ-
κομισθέντα εἰς αὐτὸν ῥαδίως εἰς τὴν Ὑρκανίαν
κατάγεσθαι καὶ τοὺς ἐφεξῆς τόπους μέχρι τοῦ
Πόντου διὰ τῶν ποταμῶν.

16. Τίν' ἂν οὖν τοιαύτην εὕροις εὐδαιμονίαν
περὶ Βορυσθένη καὶ τὴν Κελτικὴν τὴν παρωκεανῖτιν, ὅπου μηδὲ φύεται ἄμπελος ἢ μὴ
τελεσφορεῖ; ἐν δὲ τοῖς νοτιωτέροις τούτων καὶ

---

[1] τριγονίαν, Cobet, for τριγένειαν; Bernadakis, Cascorbi,
approving.
[2] Βαγαδαονία, Casaubon, for Βαγαδανία; Corais following;
W. M. Ramsay approving.

vintage, since there, at all events, the wine actually keeps for three generations in unpitched casks ; and that Bactriana, too, which lies on the border of Aria, produces everything except olive-oil.

15. But if all the parts of these regions that are high and mountainous are also cold, we should not be amazed ; for even in the southern latitudes the mountains are cold, and in general all high-lying lands, even if they be plateaux, are cold. At any rate, in Cappadocia the regions next to the Euxine are much farther north than those next to the Taurus ; but Bagadaonia, an enormous plain which falls between the Argaeus Mountain[1] and the Taurus Range, only scantily (if anywhere) produces fruit-trees, although it is three thousand stadia farther south than the Pontic Sea, whereas the suburbs of Sinope and Amisus and the greater part of Phanaroea are planted with olive-trees. And further, the River Oxus, which divides Bactriana from Sogdiana, is so easily navigable, they say, that the Indian merchandise packed over the mountains to it is easily brought down to the Hyrcanian Sea, and thence, on the rivers, to the successive regions beyond as far as the Pontus.[2]

16. Now what comparable blessings of nature can you find round about the Borysthenes or in the part of Celtica that lies on the ocean, where the grape either does not grow at all, or else does not bear fruit ? In the more southern districts of these

---

[1] In Cappadocia ; now Mt. Erdjias.
[2] According to this statement the Oxus, which now empties into the Aral Lake, flowed into the Caspian Sea. Thence, by the Kur and other rivers, the merchandise was carried to western points. See 11. 7. 3.

ἐπιθαλαττιδίοις[1] καὶ τοῖς κατὰ Βόσπορον τελεσφορεῖ, ἐν μικροκαρπίᾳ δέ, καὶ τοῦ χειμῶνος κατορύττεται. οἱ δὲ πάγοι παρ' αὐτοῖς τοιοῦτοί τινές εἰσιν ἐπὶ τῷ στόματι τῆς λίμνης τῆς Μαιώτιδος, ὥστ' ἐν χωρίῳ, ἐν ᾧ χειμῶνος ὁ τοῦ Μιθριδάτου στρατηγὸς ἐνίκησε τοὺς βαρβάρους ἱππομαχῶν ἐπὶ τῷ πάγῳ, τοὺς αὐτοὺς κατα-

C 74 ναυμαχῆσαι θέρους, λυθέντος τοῦ πάγου. ὁ δ' Ἐρατοσθένης καὶ τοὐπίγραμμα προφέρεται τὸ ἐν τῷ Ἀσκληπιείῳ τῷ Παντικαπαιέων ἐπὶ τῇ ῥαγείσῃ χαλκῇ ὑδρίᾳ διὰ τὸν πάγον·

> εἴ τις ἄρ' ἀνθρώπων μὴ πείθεται οἷα παρ' ἡμῖν
> γίγνεται, εἰς τήνδε γνώτω ἰδὼν ὑδρίαν·
> ἣν οὐχ ὡς ἀνάθημα θεοῦ καλόν, ἀλλ' ἐπίδειγμα
> χειμῶνος μεγάλου θῆχ' ἱερεὺς Στρατίος.[2]

ὅπου οὖν οὐδὲ τοῖς ἐν Βοσπόρῳ συγκριτέον τὰ ἐν τοῖς διαριθμηθεῖσι τόποις, ἀλλ' οὐδὲ τοῖς ἐν Ἀμισῷ καὶ Σινώπῃ (καὶ γὰρ ἐκείνων εὐκρατοτέρους ἂν εἴποι τις), σχολῇ γ' ἂν παραβάλλοιντο τοῖς κατὰ Βορυσθένη καὶ τοῖς ἐσχάτοις Κελτοῖς. μόλις γὰρ ἂν ταὐτοκλινεῖς εἶεν τοῖς κατ' Ἀμισὸν καὶ Σινώπην καὶ Βυζάντιον καὶ Μασσαλίαν, οἱ τοῦ Βορυσθένους καὶ τῶν Κελτῶν ὡμολόγηνται νοτιώτεροι σταδίοις τρισχιλίοις καὶ ἑπτακοσίοις.

---

[1] ἐπιθαλαττιδίοις, Friedemann, for ἐπιθαλαττίοις or ἐπιθαλαττιαίοις; Meineke following; Kramer, C. Müller, approving.　　[2] Στρατίος, Meineke, for Στράτιος.

---

[1] That is, to keep them from freezing. See 7. 3. 18.

countries, both on the Mediterranean Sea and in the regions about the Bosporus, the vine does bear fruit, but the grapes are small, and the vines are buried during the winter.[1] The frosts are so severe at the mouth of Lake Maeotis that, at a certain spot where, in winter time, Mithridates' general conquered the barbarians in a cavalry engagement fought on the ice, he afterwards, in summer time, when the ice had melted, defeated the same barbarians in a naval engagement.[2] And Eratosthenes brings forward, also, the following epigram from the temple of Asclepius at Panticapaeum,[3] which was inscribed on the bronze water-jar that had been burst by freezing: " If any man is incredulous in regard to what happens in our country, let him look at this water-jar and know the truth ; which, not as a fair offering unto God but as an illustration of our severe winters, has been dedicated by Stratius the priest." Since, therefore, the climatic conditions in the Asiatic regions that I have enumerated are not to be compared even with those at the Bosporus, nay, not even with those at Amisus and Sinope (which places one would call milder in climate than the regions at the Bosporus), those Asiatic regions could hardly be thrown on the same parallel with those about Borysthenes and with the country of the northernmost Celts. In fact, the Asiatic regions could hardly be in the same latitude as the regions about Amisus, Sinope, Byzantium, and Massilia, which are conceded to be thirty-seven hundred stadia farther south than the Borysthenes and the Celts.

[2] Strabo refers to battles fought on the Strait of Yenikale, or Kerch, by Neoptolemus, the general of Mithridates the Great (Eupator). Compare 7. 3. 18.

[3] Now Kerch, at the mouth of the Sea of Azov.

17. Οἱ δέ γε περὶ Δηίμαχον τοῖς τρισμυρίοις ἐὰν προσλάβωσι τὸ ἐπὶ τὴν Ταπροβάνην καὶ τοὺς ὅρους τῆς διακεκαυμένης, οὓς οὐκ ἐλάττους τῶν τετρακισχιλίων θετέον, ἐκτοπιοῦσι τά τε Βάκτρα καὶ τὴν Ἀρίαν εἰς τοὺς ἀπέχοντας τόπους τῆς διακεκαυμένης σταδίους τρισμυρίους καὶ τετρακισχιλίους, ὅσους ἀπὸ τοῦ ἰσημερινοῦ ἐπὶ Βορυσθένη φησὶν εἶναι ὁ Ἵππαρχος. ἐκπεσοῦνται ἄρα εἰς τοὺς βορειοτέρους τοῦ Βορυσθένους καὶ τῆς Κελτικῆς σταδίοις ὀκτακισχιλίοις καὶ ὀκτακοσίοις, ὅσοις νοτιώτερός ἐστιν ὁ ἰσημερινὸς τοῦ ὁρίζοντος κύκλου τὴν διακεκαυμένην καὶ τὴν εὔκρατον, ὃν φαμεν διὰ τῆς Κινναμωμοφόρου[1] μάλιστα γράφεσθαι. ἡμεῖς δέ γε ἐπεδείκνυμεν μέχρι τῆς Ἰέρνης μόλις οἰκήσιμα ὄντα τὰ ὑπὲρ τὴν Κελτικήν, ἅπερ οὐ πλείω τῶν πεντακισχιλίων ἐστίν· οὗτος δ᾽ ἀποφαίνει ὁ λόγος τῆς Ἰέρνης ἔτι βορειότερον εἶναί τινα κύκλον οἰκήσιμον σταδίοις τρισχιλίοις ὀκτακοσίοις. ἔσται[2] δὲ Βάκτρα καὶ τοῦ στόματος τῆς Κασπίας θαλάττης, εἴτε Ὑρκανίας, πάμπολύ τι ἀρκτικώτερα, ὅπερ τοῦ μυχοῦ τῆς Κασπίας καὶ τῶν Ἀρμενιακῶν καὶ Μηδικῶν ὀρῶν διέχει περὶ ἑξακισχιλίους σταδίους, καὶ δοκεῖ αὐτῆς τῆς[3] παραλίας μέχρι τῆς Ἰνδικῆς ἀρκτικώτερον εἶναι σημεῖον καὶ περίπλουν ἔχειν

---

[1] Ἰνδικῆς, before μάλιστα, is discarded by the various editors.

[2] ἔσται, Kramer, for ἐστί; Forbiger, Meineke, following.

[3] αὐτῆς τῆς, Groskurd, for τῆς αὐτῆς; Meineke, Forbiger, following; L. Kayser approving.

17. Now if Deïmachus and his followers add to
the thirty thousand stadia the distance to Taprobane
and to the boundary of the torrid zone, which must
be put at not less than four thousand stadia,[1] they
will thus be placing both Bactra and Aria outside
the inhabited world in the regions that are thirty-
four thousand stadia from the torrid zone—the
number of stadia Hipparchus gives as the distance
from the equator to the Borysthenes. And so Bactra
and Aria will be thrown outside into the regions that
are eight thousand eight hundred stadia farther
north than the Borysthenes and Celtica—the number
of stadia by which the equator is south of the circle
that divides the torrid zone from the temperate;
and this circle we say is drawn, in a general way,
through the Cinnamon-producing Country. Now I
myself was pointing out that the regions beyond
Celtica as far as Ierne were scarcely habitable, and
that this distance is not more than five thousand
stadia[2]; but this argument of Deïmachus declares
that there is a habitable parallel of latitude three
thousand eight hundred stadia still farther north
than Ierne! Thus Bactra will be a very considerable
distance farther north than even the mouth of the
Caspian (or Hyrcanian) Sea; and this mouth[3] is
about six thousand stadia distant from the inmost
part of the Caspian Sea and from the Armenian and
Median mountains (and it seems to be a more
northerly point than the coast-line itself that runs
thence to India; and to offer a practicable route of

---

[1] In § 14 Strabo said " not less than 3,000 stadia."
[2] § 13.
[3] Strabo thought that the Caspian Sea opened into "the
northern sea."

ἀπὸ τῆς Ἰνδικῆς δυνατόν, ὥς φησιν ὁ τῶν τόπων
ἡγησάμενος τούτων Πατροκλῆς. ἔτι τοίνυν ἡ
Βακτριανὴ χίλια στάδια ἐπὶ τὴν ἄρκτον ἐκτεί-
νεται· τὰ δὲ τῶν Σκυθῶν ἔθνη[1] πολὺ μείζω ταύτης ἐπέκεινα χώραν νέμεται, καὶ τελευτᾷ πρὸς
C 75 τὴν βόρειον θάλατταν, νομαδικῶς μέν, ζῶντα δ'
ὅμως. πῶς οὖν, εἴπερ καὶ αὐτὰ τὰ Βάκτρα ἤδη τῆς
οἰκουμένης ἐκπίπτει, εἴη ἂν τὸ διάστημα τοῦτο ἀπὸ
τοῦ Καυκάσου μέχρι τῆς βορείας θαλάττης τῇ
διὰ Βάκτρων ὀλίγῳ πλειόνων ἢ τετρακισχιλίων;
ταῦτα δὴ προστεθέντα τῷ ἀπὸ τῆς Ἰέρνης ἐπὶ
τὰ βόρεια σταδιασμῷ ποιεῖ τὸ πᾶν διὰ τῆς ἀοικήτου διάστημα ἐπὶ τοῦ διὰ τῆς Ἰέρνης σταδιασμοῦ
σταδίων ἑπτακισχιλίων καὶ ὀκτακοσίων· εἰ δὲ
ἐάσειέ τις τοὺς τετρακισχιλίους σταδίους, αὐτά
γε τὰ πρὸς τῷ Καυκάσῳ μέρη τῆς Βακτριανῆς
ἔσται βορειότερα τῆς Ἰέρνης σταδίοις τρισχιλίοις
καὶ ὀκτακοσίοις, τῆς δὲ Κελτικῆς καὶ τοῦ Βορυσθένους ὀκτακισχιλίοις καὶ ὀκτακοσίοις.

18. Φησὶ δέ γε ὁ Ἵππαρχος κατὰ τὸν Βορυσθένη
καὶ τὴν Κελτικὴν ἐν ὅλαις ταῖς θεριναῖς νυξὶ
παραυγάζεσθαι τὸ φῶς τοῦ ἡλίου περιϊστάμενον
ἀπὸ τῆς δύσεως ἐπὶ τὴν ἀνατολήν, ταῖς δὲ

---

[1] ἔθνη, Kramer suggests, after Σκυθῶν; Meineke following.

[1] That is, beyond the mouth of the Caspian into the
uninhabited world. This whole argument against Deïmachus
and his school is a *reductio ad absurdum*.
[2] And thus, according to Strabo, they really reach no
farther, approximately, than the mouth of the Caspian.

circumnavigation from India, according to Patrocles, who was once governor of these regions). Accordingly, Bactriana stretches out still farther [1] for a thousand stadia toward the north. But the Scythian tribes inhabit a much larger country than Bactriana, on beyond it, and they end at the northern sea [2]; who, though it be as nomads, still manage to live. How, then, if even Bactra itself is now thrown outside of the inhabited world, could this distance from the Caucasus up to the northern sea, measured on the meridian line through Bactra, be slightly more than four thousand stadia [3]? If these stadia, then, be added to the stadia-reckoning from Ierne to the northern regions,[4] they make the total distance through the uninhabitable region, on the stadia-reckoning made through Ierne, seven thousand eight hundred stadia. But if one should leave out the four thousand stadia, at least the very parts of Bactriana that are next to the Caucasus [5] will be farther north than Ierne by three thousand eight hundred stadia, and farther north than Celtica and the Borysthenes by eight thousand eight hundred stadia.

18.[6] Hipparchus says, at all events, that at the Borysthenes and Celtica, throughout the nights in summer-time, the light of the sun shines dimly, moving round from the west to the east, and at

---

[3] The figure of 4,000 is quoted from Deïmachus and his school. Strabo continues to meet them upon their own ground with his favourite form of argument.

[4] That is, the 3,800 stadia above-mentioned.

[5] Hence, not the Armenian Caucasus. The mountains from Ariana on were also called Caucasus (11. 8. 1.).

[6] In connection with this paragraph, read 2. 5. 34-43. Strabo finds another "absurdity" (compare § 12).

χειμεριναῖς τροπαῖς τὸ πλεῖστον μετεωρίζεσθαι
τὸν ἥλιον ἐπὶ πήχεις ἐννέα· ἐν δὲ τοῖς ἀπέχουσι
τῆς Μασσαλίας ἑξακισχιλίοις καὶ τριακοσίοις
(οὓς ἐκεῖνος μὲν ἔτι Κελτοὺς ὑπολαμβάνει, ἐγὼ
δ' οἶμαι Βρεττανοὺς εἶναι, βορειοτέρους τῆς Κελτικῆς σταδίοις δισχιλίοις πεντακοσίοις) πολὺ
μᾶλλον τοῦτο συμβαίνειν· ἐν δὲ ταῖς χειμεριναῖς ἡμέραις ὁ ἥλιος μετεωρίζεται πήχεις ἕξ,
τέτταρας δ' ἐν τοῖς ἀπέχουσι Μασσαλίας ἐνακισχιλίους[1] σταδίους καὶ ἑκατόν, ἐλάττους δὲ
τῶν τριῶν ἐν τοῖς ἐπέκεινα, οἳ[2] κατὰ τὸν ἡμέτερον
λόγον πολὺ ἂν εἶεν ἀρκτικώτεροι τῆς Ἰέρνης.
οὗτος δὲ Πυθέᾳ πιστεύων κατὰ τὰ νοτιώτερα[3] τῆς
Βρεττανικῆς τὴν οἴκησιν ταύτην τίθησι, καί φησιν
εἶναι τὴν μακροτάτην ἐνταῦθα ἡμέραν ὡρῶν
ἰσημερινῶν δέκα ἐννέα, ὀκτωκαίδεκα δέ, ὅπου
τέτταρας ὁ ἥλιος μετεωρίζεται πήχεις· οὓς φησιν
ἀπέχειν τῆς Μασσαλίας ἐννακισχιλίους καὶ ἑκατὸν σταδίους. ὥσθ' οἱ νοτιώτατοι τῶν Βρεττανῶν
βορειότεροι τούτων εἰσίν. ἤτοι οὖν ἐπὶ τοῦ αὐτοῦ

---

[1] ἐνακισχιλίους, Meineke, for ἐννακισχιλίους; A. Jacob
approving.
[2] καί, Penzel deletes, before κατά; Du Theil, Groskurd,
Meineke, Forbiger, Tardieu, following.
[3] νοτιώτερα, as A. Jacob proves, must not be changed to
ἀρκτικώτερα (as has been done since Du Theil's time), since the
argument is rigorously correct and in keeping with οἱ νοτιώτατοι τῶν Βρεττανῶν below. T. G. Tucker suggests τἀνώτερα.

---

[1] The astronomical cubit was two degrees.
[2] At 6,300 stadia north of Marseilles.
[3] "This inhabited country" of Hipparchus means the

the winter solstice the sun ascends at most only
nine cubits[1]; but that among the people who are
six thousand three hundred stadia distant from
Massilia (people who live two thousand five hundred
stadia north of Celtica, whom Hipparchus assumes still
to be Celts, though I think they are Britons) this
phenomenon is much more marked; and on the
winter days there[2] the sun ascends only six cubits,
and only four cubits among the people who are distant
from Massilia nine thousand one hundred stadia;
and less than three cubits among the people who
live on beyond (who, according to my argument,
would be much farther north than Ierne). But
Hipparchus, trusting Pytheas, puts this inhabited
country in the regions that are farther south than
Britain,[3] and says that the longest day there has
nineteen equinoctial hours,[4] but that the longest
day has eighteen hours where the sun ascends only
four cubits; and these people,[5] he says, are distant
from Massilia nine thousand and one hundred stadia;
and hence the most southerly of the Britons are
more northerly than these people. Accordingly,

country that is beyond 9,100 stadia north of Marseilles. To
Strabo, this country is uninhabited.

[4] The solar day is not constant; and so the ancients, being
dependent upon the sun-dial, took as a unit the hour
computed at the time of an equinox. Hence "equinoctial
hour"—a term not used in modern astronomy.

[5] That is, at 9,100 stadia north of Marseilles. By comparing this and other passages in Strabo we find that
Hipparchus' data were: Borysthenes, 9 cubits, 16 hours;
6,300 stadia north of Byzantium (or Marseilles, which
Hipparchus placed in the same latitude as Byzantium),
6 cubits, 17 hours; 9,100 stadia north of Byzantium (or
Marseilles), 4 cubits, 18 hours; the "inhabited country" on
beyond, less than 3 cubits, 19 hours.

παραλλήλου εἰσὶ τοῖς πρὸς τῷ Καυκάσῳ Βακ-
τρίοις ἢ ἐπί τινος πλησιάζοντος· εἴρηται γὰρ ὅτι
κατὰ τοὺς περὶ Δηίμαχον συμβήσεται βορειοτέρους εἶναι τῆς Ἰέρνης τοὺς πρὸς τῷ Καυκάσῳ
Βακτρίους σταδίοις τρισχιλίοις ὀκτακοσίοις· προστεθέντων δὲ τούτων τοῖς ἀπὸ Μασσαλίας εἰς
Ἰέρνην, γίνονται μύριοι δισχίλιοι πεντακόσιοι.
τίς οὖν ἱστόρηκεν ἐν τοῖς ἐκεῖ τόποις, λέγω δὲ
τοῖς περὶ Βάκτρα, τοῦτο τὸ μῆκος τῶν μεγίστων
ἡμερῶν ἢ τὸ ἔξαρμα τοῦ ἡλίου τὸ κατὰ τὰς
μεσουρανήσεις ἐν ταῖς χειμεριναῖς τροπαῖς; ὀφθαλ-
μοφανῆ γὰρ πάντα ταῦτα καὶ[1] ἰδιώτῃ καὶ οὐ
C 76 δεόμενα μαθηματικῆς σημειώσεως, ὥστε συνέγραψαν ἂν πολλοὶ καὶ τῶν παλαιῶν τῶν τὰ
Περσικὰ ἱστορούντων καὶ τῶν ὕστερον μέχρι καὶ
εἰς ἡμᾶς. πῶς δ' ἂν ἡ λεχθεῖσα εὐδαιμονία τῶν
τόπων ὡμολογεῖτο[2] τοῖς τοιούτοις ἐν τῷ οὐρανῷ
φαινομένοις; ἐκ δὲ τῶν εἰρημένων δῆλον, ὡς καὶ
σοφῶς ἀντιλέγει πρὸς τὴν ἀπόδειξιν, ὡς ἰσο-
δυναμούντων τῶν ζητουμένων λαμβάνοντος πρὸς
τὸ ἀποδεῖξαι τὸ ζητούμενον.

19. Πάλιν δ' ἐκείνου τὸν Δηίμαχον ἰδιώτην
ἐνδείξασθαι βουλομένου καὶ ἄπειρον τῶν τοιού-

---

[1] καί, Corais inserts; Groskurd, Meineke, Forbiger, Tardieu, following.
[2] ὡμολογεῖτο, A. Jacob, for ὡμολόγητο.

---

[1] Compare §§ 15–16.   [2] 4 cubits, 18 hours, etc.
[3] The fallacy is that of "begging the question" (petitio
principii). On the question of the most northerly latitude
of the inhabited world, Eratosthenes and Hipparchus are

they are either on the same parallel as the Bactrians
that live near the Caucasus or on some parallel
close to it; for, as I have stated, according to
Deïmachus and his followers our result will be
that the Bactrians that live near the Caucasus are
more northerly than Ierne by three thousand eight
hundred stadia; and if these stadia be added to
those from Massilia to Ierne, we get twelve thousand
five hundred stadia. Now who has ever reported
in these regions (I mean the regions about Bactra)
such a length of the longest days, or such a meridian
height of the sun at the winter solstice? Why,
all such phenomena are obvious to the eye even
of a layman and do not require mathematical
notation; so that many men, both of the early
writers of Persian history and of their successors
on down to our own times, could have compiled
them. Again, how could the above-mentioned [1]
happy lot of these regions be conceded to those
regions that have such celestial phenomena? [2] And
so from what I have said it is clear how very cleverly
Hipparchus contradicts the demonstration of Eratosthenes on the ground that the latter (although
their objects of inquiry are in effect equivalent)
were taking the object of inquiry for granted as an
aid to his demonstration thereof! [3]

19. And so, again, where Eratosthenes wishes to
show that Deïmachus is a layman and inexperienced

both wrong in that they place the limit too far north, Strabo
thinks. Among other things, they both assume in their
reckonings that Marseilles is as far north as Byzantium
(Strabo places Marseilles much farther south). Hence the
ironical remark, that only with poor grace could Hipparchus
meet the demonstration of Eratosthenes by accusing him of
begging the question.

των· οἴεσθαι γὰρ τὴν Ἰνδικὴν μεταξὺ κεῖσθαι τῆς
τε φθινοπωρινῆς ἰσημερίας καὶ τῶν τροπῶν τῶν
χειμερινῶν, Μεγασθένει τε ἀντιλέγειν φήσαντι ἐν
τοῖς νοτίοις μέρεσι τῆς Ἰνδικῆς τάς τε ἄρκτους
ἀποκρύπτεσθαι καὶ τὰς σκιὰς ἀντιπίπτειν· μηδέ-
τερον γὰρ τούτων μηδαμοῦ τῆς Ἰνδικῆς συμβαί-
νειν· ταῦτα δὴ φάσκοντος ἀμαθῶς λέγεσθαι· τό τε
γὰρ τὴν φθινοπωρινὴν τῆς ἐαρινῆς διαφέρειν
οἴεσθαι κατὰ τὴν διάστασιν τὴν πρὸς τὰς τροπὰς
ἀμαθές, τοῦ τε κύκλου τοῦ αὐτοῦ ὄντος καὶ τῆς
ἀνατολῆς· τοῦ τε διαστήματος τοῦ ἐπὶ τῆς γῆς
τροπικοῦ ἀπὸ τοῦ ἰσημερινοῦ, ὧν μεταξὺ τίθησι
τὴν Ἰνδικὴν ἐκεῖνος, δειχθέντος ἐν τῇ ἀναμετρήσει
πολὺ ἐλάττονος τῶν δισμυρίων σταδίων, συμβῆναι ἂν καὶ κατ' αὐτὸν ἐκεῖνον, ὅπερ αὐτὸς
νομίζει, οὐχ ὃ ἐκεῖνος· δυεῖν μὲν γὰρ ἢ καὶ τριῶν
μυριάδων οὖσαν τὴν Ἰνδικὴν οὐδὲ πεσεῖν μεταξὺ
τοσούτου διαστήματος, ὅσην δ' αὐτὸς εἴρηκε,
πεσεῖν ἄν· τῆς δ' αὐτῆς ἀγνοίας εἶναι καὶ τὸ
μηδαμοῦ τῆς Ἰνδικῆς ἀποκρύπτεσθαι φάσκειν τὰς
ἄρκτους μηδὲ τὰς σκιὰς ἀντιπίπτειν, ὅτε γε καὶ
πεντακισχιλίους προελθόντι ἀπ' Ἀλεξανδρείας
εὐθὺς συμβαίνειν ἄρχεται. ταῦτα δὴ εἰπόντα,[1]

---

[1] εἰπόντα, Corais, Du Theil, for εἰπόντας.

---

[1] Strabo's "winter tropic" and "summer tropic" correspond roughly to the tropic of Capricorn and the tropic of
Cancer. The former was placed at 24°, at Syene.

[2] That is, to the south as well as to the north—which
would be true of all points in the torrid zone.

in such matters. For he says Deïmachus thinks
that India lies between the autumnal equinox and
the winter tropic,[1] and contradicts the statement
of Megasthenes that, in the southern parts of India,
the Bears set and the shadows fall in the opposite
directions,[2] asserting that neither phenomenon takes
place anywhere in India; and so, says Eratosthenes,
when Deïmachus asserts this, he speaks ignorantly,
since it is mere ignorance to think that the autumnal
equinox differs from the vernal equinox in distance
from the tropic, because both the circle[3] and the
rising of the sun are the same at the equinoxes;
and, since the distance between the terrestrial
tropic and the equator, between which Deïmachus
places India, has been shown in the measurement
of the earth to be much less than twenty thousand
stadia,[4] the result would be, even according to
Deïmachus himself, precisely what Eratosthenes
thinks, and not what Deïmachus thinks; for if India
be twenty, or as much as thirty, thousand stadia
in breadth it could not even fall within such a
space.[5] But if India has the breadth which Eratosthenes himself has given it, then it would fall
therein; and that it is also a mark of the same
ignorance for Deïmachus to assert that in no part
of India do the Bears set or the shadows fall in
the opposite directions, since, at any rate, if you
proceed only five thousand stadia south from Alexandria the phenomena begin at once to take place.

[3] The circle in which they each lie is that of the
(celestial) equator.

[4] Counting 700 stadia to the degree, Eratosthenes' measurement of the earth being 252,000 stadia, the tropic at 24°
would be 16,800 stadia from the equator.

[5] Between the tropic and the equator.

εὐθύνει πάλιν οὐκ εὖ ὁ Ἵππαρχος, πρῶτον ἀντὶ[1]
τοῦ χειμερινοῦ τροπικοῦ τὸν θερινὸν δεξάμενος,
εἶτ' οὐκ οἰόμενος δεῖν μάρτυρι χρῆσθαι τῶν μαθηματικῶν ἀναστρολογήτῳ ἀνθρώπῳ, ὥσπερ τοῦ
Ἐρατοσθένους προηγουμένως τὴν ἐκείνου μαρ-
τυρίαν ἐγκρίνοντος, ἀλλ' οὐ κοινῷ τινι ἔθει χρω-
μένου πρὸς τοὺς ματαιολογοῦντας. εἰς γάρ τις
τῶν πρὸς τοὺς ματαίως ἀντιλέγοντας ἐλέγχων
ἐστίν, ὅταν αὐτὴν τὴν ἐκείνων ἀπόφασιν, ὁποία
ποτέ ἐστι, δείξωμεν ἡμῖν συνηγοροῦσαν.

20. Νυνὶ μὲν οὖν ὑποθέμενοι τὰ νοτιώτατα τῆς
Ἰνδικῆς ἀνταίρειν τοῖς κατὰ Μερόην, ὅπερ εἰρήκασι πολλοὶ καὶ πεπιστεύκασιν, ἐπεδείξαμεν τὰ
C 77 συμβαίνοντα ἄτοπα. ἐπεὶ δὲ ὁ Ἵππαρχος, οὐδὲν
ἀντειπὼν τῇ ὑποθέσει ταύτῃ νυνί, μετὰ ταῦτα ἐν
τῷ δευτέρῳ ὑπομνήματι οὐ συγχωρεῖ, σκεπτέον καὶ
τοῦτον τὸν λόγον. φησὶ τοίνυν, ἀνταιρόντων
ἀλλήλοις τῶν[2] ἐπὶ τοῦ αὐτοῦ παραλλήλου κειμένων, ἐπειδὰν τὸ μεταξὺ ᾖ μέγα διάστημα, μὴ
δύνασθαι γνωσθῆναι αὐτὸ τοῦτο, ὅτι εἰσὶν ἐπὶ τοῦ
αὐτοῦ παραλλήλου οἱ τόποι, ἄνευ τῆς τῶν κλιμάτων συγκρίσεως τῆς κατὰ θάτερον τῶν τόπων.[3]
τὸ μὲν οὖν κατὰ Μερόην κλίμα Φίλωνά τε τὸν
συγγράψαντα τὸν εἰς Αἰθιοπίαν πλοῦν ἱστορεῖν,
ὅτι πρὸ πέντε καὶ τεσσαράκοντα ἡμερῶν τῆς
θερινῆς τροπῆς κατὰ κορυφὴν γίνεται ὁ ἥλιος,
λέγειν δὲ καὶ τοὺς λόγους τοῦ γνώμονος πρός τε

[1] ἀντί, Corais, Penzel, Pätz, for ἀπό; Groskurd, Meineke,
Forbiger, Kärcher, Tardieu, following; C. Müller approving.
[2] τῶν, Casaubon inserts, before ἐπί; Corais, Groskurd,
Meineke, Forbiger, following; C. Müller, L. Kayser, approving.
[3] τῶν τόπων, Corais, for τὸν τόπον, on the authority of n.

So Hipparchus is again not right in correcting Eratosthenes on that statement, because, in the first
place, he interprets Deïmachus as saying "the
summer tropic" instead of "the winter tropic," and
because, in the second place, he thinks we should
not use as a source of evidence on mathematics a
man who is unversed in astronomy—just as if
Eratosthenes were reckoning in the evidence of
Deïmachus above that of other men and not
merely following a common custom used in replying
to men that talk foolishness. For one way of
refuting men who contradict foolishly is to shew
that the very declaration they make, whatever it
may be, pleads our case.

20. Up to this point, then, having taken as hypothesis that the most southerly regions of India rise
opposite the regions about Meroë—which many have
stated and believed—I have pointed out the absurdities that result from this hypothesis. But since
Hipparchus up to this point offers no objection to
this hypothesis, and yet later on, in his Second Book,
will not concede it, I must consider his argument on
this matter, too. Well, then, he says: If only the
regions that lie on the same parallel rise opposite
each other, then, whenever the intervening distance
is great, we cannot know this very thing, namely, that
the regions in question are on the same parallel,
without the comparison of the "climata[1]" as observed
at the other of the two places; now as for the
"clima" at Meroë, Philo, who wrote an account of
his voyage to Ethiopia, reports that the sun is in the
zenith forty-five days before the summer solstice and
tells also the relations of the gnomon to the shadows

[1] See footnote 2, page 22.

τὰς τροπικὰς σκιὰς καὶ τὰς ἰσημερινάς, αὐτόν τε
Ἐρατοσθένη συμφωνεῖν ἔγγιστα τῷ Φίλωνι, τὸ δ'
ἐν τῇ Ἰνδικῇ κλίμα μηδένα ἱστορεῖν, μηδ' αὐτὸν
Ἐρατοσθένη. εἰ δὲ δὴ καὶ αἱ ἄρκτοι ἐκεῖ ἀμφότεραι, ὡς οἴονται, ἀποκρύπτονται, πιστεύοντες
τοῖς περὶ Νέαρχον, μὴ δυνατὸν εἶναι ἐπὶ ταὐτοῦ
παραλλήλου κεῖσθαι τήν τε Μερόην[1] καὶ τὰ ἄκρα
τῆς Ἰνδικῆς. εἰ μὲν τοίνυν περὶ τῶν ἄρκτων
ἀμφοτέρων, ὅτι ἀποκρύπτονται, συναποφαίνεται
τοῖς εἰποῦσιν Ἐρατοσθένης, πῶς περὶ τοῦ ἐν τῇ
Ἰνδικῇ κλίματος οὐδεὶς ἀποφαίνεται, οὐδ' αὐτὸς
Ἐρατοσθένης; οὗτος γὰρ ὁ λόγος περὶ τοῦ κλί-
ματός ἐστιν. εἰ δ' οὐ συναποφαίνεται, ἀπηλλά-
χθω τῆς αἰτίας. οὐ συναποφαίνεται δέ γε, ἀλλὰ
τοῦ Δηιμάχου φήσαντος μηδαμοῦ τῆς Ἰνδικῆς
μήτ' ἀποκρύπτεσθαι τὰς ἄρκτους μήτ' ἀντιπίπτειν τὰς σκιάς, ἅπερ ὑπείληφεν ὁ Μεγασθένης,
ἀπειρίαν αὐτοῦ καταγιγνώσκει, τὸ συμπεπλεγ-
μένον νομίζων ψεῦδος, ἐν ᾧ ὁμολογουμένως καὶ
κατ' αὐτὸν τὸν Ἵππαρχον τό γε μὴ ἀντιπίπτειν
τὰς σκιὰς ψεῦδος ἐμπέπλεκται. καὶ γὰρ εἰ μὴ
τῇ Μερόῃ ἀνταίρει, τῆς γε Συήνης νοτιώτερα εἶναι
τὰ ἄκρα τῆς Ἰνδικῆς συγχωρῶν φαίνεται.

21. Καὶ ἐν τοῖς ἑξῆς δὲ περὶ τῶν αὐτῶν ἐπιχει-
ρῶν ἢ ταὐτὰ λέγει τοῖς ἐξελεγχθεῖσιν ὑφ' ἡμῶν, ἢ
λήμμασι προσχρῆται ψευδέσιν, ἢ ἐπιφέρει τὸ μὴ
ἀκολουθοῦν. οὔτε γὰρ τῷ ἀπὸ Βαβυλῶνος εἰς

_____
[1] ταῦτα, Corais deletes, before καί; Meineke following.

both in the solstices and the equinoxes, and Eratosthenes agrees very closely with Philo; whereas nobody reports the "clima" in India, not even Eratosthenes himself; however, if it is really true that in India the Bears set (both of them, as they think, relying on Nearchus and his followers), then it is impossible that Meroë and the capes of India lie on the same parallel. Now if Eratosthenes joins those who have already so stated in reporting that both Bears do set, how can it be that nobody reports about the "clima" in India, not even Eratosthenes himself? For this statement concerns the "clima." But if Eratosthenes does not join them in the report, let him be free from the accusation. No, he does not join them in the report; nay, because Deïmachus said that the Bears do not set and the shadows do not fall in the opposite direction anywhere in India (as Megasthenes assumed), Eratosthenes convicts him of inexperience, regarding as falsehood the combined statement, wherein by the acknowledgement of Hipparchus himself the false statement that the shadows do not fall in the opposite direction is combined with that about the Bears. For even if the southern capes of India do not rise opposite to Meroë, Hipparchus clearly concedes that they are at least farther south than Syene.[1]

21. In what follows, also, Hipparchus, in attempting proofs on the same questions, either states again the same things that I have already disproved, or employs additional false assumptions, or appends conclusions that do not follow. In the first place, take the state-

---

[1] 5,000 stadia directly north of Meroë. To one travelling north from the equator the Lesser Bear is first wholly visible at Meroë, according to Hipparchus (2. 5. 35).

Θάψακον εἶναι σταδίους τετρακισχιλίους ὀκτακοσίους, ἐντεῦθεν δὲ πρὸς τὴν ἄρκτον ἐπὶ τὰ Ἀρμένια ὄρη δισχιλίους ἑκατόν, ἀκολουθεῖ τὸ ἀπὸ Βαβυλῶνος ἐπὶ τοῦ δι᾽ αὐτῆς μεσημβρινοῦ ἐπὶ τὰ ἀρκτικὰ ὄρη πλείους εἶναι τῶν ἑξακισχιλίων· οὔτε τὸ ἀπὸ Θαψάκου ἐπὶ τὰ ὄρη δισχιλίων C 78 καὶ ἑκατόν φησιν Ἐρατοσθένης, ἀλλ᾽ εἶναί τι λοιπὸν ἀκαταμέτρητον, ὥσθ᾽ ἡ ἑξῆς ἔφοδος ἐκ μὴ διδομένου λήμματος οὐκ ἂν ἐπεραίνετο. οὔτ᾽ ἀπεφήνατο οὐδαμοῦ Ἐρατοσθένης τὴν Θάψακον τῆς Βαβυλῶνος πρὸς ἄρκτους κεῖσθαι πλείοσιν ἢ τετρακισχιλίοις καὶ πεντακοσίοις σταδίοις.

22. Ἑξῆς δὲ συνηγορῶν ἔτι τοῖς ἀρχαίοις πίναξιν οὐ τὰ λεγόμενα ὑπὸ τοῦ Ἐρατοσθένους προφέρεται περὶ τῆς τρίτης σφραγῖδος, ἀλλ᾽ ἑαυτῷ κεχαρισμένως πλάττει τὴν ἀπόφασιν πρὸς ἀνατροπὴν εὐφυῆ. ὁ μὲν γὰρ ἀκολουθῶν τῇ θέσει τῇ προειρημένῃ τοῦ τε Ταύρου καὶ τῆς ἀπὸ Στηλῶν θαλάττης, διελὼν τῇ γραμμῇ ταύτῃ τὴν οἰκουμένην δίχα, καὶ καλέσας τὸ μὲν βόρειον μέρος, τὸ δὲ νότιον, πειρᾶται τούτων ἑκάτερον τέμνειν πάλιν εἰς τὰ δυνατὰ μέρη· καλεῖ δὲ ταῦτα σφραγῖδας. καὶ δὴ τοῦ νοτίου μέρους πρώτην εἰπὼν σφραγῖδα τὴν Ἰνδικήν, δευτέραν δὲ τὴν Ἀριανήν, ἐχούσας τι εὐπερίγραφον, ἴσχυσεν ἀμφοτέρων ἀποδοῦναι

---

[1] See footnote, page 306.
[2] That is, which he charges to Eratosthenes.

ment of Eratosthenes that the distance from Babylon
to Thapsacus is four thousand eight hundred stadia,
and thence northwards to the Armenian Mountains
two thousand one hundred : it does not follow from
this that the distance from Babylon measured on the
meridian through it to the northern mountains is
more than six thousand stadia. Secondly, Eratosthenes does not say that the distance from Thapsacus
to the mountains is two thousand one hundred stadia,
but that there is a remainder of that distance which
has not been measured ; and hence the ensuing
attack, made from an assumption not granted, could
not result in a valid conclusion. And, thirdly,
Eratosthenes has nowhere declared that Thapsacus
lies north of Babylon more than four thousand five
hundred stadia.

22. Next, still pleading for the early maps, Hipparchus does not produce the words of Eratosthenes
in regard to the Third Section,[1] but for his own
gratification invents his statement,[2] making it easy
to overthrow. For Eratosthenes, pursuing his afore-
mentioned thesis about the Taurus and the Mediterranean Sea, beginning at the Pillars,[3] divides the
inhabited world by means of this line into two
divisions, and calls them respectively the Northern
Division and the Southern Division, and then attempts to cut each of these divisions again into such
sections as are possible ; and he calls these sections
"Sphragides." [4] And so, after calling India Section
First of the Southern Division, and Ariana Section
Second, since they had contours easy to sketch, he
was able to represent not only length and breadth of

[3] 2. 1. 1.
[4] See paragraph 35 following and footnote.

καὶ μῆκος καὶ πλάτος, τρόπον δέ τινα καὶ σχῆμα
ὡς ἂν γεωμετρικός. τὴν μὲν γὰρ Ἰνδικὴν ῥομ-
βοειδῆ φησι διὰ τὸ τῶν πλευρῶν τὰς μὲν θαλάττῃ
κλύζεσθαι τῇ τε νοτίῳ καὶ τῇ ἐῴα, μὴ πάνυ
κολπώδεις ἠόνας[1] ποιούσῃ, τὰς δὲ λοιπάς, τὴν
μὲν τῷ ὄρει, τὴν δὲ τῷ ποταμῷ, κἀνταῦθα τοῦ
εὐθυγράμμου σχήματος ὑπό τι σωζομένου· τὴν
δ᾽ Ἀριανὴν ὁρῶν τάς γε τρεῖς πλευρὰς ἔχουσαν
εὐφυεῖς πρὸς τὸ ἀποτελέσαι παραλληλόγραμμον σχῆμα, τὴν δ᾽ ἑσπέριον οὐκ ἔχων σημείοις
ἀφορίσαι διὰ τὸ ἐπαλλάττειν ἀλλήλοις τὰ ἔθνη,
γραμμῇ τινι ὅμως δηλοῖ τῇ ἀπὸ Κασπίων πυλῶν
ἐπὶ τὰ ἄκρα τῆς Καρμανίας τελευτώσῃ τὰ συνάπτοντα πρὸς τὸν Περσικὸν κόλπον. ἑσπέριον μὲν
οὖν καλεῖ τοῦτο τὸ πλευρόν, ἐῷον δὲ τὸ παρὰ
τὸν Ἰνδόν,[3] παράλληλα δ᾽ οὐ λέγει, οὐδὲ τὰ
λοιπά, τό τε τῷ ὄρει γραφόμενον καὶ τὸ τῇ
θαλάττῃ, ἀλλὰ μόνον τὸ μὲν βόρειον, τὸ δὲ νότιον.

23. Οὕτω δ᾽ ὁλοσχερεῖ τινι τύπῳ τὴν δευτέραν
ἀποδιδοὺς σφραγῖδα, πολὺ ταύτης ὁλοσχερέστε-
ρον ἀποδίδωσι τὴν τρίτην σφραγῖδα κατὰ πλείους αἰτίας. πρώτην μὲν τὴν λεχθεῖσαν, ὅτι οὐκ
εὐκρινῶς ἀφώρισται ἡ ἀπὸ Κασπίων πυλῶν ἐπὶ
Καρμανίαν, ἥτις κοινή ἐστι τῇ τρίτῃ πρὸς τὴν
δευτέραν σφραγῖδα πλευρά· ἔπειθ᾽ ὅτι εἰς τὴν

---

[1] ἠόνας, Meineke, for ἠιόνας.

---

[1] Strabo discusses this point again in 15. 1. 11.
[2] The Taurus.   [3] Indus.

In §§ 23-29 Strabo shews that Hipparchus applies the figures of Eratosthenes to rectangular dimensions (*TCKM*), placing Thapsacus at *T*, Caspian Gates at *C*, the point on the Carmanian frontiers at *K*, Babylon at *B*, and so on ; and that

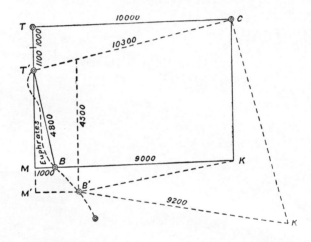

the dotted lines, including the Euphrates, represent what Eratosthenes meant in his rough estimates. Of course it is easy to show the impossibility of Eratosthenes' figures in their mutual relations if they be applied as Hipparchus applied them.

both sections, but, after a fashion, shape also, as
would a geometrician. In the first place, India, he
says, is rhomboidal,[1] because, of its four sides, two
are washed by seas (the southern and the eastern
seas) which form shores without very deep gulfs;
and because the remaining sides [are marked], one
by the mountain [2] and the other by the river,[3] and
because on these two sides, also, the rectilinear
figure is fairly well preserved. Secondly, Ariana.
Although he sees that it has at least three sides well-
suited to the formation of the figure of a parallelogram,
and although he cannot mark off the western side by
mathematical points, on account of the fact that the
tribes there alternate with one another,[4] yet he
represents that side by a sort of line [5] that begins at
the Caspian Gates and ends at the capes of Carmania
that are next to the Persian Gulf. Accordingly, he
calls this side " western " and the side along the
Indus " eastern," but he does not call them parallel;
neither does he call the other two sides parallel,
namely, the one marked by the mountain, and the
one marked by the sea, but he merely calls them
" the northern" and " the southern " sides.

23. [6] And so, though he represents the Second
Section merely by a rough outline, he represents
the Third Section much more roughly than the
Second—and for several reasons. First is the reason
already mentioned, namely, because the side be-
ginning at the Caspian Gates and running to
Carmania (the side common to the Second and
Third Sections) has not been determined distinctly;

[4] That is, they merge confusedly with one another across
the imaginary line representing the common boundary
between Section Second and Section Third.

[5] In mathematics, a dotted line.

[6] See figure and note on page 296.

νότιον πλευρὰν ὁ Περσικὸς ἐμπίπτει κόλπος, ὅπερ
καὶ αὐτός φησιν, ὥστ' ἠνάγκασται τὴν ἐκ Βαβυλῶνος λαβεῖν γραμμήν, ὡς ἂν εὐθεῖάν τινα διὰ
Σούσων καὶ Περσεπόλεως μέχρι τῶν ὅρων τῆς
C 79 Καρμανίας καὶ τῆς Περσίδος, ᾗ δυνατὸς ἦν
εὑρεῖν μεμετρημένην ὁδόν, σταδίων οὖσαν τὴν
ὅλην μικρῷ πλειόνων ἢ ἐννακισχιλίων· ἣν νότιον
μὲν καλεῖ πλευράν, παράλληλον δ' οὐ λέγει τῇ
βορείῳ. δῆλον δ' ὅτι οὐδ' ὁ Εὐφράτης, ᾧ τὸ
ἑσπέριον ἀφορίζει πλευρόν, σύνεγγύς ἐστιν εὐθείᾳ
γραμμῇ, ἀλλ' ἀπὸ τῶν ὀρῶν ἐπὶ τὴν μεσημβρίαν
ῥυείς, εἶτ' ἐπιστρέφει πρὸς ἔω καὶ πάλιν πρὸς
νότον μέχρι τῆς εἰς θάλατταν ἐκβολῆς. δηλοῖ
δὲ τὸ μὴ εὐθύπορον τοῦ ποταμοῦ, φράζων τὸ
σχῆμα τῆς Μεσοποταμίας, ὃ ποιοῦσι συμπίπ-
τοντες εἰς ἓν ὅ τε Τίγρις καὶ ὁ Εὐφράτης, ὑπηρεσίῳ παραπλήσιον, ὥς φησι. καὶ μὴν τὸ ἀπὸ
Θαψάκου μέχρι τῆς Ἀρμενίας οὐδὲ πᾶν μεμετρη-
μένον ἔχει τὸ ἑσπέριον πλευρὸν τὸ ἀφοριζόμενον
ὑπὸ τοῦ Εὐφράτου, ἀλλά φησι τὸ πρὸς τῇ Ἀρ-
μενίᾳ μέρος καὶ τοῖς ἀρκτικοῖς ὄρεσι μὴ ἔχειν
εἰπεῖν[1] πόσον ἐστὶ διὰ τὸ ἀμέτρητον εἶναι. διὰ
δὴ ταῦτα πάντα τυπωδῶς φησιν ἀποδιδόναι τὴν
τρίτην μερίδα· καὶ γὰρ καὶ τὰ διαστήματά[2] φησιν
ἐκ πολλῶν συναγαγεῖν[3] τῶν τοὺς σταθμοὺς
πραγματευσαμένων· ὧν[4] τινας καὶ ἀνεπιγράφους

---

[1] εἰπεῖν, Meineke inserts, after ἔχειν ; Corais, Kramer, had
already suggested it.
[2] ἅ. Siebenkees, Du Theil, delete, before φησιν ; Groskurd,
Meineke, Forbiger, following.
[3] συναγαγεῖν, Corais, for συνάγειν ; Meineke following.
[4] ὧν, Corais inserts, before τινάς ; Groskurd, Meineke,
Forbiger, following ; C. Müller approving.

secondly, because the Persian Gulf breaks into the
southern side, as Eratosthenes himself says, and
therefore he has been forced to take the line
beginning at Babylon as though it were a straight
line running through Susa and Persepolis to the
frontiers of Carmania and Persis, on which he was
able to find a measured highway, which was slightly
more than nine thousand stadia long, all told. This
side Eratosthenes calls " southern," but he does not
call it parallel to the northern side. Again, it is
clear that the Euphrates, by which he marks off the
western side, is nowhere near a straight line; but
after flowing from the mountains towards the south,
it then turns eastward, and then southward again to
the point where it empties into the sea. And
Eratosthenes makes clear the river's lack of straight-
ness when he indicates the shape of Mesopotamia,
which results from the confluence of the Tigris and the
Euphrates—" like a galley," as he says. And besides,
as regards the stretch from Thapsacus to Armenia—
Eratosthenes does not even know, as a distance that
has been wholly measured, the western side that is
marked off by the Euphrates; nay, he says he does
not know how great is the stretch next to Armenia
and the northern mountains, from the fact that it
is unmeasured. For all these reasons, therefore, he
says he represents the Third Section only in rough
outline; indeed, he says that he collected even the
distances from many writers who had worked out the
itineraries—some of which he speaks of as actually

καλεῖ. ἀγνωμονεῖν δὴ δόξειεν ἂν ὁ Ἵππαρχος πρὸς τὴν τοιαυτὴν ὁλοσχέρειαν γεωμετρικῶς ἀντιλέγων, ἐν ᾗ χάριν εἰδέναι δεῖ τοῖς καὶ ὁπωσοῦν ἀπαγγείλασιν ἡμῖν τὴν τῶν τόπων φύσιν. ὅταν δὲ δὴ μηδ' ἐξ ὧν ἐκεῖνος λέγει λαμβάνῃ τὰς γεωμετρικὰς ὑποθέσεις, ἀλλ' ἑαυτῷ πλάσας, ἐκφανέστερον ἂν τὸ φιλότιμον καταμηνύοιτο.

24. Ὁ μὲν δὴ οὕτως φησὶ τὴν τρίτην μερίδα τυπωδῶς ἀποδίδοσθαι μυρίων σταδίων ἀπὸ Κασπίων πυλῶν ἐπὶ τὸν Εὐφράτην, κατὰ μέρος δὲ διαιρῶν, ὡς ἀναγεγραμμένην εὗρε τὴν μέτρησιν, οὕτω τίθησιν, ἔμπαλιν τὴν ἀρχὴν ἀπὸ τοῦ Εὐφράτου ποιησάμενος καὶ τῆς κατὰ Θάψακον διαβάσεως αὐτοῦ. μέχρι μὲν δὴ τοῦ Τίγριδος, ὅπου Ἀλέξανδρος διέβη, σταδίους δισχιλίους καὶ τετρακοσίους γράφει· ἐντεῦθεν δ' ἐπὶ τοὺς ἑξῆς τόπους διὰ Γαυγαμήλων καὶ τοῦ Λύκου καὶ Ἀρβήλων καὶ Ἐκβατάνων, ᾗ Δαρεῖος ἐκ τῶν Γαυγαμήλων ἔφυγε μέχρι Κασπίων πυλῶν, τοὺς μυρίους ἐκπληροῖ, τριακοσίοις μόνον πλεονάσας. τὸ μὲν δὴ βόρειον πλευρὸν οὕτω καταμετρεῖ, οὐ παράλληλον τοῖς ὄρεσι θείς, οὐδὲ τῇ διὰ Στηλῶν καὶ Ἀθηνῶν καὶ Ῥόδου γραμμῇ· ἡ γὰρ Θάψακος πολὺ τῶν ὁρῶν ἀφέστηκε, συμπίπτει δὲ καὶ τὸ ὄρος καὶ ἡ ἀπὸ Θαψάκου ὁδὸς ἐπὶ τὰς Κασπίους πύλας. καὶ τά γε προσάρκτια μέρη τοῦ ὄρου ταῦτ' ἐστίν.

without titles. So, then, Hipparchus would seem to be acting unfairly when he contradicts with geometrical accuracy a mere rough outline of this nature, instead of being grateful, as we should be, to all those who have reported to us in any way at all the physiography of the regions. But when Hipparchus does not even take his geometrical hypotheses from what Eratosthenes says, but fabricates on his own account, he betrays his spirit of jealousy still more obviously.

24. Now Eratosthenes says that it is only thus, "in a rough-outline way," that he has represented the Third Section, with its length of ten thousand stadia from the Caspian Gates to the Euphrates. And then, in making subdivisions of this length, he sets down the measurements just as he found them already assigned by others, after beginning in the inverse order at the Euphrates and its passage at Thapsacus. Accordingly, for the distance from the Euphrates to the Tigris, at the point where Alexander crossed it, he lays off two thousand four hundred stadia; thence to the several places in succession, through Gaugamela, the Lycus, Arbela, and Ecbatana (the route by which Darius fled from Gaugamela to the Caspian Gates) he fills out the ten thousand stadia, and has a surplus of only three hundred stadia. This, then, is the way he measures the northern side, not having first put it parallel with the mountains, or with the line that runs through the Pillars, Athens, and Rhodes. For Thapsacus lies at a considerable distance from the mountains, and the mountain-range and the highway from Thapsacus meet at the Caspian Gates.—And these are the northern portions of the boundary of the Third Section.

C 80   25. Ἀποδοὺς δὲ τὸ βόρειον οὕτω πλευρόν, τὸ
δὲ νότιον, φησί, παρὰ μὲν τὴν θάλατταν οὐκ ἔστι
λαβεῖν διὰ τὸ τὸν Περσικὸν ἐμπίπτειν κόλπον,
ἀπὸ Βαβυλῶνος δὲ διὰ Σούσων καὶ Περσεπόλεως
ἕως[1] τῶν ὁρίων τῆς τε Περσίδος καὶ τῆς Καρμανίας σταδίους εἶναι ἐννακισχιλίους καὶ διακοσίους, νότιον μὲν λέγων, παράλληλον δ' οὐ
λέγων τῷ βορείῳ τὸ νότιον. τὴν δὲ διαφωνίαν
τοῦ μήκους φησὶ συμβαίνειν τοῦ τε βορείου
τεθέντος πλευροῦ καὶ τοῦ νοτίου, διὰ τὸ τὸν
Εὐφράτην μέχρι τινὸς πρὸς μεσημβρίαν ῥυέντα
πρὸς τὴν ἕω πολὺ ἐγκλίνειν.

    26. Τῶν δὲ πλαγίων πλευρῶν τὴν ἑσπερίαν
λέγει πρῶτον· ἣν ὁποία τίς ἐστιν, εἴτε μία εἴτε
δύο, ἐν μέσῳ πάρεστι σκοπεῖν. ἀπὸ γὰρ τῆς
κατὰ Θάψακον φησι διαβάσεως παρὰ τὸν Εὐφράτην εἰς μὲν Βαβυλῶνα σταδίους εἶναι τετρακισχιλίους ὀκτακοσίους, ἐντεῦθεν δ' ἐπὶ τὰς ἐκβολὰς
τοῦ Εὐφράτου καὶ πόλιν Τερηδόνα τρισχιλίους·
τὰ δ' ἀπὸ Θαψάκου πρὸς τὰς ἄρκτους μέχρι μὲν
τῶν Ἀρμενίων πυλῶν καταμεμετρῆσθαι καὶ εἶναι
ὡς χιλίους ἑκατόν, τοὺς δὲ διὰ Γορδυαίων καὶ
Ἀρμενίων μηκέτι· διὸ δὴ παραλείπειν αὐτούς.
τοῦ δὲ πρὸς ἕω πλευροῦ τὸ μὲν διὰ τῆς Περσικῆς
κατὰ μῆκος ἀπὸ τῆς Ἐρυθρᾶς ὡς ἐπὶ Μηδίαν καὶ
τὰς ἄρκτους οὐκ ἔλαττον εἶναι δοκεῖ τῶν ὀκτακισχιλίων, ἀπὸ δέ τινων ἀκρωτηρίων καὶ ὑπὲρ
τοὺς ἐννακισχιλίους, τὸ δὲ λοιπὸν διὰ τῆς Παραι-
τακηνῆς καὶ Μηδίας ἐπὶ Κασπίους πύλας ὡς

---

[1] ἕως, Cobet, for καί (for which Groskurd substitutes μέχρι;
Meineke, Dübner-Müller, Forbiger, following); Bernadakis
approving.

25. After having thus represented the northern side, Eratosthenes says it is not possible to take the southern side as along the sea, because the Persian Gulf breaks into it; but, says he, from Babylon through Susa and Persepolis to the frontiers of Persis and Carmania, it is nine thousand two hundred stadia—and this he calls "southern side," but he does not call the southern side parallel to the northern. As to the difference in the lengths of the estimated northern and southern sides, he says it results from the fact that the Euphrates, after having flowed southwards to a certain point, makes a considerable bend towards the east.

26. Of the two transverse sides Eratosthenes speaks of the western first; and what the nature of this side is, whether it is one line or two, is a matter open to consideration. For from the passage at Thapsacus, he says, along the Euphrates to Babylon, it is four thousand eight hundred stadia, and thence to the outlet of the Euphrates and the city of Teredon, three thousand; but as regards the distances from Thapsacus northward, the stadia have been measured up to the Armenian Gates and amount to about one thousand one hundred; whereas the stadia through Gordyene and Armenia are still unmeasured, and so for this reason he leaves them out of consideration. But of the side on the east, that part which runs through Persis lengthwise from the Red Sea, approximately toward Media and the north, is, he thinks, no less than eight thousand stadia (though, if reckoned from certain promontories, even above nine thousand stadia); and the remaining part, through Paraetacene [1] and Media to the Caspian

[1] For the position of Paraetacene see 15. 3. 12.

τρισχιλίων· τὸν δὲ Τίγριν ποταμὸν καὶ τὸν Εὐφράτην ῥέοντας ἐκ τῆς Ἀρμενίας πρὸς μεσημβρίαν, ἐπειδὰν παραμείψωνται τὰ τῶν Γορδυαίων ὄρη, κύκλον μέγαν περιβαλομένους καὶ ἐμπεριλαβόντας χώραν πολλὴν τὴν Μεσοποταμίαν ἐπιστρέφειν πρὸς χειμερινὴν ἀνατολὴν καὶ τὴν μεσημβρίαν, πλέον δὲ τὸν Εὐφράτην· γενόμενον δὲ τοῦτον ἔγγιον ἀεὶ τοῦ Τίγριδος κατὰ τὸ Σεμιράμιδος διατείχισμα καὶ κώμην καλουμένην Ὦπιν, διασχόντα ταύτης ὅσον διακοσίους σταδίους, καὶ ῥυέντα διὰ Βαβυλῶνος ἐκπίπτειν εἰς τὸν Περσικὸν κόλπον. γίνεται δή, φησί, τὸ σχῆμα τῆς Μεσοποταμίας καὶ Βαβυλωνίας ὑπηρεσίῳ παραπλήσιον. ὁ μὲν δὴ Ἐρατοσθένης τοιαῦτ᾽ εἴρηκε.

27. Περὶ δὲ τῆς τρίτης σφραγῖδος καὶ ἄλλα μέν τινα ἁμαρτήματα ποιεῖ, περὶ ὧν ἐπισκεψόμεθα, ἃ δὲ Ἵππαρχος προφέρει αὐτῷ, οὐ πάνυ. σκοπῶμεν δ᾽ ἃ λέγει. βουλόμενος γὰρ βεβαιοῦν τὸ ἐξ ἀρχῆς, ὅτι οὐ μεταθετέον τὴν Ἰνδικὴν ἐπὶ τὰ νοτιώτερα, ὥσπερ Ἐρατοσθένης ἀξιοῖ, σαφὲς ἂν γενέσθαι τοῦτο μάλιστά φησιν ἐξ ὧν αὐτὸς ἐκεῖνος προφέρεται· τὴν γὰρ τρίτην μερίδα κατὰ τὴν βόρειον πλευρὰν εἰπόντα ἀφορίζεσθαι ὑπὸ τῆς ἀπὸ Κασπίων πυλῶν ἐπὶ τὸν Εὐφράτην γραμμῆς σταδίων μυρίων οὔσης, μετὰ ταῦτα ἐπιφέρειν ὅτι τὸ νότιον πλευρὸν τὸ ἀπὸ Βαβυλῶνος εἰς τοὺς ὅρους τῆς Καρμανίας μικρῷ πλειόνων ἐστὶν ἢ ἐννακισχιλίων, τὸ δὲ πρὸς δύσει πλευρὸν ἀπὸ

Gates, about three thousand stadia. The Tigris and
the Euphrates, he says, flow from Armenia southwards; and then, as soon as they pass the mountains
of Gordyene, they describe a great circle and
enclose a considerable territory, Mesopotamia; and
then they turn toward the winter rising of the sun [1]
and the south, but more so the Euphrates; and the
Euphrates, after becoming ever nearer to the Tigris
in the neighbourhood of the Wall of Semiramis and
a village called Opis (from which village the
Euphrates was distant only about two hundred
stadia), and, after flowing through Babylon, empties
into the Persian Gulf. "So it comes to pass," he
says, "that the shape of Mesopotamia and Babylonia
is like that of a galley." Such, then, are the statements which Eratosthenes has made.

27. Now, as regards the Third Section, although
there are certain other errors which Eratosthenes
makes—and I shall discuss these—still he does not
err at all in the matters for which Hipparchus
reproaches him. Let us see what Hipparchus says.
In his desire to establish his initial statement,
namely, that we must not shift India farther to the
south, as Eratosthenes requires, he says it will be
particularly obvious from Eratosthenes' own utter-
ances that we must not do so; for after first saying
that the Third Section is marked off on its northern
side by the line drawn from the Caspian Gates to
the Euphrates, a distance of ten thousand stadia,
Eratosthenes adds, later on, that the southern side,
which runs from Babylon to the frontiers of Carmania,
is slightly more than nine thousand stadia in length,
and the side on the west from Thapsacus along the

[1] See footnote 2, page 105.

Θαψάκου παρὰ τὸν Εὐφράτην ἐστὶν εἰς Βαβυλῶνα
τετρακισχίλιοι ὀκτακόσιοι στάδιοι, καὶ ἑξῆς ἐπὶ
τὰς ἐκβολὰς τρισχίλιοι, τὰ δὲ πρὸς ἄρκτον ἀπὸ
Θαψάκου, τὸ μὲν ἀπομεμέτρηται μέχρι χιλίων
ἑκατόν, τὸ λοιπὸν δ' οὐκέτι. ἐπεὶ τοίνυν, φησί, τὸ
μὲν βόρειόν ἐστι πλευρὸν τῆς τρίτης μερίδος ὡς
μυρίων, ἡ δὲ τούτῳ παράλληλος ἀπὸ Βαβυλῶνος
εὐθεῖα μέχρι ἀνατολικοῦ πλευροῦ συνελογίσθη
μικρῷ πλειόνων ἢ ἐννακισχιλίων, δῆλον ὅτι ἡ
Βαβυλὼν οὐ πολλῷ πλείοσιν ἢ χιλίοις ἐστὶν
ἀνατολικωτέρα τῆς κατὰ Θάψακον διαβάσεως.

28. Ἐροῦμεν δ' ὅτι, εἰ μὲν ἐπὶ τῆς αὐτῆς μεσημβρινῆς εὐθείας ἐπ' ἀκριβὲς ἐλαμβάνοντο αἵ τε
Κάσπιοι πύλαι καὶ οἱ ὅροι τῶν Καρμανίων καὶ
Περσῶν, πρὸς ὀρθάς τε ἤγοντο ἀπὸ τῆς λεχθείσης
μεσημβρινῆς εὐθείας ἥ τε ἐπὶ Θάψακον καὶ ἡ ἐπὶ
Βαβυλῶνα, συνέβαινεν ἂν τοῦτο. ἡ γὰρ προσεκ-
βαλλομένη τῇ διὰ Βαβυλῶνος μέχρι τῆς διὰ
Θαψάκου εὐθείας μεσημβρινῆς, ἴση ἂν ἦν πρὸς
αἴσθησιν ἢ πάρισός γε τῇ ἀπὸ Κασπίων πυλῶν
εἰς Θάψακον· ὥστε τῇ ὑπεροχῇ ἐγίνετ' ἂν ἀνατολικωτέρα ἡ Βαβυλὼν τῆς Θαψάκου, ᾗ ὑπερέχει
ἡ ἐκ Κασπίων πυλῶν εἰς Θάψακον τῆς ἐκ τῶν
Καρμανίων ὅρων εἰς Βαβυλῶνα. ἀλλ' οὔτε

---

[1] Of course Hipparchus' argument is sound if his hypotheses be granted. Hipparchus assumes that Eratosthenes'
figures refer to latitudinal and longitudinal distances; and
by drawing a rectangle whose sides are formed by meridians
through Thapsacus and the Caspian Gates, respectively, and
by parallels of latitude through Thapsacus and the Caspian
Gates, and through Babylon, he easily convicts Eratosthenes
of inconsistency. That is, by a *reductio ad absurdum*,
he forces Eratosthenes' Babylon much farther west than

Euphrates to Babylon is four thousand eight hundred
stadia, and, next, from Babylon to the outlet of the
Euphrates is three thousand stadia, and as for the
distances north of Thapsacus, one of them has been
measured off as far as one thousand one hundred
stadia, while the remainder is still unmeasured.
Then, says Hipparchus, since the northern side of
the Third Section is about ten thousand stadia, and
since the line parallel thereto, straight from Babylon
to the eastern side, was reckoned by Eratosthenes at
slightly more than nine thousand stadia, it is clear
that Babylon is not much more than a thousand
stadia farther east than the passage at Thapsacus.[1]

28. My reply will be: If, with geometrical
precision, we took the Caspian Gates and the
frontiers of Carmania and Persis as upon the same
straight meridian, and if we drew the line to
Thapsacus and the line to Babylon at right angles
with the said straight meridian, then that conclusion of Hipparchus would be valid. Indeed, the
line through Babylon,[2] if further produced as far as the
straight meridian through Thapsacus, would, to the
eye, be equal—or at all events approximately equal—
to the line from the Caspian Gates to Thapsacus ; and
hence Babylon would come to be farther east than
Thapsacus by as much as the line from the Caspian
Gates to Thapsacus exceeds the line from the
Carmanian frontiers to Babylon ! But, in the first

Eratosthenes meant it to be (cp. § 36 below on this point).
Strabo proceeds to show the fallacy of Hipparchus' reasoning, and even to show that Hipparchus might have proved,
on the same premises, still greater absurdity on the part of
Eratosthenes.

[2] That is, the line drawn perpendicular to the meridian
that passes through the Carmanian frontier.

τὴν διορίζουσαν γραμμὴν ἑσπέριον πλευρὸν τῆς
Ἀριανῆς ἐπὶ μεσημβρινοῦ κειμένην εἴρηκεν Ἐρατοσθένης, οὐδὲ τὴν ἀπὸ Κασπίων πυλῶν ἐπὶ
Θάψακον πρὸς ὀρθὰς τῇ διὰ τῶν Κασπίων πυλῶι
μεσημβρινῇ, ἀλλὰ μᾶλλον τὴν τῷ ὄρει γραφο-
μένην, πρὸς ἣν ἡ ἐπὶ Θάψακον γωνίαν ποιεῖ ἀπὸ
τοῦ αὐτοῦ σημείου κατηγμένη, ἀφ' οὗ καὶ ἡ τοῦ
ὄρους γραμμή· οὔθ' ἡ ἐπὶ Βαβυλῶνα ἠγμένη ἀπὸ
τῆς Καρμανίας παράλληλος εἴρηται τῇ ἐπὶ
Θάψακον ἠγμένῃ· οὐδ' εἰ παράλληλος ἦν, μὴ
πρὸς ὀρθὰς δὲ τῇ διὰ Κασπίων πυλῶν μεσημβρινῇ,
οὐδὲν ἂν ἐγίνετο πλέον πρὸς συλλογισμόν.

29. Ὁ δὲ ταῦτα λαβὼν ἐξ ἑτοίμου καὶ δείξας,
ὡς οἴεται, διότι ἡ Βαβυλὼν κατὰ Ἐρατοσθένη
Θαψάκου ἀνατολικωτέρα ἐστὶ μικρῷ πλείοσιν ἢ
C 82 χιλίοις σταδίοις, πάλιν ἄλλως πλάττει λῆμμα
ἑαυτῷ πρὸς τὴν ἑξῆς ἀπόδειξιν, καί φησιν, ἐὰν
ἐννοηθῇ ἀπὸ Θαψάκου ἐπὶ μεσημβρίαν εὐθεῖα
ἀγομένη καὶ ἀπὸ Βαβυλῶνος ἐπὶ ταύτην κάθετος,
τρίγωνον ὀρθογώνιον ἔσεσθαι, συνεστηκὸς ἔκ τε
τῆς ἀπὸ Θαψάκου ἐπὶ Βαβυλῶνα τεινούσης
πλευρᾶς καὶ τῆς ἀπὸ Βαβυλῶνος καθέτου ἐπὶ
τὴν διὰ Θαψάκου μεσημβρινὴν γραμμὴν ἠγμένης
καὶ αὐτῆς τῆς διὰ Θαψάκου μεσημβρινῆς. τούτου
δὲ τοῦ τριγώνου τὴν μὲν ὑποτείνουσαν τῇ ὀρθῇ τὴν
ἀπὸ Θαψάκου εἰς Βαβυλῶνα τίθησιν, ἥν φησι
τετρακισχιλίων ὀκτακοσίων εἶναι· τὴν δ' ἐκ Βαβυλῶνος εἰς τὴν διὰ Θαψάκου μεσημβρινὴν γραμμὴν

place, Eratosthenes has not spoken of the line that
bounds a western side of Ariana as lying on a meridian;
nor yet of the line from the Caspian Gates to
Thapsacus as at right angles with the meridian line
through the Caspian Gates, but rather of the line
marked by the mountain-range, with which line the
line to Thapsacus forms an acute angle, since the
latter has been drawn down [1] from the same point as
that from which the mountain-line has been drawn.
In the second place, Eratosthenes has not called the
line drawn to Babylon from Carmania parallel to the
line drawn to Thapsacus; and even if it were
parallel, but not at right angles with the meridian
line through the Caspian Gates, no advantage would
accrue to the argument of Hipparchus.

29. But after making these assumptions off-hand,
and after showing, as he thinks, that Babylon, according to Eratosthenes, is farther east than Thapsacus by slightly more than a thousand stadia, Hipparchus again idly fabricates an assumption for use
in his subsequent argument; and, he says, if we
conceive a straight line drawn from Thapsacus towards the south and a line perpendicular to it from
Babylon, we will have a right-angled triangle, composed of the side that extends from Thapsacus to
Babylon, of the perpendicular drawn from Babylon
to the meridian line through Thapsacus, and of
the meridian itself through Thapsacus. Of this
triangle he makes the line from Thapsacus to
Babylon the hypotenuse, which he says is four
thousand eight hundred stadia; and the perpendicular from Babylon to the meridian line through
Thapsacus, slightly more than a thousand stadia—

---

[1] That is, with a divergence toward the south.

κάθετον μικρῷ πλειόνων ἢ χιλίων, ὅσων ἦν ἡ ὑπεροχὴ τῆς ἐπὶ Θάψακον πρὸς τὴν μέχρι Βαβυλῶνος. ἐκ δὲ τούτων καὶ τὴν λοιπὴν τῶν περὶ τὴν ὀρθὴν συλλογίζεται πολλαπλάσιον οὖσαν τῆς λεχθείσης καθέτου. προστίθησι δὲ ταύτῃ τὴν ἀπὸ Θαψάκου πρὸς ἄρκτον ἐκβαλλομένην μέχρι τῶν Ἀρμενίων ὀρῶν, ἧς τὸ μὲν ἔφη μεμετρῆσθαι Ἐρατοσθένης καὶ εἶναι χιλίων ἑκατόν, τὸ δ' ἀμέτρητον ἐᾷ. οὗτος δ' ἐπὶ τοὐλάχιστον ὑποτίθεται χιλίων, ὥστε τὸ συνάμφω δισχιλίων καὶ ἑκατὸν γίγνεσθαι· ὁ προσθεὶς τῇ ἐπ' εὐθείας πλευρᾷ τοῦ τριγώνου μέχρι τῆς καθέτου τῆς ἐκ Βαβυλῶνος πολλῶν χιλιάδων λογίζεται διάστημα τὸ ἀπὸ τῶν Ἀρμενίων ὀρῶν καὶ τοῦ δι' Ἀθηνῶν παραλλήλου μέχρι τῆς ἐκ Βαβυλῶνος καθέτου, ἥτις ἐπὶ τοῦ διὰ Βαβυλῶνος παραλλήλου ἵδρυται. τὸ δέ γε ἀπὸ τοῦ δι' Ἀθηνῶν παραλλήλου ἐπὶ τὸν διὰ Βαβυλῶνος δείκνυσιν οὐ μεῖζον ὂν σταδίων δισχιλίων τετρακοσίων, ὑποτεθέντος τοῦ μεσημβρινοῦ παντὸς τοσούτων σταδίων, ὅσων Ἐρατοσθένης φησίν. εἰ δὲ τοῦτο, οὐκ ἂν ἦν τὰ ὄρη τὰ Ἀρμένια καὶ τὰ τοῦ Ταύρου ἐπὶ τοῦ δι' Ἀθηνῶν παραλλήλου, ὡς Ἐρατοσθένης, ἀλλὰ πολλαῖς χιλιάσι σταδίων ἀρκτικώτερα κατ' αὐτὸν ἐκεῖνον. ἐνταῦθα δὴ πρὸς

---

[1] From the Caspian Gates.
[2] From the Carmanian frontier.

the amount by which the line to Thapsacus[1] ex-
ceeded the line up to Babylon[2]; and then from
these sums he figures the other of the two lines
which form the right angle to be many times longer
than the said perpendicular. And he adds to that
line the line produced northwards from Thapsacus
up to the Armenian mountains, one part of which
Eratosthenes said had been measured and was one
thousand one hundred stadia, but the other part
he leaves out of consideration as unmeasured. Hipparchus assumes for the latter part a thousand stadia
at the least, so that the sum of the two parts
amounts to two thousand one hundred stadia; and
adding this sum to his straight-line side[3] of the
triangle, which is drawn to meet its perpendicular
from Babylon, Hipparchus computes a distance of
several thousand stadia, namely, that from the
Armenian Mountains, or the parallel that runs
through Athens, to the perpendicular from Babylon
—which perpendicular he lays on the parallel
that runs through Babylon. At any rate, he points
out that the distance from the parallel through
Athens to that through Babylon is not more than
two thousand four hundred stadia, if it be assumed
that the whole meridian is the number of stadia
in length that Eratosthenes says; and if this is so,
then the mountains of Armenia and those of the
Taurus could not lie on the parallel that runs
through Athens, as Eratosthenes says they do,
but many thousand stadia farther north, according
to Eratosthenes' own statements. At this point,

---

[3] In § 26 Strabo indicates clearly that Eratosthenes did
not say the western side was one straight line. But
Hipparchus took this for granted.

τῷ τοῖς ἀνεσκευασμένοις λήμμασι προσχρῆσθαι
πρὸς τὴν τοῦ ὀρθογωνίου τριγώνου τάξιν, καὶ
τοῦτο λαμβάνει τὸ μὴ διδόμενον, τὸ τὴν ὑποτείνουσαν τῇ ὀρθῇ γωνίᾳ τὴν ἀπὸ Θαψάκου γραμμὴν
εὐθεῖαν εἶναι μέχρι Βαβυλῶνος ἐν σταδίοις τετρακισχιλίοις ὀκτακοσίοις. παρά τε γὰρ τὸν Εὐφράτην φησὶν εἶναι τὴν ὁδὸν ταύτην ὁ Ἐρατοσθένης,
καὶ τὴν Μεσοποταμίαν σὺν τῇ Βαβυλωνίᾳ μεγάλῳ
κύκλῳ περιέχεσθαι λέγων ὑπό τε τοῦ Εὐφράτου
καὶ τοῦ Τίγριδος, τὸ πλέον[1] τῆς περιοχῆς ὑπὸ τοῦ
Εὐφράτου συμβαίνειν φησίν· ὥσθ᾽ ἡ ἀπὸ Θα-
C 83 ψάκου εἰς Βαβυλῶνα εὐθεῖα οὔτ᾽ ἂν παρὰ τὸν
Εὐφράτην εἴη, οὔτ᾽ ἂν τοσούτων σταδίων οὐδ᾽
ἐγγύς. ἀνατέτραπται οὖν ὁ συλλογισμός· καὶ μὴν
εἴρηταί γε, ὅτι οὐχ οἷόν τε δυεῖν δεδομένων
γραμμῶν ἀπὸ τῶν Κασπίων πυλῶν κατάγεσθαι
τὴν μὲν ἐπὶ Θάψακον, τὴν δ᾽ ἐπὶ τὰ τῶν Ἀρμενίων
ὄρη τὰ κατάλληλα τῇ Θαψάκῳ, ἀπέχοντα τῆς
Θαψάκου τοὐλάχιστον κατ᾽ αὐτὸν τὸν Ἵππαρχον
δισχιλίους καὶ ἑκατὸν σταδίους, ἀμφοτέρας παραλλήλους εἶναι καὶ ἀλλήλαις καὶ τῇ διὰ Βαβυλῶνος,
ἣν νότιον πλευρὰν Ἐρατοσθένης ἐκάλεσεν. ἐκεῖνος
μὲν οὖν οὐκ ἔχων καταμεμετρημένην εἰπεῖν τὴν
παρὰ τὰ ὄρη ὁδόν, τὴν[2] ἀπὸ Θαψάκου ἐπὶ
Κασπίους πύλας ταύτην εἶπε, καὶ προσέθηκε τὸ
ὡς τυπωδῶς εἰπεῖν· ἄλλως τε τῷ βουλομένῳ τὸ
μῆκος εἰπεῖν τῆς μετὰ τὴν Ἀριανὴν μέχρι Εὐφράτου χώρας οὐ πολὺ διέφερε ταύτην ἢ ἐκείνην
καταμετρεῖν. ὁ δ᾽ ὡς παραλλήλους ὑπακούων

---

[1] δέ, Madvig deletes, after πλέον.
[2] δ᾽, before ἀπό, Jones deletes.

then, in addition to making further use of his now demolished assumptions for the construction of his right-angled triangle, he also assumes this point that is not granted, namely, that the hypotenuse—the straight line from Thapsacus to Babylon—is within four thousand eight hundred stadia; for Eratosthenes not only says that this route is along the Euphrates, but when he tells us that Mesopotamia, including Babylonia, is circumscribed by a great circle, by the Euphrates and the Tigris, he asserts that the greater part of the circumference is described by the Euphrates: consequently, the straight line from Thapsacus to Babylon could neither follow the course of the Euphrates, nor be, even approximately, so many stadia in length. So his argument is overthrown. And besides, I have already stated that, if we grant that two lines are drawn from the Caspian Gates, one to Thapsacus, the other to that part of the Armenian Mountains that corresponds in position to Thapsacus (which, according to Hipparchus himself, is distant from Thapsacus at the least two thousand one hundred stadia), it is impossible for both these lines to be parallel either to each other or to the line through Babylon, which Eratosthenes called " southern side." Now because Eratosthenes could not speak of the route along the mountain-range as measured, he spoke of only the route from Thapsacus to the Caspian Gates as measured, and he added the words " roughly speaking"; moreover, since he only wished to tell the length of the country between Ariana and the Euphrates, it did not make much difference whether he measured one route or the other. But Hipparchus, when he tacitly assumes

λέγεσθαι τελέως ἂν δόξειε καταγινώσκειν παιδικὴν
ἀμαθίαν τἀνθρώπου. ταῦτα μὲν οὖν ἐᾶν δεῖ ὡς
παιδικά.

30. Ἃ δ' ἄν τις αἰτιάσαιτο τοῦ Ἐρατοσθένους
τοιαῦτά ἐστι. καθάπερ γὰρ ἡ κατὰ μέλος τομὴ
τῆς ἄλλως κατὰ μέρος διαφέρει (διότι ἡ μὲν καὶ
τὰ μέρη λαμβάνει περιγραφὴν ἔχοντα φυσικήν,
ἀρθρώσει τινὶ καὶ τύπῳ σημειώδει, καθ' ὃ καὶ
τοῦτο εἴρηται,

τὸν δὲ διὰ μελεϊστὶ ταμών,
(Od. 9. 291, Il. 24. 409)

ἡ δ' οὐδὲν ἔχει τοιοῦτον), χρώμεθα δ' οἰκείως
ἑκατέρᾳ, τὸν καιρὸν καὶ τὴν χρείαν σκοποῦντες,
οὕτως ἐπὶ τῶν γεωγραφικῶν δεῖ μὲν τομὰς
ποιεῖσθαι τῶν μερῶν, τὰ καθ' ἕκαστα ἐπιόντας,
μιμεῖσθαι δὲ τὰς κατὰ μέλος τομὰς μᾶλλον ἢ
τὰς ὡς ἔτυχε. τὸ γὰρ σημειῶδες καὶ τὸ εὐπεριόριστον ἐκεῖθεν λαβεῖν ἔστιν, οὗ χρείαν ἔχει ὁ
γεωγράφος. εὐπεριόριστον δέ, ὅταν ἢ ποταμοῖς
ἢ ὄρεσιν ἢ θαλάττῃ δυνατὸν ᾖ, καὶ ἔθνει δὲ ἢ
ἔθνεσι καὶ μεγέθει ποσῷ καὶ σχήματι, ὅπου τοῦτο
δυνατόν. πανταχοῦ δὲ ἀντὶ τοῦ γεωμετρικῶς τὸ
ἁπλῶς καὶ ὁλοσχερῶς ἱκανόν. μέγεθος μὲν οὖν
ἱκανόν ἐστιν, ἂν τὸ μέγιστον εἴπῃς μῆκος καὶ
πλάτος, ὡς τῆς οἰκουμένης ἑπτὰ μυριάδων εἰ
τύχοι μῆκος, πλάτος δ' ἔλαττον ἢ ἥμισυ μικρῷ
τοῦ μήκους· σχῆμα δ', ἂν τῶν γεωμετρικῶν τινι
σχημάτων εἰκάσῃς, ὡς τὴν Σικελίαν τριγώνῳ, ἢ

that the lines are spoken of by Eratosthenes as parallel, would seem to charge the man with utterly childish ignorance. Therefore, I must dismiss these arguments of his as childish.

30. But the charges which one might bring against Eratosthenes are such as follow. Just as, in surgery, amputation at the joints differs from unnatural piece-meal amputation (because the former takes off only the parts that have a natural configuration, following some articulation of joints or a significant outline—the meaning in which Homer says, "and having cut him up limb by limb"—whereas the latter follows no such course), and just as it is proper for us to use each kind of operation if we have regard to the proper time and the proper use of each, just so, in the case of geography, we must indeed make sections of the parts when we go over them in detail, but we must imitate the limb-by-limb amputations rather than the haphazard amputations. For only thus it is possible to take off the member that is significant and well-defined, the only kind of member that the geographer has any use for. Now a country is well-defined when it is possible to define it by rivers or mountains or sea; and also by a tribe or tribes, by a size of such and such proportions, and by shape where this is possible. But in every case, in lieu of a geometrical definition, a simple and roughly outlined definition is sufficient. So, as regards a country's size, it is sufficient if you state its greatest length and breadth (of the inhabited world, for example, a length of perhaps seventy thousand stadia, a breadth slightly less than half the length); and as regards shape, if you liken a country to one of the geometrical figures (Sicily, for example, to a triangle), or to one of the

τῶν ἄλλων γνωρίμων τινὶ σχημάτων, οἷον τὴν
Ἰβηρίαν βύρσῃ, τὴν Πελοπόννησον πλατάνου
C 84 φύλλῳ· ὅσῳ δ' ἂν μεῖζον ᾖ τὸ τεμνόμενον,
τοσῷδε καὶ ὁλοσχερεστέρας πρέποι ἂν ποιεῖσθαι
τὰς τομάς.

31. Ἡ μὲν οὖν οἰκουμένη δίχα διῄρηται τῷ τε
Ταύρῳ καὶ τῇ ἐπὶ Στήλας θαλάττῃ καλῶς. καὶ
τοῦ νοτίου μέρους, ἡ μὲν Ἰνδικὴ περιώρισται
πολλοῖς· καὶ γὰρ ὄρει καὶ ποταμῷ καὶ θαλάττῃ
καὶ ἑνὶ ὀνόματι, ὡς ἂν[1] ἑνὸς ἔθνους· ὥστε καὶ
τετράπλευρος ὀρθῶς λέγεται καὶ ῥομβοειδής.
ἡ δ' Ἀριανὴ ἧττον μὲν τὸ εὐπερίγραφον ἔχει διὰ
τὸ τὴν ἑσπερίαν πλευρὰν συγκεχύσθαι, διώρισται
δ' ὅμως ταῖς τε τρισὶ πλευραῖς, ὡς ἂν εὐθείαις,
καὶ τῷ ὀνόματι, ὡς ἂν ἑνὸς ἔθνους. ἡ δὲ τρίτη
σφραγὶς τελέως ἀπερίγραφός ἐστιν, οὕτω[2] γε
ἀφορισθεῖσα· ἥ τε γὰρ κοινὴ πλευρὰ αὐτῇ τε καὶ
τῇ Ἀριανῇ συγκέχυται, ὡς προείρηται, καὶ ἡ
νότιος πλευρὰ ἀργότατα εἴληπται· οὔτε γὰρ περι-
γράφει τὴν σφραγῖδα, διὰ μέσης τε αὐτῆς βαδί-
ζουσα, καὶ πολλὰ μέρη ἀπολείπουσα πρὸς νότον,
οὔτε μῆκος ὑπογράφει τὸ μέγιστον· τὸ γὰρ
προσάρκτιον πλευρὸν μεῖζον· οὔθ' ὁ Εὐφράτης
ἑσπέριόν ἐστι πλευρόν, οὐδ' εἰ ἐπ' εὐθείας ῥέοι,
τῶν ἄκρων αὐτοῦ μὴ ἐπὶ τοῦ αὐτοῦ μεσημβρινοῦ
κειμένων. τί γὰρ μᾶλλον ἑσπέριον ἢ νότιον;
χωρὶς δὲ τούτων, ὀλίγης οὔσης τῆς ἐπὶ θάλατταν
λοιπῆς τὴν Κιλίκιον καὶ τὴν Συριακήν, τὸ μὴ
μέχρι δεῦρο προάγειν δεῖν τὴν σφραγῖδα οὐ πι-

[1] ἄν, Paetz, Groskurd, for ἔθνος.
[2] οὕτω, Spengel, for οὔπω; Meineke following; C. Müller
approving.

other well-known figures (for instance, Iberia tυ an
oxhide, the Peloponnesus to a leaf of a plane-tree).
And the greater the territory you cut into sections,
the more rough may be the sections you make.

31. Now the inhabited world has been happily
divided by Eratosthenes into two parts by means of
the Taurus Range and the sea that stretches to the
Pillars. And in the Southern Division : India, indeed,
has been well-defined in many ways, by a mountain,
a river, a sea, and by a single term, as of a single
ethnical group—so that Eratosthenes rightly calls
it four-sided and rhomboidal. Ariana, however, has
a contour that is less easy to trace because its western
side is confused,[1] but still it is defined by the three
sides, which are approximately straight lines, and also
by the term Ariana, as of a single ethnical group.
But the Third Section is wholly untraceable, at all
events as defined by Eratosthenes. For, in the first
place, the side common to it and Ariana is confused, as I have previously stated. And the southern
side has been taken very inaccurately ; for neither
does it trace a boundary of this section, since it runs
through its very centre and leaves out many districts
in the south, nor does it represent the section's
greatest length (for the northern side is longer), nor
does the Euphrates form its western side (it would
not do so even if its course lay in a straight line),
since its extremities do not lie on the same meridian.
In fact, how can this side be called western rather
than southern ?   And, quite apart from these
objections, since the distance that remains between
this line and the Cilician and Syrian Sea is slight,
there is no convincing reason why the section should

[1] See § 22, above.

θανόν, τῆς τε Σεμιράμιδος καὶ τοῦ Νίνου Σύρων
λεγομένων, ὧν τῆς μὲν ἡ Βαβυλὼν κτίσμα καὶ
βασίλειον, τοῦ δὲ Νίνος, ὡς ἂν μητρόπολις τῆς
Συρίας, καὶ τῆς διαλέκτου δὲ μέχρι νῦν διαμενούσης
τῆς αὐτῆς τοῖς τε ἐκτὸς τοῦ Εὐφράτου καὶ τοῖς
ἐντός. τὸ¹ δὲ² ἐνταῦθα μέντοι τοιούτῳ μερισμῷ
διασπᾶν ἔθνος γνωριμώτατον καὶ τὰ μέρη συνάπτειν τοῖς ἀλλοεθνέσιν ἥκιστα ἂν πρέποι. οὐδὲ
γὰρ ὑπὸ μεγέθους ἀπηναγκάσθαι λέγοι ἄν· καὶ
γὰρ τὸ μέχρι θαλάττης οὐ μήν πω ἂν ἐξισάζοιτο
τῇ Ἰνδικῇ, ἀλλ' οὐδὲ τῇ Ἀριανῇ, προσλαβὸν καὶ
τὸ μέχρι τῶν ὅρων τῆς εὐδαίμονος Ἀραβίας καὶ
τῆς Αἰγύπτου· ὥστε πολὺ κρεῖττον ἦν μέχρι
δεῦρο προελθεῖν, τῆς τρίτης εἰπόντα σφραγῖδος
τοσαύτῃ προσθήκῃ τῇ μέχρι τῆς Συριακῆς θαλάττης τὸ μὲν νότιον πλευρὸν οὐχ ὥσπερ ἐκεῖνος
εἶπεν ἔχον, οὐδ' ἐπ' εὐθείας, ἀλλ' ἀπὸ τῆς Καρμανίας εὐθὺς τὴν δεξιὰν παραλίαν εἰσπλέοντι
παρὰ³ τὸν Περσικὸν κόλπον μέχρι τῆς ἐκβολῆς
τοῦ Εὐφράτου, καὶ μετὰ ταῦτα τοῖς ὁρίοις τῆς
Μεσήνης καὶ τῆς Βαβυλωνίας συνάπτον, ἥπερ
ἐστὶν ἀρχὴ τοῦ ἰσθμοῦ τοῦ διορίζοντος τὴν εὐδαί-
C 85 μονα Ἀραβίαν ἀπὸ τῆς ἄλλης ἠπείρου, εἶτ'
ἐφεξῆς αὐτὸν τοῦτον διεξιόν, διῆκόν τε μέχρι τοῦ
μυχοῦ τοῦ Ἀραβίου κόλπου καὶ Πηλουσίου, καὶ
ἔτι τοῦ Κανωβικοῦ στόματος τοῦ Νείλου· τοῦτο

---

¹ τό, Corais, for τά, before ἐνταῦθα ; Meineke following.
² δέ, Madvig inserts, after Corais' τό.
³ παρά, Siebenkees and Corais, for γάρ, after εἰσπλέοντι,
following o.

not be extended thereto, both because Semiramis
and Ninus are called Syrians (Babylon was founded
and made the royal residence by Semiramis, and
Nineveh by Ninus, this showing that Nineveh was
the capital of Syria) and because up to the present
moment even the language of the people on both
sides of the Euphrates is the same. However, to
rend asunder so famous a nation by such a line of
cleavage in this region, and to join the parts thus
dissevered to the parts that belong to other tribes,
would be wholly improper. Neither, indeed, could
Eratosthenes allege that he was forced to do this by
considerations of size; for the addition of the territory
that extends up to the sea [1] would still not make the
size of the section equal to that of India, nor, for
that matter, to that of Ariana, not even if it were
increased by the territory that extends up to the
confines of Arabia Felix and Egypt. Therefore it
would have been much better to extend the Third
Section to these limits, and thus, by adding so small
a territory that extends to the Syrian Sea, to define
the southern side of the Third Section as running,
not as Eratosthenes defined it, nor yet as in a
straight line, but as following the coast-line that is
on your right hand as you sail from Carmania into
and along the Persian Gulf up to the mouth of the
Euphrates, and then as following the frontiers of
Mesene and Babylonia, which form the beginning of
the Isthmus that separates Arabia Felix from the rest
of the continent; then, next, as crossing this Isthmus
itself, and as reaching to the recess of the Arabian
Gulf and to Pelusium and even beyond to the
Canobic mouth of the Nile. So much for the

---

[1] The Mediterranean.

μὲν τὸ νότιον πλευρόν, τὸ δὲ λοιπὸν ἑσπέριον τὴν
ἀπὸ τοῦ Κανωβικοῦ στόματος μέχρι τῆς Κιλικίας
παραλίαν.

32. Τετάρτη δ' ἂν εἴη σφραγὶς ἡ συνεστῶσα
ἔκ τε τῆς εὐδαίμονος Ἀραβίας καὶ τοῦ Ἀραβίου
κόλπου καὶ τῆς Αἰγύπτου πάσης καὶ τῆς Αἰθιοπίας. ταύτης δὲ τῆς μερίδος μῆκος μὲν ἔσται τὸ
ἀφοριζόμενον ὑπὸ δυεῖν μεσημβρινῶν· ὁ μὲν γὰρ
γράφεται διὰ τοῦ δυσμικωτάτου σημείου τοῦ ἐπ'
αὐτῆς, ὁ δὲ διὰ τοῦ ἑωθινωτάτου· πλάτος δὲ τὸ
μεταξὺ δυεῖν παραλλήλων, ὧν ὁ μὲν γράφεται διὰ
τοῦ βορειοτάτου σημείου, ὁ δὲ διὰ τοῦ νοτιωτάτου·
ἐπὶ γὰρ τῶν ἀνωμάλων σχημάτων, ἐφ' ὧν πλευραῖς
οὐ δυνατὸν ἀφορίσαι πλάτος καὶ μῆκος, οὕτω τὸ
μέγεθος ἀφοριστέον. καθόλου δὲ νοητέον, ὅτι οὐχ
ὡσαύτως λέγεται μῆκος καὶ πλάτος ἐπὶ ὅλου καὶ
μέρους· ἀλλ' ἐφ' ὅλου μὲν τὸ μεῖζον διάστημα
καλεῖται μῆκος, τὸ δ' ἔλαττον πλάτος, ἐπὶ μέρους
δὲ μῆκος μὲν τὸ παράλληλον τῷ τοῦ ὅλου μήκει
τμῆμα ἐκείνου, ὁπότερον ἂν ᾖ μεῖζον, κἂν τὸ
ληφθὲν διάστημα ἐν τῷ πλάτει μεῖζον ᾖ τοῦ
ληφθέντος ἐν τῷ μήκει διαστήματος. διὸ καὶ τῆς
οἰκουμένης ἀπ' ἀνατολῆς ἐπὶ δύσιν μηκυνομένης,
ἀπὸ δὲ ἄρκτων ἐπὶ νότον πλατυνομένης, καὶ τοῦ
μὲν μήκους ἐπὶ παραλλήλου τινὸς τῷ ἰσημερινῷ
γραφομένου, τοῦ δὲ πλάτους ἐπὶ μεσημβρινοῦ,
δεῖ καὶ τῶν μερῶν λαμβάνεσθαι μήκη μὲν τὰ
παράλληλα τῷ μήκει τμήματα αὐτῆς, πλάτη δὲ
τὰ τῷ πλάτει. οὕτω γὰρ ἂν ἄμεινον ὑπογράφοιτο

southern side; the remaining, or western, side would be the coast-line from the Canobic mouth of the Nile up to Cilicia.

32. The Fourth Section would be the one composed of Arabia Felix, the Arabian Gulf, all Egypt, and Ethiopia. Of this section, the length will be the space bounded by two meridian lines, of which lines the one is drawn through the most western point on the section and the other through the most eastern point. Its breadth will be the space between two parallels of latitude, of which the one is drawn through the most northern point, and the other through the most southern point; for in the case of irregular figures whose length and breadth it is impossible to determine by sides, we must in this way determine their size. And, in general, we must assume that "length" and "breadth" are not employed in the same sense of a whole as of a part. On the contrary, in case of a whole the greater distance is called "length," and the lesser, "breadth"; but, in case of a part, we call "length" any section of a part that is parallel to the length of the whole—no matter which of the two dimensions is the greater, and no matter if the distance taken in the breadth be greater than the distance taken in the length. Therefore, since the inhabited world stretches lengthwise from east to west and breadthwise from north to south, and since its length is drawn on a line parallel to the equator and its breadth on a meridian line, we must also, in case of the parts, take as "lengths" all the sections that are parallel to the length of the inhabited world, and as "breadths" all the sections that are parallel to its breadth. For by this method we can better indicate,

πρῶτον μὲν τὸ μεγεθος τῆς οἰκουμένης ὅλης, ἔπειτα καὶ ἡ διάθεσις καὶ τὸ σχῆμα τῶν μερῶν, καθ' ἃ μὲν ἀπολείπειν, καθ' ἃ δὲ πλεονάζειν φαινομένων τῇ τοιαύτῃ παραθέσει.

33. Ἐρατοσθένης δὲ τὸ μὲν τῆς οἰκουμένης λαμβάνει μῆκος ἐπὶ τῆς διὰ Στηλῶν καὶ Κασπίων πυλῶν καὶ Καυκάσου γραμμῆς, ὡς ἂν εὐθείας, τὸ δὲ τῆς τρίτης μερίδος ἐπὶ τῆς διὰ Κασπίων πυλῶν καὶ Θαψάκου, τὸ δὲ τῆς τετάρτης ἐπὶ τῆς διὰ Θαψάκου καὶ Ἡρώων πόλεως μέχρι τῆς μεταξὺ τῶν στομάτων τοῦ Νείλου, ἣν ἀνάγκη καταστρέφειν εἰς τοὺς περὶ Κάνωβον καὶ Ἀλεξάνδρειαν τόπους· ἐνταῦθα γάρ ἐστι τὸ ἔσχατον στόμα τὸ καλούμενον Κανωβικόν τε καὶ Ἡρακλεωτικόν. εἴτ' οὖν ἐπ' εὐθείας ἀλλήλοις τὰ μήκη τίθησιν, εἴθ' ὡς ἂν γωνίαν ποιοῦντα κατὰ Θάψακον, ἀλλ' ὅτι γε οὐ παράλληλον οὐδέτερον τῷ τῆς οἰκουμένης μήκει, φανερόν ἐστιν ἐξ αὐτῶν ὧν εἴρηκεν C 86 αὐτός. τὸ μὲν γὰρ τῆς οἰκουμένης μῆκος διὰ τοῦ Ταύρου γράφει καὶ τῆς ἐπ' εὐθείας μέχρι Στηλῶν θαλάττης κατὰ γραμμὴν τὴν διὰ τοῦ Καυκάσου καὶ Ῥόδου καὶ Ἀθηνῶν, ἀπὸ δὲ Ῥόδου εἰς Ἀλεξάνδρειαν κατὰ τὸν δι' αὐτῶν μεσημβρινὸν οὐ πολὺ ἐλάττους τῶν τετρακισχιλίων φησὶν εἶναι σταδίων· ὥστε τοσοῦτον καὶ οἱ παράλληλοι διέχοιεν ἂν ἀλλήλων ὅ τε διὰ Ῥόδου καὶ ὁ δι' Ἀλεξανδρείας. ὁ δ' αὐτός πώς ἐστι τούτῳ ὁ διὰ τῆς Ἡρώων πόλεως, ἢ νοτιώτερός γε τούτου·

firstly, the size of the inhabited world as a whole, and, secondly, the position and the shape of its parts; because, by such comparison, it will be clear in what respects the parts are deficient and in what respects they are excessive in size.

33. Now Eratosthenes takes the length of the inhabited world on the line that runs through the Pillars, the Caspian Gates, and the Caucasus, as though on a straight line; and the length of his Third Section on the line that runs through the Caspian Gates and Thapsacus; and the length of his Fourth Section on the line that runs through Thapsacus and Heroönpolis to the region between the mouths of the Nile—a line which must needs come to an end in the regions near Canobus and Alexandria; for the last mouth of the Nile, called the Canobic or Heracleotic mouth, is situated at that point. Now whether he places these two lengths on a straight line with each other, or as though they formed an angle at Thapsacus, it is at any rate clear from his own words that he does not make either line parallel to the length of the inhabited world. For he draws the length of the inhabited world through the Taurus Range and the Mediterranean Sea straight to the Pillars on a line that passes through the Caucasus, Rhodes, and Athens; and he says that the distance from Rhodes to Alexandria on the meridian that passes through those places is not much less than four thousand stadia; so that also the parallels of latitude of Rhodes and Alexandria would be just this distance apart. But the parallel of latitude of Heroönpolis is approximately the same as that of Alexandria, or, at any rate, more to the south than the latter; and hence the line that intersects

ὥσθ' ἡ συμπίπτουσα γραμμὴ τούτῳ τε[1] τῷ
παραλλήλῳ καὶ τῷ διὰ Ῥόδου καὶ Κασπίων
πυλῶν, εἴτ' εὐθεῖα εἴτε κεκλασμένη, οὐκ ἂν εἴη
παράλληλος οὐδετέρᾳ. οὐκ εὖ γοῦν λαμβάνεται
τὰ μήκη· οὐκ εὖ δὲ οὐδὲ αἱ διαβόρειοι λαμβάνονται
μερίδες.

34. Ἀλλ' ἐπὶ τὸν Ἵππαρχον πρότερον ἐπανι-
όντες τὰ ἑξῆς ἴδωμεν. πάλιν γὰρ πλάσας ἑαυτῷ
λήμματα γεωμετρικῶς ἀνασκευάζει τὰ ὑπ' ἐκείνου
τυπωδῶς λεγόμενα. φησὶ γὰρ αὐτὸν λέγειν τὸ
ἐκ Βαβυλῶνος εἰς μὲν Κασπίους πύλας διάστημα
σταδίων ἑξακισχιλίων ἑπτακοσίων, εἰς δὲ τοὺς
ὅρους τῆς Καρμανίας καὶ Περσίδος πλειόνων
ἢ ἐνακισχιλίων,[2] ὅπερ ἐπὶ γραμμῆς κεῖται πρὸς
ἰσημερινὰς ἀνατολὰς εὐθείας ἀγομένης· γίνεσθαι
δὲ ταύτην κάθετον ἐπὶ τὴν κοινὴν πλευρὰν τῆς τε
δευτέρας καὶ τῆς τρίτης σφραγῖδος, ὥστε κατ'
αὐτὸν συνίστασθαι τρίγωνον ὀρθογώνιον, ὀρθὴν
ἔχον τὴν πρὸς τοῖς ὅροις τῆς Καρμανίας, καὶ
τὴν ὑποτείνουσαν εἶναι ἐλάττω μιᾶς τῶν περὶ
τὴν ὀρθὴν ἐχουσῶν· δεῖν οὖν τὴν Περσίδα τῆς
δευτέρας ποιεῖν σφραγῖδος. πρὸς ταῦτα δ'
εἴρηται, ὅτι οὔθ' ἡ ἐκ Βαβυλῶνος εἰς τὴν Καρμανίαν ἐπὶ παραλλήλου λαμβάνεται, οὔθ' ἡ διορί-
ζουσα εὐθεῖα τὰς σφραγῖδας μεσημβρινὴ εἴρηται·
ὥστ' οὐδὲν εἴρηται πρὸς αὐτόν. οὐδὲ τὸ ἐπι-

___
[1] τε, Meineke, for γε.
[2] ἐνακισχιλίων, Meineke, for ἐννακισχιλίων.

both the parallel of latitude of Heroönpolis and that
of Rhodes and the Caspian Gates, whether it be a
straight line or a broken line, cannot be parallel to
either. Accordingly, the lengths are not well taken
by Eratosthenes. And, for that matter, the sections
that stretch through the north are not well taken by
him.[1]

34. But let us first return to Hipparchus and see
what he says next. Again fabricating assumptions
on his own account he proceeds with geometrical precision to demolish what are merely the rough estimates
of Eratosthenes. He says that Eratosthenes calls the
distance from Babylon to the Caspian Gates six
thousand seven hundred stadia, and to the frontiers
of Carmania and Persis more than nine thousand
stadia on a line drawn straight to the equinoctial
east, and that this line comes to be perpendicular to
the side that is common to the Second and the Third
Sections, and that, therefore, according to Eratosthenes, a right-angled triangle is formed whose right
angle lies on the frontiers of Carmania and whose
hypotenuse is shorter than one of the sides that
enclose the right angle[2]; accordingly, adds Hipparchus, Eratosthenes has to make Persis a part of his
Second Section! Now I have already stated in
reply to this that Eratosthenes neither takes the
distance from Babylon to Carmania on a parallel, nor
has he spoken of the straight line that separates the
two sections as a meridian line; and so in this
argument Hipparchus has made no point against
Eratosthenes. Neither is his subsequent conclusion

[1] That is, the sections that stretch north of the Taurus
Range.

[2] See the figure and the note on page 328.

φερόμενον εὖ· εἰρηκότος γὰρ ἀπὸ Κασπίων
πυλῶν εἰς μὲν Βαβυλῶνα τοὺς λεχθέντας, εἰς δὲ
Σοῦσα σταδίους εἶναι τετρακισχιλίους ἐνακοσίους,[1]
ἀπὸ δὲ Βαβυλῶνος τρισχιλίους τετρακοσίους, πάλιν
ἀπὸ τῶν αὐτῶν ὁρμηθεὶς ὑποθέσεων ἀμβλυγώνιον τρίγωνον συνίστασθαί φησι πρός τε ταῖς
Κασπίοις πύλαις καὶ Σούσοις καὶ Βαβυλῶνι,
τὴν ἀμβλεῖαν γωνίαν ἔχον πρὸς Σούσοις, τὰ δὲ
τῶν πλευρῶν μήκη τὰ ἐκκείμενα· εἶτ' ἐπιλογί-
ζεται, διότι συμβήσεται κατὰ τὰς ὑποθέσεις
ταύτας τὴν διὰ Κασπίων πυλῶν μεσημβρινὴν
γραμμὴν ἐπὶ τοῦ διὰ Βαβυλῶνος καὶ Σούσων
παραλλήλου δυσμικωτέραν ἔχειν τὴν κοινὴν τομὴν τῆς κοινῆς τομῆς τοῦ αὐτοῦ παραλλήλου καὶ
C 87 τῆς ἀπὸ Κασπίων πυλῶν καθηκούσης εὐθείας
ἐπὶ τοὺς ὅρους τοὺς τῆς Καρμανίας καὶ τῆς
Περσίδος πλείοσι τῶν τετρακισχιλίων καὶ τετρα-
κοσίων· σχεδὸν δή τι πρὸς τὴν διὰ Κασπίων
πυλῶν μεσημβρινὴν γραμμὴν ἡμίσειαν ὀρθῆς
ποιεῖν γωνίαν τὴν διὰ Κασπίων πυλῶν καὶ τῶν
ὅρων τῆς τε Καρμανίας καὶ τῆς Περσίδος, καὶ
νεύειν αὐτὴν ἐπὶ τὰ μέσα τῆς τε μεσημβρίας
καὶ τῆς ἰσημερινῆς ἀνατολῆς· ταύτῃ δ' εἶναι
παράλληλον τὸν Ἰνδὸν ποταμόν, ὥστε καὶ τοῦτον
ἀπὸ τῶν ὁρῶν οὐκ ἐπὶ μεσημβρίαν ῥεῖν, ὥς φησιν
Ἐρατοσθένης, ἀλλὰ μεταξὺ ταύτης καὶ τῆς
ἰσημερινῆς ἀνατολῆς, καθάπερ ἐν τοῖς ἀρχαίοις
πίναξι καταγέγραπται. τίς οὖν συγχωρήσει
τὸ νῦν συσταθὲν τρίγωνον ἀμβλυγώνιον εἶναι, μὴ

[1] ἐνακοσίους, Meineke, for ἐννακοσίους.

Taking advantage of the rather loose estimates of Eratosthenes, and aided by false assumptions, Hipparchus again follows the process of *reductio ad absurdum* by applying the figures of Eratosthenes to latitudinal and longitudinal distances. Thus, Hipparchus forces Eratosthenes' Caspian Gates to be 4,400 stadia to the west of its real position; and hence Persis would fall into the Second Section. However,

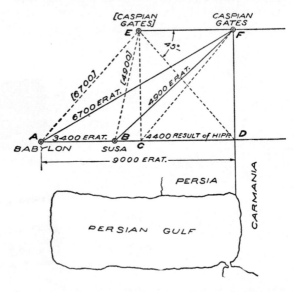

Eratosthenes' line from Babylon to Carmania, Strabo means, would not be the line *AD*, but a line drawn from *A* and diverging considerably to the south from *AD*. Of course, if Hipparchus' assumptions be granted, the Indus would have to be parallel to *ED*, and it would make an angle with the parallel *EF* of slightly more than 45°, though the Indus should really run about due south.

correct. For, because Eratosthenes had given the
distance from the Caspian Gates to Babylon as the
said six thousand seven hundred stadia, and the
distance from the Caspian Gates to Susa as four
thousand nine hundred stadia, and the distance from
Babylon to Susa as three thousand four hundred
stadia, Hipparchus, again starting from the same
hypotheses, says that an obtuse-angled triangle is
formed, with its vertices at the Caspian Gates, Susa
and Babylon, having its obtuse angle at Susa, and
having as the lengths of its sides the distances set
forth by Eratosthenes. Then he draws his conclusion,
namely, that it will follow according to these
hypotheses that the meridian line that runs through
the Caspian Gates will intersect the parallel that
runs through Babylon and Susa at a point further
west than the intersection of the same parallel with
the straight line that runs from the Caspian Gates to
the frontiers of Carmania and Persis by more than
four thousand four hundred stadia; and so the line
that runs through the Caspian Gates to the frontiers
of Carmania and Persis will form almost a half of
a right angle with the meridian line that runs
through the Caspian Gates and will lean in a
direction midway between the south and the
equinoctial east; and that the Indus River will be
parallel to this line, and that consequently this river,
also, does not flow south from the mountains as
Eratosthenes says it does, but between the south and
the equinoctial east, precisely as it is laid down on
the early maps. Who, pray, will concede that the
triangle now formed by Hipparchus is obtuse-angled
without also conceding that the triangle that

συγχωρῶν ὀρθογώνιον εἶναι τὸ περιέχον αὐτό;
τίς δ᾽ ἐπὶ παραλλήλου κειμένην τὴν ἀπὸ Βαβυλῶνος εἰς Σοῦσα μίαν τῶν τὴν ἀμβλεῖαν περιε-
χουσῶν, τὴν ὅλην μὴ συγχωρῶν τὴν μέχρι
Καρμανίας; τίς δὲ τῷ Ἰνδῷ παράλληλον τὴν ἀπὸ
Κασπίων πυλῶν ἐπὶ τοὺς ὅρους τῆς Καρμανίας;
ὧν χωρὶς κενὸς ἂν εἴη ὁ συλλογισμός. χωρὶς
δὲ τούτων κἀκεῖνος εἴρηκεν ὅτι ῥομβοειδές
ἐστι τὸ σχῆμα τῆς Ἰνδικῆς· καὶ καθάπερ ἡ
ἑωθινὴ πλευρὰ παρέσπασται πολὺ πρὸς ἔω, καὶ
μάλιστα τῷ ἐσχάτῳ ἀκρωτηρίῳ, ὃ καὶ πρὸς
μεσημβρίαν προπίπτει πλέον παρὰ τὴν ἄλλην
ἠιόνα, οὕτω καὶ ἡ παρὰ τὸν Ἰνδὸν πλευρά.

35. Πάντα δὲ ταῦτα λέγει γεωμετρικῶς, ἐλέγχων οὐ πιθανῶς. ταῦτα δὲ καὶ αὐτὸς ἑαυτῷ
ἐπενέγκας ἀπολύεται, φήσας, εἰ μὲν παρὰ μικρὰ
διαστήματα ὑπῆρχεν ὁ ἔλεγχος, συγγνῶναι ἂν ἦν·
ἐπειδὴ δὲ παρὰ χιλιάδας σταδίων φαίνεται δια-
πίπτων, οὐκ εἶναι συγγνωστά· καίτοι ἐκεῖνόν γε
καὶ παρὰ τετρακοσίους σταδίους αἰσθητὰ ἀπο-
φαίνεσθαι τὰ παραλλάγματα, ὡς ἐπὶ τοῦ δι᾽
Ἀθηνῶν παραλλήλου καὶ τοῦ διὰ Ῥόδου. ἔστι
δὲ τὸ πρὸς αἴσθησιν οὐχ ἁπλοῦν, ἀλλὰ τὸ μὲν
ἐν πλάτει μείζονι, τὸ δ᾽ ἐν ἐλάττονι. μείζονι μέν,
ἂν αὐτῷ τῷ ὀφθαλμῷ πιστεύωμεν ἢ καρποῖς ἢ

---

[1] If the line *EB* (p. 328) be produced to Eratosthenes' Susa
(on his line drawn from *A* to Carmania), we shall then have
a right-angled triangle *AEB'* that comprehends the obtuse-
angled triangle *AEB*.

comprehends it is right-angled? [1] And who will concede that one of the sides which enclose the obtuse angle (the line from Babylon to Susa) lies on a parallel of latitude, without also conceding that the whole line on to Carmania does? And who will concede that the line drawn from the Caspian Gates to the frontiers of Carmania is parallel to the Indus? Yet without these concessions the argument of Hipparchus would be void. And it is without these concessions that Eratosthenes has made his statement that the shape of India is rhomboidal; and just as its eastern side has been stretched considerably eastwards (particularly at its extreme cape, which, as compared with the rest of the sea-board, is also thrown farther southwards, so, too, the side along the Indus has been stretched considerably eastwards.

35. In all these arguments Hipparchus speaks as a geometrician, though his test of Eratosthenes is not convincing. And though he prescribed the principles of geometry for himself, he absolves himself from them by saying that if the test showed errors amounting to only small distances, he could overlook them; but since Eratosthenes' errors clearly amount to thousands of stadia, they cannot be overlooked [2]; and yet, continues Hipparchus, Eratosthenes himself declares that differences of latitude are observable even within an extent of four hundred stadia; for example, between the parallels of Athens and Rhodes. Now the practice of observing differences of latitude is not confined to a single method, but one method is used where the difference is greater, another where it is lesser; where it is greater, if we rely on the evidence of the eye itself, or of the crops,

[2] Compare § 40, following.

κράσεσιν ἀέρων πρὸς τὴν τῶν κλιμάτων κρίσιν·
ἐλάττονι δ᾽, ἂν δι᾽ ὀργάνων γνωμονικῶν ἢ διοπτρι-
κῶν. ὁ μὲν οὖν δι᾽ Ἀθηνῶν παράλληλος γνωμο-
νικῶς ληφθεὶς καὶ ὁ διὰ Ῥόδου καὶ Καρίας,
εἰκότως ἐν σταδίοις τοσούτοις αἰσθητὴν ἐποίησε
τὴν διαφοράν. ὁ δ᾽ ἐν πλάτει μὲν τρισχιλίων
σταδίων, μήκει δὲ καὶ τετρακισμυρίων ὄρους,
πελάγους δὲ τρισμυρίων λαμβάνων τὴν ἀπὸ
δύσεως ἐπ᾽ ἰσημερινὰς ἀνατολὰς γραμμήν, καὶ τὰ
C 88 ἐφ᾽ ἑκάτερον τὸ μέρος τὰ μὲν νότια ὀνομάζων,
τὰ δὲ βόρεια, καὶ ταῦτα πλινθία καλῶν καὶ
σφραγῖδας, νοείσθω πῶς καὶ ταῦτα λέγει καὶ
πλευρὰ τὰ μὲν ἀρκτικά, τὰ δὲ νότια, καὶ πῶς τὰ
μὲν ἑσπέρια, τὰ δὲ ἑωθινά· καὶ τὸ μὲν παρὰ πολὺ
διαμαρτανόμενον παρορῶν ὑπεχέτω λόγον (δίκαιον
γάρ), τὸ δὲ παρὰ μικρὸν οὐδὲ παριδὼν ἐλεγκτέος
ἐστίν. ἐνταῦθα δ᾽ οὐδετέρως αὐτῷ προσάγεταί
τις ἔλεγχος. οὔτε γὰρ τῶν ἐν τοσούτῳ πλάτει
γεωμετρική τις δύναιτ᾽ ἂν εἶναι [1] ἀπόδειξις· οὔτ᾽

---

[1] εἶναι, Casaubon inserts, after δύναιτ᾽ ἄν; Siebenkees,
Corais, Meineke, Forbiger, following ; L. Kayser approving.

[1] It was a common device of Eratosthenes and other ancient
geographers to visualize countries and sections by comparing
them to well-known objects—for example, Spain to an ox-
hide, the Peloponnesus to a plane-leaf, Sardinia to a human
foot-print. In this case the Greek words "plinthia" ("tiles")
and "sphragides" ("seals," "gems") are used in a general
sense as convenient terms for sections which presented, respectively, tile-shaped and seal-shaped appearances. (In
2. 1. 22, however, Strabo attributes only the latter word to

or of the temperature of the atmosphere, in our judgment of the "climata"; but where it is lesser, we observe the difference by the aid of sun-dials and dioptrical instruments. Accordingly, the taking of the parallel of Athens and that of Rhodes and Caria with the sun-dial showed perceptibly (as is natural when the distance is so many stadia) the difference in latitude. But when the geographer, in dealing with a breadth of three thousand stadia and with a length of forty thousand stadia of mountain plus thirty thousand stadia of sea, takes his line from west to equinoctial east, and names the two divisions thus made the Southern Division and the Northern Division, and calls their parts "plinthia" or "sphragides,"[1] we should bear in mind what he means by these terms, and also by the terms "sides that are northern" and "that are southern," and again, "sides that are western" and "that are eastern." And if he fails to notice that which amounts to a very great error, let him be called to account therefor (for that is just); but as regards that which amounts only to a slight error, even if he has failed to notice it, he is not to be condemned. Here, however, no case is made out against Eratosthenes on either ground. For no geometrical proof would be possible where the cases involve so great a breadth of latitude; nor does

Eratosthenes; and, furthermore, this is the word he himself often employs in the same sense.) Eratosthenes meant to convey by "sphragides" the notion of irregular quadrilaterals (as shows 15. 1. 11); but in his more specific description of a given section—India, for example—he refers to it as "rhomboidal," and, in the case of the Second Section, he refers to "three of its sides" as "fitting into a parallelogram" (see 2. 1. 22).

ἐν οἷς ἐπιχειρεῖ γεωμετρεῖν, ὁμολογουμένοις χρῆται λήμμασιν, ἀλλ' ἑαυτῷ πλάσας.

36. Βέλτιον δὲ περὶ τῆς τετάρτης λέγει μερίδος·
προστίθησι δὲ καὶ τὸ[1] τοῦ φιλαιτίου καὶ τοῦ
μένοντος ἐπὶ τῶν αὐτῶν ὑποθέσεων ἢ τῶν παραπλησίων. τοῦτο μὲν γὰρ ὀρθῶς ἐπιτιμᾷ, διότι
μῆκος ὀνομάζει τῆς μερίδος ταύτης τὴν ἀπὸ
Θαψάκου μέχρις Αἰγύπτου γραμμήν, ὥσπερ εἴ
τις παραλληλογράμμου τὴν διάμετρον μῆκος
αὐτοῦ φαίη. οὐ γὰρ ἐπὶ τοῦ αὐτοῦ παραλλήλου
κεῖται ἥ τε Θάψακος καὶ ἡ τῆς Αἰγύπτου παραλία, ἀλλ' ἐπὶ διεστώτων πολὺ ἀλλήλων· ἐν δὲ τῷ
μεταξὺ διαγώνιός πως ἄγεται καὶ λοξὴ ἡ ἀπὸ
Θαψάκου εἰς Αἴγυπτον. τὸ δὲ θαυμάζειν, πῶς
ἐθάρρησεν εἰπεῖν ἑξακισχιλίων σταδίων τὸ ἀπὸ
Πηλουσίου εἰς Θάψακον, πλειόνων ὄντων ἢ ὀκτακισχιλίων, οὐκ ὀρθῶς. λαβὼν γὰρ δι' ἀποδείξεως
μέν, ὅτι ὁ διὰ Πηλουσίου παράλληλος τοῦ διὰ
Βαβυλῶνος πλείοσιν ἢ δισχιλίοις καὶ πεντακοσίοις σταδίοις νοτιώτερός ἐστι, κατ' Ἐρατοσθένη δὲ (ὡς οἴεται), διότι τοῦ διὰ Βαβυλῶνος ὁ
διὰ τῆς Θαψάκου ἀρκτικώτερος τετρακισχιλίοις

[1] τό, Casaubon inserts, after καί; Siebenkees, Corais,
Meineke, following; C. Müller approving.

[1] "Lemma," the Greek word here used, is, according to
Proclus, a proposition previously proved, or hereafter to be
proved; it is, therefore, for any proposition in hand, an
assumption which requires confirmation.

Hipparchus, even where he attempts geometrical proof, use admitted assumptions,[1] but rather fabrications which he has made for his own use.

36. Hipparchus discusses Eratosthenes' Fourth Section better; though here, too, he displays his propensity for fault-finding and his persistent adherence to the same, or nearly the same, assumptions. He is correct in censuring Eratosthenes for this, namely, for calling the line from Thapsacus to Egypt the length of this section—which is as if one should call the diagonal of a parallelogram its length. For Thapsacus and the coast-line of Egypt do not lie on the same parallel of latitude, but on parallels that are far apart from each other; and between these two parallels the line from Thapsacus to Egypt is drawn somewhat diagonally and obliquely. But when he expresses surprise that Eratosthenes had the boldness to estimate the distance from Pelusium to Thapsacus at six thousand stadia, whereas the distance is more than eight thousand, he is incorrect. For having taken it as demonstrated that the parallel that runs through Pelusium is more than two thousand five hundred stadia farther south than the parallel that runs through Babylon,[2] and then saying—on the authority of Eratosthenes, as he thinks—that the parallel through Thapsacus is four thousand eight hundred stadia farther north than the parallel through Babylon, he says that the distance between Pelusium and Thapsacus amounts

[2] Both Eratosthenes and Strabo gave Pelusium a higher latitude than Babylon.

ὀκτακοσίοις, συμπίπτειν φησὶ πλείους τῶν ὀκτακισχιλίων. πῶς οὖν κατ' Ἐρατοσθένη δείκνυται
ἡ τοσαύτη ἀπόστασις τοῦ διὰ Βαβυλῶνος παραλλήλου ἀπὸ τοῦ διὰ Θαψάκου, ζητῶ. ὅτι μὲν γὰρ
ἀπὸ Θαψάκου ἐπὶ Βαβυλῶνα τοσοῦτόν ἐστιν,
εἴρηκεν ἐκεῖνος· ὅτι δὲ καὶ ἀπὸ τοῦ δι' ἑκατέρου
παραλλήλου ἐπὶ τὸν διὰ θατέρου, οὐκ εἴρηκεν·
οὐδὲ γάρ, ὅτι ἐπὶ ταὐτοῦ μεσημβρινοῦ ἐστιν ἡ
Θάψακος καὶ ἡ Βαβυλών. τἀναντία γὰρ αὐτὸς ὁ
Ἵππαρχος ἔδειξε κατ' Ἐρατοσθένη πλείοσιν ἢ
δισχιλίοις σταδίοις συμβαίνειν ἀνατολικωτέραν
εἶναι τὴν Βαβυλῶνα τῆς Θαψάκου. ἡμεῖς τε
παρετίθεμεν[1] τὰς Ἐρατοσθένους ἀποφάσεις, ἐν
αἷς τὸν Τίγριν καὶ τὸν Εὐφράτην ἐγκυκλοῦσθαι

---

[1] παρετίθεμεν, Corais, for παρατίθεμεν; Meineke, Tardieu, following.

---

[1] On the assumptions of Hipparchus, Eratosthenes' Thapsacus is made to lie at a latitude 7,300 stadia north of Pelusium (see figure, p. 337); and hence, computing the hypotenuse of the right-angled triangle for the distance between the two places, we get approximately 8,500 stadia. Hipparchus' argument is, as usual, a *reductio ad absurdum*, and his fallacy again lies, Strabo means, in his applying Eratosthenes' estimates to parallels of latitude and to meridians.

to more than eight thousand stadia.[1] I ask, then,
how is it shown on the authority of Eratosthenes
that the distance of the parallel through Babylon
from the parallel through Thapsacus is as great as
that? Eratosthenes has stated, indeed, that the
distance from Thapsacus to Babylon is four thousand
eight hundred stadia ; but he has not further stated
that this distance is measured from the parallel
through the one place to the parallel through the
other ; neither indeed has he stated that Thapsacus
and Babylon are on the same meridian. On the
contrary, Hipparchus himself pointed out that,
according to Eratosthenes, Babylon is more than
two thousand stadia farther east than Thapsacus.[2]
And I have just cited the statements of Eratosthenes
wherein he says that the Tigris and the Euphrates

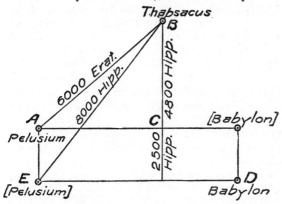

[2] Compare §§ 27-29 (above), where Hipparchus, by his
usual form of argument, forces Eratosthenes' Babylon to be
1,000 stadia farther west.

τήν τε Μεσοποταμίαν καὶ τὴν Βαβυλωνίαν, καὶ
τὸ πλέον γε τῆς ἐγκυκλώσεως τὸν Εὐφράτην
C 89 ποιεῖν· ἀπὸ γὰρ τῶν ἄρκτων ἐπὶ μεσημβρίαν
ῥυέντα ἐπιστρέφειν πρὸς τὰς ἀνατολάς, ἐκπίπτειν
δὲ ἐπὶ μεσημβρίαν. ἡ μὲν οὖν ἐπὶ μεσημβρίαν
ἀπὸ τῶν ἄρκτων ὁδὸς ὡς ἂν μεσημβρινοῦ τινός
ἐστιν, ἡ δ᾽ ἐπὶ τὰς ἀνατολὰς ἐπιστροφὴ καὶ ἐπὶ
τὴν Βαβυλῶνα ἔκνευσίς τέ ἐστιν ἀπὸ τοῦ μεσημβρινοῦ καὶ οὐκ ἐπ᾽ εὐθείας διὰ τὴν ῥηθεῖσαν ἐγκύ-
κλωσιν. τὴν δέ γε ὁδὸν εἴρηκε τετρακισχιλίων
καὶ ὀκτακοσίων σταδίων τὴν ἐπὶ Βαβυλῶνα ἀπὸ
Θαψάκου παρὰ τὸν Εὐφράτην προσθείς, καθάπερ
ἐπίτηδες, τοῦ μή τινα εὐθεῖαν αὐτὴν δέξασθαι καὶ
μέτρον τοῦ μεταξὺ δυεῖν παραλλήλων διαστήματος. μὴ διδομένου δὲ τούτου, κενόν ἐστι καὶ τὸ
ἐφεξῆς δείκνυσθαι δοκοῦν, ὅτι συνισταμένου ὀρθογωνίου τριγώνου πρός τε Πηλουσίῳ καὶ Θαψάκῳ
καὶ τῇ τομῇ τοῦ τε διὰ Θαψάκου παραλλήλου
καὶ τοῦ διὰ Πηλουσίου μεσημβρινοῦ, μία τῶν
περὶ τὴν ὀρθήν, ἡ ἐπὶ τοῦ μεσημβρινοῦ, μείζων
ἔσται τῆς ὑπὸ τὴν ὀρθήν, τῆς ἀπὸ Θαψάκου εἰς
Πηλούσιον. κενὸν δὲ καὶ τὸ συνάπτον τούτῳ,
ἀπὸ μὴ συγχωρουμένου λήμματος κατασκευαζό-
μενον. οὐ γὰρ δὴ δίδοται τὸ ἀπὸ Βαβυλῶνος ἐπὶ
τὸν διὰ Κασπίων πυλῶν μεσημβρινὸν εἶναι διάστημα τετρακισχιλίων ὀκτακοσίων. ἐλήλεγκται

---

[1] In the figure on p. 337 draw a parallel of latitude through
B (Thapsacus) and a meridian through *A* (Pelusium), and let
them intersect at a point *C'*. Then *AC'* (= *BC* = 4,800 stadia)
becomes greater than *AB* (6,000 stadia)—that is, Eratosthenes' estimates lead to this result, says Hipparchus.

[2] The Greek verb here used corresponds to the noun

encircle Mesopotamia and Babylonia, and that the
Euphrates does the greater part of the encircling,
in that, after flowing from the north towards the
south, it turns towards the east, and finally empties
southwards. Now its southward course from the
north lies approximately on some meridian, but its
bend to the east and to Babylon is not only a
deviation from the meridian but it is also not on a
straight line, owing to the said encircling. It is
true that Eratosthenes has stated the route to
Babylon from Thapsacus to be four thousand eight
hundred stadia long, though he added, as on
purpose, "following the course of the Euphrates,"
in order that no one might interpret it as a straight
line or as a measure of the distance between two
parallels. If this assumption of Hipparchus be not
granted, futile also is his subsequent proposition
which has only the appearance of being proven,
namely, that if a right-angled triangle be constructed
with vertices at Pelusium, Thapsacus, and the point
of intersection of the parallel of Thapsacus with
the meridian of Pelusium, then one of the sides of
the right angle, namely, that on the meridian, is
greater than the hypotenuse, that is, the line from
Thapsacus to Pelusium.[1] Futile also is the proposition that he links with this proposition, because
it is fabricated[2] from something that is not conceded.
For surely Eratosthenes has not granted the
assumption that the distance from Babylon to the
meridian that runs through the Caspian Gates is a
matter of four thousand eight hundred stadia. I

which, in the formal divisions of a proposition, constitutes
that division which, says Proclus, "adds what is wanting to
the data for the purpose of finding out what is sought."

γὰρ ὑφ᾽ ἡμῶν ἐκ τῶν μὴ συγχωρουμένων ὑπ᾽
Ἐρατοσθένους κατεσκευακότα τοῦτο τὸν Ἵππαρ-
χον· ἵνα δ᾽ ἀνίσχυρον ᾖ τὸ ὑπὸ ἐκείνου διδόμενον,
λαβὼν τὸ εἶναι πλείους ἢ ἐννακισχιλίους ἐκ
Βαβυλῶνος ἐπὶ τὴν ἐκ Κασπίων πυλῶν οὕτως
ἀγομένην γραμμήν, ὡς ἐκεῖνος εἴρηκεν, ἐπὶ τοὺς
ὅρους τῆς Καρμανίας, ἐδείκνυε τὸ αὐτό.

37. Οὐ τοῦτο οὖν λεκτέον πρὸς τὸν Ἐρατοσθένη, ἀλλ᾽ ὅτι τῶν ἐν πλάτει λεγομένων καὶ
μεγεθῶν καὶ σχημάτων εἶναί τι δεῖ μέτρον, καὶ
ὅπου μὲν μᾶλλον, ὅπου δὲ ἔλαττον συγχωρητέον.
ληφθέντος γὰρ τοῦ τῶν ὁρῶν πλάτους τῶν ἐπὶ
τὰς ἰσημερινὰς ἀνατολὰς ἐκτεινομένων τρισχιλίων
σταδίων, ὁμοίως δὲ καὶ τοῦ τῆς θαλάττης τῆς
μέχρι Στηλῶν, μᾶλλον ἄν τις συγχωρήσειεν ὡς
ἐπὶ μιᾶς γραμμῆς ἐξετάζεσθαι τὰς παραλλήλους
ἐκείνης ἐν τῷ αὐτῷ πλάτει ἀγομένας ἢ τὰς συμ-
πιπτούσας, καὶ τῶν συμπιπτουσῶν τὰς ἐν αὐτῷ
ἐκείνῳ τῷ πλάτει τὴν σύμπτωσιν ἐχούσας ἢ τὰς

---

[1] Strabo refers to the false conclusion in § 34.

[2] Strabo had in the main accepted Eratosthenes' map
together with his treatise thereon, inadequate though they
were. He objected to Hipparchus' criticism based upon
false assumptions and geometrical tests applied to specific
cases. He argues in this paragraph that the map requires a
"metron," or standard of measure, by means of which, as
a sort of sliding scale, we may make proportional concessions
or allowances in the matter of linear directions and geometrical magnitudes. Practically applied, this "metron" would

have proved that Hipparchus has fabricated this assumption from data that are not conceded by Eratosthenes; but in order to invalidate what Eratosthenes does grant, Hipparchus took as granted that the distance from Babylon to the line drawn from the Caspian Gates to the confines of Carmania just as Eratosthenes has proposed to draw it is more than nine thousand stadia, and then proceeded to show the same thing.[1]

37. That, therefore, is not the criticism that should be made against Eratosthenes,[2] but rather the criticism that his roughly-sketched magnitudes and figures require some standard of measure, and that more concession has to be made in one case, less in another. For example, if the breadth of the mountain-range that stretches toward the equinoctial east, and likewise the breadth of the sea that stretches up to the Pillars, be taken as three thousand stadia, one would more readily agree to regard as lying on a single line[3] the parallels of that line drawn within the same breadth than he would the lines that intersect therein[4]; and, of the intersecting lines, those that intersect within that said breadth than those that intersect without.

save us from such a mistake as placing the Caspian Gates and the mouth of the Nile on the same parallel of latitude, and again from such a mistake as estimating the actual distance between these two points to be the same as the longitudinal distance. Furthermore, Strabo shows by parallelograms that the actual distance between any two points, A and B, does not grow less in the same proportion as does their difference of longitude.

[3] That is, an assumed line drawn east and west through the length of the strip—a strip approximately 70,000 stadia in length.

[4] See the figure and the note on pages 342 and 343.

ἐκτός· ὡσαύτως καὶ τὰς διισταμένας μέχρι τοῦ
μὴ ἐκβαίνειν τοῦ πλάτους ἢ τὰς ἐκβαινούσας, καὶ
τὰς ἐν μείζονι μήκει μᾶλλον ἢ τὰς ἐν ἐλάττονι.
καὶ γὰρ ἡ ἀνισότης τῶν μηκῶν συγκρύπτοιτ᾽ ἂν
C 90 μᾶλλον καὶ ἡ ἀνομοιότης τῶν σχημάτων· οἷον ἐν
τῷ πλάτει τοῦ Ταύρου παντὸς καὶ τῆς μέχρι
Στηλῶν θαλάττης, ὑποκειμένων τρισχιλίων σταδίων, νοεῖται ἕν τι παραλληλόγραμμον χωρίον, τὸ
περιγράφον τό τε ὄρος ἅπαν καὶ τὴν λεχθεῖσαν
θάλατταν. ἐὰν οὖν διέλῃς εἰς πλείω παραλληλό-
γραμμα τὸ μῆκος, καὶ τὴν διάμετρον ὅλου τε
τούτου λάβῃς καὶ τῶν μερῶν, ῥᾷον ἂν ἡ τοῦ ὅλου
διάμετρος ἡ αὐτὴ λογισθείη,[1] παράλληλός τε καὶ
ἴση, τῇ κατὰ τὸ μῆκος πλευρᾷ ἥπερ ἡ ἐν τοῖς
μέρεσι· καὶ ὅσῳ γ᾽ ἂν ἔλαττον ᾖ τὸ παραλληλόγραμμον τὸ ληφθὲν ἐν μέρει, τοσῷδε μᾶλλον τοῦτ᾽
ἂν συμβαίνοι. ἥ τε γὰρ λοξότης τῆς διαμέτρου
ἧττον ἀπελέγχεται καὶ ἡ ἀνισότης τοῦ μήκους ἐν
τοῖς μεγάλοις, ὥστ᾽ οὐδ᾽ ἂν ὀκνήσειας ἐπ᾽ αὐτῶν
τὴν διάμετρον εἰπεῖν μῆκος τοῦ σχήματος. ἐὰν
οὖν τὴν διάμετρον λοξώσῃς μᾶλλον, ὥστε ἐκ-

---

[1] Müller and Tardieu rightly regard Meineke's deletion of
παράλληλός τε καὶ ἴση after λογισθείη as unwarranted.

Let *ABCD* be assumed strip ; let *OO'* be assumed east and
west line ; let *PP'* and *SS'* be parallel to *OO'* ; let *BK* and
KC (or *BK'* and *K'C*) be lines that intersect within, and
BK'' and *K''C* lines that intersect without. It is easier to
consider *PP'* as coincident with *OO'* than *BK* + *KC* (as ⟠ to
PK + *KP'*) as coincident with *OO'*, and easier *BK* + *KC*
than *BK''* + *K''C*.

Likewise, also, one would more readily agree to regard as lying on a single line those lines that extend within the limits of said breadth and do not reach beyond than those that reach beyond; and those lines that extend within greater lengths than those in lesser. For in such cases the inequality of the lengths and the dissimilarity of the figures would be more likely to escape notice; for instance, in the case of the breadth of the entire Taurus Range, and of the Sea up to the Pillars, if three thousand stadia be taken as hypothesis for the breadth, we can assume one single parallelogram which traces the boundary both of the entire Range and of the said Sea. Now if you divide a parallelogram lengthwise into several small parallelograms, and take the diagonal both of this whole and of its parts, then the diagonal of the whole might more easily be counted the same as (that is, both parallel and equal to) the long side than could the diagonal of any one of the small parallelograms as compared with the corresponding long side; and the smaller the parallelogram taken as a part, the more would this be true. For both the obliquity of the diagonal and the inequality of its length as compared with the long side are less easily detected in large parallelograms; so that you might not even hesitate in their case to call the diagonal the length of the figure. If, however, you make the diagonal more oblique, so that it falls exterior to both of the sides,

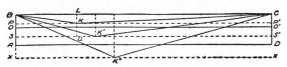

πεσεῖν ἔξω τῶν πλευρῶν ἑκατέρας ἢ τῆς γε
ἑτέρας, οὐκ ἂν ὁμοίως ἔτι ταῦτα συμβαίνοι·
τοιοῦτον δή τι λέγω τὸ μέτρον τῶν ἐν πλάτει
λεγομένων. ὁ δ' ἀπὸ τῶν Κασπίων πυλῶν τὴν
μὲν δι' αὐτῶν τῶν ὀρῶν λαμβάνων, ὡς ἂν ἐπὶ
ταὐτοῦ παραλλήλου μέχρι Στηλῶν ἀγομένην, τὴν
δ' ἀπονεύουσαν εἰς Θάψακον εὐθὺς ἔξω πολὺ τῶν
ὀρῶν, καὶ πάλιν ἐκ Θαψάκου προσεκβάλλων
ἄλλην μέχρις Αἰγύπτου τοσοῦτον ἐπιλαμβά-
νουσαν πλάτος, εἶτα τῷ μήκει τῷ ταύτης κατα-
μετρῶν τὸ τοῦ χωρίου μῆκος, διαμέτρῳ τετραγώνου καταμετρεῖν ἂν δόξειε τὸ τοῦ τετραγώνου
μῆκος. ὅταν δὲ μηδὲ διάμετρος ᾖ, ἀλλὰ κεκλασμένη ἡ γραμμή, πολὺ μᾶλλον ἂν δόξειε πλημ-
μελεῖν· κεκλασμένη γάρ ἐστιν ἡ ἀπὸ Κασπίων
πυλῶν διὰ Θαψάκου πρὸς τὸν Νεῖλον ἀγομένη.
πρὸς μὲν Ἐρατοσθένη ταῦτα.

38. Πρὸς δὲ τὸν Ἵππαρχον κἀκεῖνο, ὅτι ἐχρῆν,
ὡς κατηγορίαν πεποίηται τῶν ὑπ' ἐκείνου λεχθέντων, οὕτω καὶ ἐπανόρθωσίν τινα ποιήσασθαι
τῶν ἡμαρτημένων· ὅπερ ἡμεῖς ποιοῦμεν. ἐκεῖνος
δ' εἰ καί που τούτου πεφρόντικε, κελεύει ἡμᾶς
τοῖς ἀρχαίοις πίναξι προσέχειν, δεομένοις παμ-
πόλλῳ τινὶ μείζονος ἐπανορθώσεως, ἢ ὁ Ἐρα-

---

[1] *A'O* represents a line which falls exterior to *BG* and *AH*,
and *AO* a line which falls exterior to *BG*. Let *ABCD* be
the large parallelogram ; then the small parallelograms are
ABGH, *HGCD*, *FECD*, *JICD*—and so on indefinitely.

or at least to one of them, this would no longer, in like manner, be the case.[1] This is substantially what I mean by a standard of measurement for roughly-sketched magnitudes. But when Eratosthenes, beginning at the Caspian Gates, takes not only the line which runs through the mountains themselves, but also the line which at once diverges considerably from the mountains into Thapsacus, as though both were drawn to the Pillars on the same parallel, and when, again, he still further produces his line, on from Thapsacus to Egypt, thus taking in all this additional breadth, and then measures the length of his figure by the length of this line, he would seem to be measuring the length of his rectangle by a diagonal of a rectangle. And whenever his line is not even a diagonal but a broken line, much more he would seem to err. In fact, it is a broken line that is drawn from the Caspian Gates through Thapsacus to the Nile. So much may be said against Eratosthenes.

38. But against Hipparchus this too may be urged, that, as he criticised the statements of Eratosthenes, so also he should have made some sort of correction of Eratosthenes' errors—the thing that I am doing. But Hipparchus—if he has really ever taken thought of this matter—bids us to give heed to the old maps, although they need much more correction than the

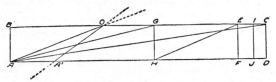

τοσθένους πίναξ προσδεῖται. καὶ τὸ ἐπιφερόμενον δ' ἐπιχείρημα τῆς αὐτῆς ἔχεται μοχθηρίας. λαμβάνει γὰρ ἐν λήμματι τὸ ἐκ τῶν μὴ διδομένων κατασκευασθέν, ὡς ἠλέγξαμεν ἡμεῖς, ὅτι Θαψάκου Βαβυλὼν ἀνατολικωτέρα ἐστὶν οὐ πλείοσιν ἢ χιλίοις σταδίοις· ὥστ' εἰ καὶ πάνυ συνάγεται τὸ πλείοσιν ἢ δισχιλίοις καὶ τετρακοσίοις σταδίοις ἀνατολικωτέραν αὐτὴν εἶναι ἐκ τῶν λεγομένων ὑπὸ τοῦ Ἐρατοσθένους, ὅτι ἐπὶ τὴν τοῦ Τίγριδος διάβασιν, ᾗ Ἀλέξανδρος διέβη, ἀπὸ Θαψάκου ἐστὶ σύντομος σταδίων δισχιλίων τετρακοσίων, C 91 ὁ δὲ Τίγρις καὶ ὁ Εὐφράτης ἐγκυκλωσάμενοι τὴν Μεσοποταμίαν, τέως μὲν ἐπ' ἀνατολὰς φέρονται, εἶτ' ἐπιστρέφουσι πρὸς νότον καὶ πλησιάζουσι τότε ἀλλήλοις τε ἅμα καὶ Βαβυλῶνι, οὐδὲν ἄτοπον συμβαίνει τῷ λόγῳ.

39. Πλημμελεῖ δὲ καὶ ἐν τῷ ἑξῆς ἐπιχειρήματι, ἐν ᾧ συνάγειν βούλεται, ὅτι τὴν ἀπὸ Θαψάκου ἐπὶ Κασπίους πύλας ὁδόν, ἣν μυρίων σταδίων Ἐρατοσθένης εἴρηκεν, οὐκ ἐπ' εὐθείας ἀναμεμετρημένην ὡς ἐπ' εὐθείας παραδίδωσι, τῆς εὐθείας πολὺ ἐλάττονος οὔσης. ἡ δ' ἔφοδός ἐστιν αὐτῷ τοιαύτη. φησὶν εἶναι καὶ κατ' Ἐρατοσθένη τὸν αὐτὸν μεσημβρινὸν τόν τε διὰ τοῦ Κανωβικοῦ στόματος καὶ τὸν διὰ Κυανέων, διέχειν δὲ τοῦτον τοῦ διὰ Θαψάκου ἑξακισχιλίους τριακοσίους

---

[1] Hipparchus' *reductio ad absurdum* again fails, Strabo says. First, he has attributed to Eratosthenes a result (1,000 stadia) not based upon Eratosthenes' statements;

map of Eratosthenes still needs. And his subsequent effort suffers from the same flaw. For, as I have shown by test, he takes as an admitted assumption what he has fabricated from data not granted by Eratosthenes, namely, that Babylon is not more than one thousand stadia farther east than Thapsacus; hence, if even a perfect inference is drawn by Hipparchus to the effect that Babylon is not more than two thousand four hundred stadia farther east than Thapsacus, from Eratosthenes' statement that there is a short route of two thousand four hundred stadia from Thapsacus to the Tigris River where Alexander crossed—yet if Eratosthenes also states that the Tigris and the Euphrates, after encircling Mesopotamia for a time, flow east, then turn toward the south, and finally draw near to each other and to Babylon, he has proved no absurdity in Eratosthenes statement.[1]

39. Hipparchus is also wrong in his next effort, in which he wishes to draw the inference that Eratosthenes gives the highway from Thapsacus to the Caspian Gates—a highway the length of which Eratosthenes has estimated at ten thousand stadia— as measured in a straight line, although it was not so measured, the straight line being much shorter. The attack he makes against Eratosthenes is to this effect: According to Eratosthenes himself the meridian through the Canobic mouth of the Nile and that through the Cyanean Rocks[2] are one and the same, and this meridian is six thousand three hundred stadia distant from the meridian through

secondly, he has drawn a false inference from an estimate that Eratosthenes did make (2,400 stadia), as Eratosthenes' description of the circuit of the Tigris and Euphrates shows.

[2] The Symplegades.

σταδίους, τὰς δὲ Κυανέας τοῦ Κασπίου ὄρους
ἑξακισχιλίους ἑξακοσίους, ὃ κεῖται κατὰ τὴν
ὑπέρθεσιν τὴν ἐπὶ τὸ Κάσπιον πέλαγος ἐκ
Κολχίδος, ὥστε παρὰ τριακοσίους σταδίους τὸ
ἴσον εἶναι διάστημα ἀπὸ τοῦ διὰ Κυανέων μεσημβρινοῦ ἐπί τε Θάψακον καὶ ἐπὶ τὸ Κάσπιον·
τρόπον δή τινα ἐπὶ τοῦ αὐτοῦ μεσημβρινοῦ κεῖσθαι
τήν τε Θάψακον καὶ τὸ Κάσπιον. τούτῳ δ᾽
ἀκολουθεῖν τὸ ἀφεστάναι ἴσον τὰς Κασπίους
πύλας Θαψάκου τε καὶ τοῦ Κασπίου· τοῦ δὲ
Κασπίου [1] πολὺ ἐλάττους ἀφεστάναι τῶν μυρίων,
ὅσους φησὶν ἀφεστάναι Ἐρατοσθένης τῆς Θαψά-
κου· τῆς Θαψάκου [2] ἄρα πολὺ ἐλάττους ἢ μυρίους
ἀφεστάναι τοὺς ἐπ᾽ εὐθείας· κυκλοπορίαν ἄρα
εἶναι τοὺς μυρίους, οὓς [3] λογίζεται ἐκεῖνος ἐπ᾽
εὐθείας ἀπὸ Κασπίων πυλῶν εἰς Θάψακον. ἐροῦμεν δὲ πρὸς αὐτόν, ὅτι τοῦ Ἐρατοσθένους ἐν
πλάτει λαμβάνοντος τὰς εὐθείας, ὅπερ οἰκεῖόν
ἐστι γεωγραφίας, ἐν πλάτει δὲ καὶ τὰς μεσημ-
βρινὰς καὶ τὰς ἐπὶ ἰσημερινὴν ἀνατολήν, ἐκεῖνος
γεωμετρικῶς αὐτὸν εὐθύνει, καὶ ὡς ἂν δι᾽ ὀργάνων
λάβοι τις τούτων ἕκαστον· οὐδὲ αὐτὸς δι᾽ ὀργάνων,

---

[1] τοῦ δὲ Κασπίου, Spengel inserts, before πολύ; Meineke,
Forbiger, following; C. Müller, H. Berger, approving.
[2] τῆς Θαψάκου, Spengel inserts, before ἄρα; Meineke, Forbiger, following; C. Müller, H. Berger, approving.
[3] οὕς, Siebenkees inserts, from Tyrwhitt's conjecture;
Forbiger, Meineke, following.

Thapsacus; and the Cyanean Rocks are six thousand six hundred stadia distant from Mt. Caspius, which lies at the mountain-pass that leads over from Colchis to the Caspian Sea; and hence the distance from the meridian through the Cyanean Rocks to Thapsacus is within three hundred stadia of being equal to the distance thence to Mt. Caspius; so then, practically speaking, both Thapsacus and Mt. Caspius lie on the same meridian. From this it follows, says Hipparchus, that the Caspian Gates are equidistant from Thapsacus and from Mt. Caspius; but the Caspian Gates are at a much less distance from Mt. Caspius than the ten thousand stadia which Eratosthenes says is the distance between the Caspian Gates and Thapsacus; therefore the Caspian Gates are at a much less distance from Thapsacus than the ten thousand stadia that are measured on a straight line; and therefore it is a roundabout way that measures the ten thousand stadia which Eratosthenes reckons on a straight line from the Caspian Gates to Thapsacus.[1] Now my reply to Hipparchus will be that, although Eratosthenes takes his straight lines only roughly, as is proper to do in geography, and roughly, too, his meridians and his lines to the equinoctial east, Hipparchus puts him to a geometrical test—just as if every one of these lines had been taken with the aid of instruments.[2] Neither does Hipparchus himself take everything by the aid of instruments, but it is rather by conjecture that he

---

[1] Even though Hipparchus takes Eratosthenes' distances as longitudinal, the error of the latter is quite obvious; and it is now obvious also that Strabo is inclined to protect Eratosthenes wherever he can.

[2] That is, instruments of observation—the sun-dial, for instance.

ἀλλὰ μᾶλλον στοχασμῷ λαμβάνων καὶ τὸ πρὸς
ὀρθὰς καὶ τὸ παραλλήλους. ἐν μὲν δὴ τοῦθ'
ἁμάρτημα· ἕτερον δὲ τὸ μηδὲ τὰ κείμενα παρ'
ἐκείνῳ διαστήματα τίθεσθαι ὑπ' αὐτοῦ, μηδὲ πρὸς
ἐκεῖνα τὸν ἔλεγχον προσάγεσθαι, ἀλλὰ πρὸς
τὰ ὑπ' αὐτοῦ πλαττόμενα. διόπερ πρῶτον μὲν
ἐκείνου τὸ ἀπὸ τοῦ στόματος ἐπὶ Φᾶσιν εἰπόντος
σταδίων ὀκτακισχιλίων, καὶ προσθέντος τοὺς εἰς
Διοσκουριάδα ἐνθένδε ἑξακοσίους, τὴν δ' ἀπὸ
Διοσκουριάδος εἰς τὸ Κάσπιον ὑπέρθεσιν ἡμερῶν
πέντε, ἥτις κατ' αὐτὸν Ἵππαρχον εἰκάζεται
λέγεσθαι ὅσον χιλίων σταδίων, ὥστε τὴν σύμ-
C 92 πασαν κατ' Ἐρατοσθένη κεφαλαιοῦσθαι ἐνακισχιλίων[1] ἑξακοσίων, αὐτὸς συντέτμηκε καὶ
φησιν ἐκ μὲν Κυανέων εἰς Φᾶσιν πεντακισχιλίους
ἑξακοσίους, εἰς δὲ Κάσπιον ἐνθένδε ἄλλους χιλίους·
ὥστ' οὐ κατ' Ἐρατοσθένη συμβαίνοι ἂν ἐπὶ τοῦ
αὐτοῦ πως μεσημβρινοῦ τό τε Κάσπιον εἶναι καὶ
τὴν Θάψακον, ἀλλὰ κατ' αὐτόν. φέρε δ' οὖν κατ'
Ἐρατοσθένη· πῶς οὖν τούτῳ ἕπεται τὸ τὴν ἀπὸ
τοῦ Κασπίου ἐπὶ Κασπίους πύλας ἴσην εἶναι τῇ
ἀπὸ Θαψάκου ἐπὶ τὸ αὐτὸ σημεῖον;

40. Ἐν δὲ τῷ δευτέρῳ ὑπομνήματι ἀναλαβὼν
πάλιν τὴν αὐτὴν ζήτησιν τὴν περὶ τῶν ὅρων τῶν
κατὰ τὸν Ταῦρον, περὶ ὧν ἱκανῶς εἰρήκαμεν,
μεταβαίνει πρὸς τὰ βόρεια μέρη τῆς οἰκουμένης·

---

[1] ἐνακισχιλίων, Sterrett, for ἐννακισχιλίων.

takes the relations of both "perpendicular" and "parallel." This, then, is one of Hipparchus' mistakes. Another mistake is this, that he does not even put down the distances that are found in Eratosthenes or apply his test to them, but to those that are fabricated by himself. So, for instance, though Eratosthenes first estimated the distance from the outlet [1] to Phasis [2] at eight thousand stadia and added to this the six hundred stadia thence to Dioscurias, and then estimated at a five days' journey the pass that leads over to Mt. Caspius (which, according to Hipparchus himself, is conjectured to mean about one thousand stadia), so that the total distance, according to Eratosthenes, amounts to nine thousand six hundred stadia, Hipparchus has made a short cut to his result, and says that from the Cyanean Rocks to Phasis the distance is five thousand six hundred stadia, and thence to Mt. Caspius, another thousand stadia. Therefore the statement that Mt. Caspius and Thapsacus are virtually situated on the same meridian could not be based on the authority of Eratosthenes, but on that of Hipparchus himself. Well, suppose it were on the authority of Eratosthenes. How, pray, can it follow therefrom that the line from Mt. Caspius to the Caspian Gates is equal in length to the line from Thapsacus to the same point?

40. In his Second Book, Hipparchus again takes up the same question of Eratosthenes' division of the inhabited world along the line of the Taurus Range, about which I have already said enough; then he passes to a discussion of the Northern

---

[1] Of the Euxine.
[2] A town at the mouth of the Phasis River.

εἶτ' ἐκτίθεται τὰ λεχθέντα ὑπὸ τοῦ Ἐρατοσθένους περὶ τῶν μετὰ τὸν Πόντον τόπων, ὅτι φησὶ τρεῖς ἄκρας ἀπὸ τῶν ἄρκτων καθήκειν· μίαν μέν, ἐφ' ἧς ἡ Πελοπόννησος, δευτέραν δὲ τὴν Ἰταλικήν, τρίτην δὲ τὴν Λιγυστικήν, ὑφ' ὧν κόλπους ἀπολαμβάνεσθαι τόν τε Ἀδριατικὸν καὶ τὸν Τυρρηνικόν. ταῦτα δ' ἐκθέμενος καθόλου πειρᾶται τὰ καθ' ἕκαστα περὶ αὐτῶν λεγόμενα ἐλέγχειν γεωμετρικῶς μᾶλλον ἢ γεωγραφικῶς. ἔστι δὲ τοσοῦτον τῶν ἁμαρτανομένων ἐν αὐτοῖς ὑπὸ τοῦ Ἐρατοσθένους τὸ πλῆθος, καὶ ὑπὸ Τιμοσθένους τοῦ τοὺς λιμένας συγγράψαντος (ὃν ἐπαινεῖ μὲν ἐκεῖνος μάλιστα τῶν ἄλλων, διαφωνῶν δ' ἐλέγχεται πρὸς αὐτὸν πλεῖστα), ὥστ' οὐκ ἄξιον ἡγοῦμαι διαιτᾶν οὔτ' ἐκείνους, ἐπὶ τοσοῦτον διαμαρτάνοντας τῶν ὄντων, οὔτε τὸν Ἵππαρχον. καὶ γὰρ οὗτος τὰ μὲν παραλείπει τῶν ἡμαρτημένων, τὰ δ' οὐκ ἐπανορθοῖ, ἀλλ' ἐλέγχει μόνον, ὅτι ψευδῶς ἢ μαχομένως εὔρηται. αἰτιάσαιτο μὲν γὰρ καὶ τοῦτ' ἂν ἴσως τις, ὅτι φησὶν ἄκρας τρεῖς τῆς Εὐρώπης, μίαν μὲν τιθεὶς τὴν ἐφ' ἧς ἡ Πελοπόννησος· ἔχει γάρ τι πολυσχιδές. καὶ γὰρ τὸ Σούνιον ἀκρωτηριάζει ὁμοίως τῇ Λακωνικῇ, οὐ πολὺ ἧττον μεσημβρινὸν[1] ὂν τῶν Μαλεῶν, καὶ κόλπον ἀπολαμβάνον ἀξιόλογον. καὶ ἡ Θρᾳκία Χερρόνησος ἀπολαμβάνει πρὸς τὸ Σούνιον τόν

---

[1] μεσημβρινόν, Madvig, for μεσημβρινώτερον.

Division; and then he sets forth what Eratosthenes
said about the countries that lie next after the
Pontus, namely, that three promontories jut down
from the north : one promontory, on which is the
Peloponnesus; a second, the Italian; and a third
the Ligurian ; and that these three promontories
enclose both the Adriatic and the Tyrrhenian
Gulfs.   After setting forth these statements of
Eratosthenes in a general way, Hipparchus undertakes to test each several statement about the
promontories, yet on the principles of geometry
rather than those of geography.   But so great is the
multitude of mistakes made in case of these promontories by Eratosthenes, and by Timosthenes who
wrote on *The Harbours* (whom Eratosthenes praises
beyond all the rest, though we find him disagreeing
with Timosthenes on most points), that I consider it
unfitting to pass judgment either upon those men,
since they both stray so very far from the facts, or
upon Hipparchus.   For even Hipparchus passes by
some of their mistakes in silence, while yet others
he does not correct, but merely shows by test that
they were made falsely or captiously.   We might
perhaps find fault with Eratosthenes on this point
too, namely, because he says " three promontories "
of Europe, putting down as " one promontory " that
on which is the Peloponnesus; for it is split, so to
speak, into a number of promontories; for example,
Sunium is a promontory just as much as is Laconia,
since it reaches almost as far south as Maleae and
embraces a gulf of considerable size.   And the
Thracian Cherronese and the promontory of Sunium
cut off, between them, not only the gulf of Melas [1] but

---

[1] The Gulf of Saros.

τε Μέλανα κόλπον καὶ τοὺς ἐφεξῆς τοὺς Μακε-
δονικούς. εἰ δ᾽ οὖν παρείημεν τοῦτο, καὶ τῶν
διαστημάτων τὰ πλεῖστα φανερῶς ψευδογρα-
φούμενα ἐλέγχει τὴν ἀπειρίαν τῶν τόπων ὑπερ-
βάλλουσαν καὶ οὐ δεομένην γεωμετρικῶν ἐλέγχων,
ἀλλὰ φανερῶν καὶ αὐτόθεν ἐκμαρτυρεῖσθαι δυνα-
μένων· οἷον ὅτι ἐξ Ἐπιδάμνου πρὸς τὸν Θερμαῖον
κόλπον ἡ ὑπέρβασίς ἐστι πλειόνων ἢ δισχιλίων
C 93   σταδίων· ὁ δ᾽ ἐνακοσίων[1] φησίν· ἐκ δὲ Ἀλεξανδρείας εἰς Καρχηδόνα ὑπὲρ μυρίους καὶ τρισχιλίους, οὐ πλείους ὄντας τῶν ἐνακισχιλίων[2]
εἴπερ ἐπὶ τοῦ αὐτοῦ μεσημβρινοῦ ἐστι κατὰ
τοῦτον τῇ μὲν Ἀλεξανδρείᾳ Καρία καὶ Ῥόδος,
τῇ δὲ Καρχηδόνι ὁ Πορθμός. πάντες γὰρ ὁμολογοῦσι μὴ πλειόνων εἶναι τὸν ἐκ Καρίας ἐπὶ
Πορθμὸν πλοῦν σταδίων ἢ ἐνακισχιλίων·[3] ὅ τε
μεσημβρινὸς ἐν μεγάλῳ μέν τινι διαστήματι
λαμβανόμενος δοθείη ἂν ὁ αὐτὸς εἶναι τῷ τοσοῦτον
δυσμικωτέρῳ[4] πρὸς τὸν ἐωθινώτερον ὅσον ἡ Καρχη-
δών ἐστι τοῦ Πορθμοῦ πρὸς δύσει μᾶλλον, ἐν
δὲ τετρακισχιλίοις[5] σταδίοις ἔχει καταφανῆ τὸν
ἔλεγχον. ὁ δὲ καὶ τὴν Ῥώμην τιθεὶς ἐπὶ ταὐτοῦ μεσημβρινοῦ τὴν τοσοῦτον καὶ Καρχηδόνος
δυσμικωτέραν, ὑπερβολὴν οὐκ ἀπολείπει τῆς τῶν
τόπων ἀπειρίας καὶ τούτων καὶ τῶν ἐφεξῆς πρὸς
δύσιν μέχρι Στηλῶν.

---

[1] ἐνακοσίων, Meineke, for ἐννακοσίων.
[2] ἐνακισχιλίων, Sterrett, for ἐννακισχιλίων.
[3] ἐνακισχιλίων, Meineke, for ἐννακισχιλίων.
[4] Kramer, Müller-Dübner, and Meineke delete τῷ before
τοσοῦτον and read δυσμικώτερος with some of the MSS. But
the MSS. also support δυσμικωτέρῳ. Capps, quite independently, suggested the above reading.

also all the Macedonian Gulfs that come after Melas. However, if we should pass over this objection, still, the most of the distances, which are obviously wrong, prove that Eratosthenes' ignorance of these regions is surpassing and that his ignorance requires no geometrical proofs, but only such proofs as are obvious and can be attested forthwith ; for instance, that the pass from Epidamnus that leads over to the Thermaic Gulf is more than two thousand stadia, though Eratosthenes says it is nine hundred ; and that the distance from Alexandria to Carthage is more than thirteen thousand stadia, though it is not more than nine thousand—if Caria and Rhodes lie, as Eratosthenes says, on the same meridian as Alexandria, and the Strait of Sicily on the same meridian as Carthage. In fact, all agree that the voyage from Caria to the Strait of Sicily is not more than nine thousand stadia ; and though, when there is some considerable distance between two places, the meridian taken for the more easterly place might be granted to be the same as the meridian which is no farther west therefrom than Carthage is west of the Strait of Sicily, yet when we are concerned with a matter of four thousand stadia the error is self-evident. And when Eratosthenes actually places Rome—which is so much farther west of the Strait of Sicily than even Carthage is—on the same meridian with Carthage, his ignorance both of these regions and of the successive regions toward the west as far as the Pillars can reach no higher extreme.

---

⁵ τετρακισχιλίοις, Bréquigny, for τρισχιλίοις ; all editors or translators following or approving.

41. Ἱππάρχῳ μὲν οὖν μὴ γεωγραφοῦντι, ἀλλ᾽ ἐξετάζοντι τὰ λεχθέντα ἐν τῇ γεωγραφίᾳ τῇ Ἐρατοσθένους, οἰκεῖον ἦν ἐπὶ πλέον τὰ καθ᾽ ἕκαστα εὐθύνειν· ἡμεῖς δ᾽, ἐν οἷς μὲν κατορθοῖ, τὸ πλέον δ᾽ ἔτι ὅπου καὶ πλημμελεῖ, τὸν καθ᾽ ἕκαστα οἰκεῖον λόγον ᾠήθημεν δεῖν προσάγειν, τὰ μὲν ἐπανορθοῦντες, ὑπὲρ ὧν δ᾽ ἀπολυόμενοι τὰς ἐπιφερομένας αἰτίας ὑπὸ τοῦ Ἱππάρχου, καὶ αὐτὸν τὸν Ἵππαρχον συνεξετάζομεν, ὅπου τι φιλαιτίως εἴρηκεν. ἐν δὲ τούτοις ὁρῶντες ἤδη τὸν μὲν τελέως παραπαίοντα, τὸν δὲ δικαίως ἐπικαλοῦντα, ἀρκεῖν ὑπολαμβάνομεν, ἂν ἐν αὐτῇ τῇ γεωγραφίᾳ τὰ ὄντα λέγοντες ἐπανορθῶμεν αὐτόν. ἐφ᾽ ὧν γὰρ συνεχῆ καὶ ἐπιπολάζοντά ἐστι τὰ ἁμαρτανόμενα, κρεῖττον μηδὲ μεμνῆσθαι, πλὴν εἰ σπάνιόν τι καὶ καθόλου· ὅπερ πειρασόμεθα ποιεῖν ἐν τοῖς καθ᾽ ἕκαστα. καὶ νῦν δ᾽ εἰρήσθω, ὅτι καὶ Τιμοσθένης καὶ Ἐρατοσθένης καὶ οἱ ἔτι τούτων πρότεροι τελέως ἠγνόουν τά τε Ἰβηρικὰ καὶ τὰ Κελτικά, μυρίῳ δὲ μᾶλλον τὰ Γερμανικὰ καὶ τὰ Βρεττανικά, ὡς δ᾽ αὕτως τὰ τῶν Γετῶν καὶ Βαστάρνων. ἐπὶ πολὺ δ᾽ ἀγνοίας ἐτύγχανον ἀφιγμένοι καὶ τῶν κατ᾽ Ἰταλίαν καὶ τὸν Ἀδρίαν καὶ τὸν Πόντον καὶ τῶν ἐφεξῆς προσαρκτίων μερῶν· εἰ καὶ τὰ τοιαῦτα ἴσως φιλαίτια. τοῦ γὰρ Ἐρατοσθένους ἐπὶ τῶν πόρρω διεστηκότων τὰ παραδεδομένα φάσκοντος ἐρεῖν διαστήματα, μὴ διισχυριζομένου δέ, καὶ λέγοντος ὡς παρέλαβε,

41. Now it would have been proper for Hipparchus, if he were not writing a work on Geography but merely a review of what Eratosthenes had said in his Geography, to go further than he did in setting right in detail the mistakes of Eratosthenes; but as for me, I have thought it right to introduce in detail the appropriate discussion both in regard to the points in which Eratosthenes is right and, still more so, in regard to those in which he is wrong; and I have not merely corrected his mistakes, but where I have acquitted him of the charges brought by Hipparchus, I have also criticised Hipparchus himself, whenever he has said anything in a censorious spirit. But since in these instances I see at a glance that Eratosthenes goes entirely astray and that Hipparchus accuses him justly, I assume that it is sufficient if I correct Eratosthenes by merely stating the facts in the course of my Geography itself. Indeed, where the errors are continuous and lie on the surface, it is better not to mention them at all, except rarely and in a general way; and this is what I shall try to do in my detailed account. However, let it be said at this moment that Timosthenes and Eratosthenes and the still earlier geographers were completely ignorant of Iberia and Celtica; and vastly more igno rant of Germany and Britain, and likewise of the countries of the Getans and the Bastarnians; and they were to a considerable extent ignorant of Italy, the Adriatic Sea, the Pontus, and the regions beyond them on the north; though perhaps such statements are censorious. For, since Eratosthenes asserts that where it is a question of very remote regions he will give merely the traditional distances without vouching for them, and admits that he got

357

προστιθέντος δ' ἔστιν ὅπου τὰ ἐπ' εὐθείας μᾶλλοι καὶ ἧττον, οὐ δεῖ προσάγειν τὸν ἀκριβῆ ἔλεγχον C 94 τοῖς μὴ ὁμολογουμένοις πρὸς ἄλληλα διαστή- μασιν· ὅπερ ποιεῖν πειρᾶται ὁ Ἵππαρχος ἔν τε τοῖς πρότερον λεχθεῖσι καὶ ἐν οἷς τὰ περὶ τὴν Ὑρκανίαν μέχρι Βακτρίων καὶ τῶν ἐπέκεινα ἐθνῶν ἐκτίθεται διαστήματα, καὶ ἔτι τὰ ἀπὸ Κολχίδος ἐπὶ τὴν Ὑρκανίαν θάλατταν. οὐ γὰρ ὁμοίως ἐπί τε τούτων ἐξεταστέον αὐτὸν καὶ ἐπὶ τῶν κατὰ τὴν ἠπειρῶτιν παραλίαν[1] καὶ τοὺς ἄλλους τοὺς οὕτω γνωρίμους τόπους· ἀλλ' οὐδ' ἐπὶ τούτων γεωμετρικῶς, ὅπερ ἔφην, ἀλλὰ γεω- γραφικῶς μᾶλλον. αἰτιασάμενος δ' οὖν τινα τῶν Αἰθιοπικῶν ἐπὶ τελει τοῦ δευτέρου ὑπομνήματος τῶν πρὸς τὴν Ἐρατοσθένους γεωγραφίαν πεποιη- μένων, ἐν τῷ τρίτῳ φησὶ τὴν μὲν πλείω θεωρίαν ἔσεσθαι μαθηματικήν, ἐπὶ ποσὸν δὲ καὶ γεω- γραφικήν· οὐδ' ἐπὶ ποσὸν μέντοι δοκεῖ μοι ποιή- σασθαι γεωγραφικήν, ἀλλὰ πᾶσαν μαθηματικήν, διδόντος καὶ τοῦ Ἐρατοσθένους τὴν τοιαύτην πρόφασιν. πολλαχοῦ γὰρ ἐκπίπτει πρὸς τὸ ἐπιστημονικώτερον τῆς προκειμένης ἱστορίας, ἐκ- πεσὼν δὲ οὐκ ἀκριβεῖς, ἀλλ' ὁλοσχερεῖς ποιεῖται τὰς ἀποφάσεις, τρόπον τινὰ ἐν μὲν τοῖς γεω- γραφικοῖς μαθηματικός, ἐν δὲ τοῖς μαθηματικοῖς γεωγραφικὸς ὤν, ὥστε πρὸς ἄμφω δίδωσιν ἀφορ-

---

[1] παραλίαν, Groskurd, for πάλιν; Meineke following.

them by tradition,—though at times he adds the words "in a line more or less straight"—it is not fair to apply the rigorous test [1] to those distances which do not agree with each other. That is precisely what Hipparchus tries to do, not only in the cases mentioned above but also where he sets forth the distances round about Hyrcania up to Bactria and to the tribes on beyond, and, besides, the distances from Colchis to the Hyrcanian Sea. Indeed, in the case of the geography of the remote countries, we should not scrutinize him in the same way as we do in that of the continental sea-board and of the other regions that are as well known; nay, not even in case of the nearer regions ought we to apply the geometrical test, as I was saying, but rather the geographical. Now toward the end of his Second Book, which he has written in refutation of the Geography of Eratosthenes, Hipparchus finds fault with some of the statements of Eratosthenes about Ethiopia, and then says that in his Third Book the greater part of his speculation will be mathematical, but "to some extent" geographical also. It seems to me, however, that he did not make his theory geographical even "to some extent," but wholly mathematical—though Eratosthenes himself gives Hipparchus a good excuse for so doing. For frequently Eratosthenes digresses into discussions too scientific for the subject he is dealing with, but, after he digresses, the declarations he makes are not rigorously accurate but only vague, since, so to speak, he is a mathematician among geographers, and yet a geographer among mathematicians; and consequently on both sides he offers his opponents occasions for

[1] That is, of geometry.

μὰς τοῖς ἀντιλέγουσιν· ἐν δὲ τούτῳ τῷ ὑπομνήματι καὶ δικαίας καὶ οὗτος καὶ ὁ Τιμοσθένης,
ὥστ' οὐδ' ἡμῖν καταλείπεται συνεπισκοπεῖν, ἀλλ'
ἀρκεῖσθαι τοῖς ὑπὸ τοῦ Ἱππάρχου λεχθεῖσιν.

II

1. Ἴδωμεν δὲ καὶ Ποσειδώνιον, ἅ φησιν ἐν τοῖς
περὶ ὠκεανοῦ· δοκεῖ γὰρ ἐν αὐτοῖς τὰ πολλὰ
γεωγραφεῖν, τὰ μὲν οἰκείως, τὰ δὲ μαθηματικώ-
τερον. οὐκ ἄτοπον οὖν ἔνια καὶ τῶν ὑπὸ τούτου
λεγομένων διαιτῆσαι, τὰ μὲν νῦν, τὰ δ' ἐν τοῖς
καθ' ἕκαστα, ὡς ἂν ὑποπίπτῃ, μέτρου τινὸς
ἐχομένους. ἔστιν οὖν τι τῶν πρὸς γεωγραφίαν
οἰκείων τὸ τὴν γῆν ὅλην ὑποθέσθαι σφαιροειδῆ,
καθάπερ καὶ τὸν κόσμον, καὶ τὰ ἄλλα παρα-
δέξασθαι τὰ ἀκόλουθα τῇ ὑποθέσει ταύτῃ· τούτων
δ' ἐστὶ καὶ τὸ πεντάζωνον αὐτὴν εἶναι.

2. Φησὶ δὴ ὁ Ποσειδώνιος τῆς εἰς πέντε ζώνας
διαιρέσεως ἀρχηγὸν γενέσθαι Παρμενίδην· ἀλλ'
ἐκεῖνον μὲν σχεδόν τι διπλασίαν ἀποφαίνειν
τὸ πλάτος τὴν διακεκαυμένην,[1] ὑπερπίπτουσαν

---

[1] The words τῆς μεταξὺ τῶν τροπικῶν after διακεκαυμένην
are omitted by Kramer and succeeding editors.

---

[1] That is, some such standard as Strabo himself has defined
in 2. 1. 37. [2] See footnote 2 on p. 40.
[3] But, according to Plutarch, Thales and Pythagoras had
divided the heavens into five zones, and Pythagoras had
divided the earth into five corresponding zones (*De Placitis
Philosophorum* 2. 12 and 3. 14).
[4] That is, double the breadth assigned to the torrid
zone by Poseidonius and Strabo—namely, 2 × 17,600 stadia

contradiction; and the occasions which both he and
Timosthenes offer Hipparchus in this Third Book are
so just that it remains for me not even to join my
observations to those of Hipparchus, but merely to
content myself with what Hipparchus has said about
them.

II

1. Now let us see what Poseidonius has to say in
his treatise on Oceanus. For in it he seems to deal
mainly with geography, treating it partly from the
point of view of geography properly so called, and
partly from a more mathematical point of view. And
so it will not be out of place for me to pass judgment
upon a few of Poseidonius' statements, some of them
now, and others in my discussion of the individual
countries, as occasion offers, always observing a kind
of standard.[1] Now it is one of the things proper to
geography to take as an hypothesis that the earth
as a whole is sphere-shaped,[2]— just as we do in the case
of the universe—and accept all the conclusions that
follow this hypothesis, one of which is that the earth
has five zones.

2. Poseidonius, then, says that Parmenides was
the originator of the division into five zones,[3] but that
Parmenides represents the torrid zone as almost
double its real breadth,[4] inasmuch as it falls beyond

= 35,200; and thus the torrid zone would reach to 25° 8′ 34⅔″
(counting 700 stadia to the degree). Thus the difference between Aristotle and Parmenides is not great, if we assume
that the former places the tropics at about 24°. The reading
of the manuscripts (see critical note on opposite page) makes
Parmenides say that the torrid zone is double the zone between the tropics, but it is inconceivable that he did so.

ἑκατέρων τῶν τροπικῶν εἰς τὸ ἐκτὸς καὶ πρὸς ταῖς
εὐκράτοις· Ἀριστοτέλη δὲ αὐτὴν καλεῖν τὴν
μεταξὺ τῶν τροπικῶν, τὰς δὲ μεταξὺ τῶν τροπικῶν[1] καὶ τῶν ἀρκτικῶν εὐκράτους. ἀμφοτέροις
C 95 δ᾽ ἐπιτιμᾷ δικαίως. διακεκαυμένην γὰρ λέγεσθαι
τὸ ἀοίκητον διὰ καῦμα· τῆς δὲ μεταξὺ τῶν τροπικῶν πλέον ἢ τὸ ἥμισυ τοῦ πλάτους οὐκ[2]
οἰκήσιμόν ἐστιν ἐκ τῶν ὑπὲρ Αἰγύπτου στοχα-
ζομένοις Αἰθιόπων, εἴπερ τὸ μὲν ἥμισυ τοῦ παντὸς
πλάτους ἐστίν, ὃ διαιρεῖ ἐφ᾽ ἑκάτερα ὁ ἰσημερινός·
τούτου δὲ τὸ μὲν ἀπὸ τῆς Συήνης, ἥπερ ἐστὶν
ὅριον τοῦ θερινοῦ τροπικοῦ, εἰς Μερόην εἰσὶ
πεντακισχίλιοι· τὸ δ᾽ ἐνθένδε ἕως τοῦ τῆς Κινναμωμοφόρου παραλλήλου, ὅσπερ ἐστὶν ἀρχὴ τῆς
διακεκαυμένης, τρισχίλιοι. τοῦτο μὲν οὖν τὸ
διάστημα πᾶν ἐστι μετρητόν, πλεῖταί τε γὰρ
καὶ ὁδεύεται· τὸ δ᾽ ἑξῆς, μέχρι τοῦ ἰσημερινοῦ,
λόγῳ[3] δείκνυται κατὰ τὴν ὑπ᾽ Ἐρατοσθένους
γενομένην ἀναμέτρησιν τῆς γῆς, ὅτι ἐστὶ σταδίων
ὀκτακισχιλίων ὀκτακοσίων· ὃν δὴ λόγον ἔχει
τὰ μύρια ἑξακισχίλια ὀκτακόσια[4] πρὸς τὰ

---

[1] τὰς δὲ μεταξὺ τῶν τροπικῶν, Casaubon inserts; all editors
following.

[2] οὐκ, Kramer inserts, before οἰκήσιμον; Forbiger, C. Müller,
Tardieu, following.

[3] ἰσημερινοῦ, λόγῳ δείκνυται, Corais, for ἰσημερινοῦ λέγω,
δείκνυται; Groskurd, Meineke, Tardieu, following; C. Müller,
H. Berger, approving.

[4] ἑξακισχίλια ὀκτακόσια, Kramer, for τρισχίλια; Meineke,
Forbiger, Tardieu, C. Müller, following.

---

[1] De Meteorologicis 2. 5.
[2] Poseidonius insists on taking literally the Greek word
διακεκαυμένην, "scorched."

both the tropics and extends into the two temperate zones, while Aristotle[1] calls "torrid" the region between the tropics, and "temperate" the regions between the tropics and the "arctic circles." But Poseidonius censures both systems, and with justice, for by "torrid,"[2] he says, is meant only the region that is uninhabitable on account of heat; and, of the zone between the tropics, more than half is uninhabitable if we may base a conjecture upon the Ethiopians who live south of Egypt—if it be true, first, that each division of the torrid zone made by the equator is half the whole breadth of that zone[3] and, secondly, that, of this half, the part that reaches to Meroë from Syene (which is a point on the boundary line of the summer tropic[4]) is five thousand stadia in breadth, and the part from Meroë to the parallel of the Cinnamon-producing Country, on which parallel the torrid zone begins, is three thousand stadia in breadth. Now the whole of these two parts can be measured, for they are traversed both by water and by land; but the rest of the distance, up to the equator, is shown by calculation based upon the measurement which Eratosthenes made of the earth[5] to be eight thousand eight hundred stadia. Accordingly, as is the ratio of the sixteen thousand eight hundred stadia[6] to the eight thousand eight

[3] Strabo proceeds to give a definite estimate of the inhabited and uninhabited portions of the torrid zone north of the equator. But, for the division of the zone south of the equator, he can only assume that a similar estimate applies. By so assuming he reaches a conclusion for the whole zone, in the form of a ratio.

[4] The north and south temperate zones had also the name of summer and winter zones ; and hence the summer tropic is the northern tropic.   [5] 252,000 stadia.

[6] The distance between the northern tropic and the equator.

ὀκτακισχίλια ὀκτακόσια, τοῦτον ἂν ἔχοι τὸ
μεταξὺ τῶν τροπικῶν διάστημα πρὸς τὸ τῆς
διακεκαυμένης πλάτος. κἂν τῶν νεωτέρων δὲ
ἀναμετρήσεων εἰσάγηται ἡ ἐλαχίστην ποιοῦσα τὴν
γῆν, οἵαν ὁ Ποσειδώνιος ἐγκρίνει περὶ ὀκτωκαίδεκα
μυριάδας οὖσαν, περὶ ἥμισύ που ἀποφαίνει τὴν
διακεκαυμένην τῆς μεταξὺ τῶν τροπικῶν, ἢ μικρῷ
τοῦ ἡμίσους μείζονα· ἴσην δὲ καὶ τὴν αὐτὴν
οὐδαμῶς. τοῖς τε ἀρκτικοῖς, οὔτε παρὰ πᾶσιν
οὖσιν, οὔτε τοῖς αὐτοῖς πανταχοῦ, τίς ἂν διορίζοι
τὰς εὐκράτους, αἵπερ εἰσὶν ἀμετάπτωτοι; τὸ μὲν
οὖν μὴ παρὰ πᾶσιν εἶναι τοὺς ἀρκτικούς, οὐδὲν
ἂν εἴη πρὸς τὸν ἔλεγχον· δεῖ γὰρ παρὰ τοῖς τὴν
εὔκρατον οἰκοῦσιν εἶναι πᾶσι, πρὸς οὕσπερ καὶ
λέγεται μόνους εὔκρατος. τὸ δὲ μὴ πανταχοῦ
τὸν αὐτὸν τρόπον, ἀλλὰ μεταπίπτειν, καλῶς
εἴληπται.

3. Αὐτὸς δὲ διαιρῶν εἰς τὰς ζώνας, πέντε μέν
φησιν εἶναι χρησίμους πρὸς τὰ οὐράνια. τούτων
δὲ περισκίους δύο τὰς ὑπὸ τοῖς πόλοις μέχρι τῶν
ἐχόντων τοὺς τροπικοὺς ἀρκτικούς, ἑτεροσκίους δὲ

---

[1] That is, 16,800 : 8,800 :: 33,600 : 17,600. The ratio is
21 : 11, and the breadth of the torrid zone 17,600 stadia
(compare 2. 1. 13).

[2] The Greeks in general used the term "arctic circle" of a
celestial circle, and not of a terrestrial circle as we do to-
day. Our arctic circle is fixed; theirs varied according
to the standpoint of the observer. Their arctic circle was
drawn on the celestial sphere parallel to the equator and
tangent to the observer's horizon, and it therefore separated
the circumpolar stars that are always above the horizon from
the stars that rise and set with respect to his horizon. Since

hundred stadia, so would be the ratio of the distance between the two tropics to the breadth of the torrid zone.[1] And if, of the more recent measurements of the earth, the one which makes the earth smallest in circumference be introduced—I mean that of Poseidonius, who estimates its circumference at about one hundred and eighty thousand stadia—this measurement, I say, renders the breadth of the torrid zone somewhere about half the space between the tropics, or slightly more than half, but in no wise equal to, or the same as, that space. And again, Poseidonius asks how one could determine the limits of the temperate zones, which are non-variable, by means of the "arctic circles," which are neither visible among all men nor the same everywhere. Now the fact that the "arctic circles" are not visible to all could be of no aid to his refutation of Aristotle, because the "arctic circles" must be visible to all who live in the temperate zone, with reference to whom alone the term "temperate" is in fact used. But his point that the "arctic circles" are not everywhere visible in the same way, but are subject to variations, has been well taken.[2]

3. When Poseidonius himself divides the earth into the zones,[3] he says that five of them are useful with reference to the celestial phenomena; of these five, two—those that lie beneath the poles and extend to the regions that have the tropics as arctic

the altitude of the celestial pole is always the same as the latitude of the observer, the arctic circles would become zero for him at the equator; and, again, he would have no arctic circles if stationed south of the equator, nor would he have any antarctic circles if stationed north of the equator. Strabo insists that the boundaries of the temperate zones shall be fixed, not variable.   [3] Seven.

τὰς ἐφεξῆς ταύταις δύο μέχρι τῶν ὑπὸ τοῖς
τροπικοῖς οἰκούντων, ἀμφίσκιον δὲ τὴν μεταξὺ
τῶν τροπικῶν. πρὸς δὲ τὰ ἀνθρώπεια ταύτας τε
καὶ δύο ἄλλας στενὰς τὰς ὑπὸ τοῖς τροπικοῖς,
καθ᾽ ἃς ἥμισύ πως μηνὸς κατὰ κορυφήν ἐστιν
ὁ ἥλιος, δίχα διαιρουμένας ὑπὸ τῶν τροπικῶν.
ἔχειν γάρ τι ἴδιον τὰς ζώνας ταύτας, αὐχμηράς τε
ἰδίως καὶ ἀμμώδεις ὑπαρχούσας καὶ ἀφόρους πλὴν
σιλφίου καὶ πυρωδῶν τινων καρπῶν συγκεκαυ-
μένων. ὄρη γὰρ μὴ εἶναι πλησίον, ὥστε τὰ νέφη
προσπίπτοντα ὄμβρους ποιεῖν, μηδὲ δὴ ποταμοῖς
C 96 διαρρεῖσθαι. διόπερ οὐλότριχας καὶ οὐλόκερως
καὶ προχείλους καὶ πλατύρρινας γεννᾶσθαι· τὰ
γὰρ ἄκρα αὐτῶν συστρέφεσθαι· καὶ τοὺς ἰχθυο-
φάγους δὲ κατὰ ταύτας τὰς ζώνας οἰκεῖν. ὅτι
δὲ ταῦτ᾽ ἴδια τῶν ζωνῶν τούτων δηλοῦν φησι
τὸ τοὺς νοτιωτέρους αὐτῶν ἔχειν τὸ περιέχον
εὐκρατότερον καὶ τὴν γῆν καρπιμωτέραν καὶ
εὐυδροτέραν.

III

1. Πολύβιος δὲ ποιεῖ ζώνας ἕξ· δύο μὲν τὰς τοῖς
ἀρκτικοῖς ὑποπιπτούσας, δύο δὲ τὰς μεταξὺ
τούτων τε καὶ τῶν τροπικῶν, καὶ δύο τὰς μεταξὺ

---

[1] That is, the frigid zones, where the shadows describe an
oval in the summer-time.
[2] That is, the temperate zones, where the shadows are

circles—are "periscian[1]"; and the two that come next and extend to the people who live beneath the tropics are "heteroscian[2]"; and the zone between the tropics, "amphiscian[3]". But for purposes of human interest there are, in addition to these five zones, two other narrow ones that lie beneath the tropics and are divided into two parts by the tropics; these have the sun directly overhead for about half a month each year. These two zones, he says, have a certain peculiarity, in that they are parched in the literal sense of the word, are sandy, and produce nothing except silphium and some pungent fruits that are withered by the heat; for those regions have in their neighbourhood no mountains against which the clouds may break and produce rain, nor indeed are they coursed by rivers; and for this reason they produce creatures with woolly hair, crumpled horns, protruding lips, and flat noses (for their extremities are contorted by the heat); and the "fish-eaters" also live in these zones. Poseidonius says it is clear that these things are peculiar to those zones from the fact that the people who live farther south than they do have a more temperate atmosphere, and also a more fruitful, and a better-watered, country.

III

1. POLYBIUS makes six zones: two that fall beneath the arctic circles, two between the arctic circles and the tropics, and two between the tropics and the

thrown in opposite directions at noon; the shadow in the northern zone falling north and in the southern falling south.

[3] That is, the torrid zone, where the shadow for any point at noon is north part of the year and south part of the year.

τούτων καὶ τοῦ ἰσημερινοῦ. ἡ μὲν οὖν εἰς πέντε διαίρεσις δοκεῖ μοι καὶ φυσικῶς ἅμα καὶ γεωγραφικῶς εἰρῆσθαι. φυσικῶς μέν, ὅτι καὶ πρὸς τὰ οὐράνια καὶ πρὸς τὴν τοῦ περιέχοντος κρᾶσιν· πρὸς μὲν τὰ οὐράνια, ὅτι τοῖς περισκίοις καὶ τοῖς ἑτεροσκίοις [1] καὶ τοῖς ἀμφισκίοις, οὕτως ἂν ἄριστα διοριζομένοις, συνδιορίζεται καὶ τὰ περὶ τὴν θέαν τῶν ἄστρων, ὁλοσχερεῖ τινι μερισμῷ λαμβάνοντα τὴν ἐξάλλαξιν· πρὸς δὲ τὴν τοῦ περιέχοντος κρᾶσιν, ὅτι τῆς τούτου κράσεως πρὸς τὸν ἥλιον κρινομένης διαφοραὶ τρεῖς εἰσιν αἱ γενικώταται καὶ συντείνουσαι πρός τε τὰς τῶν ζώων καὶ φυτῶν συστάσεις καὶ τῶν ἄλλων ἡμισυστάσεις [2] τῶν ὑπὸ τῷ ἀέρι καὶ ἐν αὐτῷ ἐκείνῳ, ὑπερβολὴ θάλπους καὶ ἔλλειψις καὶ μεσότης. αὕτη δὲ τῷ εἰς τὰς ζώνας μερισμῷ λαμβάνει τὴν οἰκείαν διάκρισιν· αἵ τε γὰρ κατεψυγμέναι δύο τὴν ἔλλειψιν τοῦ θάλπους ὑπαγορεύουσιν, εἰς μίαν τοῦ περιέχοντος φύσιν συναγόμεναι, αἵ τε εὔκρατοι παραπλησίως εἰς μίαν τὴν μεσότητα ἄγονται, εἰς δὲ τὴν λοιπὴν ἡ λοιπὴ μία καὶ διακεκαυμένη. ὅτι δὲ καὶ γεωγραφικός ἐστιν ὁ μερισμός, δῆλον.

---

[1] καὶ τοῖς ἑτεροσκίοις, Groskurd inserts, after περισκίοις; Meineke, Forbiger, Tardieu, following; Gosselin, Kramer, C. Müller, approving, but not inserting.

[2] ἡμισυστάσεις, Madvig, for ἡμισυσταλεῖς; A. Vogel, Sterrett, approving.

equator. However, the division into five zones seems to me to be in harmony with physics as well as geography; with physics, in relation both to the celestial phenomena and to the temperature of the atmosphere; in relation to the celestial phenomena, because, by means of the "periscian" and the "heteroscian" and the "amphiscian"[1] regions (the best way to determine the zones), the appearance of the constellations to our sight is at the same time determined; for thus, by a kind of rough-outline division,[2] the constellations receive their proper variations; and in relation to the temperature of the atmosphere, because the temperature of the atmosphere, being judged with reference to the sun, is subject to three very broad differences—namely, excess of heat, lack of heat, and moderate heat, which have a strong bearing on the organisations of animals and plants, and the semi-organisations[3] of everything else beneath the air or in the air itself. And the temperature of the atmosphere receives its proper determination by this division of the earth into five zones: for the two frigid zones imply the absence of heat, agreeing in the possession of one characteristic temperature; and in like manner the two temperate zones agree in one temperature, that of moderate heat; while the one remaining is consistent in having the remaining characteristic, in that it is one and torrid in temperature. And it is clear that this division is in harmony with geography.

[1] See 2. 2. 3, and footnotes.

[2] Strabo, like Pythagoras, has in mind celestial zones corresponding to his terrestrial zones. The former would not be so accurate as the latter, but they would afford a consistent basis for astronomical observation.

[3] Seeds, for example.

ζητεῖ γὰρ ἡ γεωγραφία τῇ ἑτέρᾳ[1] τῶν εὐκράτων
ἀφορίσαι τὸ οἰκούμενον ὑφ' ἡμῶν τμῆμα· πρὸς
δύσει μὲν οὖν καὶ ἀνατολῇ θάλαττά ἐστιν ἡ περα-
τοῦσα, πρὸς δὲ τὰ νότια καὶ τὰ βόρεια ὁ ἀήρ, ὁ
μὲν μέσος εὔκρατος ὢν καὶ φυτοῖς καὶ ζῴοις, ὁ
δ' ἐφ' ἑκάτερα δύσκρατος ὑπερβολῇ καὶ ἐλλείψει
τοῦ θάλπους. εἰς δὲ τὰς τρεῖς διαφορὰς ταύτας
ἐδέησε τῆς εἰς πέντε ζώνας διαιρέσεως· τῷ γὰρ
ἰσημερινῷ τμηθεῖσα δίχα ἡ σφαῖρα τῆς γῆς εἴς τε
τὸ βόρειον ἡμισφαίριον, ἐν ᾧ ἡμεῖς ἐσμεν, καὶ τὸ
νότιον, ὑπέγραψε τὰς τρεῖς διαφοράς· τὰ μὲν
γὰρ πρὸς τῷ ἰσημερινῷ καὶ τῇ διακεκαυμένῃ ζώνῃ
διὰ καῦμα ἀοίκητά ἐστι, τὰ δὲ πρὸς τῷ πόλῳ διὰ
ψῦχος, τὰ δὲ μέσα τὰ εὔκρατα καὶ τὰ οἰκήσιμα.
ὁ δὲ τὰς ὑπὸ τοῖς τροπικοῖς προστιθεὶς οὐκ ἀνὰ
λόγον ταῖς πέντε ταύτας[2] προστίθησιν, οὐδ' ὁμοίᾳ
C 97 κεχρημένος[3] διαφορᾷ, ἀλλ' ὡς ἂν εἰ καὶ ταῖς
ἐθνικαῖς διαφοραῖς ἀπέφαινε ζώνας, ἄλλην μὲν
τὴν Αἰθιοπικήν, ἄλλην δὲ τὴν Σκυθικὴν καὶ
Κελτικήν, τρίτην δὲ τὴν ἀνὰ μέσον.

2. Ὁ δὲ Πολύβιος τοῦτο μὲν οὐκ εὖ, τὸ ποιεῖν
τινας ζώνας τοῖς ἀρκτικοῖς διοριζομένας, δύο μὲν
τὰς ὑποπιπτούσας αὐτοῖς, δύο δὲ τὰς μεταξὺ
τούτων καὶ τῶν τροπικῶν· εἴρηται γὰρ ὅτι τοῖς
μεταπίπτουσι σημείοις οὐχ ὁριστέον τὰ ἀμετάπτωτα. οὐδὲ τοῖς τροπικοῖς δὲ τῆς διακεκαυ-

---

[1] τῇ ἑτέρᾳ, Madvig, for τῆς ἑτέρας.
[2] ταύτας, Corais, for ταύταις ; Meineke following.
[3] κεχρημένος, Corais, for κεχρημένας.

For geography seeks to define by boundaries that section of the earth which we inhabit by means of the one of the two temperate zones. Now on the west and on the east it is the sea that fixes its limits, but on the south and the north the nature of the air; for the air that is between these limits is well-tempered both for plants and for animals, while the air on both sides of these limits is harsh-tempered, because of excess of heat or lack of heat. It was necessary to divide the earth into five zones corresponding to these three differences of temperature; indeed, the cutting of the sphere of the earth by the equator into two hemispheres, the northern hemisphere in which we live, and the southern hemisphere, suggested the three differences of temperature. For the regions on the equator and in the torrid zone are uninhabitable because of the heat, and those near the pole are uninhabitable because of the cold; but it is the intermediate regions that are well-tempered and inhabitable. But when he adds the two zones beneath the tropics, Poseidonius does not follow the analogy of the five zones, nor yet does he employ a like criterion; but he was apparently representing zones by the ethnical criteria also, for he calls one of them the "Ethiopic zone," another the "Scythico-Celtic zone," and a third the "intermediate zone."

2. Polybius is not right in this, namely, in that he defines some of his zones by means of the arctic circles: two that fall under the arctic circles themselves, and two between the arctic circles and the tropics; for, as I have already said, non-variables must not be defined by points that are variable.[1] And we must also not employ the tropics as boundaries of the

[1] See page 365, and footnote 2.

μένης ὅροις χρηστέον· καὶ γὰρ τοῦτ' εἴρηται. τὴν διακεκαυμένην μέντοι δίχα διαιρῶν πρὸς οὐ φαύλην ἐπίνοιαν φαίνεται κεκινημένος, πρὸς ἣν καὶ ὅλην δίχα διαιροῦμεν εὐφυῶς τὴν γῆν εἴς τε τὸ βόρειον ἡμισφαίριον καὶ τὸ νότιον τῷ ἰσημερινῷ· δῆλον γὰρ ὅτι, εἰ[1] διαιρεῖται κατὰ ταύτην τὴν τομὴν καὶ ἡ διακεκαυμένη, καὶ ποιεῖ τινα ἐπιτηδειότητα ὥστε καὶ τὸ ἡμισφαίριον ἑκάτερον ἐξ ὅλων συνετάχθαι τριῶν ζωνῶν ὁμοιοειδῶν τῶν ἐν θατέρῳ. ἡ μὲν οὖν τοιαύτη τομὴ δέχεται τὴν εἰς ἓξ ζώνας διαίρεσιν, ἡ δ' ἑτέρα οὐ πάνυ. εἰ γοῦν τῷ διὰ τῶν πόλων δίχα τέμνοις τὴν γῆν, οὐκ ἂν εἰκότως ἑκάτερον τῶν ἡμισφαιρίων, τό τε ἑσπέριον καὶ τὸ ἀνατολικόν, τέμνοις εἰς ζώνας ἕξ, ἀλλὰ ἡ εἰς πέντε ἀρκοῦσα ἂν εἴη· τὸ γὰρ ὁμοιοπαθὲς τῶν τμημάτων ἀμφοτέρων τῆς διακεκαυμένης, ἃ ποιεῖ ὁ ἰσημερινός, καὶ τὸ συγκεῖσθαι περιττὴν καὶ περίεργον ἀποφαίνει τὴν τομήν, ὁμοιοειδῶν μὲν οὐσῶν καὶ τῶν εὐκράτων καὶ τῶν κατεψυγμένων, ἀλλ' οὐ συγκειμένων· οὕτως οὖν καὶ τὴν ὅλην γῆν ἐκ τῶν τοιούτων ἡμισφαιρίων ἐπινοουμένην ἀρκούντως ἂν εἰς πέντε διαιροίης. εἰ δ', ὥσπερ Ἐρατοσθένης φησίν, ἡ ὑποπίπτουσα τῷ ἰσημερινῷ ἐστιν εὔκρατος, καθάπερ καὶ Πολύβιος ὁμοδοξεῖ (προστίθησι δ' οὗτος καὶ διότι ὑψηλοτάτη ἐστί· διόπερ καὶ κατομβρεῖται, τῶν βορείων νεφῶν κατὰ τοὺς ἐτησίας ἐκεῖ τοῖς ἀναστήμασι προσπιπ-

[1] γάρ, ὅτι, εἰ διαιρεῖται, Madvig, for γὰρ ὅτι διαιρεῖται.

torrid zone ; this, too, I have already said.   However,
when he divides the torrid zone into two parts, it is
clearly no foolish notion that has moved him to do
so ; for it is by this notion that we very suitably use
the equator to divide the whole earth into two parts,
namely, the northern and the southern hemispheres.
For it is clear that, if the torrid zone as well is
divided according to this method of partition,
Polybius reaches a convenient result ; that is, each of
the two hemispheres is composed of three whole
zones, each of which is like in form to its corresponding zone in the other hemisphere.   Now a partition
of this kind admits of the division into six zones ; but
the other partition does not altogether admit of it.
At all events, if you should cut the earth into two
parts by means of the circle that runs through the
poles, you could not reasonably divide each of the
two hemispheres, the western and the eastern, into
six zones, but the division into five zones would be
sufficient; for the homogeneousness of the two
sections of the torrid zone that are made by the
equator, and the fact that they are contiguous to each
other, render their partition useless and superfluous,
while the two temperate and the two frigid zones are,
indeed, alike in form respectively, though they are
not contiguous.   So, therefore, if you conceive of the
whole earth as composed of hemispheres of this kind
it will be sufficient to divide it into five zones.   But
if the country that lies under the equator is temperate, as Eratosthenes says it is (an opinion with which
Polybius agrees, though he adds this, that it is the
highest part of the earth, and for that reason is
subject to rains, because at the season of the Etesian
Winds the clouds from the north strike in great

τόντων πλείστων), πολὺ κρεῖττον τρίτην[1] εὔκρατον
ταύτην ποιεῖν στενήν τινα, ἢ τὰς ὑπὸ τοῖς τροπικοῖς εἰσάγειν. συνηγορεῖ δὲ τούτοις καὶ τὰ
τοιαῦτα, ὧν μέμνηται καὶ Ποσειδώνιος, τὸ ἐκεῖ
τὰς μεταστάσεις ὀξυτέρας εἶναι τὰς εἰς τὰ πλάγια,
ὡς δ' αὕτως καὶ τὰς ἀπ' ἀνατολῆς ἐπὶ δύσιν τοῦ
ἡλίου· ὀξύτεραι γὰρ αἱ κατὰ μεγίστου κύκλου
τῶν ὁμοταχῶν κινήσεων.

3. Ἐνίσταται δ' ὁ Ποσειδώνιος τῷ Πολυβίῳ,
διότι φησὶ τὴν ὑπὸ τῷ ἰσημερινῷ οἴκησιν ὑψηλο-
τάτην· οὐδὲν γὰρ εἶναι κατὰ τὴν σφαιρικὴν
C 98 ἐπιφάνειαν ὕψος διὰ τὴν ὁμαλότητα, οὐδὲ δὴ
ὀρεινὴν εἶναι τὴν ὑπὸ τῷ ἰσημερινῷ, ἀλλὰ μᾶλλον
πεδιάδα ἰσόπεδόν πως τῇ ἐπιφανείᾳ τῆς θαλάττης·
τοὺς δὲ πληροῦντας τὸν Νεῖλον ὄμβρους ἐκ τῶν
Αἰθιοπικῶν ὀρῶν συμβαίνειν. ταῦτα δ' εἰπὼν
ἐνταῦθα ἐν ἄλλοις συγχωρεῖ, φήσας ὑπονοεῖν
ὄρη εἶναι τὰ ὑπὸ τῷ ἰσημερινῷ, πρὸς ἃ ἑκατέρωθεν ἀπὸ τῶν εὐκράτων ἀμφοῖν προσπίπτοντα
τὰ νέφη ποιεῖν τοὺς ὄμβρους. αὕτη μὲν οὖν ἡ ἀν-
ομολογία φανερά· ἀλλὰ καὶ δοθέντος τοῦ ὀρεινὴν
εἶναι τὴν ὑπὸ τῷ ἰσημερινῷ, ἄλλη τις ἀνακύπτειν
ἂν δόξειεν· οἱ γὰρ αὐτοὶ σύρρουν φασὶν εἶναι τὸν

_____
[1] τήν, Kramer suspects and Meineke deletes, before
εὔκρατον.

_____
[1] That is, the circumstances just quoted from Polybius.
[2] That is, the equator and adjacent circles of latitude.
Strabo means simply that the sun passes more rapidly with

374

numbers against the mountain peaks in that region), it would be much better to regard it as a third temperate zone, although a narrow one, than to introduce the two zones beneath the tropics. And in accord with these circumstances [1] are the following (which Poseidonius has already mentioned), namely, that in those regions the oblique motion of the sun is more rapid, and in the same way its daily motion from east to west; for when revolutions are accomplished within the same period of time, those on the greatest circles [2] are the more rapid.

3. But Poseidonius objects to the statement of Polybius that the inhabited region under the equator is the highest. For, says Poseidonius, there can be no high point on a spherical surface, because the surface of a sphere is uniform all round; and indeed the country under the equator is not mountainous, but rather is it a plain that is approximately on a level with the surface of the sea; and the rains that flood the Nile come together from the mountains of Ethiopia. But although Poseidonius thus expresses himself in this passage, he concedes the view of Polybius in other passages, saying he suspects that there are mountains beneath the equator and that the clouds from the two temperate zones strike against those mountains on both sides and cause the rains. Now here the lack of consistency is obvious; but even if it be admitted that the country beneath the equator is mountainous, another inconsistency, as it seems, would arise; for these same men assert that the ocean is one continuous stream round the earth. How, pray,

respect to points in this third temperate zone than in the new torrid zone on either side of that zone; hence a temperate climate on and near the equator.

ὠκεανόν. πῶς οὖν ὄρη κατὰ μέσον ἱδρύουσιν
αὐτόν, πλὴν εἰ νήσους τινὰς βούλονται λέγειν;
ὅπως δὲ δή ποτε τοῦτ' ἔχει, τῆς γεωγραφικῆς
μερίδος ἔξω πίπτει· δοτέον δ' ἴσως τῷ προθεμένῳ
τὴν περὶ ὠκεανοῦ πραγματείαν ταῦτ' ἐξετάζειν.

4. Μνησθεὶς δὲ τῶν περιπλεῦσαι λεγομένων
τὴν Λιβύην Ἡρόδοτον μὲν οἴεσθαί φησιν ὑπὸ
Νεκῶ[1] πεμφθέντας τινὰς τελέσαι τὸν περί-
πλουν· Ἡρακλείδην δὲ τὸν Ποντικὸν ἐν διαλόγῳ
ποιεῖν ἀφιγμένον παρὰ Γέλωνα[2] μάγον τινὰ
περιπλεῦσαι φάσκοντα. ἀμάρτυρα δὲ ταῦτ' εἶναι
φήσας καὶ Εὔδοξόν τινα Κυζικηνὸν θεωρὸν καὶ
σπονδοφόρον τοῦ τῶν Κορείων ἀγῶνος ἐλθεῖν εἰς
Αἴγυπτον ἱστορεῖ κατὰ τὸν δεύτερον Εὐεργέτην·
συσταθῆναι δὲ καὶ τῷ βασιλεῖ καὶ τοῖς περὶ
αὐτόν, καὶ μάλιστα κατὰ τοὺς ἀνάπλους τοῦ
Νείλου θαυμαστικὸν ὄντα τῶν τοπικῶν ἰδιω-
μάτων ἅμα καὶ οὐκ ἀπαίδευτον. τυχεῖν δή
τινα Ἰνδὸν κομισθέντα ὡς τὸν βασιλέα ὑπὸ
τῶν φυλάκων τοῦ Ἀραβίου μυχοῦ, λεγόντων
εὑρεῖν ἡμιθανῆ καταχθέντα μόνον ἐν νηί, τίς δ'
εἴη καὶ πόθεν, ἀγνοεῖν, μὴ συνιέντας τὴν διά-
λεκτον· τὸν δὲ παραδοῦναι τοῖς διδάξουσιν ἑλλη-
νίζειν. ἐκμαθόντα δὲ διηγήσασθαι, διότι ἐκ τῆς

---

[1] All scholars agree that Strabo or Poseidonius made a mistake in giving the name of Darius here. It was Neco who ordered the circumnavigation of Africa, while Darius ordered that of Arabia. (Herod. 4. 42).

[2] Γέλωνα, Corais, for Γέλωνι Meineke approving.

can they place mountains in the centre of the ocean—
unless by "mountains" they refer to certain islands?
But however this may be, it falls outside the province
of geography; and perhaps we should give over these
matters for examination to some one who proposes to
write a treatise on the ocean.

4. In giving the names of those who are said to
have circumnavigated Libya Poseidonius says that
Herodotus believes that certain men commissioned
by Neco accomplished the circumnavigation of
Libya; and adds that Heracleides of Pontus in one of
his *Dialogues* makes a certain Magus who had come
to the court of Gelo assert that he had circumnavigated
Libya. And, after stating that these reports are
unsupported by testimony, he tells the story of a
certain Eudoxus of Cyzicus, a sacred ambassador and
peace herald at the festival of Persephone. Eudoxus,
the story goes, came to Egypt in the reign of
Euergetes the Second[1]; and he became associated
with the king and the king's ministers, and
particularly in connection with the voyages up the
Nile; for he was a man inclined to admire the
peculiarities of regions and was also not uninformed
about them. Now it so happened, the story
continues, that a certain Indian was brought to the
king by the coast-guards of the recess of the Arabian
Gulf, who said that they had found him half-dead
and alone on a stranded ship, but that they did not
know who he was or where he came from, since they
did not understand his language; and the king gave
the Indian into the charge of men who would teach
him Greek; and when the Indian had learnt Greek,
he related that on his voyage from India he by a

[1] Ptolemy Physcon, who reigned B.C. 146-117.

Ἰνδικῆς πλέων περιπέσοι πλάνῃ καὶ σωθείη
δεῦρο, τοὺς σύμπλους ἀποβαλὼν λιμῷ· ὑπο-
ληφθέντα δὲ ὑποσχέσθαι τὸν εἰς Ἰνδοὺς πλοῦν
ἡγήσασθαι τοῖς ὑπὸ τοῦ βασιλέως προχειρισθεῖσι·
τούτων δὲ γενέσθαι καὶ[1] τὸν Εὔδοξον.

Πλεύσαντα δὴ μετὰ δώρων ἐπανελθεῖν ἀντιφορ-
τισάμενον ἀρώματα καὶ λίθους πολυτελεῖς, ὧν τοὺς
μὲν καταφέρουσιν οἱ ποταμοὶ μετὰ τῶν ψήφων,
τοὺς δ' ὀρυκτοὺς εὑρίσκουσι, πεπηγότας ἐξ ὑγροῦ,
C 99 καθάπερ τὰ κρυστάλλινα παρ' ἡμῖν· διαψευ-
σθῆναι δὲ τῶν ἐλπίδων· ἀφελέσθαι γὰρ αὐτὸν
ἅπαντα τὸν φόρτον τὸν Εὐεργέτην. τελευτή-
σαντος δ' ἐκείνου τὸν βίον, Κλεοπάτραν τὴν
γυναῖκα διαδέξασθαι τὴν ἀρχήν· πάλιν οὖν καὶ
ὑπὸ ταύτης πεμφθῆναι τὸν Εὔδοξον μετὰ μείζονος
παρασκευῆς. ἐπανιόντα δ' ἀνέμοις παρενεχθῆναι
ὑπὲρ τὴν Αἰθιοπίαν· προσφερόμενον δέ τισι
τόποις ἐξοικειοῦσθαι τοὺς ἀνθρώπους μεταδόσει
σιτίων τε καὶ οἴνου καὶ παλαθίδων, ὧν ἐκείνοις
οὐ μετῆν, ἀντὶ δὲ τούτων ὑδρείας τε τυγχάνειν
καὶ καθοδηγίας, ἀπογράφεσθαί τε τῶν ῥημάτων
ἔνια. εὑρόντα δ' ἀκρόπρωρον ξύλινον ἐκ ναυαγίου
ἵππον ἔχον ἐγγεγλυμμένον, πυθόμενον ὡς ἀπὸ
τῆς ἑσπέρας πλεόντων τινῶν εἴη τὸ ναυάγιον
τοῦτο, κομίζειν αὐτὸ ἀναστρέψαντα πρὸς τὸν
οἰκεῖον πλοῦν. σωθέντα δ' εἰς Αἴγυπτον, οὐκέτι
τῆς Κλεοπάτρας ἡγουμένης, ἀλλὰ τοῦ παιδός,

[1] καί, Meineke proposes to insert, after γενέσθαι.

378

strange mischance[1] mistook his course and reached
Egypt in safety, but only after having lost all his
companions by starvation; and when his story was
doubted, he promised to act as guide on the trip to
India for the men who had been previously selected
by the King; and of this party Eudoxus, also, became
a member.

So Eudoxus sailed away with presents; and he
returned with a cargo of perfumes and precious
stones (some of which the rivers bring down with the
sands, while others are found by digging, being
solidified from a liquid state, just as our crystals are).
But Eudoxus was wholly deceived in his expectations,
for Euergetes took from him his entire cargo. And
after the death of Euergetes, his wife, Cleopatra,
succeeded him on the throne; and so Eudoxus was
again sent out, by her also, and this time with a
larger outfit. But on his return voyage he was
driven out of his course by the winds to the south of
Ethiopia, and being driven to certain places he
conciliated the people by sharing with them bread,
wine, and dried figs (for they had no share of such
things), and in return therefor he received a supply
of fresh water and the guidance of pilots, and he also
made a list of some of their words. And he found
an end of a wooden prow that had come from a
wrecked ship and had a horse carved on it; and when
he learned that this piece of wreckage belonged to
some voyagers who had been sailing from the west,
he took it with him when he turned back upon his
homeward voyage. And when he arrived safely in
Egypt, inasmuch as Cleopatra no longer reigned but

---

[1] In §5 following Strabo makes sport of this "strange
mischance."

ἀφαιρεθῆναι πάλιν πάντα· φωραθῆναι γὰρ νενο-
σφισμένον πολλά. τὸ δ' ἀκρόπρῳρον προφέροντα
εἰς[1] τὸ ἐμπόριον, δεικνύναι τοῖς ναυκλήροις, γνῶναι
δὲ Γαδειριτῶν ὄν· τούτων γὰρ τοὺς μὲν ἐμπό-
ρους μεγάλα στέλλειν πλοῖα, τοὺς δὲ πένητας
μικρά, ἃ καλεῖν ἵππους, ἀπὸ τῶν ἐν ταῖς πρῴραις
ἐπισήμων· τούτοις[2] δὲ πλεῖν μέχρι τοῦ Λίξου
ποταμοῦ περὶ τὴν Μαυρουσίαν ἁλιευομένους·
ἀλλὰ τῶν δὴ ναυκλήρων τινὰς γνωρίσαι τὸ
ἀκρόπρῳρον ἑνὸς τῶν ἀπὸ τοῦ Λίξου ποταμοῦ
πορρώτερον πλευσάντων καὶ μὴ σωθέντων ὑπάρξαν.

Ἐκ δὲ τούτου συμβαλόντα τὸν Εὔδοξον ὡς
δυνατὸς εἴη ὁ περίπλους ὁ Λιβυκός, πορευθέντα
οἴκαδε τὴν οὐσίαν ἐνθέμενον πᾶσαν ἐξορμῆσαι.
καὶ πρῶτον μὲν εἰς Δικαιαρχείαν,[3] εἶτ' εἰς Μασσαλίαν ἐλθεῖν, καὶ τὴν ἑξῆς παραλίαν μέχρι
Γαδείρων, πανταχοῦ δὲ διακωδωνίζοντα ταῦτα καὶ
χρηματιζόμενον κατασκευάσασθαι πλοῖον μέγα
καὶ ἐφόλκια δύο λέμβοις λῃστρικοῖς ὅμοια, ἐμβιβάσαι τε[4] μουσικὰ παιδισκάρια καὶ ἰατροὺς καὶ
ἄλλους τεχνίτας, ἔπειτα πλεῖν ἐπὶ τὴν Ἰνδικὴν
μετέωρον ζεφύροις συνεχέσι. καμνόντων δὲ τῷ
πλῷ τῶν συνόντων, ἄκοντα ἐπουρίσαι πρὸς γῆν,
δεδοικότα τὰς πλημμυρίδας καὶ τὰς ἀμπώτεις.
καὶ δὴ καὶ συμβῆναι ὅπερ ἐδεδίει· καθίσαι γὰρ τὸ

---

[1] εἰς, Meineke, for ἐς.
[2] τούτοις, Casaubon, for τούτους; Siebenkees, Corais,
Meineke, following.
[3] Δικαιαρχείαν, Meineke, for Δικαιαρχίαν; C. Müller approving.
[4] ἐμβιβάσαι τε, Meineke, for ἐμβιβάσασθαι; Forbiger following, L. Kayser approving.

her son in her stead, he was again deprived of everything, for it was discovered that he had stolen much
property. But he brought the figure-head to the
market-place and showed it to the shipmasters, and
learned from them that it was a figure-head from
Gades; for he was told that whereas the merchants
of Gades fit out large ships, the poor men fit out small
ships which they call "horses" from the devices on
the prows of their ships, and that they sail with
these small ships on fishing voyages around the coast
of Maurusia as far as the river Lixus; but some of
the shipmasters, indeed, recognized the figure-head
as having belonged to one of the ships that had sailed
rather too far beyond the Lixus River and had not
returned home safely.

And from the above-mentioned fact Eudoxus
conjectured that the circumnavigation of Libya was
possible, went home,[1] placed all his property on a
ship, and put out to sea. First he put in at
Dicaearchia, then at Massilia, and then at the
successive points along the coast until he came to
Gades; and everywhere noisily proclaiming his
scheme and making money by trafficking, he built a
great ship and also two tow-boats like those used
by pirates; and he put music-girls on board, and
physicians, and other artisans, and finally set sail on
the high sea on the way to India, favoured by
constant western breezes. But since his companions
became tired of the voyage, he sailed with a fair wind
towards the land; though he did it against his will,
for he feared the ebb and flow of the tides. And,
indeed, what he feared actually came to pass: the

---

[1] To Cyzicus.

πλοῖον, ἡσυχῇ δέ, ὥστε μηδ' ἀθροῦν διαλυθῆναι,
ἀλλὰ φθῆναι τὰ φορτία σωθέντα εἰς γῆν καὶ τῶν
ξύλων τὰ πλεῖστα· ἐξ ὧν τρίτον λέμβον συμπη-
ξάμενον πεντηκοντόρῳ πάρισον πλεῖν, ἕως ἀνθρώποις συνέμιξε τὰ αὐτὰ ῥήματα φθεγγομένοις,
C 100 ἅπερ πρότερον ἀπεγέγραπτο.[1] ἅμα δὲ τοῦτό γε
γνῶναι, ὅτι τε οἱ ἐνταῦθα ἄνθρωποι ὁμοεθνεῖς εἶεν
τοῖς Αἰθίοψιν ἐκείνοις, καὶ ὅτι ὁμοροῖεν τῇ Βόγου
βασιλείᾳ.

Ἀφέντα δὴ τὸν ἐπὶ Ἰνδοὺς πλοῦν ἀναστρέφειν· ἐν
δὲ τῷ παράπλῳ νῆσον εὔυδρον καὶ εὔδενδρον ἐρήμην ἰδόντα σημειώσασθαι. σωθέντα δὲ εἰς τὴν Μαυρουσίαν, διαθέμενον τοὺς λέμβους πεζῇ κομισθῆναι
πρὸς τὸν Βόγον καὶ συμβουλεύειν αὐτῷ τὴν ναυστολίαν ἐπανελέσθαι ταύτην, ἰσχῦσαι δ' εἰς τἀναντία
τοὺς φίλους ὑποτείνοντας φόβον, μὴ συμβῇ τὴν
χώραν εὐεπιβούλευτον γενέσθαι, δειχθείσης παρ-
όδου τοῖς ἔξωθεν ἐπιστρατεύειν ἐθέλουσιν. ὡς
δ' ἐπύθετο λόγῳ μὲν πεμπόμενον ἑαυτὸν ἐπὶ τὴν
ἀναδειχθεῖσαν ναυστολίαν, ἔργῳ δ' ἐκτεθησόμενον
εἰς ἐρήμην τινὰ νῆσον, φυγεῖν εἰς τὴν Ῥωμαίων
ἐπικράτειαν, κἀκεῖθεν εἰς τὴν Ἰβηρίαν διᾶραι·
πάλιν δὲ κατασκευασάμενον στρογγύλον πλοῖον
καὶ μακρὸν πεντηκόντορον, ὥστε τῷ μὲν πελαγίζειν, τῷ δὲ πειρᾶσθαι τῆς γῆς, ἐνθέμενον γεωργικὰ
ἐργαλεῖα καὶ σπέρματα καὶ οἰκοδόμους ὁρμῆσαι
πρὸς τὸν αὐτὸν περίπλουν· διανοούμενον, εἰ

---

[1] ἀπεγέγραπτο, Corais, for ἀπογέγραπται; Meineke following.

ship ran aground,—though so gently that it was not broken up all at once, and they succeeded in bringing safely to land the cargo and also most of the ship's timbers; and from these timbers he constructed a third boat about as large as a ship of fifty oars; and he continued his voyage, until he came to people who spoke the same words that he had made a list of on the former occasion; and forthwith he learnt this, at least, that the men in that region belonged to the same nation as those other Ethiopians, and also that they were neighbours to the kingdom of Bogus.

Accordingly, he abandoned the voyage to India and turned back; and on the voyage along the coast, he espied and made note of an island that was well-watered and well-wooded but uninhabited. And when he reached Maurusia safely he disposed of his boats, travelled on foot to the court of Bogus, and advised him to take up this expedition on his own account; but the friends of Bogus prevailed to the contrary, inspiring in him the fear that Maurusia might in consequence be easily exposed to hostile intrigue if the way thither had once been pointed out to outsiders who wished to attack it. And when Eudoxus heard that he was being sent out, ostensibly, on the expedition as proposed by him, but in reality was going to be placed out on some desert island, he fled to the territory that was under Roman dominion, and thence crossed over to Iberia. And again he built a round ship and a long ship of fifty oars, his purpose being to keep to the open sea with his long ship and to explore the coast with the round ship. He put on board agricultural implements, seeds, and carpenters, and again set out with a view to the same circumnavigation; his intention being, in case the

βραδύνοιτο ὁ πλοῦς, ἐνδιαχειμάσαι τῇ προεσκεμμένῃ νήσῳ, καὶ σπείραντα καὶ ἀνελόμενον τοὺς καρποὺς τελέσαι τὸν ἐγνωσμένον ἐξ ἀρχῆς πλοῦν.

5. Ἐγὼ μὲν οὖν, φησί, μέχρι δεῦρο[1] τῆς περὶ τὸν Εὔδοξον ἱστορίας ἥκω· τί δ' ὕστερον συνέβη, τοὺς ἐκ Γαδείρων καὶ τῆς Ἰβηρίας εἰκὸς εἰδέναι. ἐκ πάντων δὴ τούτων φησὶ δείκνυσθαι, διότι ἡ οἰκουμένη κύκλῳ περιρρεῖται τῷ ὠκεανῷ·

οὐ γάρ μιν δεσμὸς περιβάλλεται ἠπείροιο,
ἀλλ' ἐς ἀπειρεσίην κέχυται· τό μιν οὔτι μιαίνει.

(Müller, *fr.* iii. 281).

θαυμαστὸς δὴ κατὰ πάντα ἐστὶν ὁ Ποσειδώνιος, τὸν μὲν τοῦ μάγου περίπλουν, ὃν Ἡρακλείδης εἶπεν, ἀμάρτυρον νομίσας, καὶ αὐτῶν τῶν ὑπὸ Νεκῶ πεμφθέντων, ὃν Ἡρόδοτος ἱστορεῖ, τὸ δὲ Βεργαῖον διήγημα τοῦτο ἐν πίστεως μέρει τιθείς, εἴθ' ὑπ' αὐτοῦ πεπλασμένον, εἴτ' ἄλλων πλασάντων πιστευθέν. τίς γὰρ ἡ πιθανότης πρῶτον μὲν τῆς κατὰ τὸν Ἰνδὸν περιπετείας· ὁ γὰρ Ἀράβιος κόλπος ποταμοῦ δίκην στενός ἐστι καὶ μακρὸς πεντακισχιλίους ἐπὶ τοῖς[2] μυρίοις που σταδίους μέχρι τοῦ στόματος, καὶ τούτου στενοῦ παντάπασιν ὄντος· οὐκ εἰκὸς δ' οὔτ' ἔξω που τὸν πλοῦν ἔχοντας εἰς τὸν κόλπον παρωσθῆναι τοὺς Ἰνδοὺς κατὰ πλάνην (τὰ γὰρ στενὰ ἀπὸ τοῦ στόματος δηλώσειν ἔμελλε τὴν πλάνην), οὔτ' εἰς τὸν κόλπον ἐπίτηδες καταχθεῖσιν ἔτι πλάνης ἦν πρόφασις καὶ ἀνέμων ἀστάτων.

---

[1] δεῦρο, Meineke inserts, after μέχρι ; C. Müller approving.
[2] τοῖς, Cascorbi inserts, before μυρίοις ; following the usage of Strabo. C. Frick cites.

voyage should be delayed, to spend the winter on the island he had previously observed, to sow the seed, reap the harvest therefrom, and then finish the voyage which he had decided upon at the outset.

5. "Now I," says Poseidonius, "have traced the story of Eudoxus to this point, but what happened afterwards probably the people of Gades and Iberia know." So from all these indications he says it is shown that the ocean flows in a circle round the inhabited world: "For him no fetters of continent encompass; but he pours forth his waters boundlessly, and nothing ever sullies their purity."[1] Now Poseidonius is a wonderful fellow in all this; for although he considers as unsupported by testimony the story of the voyage of the Magus, which Heracleides told, and of the voyage even of the emissaries of Neco, of which Herodotus gives an account, he puts down as real evidence this Bergaean[2] story, though he either invented it himself or accepted it from others who were its inventors. For, in the first place, what plausibility is there in the "strange mischance" which the Indian tells about? Why, the Arabian Gulf is like a river in its narrowness, and it is about fifteen thousand stadia long up to its mouth, which, in its turn, is narrow throughout its entire length; and so it is not likely that the Indians who were voyaging outside this gulf were pushed out of their course into it by mistake (for its narrowness at its mouth would have shown their mistake), nor, if they sailed into the gulf on purpose, did they any longer have the excuse that they mistook their course or encountered inconstant

[1] The authorship of these verses is unknown.
[2] See footnote, p. 172.

C 101 λιμῷ τε πῶς περιεῖδον ἅπαντας ἀπολλυμένους[1]
σφᾶς πλὴν ἑνός; περιγενόμενός τε πῶς ἱκανὸς ἦν
μόνος κατευθύνειν τὸ πλοῖον οὐ μικρὸν ὄν, τά γε
τηλικαῦτα πελάγη διαίρειν δυνάμενον; τίς δ᾽ ἡ
ὀξυμάθεια τῆς διαλέκτου, ἀφ᾽ ἧς ἱκανὸς ἦν πεῖσαι
τὸν βασιλέα, ὡς δυνάμενος τοῦ πλοῦ καθη-
γήσασθαι; τίς δ᾽ ἡ σπάνις τῷ Εὐεργέτῃ τῶν
τοιούτων καθηγεμόνων, ἤδη γνωριζομένης ὑπὸ
πολλῶν τῆς ταύτῃ θαλάττης; ὁ δὲ δὴ σπονδο-
φόρος καὶ θεωρὸς τῶν Κυζικηνῶν πῶς ἀφεὶς
τὴν πόλιν εἰς Ἰνδοὺς ἔπλει; πῶς δὲ ἐπιστεύθη
τηλικαύτην χρείαν; πῶς δ᾽ ἐπανιὼν ἀφαιρεθεὶς
πάντα παρὰ τὴν ἐλπίδα καὶ ἀτιμωθεὶς ἔτι μείζονα
ἐπιστεύθη παρασκευὴν δώρων; ἐπανιὼν δὲ καὶ
παρενεχθεὶς εἰς τὴν Αἰθιοπίαν, τίνος χάριν ἢ τὰς
διαλέκτους ἀπεγράφετο, ἢ τὸ ἀκρόπρωρον ἐπυνθά-
νετο τῆς ἁλιάδος πόθεν ἐκπέσοι; τὸ γὰρ μαθεῖν
ὅτι ἀπὸ δύσεως πλεόντων ἦν ναυάγιον, οὐδενὸς
ἔμελλεν ὑπάρξειν σημεῖον, ἐπεὶ καὶ αὐτὸς ἔμελλεν
ἀπὸ δύσεως πλεῖν κατὰ τὴν ἐπάνοδον. ἐλθὼν
δ᾽ οὖν εἰς Ἀλεξάνδρειαν, φωραθεὶς ὡς νενοσφι-
σμένος πολλά, πῶς οὐκ ἐκολάσθη, ἀλλὰ καὶ
περιῄει τοὺς ναυκλήρους διαπυνθανόμενος, δεικνὺς
ἅμα τὸ ἀκρόπρωρον; ὁ δὲ γνωρίσας οὐχὶ θαυμα-

1 ἀπολλυμένους, Xylander, for ἀπολομένους; all editors
except Kramer, following; C. Müller approving.

winds. And how can it be that they permitted all their number to die of starvation with the exception of one man? And if he survived, how could he single-handed have guided the ship, which was not a small one, since at all events it could sail over open seas of so great extent? And how strange his speedy mastery of the Greek language, which enabled him to convince the king that he was competent to act as pilot of the expedition? And how strange Euergetes' scarcity of competent pilots, since the sea in that region was already known by many men? And as for that peace herald and sacred ambassador of the people of Cyzicus, how came he to abandon his native city and go sailing to India? And how did he come to be entrusted with so great an office? And although on his return everything was taken away from him, contrary to his expectation, and he was in disgrace, how did he come to be entrusted with a still greater equipment of presents? And when he returned from this second voyage and was driven out of his course to Ethiopia, why did he write down those lists of words, and why did he enquire from what source the beak of that fishing-smack had been cast ashore? For the discovery that this bit of wreckage had belonged to men who sailed from the west could have signified nothing, since he himself was to sail from the west on his homeward voyage. And so, again, upon his return to Alexandria, when it was discovered that he had stolen much property, how is it that he was not punished, and that he even went about interviewing shipmasters, at the same time showing them the figure-head of the ship? And wasn't the man that recognized the figure-head a wonderful fellow? And

387

στός; ὁ δὲ πιστεύσας οὐ θαυμασιώτερος, καὶ
κατ' ἐλπίδα τοιαύτην ἐπανιὼν εἰς τὴν οἰκείαν,
καὶ μετοικισμὸν ἐκεῖθεν ποιησάμενος εἰς τὰ ἔξω
Στηλῶν; ἀλλ' οὐδ' ἐξῆν[1] ἄνευ προστάγματος
ἐξ Ἀλεξανδρείας ἀνάγεσθαι, καὶ ταῦτα νενο-
σφισμένῳ βασιλικὰ χρήματα. οὐδέ γε λαθεῖν
ἐκπλεύσαντα ἐνεδέχετο, τοσαύτῃ φρουρᾷ κε-
κλεισμένου τοῦ λιμένος καὶ τῶν ἄλλων ἐξόδων,
ὅσην καὶ νῦν ἔτι διαμένουσαν ἔγνωμεν ἡμεῖς
ἐπιδημοῦντες τῇ Ἀλεξανδρείᾳ πολὺν χρόνον,
καίτοι τὰ νῦν πολὺ ἀνεῖται, Ῥωμαίων ἐχόντων·
αἱ βασιλικαὶ δὲ φρουραὶ πολὺ ἦσαν πικρότεραι.
ἐπειδὴ δὲ καὶ ἀπῆρεν εἰς τὰ Γάδειρα καὶ ναυπηγη-
σάμενος ἔπλει βασιλικῶς, καὶ[2] διαλυθέντος αὐτῷ
τοῦ πλοίου, πῶς μὲν ἐναυπηγήσατο τρίτον λέμβον
ἐν τῇ ἐρήμῳ; πῶς δὲ πλέων πάλιν καὶ εὑρὼν τοὺς
ἑσπερίους Αἰθίοπας τοῖς ἑῴοις ὁμογλώττους οὐκ
ὠρέχθη διανύσαι τὸν ἑξῆς πλοῦν, οὕτω χαῦνος
ὢν πρὸς τὸ φιλέκδημον, μικρὸν ἔχειν ἐλπίσας
λοιπὸν τὸ ἄγνωστον, ἀλλ' ἀφεὶς ταῦτα τῆς διὰ
Βόγου ναυστολίας ἐπεθύμησε; πῶς δ' ἔγνω τὴν
C 102 λάθρα κατ' αὐτοῦ συνισταμένην ἐπιβουλήν; τί
δὲ τοῦτ' ἦν τῷ Βόγῳ πλεονέκτημα, ὁ τἀνθρώπου
ἀφανισμός, ἐξὸν ἄλλως ἀποπέμψασθαι; γνοὺς

---

[1] ἐξῆν, Cobet, for ἐξὸν ἦν.
[2] καί, is retained against Corais and Meineke, who delete it

wasn't the man that believed him a still more
wonderful fellow—the man who on the strength of a
hope of that sort returned to his home land, and then
changed his home to the regions beyond the Pillars?
But it would not even have been permitted him to put
to sea from Alexandria without a passport, least of all
after he had stolen property belonging to the king.
Neither could he have sailed out of the harbour
secretly, since not only the harbour, but also all the
other ways of issue from the city had always been
kept closed under just as strong guard as I know is
still kept up to this day (for I have lived a long time
in Alexandria)—though at the present time, under
Roman control, the watch is considerably relaxed:
but under the kings, the guards were much more
strict. And, again, when Eudoxus had sailed away
to Gades, and in royal style had built himself ships
and continued on his voyage, after his vessel had been
wrecked, how could he have built a third boat in the
desert? And how is it, when once more he put out
to sea and found that those western Ethiopians spoke
the same language as the eastern Ethiopians, that he
was not eager to accomplish the rest of his voyage
(inasmuch as he was so foolish in his eagerness for
travels abroad, and since he had a good hope that
the unexplored remainder of his voyage was but
small)—but instead gave up all this and conceived a
longing for the expedition that was to be carried out
through the aid of Bogus? And how did he come to
learn about the plot that was secretly framed against
him? And what advantage could this have been to
Bogus—I mean his causing the disappearance of the
man when he might have dismissed him in other
ways? But even if the man learned about the plot,

δὲ τὴν ἐπιβουλὴν πῶς ἔφθη φυγὼν εἰς ἀσφαλεῖς
τόπους; ἕκαστον γὰρ τῶν τοιούτων οὐκ ἀδύνατον
μέν, ἀλλὰ χαλεπὸν καὶ σπανίως γινόμενον μετὰ
τύχης τινός· τῷ δ' εὐτυχεῖν ἀεὶ συνέβαινεν, εἰς
κινδύνους καθισταμένῳ συνεχεῖς. πῶς δ' οὐκ
ἔδεισεν ἀποδρὰς τὸν Βόγον πλεῖν πάλιν παρὰ
τὴν Λιβύην σὺν παρασκευῇ δυναμένῃ συνοικίσαι
νῆσον;

Οὐ πολὺ οὖν ἀπολείπεται ταῦτα τῶν Πυθέου
καὶ Εὐημέρου καὶ Ἀντιφάνους ψευσμάτων. ἀλλ'
ἐκείνοις μὲν συγγνώμη, τοῦτ' αὐτὸ ἐπιτηδεύουσιν,
ὥσπερ τοῖς θαυματοποιοῖς· τῷ δ' ἀποδεικτικῷ καὶ
φιλοσόφῳ, σχεδὸν δέ τι καὶ περὶ πρωτείων ἀγωνι-
ζομένῳ, τίς ἂν συγγνοίη; ταῦτα μὲν οὖν οὐκ εὖ.

6. Τὸ δὲ ἐξαίρεσθαι τὴν γῆν ποτε καὶ ἱζήματα
λαμβάνειν καὶ μεταβολὰς τὰς ἐκ τῶν σεισμῶν καὶ
τῶν ἄλλων τῶν παραπλησίων, ὅσα διηριθμησά-
μεθα καὶ ἡμεῖς, ὀρθῶς κεῖται παρ' αὐτῷ· πρὸς ὃ
καὶ τὸ τοῦ Πλάτωνος εὖ παρατίθησιν, ὅτι ἐνδέχεται καὶ μὴ πλάσμα εἶναι τὸ περὶ τῆς νήσου τῆς
Ἀτλαντίδος, περὶ ἧς ἐκεῖνος ἱστορῆσαι Σόλωνά
φησι πεπυσμένον παρὰ τῶν Αἰγυπτίων ἱερέων,
ὡς ὑπάρχουσά ποτε ἀφανισθείη, τὸ μέγεθος οὐκ
ἐλάττων ἠπείρου· καὶ τοῦτο οἴεται βέλτιον εἶναι

---

[1] The only direct reference extant in Plato to the truth or
falsity of the story is made by Socrates to Critias : " And
what other narrative " (but the Atlantis story) " has the
very great advantage of being a fact and not a fiction ? "
(*Timaeus* 26 E.)

[2] In Plato, one of the Egyptian priests is credited with

how could he have made his escape to places of
safety? For, although there is nothing impossible
in any escapes of that sort, yet every one of them is
difficult and rarely made even with a streak of luck;
but Eudoxus is always attended by good luck, although
he is placed in jeopardies one after another. And,
again, after he had escaped from Bogus, why was he
not afraid to sail once more along the coast of Libya
when he had an outfit large enough to colonize an
island?

Now, really, all this does not fall far short of
the fabrications of Pytheas, Euhemerus and Antiphanes. Those men, however, we can pardon for their
fabrications—since they follow precisely this as their
business—just as we pardon jugglers; but who could
pardon Poseidonius, master of demonstration and
philosopher, whom we may almost call the claimant
for first honours. So much, at least, is not well
done by Poseidonius.

6. On the other hand, he correctly sets down in
his work the fact that the earth sometimes rises and
undergoes settling processes, and undergoes changes
that result from earthquakes and the other similar
agencies, all of which I too have enumerated above.
And on this point he does well to cite the statement
of Plato that it is possible that the story about the
island of Atlantis is not a fiction.[1] Concerning
Atlantis Plato relates that Solon, after having made
inquiry of the Egyptian priests, reported that Atlantis
did once exist, but disappeared—an island no smaller
in size than a continent[2]; and Poseidonius thinks

saying to Solon that Atlantis was larger than Libya and Asia
put together, and that, as a result of violent earthquakes
and floods, it sank beneath the sea in a single day and night
(see *Timaeus* 24-25, and *Critias* 108 E, 113 C).

λέγειν ἢ διότι ὁ πλάσας αὐτὴν ἠφάνισεν, ὡς ὁ
ποιητὴς τὸ τῶν Ἀχαιῶν τεῖχος. εἰκάζει δὲ καὶ
τὴν τῶν Κίμβρων καὶ τῶν συγγενῶν ἐξανάστασιν
ἐκ τῆς οἰκείας γενέσθαι κατὰ θαλάττης ἔφοδον,
ἀθρόαν συμβᾶσαν. ὑπονοεῖ δὲ τὸ τῆς οἰκουμένης μῆκος ἑπτά που μυριάδων σταδίων ὑπάρχον
ἥμισυ εἶναι τοῦ ὅλου κύκλου, καθ' ὃν εἴληπται,
ὥστε, φησίν, ἀπὸ τῆς δύσεως εὐθυπλοῶν[1] ἐν
τοσαύταις μυριάσιν ἔλθοις[2] ἂν εἰς Ἰνδούς.

7. Ἐπιχειρήσας δὲ αἰτιᾶσθαι τοὺς οὕτω τὰς
ἠπείρους διορίσαντας, ἀλλὰ μὴ παραλλήλοις τισὶ
τῷ ἰσημερινῷ, δι' ὧν ἔμελλον ἐξαλλάξεις δείκνυσθαι ζῴων τε καὶ φυτῶν καὶ ἀέρων, τῶν μὲν τῇ
κατεψυγμένῃ συναπτόντων, τῶν δὲ τῇ διακεκαυμένῃ, ὥστε οἱονεὶ ζώνας εἶναι τὰς ἠπείρους,
ἀνασκευάζει πάλιν καὶ ἐν ἀναλύσει δίκης γίνεται,
ἐπαινῶν πάλιν τὴν οὖσαν διαίρεσιν, θετικὴν
ποιούμενος τὴν ζήτησιν πρὸς οὐδὲν χρήσιμον.[3] αἱ
γὰρ τοιαῦται διατάξεις οὐκ ἐκ προνοίας γίνονται,
καθάπερ οὐδὲ αἱ κατὰ τὰ ἔθνη διαφοραί, οὐδὲ
C 103 αἱ διάλεκτοι, ἀλλὰ κατὰ ἐπίπτωσιν καὶ συν-
τυχίαν· καὶ τέχναι δὲ[4] καὶ δυνάμεις καὶ ἐπιτη-

---

[1] εὐθυπλοῶν, Cobet, for Εὔρῳ πλέων ; Bernadakis, A. Vogel,
approving.
[2] ἔλθοις, Corais, for ἔλθοι ; Cobet independently ; Berna
dakis, C. Müller, A. Vogel, approving.
[3] χρήσιμον, Cobet, for χρησίμως.
[4] δέ, Corais, for τε ; Meineke following.

that it is better to put the matter in that way than to say of Atlantis: "Its inventor caused it to disappear, just as did the Poet the wall of the Achaeans."[1] And Poseidonius also conjectures that the migration of the Cimbrians and their kinsfolk from their native country occurred as the result of an inundation of the sea that came on all of a sudden. And he suspects that the length of the inhabited world, being about seventy thousand stadia, is half of the entire circle on which it has been taken, so that, says he, if you sail from the west in a straight course you will reach India within the seventy thousand stadia.

7. Then, after an attempt to find fault with those who divided the inhabited world into continents in the way they did,[2] instead of by certain circles parallel to the equator (through means of which they could have indicated variations in animals, plants, and climates, because some of these belong peculiarly to the frigid zone and others to the torrid zone), so that the continents would be practically zones, Poseidonius again revises his own plea and withdraws his indictment, in that he again approves of the prevailing division into three continents, and thus he makes the question a mere matter of argument with no useful end in view. For such a distribution of animals, plants, and climates as exists is not the result of design—just as the differences of race, or of language, are not, either—but rather of accident and chance. And again, as regards the various arts and faculties and institutions of mankind, most of them,

[1] That is, Solon avoided the historical consequences of his fiction by sinking Atlantis, just as Homer did by making Poseidon and Apollo sweep away with a flood the wall built by the Achaeans in front of their ships (see *Iliad* 7. 433, 441, and 12. 1–33). [2] See pp. 119 and 129.

δεύσεις, ἀρξάντων τινῶν, κρατοῦσιν αἱ πλείους
ἐν ὁποιῳοῦν· κλίματι ἔστι δέ τι καὶ παρὰ τὰ
κλίματα, ὥστε τὰ μὲν φύσει ἐστὶν ἐπιχώριά
τισι, τὰ δ' ἔθει καὶ ἀσκήσει. οὐ γὰρ φύσει
Ἀθηναῖοι μὲν φιλόλογοι, Λακεδαιμόνιοι δ' οὔ,
καὶ οἱ ἔτι ἐγγυτέρω Θηβαῖοι, ἀλλὰ μᾶλλον ἔθει·
οὕτως οὐδὲ Βαβυλώνιοι φιλόσοφοι φύσει καὶ
Αἰγύπτιοι, ἀλλ' ἀσκήσει καὶ ἔθει· καὶ ἵππων τε
καὶ βοῶν ἀρετὰς καὶ ἄλλων ζῴων, οὐ τόποι μόνον,
ἀλλὰ καὶ ἀσκήσεις ποιοῦσιν· ὁ δὲ συγχεῖ ταῦτα.
ἐπαινῶν δὲ τὴν τοιαύτην διαίρεσιν τῶν ἠπείρων,
οἵα νῦν ἐστι, παραδείγματι χρῆται τῷ τοὺς Ἰνδοὺς
τῶν Αἰθιόπων διαφέρειν τῶν ἐν τῇ Λιβύῃ·
εὐερνεστέρους γὰρ εἶναι καὶ ἧττον ἕψεσθαι τῇ
ξηρασίᾳ τοῦ περιέχοντος· διὸ καὶ Ὅμηρον πάντας
λέγοντα Αἰθίοπας δίχα διελεῖν,

οἱ μὲν δυσομένου Ὑπερίονος, οἱ δ' ἀνιόντος·

(Od. 1. 24)

Κράτητα δ',[1] εἰσάγοντα τὴν ἑτέραν οἰκουμένην,
ἣν οὐκ οἶδεν Ὅμηρος, δουλεύειν ὑποθέσει· καὶ ἔδει,
φησί, μεταγράφειν οὕτως.

ἠμὲν ἀπερχομένου Ὑπερίονος,

οἷον ἀπὸ τοῦ μεσημβρινοῦ περικλίνοντος.

8. Πρῶτον μὲν οὖν οἱ πρὸς Αἰγύπτῳ Αἰθίοπες

---

[1] Κράτητα δέ, Casaubon inserts; Corais, Groskurd, Meineke,
Forbiger, Tardieu, following; Kramer, C. Müller, approving.

when once men have made a beginning, flourish in any latitude whatsoever and in certain instances even in spite of the latitude ; so that some local characteristics of a people come by nature, others by training and habit. For instance, it was not by nature that the Athenians were fond of letters, whereas the Lacedaemonians, and also the Thebans, who are still closer to the Athenians, were not so ; but rather by habit. So, also, the Babylonians and the Egyptians are philosophers, not by nature, but by training and habit. And further, the excellent qualities of horses, cattle, and other animals, are the result, not merely of locality, but of training also. But Poseidonius confounds all this. And when he approves of such a division into three continents as is now accepted, he uses as an illustration the fact that the Indians differ from the Ethiopians of Libya, for the Indians are better developed physically and less parched by the dryness of the atmosphere. And, says he, that is the reason why Homer, in speaking of the Ethopians as a whole, divides them into two groups, " some where Hyperion sets and some where he rises." But, says Poseidonius, Crates, in introducing into the discussion the question of a second inhabited world, about which Homer knows nothing, is a slave to a hypothesis,[1] and, says Poseidonius, the passage in Homer should have been emended to read : " both where Hyperion departs," meaning where he declines from the meridian.

8. Now, in the first place, the Ethiopians that border on Egypt are themselves, also, divided into

---

[1] That is, his hypothesis that one division of the Ethiopians lived south of the equator, on the other side of Oceanus (see pp. 117 ff.).

καὶ αὐτοὶ δίχα διαιροῦνται· οἱ μὲν γὰρ ἐν τῇ
Ἀσίᾳ εἰσίν, οἱ δ' ἐν τῇ Λιβύῃ, οὐδὲν διαφέροντες
ἀλλήλων. ἔπειθ' Ὅμηρος οὐ διὰ τοῦτο διαιρεῖ
τοὺς Αἰθίοπας,[1] ὅτι τοὺς Ἰνδοὺς ᾔδει τοιούτους
τινὰς τοῖς σώμασιν (οὐδὲ γὰρ ἀρχὴν εἰδέναι τοὺς
Ἰνδοὺς εἰκὸς Ὅμηρον, ὅπου γε οὐδ' ὁ Εὐεργέτης
κατὰ τὸν Εὐδόξειον μῦθον ᾔδει τὰ κατὰ τὴν
Ἰνδικήν, οὐδὲ τὸν πλοῦν τὸν ἐπ' αὐτήν), ἀλλὰ
μᾶλλον κατὰ τὴν λεχθεῖσαν ὑφ' ἡμῶν πρότερον
διαίρεσιν. ἐκεῖ δὲ καὶ περὶ τῆς γραφῆς τῆς
Κρατητείου διῃτήσαμεν, ὅτι οὐδὲν διαφέρει, οὕτως
ἢ ἐκείνως γράφειν· ὁ δὲ τοῦτο μὲν διαφέρειν φησί,
κρεῖττον δ' οὕτως εἶναι μεταθεῖναι "ἠμὲν ἀπερχομένου." τί οὖν διαφέρει τοῦτο τοῦ " ἠμὲν δυσομένου"; πᾶν γὰρ τὸ τμῆμα τὸ ἀπὸ τοῦ μεσημβρινοῦ ἐπὶ δύσιν δύσις καλεῖται, καθάπερ καὶ τὸ
τοῦ ὁρίζοντος ἡμικύκλιον· ὅπερ καὶ Ἄρατος ἐπισημαίνεται,

ᾗχί περ ἄκραι
μίσγονται δύσιές τε καὶ ἀντολαὶ ἀλλήλησιν.
(Arat. *Phaen.* 61)

εἰ δ' ἐπὶ τῆς Κρατητείου γραφῆς οὕτω βέλτιον,
φήσει τις καὶ ἐπὶ τῆς Ἀρισταρχείου δεῖν.

Τοσαῦτα καὶ πρὸς Ποσειδώνιον· πολλὰ γὰρ καὶ
C 104 ἐν τοῖς καθ' ἕκαστα τυγχάνει τῆς προσηκούσης
διαίτης, ὅσα γεωγραφικά· ὅσα δὲ φυσικώτερα,
ἐπισκεπτέον ἐν ἄλλοις, ἢ οὐδὲ φροντιστέον· πολὺ

[1] ἤ, Corais deletes, before ὅτι ; Meineke, Tardieu, following ; C. Müller approving.

two groups; for some of them live in Asia, others in
Libya,[1] though they differ in no respect from each
other. And, in the second place, Homer divides
the Ethiopians into two groups, not for this reason,
namely, because he knew that the Indians were
physically similar to the Ethiopians (for Homer
probably did not know of the Indians at all, in view
of the fact that even Euergetes himself, according
to that story of Eudoxus, knew nothing about India,
nor the voyage that leads thither), but rather on the
basis of the division of which I have spoken above.[2]
And in speaking on that subject I also expressed my
opinion in regard to the reading proposed by Crates,
namely, that it makes no difference whether we read
the passage one way or the other[3]; but Poseidonius
says it does make a difference, and that it is better
to emend the passage to read "both where Hyperion
departs." Now wherein does this differ from "both
where Hyperion sets"? For the whole segment of
the circle from the meridian to the setting is called
"the setting,"[4] just as the semi-circle of the horizon
is so called. This is what Aratus means when he says:
"There where the extremities of the west and of
the east join with each other." And if the passage
is better as Crates reads it, then one may say that it
must also be better as Aristarchus reads it.

So much for Poseidonius. For in my detailed
discussions many of his views will meet with fitting
criticism, so far as they relate to geography; but so
far as they relate to physics, I must inspect them
elsewhere or else not consider them at all. For in

[1] See pp. 119 ff. and 129.
[2] See p. 129.   [3] See p. 117.
[4] That is, the west.

γάρ ἐστι τὸ αἰτιολογικὸν παρὰ αὐτῷ καὶ τὸ
Ἀριστοτελίζον, ὅπερ ἐκκλίνουσιν οἱ ἡμέτεροι διὰ
τὴν ἐπίκρυψιν τῶν αἰτιῶν.

IV

1. Πολύβιος δὲ τὴν Εὐρώπην χωρογραφῶν τοὺς
μὲν ἀρχαίους ἐᾶν φησι, τοὺς δ᾽ ἐκείνους ἐλέγχον-
τας ἐξετάζειν Δικαίαρχόν τε καὶ Ἐρατοσθένη,
τὸν τελευταῖον πραγματευσάμενον περὶ γεωγραφίας, καὶ Πυθέαν, ὑφ᾽ οὗ παρακρουσθῆναι πολλούς, ὅλην μὲν τὴν Βρεττανικὴν τὴν¹ ἐμβατὸν
ἐπελθεῖν φάσκοντος, τὴν δὲ περίμετρον πλειόνων
ἢ τεττάρων μυριάδων ἀποδόντος τῆς νήσου, προσ-
ιστορήσαντος δὲ καὶ τὰ περὶ τῆς Θούλης καὶ τῶν
τόπων ἐκείνων ἐν οἷς οὔτε γῆ καθ᾽ αὑτὴν ὑπῆρχεν
ἔτι οὔτε θάλαττα οὔτ᾽ ἀήρ, ἀλλὰ σύγκριμά τι ἐκ
τούτων πλεύμονι θαλαττίῳ ἐοικός, ἐν ᾧ φησι τὴν
γῆν καὶ τὴν θάλατταν αἰωρεῖσθαι καὶ τὰ σύμ-
παντα, καὶ τοῦτον ὡς ἂν δεσμὸν εἶναι τῶν ὅλων,
μήτε πορευτὸν μήτε πλωτὸν ὑπάρχοντα· τὸ μὲν
οὖν τῷ πλεύμονι ἐοικὸς αὐτὸς ἑωρακέναι, τἆλλα
δὲ λέγειν ἐξ ἀκοῆς. ταῦτα μὲν τὰ τοῦ Πυθέου,
καὶ διότι ἐπανελθὼν ἐνθένδε πᾶσαν ἐπέλθοι τὴν
παρωκεανῖτιν τῆς Εὐρώπης ἀπὸ Γαδείρων ἕως
Τανάϊδος.

2. Φησὶ δ᾽ οὖν ὁ Πολύβιος ἄπιστον καὶ αὐτὸ
τοῦτο, πῶς ἰδιώτῃ ἀνθρώπῳ καὶ πένητι τὰ τοσ-

---

¹ τήν, A. Jacob inserts, before ἐμβατόν.

Poseidonius there is much inquiry into causes and much imitating of Aristotle—precisely what our school[1] avoids, on account of the obscurity of the causes.

IV

1. POLYBIUS, in his account of the geography of Europe, says he passes over the ancient geographers but examines the men who criticise them, namely, Dicaearchus, and Eratosthenes, who has written the most recent treatise on Geography; and Pytheas, by whom many have been misled; for after asserting that he travelled over the whole of Britain that was accessible Pytheas reported that the coast-line of the island was more than forty thousand stadia, and added his story about Thule and about those regions in which there was no longer either land properly so-called, or sea, or air, but a kind of substance concreted from all these elements, resembling a sea-lungs[2]—a thing in which, he says, the earth, the sea, and all the elements are held in suspension; and this is a sort of bond to hold all together, which you can neither walk nor sail upon. Now, as for this thing that resembles the sea-lungs, he says that he saw it himself, but that all the rest he tells from hearsay. That, then, is the narrative of Pytheas, and to it he adds that on his return from those regions he visited the whole coast-line of Europe from Gades to the Tanaïs.

2. Now Polybius says that, in the first place, it is incredible that a private individual—and a poor

[1] That is, the Stoic school of philosophy. Compare the same Greek phrase on p. 55; and " our Zeno," p. 151.

[2] An acaleph of the ctenophora.

αὖτα διαστήματα πλωτὰ καὶ πορευτὰ γένοιτο·
τὸν δ' Ἐρατοσθένη διαπορήσαντα, εἰ χρὴ πιστεύειν τούτοις, ὅμως περί τε τῆς Βρεττανικῆς
πεπιστευκέναι καὶ τῶν κατὰ Γάδειρα καὶ τὴν
Ἰβηρίαν. πολὺ δέ φησι βέλτιον τῷ Μεσσηνίῳ
πιστεύειν ἢ τούτῳ. ὁ μέντοι γε εἰς μίαν χώραν
τὴν Παγχαίαν λέγει πλεῦσαι· ὁ δὲ καὶ μέχρι
τῶν τοῦ κόσμου περάτων κατωπτευκέναι τὴν
προσάρκτιον τῆς Εὐρώπης πᾶσαν, ἣν οὐδ' ἂν τῷ
Ἑρμῇ πιστεύσαι τις λέγοντι. Ἐρατοσθένη δὲ
τὸν μὲν Εὐήμερον Βεργαῖον καλεῖν, Πυθέᾳ δε
πιστεύειν, καὶ ταῦτα μηδὲ Δικαιάρχου πιστεύ-
σαντος. τὸ μὲν οὖν μηδὲ Δικαιάρχου πιστεύ-
σαντος, γελοῖον· ὥσπερ ἐκείνῳ κανόνι χρήσασθαι
προσῆκον, καθ' οὗ τοσούτους ἐλέγχους αὐτὸς
προφέρεται· Ἐρατοσθένους δὲ εἴρηται ἡ περὶ τὰ
ἑσπέρια καὶ τὰ ἀρκτικὰ τῆς Εὐρώπης ἄγνοια.
ἀλλ' ἐκείνῳ μὲν καὶ Δικαιάρχῳ συγγνώμη, τοῖς
μὴ κατιδοῦσι τοὺς τόπους ἐκείνους· Πολυβίῳ δὲ
καὶ Ποσειδωνίῳ τίς ἂν συγγνοίη; ἀλλὰ μὴν
Πολύβιός γέ ἐστιν ὁ λαοδογματικὰς καλῶν ἀποφάσεις, ἃς ποιοῦνται περὶ τῶν ἐν τούτοις τοῖς
τόποις διαστημάτων καὶ ἐν ἄλλοις πολλοῖς, ἀλλ'
C 105 οὐδ' ἐν οἷς ἐκείνους ἐλέγχει καθαρεύων. τοῦ γοῦν
Δικαιάρχου μυρίους μὲν εἰπόντος τοὺς ἐπὶ Στήλας

---

[1] That is, Hermes in his capacity as god of travel.

man too—could have travelled such distances by sea
and by land; and that, though Eratosthenes was
wholly at a loss whether he should believe these
stories, nevertheless he has believed Pytheas' account of Britain, and of the regions about Gades,
and of Iberia; but he says it is far better to believe
Euhemerus, the Messenian, than Pytheas. Euhemerus, at all events, asserts that he sailed only to
one country, Panchaea, whereas Pytheas asserts that
he explored in person the whole northern region of
Europe as far as the ends of the world—an assertion
which no man would believe, not even if Hermes [1]
made it. And as for Eratosthenes—adds Poseidonius
—though he calls Euhemerus a Bergaean,[2] he believes Pytheas, and that, too, though not even
Dicaearchus believed him. Now that last remark,
"though not even Dicaearchus believed him," is
ridiculous; as if it were fitting for Eratosthenes to
use as a standard the man against whom he himself
directs so many criticisms. And I have already
stated that Eratosthenes was ignorant concerning
the western and northern parts of Europe. But
while we must pardon Eratosthenes and Dicaearchus, because they had not seen those regions with
their own eyes, yet who could pardon Polybius and
Poseidonius? Nay, it is precisely Polybius who
characterises as "popular notions" the statements
made by Eratosthenes and Dicaearchus in regard to
the distances in those regions and many other
regions, though he does not keep himself free from
the error even where he criticises them. At any
rate, when Dicaearchus estimates the distance from

[2] That is, like Antiphanes, the notorious romancer of
Berge, in Thrace; see p. 173, and footnote.

ἀπὸ τῆς Πελοποννήσου σταδίους, πλείους δὲ τούτων τοὺς ἐπὶ τὸν Ἀδρίαν μέχρι τοῦ μυχοῦ, τοῦ
δ' ἐπὶ Στήλας τὸ μέχρι τοῦ Πορθμοῦ τρισχιλίους
ἀποδόντος, ὡς γίνεσθαι τὸ λοιπὸν ἑπτακισχιλίους
τὸ ἀπὸ Πορθμοῦ μέχρι Στηλῶν· τοὺς μὲν τρισχιλίους ἐᾶν φησιν, εἴτ' εὖ λαμβάνονται εἴτε μή,
τοὺς δ' ἑπτακισχιλίους οὐδετέρως, οὐδὲ τὴν παραλίαν ἐκμετροῦντι, οὔτε τὴν διὰ μέσου τοῦ πελάγους. τὴν μὲν γὰρ παραλίαν ἐοικέναι μάλιστ'
ἀμβλείᾳ γωνίᾳ, βεβηκυίᾳ ἐπί τε τοῦ Πορθμοῦ
καὶ τῶν Στηλῶν, κορυφὴν δ' ἐχούσῃ Νάρβωνα·
ὥστε συνίστασθαι τρίγωνον βάσιν ἔχον τὴν διὰ
τοῦ πελάγους εὐθεῖαν, πλευρὰς δὲ τὰς τὴν γωνίαν
ποιούσας τὴν λεχθεῖσαν, ὧν ἡ μὲν ἀπὸ τοῦ
Πορθμοῦ μέχρι Νάρβωνος μυρίων ἐστὶ καὶ πλειόνων ἢ διακοσίων ἐπὶ τοῖς χιλίοις, ἡ δὲ λοιπὴ
μικρῷ[1] ἐλαττόνων ἢ ὀκτακισχιλίων· καὶ μὴν
πλεῖστον μὲν διάστημα ἀπὸ τῆς Εὐρώπης ἐπὶ τὴν
Λιβύην ὁμολογεῖσθαι κατὰ τὸ Τυρρηνικὸν πέλαγος σταδίων οὐ πλειόνων ἢ τρισχιλίων, κατὰ τὸ
Σαρδόνιον[2] δὲ λαμβάνειν συναγωγήν. ἀλλ' ἔστω,
φησί, καὶ ἐκεῖνο τρισχιλίων, προειλήφθω δ' ἐπὶ
τούτοις δισχιλίων σταδίων τὸ τοῦ κόλπου βάθος
τοῦ κατὰ Νάρβωνα, ὡς ἂν κάθετος ἀπὸ τῆς κορυφῆς ἐπὶ τὴν βάσιν τοῦ ἀμβλυγωνίου· δῆλον οὖν,

---

[1] λοιπόν, Corais suspects, after μικρῷ; Groskurd deletes;
Meineke, Forbiger, Tardieu, following; C. Müller approving.
[2] Σαρδόνιον, Meineke, for Σαρδώνιον.

---

[1] That is, the altitude of the triangle drawn from the
vertex at Narbo to the base line; thus an allowance of

the Peloponnesus to the Pillars at ten thousand
stadia, and from the Peloponnesus to the recess of
the Adriatic Sea at more than this, and when, of
the distance to the Pillars, he reckons the part up
to the Strait of Sicily at three thousand stadia, so
that the remaining distance—the part from the
Strait to the Pillars—becomes seven thousand stadia,
Polybius says that he will let pass the question
whether the estimate of three thousand is correctly
taken or not, but, as for the seven thousand stadia, he
cannot let the estimate pass from either of two
points of view, namely, whether you take the
measure of the coast-line or of the line drawn
through the middle of the open sea. For, says he,
the coast-line is very nearly like an obtuse angle,
whose sides run respectively to the Strait and to
the Pillars, and with Narbo as vertex; hence a triangle is formed with a base that runs straight through
the open sea and with sides that form the said angle,
of which sides the one from the Strait to Narbo
measures more than eleven thousand two hundred
stadia, the other a little less than eight thousand
stadia; and, besides, it is agreed that the maximum
distance from Europe to Libya across the Tyrrhenian
Sea is not more than three thousand stadia, whereas
the distance is reduced if measured across the
Sardinian Sea. However, let it be granted, says
Polybius, that the latter distance is also three
thousand stadia, but let it be further assumed as
a prior condition that the depth of the gulf opposite
Narbo is two thousand stadia, the depth being, as it
were, a perpendicular let fall from the vertex upon
the base of the obtuse-angled triangle [1]; then, says

1,000 stadia is made for the remaining distance to Libya,
measured on the produced altitude.

φησίν, ἐκ τῆς παιδικῆς μετρήσεως, ὅτι ἡ σύμπασα
παραλία ἡ ἀπὸ τοῦ Πορθμοῦ ἐπὶ Στήλας ἔγγιστα
ὑπερέχει τῆς διὰ τοῦ πελάγους εὐθείας πεντακοσίοις σταδίοις. προστεθέντων δὲ τῶν ἀπὸ τῆς
Πελοποννήσου ἐπὶ τὸν Πορθμὸν τρισχιλίων, οἱ
σύμπαντες ἔσονται στάδιοι, αὐτοὶ οἱ ἐπ᾽ εὐθείας,
πλείους ἢ διπλάσιοι ὧν Δικαίαρχος εἶπε· πλείους
δὲ τούτων τοὺς ἐπὶ τὸν μυχὸν τὸν Ἀδριατικὸν
δεήσει, φησί, τιθέναι κατ᾽ ἐκεῖνον.

3. Ἀλλ᾽ ὦ φίλε Πολύβιε, φαίη τις ἄν, ὥσπερ
τούτου τοῦ ψεύσματος ἐναργῆ παρίστησι τὸν
ἔλεγχον ἡ πεῖρα ἐξ αὐτῶν, ὧν εἴρηκας αὐτός,
εἰς μὲν Λευκάδα ἐκ Πελοποννήσου ἑπτακοσίους,
ἐντεῦθεν δὲ τοὺς ἴσους εἰς Κόρκυραν, καὶ πάλιν
ἐντεῦθεν εἰς τὰ Κεραύνια τοὺς ἴσους, καὶ ἐν
δεξιᾷ εἰς τὴν Ἰαπυδίαν,[1] ἀπὸ δὲ τῶν Κεραυ-
νίων, τὴν Ἰλλυρικὴν παραλίαν σταδίων ἑξακισχιλίων ἑκατὸν πεντήκοντα· οὕτως κἀκεῖνα
ψεύσματά ἐστιν ἀμφότερα, καὶ ὁ Δικαίαρχος
εἶπε, τὸ ἀπὸ Πορθμοῦ ἐπὶ Στήλας εἶναι σταδίων
ἑπτακισχιλίων, καὶ ὃ σὺ δοκεῖς ἀποδεῖξαι. ὁμολογοῦσι γὰρ οἱ πλεῖστοι λέγοντες τὸ διὰ πελάγους
μυρίων εἶναι καὶ δισχιλίων, συμφωνεῖ δὲ τοῦτο καὶ

[1] Ἰαπυδίαν, Jones, for Ἰαπυγίαν; Müller-Dübner suggest
Ἰαποδίαν; see Groskurd's critical note on 6. 3. 10 (vol. i.
p. 502).

---

[1] By computation the actual result is 436 stadia.
[2] By computation the actual result is 21.764 stadia.
[3] That is, more than 21,764 stadia; for Dicaearchus had
reckoned the recess of the Adriatic to be farther away from
the Peloponnesus than the Pillars were.

Polybius, it is clear from the principles of elementary geometry that the total length of the coast-line from the Strait to the Pillars exceeds the length of the straight line through the open sea by very nearly five hundred [1] stadia. And if to this we added the three thousand stadia from the Peloponnesus to the Strait, the sum total of the stadia, merely those measured on a straight line, will be more than double [2] the estimate given by Dicaearchus. And, according to Dicaearchus, says Polybius, it will be necessary to put the distance from the Peloponnesus to the recess of the Adriatic at more than this sum. [3]

3. But, my dear Polybius, one might reply, just as the test based upon your own words makes evident the error of these false reckonings, namely, "from the Peloponnesus to Leucas, seven hundred stadia; from Leucas to Corcyra the same; and, again, from Corcyra to the Ceraunian Mountains the same; and the Illyrian coast-line to Iapydia on your right hand side, [4] if you measure from the Ceraunian Mountains, six thousand one hundred and fifty stadia," so also those other reckonings are both false—both that made by Dicaearchus when he makes the distance from the Strait of Sicily to the Pillars seven thousand stadia, and that which you think you have demonstrated; for most men agree in saying that the distance measured straight across the Sea is twelve thousand stadia, and this estimate agrees with the

[4] Polybius thus characterises the distance from the Ceraunian Mountains to the head of the Adriatic Gulf—apparently disregarding the Istrian coast, just as does Strabo in 6. 3. 10. Iapydia was the name both of the country and the chief city of the Iapydes. Strabo thinks Polybius' estimate is too large.

τῇ ἀποφάσει τῇ περὶ τοῦ μήκους τῆς οἰκουμένης.
C 106 μάλιστα γὰρ εἶναί φασι μυριάδων ἑπτά· τούτου
δὲ τὸ ἑσπέριον τμῆμα τὸ ἀπὸ τοῦ Ἰσσικοῦ κόλπου
μέχρι τῶν ἄκρων τῆς Ἰβηρίας, ἅπερ δυσμικώτατά[1]
ἐστι, μικρὸν ἀπολείπειν τῶν τρισμυρίων. συντι-
θέασι δ' οὕτως· ἀπὸ μὲν τοῦ Ἰσσικοῦ κόλπου
μέχρι τῆς Ῥοδίας πεντακισχιλίους· ἐνθένδ' ἐπὶ
Σαλμώνιον τῆς Κρήτης, ὅπερ ἐστὶ τὸ ἑῷον ἄκρον,
χιλίους· αὐτῆς δὲ τῆς Κρήτης μῆκος πλείους ἢ
δισχιλίους ἐπὶ Κριοῦ μέτωπον· ἐντεῦθεν δ' ἐπὶ
Πάχυνον τῆς Σικελίας τετρακισχιλίους καὶ πεντακοσίους,[2] ἀπὸ Παχύνου δὲ ἐπὶ Πορθμὸν πλείους
ἢ χιλίους· εἶτα τὸ δίαρμα τὸ ἐπὶ Στήλας ἀπὸ
Πορθμοῦ μυρίους δισχιλίους·[3] ἀπὸ Στηλῶν δὲ ἐπὶ
τὰ τελευταῖα τοῦ Ἱεροῦ ἀκρωτηρίου τῆς Ἰβηρίας
περὶ τρισχιλίους. καὶ ἡ κάθετος δὲ οὐ καλῶς
εἴληπται, εἴπερ ἡ μὲν Νάρβων ἐπὶ τοῦ αὐτοῦ
παραλλήλου σχεδόν τι ἵδρυται τῷ διὰ Μασσαλίας, αὕτη τε τῷ διὰ Βυζαντίου, καθάπερ καὶ
Ἵππαρχος πείθεται, ἡ δὲ διὰ τοῦ πελάγους ἐπὶ
τοῦ αὐτοῦ ἐστι τῷ διὰ Πορθμοῦ καὶ τῆς Ῥοδίας,
ἀπὸ δὲ τῆς Ῥοδίας εἰς Βυζάντιον ὡς ἂν ἐπὶ τοῦ
αὐτοῦ μεσημβρινοῦ κειμένων ἀμφοῖν περὶ πεντακισχιλίους[4] εἰρήκασι σταδίους· τοσοῦτοι γὰρ ἂν
εἶεν καὶ οἱ τῆς εἰρημένης καθέτου. ἐπεὶ δὲ καὶ

---

[1] δυσμικώτατα, Corais, for δυσμικώτερα; editors following.
[2] καί, Meineke deletes, before ἀπό; C. Müller approving.
[3] δισχιλίους, Gosselin, for τρισχιλίους; editors following.
[4] ὡς, Madvig deletes, before εἰρήκασι, and punctuates as in the text.

opinion rendered in regard to the length of the
inhabited world.[1] For they say that this length is
about seventy thousand stadia, and that the western
section thereof, that is, from the Gulf of Issus to the
capes of Iberia, which are the most westerly points,
is a little less than thirty thousand stadia. They
arrive at this result in the following way : From the
Gulf of Issus to Rhodes the distance is five thousand
stadia ; thence to Salmonium, which is the eastern
Cape of Crete, one thousand stadia ; and the length
of Crete itself, from Salmonium to Criumetopon,
more than two thousand stadia ; thence, from Criumetopon to Pachynum in Sicily, four thousand five
hundred stadia ; and from Pachynum to the Strait of
Sicily, more than one thousand stadia ; then, the sea-
passage from the Strait of Sicily to the Pillars, twelve
thousand stadia ; and from the Pillars to the extreme
end of the Sacred Cape [2] of Iberia, about three
thousand stadia. And Polybius has not taken even
his perpendicular properly, if it be true that Narbo
is situated approximately on the same parallel as that
which runs through Massilia and (as Hipparchus also
believes) Massilia on the same as that through
Byzantium, and that the line which runs through
the open Sea is on the same parallel as that through
the Strait and Rhodes, and that the distance from
Rhodes to Byzantium has been estimated at about
five thousand stadia on the assumption that both
places lie on the same meridian ; for the perpendicular
in question would also be five thousand stadia in
length.[3] But when they say that the longest passage

---

[1] 1. 4. 5.   [2] Cape St. Vincent.
[3] For "parallels comprehended between parallels are
equal."

τὸ μέγιστον δίαρμα τοῦ πελάγους τούτου τὸ ἀπὸ
τῆς Εὐρώπης ἐπὶ τὴν Λιβύην πεντακισχιλίων
που σταδίων λέγουσιν ἀπὸ τοῦ μυχοῦ τοῦ Γαλατικοῦ κόλπου, δοκεῖ μοι πεπλανημένως λέγεσθαι
τοῦτο, ἢ πολὺ τὴν Λιβύην κατὰ τοῦτο τὸ μέρος
προνεύειν[1] ἐπὶ τὴν ἄρκτον καὶ συνάπτειν τῷ διὰ
τῶν Στηλῶν παραλλήλῳ. καὶ τοῦτο οὐκ εὖ
λέγεται, τὸ πλησίον τῆς Σαρδόνος τὴν λεχθεῖσαν
κάθετον τελευτᾶν· οὐ γὰρ παραπλήσιον, ἀλλὰ
πολὺ δυσμικώτερόν ἐστι[2] τὸ δίαρμα τοῦτο τῆς
Σαρδόνος, ὅλον σχεδόν τι ἀπολαμβάνον ἐν τῷ
μεταξὺ πρὸς τῷ Σαρδονίῳ τὸ Λιγυστικὸν πέλαγος.
καὶ τῆς παραλίας δὲ τὰ μήκη πεπλεόνασται,
πλὴν οὐκ ἐπὶ τοσοῦτόν γε.

4. Ἑξῆς δὲ τὰ τοῦ Ἐρατοσθένους ἐπανορθοῖ, τὰ
μὲν εὖ, τὰ δὲ χεῖρον λέγων ἢ ἐκεῖνος. ἐξ Ἰθάκης
μὲν γὰρ εἰς Κόρκυραν τριακοσίους εἰπόντος,
πλείους φησὶν εἶναι τῶν ἐννακοσίων· ἐξ Ἐπιδάμνου δὲ εἰς Θεσσαλονίκειαν ἐννακοσίους ἀποδόντος, πλείους τῶν δισχιλίων φησί· ταῦτα μὲν
εὖ. ἀπὸ δὲ Μασσαλίας ἐπὶ Στήλας λέγοντος
ἑπτακισχιλίους, ἀπὸ δὲ Πυρήνης ἑξακισχιλίους,
αὐτὸς λέγει χεῖρον πλείους ἢ ἐννακισχιλίους τοὺς
ἀπὸ Μασσαλίας, ἀπὸ δὲ Πυρήνης μικρὸν ἐλάττους
ἢ ὀκτακισχιλίους· ἐγγυτέρω γὰρ τῆς ἀληθείας
ἐκεῖνος εἴρηκεν. οἱ γὰρ νῦν ὁμολογοῦσιν, εἴ τις
τὰς τῶν ὁδῶν ἀνωμαλίας ὑποτέμνοιτο, μὴ μείζω
τῶν ἑξακισχιλίων σταδίων εἶναι τὸ μῆκος τὴν
C 107   σύμπασαν Ἰβηρίαν ἀπὸ Πυρήνης ἕως τῆς ἑσπε-

---

[1] προνεύειν, Cascorbi, for προσνεύειν; A. Vogel, C. Frick,
approving.
[2] ἐστι, Madvig, for εἶναι.

across this sea from Europe to Libya, reckoned from the head of the Galatic Gulf, is approximately five thousand stadia, it seems to me that they make an erroneous statement, or else that in that region Libya projects far to the north and reaches the parallel that runs through the Pillars. And Polybius is again not right when he says that the perpendicular in question ends near Sardinia; for the line of this sea-passage is nowhere near Sardinia, but much farther west, leaving between it and Sardinia not only the Sardinian Sea, but almost the whole of the Ligurian Sea as well. And Polybius has exaggerated the length of the seaboard also, only in a lesser degree.

4. Next in order, Polybius proceeds to correct the errors of Eratosthenes; sometimes rightly, but sometimes he is even more in error than Eratosthenes. For instance, when Eratosthenes estimates the distance from Ithaca to Corcyra at three hundred stadia, Polybius says it is more than nine hundred; when Eratosthenes gives the distance from Epidamnus to Thessalonica as nine hundred stadia, Polybius says more than two thousand; and in these cases Polybius is right. But when Eratosthenes says the distance from Massilia to the Pillars is seven thousand stadia and from the Pyrenees to the Pillars six thousand stadia, Polybius himself makes a greater error in giving the distance from Massilia as more than nine thousand stadia and that from the Pyrenees a little less than eight thousand stadia; for Eratosthenes' estimates are nearer the truth. Indeed, modern authorities agree that if one cut off an allowance for the irregular windings of the roads, the whole of Iberia is not more than six thousand stadia in length from the Pyrenees to its western

ρίου πλευρᾶς. ὁ δ' αὐτὸν τὸν Τάγον ποταμὸν ὀκτακισχιλίων τίθησι τὸ μῆκος ἀπὸ τῆς πηγῆς μέχρι τῶν ἐκβολῶν, οὐ δή που τὸ σὺν τοῖς σκολιώμασιν (οὐ γὰρ γεωγραφικὸν τοῦτο), ἀλλ' ἐπ' εὐθείας λέγων, καίτοι γε ἀπὸ Πυρήνης αἱ τοῦ Τάγου πηγαὶ πλέον διέχουσιν ἢ χιλίους σταδίους. πάλιν δὲ τοῦτο μὲν ὀρθῶς ἀποφαίνεται, ὅτι ἀγνοεῖ τὰ Ἰβηρικὰ ὁ Ἐρατοσθένης, καὶ διότι περὶ αὐτῆς ἔσθ' ὅπου τὰ μαχόμενα ἀποφαίνεται· ὅς γε μέχρι Γαδείρων ὑπὸ Γαλατῶν περιοικεῖσθαι φήσας τὰ ἔξωθεν αὐτῆς, εἴ γε τὰ πρὸς δύσιν τῆς Εὐρώπης μέχρι Γαδείρων ἔχουσιν ἐκεῖνοι, τούτων ἐκλαθόμενος κατὰ τὴν τῆς Ἰβηρίας περίοδον τῶν Γαλατῶν οὐδαμοῦ μέμνηται.

5. Τό τε μῆκος τῆς Εὐρώπης ὅτι ἔλαττόν ἐστι τοῦ συνάμφω τῆς τε Λιβύης καὶ τῆς Ἀσίας ἐκθείς, οὐκ ὀρθῶς τὴν σύγκρισιν ποιεῖται· τὸ μὲν γὰρ στόμα τὸ κατὰ Στήλας φησίν, ὅτι κατὰ τὴν ἰσημερινὴν δύσιν ἐστίν, ὁ δὲ Τάναϊς ῥεῖ ἀπὸ θερινῆς ἀνατολῆς· ἐλαττοῦται δὴ τοῦ συνάμφω μήκους τῷ μεταξὺ τῆς θερινῆς ἀνατολῆς καὶ τῆς ἰσημερινῆς· τοῦτο γὰρ ἡ Ἀσία προλαμβάνει πρὸς τὴν ἰσημερινὴν ἀνατολὴν τοῦ πρὸς τὰς ἄρκτους ἡμικυκλίου. χωρὶς γὰρ τοῦ περισκελοῦς ἐν πραγ-

---

[1] The Don.

[2] Polybius' abstruse comparison of the length of Europe with that of Libya and Asia combined is not extant, but his general method is clear enough. Draw a line (*PP'*) parallel to the equator from the Pillars to the eastern coast of India —that is, at about 36½° latitude. On this line as a chord describe a semicircle which will have for diameter a line (*OO'*) drawn on the equator. From some point (*A*) west of Asia on the chord (Strabo says in § 7 below that this point is a variable) draw a line to the outlet (*T*) of the Tanaïs River; produce this line in a north-easterly direction along the

side. But Polybius reckons the river Tagus alone at
eight thousand stadia in length from its source to its
mouth—without reckoning in the windings of the
river, of course (for this is a thing geography does
not do)—but estimating the distance on a straight
line. And yet from the Pyrenees the sources of the
Tagus are more than one thousand stadia distant.
On the other hand, Polybius is right when he asserts
that Eratosthenes is ignorant of the geography of
Iberia, that is, for the reason that he sometimes makes
conflicting statements ; at any rate, after he has said
that the exterior coast of Iberia as far as Gades is
inhabited by Gauls—if they really hold the western
regions of Europe as far as Gades—he forgets that
statement and nowhere mentions the Gauls in his
description of Iberia.

5. Again, when Polybius sets forth that the length
of Europe is less than the combined length of Libya
and Asia, he does not make his comparison
correctly. The outlet at the Pillars, he says, is in
the equinoctial west, whereas the Tanaïs [1] flows from
the summer rising of the sun, and therefore Europe
is less in length than the combined length of Libya
and Asia by the space between the summer sunrise
and the equinoctial sunrise ; for Asia has a prior
claim to this space of the northern semicircle that
lies toward the equinoctial sunrise. [2] Indeed, apart

course of the river to the source (T'') of it (but the source is
unexplored) ; then produce the river line (TT') to the circumference at S, which may represent the summer rising.
Drop a perpendicular ($T''B$) upon the chord PP'. Then we
have a segment ($BT''SP'$) of the semicircle, which belongs to
Asia (but we are compelled to fix T'' and B inaccurately,
inasmuch as the source of the Tanaïs was unexplored).
According to Polybius, Europe is less in length than Libya
and Asia combined by the line BP' (which is a variable).

μασιν εὐαποδότοις καὶ ψεῦδός ἐστι τὸ ἀπὸ θερινῆς
ἀνατολῆς τὸν Τάναϊν ῥεῖν· ἅπαντες γὰρ οἱ ἔμ-
πειροι τῶν τόπων ἀπὸ τῶν ἄρκτων ῥεῖν φασιν εἰς
τὴν Μαιῶτιν, ὥστε τὰ στόματα τοῦ ποταμοῦ καὶ
τὸ τῆς Μαιώτιδος καὶ αὐτὸν τὸν ποταμόν, ἐφ'
ὅσον γνώριμός ἐστιν, ἐπὶ τοῦ αὐτοῦ μεσημβρινοῦ
κεῖσθαι.

6. Οὐκ ἄξιοι δὲ λόγου οἵτινες[1] εἶπον ἀπὸ
τῶν κατὰ τὸν Ἴστρον τόπων αὐτὸν τὰς ἀρχὰς
ἔχειν καὶ ἀπὸ τῆς ἑσπέρας, οὐκ ἐνθυμηθέντες ὡς
μεταξὺ ὁ Τύρας καὶ Βορυσθένης καὶ Ὕπανις,
μεγάλοι ποταμοί, ῥέουσιν εἰς τὸν Πόντον, ὁ μὲν
τῷ Ἴστρῳ παράλληλος, οἱ δὲ τῷ Τανάϊδι· οὔτε δὲ
τοῦ Τύρα τῶν πηγῶν κατωπτευμένων, οὔτε τοῦ
Βορυσθένους, οὔτε[2] τοῦ Ὑπάνιος, πολὺ ἂν εἴη
ἀγνωστότερα τὰ ἐκείνων ἀρκτικώτερα· ὥσθ' ὁ
δι' ἐκείνων ἄγων τὸν Τάναϊν, εἶτ' ἐπιστρέφων ἀπ'
αὐτῶν ἐπὶ τὴν Μαιῶτιν[3] (αἱ γὰρ ἐκβολαὶ φανερῶς
ἐν τοῖς προσαρκτίοις μέρεσι τῆς λίμνης δείκνυνται,
καὶ τούτοις τοῖς ἑωθινωτάτοις), πλαστὸς ἄν τις
εἴη καὶ ἀπέραντος λόγος. ὡς δ' αὕτως ἀπέραντος
καὶ ὁ διὰ τοῦ Καυκάσου πρὸς ἄρκτον φήσας ῥεῖν,
εἶτ' ἐπιστρέφειν εἰς τὴν Μαιῶτιν· εἴρηται γὰρ
καὶ τοῦτο. ἀπὸ μέντοι τῆς ἀνατολῆς οὐδεὶς εἴρηκε
τὴν ῥύσιν· καὶ γὰρ εἰ ἔρρει οὕτως, οὐκ ἂν ὑπεν-

[1] οἵτινες εἶπον for τινὲς εἶπον οἱ μέν; so lno; Siebenkees,
Corais, following.
[2] οὔτε... οὔτε, Corais, for οὐδέ... οὐδέ; Meineke following;
C. Müller approving.
[3] ἄγων τὸν Τάναϊν, εἶτ' ἐπιστρέφων ἀπ' αὐτῶν ἐπὶ τὴν Μαιῶτιν,
Sterrett, for ἄγων ἐπὶ τὴν Μαιῶτιν τὸν Τάναϊν, εἶτ' ἐπιστρέφων
ἐπ' αὐτήν.

from the abstruseness which characterises Polybius when he is discussing matters that are easy of explanation, his statement that the Tanaïs flows from the summer rising of the sun is also false; for all who are acquainted with those regions say that the Tanaïs flows from the north into Lake Maeotis, and in such wise that the mouth of the river, the mouth of Lake Maeotis, and the course of the Tanaïs itself, so far as it has been explored, all lie on the same meridian.

6. Unworthy of mention are those writers who have stated that the Tanaïs rises in the regions on the Ister [1] and flows from the west, because they have not reflected that the Tyras,[2] the Borysthenes,[3] and the Hypanis,[4] all large rivers, flow between those two rivers into the Pontus, one of them parallel to the Ister and the others parallel to the Tanaïs. And since neither the sources of the Tyras, nor of the Borysthenes, nor of the Hypanis, have been explored, the regions that are farther north than they would be far less known; and therefore the argument that conducts the Tanaïs through those regions and then makes it turn from them to the Maeotis Lake (for the mouths of the Tanaïs are obviously to be seen in the most northerly parts of the Lake, which are also the most easterly parts)—such an argument, I say, would be false and inconclusive. Equally inconclusive is the argument that the Tanaïs flows through the Caucasus towards the north and then turns and flows into Lake Maeotis; for this statement has also been made. However, no one has stated that the Tanaïs flows from the east; for if it flowed from the east the more accomplished geographers would not

---

[1] The Danube. [2] The Dniester.
[3] The Dnieper. [4] The Bog.

C 108 αντίως τῷ Νείλῳ καὶ τρόπον τινὰ κατὰ δια-
μετρον ῥεῖν αὐτὸν ἀπεφαίνοντο οἱ χαριέστεροι, ὡς
ἂν ἐπὶ ταὐτοῦ μεσημβρινοῦ ἢ παρακειμένου τινὸς
τῆς ῥύσεως οὔσης ἑκατέρῳ ποταμῷ.

7. Ἥ τε τοῦ μήκους τῆς οἰκουμένης μέτρησις
κατὰ παράλληλον τῷ ἰσημερινῷ ἐστιν, ἐπειδὴ
καὶ αὐτὴ ἐπὶ μῆκος οὕτως ἐκτέταται· ὥστε καὶ
τῶν ἠπείρων ἑκάστης οὕτω δεῖ λαμβάνειν τὸ
μῆκος μεταξὺ μεσημβρινῶν δυεῖν κείμενον. τά
τε μέτρα τῶν μηκῶν σταδιασμοί εἰσιν, οὓς θη-
ρεύομεν ἢ δι' αὐτῶν ἐκείνων ἰόντες ἢ τῶν παραλλήλων ὁδῶν ἢ πόρων. ὁ δὲ τοῦτον ἀφεὶς τὸν
τρόπον καινὸν εἰσάγει τὸ μεταξὺ τῆς τε θερινῆς
ἀνατολῆς καὶ τῆς ἰσημερινῆς τμῆμά τι[1] τοῦ ἀρκτικοῦ ἡμικυκλίου. πρὸς δὲ τὰ ἀμετάπτωτα οὐδεὶς
κανόσι καὶ μέτροις χρῆται τοῖς μεταπτώτοις οὐδὲ
τοῖς κατ' ἄλλην καὶ ἄλλην σχέσιν λεγομένοις
πρὸς τὰ καθ' αὑτὰ καὶ ἀδιάφορα.[2] τὸ μὲν οὖν
μῆκος ἀμετάπτωτον καὶ καθ' αὑτὸ λέγεται, ἀνα-
τολὴ δ' ἰσημερινὴ καὶ δύσις, ὡς δ' αὕτως θερινὴ
τε καὶ χειμερινή, οὐ καθ' αὑτήν, ἀλλὰ πρὸς ἡμᾶς·
ἡμῶν δ' ἄλλοτ' ἄλλῃ μεταχωρούντων, ἄλλοτ'
ἄλλοι τόποι καὶ δύσεών εἰσι καὶ ἀνατολῶν ἰσημερινῶν τε καὶ τροπικῶν, τὸ δὲ μῆκος μένει ταὐτὸν
τῆς ἠπείρου. Τάναϊν μὲν οὖν καὶ Νεῖλον οὐκ

---

[1] τμῆμά τι, Tyrwhitt, for τμήματι; Müller-Dübner, Meineke,
following.
[2] ἀδιάφορα, Kramer, for διαφορὰν (οὐκ ἔχοντα?); A. Vogel
approving.

be asserting that it flows in a direction contrary to, and in a sense diametrically opposed to, that of the Nile—meaning that the courses of the two rivers are on the same meridian or else on meridians that lie close to each other.[1]

7. The measurement of the length of the inhabited world is made along a line parallel to the equator, because the inhabited world, in its length, stretches in the same way the equator does; and in the same way, therefore, we must take as the length of each of the continents the space that lies between two meridians. Again, the measure employed for these lengths is that by stadia; and we seek to discover the number of the stadia either by travelling through the continents themselves, or else along the roads or waterways parallel to them. But Polybius abandons this method and introduces something new, namely, a certain segment of the northern semicircle, which lies between the summer sunrise and the equinoctial sunrise. But no one employs rules and measures that are variable for things that are non-variable, nor reckonings that are made relative to one position or another for things that are absolute and unchanging. Now while the term "length" is non-variable and absolute, "equinoctial rising" and "setting" and, in the same way, "summer sunrise" and "winter sunrise," are not absolute, but relative to our individual positions; and if we shift our position to different points, the positions of sunset and sunrise, whether equinoctial or solstitial, are different, but the length of the continent remains the same. Therefore, while it is not out of place to make the Tanaïs and the Nile limits of continents, it is some-

[1] Compare 11. 2. 2.

ἄτοπον πέρας ποιεῖσθαι, θερινὴν δ' ἀνατολὴν ἢ
ἰσημερινὴν καινόν.

8. Προπεπτωκυίας δὲ τῆς Εὐρώπης ἄκραις
πλείοσι, βέλτιον μὲν οὗτος εἴρηκεν περὶ αὐτῶν
Ἐρατοσθένους, οὔπω δὲ ἱκανῶς. ἐκεῖνος μὲν γὰρ
τρεῖς ἔφη, τὴν ἐπὶ τὰς Στήλας καθήκουσαν, ἐφ'
ἧς ἡ Ἰβηρία, καὶ τὴν ἐπὶ τὸν Πορθμόν, ἐφ' ἧς ἡ
Ἰταλία, καὶ τρίτην τὴν κατὰ Μαλέας, ἐφ' ἧς
τὰ μεταξὺ τοῦ Ἀδρίου καὶ τοῦ Εὐξείνου πάντ'
ἔθνη καὶ τοῦ Τανάϊδος. οὗτος δὲ τὰς μὲν δύο
τὰς πρώτας ὁμοίως ἐκτίθεται, τρίτην δὲ τὴν κατὰ
Μαλέας καὶ Σούνιον, ἐφ' ἧς ἡ Ἑλλὰς πᾶσα καὶ
ἡ Ἰλλυρὶς καὶ τῆς Θρᾴκης τινά, τετάρτην δὲ τὴν
κατὰ Θρᾳκίαν χερρόνησον, ἐφ' ἧς τὰ κατὰ Σηστὸν
καὶ Ἄβυδον στενά, ἔχουσι δ' αὐτὴν Θρᾷκες·
πέμπτην δὲ τὴν κατὰ τὸν Κιμμερικὸν βόσπορον
καὶ τὸ στόμα τῆς Μαιώτιδος. τὰς μὲν οὖν δύο
τὰς πρώτας δοτέον· ἁπλοῖς γάρ τισι περιλαμβά-
νονται κόλποις, ἡ μὲν τῷ μεταξὺ τῆς Κάλπης
καὶ τοῦ Ἱεροῦ ἀκρωτηρίου, ἐν ᾧ τὰ Γάδειρα,
καὶ τῷ μεταξὺ Στηλῶν καὶ τῆς Σικελίας πελά-
γει· ἡ δὲ τούτῳ τε καὶ τῷ Ἀδρίᾳ, καίτοι ἥ γε
C 109   τῶν Ἰαπύγων ἄκρα παρεμπίπτουσα καὶ τὴν
Ἰταλίαν δικόρυφον ποιοῦσα ἔχει τινὰ ἀντέμφα-
σιν· αἱ λοιπαὶ δ' ἔτι ἐναργέστερον ποικίλαι καὶ
πολυμερεῖς οὖσαι ζητοῦσιν ἄλλην διαίρεσιν. ὡς
δ' αὕτως ἔχει καὶ ἡ εἰς ἓξ διαίρεσις τὴν ὁμοίαν

thing new to use the summer, or the equinoctial, sunrise for this purpose.

8. Since Europe runs out into several promontories, Polybius' account of them is better than that of Eratosthenes, but it is still inadequate. For Eratosthenes spoke of only three promontories:[1] first, the promontory that juts down to the Pillars, on which is Iberia; secondly, that to the Strait of Sicily, on which is Italy; and, thirdly, that which ends at Cape Malea, on which are all the nations that dwell between the Adriatic, the Euxine, and the Tanaïs. But Polybius explains the first two promontories in the same way and then makes a third of the promontory which ends at Cape Malea and Sunium, on which are all Greece, and Illyria, and certain parts of Thrace, and a fourth of the Thracian Chersonese, where the strait between Sestus and Abydus is, inhabited by Thracians; and still a fifth of the promontory in the region of the Cimmerian Bosporus and of the mouth of Lake Maeotis. Now we must grant the first two, because they are encompassed by simple gulfs: one of them, by the gulf that lies between Calpe and the Sacred Cape (the gulf on which Gades is situated) and also by that portion of the sea that lies between the Pillars and Sicily; the other, by the last-mentioned sea and the Adriatic—although, of course, the promontory of Iapygia, since it thrusts itself forward on the side and thus makes Italy have two crests, presents a sort of contradiction to my statement; but the remaining three promontories, which still more clearly are complex and composed of many members, require further division. Likewise, also, the division of Europe into six parts

[1] See 2. 1. 40.

ἔνστασιν ἀκολούθως ταῖς ἄκραις διειλημμένη.
ποιησόμεθα δ' ἡμεῖς ἐν τοῖς καθ' ἕκαστα τὴν
προσήκουσαν ἐπανόρθωσιν καὶ τούτων καὶ τῶν
ἄλλων, ὅσα ἔν τε τῇ Εὐρώπῃ διημάρτηται καὶ
ἐν τῇ τῆς Λιβύης περιοδείᾳ. νῦν δ' ἀρκέσει ταῦτα
λεχθέντα πρὸς τοὺς πρὸ ἡμῶν, ὅσους ᾠήθημεν
ἱκανοὺς εἶναι παρατεθέντας ἐκμαρτυρεῖν ἡμῖν,
ὅτι δικαίως προειλόμεθα καὶ αὐτοὶ τὸ αὐτὸ τοῦτο
ἔργον, τοσαύτης ἐπανορθώσεως καὶ προσθήκης
δεόμενον.

V

1. Ἐπεὶ δὲ τοῖς πρὸς ἐκείνους λόγοις συνεχὴς
ἐστιν ἡ ἐγχείρησις τῆς ἡμετέρας ὑποσχέσεως,
λαβόντες ἀρχὴν ἑτέραν λέγωμεν ὅτι δεῖ τὸν
χωρογραφεῖν ἐπιχειροῦντα πολλὰ τῶν φυσικῶς
τε καὶ μαθηματικῶς λεγομένων ὑποθέσθαι, καὶ
πρὸς τὴν ἐκείνων ὑπόνοιάν τε καὶ πίστιν τὰ
ἑξῆς πραγματεύεσθαι. εἴρηται γὰρ ὅτι οὐδ' οἰκοδόμος, οὐδ' ἀρχιτέκτων οἰκίαν ἢ πόλιν ἱδρῦσαι
καλῶς οἷός τε γένοιτ' ἄν, ἀπρονοήτως ἔχων κλιμάτων τε καὶ[1] τῶν κατὰ τὸν οὐρανὸν καὶ σχημάτων τε καὶ μεγεθῶν καὶ θάλπους καὶ ψύχους καὶ
ἄλλων τοιούτων, μή τί γε τὴν ὅλην οἰκουμένην
τοποθετῶν. αὐτὸ γὰρ τὸ εἰς ἐπίπεδον γράφειν
ἐπιφάνειαν μίαν καὶ τὴν αὐτὴν τά τε Ἰβηρικὰ

[1] τε καί, Groskurd, for τε ; Forbiger following.

is open to similar objection, since it has been made in accordance with the promontories. However, in my detailed account I shall make the suitable corrections, not only of these mistakes, but also of all the other serious mistakes that Polybius has made, both in the matter of Europe and in his circuit of Libya. But, for the present, I shall rest satisfied with what I have here said in criticism of my predecessors —that is, of so many of them as I have thought would, if cited, make enough witnesses to prove that I too am justified in having undertaken to treat this same subject, since it stands in need of so much correction and addition.

V

1. Since the taking in hand of my proposed task naturally follows the criticisms of my predecessors, let me make a second beginning by saying that the person who attempts to write an account of the countries of the earth must take many of the physical and mathematical principles as hypotheses and elaborate his whole treatise with reference to their intent and authority. For, as I have already said,[1] no architect or engineer would be competent even to fix the site of a house or a city properly if he had no conception beforehand of "climata" and of the celestial phenomena, and of geometrical figures and magnitudes and heat and cold and other such things—much less a person who would fix positions for the whole of the inhabited world. For the mere drawing on one and the same plane surface of Iberia and India and the

[1] Page 25.

καὶ τὰ Ἰνδικὰ καὶ τὰ μέσα τούτων, καὶ μηδὲν
ἧττον δύσεις καὶ ἀνατολὰς ἀφορίζειν καὶ μεσουρανήσεις, ὡς ἂν κοινὰς πᾶσι, τῷ μὲν προεπινοή-
σαντι τὴν τοῦ οὐρανοῦ διάθεσίν τε καὶ κίνησιν,
καὶ λαβόντι ὅτι σφαιρικὴ μέν ἐστιν ἡ κατ᾽ ἀλήθειαν τῆς γῆς ἐπιφάνεια, πλάττεται δὲ νῦν ἐπί-
πεδος πρὸς τὴν ὄψιν, γεωγραφικὴν ἔχει τὴν
παράδοσιν, τῷ δ᾽ ἄλλως, οὐ γεωγραφικήν. οὐ
γάρ, ὥσπερ διὰ πεδίων ἰοῦσι μεγάλων, οἷον τῶν
Βαβυλωνίων, ἢ διὰ πελάγους παρίσταται τὰ
πρόσω πάντα καὶ τὰ κατόπιν καὶ ἐκ πλαγίων
ἐπίπεδα, καὶ οὐδεμίαν ἀντέμφασιν παρέχει πρὸς
τὰ οὐράνια καὶ τὰς τοῦ ἡλίου κινήσεις καὶ σχέσεις
πρὸς ἡμᾶς καὶ τῶν ἄλλων ἄστρων, οὕτω καὶ
γεωγραφοῦσιν παρίστασθαι ἀεὶ δεῖ τὰ ὅμοια. ὁ
μὲν γὰρ πελαγίζων ἢ[1] ὁδεύων διὰ χώρας πεδιά-
δος κοιναῖς τισι φαντασίαις ἄγεται, καθ᾽ ἃς καὶ
ὁ ἀπαίδευτος καὶ ὁ πολιτικὸς ἐνεργεῖ ταὐτά, ἄπειρος ὢν τῶν οὐρανίων, καὶ τὰς πρὸς ταῦτα ἀντεμ-
C 110 φάσεις ἀγνοῶν. ἀνατέλλοντα μὲν γὰρ ὁρᾷ ἥλιον
καὶ δύνοντα καὶ μεσουρανοῦντα, τίνα δὲ τρόπον,
οὐκ ἐπισκοπεῖ· οὐδὲ γὰρ χρήσιμον αὐτῷ πρὸς τὸ
προκείμενον, ὥσπερ οὐδὲ τὸ παράλληλον ἑστάναι

---

[1] ἤ, Corais, for καί before ὁδεύων; Meineke following;
C. Müller approving.

countries that lie between them and, in spite of its
being a plane surface, the plotting of the sun's
position at its settings, risings, and in meridian, as
though these positions were fixed for all the people
of the world—merely this exercise gives to the man
who has previously conceived of the arrangement
and movement of the celestial bodies and grasped
the fact that the true surface of the earth is spherical
but that it is depicted for the moment as a plane
surface for the convenience of the eye—merely this
exercise, I say, gives to that man instruction that is
truly geographical, but to the man not thus qualified
it does not. Indeed, the case is not the same with
us when we are dealing with geography as it is when
we are travelling over great plains (those of Babylonia,
for example) or over the sea : then all that is in front
of us and behind us and on either side of us is presented
to our minds as a plane surface and offers no varying
aspects with reference to the celestial bodies or the
movements or the positions of the sun and the other
stars relatively to us ; but when we are dealing with
geography the like parts must never present themselves
to our minds in that way. The sailor on the open sea,
or the man who travels through a level country, is
guided by certain popular notions (and these notions
impel not only the uneducated man but the man of
affairs as well to act in the self-same way), because he
is unfamiliar with the heavenly bodies and ignorant
of the varying aspects of things with reference to
them. For he sees the sun rise, pass the meridian,
and set, but how it comes about he does not consider ; for, indeed, such knowledge is not useful to
him with reference to the task before him, any more
than it is useful for him to know whether or not his

τῷ παρεστῶτι ἢ μη· ταχα δ᾽ ἐπισκοπεῖ μέν, ἀντιδοξεῖ δὲ¹ τοῖς μαθηματικῶς λεγομένοις, καθάπερ
οἱ ἐπιχώριοι· ἔχει γὰρ ὁ τόπος τοιαῦτα διαπτώ-
ματα. ὁ δὲ γεωγραφικὸς οὐκ ἐπιχωρίῳ γεωγραφεῖ, οὐδὲ πολιτικῷ τοιούτῳ, ὅστις μηδὲν ἐφρόντισε
τῶν λεγομένων ἰδίως μαθημάτων· οὐδὲ γὰρ θερι-
στῇ καὶ σκαπανεῖ, ἀλλὰ τῷ πεισθῆναι δυναμένῳ
τὴν γῆν ἔχειν οὕτω τὴν ὅλην, ὡς οἱ μαθηματικοί
φασι, καὶ τὰ ἄλλα τὰ πρὸς τὴν ὑπόθεσιν τὴν
τοιαύτην. κελεύει τε τοῖς προσιοῦσιν, ἐκεῖνα
προενθυμηθεῖσι τὰ ἑξῆς ἐφορᾶν· ἐκείνοις γὰρ τὰ
ἀκόλουθα ἐρεῖν, ὥστε μᾶλλον ποιήσασθαι τῶν
παραδιδομένων ἀσφαλῆ τὴν χρῆσιν τοὺς ἐντυγχά-
νοντας, ἂν ἀκούσωσι μαθηματικῶς, τοῖς δ᾽ ἄλλως
ἔχουσιν οὔ φησι γεωγραφεῖν.

2. Τὸν μὲν δὴ γεωγραφοῦντα πιστεῦσαι δεῖ
περὶ τῶν ἐχόντων αὐτῷ τάξιν ἀρχῆς τοῖς ἀνα-
μετρήσασι τὴν ὅλην γῆν γεωμέτραις, τούτους δὲ
τοῖς ἀστρονομικοῖς, ἐκείνους δὲ τοῖς φυσικοῖς. ἡ
δὲ φυσικὴ ἀρετή τις· τὰς δ᾽ ἀρετὰς ἀνυποθέτους
φασὶν ἐξ αὐτῶν² ἠρτημένας, καὶ ἐν αὐταῖς² ἐχού-

¹ ἐπισκοπεῖ μέν, ἀντιδοξεῖ δέ, Madvig, for ἐπισκοποῖ μὲν ἄν τι,
δόξει δ᾽ ἐν; Cobet, A. Vogel, approving.
² αὐτῶν and αὐταῖς, Corais, for αὑτῶν and αὑταῖς; Groskurd,
Meineke, Forbiger, Tardieu, following; C. Müller approving.

¹ That is, a kind of "supreme excellence." Plutarch says
that the Stoics recognized three "supreme excellences"
(*Aretai*) among the sciences—namely, physics, ethics, and

body stands parallel to that of his neighbour. But perhaps he does consider these matters, and yet holds opinions opposed to the principles of mathematics—just as the natives of any given place do; for a man's place occasions such blunders. But the geographer does not write for the native of any particular place, nor yet does he write for the man of affairs of the kind who has paid no attention to the mathematical sciences properly so-called; nor, to be sure, does he write for the harvest-hand or the ditch-digger, but for the man who can be persuaded that the earth as a whole is such as the mathematicians represent it to be, and also all that relates to such an hypothesis. And the geographer urges upon his students that they first master those principles and then consider the subsequent problems; for, he declares, he will speak only of the results which follow from those principles; and hence his students will the more unerringly make the application of his teachings if they listen as mathematicians; but he refuses to teach geography to persons not thus qualified.

2. Now as for the matters which he regards as fundamental principles of his science, the geographer must rely upon the geometricians who have measured the earth as a whole; and in their turn the geometricians must rely upon the astronomers; and again the astronomers upon the physicists. Physics is a kind of *Arete*[1]; and by *Aretai* they mean those sciences that postulate nothing but depend upon themselves, and contain within themselves their own

logic; and that they regarded all three as the expedient arts for the exercise of philosophy in the acquirement of knowledge—which is wisdom.

σας τάς τε ἀρχὰς καὶ τὰς περὶ τούτων πίστεις. τὰ μὲν οὖν παρὰ τῶν φυσικῶν δεικνύμενα τοιαῦτά ἐστι· σφαιροειδὴς μὲν ὁ κόσμος καὶ ὁ οὐρανός, ἡ ῥοπὴ δ' ἐπὶ τὸ μέσον τῶν βαρέων· περὶ τοῦτό τε συνεστῶσα ἡ γῆ σφαιροειδῶς ὁμόκεντρος τῷ μὲν οὐρανῷ μένει καὶ αὐτὴ καὶ ὁ δι' αὐτῆς ἄξων καὶ τοῦ οὐρανοῦ μέσου τεταμένος, ὁ δ' οὐρανὸς περιφέρεται περί τε αὐτὴν καὶ περὶ τὸν ἄξονα ἀπ' ἀνατολῆς ἐπὶ δύσιν, σὺν αὐτῷ δὲ οἱ ἀπλανεῖς ἀστέρες ὁμοταχεῖς τῷ πόλῳ. οἱ μὲν οὖν ἀπλανεῖς ἀστέρες κατὰ παραλλήλων φέρονται κύκλων· παράλληλοι δ' εἰσὶ γνωριμώτατοι ὅ τε ἰσημερινὸς καὶ οἱ τροπικοὶ δύο καὶ οἱ ἀρκτικοί· οἱ δὲ πλάνητες ἀστέρες καὶ ἥλιος καὶ σελήνη κατὰ λοξῶν τινων, τῶν τεταγμένων ἐν τῷ ζῳδιακῷ. τούτοις δὲ πιστεύσαντες ἢ πᾶσιν ἤ τισιν οἱ ἀστρονομικοὶ τὰ ἑξῆς πραγματεύονται, κινήσεις καὶ περιόδους καὶ ἐκλείψεις καὶ μεγέθη καὶ ἀποστάσεις καὶ ἄλλα μυρία· ὡς δ' αὕτως οἱ τὴν γῆν ὅλην ἀναμετροῦντες γεωμέτραι προστίθενται ταῖς τῶν φυσικῶν καὶ τῶν ἀστρονομικῶν δόξαις, ταῖς δὲ τῶν γεωμετρῶν πάλιν οἱ γεωγράφοι.

C 111   3. Πεντάζωνον μὲν γὰρ ὑποθέσθαι δεῖ τὸν οὐρανόν, πεντάζωνον δὲ καὶ τὴν γῆν, ὁμωνύμους δὲ καὶ τὰς ζώνας τὰς κάτω ταῖς ἄνω· τὰς δ' αἰτίας εἰρήκαμεν τῆς εἰς τὰς ζώνας διαιρέσεως. διορίζοιντο δ' ἂν αἱ ζῶναι κυκλοις παραλλήλοις τῷ ἰσημερινῷ γραφομένοις ἑκατέρωθεν αὐτοῦ, δυσὶ

principles as well as the proofs thereof. Now what we are taught by the physicists is as follows: The universe and the heavens are sphere-shaped. The tendency of the bodies that have weight is towards the centre. And, having taken its position about this centre in the form of a sphere, the earth remains homocentric with the heavens, as does also the axis through it, which axis extends also through the centre of the heavens. The heavens revolve round both the earth and its axis from east to west; and along with the heavens revolve the fixed stars, with the same rapidity as the vault of the heavens. Now the fixed stars move along parallel circles, and the best known parallel circles are the equator, the two tropics, and the arctic circles; whereas the planets and the sun and the moon move along certain oblique circles whose positions lie in the zodiac. Now the astronomers first accept these principles, either in whole or in part, and then work out the subsequent problems, namely, the movements of the heavenly bodies, their revolutions, their eclipses, their sizes, their respective distances, and a host of other things. And, in the same way, the geometricians, in measuring the earth as a whole, adhere to the doctrines of the physicists and the astronomers, and, in their turn, the geographers adhere to those of the geometricians.

3. Thus we must take as an hypothesis that the heavens have five zones, and that the earth also has five zones, and that the terrestrial zones have the same names as the celestial zones (I have already stated the reasons for this division into zones [1]). The limits of the zones can be defined by circles drawn on both sides of the equator and parallel to it,

[1] See 2. 3. 1.

μὲν τοῖς ἀπολαμβάνουσι τὴν διακεκαυμένην, δυσὶ
δὲ τοῖς μετὰ τούτους, οἳ πρὸς μὲν τῇ διακεκαυμένῃ
τὰς εὐκράτους δύο ποιοῦσι, πρὸς δὲ ταῖς εὐκράτοις
τὰς κατεψυγμένας. ὑποπίπτει δ' ἑκάστῳ τῶν
οὐρανίων κύκλων ὁ ἐπὶ γῆς ὁμώνυμος αὐτῷ, καὶ ἡ
ζώνη δὲ ὡσαύτως τῇ ζώνῃ. εὐκράτους μὲν οὖν
φασι τὰς οἰκεῖσθαι δυναμένας, ἀοικήτους δὲ τὰς
ἄλλας, τὴν μὲν διὰ καῦμα, τὰς δὲ διὰ ψῦχος.
τὸν δ' αὐτὸν τρόπον καὶ περὶ τῶν τροπικῶν καὶ
τῶν ἀρκτικῶν, παρ' οἷς εἰσιν ἀρκτικοί, διορίζουσιν
ὁμωνύμους[1] τοῖς ἄνω τοὺς ἐπὶ γῆς ποιοῦντες, καὶ
τοὺς ἑκάστοις ὑποπίπτοντας. τοῦ δ' ἰσημερινοῦ
δίχα τέμνοντος τὸν ὅλον οὐρανόν, καὶ τὴν γῆν
ἀνάγκη διαιρεῖσθαι ὑπὸ τοῦ ἐν αὐτῇ ἰσημερινοῦ.
καλεῖται δὲ τῶν ἡμισφαιρίων ἑκάτερον τῶν τε
οὐρανίων καὶ τῶν ἐπὶ γῆς τὸ μὲν βόρειον, τὸ δὲ
νότιον· οὕτως δὲ καὶ τῆς διακεκαυμένης ὑπὸ τοῦ
αὐτοῦ κύκλου δίχα διαιρουμένης τὸ μὲν ἔσται
βόρειον αὐτῆς μέρος, τὸ δὲ νότιον. δῆλον δ' ὅτι
καὶ τῶν εὐκράτων ζωνῶν ἡ μὲν ἔσται βόρειος, ἡ
δὲ νότιος, ὁμωνύμως τῷ ἡμισφαιρίῳ ἐν ᾧ ἐστι.
καλεῖται δὲ βόρειον μὲν ἡμισφαίριον τὸ τὴν εὔκρατον ἐκείνην περιέχον ἐν ᾗ ἀπὸ τῆς ἀνατολῆς
βλέποντι ἐπὶ τὴν δύσιν ἐν δεξιᾷ μέν ἐστιν ὁ
πόλος, ἐν ἀριστερᾷ δ' ὁ ἰσημερινός, ἢ ἐν ᾧ πρὸς

---

[1] ὁμωνύμους, Corais, for ὁμωνύμως; Groskurd following.

namely, by two circles which enclose the torrid zone, and by two others, following upon these, which form the two temperate zones next to the torrid zone and the two frigid zones next to the temperate zones. Beneath each of the celestial circles falls the corresponding terrestrial circle which bears the same name: and, in like manner, beneath the celestial zone, the terrestrial zone. Now they call "temperate" the zones that can be inhabited; the others they call uninhabitable, the one on account of the heat, and the other two on account of the cold. They proceed in the same manner with reference to the tropic and the arctic circles (that is, in countries that admit of arctic circles [1]): they define their limits by giving the terrestrial circles the same names as the celestial—and thus they define all the terrestrial circles that fall beneath the several celestial circles. Since the celestial equator cuts the whole heavens in two, the earth also must of necessity be cut in two by the terrestrial equator. Of the two hemispheres—I refer to the two celestial as well as the two terrestrial hemispheres — one is called "the northern hemisphere" and the other "the southern hemisphere"; so also, since the torrid zone is cut in two by the same circle, the one part of it will be the northern and the other the southern. It is clear that, of the temperate zones also, the one will be northern and the other southern, each bearing the name of the hemisphere in which it lies. That hemisphere is called "northern hemisphere" which contains that temperate zone in which, as you look from the east to the west, the pole is on your right hand and the equator on your left, or in which, as you look towards

[1] See 2. 2. 2 and footnote.

μεσημβρίαν βλέπουσιν ἐν δεξιᾷ μέν ἐστι δύσις,
ἐν ἀριστερᾷ δ' ἀνατολή, νότιον δὲ τὸ ἐναντίως
ἔχον· ὥστε δῆλον ὅτι ἡμεῖς ἐσμεν ἐν θατέρῳ τῶν
ἡμισφαιρίων, καὶ τῷ βορείῳ γε, ἐν ἀμφοτέροις δ'
οὐχ οἷόν τε.

> μέσσῳ γὰρ μεγάλοι ποταμοί,
> Ὠκεανὸς μὲν πρῶτα,   (Od. 11. 157)

ἔπειτα ἡ διακεκαυμένη. οὔτε δὲ ὠκεανὸς ἐν μέσῳ
τῆς καθ' ἡμᾶς οἰκουμένης ἐστὶ τέμνων ὅλην, οὔτ'
οὖν διακεκαυμένον χωρίον· οὐδὲ δὴ μέρος αὐτῆς
εὑρίσκεται τοῖς κλίμασι ὑπεναντίως ἔχον τοῖς
λεχθεῖσιν ἐν τῇ βορείῳ εὐκράτῳ.

4. Λαβὼν οὖν ταῦθ' ὁ γεωμέτρης, προσχρησά-
μενος τοῖς γνωμονικοῖς καὶ τοῖς ἄλλοις[1] τοῖς ὑπὸ
τοῦ ἀστρονομικοῦ δεικνυμένοις, ἐν οἷς οἵ τε παράλληλοι τῷ ἰσημερινῷ εὑρίσκονται οἱ καθ' ἑκάστην
τὴν οἴκησιν καὶ οἱ πρὸς ὀρθὰς τέμνοντες τούτους,
γραφόμενοι δὲ διὰ τῶν πόλων, καταμετρεῖ τὴν μὲν
οἰκήσιμον ἐμβατεύων, τὴν δ' ἄλλην ἐκ τοῦ λόγου
τῶν ἀποστάσεων. οὕτω δ' ἂν εὑρίσκοι, πόσον ἂν
C 112 εἴη τὸ ἀπὸ τοῦ ἰσημερινοῦ μέχρι πόλου, ὅπερ
ἐστὶ τεταρτημόριον τοῦ μεγίστου κύκλου τῆς γῆς·
ἔχων δὲ τοῦτο ἔχει καὶ τὸ τετραπλάσιον αὐτοῦ,
τοῦτο δ' ἔστιν ἡ περίμετρος τῆς γῆς. ὥσπερ οὖν
ὁ μὲν τὴν γῆν ἀναμετρῶν παρὰ τοῦ ἀστρονομοῦν-
τος ἔλαβε τὰς ἀρχάς, ὁ δὲ ἀστρονόμος παρὰ τοῦ
φυσικοῦ, τὸν αὐτὸν τρόπον χρὴ καὶ τὸν γεωγράφον

---

[1] The words τοῖς γνωμονικοῖς καὶ τοῖς ἄλλοις were omitted
by Kramer and Meineke without comment.

the south, the west is on your right hand and the
east on your left; and that hemisphere is called
" southern hemisphere," in which the opposite is
true; and hence it is clear that we are in one of the
two hemispheres (that is, of course, in the northern),
and that it is impossible for us to be in both. " Between them are great rivers; first, Oceanus", and
then the torrid zone. But neither is there an Oceanus
in the centre of our whole inhabited world, cleaving
the whole of it, nor, to be sure, is there a torrid spot
in it; nor yet, indeed, is there a portion of it to
be found whose " climata " are opposite to the
" climata " [1] which I have given for the northern
temperate zone.[2]

4. By accepting these principles, then, and also by
making use of the sun-dial and the other helps given
him by the astronomer—by means of which are found,
for the several inhabited localities, both the circles
that are parallel to the equator and the circles that
cut the former at right angles, the latter being
drawn through the poles — the geometrician can
measure the inhabited portion of the earth by visiting it and the rest of the earth by his calculation
of the intervals. In this way he can find the distance from the equator to the pole, which is a fourth
part of the earth's largest circle; and when he has
this distance, he multiplies it by four; and this is
the circumference of the earth. Accordingly, just
as the man who measures the earth gets his principles
from the astronomer and the astronomer his from
the physicist, so, too, the geographer must in the

---

[1] See footnote 2, page 22.
[2] If such were the case, such a portion would have to fall
within the southern hemisphere.

παρὰ τοῦ ἀναμεμετρηκότος ὅλην τὴν γῆν ὁρμηθέντα, πιστεύσαντα τούτῳ καὶ οἷς ἐπίστευσεν
οὗτος, πρῶτον μὲν ἐκθέσθαι τὴν οἰκουμένην καθ'
ἡμᾶς, πόση τις καὶ ποια τὸ σχῆμα καὶ τὴν φύσιν
οἵα ἐστὶ καὶ πῶς ἔχουσα πρὸς τὴν ὅλην γῆν·
ἴδιον γὰρ τοῦ γεωγράφου τοῦτο· ἔπειτα περὶ τῶν
καθ' ἕκαστα τῶν τε κατὰ γῆν καὶ τῶν κατὰ
θάλατταν ποιήσασθαι τὸν προσήκοντα λόγον,
παρασημαινόμενον ὅσα μὴ ἱκανῶς εἴρηται τοῖς
πρὸ ἡμῶν τοῖς μάλιστα πεπιστευμένοις ἀρίστοις
γεγονέναι περὶ ταῦτα.

5. Ὑποκείσθω δὴ σφαιροειδὴς ἡ γῆ σὺν τῇ
θαλάττῃ, καὶ[1] μίαν καὶ τὴν αὐτὴν ἐπιφάνειαν
ἴσχουσα τοῖς πελάγεσι. συγκρύπτοιτο γὰρ ἂν τὸ
ἐξέχον τῆς γῆς ἐν τῷ τοσούτῳ μεγέθει μικρὸν ὂν
καὶ λανθάνειν δυνάμενον, ὥστε τὸ σφαιροειδὲς ἐπὶ
τούτων οὐχ ὡς ἂν ἐκ τόρνου φαμέν, οὐδ' ὡς ὁ
γεωμέτρης πρὸς λόγον, ἀλλὰ πρὸς αἴσθησιν, καὶ
ταύτην παχυτέραν. νοείσθω δὴ πεντάζωνος, καὶ ὁ
ἰσημερινὸς τεταγμένος ἐν αὐτῇ κύκλος, καὶ ἄλλος
τούτῳ παράλληλος, ὁρίζων τὴν κατεψυγμένην ἐν
τῷ βορείῳ ἡμισφαιρίῳ, καὶ διὰ τῶν πόλων τις
τέμνων τούτους πρὸς ὀρθάς. τοῦ δὴ βορείου ἡμισφαιρίου δύο περιέχοντος τεταρτημόρια τῆς γῆς,
ἃ ποιεῖ ὁ ἰσημερινὸς πρὸς τὸν διὰ τῶν πόλων, ἐν

---

[1] καί, Groskurd inserts, before μίαν.

same way first take his point of departure from the man who has measured the earth as a whole, having confidence in him and in those in whom he, in his turn, had confidence, and then explain, in the first instance, our inhabited world—its size, shape, and character, and its relations to the earth as a whole; for this is the peculiar task of the geographer. Then, secondly, he must discuss in a fitting manner the several parts of the inhabited world, both land and sea, noting in passing wherein the subject has been treated inadequately by those of our predecessors whom we have believed to be the best authorities on these matters.

5. Now let us take as hypothesis that the earth together with the sea is sphere-shaped and that the surface of the earth is one and the same with that of the high seas; for the elevations on the earth's surface would disappear from consideration, because they are small in comparison with the great size of the earth and admit of being overlooked; and so we use "sphere-shaped" for figures of this kind, not as though they were turned on a lathe, nor yet as the geometrician uses the sphere for demonstration, but as an aid to our conception of the earth—and that, too, a rather rough conception. Now let us conceive of a sphere with five zones, and let the equator be drawn as a circle upon that sphere, and let a second circle be drawn parallel thereto, bounding the frigid zone in the northern hemisphere, and let a third circle be drawn through the poles, cutting the other two circles at right angles. Then, since the northern hemisphere contains two-fourths of the earth, which are formed by the equator with the circle that passes through the poles, a quadrilateral area is

ἑκατέρῳ τούτων ἀπολαμβάνεται τετράπλευρον
χωρίον, οὗ ἡ μὲν βόρειος πλευρὰ ἥμισυ τοῦ πρὸς
τῷ πόλῳ παραλλήλου ἐστίν, ἡ δὲ νότιος τοῦ ἰσημερινοῦ ἥμισυ, αἱ δὲ λοιπαὶ πλευραὶ τμήματά
εἰσι τοῦ διὰ τῶν πόλων, ἀντικείμενα ἀλλήλοις,
ἴσαι τὸ μῆκος. ἐν θατέρῳ δὴ τῶν τετραπλεύρων
τούτων (ὁποτέρῳ δ᾽ οὐδὲν ἂν διαφέρειν δόξειεν)
ἱδρῦσθαί φαμεν τὴν καθ᾽ ἡμᾶς οἰκουμένην, περίκλυστον θαλάττῃ καὶ ἐοικυῖαν νήσῳ· εἴρηται γὰρ
ὅτι καὶ τῇ αἰσθήσει καὶ τῷ λόγῳ δείκνυται τοῦτο.
εἰ δ᾽ ἀπιστεῖ τις τῷ λόγῳ τούτῳ, διαφέροι ἂν
πρὸς τὴν γεωγραφίαν οὐδὲν νῆσον ποιεῖν, ἢ ὅπερ
ἐκ τῆς πείρας ἐλάβομεν, τούτῳ συγχωρεῖν, ὅτι
καὶ ἀπὸ τῆς ἠοῦς ἑκατέρωθεν περίπλους ἐστὶ καὶ
ἀπὸ τῆς ἑσπέρας, πλὴν ὀλίγων τῶν μέσων χωρίων.
ταῦτα δ᾽ οὐ διαφέρει θαλάττῃ περατοῦσθαι ἢ γῇ
ἀοικήτῳ· ὁ γὰρ γεωγραφῶν ζητεῖ τὰ γνώριμα
μέρη τῆς οἰκουμένης εἰπεῖν, τὰ δ᾽ ἄγνωστα ἐᾷ,
C 113 καθάπερ καὶ τὰ ἔξω αὐτῆς. ἀρκέσει δ᾽ ἐπιζεύ-
ξασιν εὐθεῖαν γραμμὴν ἐπὶ τὰ ὕστατα σημεῖα τοῦ
ἑκατέρωθεν παράπλου τὸ πᾶν ἐκπληρῶσαι σχῆμα
τῆς λεγομένης νήσου.

6. Προκείσθω δὴ[1] ἡ μὲν νῆσος ἐν τῷ λεχθέντι
τετραπλεύρῳ. δεῖ δὲ λαβεῖν τὸ μέγεθος αὐτῆς

---

[1] δή, Spengel, for δέ; Meineke following.

---

[1] See page 17.
[2] That is, one could circumnavigate the inhabited world
by setting out in any one of four ways—either north or south,

cut off in each of the two fourths. The northern side of the quadrilateral is half of the parallel next to the pole; the southern side is half of the equator; and the two remaining sides are segments of the circle that runs through the poles, these segments lying opposite to each other and being equal in length. Now in one of these two quadrilaterals (it would seem to make no difference in which one) we say that our inhabited world lies, washed on all sides by the sea and like an island; for, as I have already said above,[1] the evidence of our senses and of reason prove this. But if anyone disbelieves the evidence of reason, it would make no difference, from the point of view of the geographer, whether we make the inhabited world an island, or merely admit what experience has taught us, namely, that it is possible to sail round the inhabited world on both sides, from the east as well as from the west,[2] with the exception of a few intermediate stretches. And, as to these stretches, it makes no difference whether they are bounded by sea or by uninhabited land; for the geographer undertakes to describe the known parts of the inhabited world, but he leaves out of consideration the unknown parts of it—just as he does what is outside of it. And it will suffice to fill out and complete the outline of what we term " the island " by joining with a straight line the extreme points reached on the coasting-voyages made on both sides of the inhabited world.

6. So let us presuppose that the island lies in the aforesaid quadrilateral. We must then take as its

from either the Pillars or the eastern coast of India—were it not for the few intermediate stretches that prevent it. Compare page 17.

τὸ φαινόμενον, ἀφελόντας ἀπὸ μὲν τοῦ ὅλου μεγέθους τῆς γῆς τὸ ἡμισφαίριον τὸ καθ' ἡμᾶς, ἀπὸ
δὲ τούτου τὸ ἥμισυ, ἀπὸ δ' αὖ τούτου πάλιν τὸ
τετράπλευρον, ἐν ᾧ δὴ τὴν οἰκουμένην κεῖσθαί
φαμεν. ἀνάλογον δὲ καὶ περὶ τοῦ σχήματος
ὑπολαβεῖν δεῖ, τὸ φαινόμενον τοῖς ὑποκειμένοις
ἐφαρμόττοντα. ἀλλ' ἐπειδὴ τὸ[1] μεταξὺ τοῦ
ἰσημερινοῦ καὶ τοῦ ληφθέντος παραλλήλου τούτῳ
πρὸς τῷ πόλῳ τμῆμα τοῦ βορείου ἡμισφαιρίου
σπόνδυλός ἐστι τὸ σχῆμα, ὁ δὲ διὰ τοῦ πόλου
δίχα τέμνων τὸ ἡμισφαίριον δίχα τέμνει καὶ τὸν
σπόνδυλον καὶ ποιεῖ τὸ τετράπλευρον, ἔσται
δηλονότι σπονδύλου ἐπιφανείας ἥμισυ τὸ τετράπλευρον ᾧ ἐπίκειται τὸ Ἀτλαντικὸν πέλαγος·
ἡ δ' οἰκουμένη χλαμυδοειδὴς ἐν τούτῳ νῆσος,
ἐλάττων[2] ἢ ἥμισυ τοῦ τετραπλεύρου μέρος οὖσα.
φανερὸν δὲ τοῦτο ἔκ τε γεωμετρίας καὶ τοῦ πλήθους τῆς περικεχυμένης θαλάττης, καλυπτούσης
τὰ ἄκρα τῶν ἠπείρων ἑκατέρωθεν καὶ συναγούσης
εἰς μύουρον[3] σχῆμα, καὶ τρίτου τοῦ μήκους καὶ

---

[1] τὸ . . . τμῆμα, Kramer, for τοῦ . . . τμήματος; editors
following.
[2] ἐλάττων, Casaubon, for ἔλαττον; Siebenkees, Corais,
following.
[3] μύουρον, Meineke restores, the reading before Kramer;
C. Müller approving.

---

[1] Strabo has assumed that the earth is sphere-shaped and
that the inhabited world is an island within a certain
spherical quadrilateral. Then, after conforming the inhabited world to the limits of the quadrilateral, which
represents only the obvious, or apparent, size and shape, he
proceeds by argument to define more accurately both the
size and the shape within the limits of the quadrilateral.

size the figure that is obvious to our senses, which is obtained by abstracting from the entire size of the earth our hemisphere, then from this area its half, and in turn from this half the quadrilateral in which we say the inhabited world lies; and it is by an analogous process that we must form our conception of the shape of the island, accommodating the obvious shape to our hypotheses.[1] But since the segment of the northern hemisphere that lies between the equator and the circle drawn parallel to it next to the pole is a spinning-whorl[2] in shape, and since the circle that passes through the pole, by cutting the northern hemisphere in two, also cuts the spinning-whorl in two and thus forms the quadrilateral, it will be clear that the quadrilateral in which the Atlantic Sea lies is half of a spinning-whorl's surface; and that the inhabited world is a chlamys-shaped[3] island in this quadrilateral, since it is less in size than half of the quadrilateral. This latter fact is clear from geometry, and also from the great extent of the enveloping sea which covers the extremities of the continents both in the east and west and contracts them to a tapering shape; and, in the third place, it

[2] Approximately a truncated cone.

[3] That is, mantle-shaped—a common designation for the shape of the inhabited world in Strabo's time. The skirt of the chlamys was circular; and the collar was cut in a straight line, or else in a circle with a larger radius and a shorter arc than the skirt. If the comparison be fairly accurate, then according to Strabo's description of the inhabited world we must think of the ends of the chlamys (which represent the eastern and western extremities of the inhabited world) as tapering, and so much so that a line joining the corners of the skirt passes through the middle of the chlamys. (See Tarbell, *Classical Philology*, vol. i. page 283.)

πλάτους τοῦ μεγίστου· ὧν τὸ μὲν ἑπτὰ μυριάδων
σταδίων ἐστίν, ὡς ἐπὶ τὸ πολὺ περατούμενον
θαλάττῃ μηκέτι πλεῖσθαι δυναμένῃ διὰ τὸ μέγεθος καὶ τὴν ἐρημίαν, τὸ δ᾽ ἔλαττον τριῶν μυριάδων ὁριζόμενον τῷ ἀοικήτῳ διὰ θάλπος ἢ ψῦχος.
αὐτὸ γὰρ τὸ διὰ θάλπος ἀοίκητον τοῦ τετραπλεύρου, πλάτος μὲν ἔχον ὀκτακισχιλίων καὶ
ὀκτακοσίων σταδίων, μῆκος δὲ τὸ μέγιστον
μυριάδων δώδεκα καὶ ἑξακισχιλίων, ὅσον ἐστὶν
ἥμισυ τοῦ ἰσημερινοῦ, [μεῖζόν ἐστι τοῦ ἡμίσους
τῆς οἰκουμένης, καὶ ἔτι][1] πλέον ἂν εἴη τὸ λοιπόν.

7. Τούτοις δὲ συνῳδά πώς ἐστι καὶ τὰ ὑπὸ
Ἱππάρχου λεγόμενα· φησὶ γὰρ ἐκεῖνος, ὑποθέ-
μενος τὸ μέγεθος τῆς γῆς ὅπερ εἶπεν Ἐρατοσθένης, ἐντεῦθεν δεῖν ποιεῖσθαι τὴν τῆς οἰκουμένης ἀφαίρεσιν· οὐ γὰρ πολὺ διοίσειν πρὸς τὰ
φαινόμενα τῶν οὐρανίων καθ᾽ ἑκάστην τὴν οἴκησιν
οὕτως ἔχειν τὴν ἀναμέτρησιν, ἢ ὡς οἱ ὕστερον
ἀποδεδώκασιν. ὄντος δὴ κατ᾽ Ἐρατοσθένη τοῦ
ἰσημερινοῦ κύκλου σταδίων μυριάδων πέντε καὶ
εἴκοσι καὶ δισχιλίων, τὸ τεταρτημόριον εἴη ἂν ἐξ

---

[1] The words in brackets are inserted by Groskurd;
Kramer, C. Müller, Tardieu, approving.

---

[1] The large quadrilateral in question is composed of (1) the
inhabited world, (2) a strip one half the width of the torrid
zone and 180° long, and (3) "the remainder." "The remainder" consists of two small quadrilaterals, one of which
is east, the other west, of the inhabited world. By actual
computation the strip of the torrid zone is more than half
of the inhabited world, and "the remainder" is still more.
Therefore the inhabited world covers less than half of the
large quadrilateral in question. To illustrate the argument,
draw a figure on a sphere as follows: Let *AB* be 180° of the

is clear from the maximum length and breadth. Now the length of the inhabited world is seventy thousand stadia, being for the most part limited by a sea which still cannot be navigated because of its vastness and desolation; the breadth is less than thirty thousand stadia, being bounded by the regions that are un-inhabitable on account either of heat or cold. For merely the part of the quadrilateral that is un-inhabitable on account of the heat—since it has a breadth of eight thousand eight hundred stadia and a maximum length of one hundred and twenty six thousand stadia, that is, half the length of the equator—is more than half the inhabited world, and the remainder of the quadrilateral would be still more than that.[1]

7. In essential accord with all this are the views of Hipparchus. He says that, having taken as hypothesis the measurement of the earth as stated by Eratosthenes, he must then abstract the inhabited world from the earth in his discussion; for it will not make much difference with respect to the celestial phenomena for the several inhabited places whether the measurement followed is that of Eratosthenes or that given by the later geographers. Since, then, according to Eratosthenes, the equator measures two hundred and fifty two thousand stadia, the fourth

equator; let *CD* be 180° of the parallel through the northern limit of the inhabited world; join *A* and *C*, and *B* and *D*; and then draw an arc of 180° parallel to the equator at 8,800 stadia north of the equator, and also two meridian-arcs from *CD* to *AB* through the eastern and western limits, respectively, of the inhabited world. Thus we have the large quadrilateral *ACDB*, and, within it, four small quadri-laterals, which constitute the three divisions above-mentioned.

μυριάδες καὶ τρισχίλιοι· τοῦτο δέ ἐστι τὸ ἀπὸ
τοῦ ἰσημερινοῦ ἐπὶ τὸν πόλον πεντεκαίδεκα ἑξηκοντάδων, οἵων ἐστὶν ὁ ἰσημερινὸς ἑξήκοντα. τὸ
δ' ἀπὸ τοῦ ἰσημερινοῦ ἐπὶ τὸν θερινὸν τροπικὸν
C 114 τεττάρων· οὗτος δ' ἐστὶν ὁ διὰ Συήνης γραφό-
μενος παράλληλος. συλλογίζεται δὴ τὰ καθ'
ἕκαστα διαστήματα ἐκ τῶν φαινομένων μέτρων·
τὸν μὲν γὰρ τροπικὸν κατὰ Συήνην κεῖσθαι συμβαίνει, διότι ἐνταῦθα κατὰ τὰς θερινὰς τροπὰς
ἄσκιός ἐστιν ὁ γνώμων μέσης ἡμέρας. ὁ δὲ διὰ
τῆς Συήνης μεσημβρινὸς γράφεται μάλιστα διὰ
τῆς τοῦ Νείλου ῥύσεως ἀπὸ Μερόης ἕως Ἀλεξαν-
δρείας· στάδιοι δ' εἰσὶν οὗτοι περὶ μυρίους· κατὰ
μέσον δὲ τὸ διάστημα τὴν Συήνην ἱδρῦσθαι συμβαίνει, ὥστ' ἐντεῦθεν ἐπὶ Μερόην πεντακισχίλιοι·
προϊόντι δ' ἐπ' εὐθείας ὅσον τρισχιλίους σταδίους
ἐπὶ μεσημβρίαν, οὐκέτ' οἰκήσιμα τἆλλά ἐστι διὰ
καῦμα· ὥστε τὸν διὰ τούτων τῶν τόπων παράλληλον, τὸν αὐτὸν ὄντα τῷ διὰ τῆς Κινναμωμοφόρου, πέρας καὶ ἀρχὴν δεῖ τίθεσθαι τῆς καθ'
ἡμᾶς οἰκουμένης πρὸς μεσημβρίαν. ἐπεὶ οὖν
πεντακισχίλιοι μέν εἰσιν οἱ ἀπὸ Συήνης εἰς
Μερόην, ἄλλοι δὲ προσγεγόνασι τρισχίλιοι, εἶεν
ἂν οἱ πάντες ἐπὶ τοὺς ὅρους τῆς οἰκουμένης
ὀκτακισχίλιοι. ἐπὶ δέ γε τὸν ἰσημερινὸν ἀπὸ
Συήνης μύριοι ἑξακισχίλιοι ὀκτακόσιοι (τοσοῦτοι
γάρ εἰσιν οἱ τῶν τεττάρων ἑξηκοντάδων, τε-

---

[1] Eratosthenes divided the circumference of the earth into sixty intervals, one interval being equal to 6°. Hipparchus

part of it would be sixty three thousand stadia ; and
this is the distance from the equator to the pole,
namely, fifteen sixtieths of the sixty intervals into
which the equator is divided.[1] And the distance
from the equator to the summer tropic is four
sixtieths ; and the summer tropic is the parallel
drawn through Syene. Now the several distances
are computed from the standard measures that are
obvious to our senses. The summer tropic, for
instance, must pass through Syene, because there,
at the time of the summer solstice, the index of the
sun-dial does not cast a shadow at noon. And the
meridian through Syene is drawn approximately along
the course of the Nile from Meroë to Alexandria, and
this distance is about ten thousand stadia ; and Syene
must lie in the centre of that distance ; so that the
distance from Syene to Meroë is five thousand stadia.
And when you have proceeded about three thousand
stadia in a straight line south of Meroë, the country is
no longer inhabitable on account of the heat, and therefore the parallel through these regions, being the
same as that through the Cinnamon-producing
Country, must be put down as the limit and the
beginning of our inhabited world on the South.
Since, then, the distance from Syene to Meroë is five
thousand stadia, to which we have added the other
three thousand stadia, the total distance from Syene
to the confines of the inhabited world would be eight
thousand stadia. But the distance from Syene to
the equator is sixteen thousand eight hundred stadia
(for that is what the four sixtieths amounts to, since
each sixtieth is estimated at four thousand two

seems to have been the first to divide the earth into three
hundred and sixty degrees.

θείσης ἑκάστης τετρακισχιλίων καὶ διακοσίων),
ὥστε λοιποὶ εἶεν ἂν ἀπὸ τῶν ὅρων τῆς οἰκουμένης ἐπὶ τὸν ἰσημερινὸν ὀκτακισχίλιοι ὀκτακόσιοι, ἀπὸ δὲ Ἀλεξανδρείας δισμύριοι χίλιοι
ὀκτακόσιοι. πάλιν δ' ἀπὸ τῆς Ἀλεξανδρείας ἐπ'
εὐθείας τῇ ῥύσει τοῦ Νείλου πάντες ὁμολογοῦσι
τὸν ἐπὶ Ῥόδον πλοῦν· κἀντεῦθεν δὲ τὸν τῆς Καρίας παράπλουν καὶ Ἰωνίας μέχρι τῆς Τρωάδος
καὶ Βυζαντίου καὶ Βορυσθένους. λαβόντες οὖν
τὰ διαστήματα γνώριμα καὶ πλεόμενα σκοποῦσι
τὰ ὑπὲρ τοῦ Βορυσθένους ἐπ' εὐθείας ταύτῃ τῇ
γραμμῇ μέχρι τίνος οἰκήσιμά ἐστι, καὶ περατοῦται[1] τὰ προσάρκτια μέρη τῆς οἰκουμένης.
οἰκοῦσι δ' ὑπὲρ τοῦ Βορυσθένους ὕστατοι τῶν
γνωρίμων Σκυθῶν Ῥωξολανοί, νοτιώτεροι ὄντες
τῶν ὑπὲρ τῆς Βρεττανικῆς ἐσχάτων γνωριζομένων·
ἤδη δὲ τἀπέκεινα διὰ ψύχος ἀοίκητά ἐστι· νοτιώτεροι δὲ τούτων καὶ οἱ ὑπὲρ τῆς Μαιώτιδος Σαυρομάται καὶ Σκύθαι μέχρι τῶν ἑῴων Σκυθῶν.

8. Ὁ μὲν οὖν Μασσαλιώτης Πυθέας τὰ περὶ
Θούλην τὴν βορειοτάτην τῶν Βρεττανίδων ὕστατα
λέγει, παρ' οἷς ὁ αὐτός ἐστι τῷ ἀρκτικῷ ὁ θερινὸς
τροπικὸς κύκλος· παρὰ δὲ τῶν ἄλλων οὐδὲν
ἱστορῶ, οὔθ' ὅτι Θούλη νῆσος ἔστι τις, οὔτ' εἰ τὰ
μέχρι δεῦρο οἰκήσιμά ἐστιν, ὅπου ὁ θερινὸς

---

[1] περατοῦται, Madvig, for περατοῖ.

[1] That is, at Thule the variable arctic circle has the fixed
value of the summer tropic Hence, according to Pytheas,
the latitude of Thule would be the complement of that of

hundred stadia), and therefore we should have eight thousand eight hundred stadia left as the distance from the confines of the inhabited world to the equator, and from Alexandria twenty-one thousand eight hundred. Again, all agree that the route by sea from Alexandria to Rhodes is in a straight line with the course of the Nile, as also the route thence along the coast of Caria and Ionia to the Troad, Byzantium, and the Borysthenes. Taking, therefore, the distances that are already known and sailed over, geographers inquire as to the regions beyond the Borysthenes that lie in a straight course with this line—as to how far they are inhabitable, and how far the northern parts of the inhabited world have their boundaries. Now the Roxolanians, the most remote of the known Scythians, live beyond the Borysthenes, though they are farther south than the most remote peoples of whom we have knowledge north of Britain; and the regions beyond the Roxolanians become at once uninhabitable because of the cold; and farther south than the Roxolanians are the Sarmatians who dwell beyond Lake Maeotis, and also the Scythians as far as the Eastern Scythians.

8. Now Pytheas of Massilia tells us that Thule, the most northerly of the Britannic Islands, is farthest north, and that there the circle of the summer tropic is the same as the arctic circle.[1] But from the other writers I learn nothing on the subject—neither that there exists a certain island by the name of Thule, nor whether the northern regions are inhabitable up to the point where the summer tropic becomes the

the terrestrial tropic. Assuming that Pytheas placed the latter at 24° (as did Eratosthenes and Strabo), he placed Thule at 66°.

τροπικὸς ἀρκτικὸς γίνεται. νομίζω δὲ πολὺ εἶναι
νοτιώτερον τούτου[1] τὸ τῆς οἰκουμένης πέρας τὸ
C 115 προσάρκτιον· οἱ γὰρ νῦν ἱστοροῦντες περαιτέρω
τῆς Ἰέρνης οὐδὲν ἔχουσι λέγειν, ἢ πρὸς ἄρκτον
πρόκειται τῆς Βρεττανικῆς πλησίον, ἀγρίων τελέως ἀνθρώπων καὶ κακῶς οἰκούντων διὰ ψῦχος,
ὥστ᾽ ἐνταῦθα νομίζω τὸ πέρας εἶναι θετέον.
τοῦ δὲ παραλλήλου τοῦ διὰ Βυζαντίου διὰ Μασσαλίας πως ἰόντος, ὥς φησιν Ἵππαρχος πιστεύσας Πυθέᾳ (φησὶ γὰρ ἐν Βυζαντίῳ τὸν αὐτὸν
εἶναι λόγον τοῦ γνώμονος πρὸς τὴν σκιάν, ὃν
εἶπεν ὁ Πυθέας ἐν Μασσαλίᾳ), τοῦ δὲ διὰ
Βορυσθένους ἀπὸ τούτου διέχοντος περὶ τρισχιλίους καὶ ὀκτακοσίους, εἴη ἂν ἐκ τοῦ διαστήματος τοῦ ἀπὸ Μασσαλίας ἐπὶ τὴν Βρεττανικὴν
ἐνταῦθά που πίπτων ὁ διὰ τοῦ Βορυσθένους κύκλος. πανταχοῦ ἀλλαχοῦ[2] δὲ παρακρουόμενος
τοὺς ἀνθρώπους ὁ Πυθέας κἀνταῦθά που διέψευ-
σται. τὸ μὲν γὰρ τὴν ἀπὸ Στηλῶν γραμμὴν ἐπὶ
τοὺς περὶ τὸν Πορθμὸν καὶ Ἀθήνας καὶ Ῥόδον
τόπους ἐπὶ τοῦ αὐτοῦ παραλλήλου κεῖσθαι
ὡμολόγηται παρὰ πολλῶν· ὁμολογεῖται δὲ ὅτι καὶ
διὰ μέσου πως τοῦ πελάγους ἐστὶν ἡ ἀπὸ Στηλῶν
ἐπὶ τὸν Πορθμόν. οἵ τε[3] πλέοντές φασι[4] τὸ
μέγιστον δίαρμα ἀπὸ τῆς Κελτικῆς ἐπὶ τὴν Λιβύην
εἶναι τὸ ἀπὸ τοῦ Γαλατικοῦ κόλπου σταδίων πεντακισχιλίων, τοῦτο δ᾽ εἶναι καὶ τὸ μέγιστον πλάτος
τοῦ πελάγους, ὥστ᾽ εἴη ἂν τὸ ἀπὸ τῆς λεχθείσης

[1] τούτου, B. Niese, for τοῦτο; A. Vogel approving.
[2] ἀλλαχοῦ, A. Jacob, for πολλαχοῦ.
[3] οἵ τε, A. Jacob, for οἱ δέ, reporting that οἵ τε is the
reading of A, B, and C.
[4] φασι, Madvig inserts, after πλέοντες.

arctic circle. But in my opinion the northern limit of
the inhabited world is much farther to the south than
where the summer tropic becomes the arctic circle.
For modern scientific writers are not able to speak of
any country north of Ierne, which lies to the north
of Britain and near thereto, and is the home of men
who are complete savages and lead a miserable existence because of the cold; and therefore, in my
opinion, the northern limit of our inhabited world
is to be placed there. But if the parallel through
Byzantium passes approximately through Massilia, as
Hipparchus says on the testimony of Pytheas (Hipparchus says, namely, that in Byzantium the relation
of the index to the shadow is the same as that which
Pytheas gave for Massilia), and if the parallel through
the mouth of the Borysthenes is about three thousand eight hundred stadia distant from that parallel,
then, in view of the distance from Massilia to Britain,[1]
the circle drawn through the mouth of the Borysthenes would fall somewhere in Britain. But
Pytheas, who misleads people everywhere else, is, I
think, wholly in error here too; for it has been
admitted by many writers that all the line drawn
from the Pillars to the regions of the Strait of Sicily
and of Athens, and of Rhodes, lies on the same
parallel; and it is admitted that the part of that line
from the Pillars to the strait runs approximately
through the middle of the sea. And further, sailors
say that the longest passage from Celtica to Libya,
namely, that from the Galatic Gulf, is five thousand
stadia, and that this is also the greatest width of the
Mediterranean sea, and therefore the distance from

---

[1] That is, 3,700 stadia.

γραμμῆς ἐπὶ τὸν μυχὸν τοῦ κόλπου σταδίων δισχιλίων πεντακοσίων, ἐπὶ δὲ Μασσαλίαν ἐλατ-
τόνων· νοτιωτέρα γάρ ἐστιν ἡ Μασσαλία τοῦ
μυχοῦ τοῦ κόλπου. τὸ δέ γε ἀπὸ τῆς Ῥοδίας ἐπὶ
τὸ Βυζάντιόν ἐστι τετρακισχιλίων που καὶ ἐννακοσίων σταδίων, ὥστε πολὺ ἀρκτικώτερος ἂν εἴη ὁ διὰ
Βυζαντίου τοῦ διὰ Μασσαλίας. τὸ δ' ἐκεῖθεν ἐπὶ
τὴν Βρεττανικὴν δύναται συμφωνεῖν τῷ ἀπὸ Βυζαντίου ἐπὶ Βορυσθένη· τὸ δ' ἐκεῖθεν ἐπὶ τὴν Ἰέρνην
οὐκέτι γνώριμον, πόσον ἄν τις θείη, οὐδ' εἰ περαιτέρω ἔτι οἰκήσιμά ἐστιν, οὐδὲ δεῖ φροντίζειν τοῖς
ἐπάνω λεχθεῖσι προσέχοντας.[1] πρός τε γὰρ ἐπιστήμην ἀρκεῖ τὸ λαβεῖν, ὅτι,[2] καθάπερ ἐπὶ τῶν νοτίων
μερῶν, ὑπὲρ Μερόης μέχρι τρισχιλίων σταδίων
προελθόντι τῆς οἰκησίμου τίθεσθαι πέρας[3] προσ-
ῆκεν (οὐχ ὡς ἂν τούτου ἀκριβεστάτου πέρατος
ὄντος, ἀλλ' ἐγγύς γε τἀκριβοῦς), οὕτω κἀκεῖ τοὺς
ὑπὲρ τῆς Βρεττανικῆς οὐ πλείους τούτων θετέον ἢ
μικρῷ πλείους, οἷον τετρακισχιλίους. πρός τε τὰς
ἡγεμονικὰς χρείας οὐδὲν ἂν εἴη πλεονέκτημα τὰς
τοιαύτας γνωρίζειν χώρας καὶ τοὺς ἐνοικοῦντας,
καὶ μάλιστα εἰ νήσους οἰκοῖεν τοιαύτας, αἳ μήτε
λυπεῖν μήτ' ὠφελεῖν ἡμᾶς δύνανται μηδὲν διὰ τὸ
ἀνεπίπλεκτον. καὶ γὰρ τὴν Βρεττανικὴν ἔχειν
δυνάμενοι Ῥωμαῖοι κατεφρόνησαν, ὁρῶντες ὅτι
οὔτε φόβος ἐξ αὐτῶν οὐδὲ εἷς ἐστιν (οὐ γὰρ

---

[1] προσέχοντας, Corais conjectures ; editors following.
[2] Groskurd transposes ὅτι from a position before ὑπέρ to a
position before καθάπερ.
[3] πέρας, Corais inserts ; editors following.

the line in question to the head of the gulf would
be two thousand five hundred stadia and less than
that to Massilia; for Massilia is farther south than
the head of the gulf. But the distance from Rhodes
to Byzantium is about four thousand nine hundred
stadia, and therefore the parallel through Byzantium
would be much farther north than that through
Massilia. And the distance from Massilia to Britain
may possibly correspond to that from Byzantium to
the mouth of the Borysthenes; but the distance that
should be set down for the stretch from Britain to
Ierne is no longer a known quantity, nor is it known
whether there are still inhabitable regions farther
on, nor need we concern ourselves about the question
if we give heed to what has been said above. For,
so far as science is concerned, it is sufficient to
assume that, just as it was appropriate in the case
of the southern regions to fix a limit of the habitable world by proceeding three thousand stadia
south of Meroë (not indeed as though this were
a very accurate limit, but as one that at least ap-
proximates accuracy), so in this case too we must
reckon not more than three thousand stadia north of
Britain, or only a little more, say, four thousand
stadia. And for governmental purposes there would
be no advantage in knowing such countries and their
inhabitants, and particularly if the people live in
islands which are of such a nature that they can
neither injure nor benefit us in any way because of
their isolation. For although they could have held
even Britain, the Romans scorned to do so, because
they saw that there was nothing at all to fear from
the Britons (for they are not strong enough to cross

C 116 ἰσχύουσι τοσοῦτον, ὥστ' ἐπιδιαβαίνειν ἡμῖν), οὔτ'
ὠφέλεια τοσαύτη τις, εἰ κατάσχοιεν. πλέον γὰρ
δὴ[1] ἐκ τῶν τελῶν δοκεῖ προσφέρεσθαι νῦν, ἢ ὁ
φόρος δύναιτ' ἂν[2] συντελεῖν, ἀφαιρουμένης τῆς
εἰς τὸ στρατιωτικὸν δαπάνης τὸ φρουρῆσον καὶ
φορολογῆσον τὴν νῆσον· πολὺ δ' ἂν ἔτι γένοιτο[3] τὸ
ἄχρηστον ἐπὶ τῶν ἄλλων τῶν περὶ ταύτην νήσων.

9. Εἰ δὲ προστεθείη τῷ ἀπὸ τῆς Ῥοδίας μέχρι
Βορυσθένους διαστήματι τὸ ἀπὸ Βορυσθένους ἐπὶ
τὰς ἄρκτους τῶν τετρακισχιλίων σταδίων διάστημα, γίνεται τὸ πᾶν μύριοι δισχίλιοι ἑπτακό-
σιοι στάδιοι, τὸ δ' ἀπὸ τῆς Ῥοδίας ἐπὶ τὸ νότιον
πέρας ἐστὶ τῆς οἰκουμένης μύριοι ἑξακισχίλιοι
ἑξακόσιοι, ὥστε τὸ σύμπαν πλάτος τῆς οἰκουμένης εἴη ἂν ἔλαττον τῶν τρισμυρίων ἀπὸ νότου
πρὸς ἄρκτον. τὸ δέ γε μῆκος περὶ ἑπτὰ μυριάδας
λέγεται, τοῦτο δ' ἐστὶν ἀπὸ δύσεως ἐπὶ τὰς ἀνατολὰς τὸ ἀπὸ τῶν ἄκρων τῆς Ἰβηρίας ἐπὶ τὰ ἄκρα
τῆς Ἰνδικῆς, τὸ μὲν ὁδοῖς, τὸ δὲ ταῖς ναυτιλίαις
ἀναμεμετρημένον. ὅτι δ' ἐντὸς τοῦ λεχθέντος τετραπλεύρου τὸ μῆκός ἐστι τοῦτο, ἐκ τοῦ λόγου τῶν
παραλλήλων[4] πρὸς τὸν ἰσημερινὸν δῆλον, ὥστε
πλέον ἢ διπλάσιόν ἐστι τοῦ πλάτους τὸ μῆκος.
λέγεται δὲ καὶ χλαμυδοειδές πως τὸ σχῆμα·
πολλὴ γὰρ συναγωγὴ τοῦ πλάτους πρὸς τοῖς
ἄκροις εὑρίσκεται, καὶ μάλιστα τοῖς ἑσπερίοις, τὰ
καθ' ἕκαστα ἐπιόντων ἡμῶν.

10. Νυνὶ μὲν οὖν ἐπιγεγράφαμεν ἐπὶ σφαιρικῆς

---

[1] δή, A. Jacob, for ἄν.
[2] δύναιτ' ἄν, Cobet, for δύναται.
[3] ἔτι γένοιτο, Corais, for ἐπιγένοιτο.
[4] τῶν, Kramer suspects, after παραλλήλων ; Meineke
deletes.

over and attack us), and that no corresponding
advantage was to be gained by taking and holding
their country. For it seems that at present more
revenue is derived from the duty on their commerce
than the tribute could bring in, if we deduct the
expense involved in the maintenance of an army
for the purpose of guarding the island and collecting
the tribute; and the unprofitableness of an occupation would be still greater in the case of the other
islands about Britain.

9. Now if to the distance from Rhodes to the
mouth of the Borysthenes we add the distance of
four thousand stadia from the mouth of the Borysthenes to the northern regions, the sum total amounts
to twelve thousand seven hundred stadia, but the
distance from Rhodes to the southern limit of the
inhabited world is sixteen thousand six hundred
stadia, and therefore the total breadth of the inhabited world would be less than thirty thousand
stadia from south to north. Its length, however, is
estimated at about seventy thousand stadia; and
this is, from west to east, the distance from the capes
of Iberia to the capes of India, measured partly by
land journeys and partly by sea voyages. And that
this length falls within the quadrilateral mentioned
above is clear from the relation of the parallels to the
equator; hence the length of the inhabited world is
more than double its breadth. Its shape is described
as about like that of a chlamys; for when we visit
the several regions of the inhabited world, we discover a considerable contraction in its width at
its extremities, and particularly at its western
extremities.

10. We have now traced on a spherical surface the

ἐπιφανείας τὸ χωρίον ἐν ᾧ φαμεν ἱδρῦσθαι τὴν
οἰκουμένην· καὶ δεῖ τὸν ἐγγυτάτω διὰ τῶν χειρο-
κμήτων σχημάτων[1] μιμούμενον τὴν ἀλήθειαν ποιήσαντα σφαῖραν τὴν γῆν, καθάπερ τὴν Κρατήτειον,
ἐπὶ ταύτης ἀπολαβόντα τὸ τετράπλευρον, ἐντὸς
τούτου τιθέναι τὸν πίνακα τῆς γεωγραφίας. ἀλλ᾽
ἐπειδὴ μεγάλης δεῖ σφαίρας, ὥστε πολλοστημό-
ριον αὐτῆς ὑπάρχον τὸ λεχθὲν τμῆμα ἱκανὸν
γενέσθαι δέξασθαι σαφῶς τὰ προσήκοντα μέρη
τῆς οἰκουμένης, καὶ τὴν οἰκείαν παρασχεῖν ὄψιν
τοῖς ἐπιβλέπουσι, τῷ μὲν δυναμένῳ κατασκευάσασθαι τηλικαύτην οὕτω ποιεῖν βέλτιον· ἔστω δὲ
μὴ μείω δέκα ποδῶν ἔχουσα τὴν διάμετρον· τῷ δὲ
μὴ δυναμένῳ τηλικαύτην ἢ μὴ πολλῷ ταύτης
ἐνδεεστέραν ἐν ἐπιπέδῳ καταγραπτέον πίνακι
τοὐλάχιστον ἑπτὰ ποδῶν. διοίσει γὰρ μικρόν, ἐὰν
ἀντὶ τῶν κύκλων, τῶν τε παραλλήλων καὶ τῶν
μεσημβρινῶν, οἷς τά τε κλίματα καὶ τοὺς ἀνέμους
διασαφοῦμεν καὶ τὰς ἄλλας διαφορὰς καὶ τὰς
σχέσεις τῶν τῆς γῆς μερῶν πρὸς ἄλληλά τε καὶ
τὰ οὐράνια, εὐθείας γράφωμεν, τῶν μὲν παραλλήλων παραλλήλους, τῶν δὲ ὀρθῶν πρὸς ἐκείνους
C 117 ὀρθάς, τῆς διανοίας ῥᾳδίως μεταφέρειν δυναμένης
τὸ ὑπὸ τῆς ὄψεως ἐν ἐπιπέδῳ θεωρούμενον ἐπιφανείᾳ σχῆμα καὶ μέγεθος ἐπὶ τὴν περιφερῆ τε
καὶ σφαιρικήν. ἀνάλογον δὲ καὶ περὶ τῶν λοξῶν
κύκλων καὶ εὐθειῶν φαμεν. εἰ δ᾽ οἱ μεσημβρινοὶ
οἱ παρ᾽ ἑκάστοις διὰ τοῦ πόλου γραφόμενοι πάντες
συννεύουσιν ἐν τῇ σφαίρᾳ πρὸς ἓν σημεῖον, ἀλλ᾽

---

[1] σχημάτων, Corais, for οἰκημάτων ; Groskurd, Meineke,
Tardieu, following ; C. Müller approving.

area in which we say the inhabited world is situated[1];
and the man who would most closely approximate
the truth by constructed figures must needs make
for the earth a globe like that of Crates, and lay off
on it the quadrilateral, and within the quadrilateral
put down the map of the inhabited world. But since
there is need of a large globe, so that the section in
question (being a small fraction of the globe) may be
large enough to receive distinctly the appropriate
parts of the inhabited world and to present the
proper appearance to observers, it is better for him
to construct a globe of adequate size, if he can do so;
and let it be no less than ten feet in diameter. But
if he cannot construct a globe of adequate size or not
much smaller, he should sketch his map on a plane
surface of at least seven feet.[2] For it will make
only a slight difference if we draw straight lines to
represent the circles, that is, the parallels and
meridians, by means of which we clearly indicate
the " climata," the winds and the other differences,
and also the positions of the parts of the earth with
reference both to each other and to the heavenly
bodies—drawing parallel lines for the parallels and
perpendicular lines for the circles perpendicular to
the parallels, for our imagination can easily transfer
to the globular and spherical surface the figure or
magnitude seen by the eye on a plane surface. And
the same applies also, we say, to the oblique circles
and their corresponding straight lines. Although
the several meridians drawn through the pole all
converge on the sphere toward one point, yet on our

---

[1] That is, the quadrilateral.
[2] In length apparently; thus the scale would suit 70,000
stadia, the length of the inhabited world.

ἐν τῷ ἐπιπέδῳ γε οὐ διοίσει πίνακι τὰς εὐθείας μικρὰ[1] συννευούσας ποιεῖν μόνον τὰς μεσημβρινάς. οὐδὲ γὰρ πολλαχοῦ τοῦτ' ἀναγκαῖον, οὐδ' ἐκφανής ἐστιν ὥσπερ ἡ περιφέρεια οὕτω καὶ ἡ σύννευσις, μεταφερομένων τῶν γραμμῶν εἰς τὸν πίνακα τὸν ἐπίπεδον καὶ γραφομένων εὐθειῶν.

11. Καὶ δὴ καὶ τὸν ἑξῆς λόγον ὡς ἐν ἐπιπέδῳ πίνακι τῆς γραφῆς γινομένης ἐκθήσομεν. ἐροῦμεν δὴ ἣν[2] μὲν ἐπελθόντες αὐτοὶ τῆς γῆς καὶ θαλάττης, περὶ ἧς δὲ πιστεύσαντες τοῖς εἰποῦσιν ἢ γράψασιν. ἐπήλθομεν δὲ ἐπὶ δύσιν μὲν ἀπὸ τῆς Ἀρμενίας μέχρι τῶν κατὰ Σαρδόνα τόπων τῆς Τυρρηνίας, ἐπὶ μεσημβρίαν δὲ ἀπὸ τοῦ Εὐξείνου μέχρι τῶν τῆς Αἰθιοπίας ὅρων· οὐδὲ τῶν ἄλλων δὲ οὐδὲ εἷς ἂν εὑρεθείη τῶν γεωγραφησάντων πολύ τι ἡμῶν μᾶλλον ἐπεληλυθὼς τῶν λεχθέντων διαστημάτων, ἀλλ' οἱ πλεονάσαντες περὶ τὰ δυσμικὰ μέρη τῶν πρὸς ταῖς ἀνατολαῖς οὐ τοσοῦτον ἥψαντο, οἱ δὲ περὶ τἀναντία τῶν ἑσπερίων ὑστέρησαν· ὁμοίως δ' ἔχει καὶ περὶ τῶν πρὸς νότον καὶ τὰς ἄρκτους. τὸ μέντοι πλέον κἀκεῖνοι καὶ ἡμεῖς ἀκοῇ παραλαβόντες συντίθεμεν καὶ τὸ[3] σχῆμα καὶ τὸ μέγεθος καὶ τὴν ἄλλην φύσιν, ὁποία καὶ ὁπόση, τὸν αὐτὸν τρόπον ὅνπερ ἡ διάνοια ἐκ τῶν αἰσθητῶν συντίθησι[4] τὰ νοητά· σχῆμα γὰρ καὶ χρόαν καὶ μέγεθος μήλου καὶ ὀδμὴν καὶ ἁφὴν καὶ χυμὸν ἀπαγγέλλουσιν αἱ αἰσθήσεις, ἐκ δὲ τούτων συντίθησιν ἡ διάνοια τὴν τοῦ μήλου νόησιν· καὶ αὐτῶν δὲ τῶν

---

[1] μικρά, Madvig, for μικράς.
[2] ἥν, Capps, for τήν.
[3] τε, Kramer suspects, before σχῆμα ; Meineke deletes.
[4] συντίθησι, Casaubon, for τίθησι ; editors following.

plane-surface chart it will not be a matter of importance merely to make the straight meridian lines converge slightly [1]; for there is no necessity for this in many cases, nor are the converging straight lines, when the lines of the sphere are transferred to the plane chart and drawn as straight lines, as easily understood as are the curved lines on the sphere.

11. And so in what I have to say hereafter I shall assume that our drawing has been made on a plane chart. Now I shall tell what part of the land and sea I have myself visited and concerning what part I have trusted to accounts given by others by word of mouth or in writing. I have travelled westward from Armenia as far as the regions of Tyrrhenia [2] opposite Sardinia, and southward from the Euxine Sea as far as the frontiers of Ethiopia. And you could not find another person among the writers on geography who has travelled over much more of the distances just mentioned than I; indeed, those who have travelled more than I in the western regions have not covered as much ground in the east, and those who have travelled more in the eastern countries are behind me in the western; and the same holds true in regard to the regions towards the south and north. However, the greater part of our material both they and I receive by hearsay and then form our ideas of shape and size and also other characteristics, qualitative and quantitative, precisely as the mind forms its ideas from sense impressions—for our senses report the shape, colour, and size of an apple, and also its smell, feel, and flavour; and from all this the mind forms the concept of apple. So, too, even

[1] That is, in view of the fact that no attempt is made to indicate curvature.   [2] Tuscany.

μεγάλων σχημάτων τὰ μέρη μὲν αἴσθησις ὁρᾷ, τὸ
δ' ὅλον ἐκ τῶν ὁραθέντων ἡ διάνοια συντίθησιν.
οὕτω δὲ καὶ οἱ φιλομαθεῖς ἄνδρες, ὥσπερ αἰσθη-
τηρίοις πιστεύσαντες τοῖς ἰδοῦσιν καὶ πλανηθεῖσιν
οὓς ἔτυχε τόπους, ἄλλοις κατ' ἄλλα μέρη τῆς γῆς,
συντιθέασιν εἰς ἓν διάγραμμα τὴν τῆς ὅλης οἰκουμένης ὄψιν. ἐπεὶ καὶ οἱ στρατηγοὶ πάντα μὲν
αὐτοὶ πράττουσιν, οὐ πανταχοῦ δὲ πάρεισιν, ἀλλὰ
πλεῖστα κατορθοῦσι δι' ἑτέρων, ἀγγέλοις πιστεύοντες καὶ πρὸς τὴν ἀκοὴν διαπέμποντες οἰκείως τὰ
προστάγματα. ὁ δ' ἀξιῶν μόνους εἰδέναι τοὺς
ἰδόντας ἀναιρεῖ τὸ τῆς ἀκοῆς κριτήριον, ἥτις πρὸς
ἐπιστήμην ὀφθαλμοῦ πολὺ κρείττων ἐστί.

12. Μάλιστα δ' οἱ νῦν ἄμεινον ἔχοιεν ἄν τι
λέγειν περὶ τῶν κατὰ Βρεττανοὺς καὶ Γερμανοὺς
C 118 καὶ τοὺς περὶ τὸν Ἴστρον τούς τε ἐντὸς καὶ τοὺς
ἐκτός, Γέτας τε καὶ Τυρεγέτας καὶ Βαστάρνας,
ἔτι δὲ τοὺς περὶ τὸν Καύκασον, οἷον Ἀλβανοὺς
καὶ Ἴβηρας. ἀπήγγελται δ' ἡμῖν καὶ ὑπὸ τῶν
τὰ Παρθικὰ συγγραψάντων, τῶν περὶ Ἀπολλό-
δωρον τὸν Ἀρτεμιτηνόν, ἃ πολλῶν ἐκεῖνοι μᾶλλον
ἀφώρισαν, τὰ περὶ τὴν Ὑρκανίαν καὶ τὴν Βακτριανήν. τῶν τε Ῥωμαίων καὶ εἰς τὴν εὐδαίμονα
Ἀραβίαν ἐμβαλόντων μετὰ στρατιᾶς νεωστί, ἧς
ἡγεῖτο ἀνὴρ φίλος ἡμῖν καὶ ἑταῖρος Αἴλιος Γάλλος, καὶ τῶν ἐκ τῆς Ἀλεξανδρείας ἐμπόρων στό-

in the case of large figures, while the senses perceive only the parts, the mind forms a concept of the whole from what the senses have perceived. And men who are eager to learn proceed in just that way: they trust as organs of sense those who have seen or wandered over any region, no matter what, some in this and some in that part of the earth, and they form in one diagram their mental image of the whole inhabited world. Why, generals, too, though they do everything themselves, are not present everywhere, but they carry out successfully most of their measures through others, trusting the reports of messengers and sending their orders around in conformity with the reports they hear. And he who claims that only those have knowledge who have actually seen abolishes the criterion of the sense of hearing, though this sense is much more important than sight for the purposes of science.

12. In particular the writers of the present time can give a better account[1] of the Britons, the Germans, the peoples both north and south of the Ister, the Getans, the Tyregetans, the Bastarnians, and, furthermore, the peoples in the regions of the Caucasus, such as the Albanians and the Iberians.[2] Information has been given us also concerning Hyrcania and Bactriana by the writers of Parthian histories (Apollodorus of Artemita and his school), in which they marked off those countries more definitely than many other writers. Again, since the Romans have recently invaded Arabia Felix with an army, of which Aelius Gallus, my friend and companion, was the commander, and since the merchants

[1] That is, better than their predecessors. Compare 1. 2. 1.   [2] The "Eastern Iberians." See page 227.

λοις[1] ἤδη πλεόντων διὰ τοῦ Νείλου καὶ τοῦ Ἀραβίου κόλπου μέχρι τῆς Ἰνδικῆς, [2]πολὺ μᾶλλον
καὶ ταῦτα ἔγνωσται τοῖς νῦν ἢ τοῖς πρὸ ἡμῶν.
ὅτε γοῦν Γάλλος ἐπῆρχε τῆς Αἰγύπτου, συνόντες
αὐτῷ καὶ συναναβάντες μέχρι Συήνης καὶ τῶν
Αἰθιοπικῶν ὅρων ἱστοροῦμεν ὅτι καὶ ἑκατὸν καὶ
εἴκοσι νῆες πλέοιεν ἐκ Μυὸς ὅρμου πρὸς τὴν
Ἰνδικήν, πρότερον ἐπὶ τῶν Πτολεμαϊκῶν βασιλέων ὀλίγων παντάπασι θαρρούντων πλεῖν καὶ
τὸν Ἰνδικὸν ἐμπορεύεσθαι φόρτον.

13. Τὰ μὲν οὖν πρῶτα καὶ κυριώτατα καὶ πρὸς
ἐπιστήμην καὶ πρὸς τὰς χρείας τὰς πολιτικὰς
ταῦτα, σχῆμα καὶ μέγεθος εἰπεῖν ὡς ἁπλούστατα
ἐγχειρεῖν τὸ πῖπτον εἰς τὸν γεωγραφικὸν πίνακα,
συμπαραδηλοῦντα καὶ τὸ ποῖόν τι καὶ πόστον
μέρος τῆς ὅλης γῆς ἐστι· τοῦτο μὲν γὰρ οἰκεῖον
τῷ γεωγράφῳ. τὸ δὲ καὶ περὶ ὅλης ἀκριβολο-
γεῖσθαι τῆς γῆς καὶ περὶ τοῦ σπονδύλου παντὸς
ἧς ἐλέγομεν[3] ζώνης ἄλλης τινὸς ἐπιστήμης ἐστίν,
οἷον εἰ περιοικεῖται καὶ κατὰ θάτερον τεταρτημόριον ὁ σπόνδυλος· καὶ γὰρ εἰ οὕτως ἔχει, οὐχ
ὑπὸ τούτων γε οἰκεῖται τῶν παρ' ἡμῖν, ἀλλ' ἐκείνην ἄλλην οἰκουμένην θετέον, ὅπερ ἐστὶ πιθανόν.
ἡμῖν δὲ τὰ ἐν αὐτῇ ταύτῃ[4] λεκτέον.

14. Ἔστι δή τι χλαμυδοειδὲς σχῆμα τῆς γῆς
τῆς οἰκουμένης, οὗ τὸ μὲν πλάτος ὑπογράφει τὸ

---

[1] στόλοις, Tyrwhitt, for στόλος; editors following.
[2] ἅ, before πολύ, Paetz deletes; editors following.
[3] ἐλέγομεν, Corais, for λέγωμεν.
[4] ταύτῃ, Tyrwhitt, for ταῦτα; editors following.

of Alexandria are already sailing with fleets by way of the Nile and of the Arabian Gulf as far as India, these regions also have become far better known to us of to-day than to our predecessors. At any rate, when Gallus was prefect of Egypt, I accompanied him and ascended the Nile as far as Syene and the frontiers of Ethiopia, and I learned that as many as one hundred and twenty vessels were sailing from Myos Hormos to India, whereas formerly, under the Ptolemies, only a very few ventured to undertake the voyage and to carry on traffic in Indian merchandise.

13. Now my first and most important concern, both for the purposes of science and for the needs of the state, is this—to try to give, in the simplest possible way, the shape and size of that part of the earth which falls within our map, indicating at the same time what the nature of that part is and what portion it is of the whole earth; for this is the task proper of the geographer. But to give an accurate account of the whole earth and of the whole "spinning-whorl" [1] of the zone of which I was speaking is the function of another science—for instance, take the question whether the "spinning-whorl" is inhabited in its other fourth also. And, indeed, if it is inhabited, it is not inhabited by men such as exist in our fourth, and we should have to regard it as another inhabited world—which is a plausible theory. It is mine, however, to describe what is in this our own inhabited world.

14. As I have said, the shape of the inhabited world is somewhat like a chlamys, [1] whose greatest breadth is represented by the line that runs through

[1] See 2. 5. 6.

μέγιστον ἡ διὰ τοῦ Νείλου γραμμή, λαβοῦσα τὴι
ἀρχὴν ἀπὸ τοῦ διὰ τῆς Κινναμωμοφόρου παραλλήλου καὶ τῆς τῶν Αἰγυπτίων τῶν φυγάδων νήσου μέχρι τοῦ διὰ τῆς Ἱέρνης παραλλήλου, τὸ
δὲ μῆκος ἡ ταυτη πρὸς ὀρθὰς ἀπὸ τῆς ἑσπέρας
διὰ Στηλῶν καὶ τοῦ Σικελικοῦ πορθμοῦ μέχρι
τῆς Ῥοδίας καὶ τοῦ Ἰσσικοῦ κόλπου, παρὰ τὸν
Ταῦρον ἰοῦσα τὸν διεζωκότα τὴν Ἀσίαν καὶ
καταστρέφοντα ἐπὶ τὴν ἑώαν θάλατταν μεταξὺ
Ἰνδῶν καὶ τῶν ὑπὲρ τῆς Βακτριανῆς Σκυθῶν.
δεῖ δὴ νοῆσαι παραλληλόγραμμόν τι, ἐν ᾧ τὸ
χλαμυδοειδὲς σχῆμα ἐγγέγραπται οὕτως, ὥστε
τὸ μῆκος τῷ μήκει ὁμολογεῖν καὶ ἴσον εἶναι τὸ
μέγιστον, καὶ τὸ πλάτος τῷ πλάτει. τὸ μὲν δὴ
χλαμυδοειδὲς σχῆμα οἰκουμένη ἐστί· τὸ δὲ πλάτος ὁρίζεσθαι ἔφαμεν αὐτῆς ταῖς ἐσχάταις πα-
C 119 ραλλήλοις πλευραῖς, ταῖς διοριζούσαις τὸ οἰκήσιμον αὐτῆς καὶ τὸ ἀοίκητον ἐφ' ἑκάτερα. αὗται
δ' ἦσαν πρὸς ἄρκτοις μὲν ἡ διὰ τῆς Ἱέρνης, πρὸς
δὲ τῇ διακεκαυμένῃ ἡ διὰ τῆς Κινναμωμοφόρου·
αὗται δὴ προσεκβαλλόμεναι ἐπί τε τὰς ἀνατολὰς
καὶ ἐπὶ τὰς δύσεις μέχρι τῶν ἀνταιρόντων μερῶν
τῆς οἰκουμένης ποιήσουσί τι παραλληλόγραμμον
πρὸς τὰς ἐπιζευγνυούσας διὰ τῶν ἄκρων αὐτάς·
ὅτι μὲν οὖν ἐν τούτῳ ἐστὶν ἡ οἰκουμένη, φανερὸν
ἐκ τοῦ μήτε τὸ πλάτος αὐτῆς τὸ μέγιστον ἔξω
πίπτειν αὐτοῦ μήτε τὸ μῆκος· ὅτι δ' αὐτῆς

___

[1] The Sembritae, who revolted from Psammetichus in the
seventh century B.C. and fled to an island of the Nile, north

the Nile, a line that begins at the parallel that runs
through the Cinnamon-producing Country and the
island of the fugitive Egyptians,[1] and ends at the
parallel through Ierne ; its length is represented by
that line drawn perpendicular thereto which runs
from the west through the Pillars and the Strait of
Sicily to Rhodes and the Gulf of Issus, passes along
the Taurus Range, which girdles Asia, and ends at
the Eastern Sea between India and the country of
those Scythians who live beyond Bactriana. Accordingly, we must conceive of a parallelogram in
which the chlamys-shaped figure is inscribed in such
a way that the greatest length of the chlamys
coincides with, and is equal to, the greatest length
of the parallelogram, and likewise its greatest breadth
and the breadth of the parallelogram. Now this
chlamys-shaped figure is the inhabited world ; and,
as I said, its breadth is fixed by the parallelogram's
outermost lines, which separate its inhabited and its
uninhabited territory in both directions.[2] And these
sides were : in the north, the parallel through Ierne ;
in the torrid region, the parallel through the Cinnamon-producing Country ; hence these lines, if produced both east and west as far as those parts of the
inhabited world that rise opposite to[3] them, will
form a parallelogram with the meridian-lines that
unite them at their extremities. Now, that the
inhabited world is situated in this parallelogram is
clear from the fact that neither its greatest breadth
nor its greatest length falls outside thereof ; and

of Meroë. See Strabo 16. 4. 8. and 17. 1. 2. Herodotus
speaks of them as " voluntary deserters" (2. 30).
  [2] North and south.
  [3] That is, that " lie on the same parallel." See page 254.

χλαμυδοειδὲς τὸ σχῆμά ἐστιν, ἐκ τοῦ τὰ ἄκρα
μυουρίζειν τὰ τοῦ μήκους ἑκατέρωθεν, κλυζόμενα
ὑπὸ[1] τῆς θαλάττης, καὶ ἀφαιρεῖν τοῦ πλάτους·
τοῦτο δὲ δῆλον ἐκ τῶν περιπλευσάντων τά τε
ἑῷα μέρη καὶ τὰ δυσμικὰ ἑκατέρωθεν. τῆς τε
γὰρ Ἰνδικῆς νοτιωτέραν πολὺ τὴν Ταπροβάνην
καλουμένην νῆσον ἀποφαίνουσιν, οἰκουμένην ἔτι,
καὶ ἀνταίρουσαν τῇ τῶν Αἰγυπτίων νήσῳ καὶ τῇ
τὸ κιννάμωμον φερούσῃ γῇ· τὴν γὰρ κρᾶσιν τῶν
ἀέρων παραπλησίαν εἶναι· τῆς τε μετὰ τοὺς
Ἰνδοὺς Σκυθίας τῆς ὑστάτης ἀρκτικώτερά ἐστι
τὰ κατὰ τὸ στόμα τῆς Ὑρκανίας θαλάττης καὶ
ἔτι μᾶλλον τὰ κατὰ τὴν Ἰέρνην. ὁμοίως δὲ καὶ
περὶ τῆς ἔξω Στηλῶν λέγεται· δυσμικώτατον μὲν
γὰρ σημεῖον τῆς οἰκουμένης τὸ τῶν Ἰβήρων
ἀκρωτήριον, ὃ καλοῦσιν Ἱερόν· κεῖται δὲ κατὰ
τὴν γραμμήν πως[2] τὴν διὰ Γαδείρων τε καὶ
Στηλῶν καὶ τοῦ Σικελικοῦ πορθμοῦ καὶ τῆς
Ῥοδίας. συμφωνεῖν γὰρ καὶ τὰ ὡροσκοπεῖα καὶ
τοὺς ἀνέμους φασὶ τοὺς ἑκατέρωσε φοροὺς καὶ τὰ
μήκη τῶν μεγίστων ἡμερῶν τε καὶ νυκτῶν· ἔστι
γὰρ τεσσαρεσκαίδεκα ὡρῶν ἰσημερινῶν καὶ ἡμίσους[3] ἡ μεγίστη τῶν ἡμερῶν τε καὶ νυκτῶν. ἔν
τε τῇ παραλίᾳ τῇ κατὰ Γάδειρα Καβείρους[4] ποτὲ
ὁρᾶσθαι. Ποσειδώνιος δ' ἔκ τινος ὑψηλῆς οἰκίας
ἐν πόλει διεχούσῃ τῶν τόπων τούτων ὅσον τετρα-

---

[1] ὑπό, Corais, for δ' ἀπό; Meineke, Forbiger, following;
C. Müller approving.

[2] πρός, Pletho, Corais, delete, before τήν; Meineke
following.

[3] καὶ ἡμίσους, Groskurd inserts, from a suggestion by
Gosselin; all subsequent editors and translators following.

[4] Καβείρους, Meineke, for καὶ Ἴβηρας; Forbiger, Tardieu,
following; A. Vogel, C. Müller, Tozer, approving.

that its shape is like a chlamys is apparent from the fact that the extremities of its length, being washed away by the sea, taper off on both sides[1] and thus diminish its width there; and this is apparent from the reports of those who have sailed around the eastern and western parts in both directions.[2] For these navigators declare that the island called Taprobane is considerably south of India, inhabited nevertheless, and that it "rises opposite to" the Island of the Egyptians and the Cinnamon-bearing Country; and that, indeed, the temperature of the atmosphere is much the same as that of these latter places; and the regions about the outlet of the Hyrcanian Sea are farther north than outermost Scythia beyond India, and the regions about Ierne are farther north still. A similar report is also made concerning the country outside the Pillars, namely, the promontory of Iberia which they call the Sacred Cape is the most westerly point of the inhabited world; and this cape lies approximately on the line that passes through Gades, the Pillars, the Strait of Sicily, and Rhodes. At all these points, they say, the shadows cast by the sun-dial agree, and the winds that blow in either direction come from the same direction,[3] and the lengths of the longest days and nights are the same; for the longest day and the longest night have fourteen and a half equinoctial hours. Again, the constellation of the Cabeiri is sometimes seen along the coast near Gades. And Poseidonius says that from a tall house in a city about four hundred stadia distant from these regions

---

[1] See note on Chlamys, § 6 (preceding).
[2] That is, north and south.
[3] Strabo is referring to the periodic winds.

κοσίους σταδίους, φησὶν ἰδεῖν ἀστέρα, ὃν τεκμαί-
ρεσθαι τὸν Κάνωβον αὐτὸν ἐκ τοῦ τε τοὺς[1] μικρὸν
ἐκ τῆς Ἰβηρίας προελθόντας ἐπὶ τὴν μεσημβρίαν
ὁμολογεῖν ἀφορᾶν αὐτόν, καὶ ἐκ τῆς ἱστορίας τῆς
ἐν Κνίδῳ· τὴν γὰρ Εὐδόξου σκοπὴν οὐ πολὺ τῶν
οἰκήσεων ὑψηλοτέραν εἶναι, λέγεσθαι δ' ὅτι ἐντεῦθεν ἐκεῖνος ἀφεώρα τὸν Κάνωβον ἀστέρα, εἶναι
δ' ἐπὶ τοῦ Ῥοδιακοῦ κλίματος τὴν Κνίδον, ἐφ'
οὗ καὶ τὰ Γάδειρα καὶ ἡ ταύτῃ παραλία.

15. Ἐντεῦθεν δὲ πρὸς μὲν τὰ νότια μέρη πλέουσιν ἡ Λιβύη κεῖται· ταύτης δὲ τὰ δυσμικώτατα
μικρῷ τῶν Γαδείρων πρόκειται μᾶλλον, εἶτ' ἄκραν
ποιήσαντα στενὴν ἀναχωρεῖ πρὸς ἕω καὶ νότον,
C 120 καὶ πλατύνεται κατ' ὀλίγον, ἕως ἂν τοῖς ἑσπερίοις Αἰθίοψι συνάψῃ. οὗτοι δ' ὑπόκεινται τῶν
περὶ Καρχηδόνα τόπων ὕστατοι, συνάπτοντες τῇ
διὰ τῆς Κινναμωμοφόρου γραμμῇ. εἰς δὲ τἀναντία
πλέουσιν ἀπὸ τοῦ Ἱεροῦ ἀκρωτηρίου μέχρι τῶν
Ἀρτάβρων καλουμένων ὁ πλοῦς ἐστι πρὸς ἄρκτον,
ἐν δεξιᾷ ἔχουσι τὴν Λυσιτανίαν· εἶτ' ὁ λοιπὸς
πρὸς ἕω πᾶς ἀμβλεῖαν γωνίαν ποιῶν μέχρι τῶν
τῆς Πυρήνης ἄκρων τῶν τελευτώντων εἰς τὸν
ὠκεανόν. τούτοις δὲ τὰ ἑσπέρια τῆς Βρεττανικῆς
ἀντίκεινται πρὸς ἄρκτον, ὁμοίως δὲ καὶ ταῖς
Ἀρτάβροις ἀντίκεινται πρὸς ἄρκτον αἱ Καττιτερίδες καλούμεναι νῆσοι πελάγιαι κατὰ τὸ
Βρεττανικόν πως κλίμα ἱδρυμέναι. ὥστε δῆλον
ἐφ' ὅσον συνάγεται τὰ ἄκρα τῆς οἰκουμένης κατὰ

---

[1] τοῦ τε τούς, Corais, for τούτου τε; Groskurd, Forbiger,
following.

he saw a star which he judged to be Canopus itself, so judging from the fact that those who had proceeded but a short distance south of Iberia were in agreement that they saw Canopus, and also from scientific observations made at Cnidus; for, says he, the observatory of Eudoxus at Cnidus is not much higher than the dwelling-houses, and from there, it is said, Eudoxus saw the star Canopus; and, adds Poseidonius, Cnidus lies on the parallel of Rhodes, on which lie both Gades and the coastline thereabouts.

15. Now as you sail to the regions of the south you come to Libya; of this country the westernmost coast extends only slightly beyond Gades; then this coast, forming a narrow promontory, recedes towards the southeast and gradually broadens out to the point where it reaches the land of the Western Ethiopians. They are the most remote people south of the territory of Carthage, and they reach the parallel that runs through the Cinnamon-producing Country. But if you sail in the opposite direction from the Sacred Cape until you come to the people called Artabrians, your voyage is northward, and you have Lusitania on your right hand. Then all the rest of your voyage is eastward, thus making an obtuse angle to your former course, until you reach the headlands of the Pyrenees that abut on the ocean. The westerly parts of Britain lie opposite these headlands towards the north; and in like manner the islands called Cassiterides,[1] situated in the open sea approximately in the latitude of Britain, lie opposite to, and north of, the Artabrians. Therefore it is clear how greatly the east and west ends of

---

[1] "Tin Islands"; now Scilly.

μῆκος ὑπὸ τοῦ περικεχυμένου πελάγους εἰς στενόν.

16. Τοιούτου δὲ ὄντος τοῦ καθόλου σχήματος, χρήσιμον φαίνεται δύο λαβεῖν εὐθείας, αἳ τέμνουσαι πρὸς ὀρθὰς ἀλλήλας, ἡ μὲν διὰ τοῦ μήκους ἥξει τοῦ μεγίστου παντός, ἡ δὲ διὰ τοῦ πλάτους, καὶ ἡ μὲν τῶν παραλλήλων ἔσται μία, ἡ δὲ τῶν μεσημβρινῶν· ἔπειτα ταύταις παραλλήλους ἐπινοοῦντας ἐφ' ἑκάτερα διαιρεῖν κατὰ ταύτας τὴν γῆν καὶ τὴν θάλατταν, ᾗ χρώμενοι τυγχάνομεν. καὶ γὰρ τὸ σχῆμα μᾶλλον ἂν καταφανὲς γένοιτο, ὁποῖον εἰρήκαμεν, κατὰ τὸ μέγεθος τῶν γραμμῶν, ἄλλα καὶ ἄλλα μέτρα ἐχουσῶν, τῶν τε τοῦ μήκους καὶ τοῦ πλάτους, καὶ τὰ κλίματα ἀποδηλωθήσεται βέλτιον, τά τε ἑωθινὰ καὶ τὰ ἑσπέρια, ὡς δ' αὕτως τὰ νότια καὶ τὰ βόρεια. ἐπεὶ δὲ διὰ γνωρίμων τόπων λαμβάνεσθαι δεῖ τὰς εὐθείας ταύτας, αἱ μὲν ἐλήφθησαν ἤδη, λέγω δὲ τὰς μέσας δύο, τήν τε τοῦ μήκους καὶ τοῦ πλάτους, τὰς λεχθείσας πρότερον, αἱ δ' ἄλλαι ῥᾳδίως γνωρίζοιντ' ἂν διὰ τούτων· τρόπον γάρ τινα στοιχείοις χρώμενοι τούτοις τὰ παράλληλα μέρη συνεχόμεθα καὶ τὰς ἄλλας σχέσεις τῶν οἰκήσεων τάς τ' ἐπὶ γῆς καὶ πρὸς τὰ οὐράνια.

17. Πλεῖστον δ' ἡ θάλαττα γεωγραφεῖ καὶ σχηματίζει τὴν γῆν, κόλπους ἀπεργαζομένη καὶ

the inhabited world have been narrowed down by
the surrounding sea.

16. Such being the general shape of the inhabited
world, it is clearly helpful to assume two straight
lines that intersect each other at right angles, one of
which will run through the entire greatest length
and the other through the entire greatest breadth of
the inhabited world ; and the first line will be one of
the parallels, and the second line one of the meridians ; then it will be helpful to conceive of lines
parallel to these two lines on either side of them
and by them to divide the land and the sea with
which we happen to be conversant. For thereby the
shape of the inhabited world will prove more clearly
to be such as I have described it, being judged by
the extent of the lines, which lines are of different
measurements, both those of the length and those of
the breadth ; and thereby too the "climata" will be
better represented, both in the east and in the west,
and likewise in the south and in the north. But
since these straight lines must be drawn through
known places, two of them have already been so
drawn, I mean the two central lines mentioned above,
the one representing the length and the other the
breadth ; and the other lines will be easily found by
the help of these two. For by using these lines as
"elements,"[1] so to speak, we can correlate the regions
that are parallel, and the other positions, both geographical and astronomical, of inhabited places.

17. It is the sea more than anything else that
defines the contours of the land and gives it its

---

[1] Or, as we would say, " axes of co-ordinates." (Strabo
has in mind something similar to our system of co-ordinates
in analytical geometry.)

πελάγη καὶ πορθμούς, ὁμοίως δὲ ἰσθμοὺς καὶ χερρονήσους καὶ ἄκρας· προσλαμβάνουσι δὲ ταύτῃ
καὶ οἱ ποταμοὶ καὶ τὰ ὄρη. διὰ γὰρ τῶν τοιούτων
ἤπειροί τε καὶ ἔθνη καὶ πόλεων θέσεις εὐφυεῖς
ἐνενοήθησαν καὶ τἆλλα ποικίλματα, ὅσων μεστός
ἐστιν ὁ χωρογραφικὸς πίναξ. ἐν δὲ τούτοις καὶ τὸ
τῶν νήσων πλῆθός ἐστι κατεσπαρμένον ἔν τε τοῖς
πελάγεσι καὶ κατὰ τὴν παραλίαν πᾶσαν. ἄλλων
δ᾽[1] ἄλλας ἀρετάς τε καὶ κακίας καὶ τὰς ἀπ᾽
C 121   αὐτῶν χρείας ἐπιδεικνυμένωι ἢ δυσχρηστίας,
τὰς μὲν φύσει, τὰς δὲ ἐκ κατασκευῆς, τὰς φύσει
δεῖ λέγειν· διαμένουσι γάρ, αἱ δ᾽ ἐπίθετοι δέχονται
μεταβολάς. καὶ τούτων δὲ τὰς πλείω χρόνον συμ-
μένειν δυναμένας ἐμφανιστέον, ἢ[2] μὴ πολὺ μέν,
ἄλλως δ᾽ ἐπιφάνειαν μὲν ἐχούσας τινὰ καὶ δόξαν,
ἢ πρὸς τὸν ὕστερον χρόνον παραμένουσα τρόπον
τινὰ συμφυῆ τοῖς τόποις ποιεῖ καὶ μηκέτι οὖσαν
κατασκευήν· ὥστε δῆλον ὅτι δεῖ καὶ τούτων
μεμνῆσθαι. περὶ πολλῶν γὰρ ἔστι πόλεων τοῦτ᾽
εἰπεῖν, ὅπερ εἶπε Δημοσθένης ἐπὶ τῶν περὶ
Ὄλυνθον, ἃς οὕτως ἠφανίσθαι φησίν, ὥστε μηδ᾽
εἰ πώποτε ᾠκήθησαν γνῶναι ἄν τινα ἐπελθόντα.
ἀλλ᾽ ὅμως καὶ εἰς τούτους τοὺς τόπους καὶ εἰς ἄλλους ἀφικνοῦνται ἄσμενοι, τά γ᾽ ἴχνη ποθοῦντες
ἰδεῖν τῶν οὕτω διωνομασμένων ἔργων, καθάπερ καὶ
τοὺς τάφους τῶν ἐνδόξων ἀνδρῶν. οὕτω δὲ καὶ νο-

---

[1] δ᾽, Corais inserts, after ἄλλων ; generally followed.
[2] ἤ, Corais inserts ; Groskurd, Kramer, Forbiger, following.

shape, by forming gulfs, deep seas, straits, and likewise isthmuses, peninsulas, and promontories; but both the rivers and the mountains assist the seas herein. It is through such natural features that we gain a clear conception of continents, nations, favourable positions of cities, and all the other diversified details with which our geographical map is filled. And among these details are the multitude of islands scattered both in the open seas and along the whole seaboard. And since different places exhibit different good and bad attributes, as also the advantages and inconveniences that result therefrom, some due to nature and others resulting from human design, the geographer should mention those that are due to nature; for they are permanent, whereas the adventitious attributes undergo changes. And also of the latter attributes he should indicate such as can persist for a long time, or else such as can not persist for long and yet somehow possess a certain distinction and fame, which, by enduring to later times, make a work of man, even when it no longer exists, a kind of natural attribute of a place; hence it is clear that these latter attributes must also be mentioned. Indeed, it is possible to say concerning many cities what Demosthenes said[1] of Olynthus and the cities round about it,[2] which have so completely disappeared, he says, that a visitor could not know even whether they had ever been founded. But nevertheless men like to visit these places as well as others, because they are eager to see at least the traces of deeds so widely famed, just as they like to visit the tombs of illustrious men. So, also, I have mentioned

[1] *Philippics* 3. 117.
[2] Methone, Apollonia, and thirty-two other cities.

μίμων καὶ πολιτειῶν μεμνήμεθα τῶν μηκετι οὐσῶν, ἐνταῦθα καὶ τῆς ὠφελείας προκαλουμένης
τὸν αὐτὸν τρόπον ὅνπερ καὶ ἐπὶ τῶν πράξεων· ἢ
γὰρ ζήλου χάριν, ἢ ἀποτροπῆς τῶν τοιούτων.

18. Λέγομεν δ' ἀναλαβόντες ἀπὸ τῆς πρώτης
ὑποτυπώσεως, ὅτι ἡ καθ' ἡμᾶς οἰκουμένη γῆ περίρρυτος οὖσα δέχεται κόλπους εἰς ἑαυτὴν ἀπὸ τῆς
ἔξω θαλάττης κατὰ τὸν ὠκεανὸν πολλούς, μεγί-
στους δὲ τέτταρας· ὧν ὁ μὲν βόρειος Κασπία
καλεῖται θάλαττα, οἱ δ' Ὑρκανίαν προσαγορεύου-
σιν· ὁ δὲ Περσικὸς καὶ Ἀράβιος ἀπὸ τῆς νοτίας
ἀναχέονται θαλάττης, ὁ μὲν τῆς Κασπίας κατ'
ἀντικρὺ μάλιστα, ὁ δὲ τῆς Ποντικῆς· τὸν δὲ
τέταρτον, ὅσπερ πολὺ τούτους ὑπερβέβληται κατὰ
τὸ μέγεθος, ἡ ἐντὸς καὶ καθ' ἡμᾶς λεγομένη θάλαττα ἀπεργάζεται, τὴν μὲν ἀρχὴν ἀπὸ τῆς ἑσπέρας
λαμβάνουσα καὶ τοῦ κατὰ τὰς Ἡρακλείους στήλας πορθμοῦ, μηκυνομένη δ' εἰς τὸ πρὸς ἕω μέρος
ἐν ἄλλῳ καὶ ἄλλῳ[1] πλάτει, μετὰ δὲ ταῦτα σχιζο-
μένη καὶ τελευτῶσα εἰς δύο κόλπους πελαγίους,
τὸν μὲν ἐν ἀριστερᾷ, ὅνπερ Εὔξεινον πόντον προσ-
αγορεύομεν, τὸν δ' ἕτερον τὸν συγκείμενον ἔκ τε
τοῦ Αἰγυπτίου πελάγους καὶ τοῦ Παμφυλίου
καὶ τοῦ Ἰσσικοῦ. ἅπαντες δ' οἱ λεχθέντες κόλποι
ἀπὸ τῆς ἔξω θαλάττης στενὸν ἔχουσι τὸν
εἴσπλουν, μᾶλλον μὲν ὅ τε Ἀράβιος καὶ ὁ
κατὰ Στήλας, ἧττον δ' οἱ λοιποί. ἡ δὲ περι-
κλείουσα αὐτοὺς γῆ τριχῇ νενέμηται, καθάπερ εἴρηται. ἡ μὲν οὖν Εὐρώπη πολυσχημονε-
στάτη πασῶν ἐστιν, ἡ δὲ Λιβύη τἀναντία
πέπονθεν, ἡ δὲ Ἀσία μέσην πως ἀμφοῖν ἔχει

---

[1] καὶ ἄλλῳ, Casaubon conjectures; editors following.

customs and constitutions that no longer exist, for
the reason that utility urges me in their case just as
it does in the case of deeds of action; that is, either
to incite emulation or else avoidance of this or that.

18. I now resume my first sketch of the inhabited
world and say that our inhabited world, being girt
by the sea, admits into itself from the exterior sea
along the ocean many gulfs, of which four are very
large. Of these four gulfs the northern one is
called the Caspian Sea (though some call it the
Hyrcanian Sea); the Persian Gulf and the Arabian
Gulf pour inland from the Southern Sea, the one
about opposite the Caspian Sea and the other about
opposite the Pontus; and the fourth, which far
exceeds the others in size, is formed by the sea
which is called the Interior Sea, or Our Sea; it takes
its beginning in the west at the strait at the Pillars
of Heracles, and extends lengthwise towards the
regions of the east, but with varying breadth, and
finally divides itself and ends in two sea-like gulfs,
the one on the left hand, which we call the Euxine
Pontus, and the other consisting of the Egyptian,
the Pamphylian, and the Issican Seas. All these
aforesaid gulfs have narrow inlets from the Exterior
Sea, particularly the Arabian Gulf and that at the
Pillars, whereas the others are not so narrow. The
land that surrounds these gulfs is divided into three
parts, as I have said. Now Europe has the most
irregular shape of all three; Libya has the most
regular shape; while Asia occupies a sort of middle

C 122 τὴν διάθεσιν· ἅπασαι δ' ἐκ τῆς ἐντὸς παραλίας ἔχουσι τὴν αἰτίαν τοῦ τε πολυσχήμονος καὶ
τοῦ μή, ἡ δ' ἐκτὸς πλὴν τῶν λεχθέντων κόλπων
ἁπλῆ καὶ χλαμυδοειδής ἐστιν, ὡς εἶπον, τὰς δ'
ἄλλας ἐν μικρῷ διαφορὰς ἐατέον· οὐδὲν γὰρ ἐν
τοῖς μεγάλοις τὸ μικρόν. ἔτι δ' ἐπεὶ κατὰ τὴν
γεωγραφικὴν ἱστορίαν οὐ σχήματα μόνον ζητοῦμεν
καὶ μεγέθη τόπων, ἀλλὰ καὶ σχέσεις πρὸς ἄλληλα
αὐτῶν, ὥσπερ ἔφαμεν, καὶ ἐνταῦθα τὸ ποικίλον ἡ
ἐντὸς παραλία παρέχεται μᾶλλον ἢ ἡ ἐκτός. πολὺ
δ' ἐστὶ καὶ τὸ γνώριμον καὶ τὸ εὔκρατον καὶ τὸ
πόλεσι καὶ ἔθνεσιν εὐνομουμένοις συνοικούμενον
μᾶλλον ἐνταῦθα ἢ ἐκεῖ. ποθοῦμέν τε εἰδέναι
ταῦτα, ἐν οἷς πλείους παραδίδονται πράξεις καὶ
πολιτεῖαι καὶ τέχναι καὶ τἆλλα, ὅσα εἰς φρόνησιν
συνεργεῖ, αἵ τε χρεῖαι συνάγουσιν ἡμᾶς πρὸς
ἐκεῖνα, ὧν ἐν ἐφικτῷ αἱ ἐπιπλοκαὶ καὶ κοινωνίαι·
ταῦτα δ' ἐστὶν ὅσα οἰκεῖται, μᾶλλον δ' οἰκεῖται
καλῶς. πρὸς ἅπαντα δὲ τὰ τοιαῦτα, ὡς ἔφην, ἡ
παρ' ἡμῖν θάλαττα πλεονέκτημα ἔχει μέγα· καὶ
δὴ καὶ ἔνθεν ἀρκτέον τῆς περιηγήσεως.

19. Εἴρηται δὲ ὅτι ἀρχὴ τοῦδε τοῦ κόλπου
ἐστὶν ὁ κατὰ τὰς Στήλας πορθμός· τὸ δὲ στενότατον τούτου περὶ ἑβδομήκοντα σταδίους λέγεται·
παραπλεύσαντι δὲ τὸν στενωπὸν ἑκατὸν καὶ εἴκοσι σταδίων ὄντα διάστασιν λαμβάνουσιν αἱ

468

position between the other two in this respect. And the cause of their irregularity or their lack of it lies in the coastline of the Interior Sea, whereas the coastline of the Exterior Sea, with the exception of that of the aforesaid gulfs, is regular and, as I have said, like a chlamys; but I must leave out of view the other slight irregularities, for a little thing is nothing when we are dealing with great things. And further, since in the study of geography we inquire not merely into the shapes and dimensions of countries, but also, as I have said, into their positions with reference to each other, herein, too, the coast-line of the Interior Sea offers for our consideration more varied detail than that of the Exterior Sea. And far greater in extent here than there is the known portion, and the temperate portion, and the portion inhabited by well-governed cities and nations. Again, we wish to know about those parts of the world where tradition places more deeds of action, political constitutions, arts, and everything else that contributes to practical wisdom; and our needs draw us to those places with which commercial and social intercourse is attainable; and these are the places that are under government, or rather under good government. Now, as I have said, our Interior Sea has a great advantage in all these respects; and so with it I must begin my description.

19. I have already stated that the strait at the Pillars forms the beginning to this gulf; and the narrowest part of the strait is said to be about seventy stadia; but after you sail through the narrows, which are one hundred and twenty stadia in length, the coasts take a divergent course all at

ἠιόνες ἀθρόαν, ἡ δ' ἐν ἀριστερᾷ μᾶλλον· εἶτ'
ὄψις μεγάλου φαίνεται πελάγους. ὁρίζεται δ'
ἐκ μὲν τοῦ δεξιοῦ πλευροῦ τῇ Λιβυκῇ παραλίᾳ
μέχρι Καρχηδόνος, ἐκ δὲ θατέρου τῇ τε Ἰβη-
ρικῇ καὶ τῇ Κελτικῇ κατὰ Νάρβωνα καὶ Μασσαλίαν, καὶ μετὰ ταῦτα τῇ Λιγυστικῇ, τελευταίᾳ
δὲ τῇ Ἰταλικῇ μέχρι τοῦ Σικελικοῦ πορθμοῦ.
τὸ δ' ἑῷον τοῦ πελάγους πλευρὸν ἡ Σικελία ἐστὶ
καὶ οἱ ἑκατέρωθεν αὐτῆς πορθμοί· ὁ μὲν πρὸς τῇ
Ἰταλίᾳ ἑπταστάδιος, ὁ δὲ πρὸς τῇ Καρχηδόνι
χιλίων καὶ πεντακοσίων σταδίων. ἡ δ' ἀπὸ[1] τῶν
Στηλῶν ἐπὶ τὸ ἑπταστάδιον γραμμὴ μέρος μέν
ἐστι τῆς ἐπὶ Ῥόδον καὶ τὸν Ταῦρον, μέσον δέ πως
τέμνει τὸ λεχθὲν πέλαγος· λέγεται δὲ σταδίων
μυρίων καὶ δισχιλίων· τοῦτο μὲν δὴ τὸ μῆκος
τοῦ πελάγους, πλάτος δὲ τὸ μέγιστον ὅσον πεντακισχιλίων σταδίων τὸ ἀπὸ τοῦ Γαλατικοῦ κόλπου
μεταξὺ Μασσαλίας καὶ Νάρβωνος ἐπὶ τὴν κατ'
ἀντικρὺ Λιβύην. καλοῦσι δὲ τὸ πρὸς τῇ Λιβύῃ
πᾶν μέρος τῆς θαλάττης ταύτης Λιβυκὸν πέλαγος, τὸ δὲ πρὸς τῇ κατ' ἀντικρὺ γῇ τὸ μὲν
Ἰβηρικόν, τὸ δὲ Λιγυστικόν, τὸ δὲ Σαρδόνιον,[2]
τελευταῖον δὲ μέχρι τῆς Σικελίας τὸ Τυρρηνικόν.
νῆσοι δ' εἰσὶν ἐν μὲν τῇ παραλίᾳ τῇ κατὰ τὸ
Τυρρηνικὸν πέλαγος μέχρι τῆς Λιγυστικῆς συχναί,
C 123 μέγισται δὲ Σαρδὼ καὶ Κύρνος μετά γε τὴν
Σικελίαν· αὕτη δὲ καὶ τῶν ἄλλων ἐστὶ μεγίστη
τῶν καθ' ἡμᾶς καὶ ἀρίστη. πολὺ δὲ τούτων

---

[1] τῆς, Kramer suspects, before τῶν Στηλῶν; Meineke
deletes; C. Müller approving.
[2] Σαρδόνιον, Corais, for Σαρδόνιον; Meineke following;
C. Müller approving.

once, though the one on the left diverges more; and
then the gulf assumes the aspect of a great sea. It
is bounded on the right side by the coastline of
Libya as far as Carthage, and on the other side,
first, by Iberia and also by Celtica in the regions of
Narbo and Massilia, and next by Liguria, and finally
by Italy as far as the Strait of Sicily. The eastern
side of this sea is formed by Sicily and the straits
on either side of Sicily; the one between Italy and
Sicily is seven stadia in width and the one between
Sicily and Carthage is fifteen hundred stadia. But
the line from the Pillars to the seven-stadia strait is
a part of the line to Rhodes and the Taurus Range;
it cuts the aforesaid sea approximately in the middle;
and it is said to be twelve thousand stadia in length.
This, then, is the length of the sea, while its greatest breadth is as much as five thousand stadia, the
distance from the Galatic Gulf between Massilia and
Narbo to the opposite coast of Libya. The entire
portion of this sea along the coast of Libya they call
the Libyan Sea, and the portion that lies along the
opposite coast they call, in order, the Iberian Sea,
the Ligurian Sea, the Sardinian Sea, and finally, to
Sicily, the Tyrrhenian Sea. There are numerous
islands along the coast of the Tyrrhenian Sea as far
as Liguria, and largest of all are Sardinia and
Corsica, except Sicily; but Sicily is the largest and
best of all the islands in our part of the world.

λειπόμεναι πελάγιαι μὲν Πανδατερία¹ τε καὶ
Ποντία, πρόσγειοι δὲ Αἰθαλία τε καὶ Πλανασία
καὶ Πιθηκοῦσσα καὶ Προχύτη καὶ Καπρίαι καὶ
Λευκωσία καὶ ἄλλαι τοιαῦται. ἐπὶ θάτερα δὲ
τῆς Λιγυστικῆς αἱ πρὸ τῆς λοιπῆς ἠιόνος μέχρι
Στηλῶν οὐ πολλαί, ὧν εἰσιν αἵ τε Γυμνήσιαι²
καὶ Ἔβυσος· οὐ πολλαὶ δ' οὐδ' αἱ³ πρὸ τῆς
Λιβύης καὶ τῆς Σικελίας, ὧν εἰσι Κόσσουρά τε
καὶ Αἰγίμουρος καὶ αἱ Λιπαραίων νῆσοι, ἃς
Αἰόλου τινὲς προσαγορεύουσι.

20. Μετὰ δὲ τὴν Σικελίαν καὶ τοὺς ἑκατέρωθεν
πορθμοὺς ἄλλα πελάγη συνάπτει· τό τε πρὸ τῶν
Σύρτεων καὶ τῆς Κυρηναίας καὶ αὐταὶ αἱ Σύρτεις
καὶ τὸ Αὐσόνιον μὲν πάλαι, νῦν δὲ καλούμενον
Σικελικόν, σύρρουν ἐκείνῳ καὶ συνεχές. τὸ μὲν
οὖν πρὸ τῶν Σύρτεων καὶ τῆς Κυρηναίας καλεῖται
Λιβυκόν, τελευτᾷ δ' εἰς τὸ Αἰγύπτιον πέλαγος.
τῶν δὲ Σύρτεων ἡ μὲν ἐλάττων ἐστὶν ὅσον χιλίων
καὶ ἑξακοσίων σταδίων τὴν περίμετρον· πρόκεινται δ' ἐφ' ἑκάτερα τοῦ στόματος νῆσοι Μήνιγξ
τε καὶ Κέρκινα· τῆς δὲ μεγάλης Σύρτεώς φησιν
Ἐρατοσθένης τὸν κύκλον εἶναι πεντακισχιλίων,
τὸ δὲ βάθος χιλίων ὀκτακοσίων ἀφ' Ἑσπερίδων
εἰς Αὐτόμαλα καὶ τὸ τῆς Κυρηναίας μεθόριον
πρὸς τὴν ἄλλην τὴν ταύτῃ Λιβύην· ἄλλοι δὲ τὸν
περίπλουν τετρακισχιλίων σταδίων εἶπον, τὸ δὲ
βάθος χιλίων πεντακοσίων, ὅσον καὶ τὸ πλάτος
τοῦ στόματος. τὸ δὲ Σικελικὸν πέλαγος πρὸ τῆς
Σικελίας ἐστὶ καὶ τῆς Ἰταλίας ἐπὶ τὸ πρὸς ἕω

---

¹ Πανδατερία, Meineke, for Πανδαρια.
² αἵ τε Γυμνήσιαι, Du Theil, Kramer, for ἥ τε Γυμνησία.
³ οὐδ' αἱ, Corais, for οὐδέ ; Meineke following.

Far behind these in size are Pandateria and Pontia, which lie in the open sea, and, lying near the land, Aethalia, Planasia, Pithecussa, Prochyta, Capreae, Leucosia, and others like them. But on the other side of the Ligurian Sea the islands off the rest of the coast up to the Pillars are not numerous, among which are the Gymnesiae and Ebysus; and those off the coasts of Libya and Sicily are not numerous, either, among which are Cossura, Aegimurus, and the Liparian Islands, which some call the Islands of Aeolus.

20. Beyond Sicily and the straits on both sides of it other seas join with the former sea. The first is the sea in front of the Syrtes and Cyrenaea and the two Syrtes themselves, and the second is the sea formerly called the Ausonian Sea, but now the Sicilian Sea, which is confluent with and a continuation of the first sea. Now the sea in front of the Syrtes and Cyrenaea is called the Libyan Sea, and it ends at the Egyptian Sea. Of the Syrtes, the lesser is about one thousand six hundred stadia in circumference; and the islands Meninx and Cercina lie at either side of its mouth. As for the Greater Syrtes, Eratosthenes says that its circuit is five thousand stadia, and its breadth eighteen hundred stadia, reckoning from the Hesperides to Automala and to the common boundary between Cyrenaea and the rest of Libya in that region; but others have estimated its circuit at four thousand stadia, and its breadth at fifteen hundred stadia, as much as the breadth of its mouth is. The Sicilian Sea lies in front of Sicily and Italy toward the regions of the

μέρος καὶ ἔτι τοῦ μεταξὺ πόρου τῆς τε Ῥηγίνης
μέχρι Λοκρῶν, καὶ τῆς Μεσσηνίας μέχρι Συ-
ρακουσῶν καὶ Παχύνου. αὔξεται δ' ἐπὶ μὲν τὸ
πρὸς ἕω μέρος μέχρι τῶν ἄκρων τῆς Κρήτης, καὶ
τὴν Πελοπόννησον δὲ περικλύζει τὴν πλείστην,
καὶ πληροῖ τὸν Κορινθιακὸν καλούμενον κόλπον·
πρὸς ἄρκτους δὲ ἐπί τε ἄκραν Ἰαπυγίαν καὶ τὸ
στόμα τοῦ Ἰονίου κόλπου, καὶ τῆς Ἠπείρου τὰ
νότια μέρη μέχρι τοῦ Ἀμβρακικοῦ κόλπου καὶ
τῆς συνεχοῦς παραλίας τῆς ποιούσης τὸν Κορινθιακὸν κόλπον πρὸς τὴν Πελοπόννησον. ὁ δ' Ἰόνιος
κόλπος μέρος ἐστὶ τοῦ νῦν Ἀδρίου λεγομένου·
τούτου δὲ τὴν μὲν ἐν δεξιᾷ πλευρὰν ἡ Ἰλλυρὶς
ποιεῖ, τὴν δ' εὐώνυμον ἡ Ἰταλία μέχρι τοῦ μυχοῦ
τοῦ κατὰ Ἀκυληίαν. ἔστι δὲ πρὸς ἄρκτον ἅμα καὶ
πρὸς τὴν ἑσπέραν ἀνέχων στενὸς καὶ μακρός,
μῆκος μὲν ὅσον ἑξακισχιλίων σταδίων, πλάτος δὲ
τὸ μέγιστον διακοσίων ἐπὶ τοῖς χιλίοις. νῆσοι δέ
εἰσιν ἐνταῦθα συχναὶ μὲν αἱ πρὸ τῆς Ἰλλυρίδος,
C 124 αἵ τε Ἀψυρτίδες καὶ Κυρικτικὴ καὶ Λιβυρνίδες·
ἔτι δ' Ἴσσα καὶ Τραγούριον καὶ ἡ Μέλαινα Κόρκυρα καὶ Φάρος· πρὸ τῆς Ἰταλίας δὲ αἱ Διο-
μήδειοι. τοῦ Σικελικοῦ δὲ τὸ ἐπὶ Κρήτην ἀπὸ
Παχύνου τετρακισχιλίων καὶ πεντακοσίων σταδίων φασί· τοσοῦτον δὲ καὶ τὸ ἐπὶ Ταίναρον τῆς
Λακωνικῆς· τὸ δὲ ἀπὸ ἄκρας Ἰαπυγίας ἐπὶ τὸν
μυχὸν τοῦ Κορινθιακοῦ κόλπου τῶν μὲν τρισχιλίων ἐστὶν ἔλαττον, τὸ δ' ἀπὸ Ἰαπυγίας εἰς
τὴν Λιβύην πλέον τῶν τετρακισχιλίων ἐστί.
νῆσοι δ' εἰσὶν ἐνταῦθα ἥ τε Κόρκυρα καὶ Σύβοτα
πρὸ τῆς Ἠπειρώτιδος, καὶ ἐφεξῆς πρὸ τοῦ Κοριν-

east, and, besides, in front of the strait that lies
between them—in front of the territory of Rhegium
as far as Locri, and of the territory of Messina as
far as Syracuse and Pachynum. Toward the regions
of the east it stretches on to the headlands of
Crete, and its waters also wash round most of the
Peloponnesus and fill what is called the Gulf of
Corinth. On the north it stretches to the Iapygian
Cape and the mouth of the Ionian Gulf and to the
southern parts of Epirus as far as the Ambracian
Gulf and the coast that adjoins it and, with the
Peloponnesus, forms the Corinthian Gulf. But the
Ionian Gulf is part of what is now called the
Adriatic Sea. The right side of this sea is formed
by Illyria, and the left by Italy up to its head at
Aquileia. It reaches up towards the north-west in a
narrow and long course; and its length is about six
thousand stadia, while its greatest breadth is twelve
hundred stadia. There are numerous islands in this
sea: off the Illyrian coast the Apsyrtides, and Cyric-
tica, and the Liburnides, and also Issa, Tragurium,
Black Corcyra, and Pharos; and off the Italian
coast the Diomedeae. The stretch of the Sicilian
Sea from Pachynum to Crete, they say, measures
four thousand five hundred stadia, and just as much
the stretch to Taenarum in Laconia; and the stretch
from the Iapygian Cape to the head of the Gulf of
Corinth is less than three thousand stadia, while
that from Iapygia to Libya is more than four
thousand. The islands of this sea are: Corcyra
and the Sybota off the coast of Epirus; and next to

475

θιακοῦ κόλπου Κεφαλληνία καὶ Ἰθάκη καὶ Ζά-
κυνθος καὶ Ἐχινάδες.

21. Τῷ δὲ Σικελικῷ συνάπτει τὸ Κρητικὸν
πέλαγος καὶ τὸ Σαρωνικὸν καὶ τὸ Μυρτῷον, ὃ
μεταξὺ τῆς Κρήτης ἐστὶ καὶ τῆς Ἀργείας καὶ τῆς
Ἀττικῆς, πλάτος ἔχον τὸ μέγιστον τὸ ἀπὸ τῆς
Ἀττικῆς ὅσον χιλίων καὶ διακοσίων σταδίων,
μῆκος δ᾽ ἔλαττον ἢ διπλάσιον. ἐν τούτῳ δὲ νῆσοι
Κύθηρά τε καὶ Καλαυρία καὶ αἱ περὶ Αἴγιναν καὶ
Σαλαμῖνα καὶ τῶν Κυκλάδων τινές. τὸ δὲ
συνεχὲς τὸ Αἰγαῖόν ἐστιν ἤδη σὺν τῷ Μέλανι
κόλπῳ καὶ τῷ Ἑλλησπόντῳ, καὶ τὸ Ἰκάριον καὶ
Καρπάθιον μέχρι τῆς Ῥόδου καὶ Κρήτης καὶ
Καρπάθου[1] καὶ τῶν πρώτων μερῶν τῆς Ἀσίας·
ἐν ᾧ αἵ τε Κυκλάδες[2] νῆσοί εἰσι καὶ αἱ Σπορ-
άδες καὶ αἱ προκείμεναι τῆς Καρίας καὶ Ἰωνίας
καὶ Αἰολίδος μέχρι τῆς Τρῳάδος, λέγω δὲ Κῶ
καὶ Σάμον καὶ Χίον καὶ Λέσβον καὶ Τένεδον·
ὡς δ᾽ αὕτως αἱ προκείμεναι τῆς Ἑλλάδος μέχρι
τῆς Μακεδονίας καὶ τῆς ὁμόρου Θρᾴκης Εὔβοιά
τε καὶ Σκῦρος καὶ Πεπάρηθος καὶ Λῆμνος καὶ
Θάσος καὶ Ἴμβρος καὶ Σαμοθράκη καὶ ἄλλαι
πλείους, περὶ ὧν ἐν τοῖς καθ᾽ ἕκαστα δηλώσομεν.
ἔστι δὲ τὸ μῆκος τῆς θαλάττης ταύτης περὶ τετρακισχιλίους ἢ μικρῷ πλείους, τὸ δὲ πλάτος περὶ
δισχιλίους. περιέχεται δὲ ὑπὸ τῶν λεχθέντων
μερῶν τῆς Ἀσίας καὶ τῆς ἀπὸ Σουνίου μέχρι
Θερμαίου κόλπου πρὸς ἄρκτον ἐχούσης τὸν πλοῦν

---

[1] Καρπάθου, Tzschucke, for Κύπρου; Groskurd, Forbiger,
following.
[2] The MSS. have: μερῶν. Τῆς δ᾽ Ἀσίας αἵ τε Κυκλάδες.
Pletho deletes the δ᾽ before Ἀσίας, and inserts ἐν ᾧ before
αἵ τε Κυκλάδες.

them, off the Gulf of Corinth, Cephallenia, Ithaca, Zacynthus, and the Echinades.

21. Adjoining the Sicilian Sea are the Cretan, the Saronic, and the Myrtoan Seas. The Myrtoan Sea is between Crete, Argeia[1] and Attica; its greatest breadth, measured from Attica, is about one thousand two hundred stadia, and its length is less than double its breadth. In this sea are the islands of Cythera, Calauria, Aegina and its neighbouring isles, Salamis, and some of the Cyclades. Next beyond the Myrtoan Sea comes immediately the Aegean Sea, with the Gulf of Melas and the Hellespont; and also the Icarian and Carpathian Seas, extending to Rhodes, Crete, Carpathus, and the first regions of Asia. In the Aegean are the Cyclades,[2] the Sporades, and the islands that lie off Caria, Ionia, and Aeolis up to the Troad —I mean Cos, Samos, Chios, Lesbos, and Tenedos; so also those that lie off Greece as far as Macedonia and Thrace the next country beyond Macedonia— namely, Euboea, Scyros, Peparethos, Lemnos, Thasos, Imbros, Samothrace, and a number of others, concerning which I shall speak in my detailed description. The length of this sea is about four thousand stadia or slightly more, and its breadth is about two thousand stadia. It is surrounded by the aforesaid regions of Asia, and by the coast-line from Sunium to the Thermaic Gulf as you sail towards the north,

[1] Argolis.
[2] Strabo has just said that "some of the Cyclades" belong to the Myrtoan Sea He elsewhere places "many of the Sporades" in the Carpathian Sea (10.5.14); and Samos, Cos, and others in the Icarian Sea (10. 5. 13). He now, apparently, makes the Aegean comprehend all these islands and many others besides. But the text is corrupt.

παραλίας καὶ τῶν Μακεδονικῶν κόλπων μέχρι
τῆς Θρᾳκίας χερρονήσου.

22. Κατὰ δὲ ταύτην ἐστὶ τὸ ἑπταστάδιον τὸ
κατὰ Σηστὸν καὶ Ἄβυδον, δι' οὗ τὸ Αἰγαῖον καὶ ὁ
Ἑλλήσποντος ἐκδίδωσι πρὸς ἄρκτον εἰς ἄλλο
πέλαγος, ὃ καλοῦσι Προποντίδα. κἀκεῖνο εἰς ἄλλο, τὸν Εὔξεινον προσαγορευόμενον πόντον. ἔστι
δὲ διθάλαττος τρόπον τινὰ οὗτος· κατὰ μέσον γάρ
πως ἄκραι δύο προπίπτουσιν, ἡ μὲν ἐκ τῆς Εὐρώπης καὶ τῶν βορείων μερῶν, ἡ δ' ἐκ τῆς Ἀσίας
ἐναντία ταύτῃ, συνάγουσαι τὸν μεταξὺ πόρον καὶ
ποιοῦσαι δύο πελάγη μεγάλα· τὸ μὲν οὖν τῆς
Εὐρώπης ἀκρωτήριον καλεῖται Κριοῦ μέτωπον, τὸ
C 125   δὲ τῆς Ἀσίας Κάραμβις, διέχοντα ἀλλήλων περὶ
δισχιλίους[1] σταδίους καὶ πεντακοσίους. τὸ μὲν
οὖν πρὸς ἑσπέραν πέλαγος μῆκός ἐστιν ἀπὸ
Βυζαντίου μέχρι τῶν ἐκβολῶν τοῦ Βορυσθένους
σταδίων τρισχιλίων ὀκτακοσίων, πλάτος δὲ δισχιλίων ὀκτακοσίων·[2] ἐν τούτῳ δ' ἡ Λευκὴ νῆσός
ἐστι· τὸ δ' ἑῷον ἐστι παράμηκες, εἰς στενὸν
τελευτῶν μυχὸν τὸν κατὰ Διοσκουριάδα, ἐπὶ πεντακισχιλίους ἢ μικρῷ πλείους σταδίους, τὸ δὲ
πλάτος περὶ τρισχιλίους· ἡ δὲ περίμετρος τοῦ
σύμπαντος πελάγους ἐστὶ δισμυρίων που καὶ
πεντακισχιλίων σταδίων. εἰκάζουσι δέ τινες τὸ
σχῆμα τῆς περιμέτρου ταύτης ἐντεταμένῳ Σκυθικῷ

---

[1] C. Müller shews that δισχιλίους must not be changed to
χιλίους, with most editors.

[2] ὀκτακοσίων, C. Müller proposes to insert, after δισχιλίων.

and by the Macedonian Gulfs up to the Thracian Chersonese.

22. Along this Chersonese lies the strait, seven stadia in breadth, between Sestus and Abydus, through which the Aegean Sea and the Hellespont empty northwards into another sea which they call the Propontis; and the Propontis empties into another sea termed the "Euxine"[1] Pontus. This latter is a double sea, so to speak: for two promontories jut out at about the middle of it, one from Europe and the northern parts, and the other, opposite to it, from Asia, thus contracting the passage between them and forming two large seas. The promontory of Europe is called Criumetopon,[2] and that of Asia, Carambis[3]; and they are about two thousand five hundred stadia distant from each other. Now the western sea has a length of three thousand eight hundred stadia, reckoning from Byzantium to the mouths of the Borysthenes, and a breadth of two thousand eight hundred stadia; in this sea the island of Leuce is situated. The eastern sea is oblong and ends in a narrow head at Dioscurias; it has a length of five thousand stadia or a little more, and a breadth of about three thousand stadia. The circumference of the whole sea is approximately twenty-five thousand stadia. Some compare the shape of this circumference to that of a bent Scythian bow,[4]

[1] On the term "Euxine" see 7. 3. 6.
[2] Cape Karadje, in Crimea
[3] Cape Kerembe, in Paphlagonia.
[4] The Scythian bow consisted of a central bar of elastic wood to whose ends were fitted the curved horns of an ibex or goat, the horns being tipped with metal and joined by a bow-string of ox-hide or sheep's hide. At the junction of the bar with each horn the curvature of the horn was concave but, at the tip, the horn had a convex curvature.

STRABO

τόξῳ, τὴν μὲν νευρὰν ἐξομοιοῦντες τοῖς δεξιοῖς
καλουμένοις μέρεσι τοῦ Πόντου (ταῦτα δ' ἐστὶν ὁ
παράπλους ὁ ἀπὸ τοῦ στόματος μέχρι τοῦ μυχοῦ
τοῦ κατὰ Διοσκουριάδα· πλὴν γὰρ τῆς Καράμβιος
ἥ γε ἄλλη πᾶσα ἠιὼν μικρὰς ἔχει εἰσοχάς [1] τε καὶ
ἐξοχάς, ὥστ' εὐθείᾳ ἐοικέναι), τὴν δὲ λοιπὴν τῷ
κέρατι τοῦ τόξου διττὴν ἔχοντι τὴν ἐπιστροφήν,
τὴν μὲν ἄνω περιφερεστέραν, τὴν δὲ κάτω εὐθυτέ-
ραν· οὕτω δὲ κἀκείνην ἀπεργάζεσθαι δύο κόλπους,
ὧν ὁ ἑσπέριος πολὺ θατέρου περιφερέστερός
ἐστιν.

23. Ὑπέρκειται δὲ τοῦ ἑωθινοῦ κόλπου πρὸς
ἄρκτον ἡ Μαιῶτις λίμνη, τὴν περίμετρον ἔχουσα
ἐννακισχιλίων σταδίων ἢ καὶ μικρῷ πλεόνων·
ἐκδίδωσι δ' αὕτη μὲν εἰς Πόντον κατὰ τὸν Κιμμερικὸν καλούμενον Βόσπορον, οὗτος δὲ κατὰ τὸν
Θράκιον εἰς τὴν Προποντίδα· τὸ γὰρ Βυζαντιακὸν
στόμα οὕτω καλοῦσι Θράκιον Βόσπορον, ὃ τετρα-
στάδιόν ἐστιν. ἡ δὲ Προποντὶς χιλίων καὶ πεντακοσίων λέγεται τὸ μῆκος σταδίων τὸ ἀπὸ τῆς
Τρωάδος ἐπὶ τὸ Βυζάντιον· πάρισον δέ πώς ἐστι
καὶ τὸ πλάτος. ἐνταῦθα δ' ἡ τῶν Κυζικηνῶν
ἵδρυται νῆσος καὶ τὰ περὶ αὐτὴν νησία.

24. Τοιαύτη μὲν ἡ πρὸς ἄρκτον τοῦ Αἰγαίου
πελάγους ἀνάχυσις καὶ τοσαύτη, πάλιν δ' ἀπὸ
τῆς Ῥοδίας ἡ τὸ Αἰγύπτιον πέλαγος ποιοῦσα καὶ
τὸ Παμφύλιον καὶ τὸ Ἰσσικὸν ἐπὶ μὲν τὴν ἔω καὶ
τῆς Κιλικίας κατὰ Ἰσσὸν ἐκτείνεται μέχρι καὶ
πεντακισχιλίων σταδίων παρά τε Λυκίαν καὶ
Παμφυλίαν καὶ τὴν Κιλίκων παραλίαν πᾶσαν.
ἐντεῦθεν δὲ Συρία τε καὶ Φοινίκη καὶ Αἴγυπτος

[1] εἰσοχάς, Meineke, for ἐσοχάς.

480

likening the bow-string to the regions on what is
called the right-hand side of the Pontus (that is, the
ship-course along the coast from the outlet to the
head at Dioscurias; for with the exception of the
promontory of Carambis the whole shore has but
small recesses and projections, so that it is like a
straight line; and the rest they liken to the horn
of the bow with its double curve, the upper curve
being rounded off, while the lower curve is straighter;
and thus they say the left coast forms two gulfs,
of which the western is much more rounded than
the other.

23. North of the eastern gulf lies Lake Maeotis,
which has a circumference of nine thousand stadia
or even a little more. It empties into the Pontus at
what is called the Cimmerian Bosporus, and the
Pontus empties into the Propontis at the Thracian
Bosporus; for they give the name of Thracian Bosporus to the outlet at Byzantium, which is four
stadia.[1] The Propontis is said to be fifteen hundred
stadia long, reckoning from the Troad to Byzantium;
and its breadth is approximately the same. In it lie
the island of Cyzicus and the little islands in its
neighbourhood.

24. Such, then, is the nature and such the size of
the arm of the Aegean Sea that extends towards the
north. Again: the arm that begins at Rhodes and
forms the Egyptian, the Pamphylian, and the Issican
Seas, stretches towards the east as far as Issus in
Cilicia for a distance of five thousand stadia along
Lycia, Pamphylia, and the whole coastline of Cilicia.
Thence, Syria, Phoenicia, and Egypt encircle the sea

---

[1] That is, in breadth; but compare 7. 6. 1.

ἐγκυκλοῖ πρὸς νότον τὴν θάλατταν καὶ πρὸς δύσιν
ἕως Ἀλεξανδρείας. ἐν δὲ τῷ Ἰσσικῷ κόλπῳ καὶ
τῷ Παμφυλίῳ κεῖσθαι συμβαίνει τὴν Κύπρον,
συνάπτουσαν τῷ Αἰγυπτίῳ πελάγει. ἔστι δ᾽ ἀπὸ
Ῥόδου δίαρμα εἰς Ἀλεξάνδρειαν βορέᾳ τετρακισχιλίων που σταδίων, ὁ δὲ περίπλους διπλάσιος.
ὁ δ᾽ Ἐρατοσθένης ταύτην μὲν τῶν ναυτικῶν εἶναί
φησι τὴν ὑπόληψιν περὶ τοῦ διάρματος τοῦ
πελάγους, τῶν μὲν οὕτω λεγόντων, τῶν δὲ καὶ
C 126 πεντακισχιλίους οὐκ ὀκνούντων εἰπεῖν, αὐτὸς δὲ
διὰ τῶν σκιοθηρικῶν γνωμόνων ἀνευρεῖν τρισχιλίους ἑπτακοσίους πεντήκοντα. τούτου δὴ τοῦ
πελάγους τὸ πρὸς τῇ Κιλικίᾳ καὶ Παμφυλίᾳ καὶ
τοῦ Ποντικοῦ τὰ καλούμενα δεξιὰ μέρη καὶ ἡ
Προποντὶς καὶ ἡ ἐφεξῆς παραλία μέχρι Παμφυλίας ποιεῖ τινα χερρόνησον μεγάλην καὶ μέγαν
ταύτης ἰσθμὸν τὸν ἀπὸ τῆς πρὸς Ταρσῷ θαλάττης
ἐπὶ πόλιν Ἀμισὸν καὶ τὸ τῶν Ἀμαζόνων πεδίον
τὴν Θεμίσκυραν. ἡ γὰρ ἐντὸς τῆς γραμμῆς ταύτης
χώρα μέχρι Καρίας καὶ Ἰωνίας καὶ τῶν ἐντὸς
Ἅλυος νεμομένων ἐθνῶν περίκλυστος ἅπασά
ἐστιν ὑπὸ τοῦ Αἰγαίου καὶ τῶν ἑκατέρωθεν λεχθέντων τῆς θαλάττης μερῶν· καὶ δὴ καὶ καλοῦμεν
Ἀσίαν ταύτην ἰδίως καὶ ὁμωνύμως τῇ ὅλῃ.

25. Συλλήβδην δ᾽ εἰπεῖν, τῆς καθ᾽ ἡμᾶς θαλάττης νοτιώτατον μέν ἐστι σημεῖον ὁ τῆς μεγάλης
Σύρτεως μυχός, καὶ μετὰ τοῦτον ἡ κατ᾽ Αἴγυπτον
Ἀλεξάνδρεια καὶ τοῦ Νείλου προχοαί, βορειότα-
τον δὲ τὸ τοῦ Βορυσθένους στόμα· εἰ δὲ καὶ τὴν
Μαιῶτιν προστιθείη τῷ πελάγει τις (καὶ γὰρ
ἔστιν ὡς ἂν μέρος), τὸ τοῦ Τανάιδος· δυσ-

on the south and west as far as Alexandria. And
Cyprus must lie both in the Issican and the Pamphylian Gulfs, since it borders on the Egyptian Sea.
The sea-passage from Rhodes to Alexandria is, with
the north wind, approximately four thousand stadia,
while the coasting-voyage is double that distance.
Eratosthenes says that this is merely the assumption
made by navigators in regard to the length of the
sea-passage, some saying it is four thousand stadia,
others not hesitating to say it is even five thousand
stadia, but that he himself, by means of the shadow-
catching sun-dial, has discovered it to be three
thousand seven hundred and fifty stadia. Now the
part of this sea that is next to Cilicia and Pamphylia,
and the side called the right-hand side of the Pontic
Sea, and the Propontis, and the sea-board next
beyond as far as Pamphylia, form a great peninsula
and a great isthmus belonging thereto that stretches
from the sea at Tarsus to the city of Amisus, and to
Themiscyra, the Plain of the Amazons. For the
country within this line, as far as Caria and Ionia
and the peoples that live on this side of the Halys
River, is all washed by the Aegean or else by the
above-mentioned parts thereof on both sides of the
peninsula. And indeed we call this peninsula by
the special name of Asia, the same name that is
given to the whole continent.

25. In short, the head of the Greater Syrtis is the
most southerly point of our Mediterranean Sea, and
next to this are Alexandria in Egypt and the mouths
of the Nile ; the most northerly point is the mouth
of the Borysthenes, though if we add Lake Maeotis
to the sea (and indeed it is a part of it, in a sense)
the mouth of the Tanaïs is the most northerly point ;

μικώτατον δὲ ὁ κατὰ τὰς Στήλας πορθμός, ἑωθι
νώτατον δ᾿ ὁ λεχθεὶς μυχὸς κατὰ Διοσκουριάδα·
Ἐρατοσθένης δ᾿ οὐκ εὖ τὸν Ἰσσικὸν κόλπον φησίν.
ὁ μὲν γὰρ ἐπὶ τοῦ αὐτοῦ μεσημβρινοῦ ἵδρυται, ἐφ᾿
οὗπερ ἥ τε Ἀμισὸς καὶ Θεμίσκυρα· εἰ δὲ βούλει,
πρόσλαβε καὶ τὴν Σιδήνην μέχρι Φαρνακείας.
ἀπὸ δὲ τούτων τῶν μερῶν πρὸς ἕω πλοῦς ἐστι
πλειόνων ἢ τρισχιλίων που σταδίων εἰς Διοσκου
ριάδα, ὡς ἔσται μᾶλλον ἐκ τῆς ἐν μέρει περιοδείας
φανερόν. ἡ μὲν δὴ καθ᾿ ἡμᾶς θάλαττα τοιαύτη
τις.

26. Ὑπογραπτέον δὲ καὶ τὰς περιεχούσας
αὐτὴν γᾶς, ἀρχὴν λαβοῦσιν ἀπὸ τῶν αὐτῶν μερῶν,
ἀφ᾿ ὧνπερ καὶ τὴν θάλατταν ὑπεγράψαμεν.
εἰσπλέουσι τοίνυν τὸν κατὰ Στήλας πορθμὸν
ἐν δεξιᾷ μέν ἐστιν ἡ Λιβύη μέχρι τῆς τοῦ Νείλου
ῥύσεως, ἐν ἀριστερᾷ δὲ ἀντίπορθμος ἡ Εὐρώπη
μέχρι τοῦ Τανάϊδος· τελευτῶσι δ᾿ ἀμφότεραι περὶ
τὴν Ἀσίαν. ἀρκτέον δ᾿ ἀπὸ τῆς Εὐρώπης, ὅτι
πολυσχήμων τε καὶ πρὸς ἀρετὴν ἀνδρῶν εὐφυε
στάτη καὶ πολιτειῶν, καὶ ταῖς ἄλλαις πλεῖστον
μεταδεδωκυῖα τῶν οἰκείων ἀγαθῶν· ἐπειδὴ σύμ
πασα οἰκήσιμός ἐστι πλὴν ὀλίγης τῆς διὰ ψῦχος
ἀοικήτου. αὕτη δ᾿ ὁμορεῖ τοῖς Ἀμαξοίκοις τοῖς
περὶ τὸν Τάναϊν καὶ τὴν Μαιῶτιν καὶ τὸν Βορυ
σθένη. τῆς δ᾿ οἰκησίμου τὸ μὲν δυσχείμερον καὶ
τὸ ὀρεινὸν μοχθηρῶς οἰκεῖται τῇ φύσει, ἐπιμελη
τὰς δὲ λαβόντα ἀγαθοὺς καὶ τὰ φαύλως οἰκούμενα

the most westerly point is the strait at the Pillars;
and the most easterly point is the above-mentioned
head of the Pontus at Dioscurias; and Eratosthenes
is wrong in saying that the Issican Gulf is the most
easterly, for it lies on the same meridian with Amisus
and Themiscyra—or, if you like, you may add in the
territory of Sidene on to Pharnacia. From these
regions the voyage to Dioscurias is, I might say,
more than three thousand stadia eastward, as will
become clearer when I describe that region in detail.[1] Such, then, is the nature of our Mediterranean
Sea.

26. I must also give a general description of the
countries that surround this sea, beginning at the
same points at which I began to describe the sea
itself. Now as you sail into the strait at the Pillars,
Libya lies on your right hand as far as the stream of
the Nile, and on your left hand across the strait lies
Europe as far as the Tanaïs. And both Europe and
Libya end at Asia. But I must begin with Europe,
because it is both varied in form and admirably
adapted by nature for the development of excellence
in men and governments, and also because it has
contributed most of its own store of good things to
the other continents; for the whole of it is inhabitable with the exception of a small region that
is uninhabited on account of the cold. This uninhabited part borders on the country of the Wagon-
Dwellers in the region of the Tanaïs, Lake Maeotis,
and the Borysthenes. Of the inhabitable part of
Europe, the cold mountainous regions furnish by
nature only a wretched existence to their inhabitants,
yet even the regions of poverty and piracy become

[1] Compare 12. 3. 17.

C 127 καὶ λῃστρικῶς ἡμεροῦται· καθάπερ οἱ "Ελληνες,
ὄρη καὶ πέτρας κατέχοντες, ᾤκουν καλῶς διὰ προ-
νοιαν τὴν περὶ τὰ πολιτικὰ καὶ τὰς τέχνας καὶ
τὴν ἄλλην σύνεσιν τὴν περὶ βίον. Ῥωμαῖοί
τε πολλὰ ἔθνη παραλαβόντες κατὰ¹ τὴν φύσιν
ἀνήμερα διὰ τοὺς τόπους ἢ τραχεῖς ὄντας ἢ ἀλι-
μένους ἢ ψυχροὺς ἢ ἀπ' ἄλλης αἰτίας δυσοική-
τους πολλοῖς τούς τε ἀνεπιπλέκτους ἀλλήλοις
ἐπέπλεξαν καὶ τοὺς ἀγριωτέρους πολιτικῶς ζῆν
ἐδίδαξαν. ὅσον δ' ἐστὶν αὐτῆς ἐν ὁμαλῷ καὶ
εὐκράτῳ τὴν φύσιν ἔχει συνεργὸν πρὸς ταῦτα,
ἐπειδὴ τὸ μὲν ἐν τῇ εὐδαίμονι χώρᾳ πᾶν ἐστιν
εἰρηνικόν, τὸ δ' ἐν τῇ λυπρᾷ μάχιμον καὶ ἀνδρικόν,
καὶ δέχεταί τινας παρ' ἀλλήλων εὐεργεσίας τὰ
γένη ταῦτα· τὰ μὲν γὰρ ἐπικουρεῖ τοῖς ὅπλοις, τὰ
δὲ καρποῖς καὶ τέχναις καὶ ἠθοποιίαις. φανεραὶ δὲ
καὶ αἱ ἐξ ἀλλήλων βλάβαι, μὴ ἐπικουρούντων·
ἔχει δέ τι πλεονέκτημα ἡ βία τῶν τὰ ὅπλα ἐχόντων, πλὴν εἰ τῷ πλήθει κρατοῖτο. ὑπάρχει δή τι
καὶ πρὸς τοῦτο εὐφυὲς τῇ ἠπείρῳ ταύτῃ· ὅλη γὰρ
διαπεποίκιλται πεδίοις τε καὶ ὄρεσιν, ὥστε πανταχοῦ καὶ τὸ γεωργικὸν καὶ² πολιτικὸν καὶ τὸ
μάχιμον παρακεῖσθαι· πλέον δ' εἶναι θάτερον, τὸ
τῆς εἰρήνης οἰκεῖον, ὥσθ' ὅλων ἐπικρατεῖ τοῦτο,

---

¹ κατά, Tyrwhitt, for καὶ ἄ; Madvig also independently.
² τό, Madvig deletes, before πολιτικόν.

civilised as soon as they get good administrators.
Take the case of the Greeks: though occupying
mountains and rocks, they used to live happily,
because they took forethought for good government,
for the arts, and in general for the science of living.
The Romans, too, took over many nations that were
naturally savage owing to the regions they inhabited, because those regions were either rocky or
without harbours or cold or for some other reason
ill-suited to habitation by many, and thus not only
brought into communication with each other peoples
who had been isolated, but also taught the more
savage how to live under forms of government. But
all of Europe that is level and has a temperate
climate has nature to coöperate with her toward
these results; for while in a country that is blessed
by nature everything tends to peace, in a dis-
agreeable country everything tends to make men
warlike and courageous; and so both kinds of
country receive benefits from each other, for the
latter helps with arms, the former with products of
the soil, with arts, and with character-building. But
the harm that they receive from each other, if they
are not mutually helpful, is also apparent; and the
might of those who are accustomed to carry arms
will have some advantage unless it be controlled by
the majority. However, this continent has a natural
advantage to meet this condition also; for the whole
of it is diversified with plains and mountains, so that
throughout its entire extent the agricultural and
civilised element dwells side by side with the warlike element; but of the two elements the one that
is peace-loving is more numerous and therefore keeps
control over the whole body; and the leading

προσλαμβανόντων καὶ τῶν ἡγεμόνων, Ἑλλήνων
μὲν πρότερον, Μακεδόνων δὲ καὶ Ῥωμαίων ὕστερον. διὰ τοῦτο δὲ καὶ πρὸς εἰρήνην[1] καὶ πρὸς
πόλεμον αὐταρκεστάτη ἐστί· καὶ γὰρ τὸ μάχιμον
πλῆθος ἄφθονον ἔχει καὶ τὸ ἐργαζόμενον τὴν γῆν
καὶ τὸ τὰς πόλεις συνέχον. διαφέρει δὲ καὶ ταύτῃ,
διότι τοὺς καρποὺς ἐκφέρει τοὺς ἀρίστους καὶ τοὺς
ἀναγκαίους τῷ βίῳ καὶ μέταλλα ὅσα χρήσιμα,
θυώματα δὲ καὶ λίθους πολυτελεῖς ἔξωθεν μέτει-
σιν, ὧν τοῖς σπανιζομένοις οὐδὲν χεῖρων ὁ βίος
ἐστὶν ἢ τοῖς εὐπορουμένοις. ὡς δ᾽ αὕτως βοσκη-
μάτων μὲν πολλῶν ἀφθονίαν παρέχει, θηρίων δὲ
σπάνιν. τοιαύτη μὲν ἡ ἤπειρος αὕτη καθόλου τὴν
φύσιν ἐστί.

27. Κατὰ μέρος δ᾽ ἐστὶ πρώτη πασῶν ἀπὸ τῆς
ἑσπέρας ἡ Ἰβηρία, βύρσῃ βοείᾳ παραπλησία,
τῶν ὡς ἂν τραχηλιμαίων μερῶν ὑπερπιπτόντων
εἰς τὴν συνεχῆ Κελτικήν· ταῦτα δ᾽ ἐστὶ τὰ πρὸς
ἕω, καὶ τούτοις ἐναποτέμνεται τὸ πλευρὸν ἑῷον[2]
ὄρος ἡ καλουμένη Πυρήνη. ἡ δ᾽ ἄλλη πᾶσα[3] ἐστι
περίρρυτος τῇ θαλάττῃ, τὸ μὲν νότιον τῇ καθ᾽
ἡμᾶς μέχρι Στηλῶν τὰ δὲ λοιπὰ τῇ Ἀτλαντικῇ
C 128 μέχρι τῶν βορείων ἄκρων τῆς Πυρήνης. μῆκος
δὲ τῆς χώρας ταύτης ἐστὶ περὶ ἑξακισχιλίους
σταδίους τὸ μέγιστον, πλάτος δὲ πεντακισχιλίους.

28. Μετὰ δὲ ταύτην ἐστὶν ἡ Κελτικὴ πρὸς
ἕω μέχρι ποταμοῦ Ῥήνου, τὸ μὲν βόρειον πλευ-

---

[1] The words καὶ πρὸς εἰρήνην are unintentionally omitted
by Kramer; also by Meineke, Müller-Dübner, Tozer, Tardieu.
[2] ἑῷον, Groskurd inserts; Kramer, Forbiger, Müller-
Dübner, following.
[3] ἡ δ᾽ ἄλλη πᾶσα, Pletho, Siebenkees, Corais, following
gpr, for αὕτη.

nations, too—formerly the Greeks and later the Macedonians and the Romans—have taken hold and helped. And for this reason Europe is most independent of other countries as regards both peace and war; for the warlike population which she possesses is abundant and also that which tills her soils and holds her cities secure. She excels also in this respect, that she produces the fruits that are best and that are necessary for life, and all the useful metals, while she imports from abroad spices and precious stones—things that make the life of persons who have only a scarcity of them fully as happy as that of persons who have them in abundance. So, also, Europe offers an abundance of various kinds of cattle, but a scarcity of wild animals. Such, in a general way, is the nature of this continent.

27. If, however, we look at the separate parts of it, the first of all its countries, beginning from the west, is Iberia, which in shape is like an ox-hide, whose "neck" parts, so to speak, fall over into the neighbouring Celtica; and these are the parts that lie towards the east, and within these parts the eastern side of Iberia is cut off by a mountain, the so-called Pyrenees, but all the rest is surrounded by the sea; on the south, as far as the Pillars, it is surrounded by our Sea, and on the other side, as far as the northern headlands of the Pyrenees, by the Atlantic. The greatest length of this country is about six thousand stadia; and breadth, five thousand.

28. Next to Iberia towards the east lies Celtica, which extends to the River Rhine. On its northern

ρὸν τῷ Βρεττανικῷ κλυζομένη πορθμῷ παντί·
ἀντιπαρήκει γὰρ αὐτῇ παράλληλος ἡ νῆσος αὕτη
πᾶσα πάσῃ, μῆκος ὅσον πεντακισχιλίους ἐπέ-
χουσα· τὸ δ' ἑωθινὸν τῷ Ῥήνῳ ποταμῷ περι-
γραφομένη, παράλληλον ἔχοντι τὸ ῥεῦμα τῇ
Πυρήνῃ· τὸ δὲ νότιον τὸ μὲν ταῖς Ἄλπεσι τὸ ἀπὸ
τοῦ Ῥήνου, τὸ δ' αὐτῇ τῇ καθ' ἡμᾶς θαλάττῃ,
καθ' ὃ χωρίον ὁ καλούμενος Γαλατικὸς κόλπος
ἀναχεῖται, καὶ ἐν αὐτῷ Μασσαλία τε καὶ Νάρβων
ἵδρυνται πόλεις ἐπιφανέσταται. ἀντίκειται δὲ τῷ
κόλπῳ τούτῳ κατ' ἀποστροφὴν ἕτερος κόλπος
ὁμωνύμως αὐτῷ καλούμενος Γαλατικός, βλέπων
πρὸς τὰς ἄρκτους καὶ τὴν Βρεττανικήν· ἐνταῦθα
δὲ καὶ στενότατον λαμβάνει τὸ πλάτος ἡ Κελτική·
συνάγεται γὰρ εἰς ἰσθμὸν ἐλαττόνων μὲν ἢ τρισχιλίων σταδίων, πλειόνων δ' ἢ δισχιλίων.
μεταξυ δέ ἐστι ῥάχις ὀρεινὴ πρὸς ὀρθὰς τῇ Πυ-
ρήνῃ, τὸ καλούμενον Κέμμενον ὄρος· τελευτᾷ δὲ
τοῦτο εἰς μεσαίτατα τὰ Κελτῶν πεδία. τῶν δὲ
Ἄλπεων, ἅ ἐστιν ὄρη σφόδρα ὑψηλὰ ποιοῦντα[1]
περιφερῆ γραμμήν, τὸ μὲν κυρτὸν ἔστραπται
πρὸς τὰ λεχθέντα τῶν Κελτῶν πεδία καὶ τὸ Κέμμενον ὄρος, τὸ δὲ κοῖλον πρὸς τὴν Λιγυστικὴν καὶ
τὴν Ἰταλίαν. ἔθνη δὲ κατέχει πολλὰ τὸ ὄρος
τοῦτο Κελτικὰ πλὴν τῶν Λιγύων· οὗτοι δ' ἑτερο-
εθνεῖς μέν εἰσι, παραπλήσιοι δὲ τοῖς βίοις· νέ-
μονται δὲ μέρος τῶν Ἄλπεων τὸ συνάπτον τοῖς
Ἀπεννίνοις ὄρεσι, μέρος δέ τι καὶ τῶν Ἀπεννίνων
ὀρῶν κατέχουσι. ταῦτα δ' ἐστὶν ὀρεινὴ ῥάχις διὰ

---

[1] ποιοῦντα, Corais, for ποιούντων; Forbiger, Meineke,
Müller-Dübner, following.

side it is washed by the whole British Channel (for the whole island of Britain lies over against and parallel to the whole of Celtica and stretches length-wise about five thousand stadia) ; on its eastern side it is bounded by the River Rhine, whose stream runs parallel to the Pyrenees; and on its southern side it is bounded, on the stretch that begins at the Rhine, by the Alps, and by our sea itself in the region where the so-called Galatic Gulf[1] widens out—the region in which Massilia and Narbo are situated, very famous cities.   Opposite this gulf, and facing in the opposite direction, lies another gulf[2] that is also called Galatic Gulf; and it looks toward the north and Britain; and it is between these two gulfs that Celtica has its least breadth; for it is contracted into an isthmus of less than three thousand, but more than two thousand, stadia.   Between these two gulfs a mountain range, the so-called Cemmenus Mountain,[3] runs at right angles to the Pyrenees and comes to an end in the very centre of the plains of Celtica.   As for the Alps (which are extremely high mountains that form the arc of a circle), their convex side is turned towards the plains of Celtica just mentioned and the Cemmenus Mountain, while their concave side is turned toward Liguria and Italy. Many tribes occupy these mountains, all Celtic except the Ligurians ; but while these Ligurians belong to a different race, still they are similar to the Celts in their modes of life.   They live in the part of the Alps that joins the Apennines, and they occupy a part of the Apennines also.   The Apen-nines form a mountain range running through the

[1] Gulf of Lyon.   [2] Gulf of Gascogne.
[3] Cevennes.

τοῦ μήκους ὅλου τῆς Ἰταλίας διαπεφυκυῖα ἀπὸ τῶν ἄρκτων ἐπὶ μεσημβρίαν, τελευτῶσα δ' ἐπὶ τὸν Σικελικὸν πορθμόν.

29. Τῆς δ' Ἰταλίας ἐστὶ τὰ μὲν πρῶτα μέρη τὰ ὑποπίπτοντα ταῖς Ἄλπεσι πεδία μέχρι τοῦ μυχοῦ τοῦ Ἀδρίου καὶ τῶν πλησίον τόπων, τὰ δ' ἑξῆς ἄκρα στενὴ καὶ μακρὰ χερρονησιάζουσα, δι' ἧς, ὡς εἶπον, ἐπὶ μῆκος τέταται τὸ Ἀπέννινον ὄρος ὅσον ἑπτακισχιλίων σταδίων,[1] πλάτος δ' ἀνώμαλον. ποιεῖ δὲ τὴν Ἰταλίαν χερρόνησον τό τε Τυρρηνικὸν πέλαγος ἀρξάμενον ἀπὸ τοῦ Λιγυστικοῦ καὶ τὸ Αὐσόνιον καὶ ὁ Ἀδρίας.

30. Μετὰ δὲ τὴν Ἰταλίαν καὶ τὴν Κελτικὴν τὰ πρὸς ἔω λοιπά ἐστι τῆς Εὐρώπης, ἃ δίχα τέμνεται τῷ Ἴστρῳ ποταμῷ. φέρεται δ' οὗτος ἀπὸ τῆς ἑσπέρας ἐπὶ τὴν ἔω καὶ τὸν Εὔξεινον πόντον, ἐν ἀριστερᾷ λιπὼν τήν τε Γερμανίαν ὅλην ἀρξαμένην ἀπὸ τοῦ Ῥήνου καὶ τὸ Γετικὸν πᾶν καὶ τὸ τῶν Τυρεγετῶν καὶ Βασταρνῶν καὶ Σαυροματῶν μέχρι Τανάϊδος ποταμοῦ καὶ τῆς Μαιώτιδος λίμνης, ἐν δεξιᾷ δὲ τήν τε Θρᾴκην ἅπασαν καὶ τὴν Ἰλλυρίδα, λοιπὴν δὲ καὶ τελευταίαν τὴν Ἑλλάδα. πρόκεινται δὲ νῆσοι τῆς Εὐρώπης, ἃς ἔφαμεν, ἔξω μὲν Στηλῶν Γάδειρά τε καὶ Καττιτερίδες καὶ Βρεττανικαί, ἐντὸς δὲ Στηλῶν αἵ τε Γυμνήσιαι καὶ ἄλλα νησίδια Φοινίκων καὶ τὰ τῶν Μασσαλιωτῶν καὶ Λιγύων καὶ αἱ πρὸ τῆς Ἰταλίας μέχρι τῶν Αἰόλου νήσων καὶ τῆς Σικελίας, ὅσαι τε περὶ τὴν Ἠπειρῶτιν καὶ Ἑλλάδα καὶ μέχρι Μακεδονίας καὶ τῆς Θρᾳκίας χερρονήσου.

C 129

---

[1] σταδίων, Pletho inserts, after ἑπτακισχιλίων; following gp.

whole length of Italy from the north to the south and ending at the Strait of Sicily

29. The first parts of Italy are the plains that lie at the foot of the Alps and extend as far as the head of the Adriatic and the regions near it, but the rest of Italy is a narrow and long promontory in the form of a peninsula, through which, as I have said, the Apennines extend lengthwise for about seven thousand stadia, but with varying breadth. The seas that make Italy a peninsula are the Tyrrhenian (which begins at the Ligurian Sea), the Ausonian, and the Adriatic.

30. After Italy and Celtica come the remaining, or eastern, countries of Europe, which are cut in two by the River Ister. This river flows from the west towards the east and the Euxine Sea; it leaves on its left the whole of Germany (which begins at the Rhine), all the country of the Getans, and the country of the Tyregetans, Bastarnians, and Sarmatians as far as the River Tanaïs and Lake Maeotis; and it leaves on its right the whole of Thrace, Illyria, and, lastly and finally, Greece. The islands which I have already mentioned [1] lie off Europe; outside the Pillars: Gades, the Cassiterides, and the Britannic islands; and inside the Pillars: the Gymnesiae and other little islands [2] of the Phoenicians,[3] and those off Massilia and Liguria, and the islands off Italy up to the Islands of Aeolus and to Sicily, and all the islands round about Epirus and Greece and as far as Macedonia and the Thracian Chersonese.

---

[1] §§ 19–21 (above).
[2] That is, the Pityussae, which, with the Gymnesiae, form the Balearic Isles.   [3] See 3. 5. 1.

31. Ἀπὸ δὲ τοῦ Τανάιδος καὶ τῆς Μαιώτιδος τῆς Ἀσίας ἐστὶ τὰ μὲν[1] ἐντὸς τοῦ Ταύρου συνεχῆ, τούτοις δ' ἐξῆς τὰ ἐκτός. διαιρουμένης γὰρ αὐτῆς ὑπὸ ὄρους τοῦ Ταύρου δίχα, διατείνοντος ἀπὸ τῶν ἄκρων τῆς Παμφυλίας ἐπὶ τὴν ἑῴαν θάλατταν κατ' Ἰνδοὺς καὶ τοὺς ταύτῃ Σκύθας, τὸ μὲν πρὸς τὰς ἄρκτους νενευκὸς τῆς ἠπείρου μέρος καλοῦσιν οἱ Ἕλληνες ἐντὸς τοῦ Ταύρου, τὸ δὲ πρὸς μεσημβρίαν ἐκτός· τὰ δὴ συνεχῆ τῇ Μαιώτιδι καὶ τῷ Τανάιδι μέρη τὰ ἐντὸς τοῦ Ταύρου ἐστί. τούτων δὲ τὰ πρῶτα μέρη τὰ μεταξὺ τῆς Κασπίας θαλάττης ἐστὶ καὶ τοῦ Εὐξείνου πόντου, τῇ μὲν ἐπὶ τὸν Τάναϊν καὶ τὸν ὠκεανὸν τελευτῶντα τόν τε ἔξω καὶ τὸν τῆς Ὑρκανίας θαλάττης, τῇ δ' ἐπὶ τὸν ἰσθμόν, καθ' ὃ ἐγγυτάτω ἐστὶν ἀπὸ τοῦ μυχοῦ τοῦ Πόντου ἐπὶ τὴν Κασπίαν. ἔπειτα τὰ ἐντὸς τοῦ Ταύρου τὰ ὑπὲρ τῆς Ὑρκανίας μέχρι πρὸς τὴν κατὰ Ἰνδοὺς καὶ Σκύθας τοὺς ταύτῃ[2] θάλατταν καὶ τὸ Ἰμάιον ὄρος. ταῦτα δ' ἔχουσι τὰ μὲν οἱ Μαιῶται Σαυρομάται[3] καὶ οἱ μεταξὺ τῆς Ὑρκανίας καὶ τοῦ Πόντου μέχρι τοῦ Καυκάσου καὶ Ἰβήρων καὶ Ἀλβανῶν Σαυρομάται καὶ Σκύθαι καὶ Ἀχαιοὶ καὶ Ζυγοὶ καὶ Ἡνίοχοι, τὰ δ' ὑπὲρ τῆς Ὑρκανίας θαλάττης Σκύθαι καὶ Ὑρκανοὶ καὶ Παρθυαῖοι καὶ Βάκτριοι καὶ Σογδιανοὶ καὶ τἆλλα τὰ ὑπερκείμενα μέρη τῶν Ἰνδῶν πρὸς ἄρκτον. πρὸς νότον δὲ τῆς Ὑρκανίας θαλάττης ἐκ μέρους

---

[1] μέν, Jones inserts.
[2] ταύτῃ, Capps, for πρὸς τὴν αὐτήν.
[3] Groskurd defends the old reading Μαιῶται Σαυρομάται, and deletes the comma after Ἀλβανῶν; Forbiger approving.

31. After the Tanaïs and Lake Maeotis come the regions of Asia—the Cis-Tauran regions which are contiguous to the Tanaïs and Lake Maeotis, and following upon these regions come the Trans-Tauran regions. For since Asia is divided in two by the Taurus Range, which stretches from the capes of Pamphylia to the eastern sea at India and farther Scythia, the Greeks gave the name of Cis-Tauran to that part of the continent which looks towards the north, and the name of Trans-Tauran to that part which looks towards the south; accordingly, the parts of Asia that are contiguous to lake Maeotis and the Tanaïs belong to the Cis-Tauran regions. The first of these regions are those that lie between the Caspian Sea and the Euxine Pontus, and they come to an end, in one direction, at the Tanaïs and the ocean, that is, both at the exterior ocean and at that part of it which forms the Hyrcanian Sea, and, in the other direction, at the isthmus, at the point where the distance from the head of the Pontus to the Caspian Sea is least. Then come those Cis-Tauran regions that are north of Hyrcania, which reach all the way to the sea at India and farther Scythia, and to Mt. Imaeus. These regions are inhabited, partly, by the Maeotic Sarmatians, and by the Sarmatians that dwell between the Hyrcanian Sea and the Pontus as far as the Caucasus and the countries of the Iberians and the Albanians, and by Scythians, Achaeans, Zygians, and Heniochians; and, partly, beyond the Hyrcanian Sea, by Scythians, Hyrcanians, Parthians, Bactrians, Sogdianians, and also by the inhabitants of the regions that lie beyond India on the north. And to the south of the Hyrcanian Sea, in part, and of the whole of the

καὶ τοῦ ἰσθμοῦ παντὸς μεταξὺ ταύτης καὶ τοῦ
Πόντου τῆς τε Ἀρμενίας ἡ πλείστη κεῖται καὶ
Κολχὶς καὶ Καππαδοκία σύμπασα μέχρι τοῦ
Εὐξείνου πόντου καὶ τῶν Τιβαρανικῶν ἐ-νῶν, ἔτι
δὲ ἡ ἐντὸς Ἅλυος χώρα λεγομένη, περιέχουσα
πρὸς μὲν τῷ Πόντῳ καὶ τῇ Προποντίδι Παφλα-
γόνας τε καὶ Βιθυνοὺς καὶ Μυσοὺς καὶ τὴν ἐφ'
Ἑλλησπόντῳ λεγομένην Φρυγίαν, ἧς ἐστι καὶ
ἡ Τρωάς, πρὸς δὲ τῷ Αἰγαίῳ καὶ τῇ ἐφεξῆς θα-
λάττῃ τήν τε Αἰολίδα καὶ τὴν Ἰωνίαν καὶ Καρίαν
καὶ Λυκίαν, ἐν δὲ τῇ μεσογαίᾳ τήν τε Φρυγίαν,
C 130 ἧς ἐστι μέρος ἥ τε τῶν Γαλλογραικῶν λεγομένη
Γαλατία καὶ ἡ Ἐπίκτητος, καὶ Λυκάονας καὶ
Λυδούς.

32. Ἐφεξῆς δὲ τοῖς ἐντὸς τοῦ Ταύρου οἵ τε
τὰ ὄρη κατέχοντες Παροπαμισάδαι καὶ τὰ Παρθυαίων τε καὶ Μήδων καὶ Ἀρμενίων καὶ[1] Κιλίκων
ἔθνη καὶ Κατάονες[2] καὶ Πισίδαι. μετὰ δὲ τοὺς
ὀρείους ἐστὶ τὰ ἐκτὸς τοῦ Ταύρου. πρώτη δ'
ἐστὶ τούτων ἡ Ἰνδική, ἔθνος μέγιστον τῶν πάντων καὶ εὐδαιμονέστατον, τελευτῶν πρός τε τὴν
ἑῴαν θάλατταν καὶ τὴν νοτίαν τῆς Ἀτλαντικῆς.
ἐν δὲ τῇ νοτίᾳ ταύτῃ θαλάττῃ πρόκειται τῆς
Ἰνδικῆς νῆσος οὐκ ἐλάττων τῆς Βρεττανικῆς ἡ
Ταπροβάνη· μετὰ δὲ τὴν Ἰνδικὴν ἐπὶ τὰ ἑσπέρια νεύουσιν, ἐν δεξιᾷ δ' ἔχουσι τὰ ὄρη χώρα
ἐστὶ συχνή, φαύλως οἰκουμένη διὰ λυπρότητα
ὑπ' ἀνθρώπων τελέως βαρβάρων, οὐχ ὁμοεθνῶν·
καλοῦσι δ' Ἀριανούς, ἀπὸ τῶν ὀρῶν διατείνοντας

---

[1] τά, after καί, Pletho deletes ; editors following.
[2] Κατάονες, Siebenkees, for Λυκάονες ; usually followed.

isthmus between this sea and the Pontus lie the
greater part of Armenia, Colchis, the whole of
Cappadocia up to the Euxine and to the Tibaranian
tribes, and also the so-called Cis-Halys country,
which embraces, first, next to the Pontus and to the
Propontis, Paphlagonia, Bithynia, Mysia, the so-called
" Phrygia on the Hellespont" (of which the Troad
is a part) ; and, secondly, next to the Aegean and to
the sea that forms its continuation, Aeolis, Ionia,
Caria, Lycia ; and, thirdly, in the interior, Phrygia
(of which both the so-called " Galatia of the Gallo-
Grecians" and " Phrygia Epictetus [1]" form a part),
Lycaonia, and Lydia.

32. Following immediately upon the Cis-Tauran
peoples come the peoples that inhabit the mountains [2] :
the Paropamisadae, the tribes of the Parthians, of
the Medes, of the Armenians, and of the Cilicians,
and the Cataonians and the Pisidians. Next after
the mountaineers come the Trans-Tauran regions.
The first of them is India,[3] which is the greatest of
all nations and the happiest in lot, a nation whose
confines reach both to the eastern sea and to the
southern sea of the Atlantic. In this southern sea,
off the coast of India, lies an island, Taprobane,[4]
which is not less than Britain. Then, if we turn from
India toward the western regions and keep the
mountains on our right, we come to a vast country,
which, owing to the poverty of the soil, furnishes
only a wretched livelihood to men who are wholly
barbarians and belong to different races. They call
this country Aria, and it extends from the mountains

[1] " Phrygia Annex " ; the name given to lesser Phrygia by
the Kings of Pergamus.   [2] Compare 11. 1. 4.
[3] For the full description of India, see 15. 1. 1 ff.
[4] Ceylon.

μέχρι Γεδρωσίας καὶ Καρμανίας. ἐξῆς δέ εἰσι
πρὸς μὲν τῇ θαλάττῃ Πέρσαι καὶ Σούσιοι καὶ
Βαβυλώνιοι, καθήκοντες ἐπὶ τὴν κατὰ Πέρσας
θάλατταν καὶ τὰ περιοικοῦντα τούτους ἔθνη
μικρά· πρὸς δὲ τοῖς ὄρεσιν ἢ[1] ἐν αὐτοῖς τοῖς
ὄρεσι Παρθυαῖοι καὶ Μῆδοι καὶ Ἀρμένιοι καὶ
τὰ τούτοις πρόσχωρα ἔθνη καὶ ἡ Μεσοπota-
μία. μετὰ δὲ τὴν Μεσοποταμίαν τὰ ἐντὸς Εὐ-
φράτου· ταῦτα δ᾽ ἐστὶν ἥ τε εὐδαίμων Ἀραβία
πᾶσα, ἀφοριζομένη τῷ τε Ἀραβίῳ κόλπῳ παντὶ
καὶ τῷ Περσικῷ, καὶ ὅσην οἱ Σκηνῖται καὶ οἱ
Φύλαρχοι κατέχουσιν οἱ ἐπὶ τὸν Εὐφράτην καθήκοντες καὶ τὴν Συρίαν· εἶθ᾽ οἱ πέραν τοῦ Ἀραβίου
κόλπου μέχρι Νείλου, Αἰθίοπές τε καὶ Ἄραβες,
καὶ οἱ μετ᾽ αὐτοὺς Αἰγύπτιοι καὶ Σύροι καὶ
Κίλικες οἵ τε ἄλλοι καὶ οἱ Τραχειῶται λεγόμενοι,
τελευταῖοι δὲ Πάμφυλοι.

33. Μετὰ δὲ τὴν Ἀσίαν ἐστὶν ἡ Λιβύη, συνεχὴς οὖσα τῇ τε Αἰγύπτῳ καὶ τῇ Αἰθιοπίᾳ, τὴν
μὲν καθ᾽ ἡμᾶς ἠιόνα ἐπ᾽ εὐθείας ἔχουσα, σχεδόν
τι μέχρι Στηλῶν ἀπὸ Ἀλεξανδρείας ἀρξαμένην,
πλὴν τῶν Σύρτεων καὶ εἴ πού τις ἄλλη κόλπων
ἐπιστροφὴ μετρία καὶ τῶν τούτους[2] ποιούντων
ἀκρωτηρίων ἐξοχή· τὴν δὲ παρωκεανῖτιν ἀπὸ τῆς
Αἰθιοπίας μέχρι τινός, ὡς ἂν παράλληλον οὖσαν
τῇ προτέρᾳ, μετὰ δὲ ταῦτα συναγομένην ἀπὸ τῶν
νοτίων μερῶν εἰς ὀξεῖαν ἄκραν, μικρὸν ἔξω Στηλῶν προπεπτωκυῖαν καὶ ποιοῦσαν τραπέζιόν πως

[1] ἤ, the reading of C, for οἱ; so Groskurd, Kramer, Müller-
Dübner, and Meineke.
[2] τούτους (namely κόλπους), Casaubon, for ταύτῃ; Du Theil,
Tardieu, following; Groskurd approving.

as far as Gedrosia and Carmania. Next after Aria, toward the sea, are Persia, Susiana, Babylonia (countries which reach down to the Persian Sea,[1]) and the small tribes that dwell on the frontiers of those countries; while the peoples who live near the mountains or in the mountains themselves are the Parthians, the Medes, the Armenians and the tribes adjoining them, and the Mesopotamians. After Mesopotamia come the countries this side of the Euphrates. These are: the whole of Arabia Felix (which is bounded by the whole extent of the Arabian Gulf and by the Persian Gulf), and all the country occupied by the Tent-Dwellers and by the Sheikh-governed tribes (which reaches to the Euphrates and Syria). Then come the peoples who live on the other side of the Arabian Gulf and as far as the Nile, namely, the Ethiopians and the Arabs, and the Egyptians who live next to them, and the Syrians, and the Cilicians (including the so-called "Trachiotae[2]"), and finally the Pamphylians.

33. After Asia comes Libya, which is a continuation of Egypt and Ethiopia. Its shore that lies opposite to us runs in a straight line almost to the Pillars, beginning at Alexandria, except for the Syrtes and perhaps other moderate bends of gulfs and projections of the promontories that form these gulfs; but its coastline on the ocean from Ethiopia to a certain point is approximately parallel to the former line, and then it draws in on the south and forms a sharp promontory, which projects slightly outside the Pillars and thus gives to Libya approximately

[1] That is, the Persian Gulf.
[2] That is, the inhabitants of " Rugged Cilicia." Compare 12. 6. 1.

τὸ σχῆμα. ἔστι δ᾽, ὥσπερ οἵ τε ἄλλοι δηλοῦσι
καὶ δὴ καὶ Γναῖος Πείσων ἡγεμὼν γενόμενος τῆς
χώρας διηγεῖτο ἡμῖν, ἐοικυῖα παρδαλῇ· κατά-
στικτος γάρ ἐστιν οἰκήσεσι περιεχομέναις ἀνύδρῳ
καὶ ἐρήμῳ γῇ· καλοῦσί τε τὰς τοιαύτας οἰκήσεις
Αὐάσεις οἱ Αἰγύπτιοι. τοιαύτη δὲ οὖσα ἔχει
C 131 τινὰς ἄλλας διαφορὰς τριχῇ διαιρουμένας· τῆς
μὲν γὰρ καθ᾽ ἡμᾶς παραλίας εὐδαίμων ἐστὶν ἡ
πλείστη σφόδρα, καὶ μάλιστα ἡ Κυρηναία καὶ
ἡ περὶ Καρχηδόνα μέχρι Μαυρουσίων καὶ τῶν
Ἡρακλείων στηλῶν· οἰκεῖται δὲ μετρίως καὶ ἡ
παρωκεανῖτις, ἡ δὲ μέση φαύλως ἡ τὸ σίλφιον φέ-
ρουσα, ἔρημος ἡ πλείστη καὶ τραχεῖα καὶ ἀμμώ-
δης. τὸ δ᾽ αὐτὸ πέπονθε καὶ ἡ ἐπ᾽ εὐθείας ταύτῃ
διά τε τῆς Αἰθιοπίας διήκουσα τῆς τε Τρωγλοδυ-
τικῆς καὶ τῆς Ἀραβίας καὶ τῆς Γεδρωσίας τῆς
τῶν Ἰχθυοφάγων. νέμεται δ᾽ ἔθνη τὴν Λιβύην
τὰ πλεῖστα ἄγνωστα· οὐ πολλὴν γὰρ ἐφοδεύεσθαι
συμβαίνει στρατοπέδοις οὐδ᾽ ἀλλοφύλοις ἀνδράσιν, οἱ δ᾽ ἐπιχώριοι καὶ ὀλίγοι παρ᾽ ἡμᾶς ἀφικνοῦνται πόρρωθεν, καὶ οὐ πιστὰ οὐδὲ πάντα λέ-
γουσιν· ὅμως δ᾽ οὖν τὰ λεγόμενα τοιαῦτά ἐστι.
τοὺς μὲν μεσημβρινωτάτους Αἰθίοπας προσαγορεύουσι, τοὺς δ᾽ ὑπὸ τούτοις τοὺς πλείστους
Γαράμαντας καὶ Φαρουσίους καὶ Νιγρίτας, τοὺς
δ᾽ ἔτι ὑπὸ τούτοις Γαιτούλους, τοὺς δὲ τῆς θαλάττης ἐγγὺς ἢ καὶ ἁπτομένους αὐτῆς πρὸς Αἰγύπτῳ
μὲν Μαρμαρίδας μέχρι τῆς Κυρηναίας, ὑπὲρ δὲ
ταύτης καὶ τῶν Σύρτεων Ψύλλους καὶ Νασαμῶνας

the shape of a trapezium. And Libya is—as the others show, and indeed as Cnaeus Piso, who was once the prefect of that country, told me—like a leopard's skin; for it is spotted with inhabited places that are surrounded by waterless and desert land. The Egyptians call such inhabited places "auases."[1] But though Libya is thus peculiar, it has some other peculiarities, which give it a threefold division. In the first place, most of its coastline that lies opposite to us is extremely fertile, and especially Cyrenaea and the country about Carthage up to Maurusia and to the Pillars of Heracles; secondly, even its coast-line on the ocean affords only moderate sustenance, and thirdly, its interior region, which produces silphium, affords only a wretched sustenance, being, for the most part, a rocky and sandy desert; and the same is also true of the straight prolongation of this region through Ethiopia, the Troglodyte Country, Arabia, and Gedrosia where the Fish-Eaters live. The most of the peoples of Libya are unknown to us; for not much of it is visited by armies, nor yet by men of outside tribes; and not only do very few of the natives from far inland ever visit us, but what they tell is not trustworthy or complete either. But still the following is based on what they say. They call the most southerly peoples Ethiopians; those who live next north of the Ethiopians they call, in the main, Garamantians, Pharusians, and Nigritans; those who live still north of these latter, Gaetulans; those who live near the sea, or even on the seacoast, next to Egypt and as far as Cyrenaea, Marmaridans; while they call those beyond Cyrenaea and the Syrtes, Psyllians, Nasamonians, and certain of the Gaetulans,

---

[1] That is, "oases."

καὶ τῶν Γαιτούλων τινάς, εἶτ' Ἀσβύστας καὶ
Βυζακίους μέχρι τῆς Καρχηδονίας. πολλὴ δ'
ἐστὶν ἡ Καρχηδονία· συνάπτουσι δ' οἱ Νομάδες
αὐτῇ· τούτων δὲ τοὺς γνωριμωτάτους τοὺς μὲν
Μασυλιεῖς, τοὺς δὲ Μασαισυλίους προσαγορεύου-
σιν· ὕστατοι δ' εἰσὶ Μαυρούσιοι. πᾶσα δ' ἡ
ἀπὸ Καρχηδόνος μέχρι Στηλῶν ἐστιν εὐδαίμων,
θηριοτρόφος δέ, ὥσπερ καὶ ἡ μεσόγαια πᾶσα.
οὐκ ἀπεικὸς δὴ¹ καὶ Νομάδας λεχθῆναί τινας
αὐτῶν, οὐ δυναμένους γεωργεῖν διὰ τὸ πλῆθος
τῶν θηρίων τὸ παλαιόν· οἱ δὲ νῦν ἅμα τῇ ἐμπειρίᾳ τῆς θήρας διαφέροντες, καὶ τῶν Ῥωμαίων
προσλαμβανόντων πρὸς τοῦτο διὰ τὴν σπουδὴν
τὴν περὶ τὰς θηριομαχίας, ἀμφοτέρων περιγίγ-
νονται καὶ τῶν θηρίων καὶ τῆς γεωργίας. τοσαῦτα
καὶ περὶ τῶν ἠπείρων λέγομεν.

34. Λοιπὸν εἰπεῖν περὶ τῶν κλιμάτων, ὅπερ καὶ
αὐτὸ ἔχει καθολικὴν ὑποτύπωσιν, ὁρμηθεῖσιν ἐκ
τῶν γραμμῶν ἐκείνων, ἃ στοιχεῖα ἐκαλέσαμεν,
λέγω δὲ τῆς τε τὸ μῆκος ἀφοριζούσης τὸ μέγιστον
καὶ τῆς τὸ πλάτος, μάλιστα δὲ τῆς τὸ πλάτος.
τοῖς μὲν οὖν ἀστρονομικοῖς ἐπὶ πλέον τοῦτο ποιη-
τέον, καθάπερ Ἵππαρχος ἐποίησεν. ἀνέγραψε
γάρ, ὡς αὐτός φησι, τὰς γιγνομένας ἐν τοῖς
οὐρανίοις διαφορὰς καθ' ἕκαστον τῆς γῆς τόπον
C 132 τῶν ἐν τῷ καθ' ἡμᾶς τεταρτημορίῳ τεταγμένων,
λέγω δὲ τῶν ἀπὸ τοῦ ἰσημερινοῦ μέχρι τοῦ
βορείου πόλου. τοῖς δὲ γεωγραφοῦσιν οὔτε τῶν

¹ δή, Jones, for δέ.

and then Asbystians and Byzacians, whose territory reaches to that of Carthage. The territory of Carthage is large, and beyond it comes that of the Nomads [1]; the best known of these are called, some of them, Masylians, and others Masaesylians. And last of all come the Maurusians. The whole country from Carthage to the Pillars is fertile, though full of wild beasts, as is also the whole of the interior of Libya. So it is not unlikely that some of these peoples were also called Nomads for the reason that in early times they were not able to cultivate the soil on account of the multitude of wild animals. But the Nomads of to-day not only excel in the skill of hunting (and the Romans take a hand in this with them because of their fondness for fights with wild animals), but they have mastered farming as well as the chase. This, then, is what I have to say about the continents.

34. It remains for me to speak about the "climata" (which is likewise a subject that involves only a general sketch), taking my beginning at those lines which I have called "elements [2]"—I mean the two lines that mark off the greatest length and breadth of the inhabited world, but more particularly the breadth-line. Astronomers, of course, must treat this subject more at length, just as Hipparchus has treated it. For, as he himself says, he recorded the different aspects of the celestial bodies for all the different regions of the earth that are found in our Fourth [3]—I mean the regions between the equator and the north pole. The geographer, however, need not busy himself with what lies outside of our

Numidians.   [2] See 2. 5. 16.
         [3] See 2. 5. 5.

ἔξω τῆς καθ᾽ ἡμᾶς οἰκουμένης φροντιστέον,
οὔτ᾽ ἐν αὐτοῖς τοῖς τῆς οἰκουμένης μέρεσι τὰς
τοιαύτας καὶ τοσαύτας διαφορὰς παραδεκτέον
τῷ πολιτικῷ· περισκελεῖς γάρ εἰσιν. ἀλλ᾽
ἀρκεῖ τὰς σημειώδεις καὶ ἁπλουστέρας ἐκθέσθαι τῶν ὑπ᾽ αὐτοῦ λεχθεισῶν, ὑποθεμένοις,
ὥσπερ ἐκεῖνος, εἶναι τὸ μέγεθος τῆς γῆς σταδίων
εἴκοσι πέντε μυριάδων καὶ δισχιλίων, ὡς καὶ
Ἐρατοσθένης ἀποδίδωσιν· οὐ μεγάλη γὰρ παρὰ
τοῦτ᾽ ἔσται διαφορὰ πρὸς τὰ φαινόμενα ἐν τοῖς
μεταξὺ τῶν οἰκήσεων διαστήμασιν. εἰ δή τις εἰς
τριακόσια ἑξήκοντα τμήματα τέμοι τὸν μέγιστον
τῆς γῆς κύκλον, ἔσται ἑπτακοσίων σταδίων ἕκαστον τῶν τμημάτων· τούτῳ δὴ χρῆται μέτρῳ πρὸς
τὰ διαστήματα τὰ [1] ἐν τῷ λεχθέντι διὰ Μερόης
μεσημβρινῷ λαμβάνεσθαι μέλλοντα. ἐκεῖνος μὲν
δὴ ἄρχεται ἀπὸ τῶν ἐν τῷ ἰσημερινῷ οἰκούντων,
καὶ λοιπὸν ἀεὶ δι᾽ ἑπτακοσίων σταδίων τὰς ἐφεξῆς
οἰκήσεις ἐπιὼν κατὰ τὸν λεχθέντα μεσημβρινὸν
πειρᾶται λέγειν τὰ παρ᾽ ἑκάστοις φαινόμενα· ἡμῖν
δ᾽ οὐκ ἐντεῦθεν ἀρκτέον. καὶ γὰρ εἰ οἰκήσιμα
ταῦτά ἐστιν, ὥσπερ οἴονταί τινες, ἰδίᾳ γέ τις
οἰκουμένη αὕτη ἐστί, διὰ μέσης τῆς ἀοικήτου διὰ
καῦμα στενὴ τεταμένη, οὐκ οὖσα μέρος τῆς καθ᾽
ἡμᾶς οἰκουμένης· ὁ δὲ γεωγράφος ἐπισκοπεῖ ταύτην μόνην τὴν καθ᾽ ἡμᾶς οἰκουμένην. αὕτη δ᾽
ἀφορίζεται πέρασι νοτίῳ μὲν τῷ διὰ τῆς Κινναμωμοφόρου παραλλήλῳ, βορείῳ δὲ τῷ διὰ Ἰέρνης·
οὔτε δὲ τὰς τοσαύτας οἰκήσεις ἐπιτέον, ὅσας ὑπα-

---

[1] τά, Corais inserts, after διαστήματα: Meineke following;
C. Müller approving.

inhabited world; and even in the case of the parts of
the inhabited world the man of affairs need not be
taught the nature and number of the different aspects
of the celestial bodies, because this is dry reading for
him.   But it will be sufficient for me to set forth the
significant and simplest differences noted by Hipparchus, taking as a hypothesis, just as he does, that the
magnitude of the earth is two hundred and fifty-two
thousand stadia, the figure rendered by Eratosthenes
also.   For the variation from this reckoning will not
be large, so far as the celestial phenomena are
concerned, in the distances between the inhabited
places.   If, then, we cut the greatest circle of the
earth into three hundred and sixty sections, each of
these sections will have seven hundred stadia.   Now
it is this that Hipparchus uses as a measure for the
distances to be fixed on the aforesaid meridian through
Meroë.   So he begins with the inhabitants of the
equator, and after that, proceeding along the said
meridian to the inhabited places, one after another,
with an interval each time of seven hundred stadia,
he tries to give the celestial phenomena for each
place; but for me the equator is not the place to
begin.   For if these regions are inhabitable, as some
think, they constitute a peculiar kind of inhabited
country, stretching as a narrow strip through the
centre of the country that is uninhabitable on account
of the heat, and not forming a part of our inhabited
world.   But the geographer takes into his purview
only this our inhabited world; and its limits are
marked off on the south by the parallel through the
Cinnamon-producing Country and on the north by
the parallel through Ierne; and, keeping in mind the
scope of my geography, I am neither required to

γορεύει τὸ λεχθὲν μεταξὺ διάστημα, οὔτε πάντα
τὰ φαινόμενα θετέον, μεμνημένοις τοῦ γεωγρα-
φικοῦ σχήματος. ἀρκτέον δ', ὥσπερ Ἵππαρχος,
ἀπὸ τῶν νοτίων μερῶν.

35. Φησὶ δὴ τοῖς οἰκοῦσιν ἐπὶ τῷ διὰ τῆς
Κινναμωμοφόρου παραλλήλῳ, ὃς ἀπέχει τῆς
Μερόης τρισχιλίους σταδίους πρὸς νότον, τούτου
δ' ὁ ἰσημερινὸς ὀκτακισχιλίους καὶ ὀκτακοσίους,
εἶναι τὴν οἴκησιν ἐγγυτάτω μέσην τοῦ τε ἰσημερινοῦ καὶ τοῦ θερινοῦ τροπικοῦ τοῦ κατὰ Συήνην·
ἀπέχειν γὰρ τὴν Συήνην πεντακισχιλίους τῆς
Μερόης· παρὰ δὲ τούτοις πρώτοις τὴν μικρὰν
ἄρκτον ὅλην ἐν τῷ ἀρκτικῷ περιέχεσθαι καὶ ἀεὶ
φαίνεσθαι· τὸν γὰρ ἐπ' ἄκρας τῆς οὐρᾶς λαμπρὸν
ἀστέρα, νοτιώτατον ὄντα, ἐπ' αὐτοῦ ἱδρῦσθαι τοῦ
ἀρκτικοῦ κύκλου, ὥστ' ἐφάπτεσθαι τοῦ ὁρίζοντος.
τῷ δὲ λεχθέντι μεσημβρινῷ παράλληλός πως
C 133 παράκειται ἔωθεν ὁ Ἀράβιος κόλπος· τούτου δ'
ἔκβασις εἰς τὸ ἔξω πέλαγος ἡ Κινναμωμοφόρος
ἐστίν, ἐφ' ἧς ἡ τῶν ἐλεφάντων γέγονε θήρα τὸ
παλαιόν. ἐκπίπτει δ' ὁ παράλληλος οὗτος τῇ
μὲν ἐπὶ τοὺς νοτιωτέρους μικρὸν τῆς Ταπροβάνης
ἢ ἐπὶ τοὺς ἐσχάτους οἰκοῦντας, τῇ δ' ἐπὶ τὰ
νοτιώτατα τῆς Λιβύης.

36. Τοῖς δὲ κατὰ Μερόην καὶ Πτολεμαΐδα τὴν

---

[1] The arctic circle as referred to by Strabo was a variable
celestial circle, and may be represented by a system of con-
centric circles, each one of which is tangent to the horizon of
the observer and has for its centre the visible celestial pole
and for its radius the altitude of that pole above the horizon.
At the equator, of course, the observer has no arctic circles
—that is, they are non-existent for him at that point. As he
proceeds toward the north pole his arctic circle expands, so

enumerate all the many inhabited places that the said intervening distance suggests to me, nor to fix all the celestial phenomena; but I must begin with the southern parts, as Hipparchus does.

35. Now Hipparchus says that the people who live on the parallel that runs through the Cinnamon-producing Country (this parallel is three thousand stadia south of Meroë and from it the equator is distant eight thousand eight hundred stadia), have their home very nearly midway between the equator and the summer tropic which passes through Syene; for Syene is five thousand stadia distant from Meroë. The Cinnamon-producing people are the first to whom the Little Bear is wholly inside the arctic circle and always visible; for the bright star at the tip of the tail, the most southerly in the constellation, is situated on the very circumference of the arctic circle, so that it touches the horizon.[1] The Arabian Gulf lies approximately parallel to the meridian in question, to the east of it; and where this gulf pours outside into the exterior sea is the Cinnamon-producing Country, where in ancient times they used to hunt the elephant. But this parallel[2] passes outside the inhabited world, running, on the one side,[3] to the south of Taprobane, or else to its farthermost inhabitants, and, on the other side, to the most southerly regions of Libya.

36. In the regions of Meroë, and of the Ptolemaïs

---

[1] that at the Cinnamon-producing Country the Little Bear is comprehended within his circle, and at Syene almost the whole of the Great Bear, and so on. The same general principle would apply to observations made by an observer in a journey from the equator to the south pole.

[2] That is, through the Cinnamon-producing Country.

[3] That is, on the east.

ἐν τῇ Τρωγλοδυτικῇ ἡ μεγίστη ἡμέρα ὡρῶν ἰσημερινῶν ἐστι τρισκαίδεκα· ἔστι δ' αὕτη ἡ οἴκησις
μέση πως τοῦ τε ἰσημερινοῦ καὶ τοῦ δι' Ἀλεξανδρείας παρὰ χιλίους καὶ ὀκτακοσίους τοὺς πλεονά-
ζοντας πρὸς τῷ ἰσημερινῷ· διήκει δ' ὁ διὰ Μερόης
παράλληλος τῇ μὲν δι' ἀγνωρίστων μερῶν, τῇ δὲ
διὰ τῶν ἄκρων τῆς Ἰνδικῆς. ἐν δὲ Συήνῃ καὶ
Βερενίκῃ τῇ ἐν τῷ Ἀραβίῳ κόλπῳ καὶ τῇ Τρωγλοδυτικῇ κατὰ θερινὰς τροπὰς ὁ ἥλιος κατὰ
κορυφῆς γίγνεται, ἡ δὲ μακροτάτη ἡμέρα ὡρῶν
ἰσημερινῶν ἐστι τρισκαίδεκα καὶ ἡμιωρίου, ἐν δὲ
τῷ ἀρκτικῷ φαίνεται καὶ ἡ μεγάλη ἄρκτος ὅλη
σχεδόν τι πλὴν τῶν σκελῶν καὶ τοῦ ἄκρου τῆς
οὐρᾶς καὶ ἑνὸς τῶν ἐν τῷ πλινθίῳ ἀστέρων. ὁ δὲ
διὰ Συήνης παράλληλος τῇ μὲν διὰ τῆς τῶν
Ἰχθυοφάγων τῶν κατὰ τὴν Γεδρωσίαν καὶ τῆς
Ἰνδικῆς διήκει, τῇ δὲ διὰ τῶν νοτιωτέρων Κυρήνης
πεντακισχιλίοις σταδίοις παρὰ μικρόν.

37. Ἅπασι δὲ τοῖς μεταξὺ κειμένοις τοῦ τε
τροπικοῦ καὶ τοῦ ἰσημερινοῦ κύκλου μεταπίπ-
τουσιν αἱ σκιαὶ ἐφ' ἑκάτερα, πρός τε ἄρκτους καὶ
μεσημβρίαν, τοῖς δ' ἀπὸ Συήνης καὶ [1] τοῦ θερινοῦ
τροπικοῦ πρὸς ἄρκτους πίπτουσιν αἱ σκιαὶ κατὰ
μεσημβρίαν· καλοῦνται δ' οἱ μὲν ἀμφίσκιοι, οἱ δ'
ἑτερόσκιοι. ἔστι δέ τις καὶ ἄλλη διαφορὰ τοῖς
ὑπὸ τῷ τροπικῷ, ἣν προείπομεν ἐν τῷ περὶ τῶν
ζωνῶν λόγῳ, αὐτὴ γάρ ἐστιν ἡ γῆ δίαμμος [2]

---

[1] καί, Madvig, for ἐκ after Συήνης.
[2] αὐτὴ γάρ ἐστιν ἡ γῆ δίαμμος, Madvig, for αὐτή τε γάρ ἐστιν
ἡ δίαμμος.

in the country of the Troglodytes, the longest day
has thirteen equinoctial[1] hours; and this inhabited
country is approximately midway between the equator
and the parallel that runs through Alexandria (the
stretch to the equator being eighteen hundred stadia
more[2]). And the parallel through Meroë passes, on
the one side, through unknown regions, and, on the
other, through the capes of India. At Syene, at
Berenice on the Arabian Gulf, and in the country
of the Troglodytes, the sun stands in the zenith at
the time of the summer solstice, and the longest day
has thirteen and one half equinoctial hours; and
almost the whole of the Great Bear is also visible in
the arctic circle, with the exception of the legs, the
tip of the tail, and one of the stars in the square.
And the parallel through Syene passes, on the one
side, through the country of the Fish-Eaters in
Gedrosia, and through India, and, on the other side,
through the regions that are almost five thousand
stadia south of Cyrene.

37. In all the regions that lie between the tropic
and the equator the shadows fall in both directions,
that is, toward the north and toward the south; but,
beginning at the regions of Syene and the summer
tropic, the shadows fall toward the north at noon;
and the inhabitants of the former region are called
Amphiscians,[3] and of the latter, Heteroscians. There
is still another distinctive characteristic of the regions
beneath the tropic, which I have mentioned before in
speaking of the zones,[4] namely, the soil itself is very

[1] On the "equinoctial hour," see footnote 4, page 283.
[2] That is, the distance from Meroë to the equator is 11,800
stadia, and to Alexandria, 10,000.
[3] See § 43 (following), and also 2. 2. 3.
[4] 2. 2. 3.

καὶ σιλφιοφόρος καὶ ξηρά, τῶν νοτιωτέρων μερῶν
εὐύδρων τε καὶ εὐκάρπων ὄντων.

38. Ἐν δὲ τοῖς τοῦ δι' Ἀλεξανδρείας καὶ
Κυρήνης νοτιωτέροις ὅσον τετρακοσίοις σταδίοις,
ὅπου ἡ μεγίστη ἡμέρα ὡρῶν ἐστιν ἰσημερινῶν
δεκατεττάρων, κατὰ κορυφὴν γίνεται ὁ ἀρκτοῦρος,
μικρὸν ἐκκλίνων πρὸς νότον. ἐν δὲ τῇ Ἀλεξανδρείᾳ
ὁ γνώμων λόγον ἔχει πρὸς τὴν ἰσημερινὴν σκιάν,
ὃν ἔχει τὰ πέντε πρὸς τρία.[1] Καρχηδόνος δὲ
νοτιώτεροί εἰσι χιλίοις καὶ τριακοσίοις σταδίοις,
εἴπερ ἐν Καρχηδόνι ὁ γνώμων λόγον ἔχει πρὸς τὴν
ἰσημερινὴν σκιάν, ὃν ἔχει τὰ ἕνδεκα πρὸς τὰ
ἑπτά. διήκει δ' ὁ παράλληλος οὗτος τῇ μὲν διὰ
Κυρήνης καὶ τῶν νοτιωτέρων Καρχηδόνος ἐνα-
κοσίοις σταδίοις, μέχρι Μαυρουσίας μέσης, τῇ
δὲ δι' Αἰγύπτου καὶ Κοίλης Συρίας καὶ τῆς ἄνω
C 134   Συρίας καὶ Βαβυλωνίας[2] καὶ Σουσιάδος, Περσίδος, Καρμανίας, Γεδρωσίας τῆς ἄνω μέχρι τῆς
Ἰνδικῆς.

39. Ἐν δὲ τοῖς περὶ Πτολεμαΐδα τὴν ἐν τῇ
Φοινίκῃ καὶ Σιδῶνα[3] καὶ Τύρον ἡ μεγίστη ἡμέρα
ἐστὶν ὡρῶν ἰσημερινῶν δεκατεττάρων καὶ τετάρ-
του· βορειότεροι δ' εἰσὶν οὗτοι Ἀλεξανδρείας μὲν
ὡς χιλίοις ἑξακοσίοις σταδίοις, Καρχηδόνος δὲ ὡς

---

[1] τρία, Gosselin, for ἑπτά ; editors following.
[2] Βαβυλωνίας, Gosselin, for Βαβυλῶνος ; Meineke, Groskurd,
following ; C. Müller approving.
[3] Σιδῶνα, Meineke, for Σιδόνα ; C. Müller approving.

---

[1] Computation on the basis of this ratio gives Alexandria's
latitude as 30° 57′ 50″, and its distance from the equator as
21,675 stadia. Of course figures based on such a ratio are
only approximate. Hipparchus gives 21,800. Let a vertical

sandy, silphium-producing, and dry, whereas the regions to the south of it are well-watered and very fruitful.

38. In the region approximately four hundred stadia farther south than the parallel through Alexandria and Cyrene, where the longest day has fourteen equinoctial hours, Arcturus stands in the zenith, though he declines a little toward the south. At Alexandria the relation of the index of the sundial to the shadow on the day of the equinox is as five to three.[1] But the region in question is thirteen hundred stadia farther south than Carthage—if it be true that at Carthage the relation of the index to the shadow on the day of the equinox is as eleven to seven.[2] But our parallel through Alexandria passes, in one direction, through Cyrene and the regions nine hundred stadia south of Carthage and central Maurusia, and, in the other direction, it passes through Egypt, Coelesyria, Upper Syria, Babylonia, Susiana, Persia, Carmania, Upper Gedrosia, and India.[3]

39. At the Ptolemaïs in Phoenicia, at Sidon, and at Tyre, and the regions thereabouts, the longest day has fourteen and one quarter equinoctial hours; and these regions are about sixteen hundred stadia farther north than Alexandria and about seven hundred stadia

line AB represent the index. Then let BC be the horizontal shadow. The angle BAC is the latitude of the point B and may be solved by trigonometry.

[2] The latitude of Carthage, therefore, would be 32° 28′ 16″, which corresponds to a distance of 22,730 stadia from the equator.

[3] To fix a parallel of latitude by the *countries* through which it runs seems loose indeed, but Strabo not infrequently does so. On Coelesyria see 16. 2. 16 ; 16. 2. 21 ; and 16. 3. 1. By Upper Syria Strabo must mean Assyria.

ἑπτακοσίοις. ἐν δὲ τῇ Πελοποννήσῳ καὶ περὶ τὰ
μέσα τῆς Ῥοδίας καὶ περὶ Ξάνθον τῆς Λυκίας ἢ τὰ
μικρῷ νοτιώτερα καὶ ἔτι τὰ Συρακουσίων νοτιώτερα τετρακοσίοις σταδίοις, ἐνταῦθα ἡ μεγίστη
ἡμέρα ἐστὶν ὡρῶν ἰσημερινῶν δεκατεττάρων καὶ
ἡμίσους· ἀπέχουσι δ' οἱ τόποι οὗτοι Ἀλεξανδρείας
μὲν τρισχιλίους ἑξακοσίους τετταράκοντα, διήκει
δ' ὁ παράλληλος οὗτος κατ' Ἐρατοσθένη διὰ
Καρίας, Λυκαονίας, Καταονίας, Μηδίας, Κασπίων
πυλῶν, Ἰνδῶν τῶν κατὰ Καύκασον.

40. Ἐν δὲ τοῖς περὶ Ἀλεξάνδρειαν μέρεσι τῆς
Τρωάδος, κατ' Ἀμφίπολιν καὶ Ἀπολλωνίαν τὴν
ἐν Ἠπείρῳ καὶ τοὺς Ῥώμης μὲν νοτιωτέρους, βορειοτέρους δὲ Νεαπόλεως ἡ μεγίστη ἡμέρα ἐστὶν
ὡρῶν ἰσημερινῶν δεκαπέντε· ἀπέχει δὲ ὁ παράλληλος οὗτος τοῦ μὲν δι' Ἀλεξανδρείας τῆς πρὸς
Αἰγύπτῳ ὡς ἑπτακισχιλίους σταδίους πρὸς ἄρκτον, τοῦ δ' ἰσημερινοῦ ὑπὲρ δισμυρίους ὀκτακισχιλίους ὀκτακοσίους, τοῦ δὲ διὰ Ῥόδου τρισχιλίους τετρακοσίους, πρὸς νότον δὲ Βυζαντίου καὶ
Νικαίας καὶ τῶν περὶ Μασσαλίαν χιλίους πεντακοσίους, μικρὸν δ' ἀρκτικώτερός ἐστιν ὁ διὰ Λυσιμαχείας,[1] ὅν φησιν Ἐρατοσθένης διὰ Μυσίας
εἶναι καὶ Παφλαγονίας καὶ τῶν περὶ Σινώπην καὶ
Ὑρκανίαν καὶ Βάκτρα.

41. Ἐν δὲ τοῖς περὶ τὸ Βυζάντιον ἡ μεγίστη
ἡμέρα ὡρῶν ἐστιν ἰσημερινῶν δεκαπέντε καὶ τε-
τάρτου, ὁ δὲ γνώμων πρὸς τὴν σκιὰν λόγον ἔχει
ἐν τῇ θερινῇ τροπῇ, ὃν τὰ ἑκατὸν εἴκοσι πρὸς
τετταράκοντα δύο, λείποντα πέμπτῳ. ἀπέχουσι

[1] Λυσιμαχείας, Meineke, for Λυσιμαχίας; C. Müller approving.

farther north than Carthage. But in the Peloponnesus, in the regions about the centre of Rhodes, about Xanthus of Lycia or a little south of Xanthus, and also in the regions four hundred stadia south of Syracuse,— here, I say, the longest day has fourteen and one half equinoctial hours. These regions are three thousand six hundred and forty stadia distant in latitude from Alexandria; and, according to Eratosthenes, this parallel runs through Caria, Lycaonia, Cataonia, Media, the Caspian Gates, and the parts of India along the Caucasus.

40. At the Alexandria in the Troad and the regions thereabouts, at Amphipolis, at the Apollonia in Epirus, and in the regions south of Rome but north of Neapolis, the longest day has fifteen equinoctial hours. This parallel is about seven thousand stadia north of the parallel through the Alexandria in Egypt, and more than twenty-eight thousand eight hundred stadia distant from the equator, and three thousand four hundred stadia distant from the parallel through Rhodes, and one thousand five hundred stadia south of Byzantium, Nicaea, Massilia, and the regions thereabouts; and a little north of it lies the parallel through Lysimachia, which, says Eratosthenes, passes through Mysia, Paphlagonia, Sinope, and the regions thereabouts, Hyrcania, and Bactra.

41. At Byzantium and the regions thereabouts the longest day has fifteen and one quarter equinoctial hours, and the ratio of the index of the sun-dial to the shadow at the time of the summer solstice is that of one hundred and twenty to forty-two minus one fifth. These regions are about four thousand nine

δ' οἱ τόποι οὗτοι τοῦ διὰ μέσης τῆς Ῥοδίας περὶ τετρακισχιλίους καὶ ἐννακοσίους, τοῦ δ' ἰσημερινοῦ ὡς τρισμυρίους τριακοσίους. εἰσπλεύσασι δ' εἰς τὸν Πόντον καὶ προελθοῦσιν ἐπὶ τὰς ἄρκτους ὅσον χιλίους καὶ τετρακοσίους ἡ μεγίστη ἡμέρα γίνεται ὡρῶν ἰσημερινῶν δεκαπέντε καὶ ἡμίσους· ἀπέχουσι δ' οἱ τόποι οὗτοι ἴσον ἀπό τε τοῦ πόλου καὶ τοῦ ἰσημερινοῦ κύκλου, καὶ ὁ ἀρκτικὸς κύκλος κατὰ κορυφὴν αὐτοῖς ἐστιν, ἐφ' οὗ κεῖται ὅ τ' ἐν τῷ τραχήλῳ τῆς Κασσιεπείας καὶ ὁ ἐν τῷ δεξιῷ ἀγκῶνι τοῦ Περσέως μικρῷ βορειότερος ὤν.

42. Ἔν τε τοῖς ἀπέχουσι Βυζαντίου πρὸς ἄρκτον ὅσον τρισχιλίους ὀκτακοσίους ἡ μεγίστη ἡμέρα ἐστὶν ὡρῶν ἰσημερινῶν δεκαέξ· ἡ οὖν δὴ Κασσιέπεια ἐν τῷ ἀρκτικῷ φέρεται. εἰσὶ δ' οἱ τόποι οὗτοι περὶ Βορυσθένη καὶ τῆς Μαιώτιδος τὰ νότια· ἀπέχουσι δὲ τοῦ ἰσημερινοῦ περὶ τρισμυρίους τετρακισχιλίους ἑκατόν. ὁ δὲ κατὰ τὰς ἄρκτους τόπος τοῦ ὁρίζοντος ἐν ὅλαις σχεδόν τι ταῖς θεριναῖς νυξὶ παραυγάζεται ὑπὸ τοῦ ἡλίου ἀπὸ δύσεως ἕως καὶ ἀνατολῆς ἀντιπεριισταμένου τοῦ φωτός· ὁ γὰρ θερινὸς τροπικὸς ἀπέχει ἀπὸ τοῦ ὁρίζοντος, ἑνὸς ζῳδίου ἥμισυ καὶ δωδέκατον· τοσοῦτον οὖν καὶ ὁ ἥλιος ἀφίσταται τοῦ ὁρίζοντος κατὰ τὸ μεσονύκτιον. καὶ παρ' ἡμῖν δὲ τοσοῦτον τοῦ ὁρίζοντος ἀποσχὼν πρὸ τοῦ ὄρθρου καὶ μετὰ τὴν ἑσπέραν ἤδη καταυγάζει τὸν περὶ τὴν ἀνατολὴν ἢ τὴν δύσιν ἀέρα. ἐν δὲ ταῖς χειμεριναῖς ὁ ἥλιος τὸ πλεῖστον μετεωρίζεται πήχεις ἐννέα.

C 135

hundred stadia distant from the parallel through the centre of Rhodes and about thirty thousand three hundred stadia distant from the equator.[1] If you sail into the Pontus and proceed about fourteen hundred stadia toward the north, the longest day becomes fifteen and one half equinoctial hours. These regions are equidistant from the pole and from the equator, and there the arctic circle is in the zenith; and the star on the neck of Cassiopeia lies on the arctic circle, while the star on the right elbow of Perseus is a little north of it.

42. In the regions about three thousand eight hundred stadia north of Byzantium[2] the longest day has sixteen equinoctial hours; and therefore Cassiopeia moves within the arctic circle. These are the regions about the Borysthenes and the southern parts of Lake Maeotis, and they are about thirty-four thousand one hundred stadia distant from the equator. There the northern part of the horizon is dimly illumined by the sun throughout almost the entire night in the summer-time, the sun's light making a reverse movement from west back to east.[3] For the summer tropic is seven-twelfths of a zodiacal sign[4] distant from the horizon; and accordingly the sun at midnight is just that distance below the horizon. And in our own regions also, when the sun is so far as that from the horizon before sunrise and after sunset, it illumines the skies in the east and in the west. And in those regions in the winter-days the sun attains an elevation of at most nine cubits.[5]

---

[1] That is, a latitude of 43° 17′ 9″.
[2] Which corresponds to 48° 42′ 51″.   [3] Compare 2. 1. 18.
[4] That is, seven-twelfths of 30°, or 17° 30′.
[5] The astronomical cubit of the ancients was two degrees.

φησὶ δ' Ἐρατοσθένης τούτους τῆς Μερόης διέχειν μικρῷ πλείους ἢ δισμυρίους τρισχιλίους, διὰ γὰρ Ἑλλησπόντου εἶναι μυρίους ὀκτακισχιλίους, εἶτα πεντακισχιλίους εἰς Βορυσθένη. ἐν δὲ τοῖς ἀπέχουσι τοῦ Βυζαντίου σταδίους περὶ ἑξακισχιλίους τριακοσίους, βορειοτέροις οὖσι τῆς Μαιώτιδος, κατὰ τὰς χειμερινὰς ἡμέρας μετεωρίζεται τὸ πλεῖστον ὁ ἥλιος ἐπὶ πήχεις ἕξ, ἡ δὲ μεγίστη ἡμέρα ἐστὶν ὡρῶν ἰσημερινῶν δεκαεπτά.

43. Τὰ δ' ἐπέκεινα, ἤδη πλησιάζοντα τῇ ἀοικήτῳ διὰ ψῦχος, οὐκέτι χρήσιμα τῷ γεωγράφῳ ἐστίν. ὁ δὲ βουλόμενος καὶ ταῦτα μαθεῖν καὶ ὅσα ἄλλα τῶν οὐρανίων Ἵππαρχος μὲν εἴρηκεν, ἡμεῖς δὲ παραλείπομεν διὰ τὸ τρανότερα εἶναι τῆς νῦν προκειμένης πραγματείας,[1] παρ' ἐκείνου λαμβανέτω. τρανότερα δ' ἐστὶ καὶ τὰ περὶ τῶν περισκίων καὶ ἀμφισκίων καὶ ἑτεροσκίων, ἅ φησι Ποσειδώνιος. ὅμως γε καὶ τούτων τό γε τοσοῦτον ἐπιμνηστέον, ὥστε τὴν ἐπίνοιαν διασαφῆσαι, καὶ πῇ χρήσιμον πρὸς τὴν γεωγραφίαν, καὶ πῇ ἄχρηστον. ἐπεὶ δὲ περὶ τῶν ἀφ' ἡλίου σκιῶν ὁ λόγος ἐστίν, ὁ δ' ἥλιος πρὸς αἴσθησιν κατὰ παραλλήλου φέρεται, καθ' οὗ καὶ ὁ κόσμος, παρ' οἷς καθ' ἑκάστην κόσμου περιστροφὴν ἡμέρα γίνεται καὶ νύξ, ὅτε μὲν ὑπὲρ γῆς τοῦ ἡλίου φερομένου, ὅτε δ' ὑπὸ γῆν, παρὰ τούτοις οἵ τε ἀμφίσκιοι ἐπινοοῦνται καὶ οἱ ἑτερόσκιοι. ἀμφίσκιοι μέν, ὅσοι κατὰ

---

[1] πραγματείας, Jones, for γραμματείας.

Eratosthenes says that these regions are a little more than twenty-three thousand stadia from Meroë, since the distance from Meroë to the parallel through the Hellespont is eighteen thousand stadia, and thence to the Borysthenes, five thousand. In the regions about six thousand three hundred stadia distant from Byzantium [1] north of Lake Maeotis, in the winter-days, the sun attains an elevation of at most six cubits, and there the longest day has seventeen equinoctial hours.

43. Since the regions beyond already lie near territory rendered uninhabitable by the cold, they are without value to the geographer. But if any one wishes to learn about these regions also, and about all the other astronomical matters that are treated by Hipparchus, but omitted by me as being already too clearly treated to be discussed in the present treatise, let him get them from Hipparchus. And what Poseidonius says about the Periscians and Amphiscians and Heteroscians [2] is too clear to be repeated here ; nevertheless, I must mention these terms at sufficient length to explain the idea and to show wherein it is useful for geography and wherein useless. Now since the point in question concerns the shadows cast by the sun, and since, on the evidence of our senses, the sun moves along a circle parallel to the revolution of the universe, it follows that, wherever each revolution of the universe produces a day and a night (because at one time the sun moves beneath the earth and at another time above the earth), the people are thought of as either Amphiscians or Heteroscians,—as Amphiscians, all

---

[1] Corresponding to 52° 17′ 9″.
[2] See 2. 2. 3 and 2. 5. 37.

μέσον ἡμέρας τοτὲ μὲν ἐπὶ τάδε πιπτούσας ἔχουσι
τὰς σκιάς, ὅταν ὁ ἥλιος ἀπὸ μεσημβρίας τῷ γνώ-
μονι προσπίπτῃ τῷ ὀρθῷ πρὸς τὸ ὑποκείμενον
ἐπίπεδον, τοτὲ δ᾽ εἰς τοὐναντίον, ὅταν ὁ ἥλιος εἰς
τοὐναντίον περιστῇ· τοῦτο δὲ συμβέβηκε μόνοις
τοῖς μεταξὺ τῶν τροπικῶν οἰκοῦσιν. ἑτερόσκιοι
δ᾽ ὅσοις ἢ ἐπὶ τὴν ἄρκτον ἀεὶ πίπτουσιν, ὥσπερ
ἡμῖν, ἢ ἐπὶ τὰ νότια, ὥσπερ τοῖς ἐν τῇ ἑτέρᾳ
C 136 εὐκράτῳ ζώνῃ οἰκοῦσι. τοῦτο δὲ συμβαίνει πᾶσι
τοῖς ἐλάττονα ἔχουσι τοῦ τροπικοῦ τὸν ἀρκτικόν.
ὅταν δὲ τὸν αὐτὸν ἢ μείζονα, ἀρχὴ τῶν περισκίων
ἐστὶ μέχρι τῶν οἰκούντων ὑπὸ τῷ πόλῳ. τοῦ γὰρ
ἡλίου καθ᾽ ὅλην τὴν τοῦ κόσμου περιστροφὴν
ὑπὲρ γῆς φερομένου, δηλονότι καὶ ἡ σκιὰ κύκλῳ
περιενεχθήσεται περὶ τὸν γνώμονα. καθ᾽ ὃ δὴ καὶ
περισκίους αὐτοὺς ἐκάλεσεν, οὐδὲν ὄντας πρὸς τὴν
γεωγραφίαν· οὐ γάρ ἐστιν οἰκήσιμα ταῦτα τὰ
μέρη διὰ ψῦχος, ὥσπερ ἐν τοῖς πρὸς Πυθέαν
λόγοις εἰρήκαμεν. ὥστ᾽ οὐδὲ τοῦ μεγέθους τῆς
ἀοικήτου ταύτης φροντιστέον ἐκ τοῦ λαβεῖν ὅτι
οἱ ἔχοντες ἀρκτικὸν τὸν τροπικὸν ὑποπεπτώκασι
τῷ γραφομένῳ κύκλῳ ὑπὸ τοῦ πόλου τοῦ ζῳδιακοῦ

---

[1] From the equator to 66° every man is either Amphiscian
or Heteroscian.

[2] From 66° to 90°.

[3] Strabo places the tropic of Cancer at 24° (4/60 or 24/360
of the greatest circle) ; and he places the beginning of the
frigid zone at 66°. The radius of the tropic, therefore, is
constant, and is 66°, while the radius of the arctic circle

whose shadows at noon sometimes fall toward the
north, namely, when the sun strikes from the south
the index (which is perpendicular to the horizontal
surface beneath), and, at other times, fall in the
opposite direction, namely, when the sun revolves
round to the opposite side (this is the result for only
those who live between the tropics), but as Heteroscians, all whose shadows either always fall toward
the north, as is the case with us, or always toward
the south, as is the case with the inhabitants of
the other temperate zone. And this is the result
for every man whose arctic circle is smaller than
the tropic circle.[1] But wherever the arctic circle is
the same as, or larger than, the tropic,[2] there the
Periscians begin and they extend to the people who
live beneath the pole. For since, in those regions,
the sun moves above the earth throughout the
whole revolution of the universe, it is clear that
the shadow will move in a circle round the index of
the sun-dial; and that is the reason why Poseidonius
called them Periscians, although they are non-existent
so far as geography is concerned; for all those
regions are uninhabitable on account of the cold, as
I have already stated in my criticism of Pytheas.
Therefore I need not concern myself, either, with
the extent of this uninhabited region, apart from
assuming that those regions which have the tropic-
arctic circle[3] lie beneath the circle described by

is a variable, and is 66° only when the observer stands at
the beginning of the frigid zone. Accordingly, when the
observer is within the frigid zone the radius is greater than
66°, and less than 66° when he is this side of it. By "the
tropic-arctic circle" Strabo refers to the case where the
arctic circle becomes equal to the tropic circle, namely, at
latitude 66°.

κατὰ τὴν τοῦ κόσμου περιστροφήν, ὑποκειμένου
τοῦ μεταξὺ διαστήματος τοῦ τε ἰσημερινοῦ καὶ
τοῦ τροπικοῦ τεττάρων ἑξηκοστῶν τοῦ μεγίστου
κύκλου.

---

[1] That is, the pole of the ecliptic, which daily appears to
describe a circle in the heavens about the pole of the equator.

the pole of the zodiac [1] in the diurnal revolution of the universe—that is, on the hypothesis that the distance between the equator and the tropic is four-sixtieths of the greatest circle.

The projection of this circle upon the earth marks off the frigid zone, and is practically what we mean to-day by the term "arctic circle."

A PARTIAL DICTIONARY OF
PROPER NAMES [1]

A

Aea, a city of Medea, compared with the Aeaea of Circe, 75

Aeolus, 73, 85; mythical king of the Aeolian Islands and ruler of the winds, residing on the isle now called Stromboli

Aelius Gallus, 453; Roman prefect of Egypt about 25 B.C. and personal friend of Strabo

Aeschylus, 123, 157; the tragic poet, 525–456 B.C.

Agamemnon, 35; commander-in-chief of the Greek forces in the Trojan War

Albis (Elbe), the, 51

Alcaeus of Mitylene in Lesbos (fl. about 600 B.C.), 135; the famous lyric poet

Alcman of Sardis (fl. about 625 B.C.), 157; the founder of Doric lyric poetry

Alexander the Great (356–323 B.C.), 49, 249, 259, 347

Amisus (Samsun), 255, town on the southern coast of the Euxine

Ammon, the temple of, in Egypt, 185

Anaximander of Miletus (b. 610 B.C.) 3; an Ionian philosopher, and pupil of Thales. He introduced the gnomon into Greece, and was said to have been the inventor of geographical maps, 23

Andromeda, 157; daughter of Cepheus, king of Ethiopia; her story was made the subject of tragedies (now lost) by Sophocles and Euripides

Antiphanes of Berga in Thrace (fl. not later than the third century B.C.), 391; traveller, and typical romancer. "Bergaean" became a proverbial epithet for romancers

Apelles (fl. about 330 B.C.), 53; the most famous of Greek painters

Apollodorus of Artemita (fl. apparently about the middle of the first century B.C.), 453; author of a history of Parthia

Apollodorus of Athens (fl. about 140 B.C.), 117, 157, 163, 227; grammarian, pupil of Aristarchus, and prolific writer on various subjects

Arabian Gulf (Red Sea), the Ethiopians "sundered in twain" by, 129

Aratus of Soli in Cilicia (b. about 315 B.C.), 11, 397; the astronomical poet, of whose works there remain two short poems and some recently discovered fragments

Arcesilaus of Pitane in Aeolis (b. about 316 B.C.), 53; founder of the Middle Academy of Philosophy

Archimedes of Syracuse (287–212 B.C.), 201; the great mathematician and inventor. Nine of his treatises are extant

Aristarchus of Samothrace (fl. about 155 B.C.), 113, 397; grammarian and critic, and librarian at Alexandria

---

[1] A complete index will appear in the last volume.

A PARTIAL DICTIONARY OF PROPER NAMES

Aristeas of Proconnesus, 79; an epic poet, author of the Arimaspian Epic; all accounts of him are uncertain

Ariston of Chios (fl. about 260 B.C.) 53; a Stoic philosopher, and pupil of Zeno

Aristonicus of Alexandria, 139; grammarian and contemporary of Strabo

Aristotle of Stagira (384–322 B.C.), prince of ancient philosophers; on the winds, 107, the zones, 363

Aristoxenus of Tarentum (fl. about 330 B.C.), 57; pupil of Aristotle, philosopher, musician, and author of *Elements of Harmony*, of which three incomplete books are preserved

Artabrians, the, 461; a district at the north-western corner of Spain

Asteria (the Homeric Asteris), 221; a small island between Ithaca and Cephallenia

Atalanta (now Talanta), 225; an island between Euboea and Locris

Athenodorus of Canana near Tarsus (about 74 B.C.–A.D. 7), 19; pupil of Poseidonius, friend of Strabo, learned scientist; none of his works are extant. On the tides, 203

Atlantic Ocean, not divided by isthmuses into two seas, 17, 121

Atreus, father of Agamemnon, discovered that the sun and heavens moved in contrary directions, 87

Axius (Vardar), the, 21

B

Bear, the Great, 11, 45, 509; the Little, 507

Bion, "the astrologer," 107, by whom is meant, probably, Bion of Abdera, a philosopher and mathematician who flourished about 400 B.C.

Bion, the philosopher, 53, born near the mouth of the Dnieper River and flourished about 250 B.C. He was long at the court of Antigonus Gonatas in Macedonia

Bistonis (Lagos), Lake, 221, in Thrace

Bizone, 199, on the Thracian coast of the Euxine, identical with the Kavarna of to-day

Boagrius, the, 225; a torrent near Thronium in Locris

Bogus (Bocchus), 383, King of Maurusia in Libya about 110 B.C.

Boreas, the north wind, 105

Borysthenes (Dnieper), the, 235, 413; Strabo often refers to the *mouth* of the Borysthenes simply as Borysthenes

Bosporus, the Cimmerian, 21, 75; the Strait of Yenikale

Britain, its position and length, 235

Bura, 199, 219; a town on the Corinthian Gulf

C

Cadmus of Miletus (fl. about 550 B.C.), 65; probably the earliest Greek prose-writer. A work *On the Foundation of Miletus*, in four books, was attributed to him

Callimachus of Cyrene (fl. about 250 B.C.), 163, 169; Greek poet and grammarian, librarian at Alexandria, cataloguer of the library, and said to have written about 800 works, in prose and verse. Only 6 hymns, 64 epigrams and some fragments are extant

Calpe, 189, the Rock of Gibraltar

Celts, campaign of the Romans against the, 37

Ceraunian Mountains (the Kimara Mountains in Albania), 75

Chersonese, the Thracian, 353; the Gallipoli peninsula

Choaspes (Kerah); a river emptying into the Tigris, 175

Cimbrians, the, a Teutonic tribe, who, before their appearance in Roman history (113 B.C.), lived on the North Sea (in Jutland, apparently), but later migrated on account of an inundation, 393

Clazomenae, an important city on the Gulf of Smyrna; once an island, 217

A PARTIAL DICTIONARY OF PROPER NAMES

Cleopatra, 379, wife of Ptolemy Euergetes II, king of Egypt, 146–117 B.C.

Clytaemnestra, wife of Agamemnon, 57

Cnaeus Piso, 501; fought against Caesar in Libya (46 B.C.), and later (23 B.C.) was raised to the consulship

Cobus, the Treran chief, 227

Copaïs (Topolia), Lake, 219, in Boeotia

Corcyra (Corfu), island of, 163

Corinth, an attempt to cut through the Isthmus of, 201

Crates of Mallus in Cilicia (fl. about 150 B.C.), 11; a Stoic philosopher, author of a commentary on Homer, and the leading exponent of the allegorical theory of exegesis. Concerning the tides, 15; his misunderstanding of Homer, 113; his theory of Menelaus' wanderings, 139; his globe and map, 449

Ctesias of Cnidus in Caria (fl. in the fifth century B.C.), 159; historian, physician to Artaxerxes, and author of a *Persian History* in 23 books

Cumae, Gulf of, (Bay of Naples), 81

Cyaneae ("Dark Blue Rocks"), two isles near the mouth of the Bosporus, 75, 349; also called Symplegades ("Clashing Rocks")

Cyrus (Kur), 227; a large river in Asiatic Russia, emptying into the Caspian Sea

D

Damastes of Sigeum, 173; Greek historian, contemporary of Herodotus, and discredited by Strabo. His works are lost

Danaüs, discoverer of the reservoirs of Argos, 87

Darius Codomannus, King of Persia, 301; defeated by Alexander near Gaugamela in 331 B.C. ("the battle of Arbela")

Deïmachus, 257, ambassador of Antiochus Soter (reigned 281–262 B.C.) to Allitrochades, King of Palimbothra in India. He

wrote a work on India, which was thoroughly distrusted by Strabo because of its fabulous stories

Demetrius of Callatis (fl. about 200 B.C.), 223; historian, and author of a work on the geography and ethnography of the Euxine regions

Demetrius Poliorcetes (334–283 B.C.) 201; son of Antigonus the king of Asia; a noted engineer, general, and admiral

Demetrius of Scepsis (fl. about 150 B.C.), 165, 215; grammarian, and author of a historical and geographical work, in 30 books, on the Trojan allies

Democles of Pygela in Lydia (fourth or fifth century B.C.), 217; a cataloguer of earthquakes, of whom little is known

Democritus of Abdera (b. about 460 B.C.), 3, 227, 245; a celebrated philosopher, traveller, and lecturer

Demosthenes (about 383–322 B.C.), 465; the great Athenian orator

Dicaearchia (Puteoli), 95

Dicaearchus of Messene in Sicily (fl. about 320 B.C.), 3, 399; a peripatetic philosopher and pupil of Aristotle, historian, and geographer. Besides other works he wrote a *Periegesis*, and he was the first to measure the altitude of mountains, a subject upon which he wrote a treatise

Dioscuri (Castor and Pollux), 177

Duris of Samos (fl. about 350 B.C.), 223; author of a number of historical works, of which only fragments remain. Among them was a *History of Greece and Macedon*

Dyris, the Atlas Mountains, 121

E

Echinus (now Echino), 225; a town in Thessaly near the sea

Ephialtes, the traitor at Thermopylae, 35

Ephorus of Cyme in Aeolis, 3, 121, 125; a pupil of Isocrates, and

A PARTIAL DICTIONARY OF PROPER NAMES

author of a history dating from the Dorian Invasion to 340 B.C., the year of his death

Epidamnus, 355, 409, now Durazzo, on the coast of Albania

Eratosthenes of Cyrene (about 276–194 B.C.), 3, 49; the learned mathematician and geographer, writer on philosophy, and for years librarian at Alexandria. His opinion of Homer, 93; concerning currents of straits, 201; the dimensions of the inhabited world, 237, 437; his map, 253; the size of the earth, 505

Ethiopians, the, "sundered in twain," 109, 119, 397

Eudoxus of Cnidus (fl. about 366 B.C.), 3, 461; an astronomer, who also wrote a geographical work, to which Strabo frequently refers

Eudoxus of Cyzicus (fl. about 130 B.C.); a navigator and adventurer. His voyages about Libya were described at length by Poseidonius, and discussed by Strabo, 377

Euhemerus of Messene (fl. about 310 B.C.), 173, 391, 401; author of a work on *Sacred History*, which was discredited by Strabo

Euripides (480–406 B.C.), 99, 123; the tragic poet

Euripus, the narrow strait between Boeotia and Euboea, 133

Euxine (Black) Sea, 21; its bed higher than that of the Propontis, 189

G

Gades (now Cadiz), 381

Galatic Gulf (Gulf of Lyon), 409

Gaudos (Gozo), 163; an island south of Sicily

Gelo, 377, who became tyrant of Gela in 491 B.C., of Syracuse in 485 B.C., and, later, lord of all Sicily. He died in the year 478 B.C.

Germans, campaign of the Romans against the, 37

Gerrha, 185, 207; a town in Egypt between Pelusium and Mt. Casius

H

Hecataeus of Miletus (b. about 540 B.C.), 3, 23, 65; a historian and geographer. His geographical work was called *Periegesis*, which embodied about all the Greeks of his time knew on the subject

Hellanicus of Lesbos (fl. about 430 B.C.), 159; the first scientific chronicler among the Greeks, and author of a number of works, among them histories of Troy and Persia

Heracleia Trachinia, 225; a town in Thessaly about eight miles from Thermopylae and three miles from the sea

Heracleides of Pontus (b. about 380 B.C.); pupil of Plato and Aristotle, philosopher, and author of numerous works on a variety of subjects, including certain *Dialogues* mentioned by Strabo, 377

Heracleitus of Ephesus (about 535–475 B.C.), 11; the founder of metaphysics, and called the "Dark Philosopher" because of the obscurity of his writings

Herodotus (about 484–425 B.C.), the "Father of History"; concerning the Nile, 111, 131; narrator of myths, 159; the silting process, 221; the Hyperboreans, 229; the circumnavigation of Libya, 377

Hesiod of Ascra in Boeotia (fl. in the eighth century B.C.), 85; the father of Greek didactic poetry. The extant works under his name are *Works and Days*, *Theogony*, and the *Shield of Heracles*. Concerning the Nile, 107; his mythical stories, 157

Hesperides, 473; a city of Cyrenaica in Libya, renamed Berenicē by Ptolemy III, now called Bengazi

Hipparchus of Nicaea in Bithynia (fl. about 150 B.C.), 5; the famous astronomer. He made the discovery of the precession of the equinoxes, was the first to divide

A PARTIAL DICTIONARY OF PROPER NAMES

the inhabited world into zones of latitude ("climata"), and invented a method of fixing terrestrial positions by circles of longitude and latitude. On the tides, 19; the inhabited world, 269, 437; the "climata," 505

Homer, the great epic poet; philosopher, 3; founder of the science of geography, 5, 23; his conception of Oceanus, 13; his wide knowledge, 59; his use of myth, 67, 71, 75, 159

Hypanis (Bog), the, 413

I

Ierne (Ireland), 237, 279, 443
Ister (Danube), the, 21, 169, 211, 413

J

Jason, 21, 39, 167; leader of the Argonautic expedition, who went to Colchis in quest of the golden fleece

L

Lapithae, the, 29; a mythical race of Thessaly, akin to the Centaurs
Lelantine Plain, 215, in Euboea, between the cities of Eretria and Chalcis
Leonidas, 37, the hero of Thermopylae (480 B.C.)

M

Madys, the Scythian chief, 227, who overran portions of Asia Minor, conquering Cyaxares in 623 B.C.
Maeotis (Sea of Azov), the, 51, 277, 413
Malea, a promontory on the S.E. coast of Laconia, 93
Massilia (Marseilles), 237, 283
Maurusia (Morocco, approximately), 7
Megasthenes, 257, ambassador of Seleucus Nicator (reigned 312–281 B.C.) to Sandrocottus, king of Palimbothra in India. He wrote a historical and geographical work on India, which was discredited by Strabo because of its fabulous stories
Melas (Saros), Gulf of, 103

Meninx (now Isle of Jerba), home of the Lotus-Eaters, 91
Meroë, 119, 233, 255, 439; metropolis of the Ethiopians, on the Nile
Midas, ancient king of Phrygia, 229
Mimnermus of Colophon (fl. about 625 B.C.), 171; the Greek elegiac poet
Minos, 177, ancient king of Crete
Mithridates Eupator, 277, king of Pontus (120–63 B.C.), and most formidable enemy of the Romans in the East
Moeris (Birket-el-Kerun), Lake, 185
Myrsilus of Lesbos, 223; a historical writer of uncertain date

N

Narbo (Narbonne), 403
Neanthes of Cyzicus (fl. in the third century B.C.), 165; a voluminous writer on historical subjects, though only a few fragments of his works are extant
Neapolis (Naples), 83
Nearchus, 263; an admiral of Alexander the Great; in 325 B.C. he made a voyage with his fleet from the mouth of the Indus to the Persian Gulf. An abstract of his voyage is contained in the *Indica* of Arrian. Strabo discredited his work
Neco, 377, king of Egypt, who began his reign in 612 B.C.
Nile, the, and its mouths, 107; boundary-line between Asia and Libya, 119, 243; the silting process at its mouth, 193
Notus, the south wind, 105, 229

O

Olynthus, 465; a Greek city near the head of the Gulf of Torone. It was destroyed and its inhabitants sold as slaves by Philip of Macedon in 347 B.C.
Onesicritus, 263; wrote a biography of Alexander the Great, including a description of Asiatic Countries traversed by Alexander, particularly India. He accom-

A PARTIAL DICTIONARY OF PROPER NAMES

panied the admiral Nearchus on a voyage from the Indus to the Persian Gulf. His work was discredited by Strabo

P

Panchaea, 401; a fabulous land which Euhemerus professed to have visited

Parmenides of Elea in Italy (b. about 510 B.C.), 361; philosopher and poet; and author of a didactic poem *On Nature*, of which only fragments remain

Parthenope, one of the sirens, monument of, 83

Parthians, campaign of the Romans against the, 37; spread of the empire of, 49

Patrocles (about 312–261 B.C.), 255; Macedonian general under Seleucus I and Antiochus I; explorer, and author of geographical treatises (now lost). He regarded the Caspian Sea as a gulf of the "Northern Ocean." Strabo had the utmost faith in his statements

Peiraeus, the most important harbour of Athens; once an island, 217

Pelorias (Faro), Cape, 81

Pelorus, the pilot who was put to death by the Carthaginians, 35

Peneus (Salambria), the, 21

Phalara, 225; now Stillida, on the Maliac Gulf

Pharos, 109, 135, 217, an island off Alexandria, which Alexander united by a mole to the coast

Phasis, 167, 193, river, and town, at the eastern end of the Euxine

Pherecydes of Syros (fl. about 560 B.C.), 65; a philosophical theologian, author of a work concerning nature and the gods, and possibly the earliest prose-writer

Phrixus, 167; the mythical son-in-law of Aeëtes the king of Colchis

Pillars of Heracles, the Straits of Gibraltar, 19, 119, 141

Plato (427–347 B.C.), 391; the great Athenian philosopher

Polemon of Troas (fl. about 200 B.C.), 53; among other works he wrote one on Athens. His works, now lost, were of great value to later times, being rich in information for travellers and students of art and archaeology

Polybius of Megalopolis in Arcadia (b. about 204 B.C.), 3, 73, 85, 367, 399; of his *Histories* in 40 books only the first five have come down to us in complete form. His geographical treatise, referred to by Geminus, is thought to be identical with the 34th book of the *Histories*, of which only a few fragments remain

Pontus (*see* Euxine), the, 75, 77

Poseidonia (Salerno), Gulf of, 75, 81

Poseidonius of Apamea in Syria (b. about 130 B.C.), 3; the author of a history in 52 books, now lost. His researches in geography and astronomy were of the greatest value to Strabo and other scientific writers. Concerning the tides, 15; the winds, 107; the Erembians, 151; the silting process, 199; the tides, 203; Oceanus and the zones, 361

Psammitichus, king of Egypt, 227; one of the Psammitichi of the sixth and seventh centuries, B.C.

Ptolemy Euergetes II (Physcon), 379, 397; king of Egypt 146–117 B.C.

Pygmies, geographical position of, 127

Pytheas of Massilia (Marseilles), 233, 391, 399; navigator, and author of a geographical treatise (now lost). He was the first, apparently, to give definite information on Western Europe and especially the British Islands. Though pronounced by Strabo as unworthy of belief, he is now regarded with greater favour. His date is uncertain, but he flourished at some time before 285 B.C.

R

Romans, campaigns of the, against the Parthians, Germans, and Celts, 37; spread of the empire of, 49

528

A PARTIAL DICTIONARY OF PROPER NAMES

S

Sacred Cape (St. Vincent), of Iberia, 407

Salganeus, the pilot who was executed by the Persians, 35

Salmydessus, 193; the coast of Thrace to the north of the Bosporus

Sappho of Lesbos (fl. about 600 B.C.) 149; Greek poetess, and contemporary of Alcaeus

Scironian Rocks (Derveni Bouno), 103; large rocks on the eastern coast of Megaris

Scylla and Charybdis, 73, 77

Seleucus, king of Babylonia, 19; b. about 358 B.C. and assassinated 281 B.C.

Semiramis and Ninus, 319; the mythical founders of the Assyrian Empire of Nineveh

Sesostris, 141, a legendary king of Egypt; the name is regarded as a corruption of Senwosri, but which one of the Senwosri is meant is unknown, 227

Sipylus, Mt., 217, in Lydia; a branch of the Tmolus.

Sirbonis, 185, a lake on the coast of Lower Egypt

Sirenussae (Siren Rocks), a three-peaked rock between the Bay of Naples and the Gulf of Salerno, 81

Solon (b. about 638 B.C.), 391; the great Athenian legislator

Solymi, the territory of the, 19, 77, 127

Sophocles (495–406 B.C.), 99; the tragic poet

Sphercheius (Hellada), the, 225

Stesichorus of Himera in Sicily (fl. about 600 B.C.), 155; there remain only about thirty fragments of his lyric poetry

Strato of Lampsacus in Mysia in Asia Minor, 181; became head of the Peripatetic school of philosophy in 287 B.C., and was surnamed "the physicist"

Sunium (Colonna), Cape, 353

Syene (now Assuan), at the "summer tropic," 439

T

Tanaïs (Don), the, 243, 411

Taprobane (now Ceylon), 235, 271, 497

Tartessians, the, 121; a people in Spain, west of Gibraltar

Tearko, the Ethiopian Chief, 227

Thebes in Egypt, 31, 109, 147

Theopompus of Chios (b. about 380 B.C.), 159; pupil of Isocrates, and historian of Greece (411–394 B.C.) and of Philip of Macedonia (360–336 B.C.)

Thermaic Gulf (Gulf of Saloniki),355

Thermodon, and Iris, 193, rivers emptying from the south into the Euxine

Thermopylae, the pass of, 35, 133, the spring at, 223

Theseus, 177, a legendary Attic hero

Thessalonica (Saloniki), 409

Thrasyalces the Thasian, 105; one of the earliest writers on natural philosophy, and quoted by Aristotle

Thule, the island of, 233, 441; first referred to by Pytheas, and regarded as the most northerly point of the inhabited world. Strabo denied the existence of such an island

Timosthenes of Rhodes (fl. about 280 B.C.), 107, 353; an admiral under Ptolemy Philadelphus, and author of a work on *The Harbours* in ten books

Troglodytes, the, 5, 153

Tyras (Dniester), the, 51, 413

X

Xanthus of Lydia (fl. about 480 B.C.), 181; a writer of Lydian history

Xenocles, 261; Alexander's treasurer

Xerxes, 35; king of Persia (485–465 B.C.)

Z

Zeno of Citium in Cyprus (about 345–265 B.C.), 53, 151; the founder of the Stoic school of philosophy